S0-AKJ-024

THE HISTORY OF POMONA COLLEGE 1887-1969

CHARLES BURT SUMNER

THE HISTORY
OF
POMONA COLLEGE

1887–1969

By E. Wilson Lyon

POMONA COLLEGE, CLAREMONT, CALIFORNIA
1977

Printed in the United States of America by
Grant Dahlstrom at The Castle Press

To the memory of
George White Marston
Trustee of Pomona College
1887 - 1946

Table of Contents

PART THREE—*Pomona in an Era of International Conflict*

Foreword

POMONA COLLEGE, although still a young member of the international company of colleges and universities, has had from its beginnings a strong sense of history. For example, as early as 1898, eleven years after the college's founding, a portrait of its first president, Cyrus Grandison Baldwin, was commissioned soon after he was forced to resign. One is impressed by the care with which both important documents and ephemera were preserved from the earliest days. Evidently the Founders' sense of destiny impelled them to keep their records for the benefit of future students of the history of education.

Nor has the college neglected its historical self-consciousness in the intervening years. Charles B. Sumner's *The Story of Pomona College* was published in 1914. Professor Frank P. Brackett's engaging volume of reminiscences, *Granite and Sagebrush,* appeared in 1944, and Dean Norton's papers, diaries, letters, and famed witticisms were collected in *The Dean Speaks Again,* which was published in 1955. Accounts of the lives of the college's great benefactors include Professor Hubert Herring's *The Education of George W. Marston,* and Miss Mary Gilman Marston's two-volume edition of *George White Marston: A Family Chronicle,* published in 1956. Professor Clifford Drury's *Rudolph James Wig,* published in 1968, gives a comprehensive account of the life and times of this stalwart and creative man. In 1960, Pomona College published Mrs. Jane Werner Watson's *The Seaver Story,* commemorating the magnanimous work and philanthropy of Mr. and Mrs. Frank Roger Seaver.

President Emeritus E. Wilson Lyon has devoted much of his time since his retirement to the preparation of a formal history of the college. He has skillfully collected and analyzed the extensive documents of the college to write a comprehensive history of Pomona from 1887 through his own tenure as president. Dr. Lyon is a professional historian who has published two books in French history and Franco-American relations. He has served on the editorial board of the *Journal of Modern History*, and he was a member of the Pacific Coast Committee for the Humanities of the American Council of Learned Societies which founded and published the quarterly journal, *The Pacific Spectator*, from 1947 to 1956. A former Rhodes Scholar, he edited *The American Oxonian* from 1956 to 1962. The reader of *The History of Pomona College* will quickly sense the sure touch of a master historian.

What is especially praiseworthy about this book, in my view, is the even-handed manner of the treatment of his own time. He avoids the pitfalls of either the apologist or the memoirist, and he is able to write about himself and his colleagues and the events from 1941 to 1969 with the same graceful detachment he exemplified in his handling of the tenures of his predecessors. Such an accomplishment is an ornament to the career of a man whose transcendent devotion to Pomona College guided his life here.

What Dr. Lyon could not do is praise himself for the extraordinary growth of Pomona College under his leadership. He and Mrs. Lyon, Carolyn Bartel, Wellesley '28, brought to the college the charm and distinction of a presidential couple whose reverence for moral learning and well-informed public service helped maintain the character of the college. They gave themselves selflessly to advancing Pomona College and its ideals. All who love Pomona College owe them a great debt of gratitude and the commitment to carry forward the unbroken traditions of the college.

DAVID ALEXANDER

Preface

POMONA COLLEGE, founded in 1887, was one of the earliest institutions of higher education in the American Southwest. Overcoming major and repeated financial difficulties, it became the first college or university in its region to win national academic recognition. Its graduates and former students, now numbering 23,441, have contributed greatly to the professions, to business and industry, and to many other aspects of American life.

Led by its president and trustees, Pomona initiated in 1925 a plan for academic organization, then unique in the United States and destined to make Claremont an educational center of national and international interest. Today, Pomona College is the senior of six associated institutions which have developed under the group plan which it inaugurated.

The history of Pomona College is thus that of both a leading liberal arts college and an innovator in the organization of higher education in the United States. The story of the college is cherished by those who have studied or taught on the campus. It is also of value to students of the history of California and the history of American higher education.

My own association with Pomona College extends over the past thirty-six years. When a professor of history at Colgate University, I was privileged to be called to the presidency of Pomona, and assumed office in September 1941. I served for twenty-eight years, through World War II, the return of the veterans, the Korean War, the astounding growth in population and resources of Southern California, during the Vietnam War with all its wide-ranging problems, and into the period of fuller participation of minorities in higher education and American life. As president emeritus since 1969 I have followed the current work of the college and have studied Pomona's history.

It was my good fortune to know intimately one of the original Pomona trustees, two of the first faculty, several members of the first graduating class, and other alumni from the earliest years to the present. From them I have come to understand much and to share deeply the respect and devotion which they hold for Pomona. As the years passed I learned increasingly of the courage and sacrificial work of generations of trustees, faculty, and alumni in building a college of academic distinction and high moral purpose. When the trustees asked me to write a history of the college, I accepted enthusiastically. In this history of Pomona I hope to present its values and achievements and to affirm my own abiding faith in the American liberal arts college.

While excellent accounts of the college, through 1912 and 1937 respectively, had been written by Dr. Charles B. Sumner, founder, trustee, and faculty member, and by Professor Frank P. Brackett, a member of the original faculty, the college was in need of a book giving a comprehensive account of its history. This I have undertaken to provide, beginning the story in 1887 and continuing it to my retirement in 1969. I am pleased that my book can appear in Pomona's Ninetieth Anniversary Year and provide a view of the past as the college looks to its future.

A history of Pomona College must give consideration to the group plan which its trustees established in 1925. I have prepared, therefore, succinct accounts of the development of the central coordinating institution, the founding of the respective undergraduate colleges, and the evolution of practices and precedents that eventuated in a constitution for the group. I hope these accounts will contribute to better understanding of the complex relationships of the Claremont Colleges.

Throughout the book I have emphasized the people and the forces that made Pomona a college of academic distinction. This has required the omission of much that I would like to have included. I trust that I shall be forgiven by the reader who fails to find mention of a cherished event or a favorite faculty member.

While I have sought many interviews and have queried my Pomona friends on countless occasions, this book is primarily a work of historical research. I have read the minutes of the Board of Trustees and of its Executive Committee, the minutes of the Faculty and the Cabinet of the Faculty, the files of the student paper from its beginning in 1889, all copies of the yearbook since its first appearance in 1894, printed reports of the presidents, most of the literature put out by the college, and countless items which throw light on the role of individuals in the college. For my own administration I have also drawn upon the office records, aided by my personal knowledge and recollection of events.

My research has been made possible by the careful preservation of records by the college administrative officials and the alumni office, and by the systematic deposit of many of these materials in the college library—earlier in the Carnegie Library at Pomona, and after 1952 in the Honnold Library of the Claremont Colleges, where they are now housed and conveniently available within one room in the Special Collections department. I am greatly indebted to Miss Ruth M. Hauser and Mrs. Morton O. Beckner of this department for their assistance and many kindnesses during my years of research.

There is not space to list the host of individuals who have assisted and advised me, and I can thank only a few to whom I am especially indebted. Miss Agnes M. Johnson, my secretary for twenty-six years, read two versions of the manuscript and saved me from errors. President David Alexander read the manuscript and made helpful suggestions. George C. S. Benson '28, president emeritus of Claremont Men's College, read the manuscript and shared his personal knowledge of Pomona. Three of my long-time friends from the Pomona faculty, Ernest A. Strathmann, dean emeritus of the faculty, W. T. Jones, professor emeritus of philosophy, and Ray Frazer, professor of English, read and made detailed comments on the entire manuscript. Guided by their suggestions and corrections, I revised and reduced the manuscript. This version was then read by Robert B. Coons, former chairman of the Board of Trustees, and John H. Kemble, professor of history, who made much appreciated suggestions. I am deeply indebted to the two secretaries who helped me with the book: Mrs. Eva S. Ballard, who typed the individual chapters, and Mrs. Gladys S. Burton, who twice typed the entire manuscript. George F. Sweeney, former director of the Pomona College News Bureau, generously provided valuable photographs. I am grateful to Mrs. Margaret Mulhauser for her expert proofreading. The book owes much to the editorial skill and concern of Grant Dahlstrom of The Castle Press. I owe most to my wife,Carolyn Bartel Lyon, who has read and advised on every part and version of this history of Pomona. None of my generous helpers should be held accountable for any errors or omissions the reader may note. These are my responsibility alone.

E. WILSON LYON

Claremont, California
July 18, 1977

THE HISTORY OF POMONA COLLEGE 1887-1969

CHAPTER I

Congregationalists Establish a College in the Pacific Southwest

THE FOUNDING of Pomona College in 1887 was a part of the economic and cultural change that transformed Southern California in the last decades of the nineteenth century. This change had been foreshadowed as early as 1865 by the decline of the great cattle ranches and an increasing interest in the development of agriculture. The land from San Diego to Santa Barbara was well suited to field crops, vineyards, and orchards. South of the Tehachapi Mountains were a number of fertile valleys where the climate was mild, even in winter. Furthermore, there was an abundant supply of water for irrigation in the dry summer months. The winter rains and snow from the mountains, some with an elevation of over 10,000 feet, created streams that flowed through the valleys throughout the year. In addition, the underground water table was high, and wells, often artesian, could be developed successfully in most of the area.

The climate, in which frost was rare, was ideal for citrus, and in the 1870's two varieties of oranges, introduced from abroad, laid the foundations for a great industry. The Valencia from Spain, which ripened from spring through late autumn, and the Washington Navel from Brazil, ripening from early winter to late spring, provided a year round supply of delicious fruit. Shipments of oranges to the east began in 1877 and helped to develop national interest in Southern California.

Most accessible for settlement were the valleys that reached for a hundred miles from the mountains to the ocean. Twenty miles inland from the Pacific was Los Angeles, founded by Spain in 1781. To the east were San Bernardino, which the Mormons had settled in 1851, and Riverside, founded in 1870, where the Navel orange had been planted. Easterners in search of health and a milder climate were lured by writings portraying a fabulous land of opportunity. The land beckoned and the way to get there was opening up. Railroads were coming to Southern California.

The joining of the Central Pacific and the Union Pacific in 1869, which established a transcontinental railroad to the San Francisco Bay area, raised hopes for a railroad into Los Angeles. This was achieved in 1876 when the Southern Pacific, of which Leland Stanford was president, constructed a line from San Francisco to Los Angeles, via the San Joaquin Valley. The Southern Pacific was conceived as a transcontinental line to the southern states, and, by building across the southwest to El Paso, where it joined the Texas and Pacific, it opened railway transportation from Los Angeles to New Orleans in 1883.

But the public chafed under this monopoly and ardently desired competition. There was rejoicing, therefore, when another line, the Atchison, Topeka and Santa Fe, building from the heart of the Middle West, entered Los Angeles, first over leased trackage in 1885, and on its own line in 1887. The way was open for easy and economical travel to Southern California from other parts of the United States, and the region became for many an attainable future home or winter residence. Los Angeles, which in 1880 had a population of only 11,183, would grow to 50,395 by 1890. In the same decade San Diego grew from 2637 to 16,159, and Santa Barbara from 3460 to 5864. The population of the fourteen counties of Southern California increased from 54,184 to 158,530.

The Southern Pacific and the Santa Fe entered into feverish competition in 1886 and 1887, laying out prospective towns along their lines, and attracting travellers from Chicago and Kansas City by fares which at one time were as low as one dollar. Aggressive developers offered the newly opened land with extravagant descriptions of potential benefits. Typical was the presentation of Burbank, in the Los Angeles area, as a place where "land and ocean, mountain and valley, sunshine and shade offer their choicest benefactions to prolong the lives of the feeble and enhance the enjoyment of the robust."

The unprecedented influx of new people led in 1886 and 1887 to one of the most spectacular economic booms in American history. Lured by the cheap railway excursions, thousands eagerly bought the newly available lands. As the historian of this movement, Glenn S. Dumke, wrote in his book, *The Boom of the Eighties:*

> Men stood excitedly in line for days at a time in order to get first choice of lots in a new subdivision. Flag-draped trains hauled flatcars jammed with enthusiastic prospects to undeveloped tracts far from centers of settlement. Exuberant auction sales, accompanied by brass bands and free lunches, helped sell $100,000,000 of Southern California real estate during the boom's peak year.

While there was much speculation in recently purchased real estate during the boom, most of the immigrants expected to establish homes in "the new Italy." One of their first concerns was the building of churches, and soon these began to found colleges. The Methodists took the lead in 1880 with the University of Southern California, and the Presbyterians and the Congregationalists followed with the incorporation of Occidental College and Pomona College in 1887. Among the new settlers were a number of Congregationalists — some directly from New England and larger numbers from Middle Western communities of New England origin. The newcomers found their denomination already established and gaining strength in Southern California. From the foundation of their original church in San Bernardino in 1866, the number of Congregationalists had steadily increased and by 1883 they were able to organize a District Association of their churches.

Congregationalists had begun higher education in colonial America by founding Harvard College, and they had been leaders in founding colleges across the country as their members moved west. In this tradition Southern California Congregationalists took early steps to advance higher education in the Pacific Southwest. With the organization of their District Association they also authorized the formation of a representative education committee "to establish a Christian Academy or College." Little was achieved, however, until 1887, when the increase in the number of their churches in California led Congregationalists to establish two General Associations, one in each of the two major areas of the state.

When the General Association of Southern California was organized on May 3, 1887, the way was opened for the foundation of a college. Provision was made for a permanent Committee on Education, and eight ministers were named as its members. Two days later the membership of the committee was increased to twelve and the Association voted that "the Committee on Education have full power to act in regard to propositions looking toward the establishment of a Christian College in Southern California and if need be in the appointment of trustees — the committee to be requested to take final action within thirty days." These were bold steps for a denomination which then had only twenty-one churches and twelve hundred members in Southern California. However, the influx of new people and the economic activity of 1886 and 1887 gave them confidence that the college could be established immediately.

The Committee on Education vigorously undertook its mission, looking to the completion of its responsibility within the required thirty days. Its first task was to determine a location for the college and to secure local financial support. A number of communities were interested in attracting the college, and to a degree the final decision would be affected by the best financial offer. Visits were made to Beaumont and to Lugonia (today a part of Redlands), and each community offered land and money if the college were to come there. However, both communities were near the desert and far from the main centers of population, and there was a growing feeling that the college should be placed in a better climate and at a site more accessible to all of Southern California.

The Committee on Education then turned its attention to the city of Pomona. Founded in 1874 by the Los Angeles Immigration and Land Cooperative Association, which had acquired and subdivided 2500 acres of the Rancho San Jose, the settlement became a shipping point for Riverside when the Southern Pacific arrived in 1875. Following a disastrous drought in 1876-77 and a fire in 1877, the population had declined to 130 by 1880, but the great boom of 1886 brought such a revival that by 1887 Pomona had become a community with a population of 3500. Located in a beautiful valley at the foot of the San Gabriel Mountains, it was served by both the Southern Pacific and the Santa Fe. Its economic base and its hopes for the future were indicated when the city was named for Pomona, the Roman goddess of fruit trees.

Pilgrim Congregational Church in Pomona, organized in 1887, soon had a hundred members. Its pastor, Charles Burt Sumner, would play a determining role in the location and development of the college. Sumner brought to Pilgrim Church an appreciation of higher education, a deep sense of purpose, and unrelenting perseverance. Born in Southbridge, Massachusetts, on August 17, 1837, he had graduated from Yale in 1862 with election to Phi Beta Kappa. After military service in the Union Army he returned to civilian life and entered Andover Theological Seminary, from which he graduated in 1867. Ordained as a Congregational minister, he held a twelve-year pastorate at Monson, Massachusetts. The illness of his wife led him to resign a second Massachusetts pastorate and to take his family to the dry climate of the Southwest, where he first served a newly organized Congregational church in Tucson, Arizona Territory, from 1882 to 1884. He then became Superintendent for the American Home Missionary Society in Arizona and New Mexico Territories, residing at Las Vegas, New Mexico, whence he was called to California.

As pastor of Pilgrim Church, Sumner enthusiastically supported the founding of a college in Southern California by the Congregational churches. He was drawn into the discussions soon after his arrival in the state, and as a friend of J. T. Ford, pastor of the San Bernardino Church, he was invited to some of the meetings of the Education Committee and he accompanied the members on their site visitations. When the search for a location nearer the centers of population led to the discovery of a beautiful mesa at the mouth of Live Oak Canyon in the foothills five miles north of Pomona, Sumner determined to see if Pomona could make a bid for the college. The mesa had just been acquired by H. A. Palmer, a leader in the establishment of Pilgrim Church, and he agreed to give a tract of eighty acres. Two ladies from Boston, the Misses Wheeler who were spending the winter in Pomona, added forty adjoining acres, and others contributed one thousand dollars in money. These gifts were secured in the course of a Saturday evening; after the church service the following morning the matter was placed before the congregation of Pilgrim Church and approved "kindly and heartily." Pomona could offer for the college subscriptions of land and money estimated at $160,000.

The crucial decision on location was made by the Education Committee in a meeting held on May 19 at the First Congregational Church of Los Angeles. After full discussion and consideration of Lugonia, Pasadena, Riverside, and Pomona, the Committee voted 8 to 2, and then unanimously to "accept the Pomona proposition provided water is guaranteed for domestic and irrigating purposes in the principal tracts"—a guarantee which H. A. Palmer was able to provide.

Following selection of the site, the Education Committee fulfilled its second mandate by electing trustees for the college. Nine trustees were named by the Committee on May 19. In bequeathing its authority to the newly constituted Board of Trustees, the Education Committee stipulated that "one condition of transfer be that a majority of the trustees now and forever shall be members of evangelical Congregational churches. This condition to be incorporated in the deeds [of property]." At its own first meeting, on June 3, the Board altered this provision by voting "that a majority of the Board shall be members of Congregational churches, and that two-thirds of the Board shall be members of evangelical churches."

Within a few weeks, the Board of Trustees took the form and membership that were to characterize it in the early years of the college. On June 3 the number of trustees was increased to twelve and on June 15 to fifteen — the number which continued until 1907. Two of those first elected resigned in 1888, but thirteen of the original trustees gave long service to the Board. Eight were Congregational ministers and five were leading laymen from the Congregational churches. Eleven of the original trustees resided in Southern California, one in Oakland, and another in Berkeley.

On matters of educational theory and academic organization the Board relied upon its ministerial members. Without exception, the ministers were graduates of liberal arts colleges and also of theological seminaries. Typical were Sumner, James T. Ford, of the San Bernardino Church, and T. C. Hunt, pastor at Riverside. Ford was a graduate of Williams College and Andover Seminary. After home missionary work in South Carolina, he had come to California to conclude his career as Home Missionary Superintendent of Southern California. Hunt was a graduate of Dartmouth College and the Chicago Theological Seminary, who had come to Riverside from the pastorate of the Congregational Church at Prescott, Arizona.

A banker, a rancher, a real estate man, a judge, and a merchant completed the membership of the Board. Although none of the five was a college graduate, they shared the zeal for higher education which characterized American life at the end of the nineteenth century. The four businessmen were destined to play a large part in the development of the college. Henry A. Palmer, whose gift of land did so much to make the college possible, was a native of Connecticut, who had moved to California in 1861 at the age of nineteen. After long residence in the Bay Area, he had opened a bank in the new city of Pomona just before the plans for the college took form. Nathan W. Blanchard, born of Huguenot stock in Maine in 1831, had attended Colby College for two years. When lack of funds had forced him to discontinue his studies, he decided to go to California. By 1887, he was a prosperous citrus rancher in Santa Paula, and destined to play a large part in establishing the new college. Henry Kirke White Bent, the son of a Massachusetts Congregational pastor, had relinquished the prospect of the ministry because of trouble with his eyes in his youth, and had followed the outdoor life of a railroad and mining engineer. When his health forced him to abandon this work, he began a real estate business and in 1867 came to Los Angeles where by 1887 he had become a leader in civic affairs and in the Congregational church. George W. Marston, the youngest of the trustees, who was born in Wisconsin in 1850, had graduated from the preparatory department of Beloit College. After a brief business experience and a special scientific course at the University of Michigan, he came to San Diego where his successful dry goods and clothing business and his service to church and city had early marked him as an outstanding citizen. Judge Anson Brunson assisted the Board in the preparation of the Articles of Incorporation, the By-Laws, and the lease papers required for the acquisition and management of property. He was the first of the long line of lawyer members to whom the Board would be greatly indebted.

The choice of a name for the college required more time than the selection of the trustees. The Board voted on June 15, 1887 to ask each trustee to submit three choices within five days, "three names marked 1st, 2nd, and 3rd choice." The secretary of the Board would then send these choices to each trustee with the request that the trustee in returning the names indicate any he considered "especially objectionable." The trustee action provided that when this procedure was completed, "the name not especially objectionable to any and receiving the highest number of votes to be the name for the College." The balloting resulted in the choice of "Piedmont." However, at a trustee meeting on the Scanlon mesa on September 5, 1887 it was reported that the village lying between the college site and Pomona would have a Santa Fe station which would be named North Pomona. On the basis of this information it was voted to reconsider the former choice of "Piedmont." Appreciative of the value of the railroad station and of the assistance of Pomona, the trustees voted "that the name of the College be Pomona College."

After agreement on the name, the trustees took steps to incorporate the college under the laws of the State of California. Articles of Incorporation, which had been first considered by the Board on August 5, were filed and approved in Sacramento on October 14, 1887. The legal name was "The Pomona College," and it so remained until 1909. As set forth in the Articles of Incorporation, the purposes for which the college was formed were: "to establish, maintain, and conduct a College and Seminary of Learning, with all the powers and privileges conferred by law upon such corporations. The College shall be distinctly Christian in harmony with evangelical churches, but non-sectarian and shall be open to students of both sexes."

The decision for coeducation, which followed the pattern of

Congregational colleges in the Middle West, was accepted as a matter of course by Pomona's founders. While the Articles of Incorporation stipulated that "the location of the College shall be near North Pomona, San Jose Township, Los Angeles Co., Cal.," the corporation was authorized to establish a "preparatory or academical school or schools which may be located at such other places within the State of California as may be designated by the Board of Trustees." The final article listed the donors and the properties and sum of money they had subscribed "to assist in founding the College and Seminary."

While the Articles of Incorporation were being drafted, the trustees prepared the By-Laws to govern the organization and operation of the college. The duties of the Board were set forth, and provision was made for an Executive Committee of five which would control the business affairs of the college, oversee the college property, and prepare recommendations for action by the Board. The government of the college was entrusted to "the President, Professors and Tutors who shall be styled The Faculty of Pomona College," and careful procedures were established for the handling of faculty meetings and the keeping of faculty records. A large responsibility was placed on faculty members in their relations to students for, in addition to teaching, the faculty were charged

> to exercise a thorough and parental supervision of the habits and deportment of students, to inculcate the lessons of morality and piety, to admonish them of their duties to God and man, and to administer impartially the laws of the College, enforcing them by admonition, suspension, dismission or expulsion, as the nature of offenses may require.

For their part, students admitted to the privileges of the college were "regarded as pledged to the faithful performance of the duties assigned to them and a cheerful conformity to the regulations prescribed." These regulations included daily devotional exercises and church on Sunday. The baccalaureate degree would be awarded upon recommendation of the faculty, the vote of the trustees, and after the student had paid all college bills.

Following incorporation and adoption of the By-Laws, the Board of Trustees set up its permanent organization. H. A. Palmer, who had been temporary chairman, was elected President of the Board. Nathan W. Blanchard was named Vice-President; C. B. Sumner, Secretary; and C. B. Shelton, Treasurer. Shelton, a Congregational minister and an 1847 graduate of Williams College, had moved to California for his health, settling in North Pomona. The original Executive Committee consisted of Palmer, Bent, Ford, Shelton, and Sumner.

Immediate problems were plans for the physical plant of the college, and the raising of funds for all aspects of the institution's anticipated program. The Board, on October 6, 1887, "specially commissioned" the Executive Committee "to arrange for the plotting of the grounds of the college . . . and to secure plans for a college building." At its own first meeting on November 25, 1887, the Executive Committee determined that a financial agent should be appointed immediately and that Sumner was "the available man." After two months of agonizing deliberation Sumner accepted on January 20, 1888 but only on condition that Pilgrim Church "first be provided with a satisfactory pastor." When he had secured an old friend, L. H. Frary, for the church, Sumner took the appointment as "Financial Agent," effective April 1, "with general supervisory authority" for one year at a salary of $1,500.

Had the situation been less grave, Sumner would not have considered relinquishing a pastorate in which he was so happy. He had been asked, in fact, to save the college. During the six months following incorporation hardly a hand had been lifted, "not even to collect subscriptions." The feverish stimulus of the boom had over-shadowed less exciting matters. But by April 1888 ominous signs had begun to appear. Sales of real estate decreased, interest rates rose, and the consequent widespread desire to sell brought a catastrophic collapse of the boom by the end of the summer. While the conservative policy of the banks prevented financial ruin for the region, the end of the boom left Southern California with high interest charges, low prices, and very hard times indeed. "For the college," as Sumner later wrote, "matters were already bad enough and growing worse and worse. Money subscribed could be collected only with difficulty. New gifts were out of the question. No money could be raised on land." In the face of such conditions,

Architect's sketch for the first building

Sumner, as Financial Agent, was given the threefold task of laying out a town where by the sale of lots a community would be established around the college, constructing a "Central Building," and preparing for the beginning of instruction in September 1888. In close cooperation with Palmer, Bent, Ford, and Shelton, Sumner went forward with these large responsibilities.

The opening of school meant beginning instruction at the high school level, for there were few students in the region ready for college. Although the institution was incorporated as a college, the trustees envisaged a preparatory department as an important and continuing part of the enterprise. In accordance with this concept, Sumner had been empowered by the trustees, on May 11, 1888 to engage teachers and to open school in Pomona in the autumn. His completed plans were released in the college's first piece of printed literature. "Pomona College of Pomona, California, an unsectarian Christian College for the education of both sexes" announced its opening for the academic year 1888-89, with three terms of twelve weeks each, offering an "English course" and a "Classical and Literary course," in the Preparatory Department, and a freshman year in the Collegiate Department. Tuition for the year was $45 in the Preparatory Department and $60 in the Collegiate Department. The center of instruction was the Ayer Cottage, a five-room house on the corner of Fifth Street and White Avenue, a pleasant building set in spacious grounds, with lawns, flowers, and ornamental trees. Six teachers were listed, and the subjects to be taught included Greek, Latin, mathematics, science, English, German, drawing and painting, piano, harmony and music theory. Some thirty students, three of them of college standing, were to constitute the first classes.

The trustees, parents of students, and visitors who attended the simple exercises in the Ayer Cottage on September 12 looked to the future in expectation and faith. After Reverend Hunt had opened the chapel service with a reading from the Psalms and prayer, Sumner spoke of this founding of a Christian College of the New England type as "the realization of a great purpose formed under divine guidance and carried forward through strenuous efforts and in the face of difficulties, for the furtherance of Christian civilization."

The faculty members whom Sumner had chosen were imbued with his own high purpose. They were deeply committed Christians, challenged by the frontier, and devoted to learning. Two of the faculty were young men who were to give their entire lives to Pomona College and to provide enlightened leadership of incalculable value. By their selection Sumner made one of his greatest contributions to the future of the college.

Edwin Clarence Norton, Principal of the Preparatory Department and teacher of Greek, combined an excellent education with teaching experience in another frontier college. Born in Bradford, Pennsylvania, in 1856, Norton spent his childhood in New York State and Wisconsin, as his father, a Congregational minister, moved westward serving frontier churches. After completing his sophomore year at Carleton College, Norton transferred to Amherst, where he was elected to Phi Beta Kappa and received his B.A. degree in 1879. The decision to teach Greek which he had made at Carleton was confirmed at Amherst, where he studied with the much-beloved Professor William Tyler. After a year as a school principal in Minnesota, Norton went to Johns Hopkins University for a semester and then to Yale, where along with Greek, he took Sanskrit and theology, graduating from the theological department in 1883.

Norton had earlier decided that his lot was to be cast with a new frontier college, and he was delighted in 1883 when he received an invitation to be Professor of Greek at Yankton College, in South Dakota, then beginning its second year. There he had four valuable years. In 1884 he was married to Miss Fannie Rice, a teacher from New Haven, whom he had met while at Yale. Norton was spending the academic year 1887-88 in rest and study among old friends in Northfield, Massachusetts, when he read in *Advance,* a Congregational publication in Chicago, that the Congregational Churches in Southern California were planning a college of the New England type. Norton wrote to Hunt, pastor of the Riverside Church, whom he knew through Carleton, expressing his interest in a position with the new college. Hunt turned Norton's letter over to Sumner, and on July 27, 1888, the trustees approved Norton's appointment for a year at a salary of $1350.

Frank Parkhurst Brackett, who was appointed teacher of mathematics and Latin, was nine years younger than Norton. Following his graduation in 1887 from Dartmouth College, where he had earned his way by summer jobs and winter teaching in rural schools, Brackett came to Los Angeles and took a teaching position in McPherson Academy. Sumner persuaded him to open a private school in Pomona in January 1888 and made available for Brackett's use a small chapel room in Pilgrim Church. Some of the students who attended this school formed a nucleus for the preparatory classes at Ayer Cottage.

Much of 1888 was given to planning the college building. The Executive Committee on January 20 had invited Clinton Day, an architect in San Francisco, to visit the college grounds at an early date, "to confer with the committee and draw plans for our first college building." A month later, Day met with the committee at Sumner's home, and he and the committee studied the site. His preliminary plans were approved by the Executive Committee on April 11 and he was requested to prepare "working plans and specifications for a brick building after this model." In approving the plans with some modifications on May 11, the Board of Trustees asked the Executive Committee "to go forward with the construction as rapidly as they can secure the money to pay the bills....The names of prominent New England institutions of learning" were to be given to the streets of the College Tract.

The Executive Committee found it difficult to execute its mandate. The building was expected to cost $45,000, and few gifts were forthcoming. The laying of the cornerstone and the annual meeting of the Board of Trustees, first set for July 20, had to be postponed to September 26. By this time the foundation of the building had been prepared, largely by ranchers who had contributed their teams and labor, and a quantity of bricks sufficient for the building had been made on the site.

As the laying of the cornerstone was the first public exercise of Pomona College, the trustees sought to make the day an occasion for Congregationalists throughout Southern California, and five hundred people were in attendance. The main address was given by R. G. Hutchins, pastor of the First Congregational Church of Los Angeles, the scripture was read by Ford, and Hunt led in prayer. Palmer presided and, after stating the purpose of the college and the hopes of the trustees, he laid the cornerstone. Sumner gave the benediction. It was a humid September day that had begun with rain and "it was a test of loyalty to go out into the country and stand under the broiling sun." Happily, there was a shady place for the basket lunch that concluded the assembly.

Those who enjoyed the pleasant sociability of the occasion would have been astounded to know that they were participating in not only the first but the last meeting of Pomona College on the mesa campus. After the trustees in their annual meeting that afternoon at the Palomares Hotel in Pomona had re-elected their current officers for the following year, Hunt on behalf of four associates in real estate presented an offer to the college of the newly constructed, but unoccupied, hotel building in Claremont and certain property at that locality. A special committee of Hunt,

Laying the cornerstone

The Ayer cottage in Pomona

Bent and Blanchard was appointed to consider the matter and, in conjunction with the Executive Committee, given power to act. From their negotiations came a new and permanent course for the nascent college.

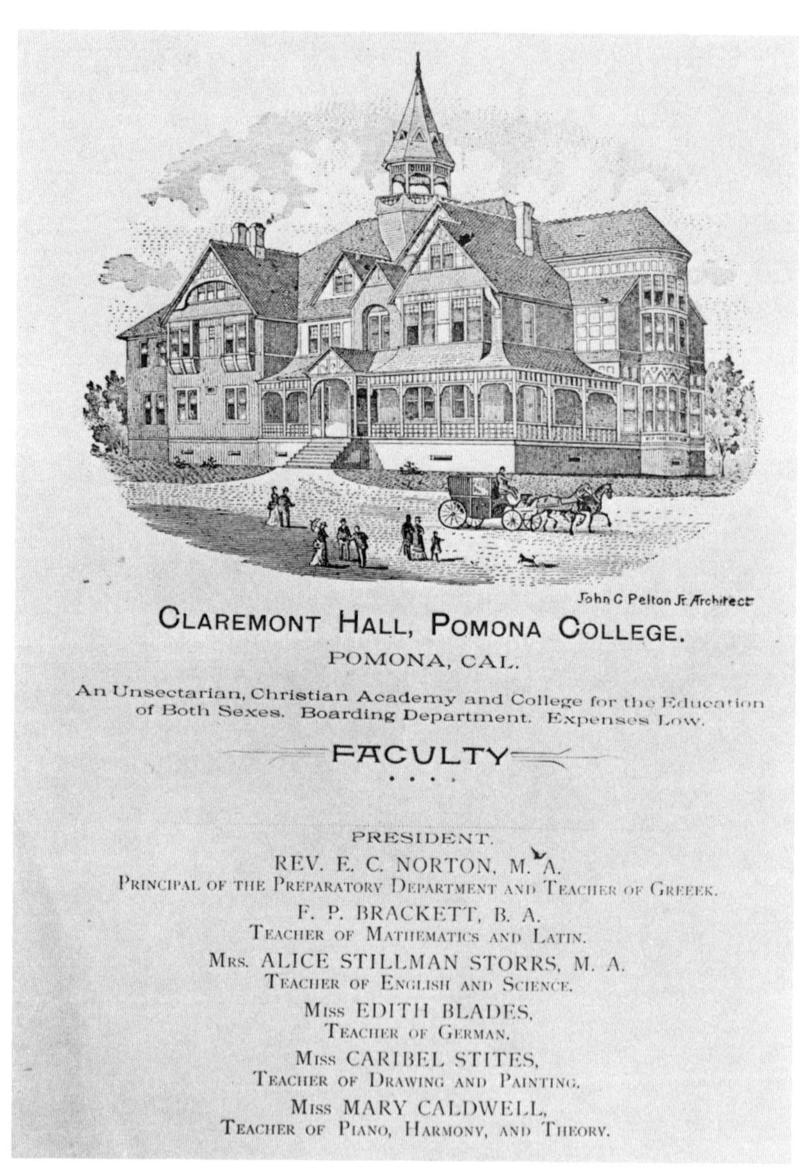

John C Pelton Jr. Architect

CLAREMONT HALL, POMONA COLLEGE.

POMONA, CAL.

An Unsectarian, Christian Academy and College for the Education of Both Sexes. Boarding Department. Expenses Low.

FACULTY

PRESIDENT.

REV. E. C. NORTON, M. A.

PRINCIPAL OF THE PREPARATORY DEPARTMENT AND TEACHER OF GREEK.

F. P. BRACKETT, B. A.

TEACHER OF MATHEMATICS AND LATIN.

MRS. ALICE STILLMAN STORRS, M. A.

TEACHER OF ENGLISH AND SCIENCE.

MISS EDITH BLADES,

TEACHER OF GERMAN.

MISS CARIBEL STITES,

TEACHER OF DRAWING AND PAINTING.

MISS MARY CALDWELL,

TEACHER OF PIANO, HARMONY, AND THEORY.

Announcement of the move to Claremont

CHAPTER II

The Move to Claremont

WHILE POMONA COLLEGE was the expression of earlier plans, Claremont was a product of the boom. It would have been difficult to find a locality more expressive, in so short a period, of the exaggerated claims of real estate agents, the height of dazzling hopes, and the collapse of frenzied speculation. Claremont was one of many townsites located along the Santa Fe Railroad, and it reflected the common pattern of such ventures. A few persons would form a company, secure options on land, and upon being assured of a railroad station, would build a hotel and a cheap house or two within their holdings. The next step was a widely advertised auction, with reduced transportation fares, a free luncheon, and band music.

In the spring of 1887, workmen were busy clearing the undergrowth and trees in preparation for streets, avenues, parks, and the grand plaza of prospective Claremont, where optimists envisaged "a large sized town" by the time the railroad from San Bernardino reached that site. A writer in the *Pomona Progress* portrayed a back country already settled with "an intelligent set of thrifty fruitgrowers" happy with a "shipping point on a transcontinental railway at their very doors," and held forth the further advantages of "the delightful trout streams of San Antonio Canyon . . . and the deep pine woods, which welcome the hunter to his big game of deer and bear." The Pacific Land Improvement Company, which was developing the townsite, eloquently described it as a place "of clear mountain air; clear mountain water; clear from malaria, frost, fogs and most of 'the ills that flesh is heir to.'" The townsite of Claremont was not laid out in proportion to such anticipations. Residential lots were generally fifty by a hundred and fifty feet, and business lots had a frontage of only twenty-five feet. One wide, north-south street, Warren Avenue, ran through the center of the townsite, and on this the Hotel Claremont had been located.

Describing their locality as "Claremont the Beautiful," the Pacific Land Improvement Company enjoyed a brief success, selling lots in an amount exceeding $80,000 and constructing the Hotel Claremont. The purchasers were generally speculators, and often resold immediately at a profit. When the boom burst in the summer of 1888, land in Claremont became of little value. The Hotel Claremont, completed but unfurnished, stood in a locality which included only the railroad station, a single farm house, and two or three small houses in the brush.

The prospects for the townsite and the college building on the Piedmont mesa were equally bleak when T. C. Hunt, on September 26, presented to the trustees the offer of the four owners of the land company to give the Hotel Claremont and its surrounding property to Pomona College. After negotiation, the college under date of October 21, 1888 entered into an agreement with Frank A. Miller, E. F. Kingman, and George H. Fullerton, all of Riverside, and H. A. Palmer of Berkeley, who was chairman of the college Board of Trustees, to transfer to Pomona College the Hotel Claremont, the block of land on which it stood, and 260 additional lots, as shown on the map of Claremont in the office of the Recorder of Los Angeles County. The college was to sell the lots at its discretion, giving one half the proceeds to the four donors until $5,000 had been paid them. By this transaction the college acquired real estate not only for the institution but also for developing a residential and business community around it.

Most significant was the commitment of the trustees to establish and maintain in the Hotel Claremont "a school, which shall be a department of the educational work for which the College is organized, or allied thereto, as a Preparatory School of the College." This agreement met the immediate need and kept open the possibility of completing the building begun on the mesa.

While conducting classes in Pomona Norton and his staff began planning for the move to Claremont. The trustees asked Sumner to

Edwin Clarence Norton and Frank Parkhurst Brackett

secure estimates of the repairs needed to make secure the foundations and roof of "the newly acquired School Building," and to insure it for $12,000. Sumner was also authorized to advertise in both the local and Eastern papers the opening of a boarding department for the term beginning in January, 1889. A four-page leaflet with an artist's sketch of the hotel, rechristened as "Claremont Hall," announced that after a "highly satisfactory and auspicious" twelve weeks in Pomona, the college was moving to Claremont, where "through the kindly interest and generosity of friends" the college would have "its own new, convenient, and commodious building, healthfully and delightfully located." "Two things are emphasized," the announcement states, "the quality of the work; the distinctly Christian character of the institution."

Claremont Hall, to which the meager possessions of the college were moved during the Christmas vacation of 1888, was in many ways well suited to the college's needs. The first floor provided recitation rooms, the assembly room and parlor, a library alcove, the dining room, kitchen, and storage rooms. On the second floor

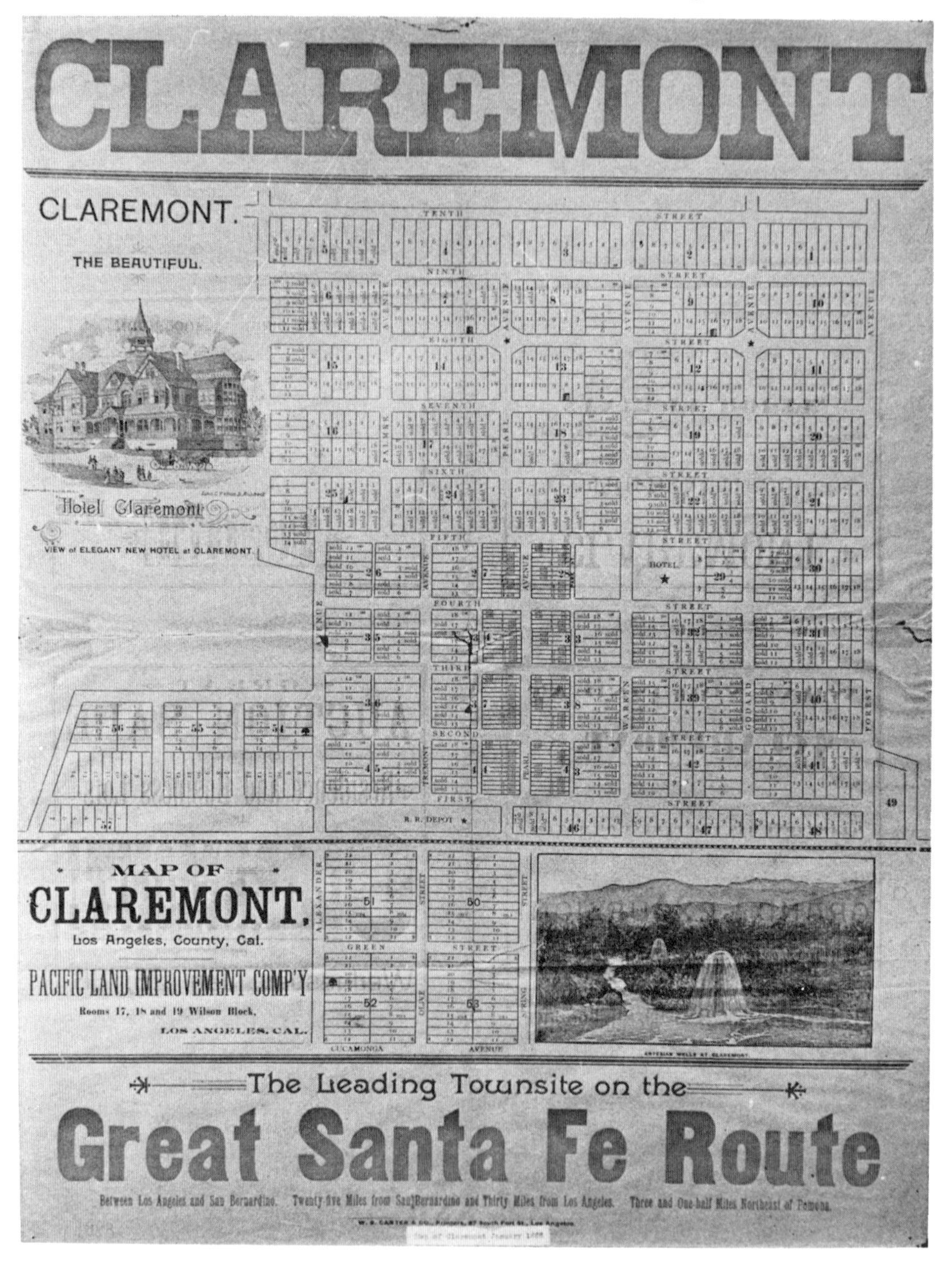

Map of Claremont

were a suite for the President, guest rooms, and rooms for resident students, the girls in the south section and the boys in the north. The Norton family and the other faculty members not only roomed in the building but took their meals in the dining hall with the students and presided over the tables. Claremont Hall was a college home and students and faculty came to cherish the close relationships they enjoyed. Led by Mrs. Sumner, the women of the faculty secured curtains and other amenities to relieve the starkness of the vacant building and a certain comfort developed amidst frugality.

The greatest inconvenience was the distance from Pomona, which was the base for supplies, the center for medical services, and the location of the church for faculty and students. Public transportation was a flat top bus with two rows of people facing each other on poorly padded seats, the conveyance drawn by two horses. The bus, which made daily morning and afternoon trips to Claremont Hall, connected at North Pomona, a Santa Fe station, with the "dummy," a one-car conveyance, half steam engine and half passenger compartment. A smoky and bumpy ride then completed the journey to Pomona.

In their first eighteen months in Claremont, Norton and his staff worked zealously to establish the school in its new home. Landscaping of Claremont Hall was much facilitated by an Arbor Day in which faculty, students, and friends joined in the planting of trees and shrubs; the long growing season of California soon provided flowers most of the year. As a sense of home and community developed, instruction progressed and enrollment increased. While the academic program was essentially that of a preparatory school, the principal and his colleagues looked to an early beginning of the collegiate department and shaped their plans to this end when choosing new faculty members. The literature of the institution was always issued under the name of "Pomona College."

Two of the faculty who came in the first year after the move to Claremont were destined, like Norton and Brackett, to give great service and the remainder of their careers to the institution. Phebe Estelle Spalding, a graduate of Carleton College where she had known Norton, was appointed "teacher of English literature, history, and modern languages," effective September 1889. In addition, she was to be in charge of the women students in Claremont Hall, where she would reside. For all these responsibilities she received an annual salary of $400 and room and board. Her teaching duties were more concentrated in 1890-91 when she became teacher of "English literature and rhetoric." In March 1890, D. H. Colcord, then pastor of the Congregational Church in Monrovia, California, was appointed to teach "Latin and the Modern Languages," at a salary of $1,100. A graduate of Amherst in 1878, where he had known Norton, he had then gone to Andover Theological Seminary, where he graduated in 1881. After a pastorate in Bedford, New Hampshire, Colcord had been called to the Monrovia church in 1887 at the height of the boom. An able scholar, a splendid speaker, a lover of people, and a man deeply loyal to the college, Colcord brought much strength to the faculty.

The earliest catalogues show how eagerly the trustees and faculty looked to beginning the college program. For example, the first catalogue, which carried the records of 1888-89 and listed the faculty for 1889-90, announced that three degrees would be offered in the collegiate department: Bachelor of Arts, in which emphasis was placed on Greek and Latin; Bachelor of Literature, for which the classics were not required; and Bachelor of Science. The second catalogue, announcing the faculty and program for 1890-91, set forth the ideal which underlay and guided the founders of the institution. "Pomona College," it states, "aims to give a regular college course simply, leaving professional training to a post-graduate school equipped for that purpose. It requires for admission a course of study substantially identical with the old academies of New England. . . . It relies upon the patronage of those who know what good work requires. It is a Christian college. Its teachers are appointed with reference to their large personal influence in the foundation of character."

To help in achieving these high purposes, the college required a president, and in the spring of 1890, the trustees sought a candidate. It went without saying that the president must be a Congregational minister, but it was hoped that a man could be secured who also would have some experience in college work. The trus-

President Cyrus Grandison Baldwin

tees found such a man and happily he was already in Los Angeles. Cyrus Grandison Baldwin, born in Napoli, New York, in 1852, had graduated from Oberlin College in 1873 and from Andover Theological Seminary in 1876. He was then called to Ripon College, in Wisconsin, where he taught Latin for nine years, and was ordained as a Congregational minister in 1881. Baldwin resigned at Ripon to become state secretary for the Young Men's Christian Association in Iowa, and four years later he relinquished this office and accepted a fund-raising position for the Y.M.C.A. in Des Moines. Successful in this undertaking, he had been called to raise funds for a Y.M.C.A. building in Los Angeles, where he came to the attention of the Pomona trustees. Baldwin's scholarly background, interest in college teaching, devotion to the church, and experience in fund-raising constituted an ideal preparation for the presidency of Pomona College.

When approached by the trustees Baldwin immediately won their confidence and respect, and a committee was appointed to consult with him and "see on what terms his services can be secured." The terms agreed upon provided a salary of $1,500 a year, full expenses for Mr. Baldwin and his family in Claremont Hall, and the travelling expenses of his office. Mrs. Baldwin, an experienced teacher and like her husband an Oberlin graduate, was employed to teach part time and to be in charge of Claremont Hall, at an annual salary of $500. President and Mrs. Baldwin, their young daughter, Florence, and Mrs. Baldwin's half-sister, Frances Billings, moved into Claremont Hall in August, taking for their apartment a suite of rooms on the second floor, made up of the large bay-window room and adjoining rooms opening off it. Thirty-two years later when the building would be moved and renovated, this area would become the president's office, and thereafter until the present the college would be administered from the rooms where the first president and his family began their life in Claremont in 1890.

The First President

With the appointment of President Baldwin interest quickened among supporters of the institution, which then moved toward becoming a college in fact as well as in name. His magnetic personality, broad human sympathies, and high ideals immediately won the loyalty of all concerned with the college. Thoroughly at home in academic life, Baldwin moved easily and congenially with members of the faculty, and he was to enjoy a close relationship with the students, many of whom held him in great affection. Equally at home in the church, he was an able and eloquent spokesman for the college among Congregationalists, both in Southern California and the East. Forgetful of self and with great faith in the future of Southern California, he was a leader who inspired confidence.

Evidence of this was shown by the enrollment in September, 1890 of a freshman college class of sixteen. These students, ten of them from the Preparatory Department, constituted a remarkable group who were to play an outstanding part in making Pomona a college, and whose distinctions after graduation would bring great honor to their alma mater.

President Baldwin was received enthusiastically by the Congregational churches of Southern California and he entered actively into their life. He attended the annual meetings of the General Congregational Association of Southern California, and preached repeatedly in the individual churches, looking to them both for students and funds for the college. As he went from church to church, preaching, staying in homes, and talking with church members, he constantly sought the required human and material resources. The General Association of Southern California consistently strengthened the President's hand. In a typical resolution it stated,

> Pomona College, the child of our begetting, lies in our hearts, claiming our tender fostering and sustaining care. . . . It is clearly and imperatively the privilege and duty of our pastors to preach or have preached in every church, each year, a sermon on Christian education in which should be fully set forth the advantages and claims of Pomona College. . . . [It] should be on the Benevolent List of every church in this Association, and once a year there should be taken for it a collection. Our Missionary Unions and Young People's Societies of Christian Endeavor should be encouraged to provide scholarships for the payment of the tuition, and for the full support of deserving students.

After 1891, such local support was to be supplemented significantly by the national organization of Congregational churches. Although the college had been founded on the assumption that the Southern California churches could finance it themselves, the collapse of the local boom and the continuation of a national depression showed that outside financial support was necessary for survival. The avenue of hope was the American College and Education Society in Boston. Originally organized in 1816 to assist young men in entering the ministry, the Society had broadened its scope to support new institutions as the frontier moved westward. The basis for the Society's efforts was its conviction that the growth of wealth and population had not been matched by educational institutions based upon the principles of Christianity.

When Pomona in 1892 received a grant of $4,000 on the condition that it raise $7,000 in matching funds, other Western colleges then being aided by the Society were Doane in Nebraska, Pacific in Oregon, Whitman in Washington, Yankton in South Dakota, and Fargo in North Dakota. The courses of instruction in these institutions were based on those in the East and most of the teachers came from Eastern institutions. Religion and learning were considered inseparable and the stated purpose of these home missionary institutions was to "bring the students under the influence of true Christian example and into the experience of a true Christian life." While the normal matching grant for a college came to be $5,000, larger appropriations were occasionally available. *The Congregational Year Book* listed Pomona as a continuing recipient of aid from the Society from 1892 through 1901, and the Society and its officers played a large role in the college over those years.

In addition to its more general problems the college was handicapped in seeking financial aid by the continuing uncertainty of its permanent location. While work on the brick building on the Scanlon mesa had ceased with the move to Claremont, the property on the mesa was retained and still envisaged as the ultimate site of the College Department. The Preparatory Department would then remain in Claremont Hall. However, doubts about this plan were voiced even before instruction had begun in Claremont. On September 1, 1890, the faculty officially asked the trustees about "the advisability of planning for the erection of new buildings in Claremont," and on September 16, the trustees appointed a committee to consider the matter. The catalogue of 1890-91 announced that the most pressing need of the college was a recitation building which, fully equipped, would cost about $20,000, saying that "a memorial building would be a fitting gift from a Christian man or woman to a Christian College."

As if this appeal had been made to them directly, Mrs. S. B. Holmes and Miss Esther R. Holmes, the widow and daughter of the late Cyrus W. Holmes, Jr., of Monson, Massachusetts, offered in October 1891 to give $25,000 in annual payments of not less than $5,000 for a building in his memory. But the donors had in mind the completion of the building on the mesa and the installation of the College Department there. The gift had been secured by Sumner, who retained a warm friendship with the Holmes family from the years when he was their pastor in Monson, and the trustees asked him to ascertain if the donors would modify their proposal and leave the date for removal of the College Department to the discretion of the Board of Trustees.

The prospect of a new building forced a fundamental discussion, and led to one of the most important decisions in the history of Pomona College. The issue was decided at a trustee meeting on April 13, 1892. The question as posed in the Board of Trustees was whether the Preparatory Department and the College Department would be in separate locations. In a vigorous debate, Sumner argued for separation and for locating the College Department on the Scanlon mesa, while Baldwin and McLean spoke for union and location in Claremont. After the debate, the trustees voted, seven to four, to establish "the permanent location of the Preparatory and College Departments of Pomona College in the same place." Then with no one opposing, the Board voted "that the College remain permanently at Claremont." These actions determined that Claremont would be an academic community, and opened the way for developments of unprecedented magnitude in the years ahead.

For the moment, practical questions of human cooperation and institutional reorganization precluded great dreams of the future. The Holmes family generously conformed to the decision of the trustees to build in Claremont and made their gift available accordingly. The trustees also had to face the consequences of their decision *not* to build on the Scanlon mesa, and this they did forthrightly. By a formal vote on July 12, 1892, the property there was returned to H. A. Palmer. Others who had made donations of any kind with the expectation of location of the institution on the mesa were offered the return of their property or the cancellation of their pledges. This delicate and arduous work fell to Sumner who performed it in masterful fashion. Although he had been disappointed by the decision to maintain the institution permanently in Claremont, he accepted the decision in fine spirit, giving his full energy and thought to the tasks at hand and, in his liquidation of the undertaking on the mesa, earned added respect for the integrity of the college.

Meanwhile preparations went forward for the recitation building in Claremont. On June 14, 1892, the Board appointed Chairman Bent and Sumner as a committee to canvass plans and details "pertaining to the erection of a college recitation building." C. H. Brown was engaged as architect, and when the plans were ready the committee advertised for bids. John Hanlon, the lowest of the four bidders, was awarded the contract for $22,400 on July 12, 1892. As brick would be too expensive, redwood had been chosen as the material for the building. Sumner, Bent, and Baldwin were named as a building committee and authorized to make any needed changes "provided the whole cost of the building and fixtures does not exceed $25,000." Construction moved ahead and the building was ready for occupancy in January 1893.

Later generations can only faintly imagine what this first classroom building meant to the faculty and students of the young college. Cyrus W. Holmes, Jr., Hall, as first constructed, was a two-story building with a basement, and a chapel wing attached on the northeast. The basement contained a chemical laboratory and the hot water heating system, and each of the two floors contained seven recitation rooms and two offices. The chapel had a seating capacity of 300. Light was from kerosene lamps. Furnishings for the hall were secured by solicitation, and long to be remembered would be the bell placed in the tower. The building was placed on the east side of Warren Avenue just north of Claremont Hall, with its main entrance from the south. Two tall palms continue to mark this early approach to Holmes.

The dedication of Holmes Hall on January 27, 1893 was a joyous event of great promise. Despite heavy rain, large numbers of guests came from Los Angeles, Riverside, Ontario, and Pomona, and the chapel was filled for the exercises. The main address was given by the Reverend C. O. Brown of San Francisco, Sumner presented the building on behalf of the donors, and Henry Kirke White Bent received the keys for the trustees. The faculty had arranged for "a collation to be served at 12:30" at which the Reverend Hutchins of Los Angeles acted as toastmaster. Brief luncheon talks, "Now the Auspicious Moment for a College in Southern California" by President Baldwin, "Our Plan" by Professor Norton, "The Ladies' Department" by Professor Colcord, "The Conservancy of Music" by Professor Bissell, and "The Library" by Miss Spalding, gave the hopes and aims of the faculty. In the minds and hearts of all present that day Pomona College had moved from the provisional to the permanent.

Warren Avenue with Sumner and Holmes Halls, 1893-94

Sumner Hall in 1894

The completion of Holmes Hall brought a new stage in the role of Claremont Hall in the life of the college. Class work was discontinued there, and the building became the residence hall for young ladies and the dining room for all the students. The reorganization of its uses was also accompanied by a change of name. The Board of Trustees on May 10, 1893 rechristened the building as Mary L. Sumner Hall in honor of the wife of Charles Burt Sumner. In a resolution expressing its indebtedness for the great work of Mr. Sumner, the Board of Trustees stated its appreciation for "the valuable services of his beloved wife, whose sympathy and earnest cooperation in all his efforts have been a constant support and inspiration. . . . We would perpetuate the name and memory of this noble woman and trust that they may be an inspiration to the young women who from generation to generation shall occupy our Ladies Hall." This recognition of Mrs. Sumner, who had been an invalid for some time, came shortly before her death. She had been indeed a leader among the heroic women who supported their husbands so valiantly in the difficult early years of Pomona College.

With the growth in enrollment and with faith in the permanency of the college, organizational forms of the faculty and the student body began to emerge. While for many years the enrollment of the Preparatory Department would exceed that of the College Department, important steps emphasized the college concept. Norton, Principal of the Preparatory Department, who on June 19, 1890 had been elected also "professor of the Greek Language and Literature in Pomona College," resigned as principal on May 10, 1893 and was elected that day to the newly created office of "Dean of the College Department." Henceforth in his long career at Pomona, "Greek" and "the Dean" would be synonyms for "Norton." Brackett had been elected professor of mathematics on June 19, 1890. Charles Burt Sumner, trustee and secretary of the Board and sometime "Financial Agent," was elected professor of Biblical Literature on July 8, 1890, a cherished position for which unfortunately the financial exigencies of the college and his duty as a trustee would leave him very limited time. Miss Spalding was elected professor of English Literature on April 13, 1892.

"The Old Guard," top row, left to right: Daniel H. Colcord, Frank A. Bissell, George G. Hitchcock, George S. Sumner '94; bottom row: C. B. Sumner, Edwin C. Norton, Frank P. Brackett, Phebe Estelle Spalding

Two other members of the faculty who were to give the remainder of their careers to Pomona were appointed in 1892: Arthur Dart Bissell as professor of Modern Languages, and George Gale Hitchcock, as professor of Physics and Chemistry. Bissell, born of missionary parents in India, had graduated from Amherst with Norton in 1879; taking an M.A. at Amherst he had gone to Yale where he graduated from the Theological Seminary in 1882. After teaching some years in Hawaii, he had come to California shortly before his appointment at Pomona. In the beginning, Bissell was asked to give one-fourth of his time to music, a field in which he was gifted and through which he was to make a lasting contribution to the musical tradition of the college. Hitchcock, a graduate of the University of Nebraska in 1883, with graduate work at Johns Hopkins and Cornell, was called to Pomona from the Agricultural College of the State of Washington. A grandson of the Reverend Gale who founded Knox College and the son of a professor at that institution, Hitchcock had grown up in the tradition of the church-related college. The coming of Bissell and Hitchcock brought both new areas of instruction and the devotion of two men who would build themselves into the life of the college and the community.

As Pomona acquired strength and experience in its faculty and student body, expanding responsibilities required greater and more continuous concern on the part of the trustees. The Board, which had been organized in the great optimism of 1887, was not prepared for the arduous task that the founding of a college in Southern California proved to be. The collapse of the boom was disastrous for many supporters of the college, particularly for H. A. Palmer, president of the Board and the college's major donor, who suffered such overwhelming financial reverses that he could no longer assist the institution and in 1892 felt compelled to resign as a trustee. Palmer's services would not be forgotten, for as the trustees resolved, "his generosity made the genesis of the college possible." Moreover, his experience on other boards of trust, his knowledge of parliamentary procedure, and his ability to draft legal papers had made him an exceptionally able president of the Board. Happily, in later years he improved his financial position, and lived to see at the college the fruition of his early labors. Palmer was succeeded by Henry Kirke White Bent, whose devotion led him to give time not only to the consideration of policy, but also to the details of finance. He and Sumner were a hard working and compatible team, setting an example for others. Supported by Blanchard, the vice president and the most prosperous trustee, Bent and Sumner educated their associates in the organization and functioning of a college board.

With the appointment of Baldwin, the trustees established their relation to the "President of the Faculty," a title designed to separate his functions from those of the "President of the Board of Trustees." Although Baldwin attended most trustee meetings, he was not a member of the Board and there does not seem to have been any consideration of electing him. The relationship of the President of the Faculty and the Board throughout Baldwin's administration was determined by the trustee action of July 15, 1891, "that the President of the Faculty be and is hereby invited to sit with the Board of Trustees at all its meetings and upon all questions to be accorded the privilege of participating in debate." There is no evidence that Baldwin was ever invited to cast a vote.

In Baldwin's first year the trustees addressed themselves to the formulation and adoption of a college seal. As the seal would epitomize the purpose and outlook of the institution, it received long and careful attention, first by a special committee and then in sessions of the Board on April 14 and July 15, 1891. For the founding date the trustees used "1888", the year classes began, and this remained on the seal until the Board, on April 10, 1913 voted to substitute "1887", the year of incorporation. In placing the words "Pomona College, Our Tribute to Christian Civilization" on the seal the trustees expressed their faith and their ideal. They hoped to make Pomona College an example of the best of which men and women were capable. "Christian Civilization" was not a restrictive ideal but the most comprehensive term the founders could conceive. They would have understood well "the quest for truth" and "the pursuit of excellence" which were to animate later generations.

To place their concept of the college and its needs before its constituency, the Pomona trustees arranged an Educational Convention of the Congregational Churches of Southern California in

Los Angeles on April 13-14, 1892. The response was excellent and thirty-six churches were represented. The papers presented at the convention were published in a 128-page pamphlet and widely distributed with "Compliments of Pomona College." Nowhere else is the thinking about the college in its early years so cogently set forth. "The object of the Convention was to confer together early in the history of the College, that the best ideas of the constituency might reach the ears of the Board of Trustees." In his address, "The Building of a Christian College," trustee John Knox McLean held a high standard before his fellow trustees and fellow pastors. "If we are going to enter the educational field with any hope at all, we must be prepared, as regards at least the quality of our equipment, to stand comparison with other institutions. . . . The Christian college of tomorrow must be thoroughly a college."

President Baldwin, in an address entitled "The Christian College We Are Undertaking" recognized that Pomona College

> by force of circumstances is a Christian Academy and Christian College combined. It is not intended to cover more than seven years from the beginning Latin. It does not propose to make university provision through advanced electives for those who wish to begin in part their graduate courses at the close of the sophomore year, but to give a full general course of undergraduate study in Literature, Philosophy and Science. It believes that these seven years of general work constitute a worthy preparation for special studies in professional lines of the universities.

Speaking on "The Student Material For College Building" Dean Norton told the churchmen that the tone of the student body would determine the nature of the college, and he besought their support. "In these days of beginnings," he urged, "you, pastors, are largely responsible for the students we receive or fail to receive."

The spirit of the pastors and of the meeting was expressed by the Reverend E. R. Brainerd of Mentone: "Let us be especially loyal to Pomona College, the child of our prayers and earnest desires and worthy of our fondest hopes. Let us make her the Yale of the West, sending forth her great men to dominate the land." In a closing resolution the convention offered its full support, approving "the faith of the Board of Trustees of Pomona College in going forward in the face of financial depression to carry out a plan of a college of the highest grade," and recommending that the members of the churches support the college "in sums from twenty-five cents to one hundred dollars" thereby enabling children to add their names "to the roll of the builders of Pomona College."

Campus Life In The Nineties

Faculty minutes, which are extant from January 2, 1890 to the present, give a revealing picture of those early days. The meetings were held weekly and always began with prayer by one of the members. Norton presided until the election of Baldwin, and thereafter when the president was absent; Miss Spalding was the first secretary. Business was handled very democratically and in many ways the faculty served as a committee of the whole. A favorite device was the referring of a matter, after discussion, to a "committee" of one person, with curricular questions and student conduct claiming most attention. Matters from President Baldwin's first meeting included "the appointment of Professor Sumner to secure a repair of the college hack for the Sunday use of teachers and students," the decision to seek "arrangements with the Santa Fe R.R. for cheap conveyance of students during the week," arrangements for a study hall for boys under Norton, and one for girls under Miss Spalding, fixing "the tardy limit for classes at three minutes," and authorization to President Baldwin "to arrange for College stationery, the amount to be determined in a measure by the expense." In developing the college catalogue in 1890-91 the faculty instituted the helpful and since continued practice of placing the date of appointment after the name of the individual faculty member. For the prize debate at the end of 1891-92 the topic selected by the faculty was: "Should the government own the railroads and telegraph?" Professor Colcord was appointed to aid the freshman class in their decoration of the Methodist Church, in Pomona, for the closing exercises in June 1892. Significant were the pleas of the Preparatory Department and the College Department regarding "the necessity of owning individually a dictionary."

The early regulations for student conduct reflected both the spirit of the times and also the fact that most of the students were of high school age. "A lengthy discussion regarding the association of ladies and gentlemen at the College" occupied much of the time of the faculty meeting on October 17, 1890. Townspeople who asked permission to give parties for students were to be informed by the Lady Principal "that 10 o'clock is the hour limit for evening entertainment." For some years after 1891-92, the college set forth in the catalogue its policy on cards and tobacco:

> To secure the best results, it has been deemed wise to forbid card playing and the use of tobacco. Any student finding upon trial that he can not give up these indulgences will, upon such statement to the faculty, receive an honorable dismissal. Those who indulge in these practices wilfully and persistently will be dismissed from school.

While students were expelled for offenses, the faculty and the dean, who dealt with them in disciplinary cases, endeavored to save students by admonition and probation. When these failed, the student, by faculty action "was placed on the last course of discipline," in which the records indicate many were saved. The sanctity of Sunday was respected, and in order to free that day from work and for worship classes were held on Saturdays. Mondays were holidays. The students took pleasure in December 1889 in observing that "Pomona ranks with Carleton and and Wellesley in having Monday as a holiday . . . Tuesday's lessons are well prepared and the temptation to study Sunday is removed." With regard for the Sabbath, the faculty in October 1892 voted "that the Sunday daily paper should not be delivered until Monday morning."

Life was not as stern, however, as the college regulations indicated. Informal occasions provided pleasant entertainment, and from a Hallowe'en party came the refrain that would be the basis for Pomona's most noted song. In the summer of 1890 Professor Brackett and David Barrows, who had just graduated from the preparatory department, attended a fiesta of the Coahuilla Indians in the San Jacinto mountains. There late at night they watched the ancient war dance of the Coahuillas and heard its haunting refrain, "He-ne-terra-toma, he-ne-terra-toma." Later Barrows gave an exhibition of the dance as a stunt at a Hallowe'en party. As Brackett tells us, "the air caught, and all went out singing it." In 1896 Frances Fulkerson wrote the verses and Professor Bissell composed the music for a song entitled *Ghost Dance.* Years later a new

The Ghost Dance 1896

arrangement and new words transformed *Ghost Dance* into *Torchbearers,* Pomona's most cherished song.

Student publications and institutions developed in the early years in Claremont were to have a permanent influence. The first publication was *The Pomona Student,* a monthly begun in October 1889 and sponsored by the two literary societies. The first editor of *The Pomona Student* was David Prescott Barrows, then a senior in the Preparatory Department, who in news matter and editorials in these early years gave evidence of the intellectual vigor which would make him one of the great Californians of the twentieth century. Editorially, *The Pomona Student* called for the organization of an oratorical association, the development of the library, and work to beautify the grounds, reminding its readers that in this formative period their "bearing and scholarship" would "determine to an alarming extent the character and consequently the reputation of Pomona for years to come." In its first year *The Pomona Student* urged the formation of a glee club, and was rewarded by the establishment of a men's glee club in 1891, which soon took the name of Pomona to many audiences in California. Fifteen concerts in cities from San Diego to Santa Barbara were given in 1892-93, and the following year the concert tour was extended as far north as San Francisco.

In this spirit, and by Baldwin's and Sumner's efforts, funds were provided to meet the needs of the early Nineties, and life on the campus reflected growing strength and confidence. *The Pomona Student* published annual issues with illustrated records of the year in the springs of 1892 and 1893. In the latter, the editors called upon the junior class, "as in colleges of long experience," to assume the financial and editorial responsibility for producing a college annual. In the spirit of this appeal, *The Pomona Student* itself expanded from a four-page to a twelve-page monthly and changed its name to *The Student Life,* with its first number for 1893-94.

The juniors responded by publishing *Speculum,* the first Pomona College annual, in the spring of 1894. The book was dedicated to Professor Brackett, and there was a three-page tribute to President Baldwin.

Speculum presented a valuable record and interpretation of the

The Glee Club 1896-97

college in its fourth year in Claremont. It showed the development of class spirit and the emergence of classes as the major social organizations within the student body. The Glee Club's trips were hailed proudly as a field in which "Pomona College has held her own with Berkeley and Stanford." Other functioning student organizations were the Y.M.C.A., a science club, a social science club, and an oratorical association. Above all, *Speculum* celebrated Pomona's coming of age with the graduation of its first class. It hailed the great class of '94, which was as famous to the students of that day as it later came to be among the alumni.

Early in 1893-94 the faculty had begun to look forward to the graduation of Pomona's first College class. The revered term "Commencement," never before used for the closing exercises at Pomona, first appeared in the faculty minutes of October 13, 1893. The desirable form for diplomas was discussed and on April 10 the faculty voted that the diplomas be written in Latin. The faculty considered and denied a petition from the seniors "that a speaker from abroad be substituted for the proposed orations of the members of the class." Professor Colcord was named General Director of the Commencement. The date chosen, June 27, was some weeks later than that of both Stanford and the University of California, and *The Student Life* noted that "Pomona will hold on until the last blast is blown."

In the historic exercises ten degrees were awarded and an eleventh was held over for a month until the student could complete certain tests. The Bachelor of Arts degree was conferred on seven students, the Bachelor of Letters on two, and the Bachelor of Science degree on one. The strength of the class and its significance within the college inspired an editorial, "The Hole That Confronts Us," in *The Student Life:* "We have at last to fairly confront and estimate the overpowering cavity which is to be left in us by the graduation of the Class of '94. Ever since there has been a Pomona College, there has been a class of '94. It was the foundation of the student body, and we are sorry to say it now, it has always remained so much a foundation that its removal makes us particularly apprehensive."

In the years immediately after this first commencement, there was notable development of student institutions and activities. The annual became a permanent record of college life, and its name was changed from *Speculum* to *Metate.* Upon discovering that *Speculum* was a title used by at least two other colleges, the juniors in 1895 sought a name "as distinctive as possible and one that would not be duplicated." "We have adopted the name *Metate,*" the class reported, "after thorough discussion and assurances from '97 and '98 that they would continue the name. *Metate* is an Indian word meaning mortar or grinding stone. It has accordingly been our effort to grind up and get into mentally digestible condition, the year's doings."

The dedications of the *Metates* of 1895 and 1896 to faculty members, and that of 1897 to the class of 1895, reveal much of the sense of community which characterized the college of the late Nineties. Professor Hitchcock in 1895 was acclaimed as "the man to whom we owe all respect for his ability, and admire because he is unassuming; the man who is never out of patience." The *Metate* in 1896 hailed Norton as "The other Patriarch of Pomona College;

the man who teaches Greek and guides the Prep into paths of peace and prosperity; the man of the pink carnation and the twinkling eye; the man who knows how to puncture inflated knowledge, and to pick up lagging energy; the best feared and best loved, the Dean of the Faculty." The following quatrain in the succeeding *Metate* gives a lighter insight into Dean Norton's life and work in and around Sumner and Holmes Halls:

> 'My gait is just the thing I want,
> 'Tis very smooth and gliding.
> I sneak around and spy out sin
> No matter where it's hiding.'

The Class of '95 is also to be remembered in Pomona history for preserving on the permanent campus of the college a reminder of the building projected for the Scanlon mesa. To mark their Class Day, '95 secured the neglected red sandstone cornerstone of the abandoned structure. In secret the class polished the stone, trimmed its edges, and prepared it for erection on a pedestal of seven stones, one for each member of the class. Upon the cornerstone they carved their class numerals, and in Greek, the class motto: which in translation reads "Not to live but to live well." Beneath the stone were placed duplicates of some of the papers that were laid under the stone originally in 1888. As "the clandestine movements of the class had aroused an intense curiosity among Preps and Faculty, a large number on Class Day gathered to witness the unveiling." Placed across the street from Sumner Hall and on a site south of the later Carnegie Library, this stone has carried to subsequent generations a sense of Pomona's beginnings.

Much of campus life and thought centered in the Pomona College Literary Society, which after the completion of Holmes Hall enjoyed its own rooms in that building. Coeducational and meeting fortnightly, the society was in the tradition of the literary societies of New England, the Middle West, and the South, which fostered study of current political, economic, and social issues, oratory, debating, and parliamentary procedure, and maintained libraries at times more significant than the official institutional ones. Except for the extent of its library, the Pomona Literary Society followed the customary interests of literary societies elsewhere.

Public speaking was encouraged by the Oratorical Association and the Debating Club, organized during 1894-95. The two organizations played major roles in the creation of the intercollegiate community that took form in Southern California by the mid-Nineties among Pomona, the University of Southern California, and Occidental College. The annual Southern California Intercollegiate Oratorical Contest conducted by an Oratorical Association of the three student bodies aroused tremendous interest. Each institution was represented by a single entrant who had been chosen by arduous campus competition prior to the big intercollegiate meeting. These contests were great occasions for students. Pomona, for example, had an excursion train to Los Angeles in May 1895, for the fourth annual Oratorical Contest. Defeated as before, Pomona took consolation in the fact that she had "never been disgraced." But victory came in '96 when Edwin F. Hahn, a sophomore, later to be a distinguished judge and a Pomona trustee, triumphed impressively with his oration, "Anglo-Saxon Freedom." When the result was announced, the cheering Pomona section sang the college hymn, "How Firm a Foundation." As the *Metate* recorded, "Every loyal son and daughter was thrilled to his very capillaries and expressed his patriotism by every method known to psychology." Rarely has a Pomona student been so lionized on the campus. The college gave him a reception in Sumner Hall, *The Student Life* saluted him in an editorial, and his class honored him with "one of the neatest and prettiest receptions of the season."

Enthusiasm and support for intercollegiate contests were shown by wearing the blue and white colors, which in 1893-94 replaced the earlier orange and green and were soon established as the traditional colors of the college. The blue was the "Yale blue," emphasizing the role of Yale men in founding Pomona. The colors and the college pins which appeared at the same time were first worn at an athletic event and were soon featured at all intercollegiate contests.

The Nineties were a period when the American college and university discovered the appeal of intercollegiate athletics, and Pomona was early caught up in this enthusiasm for sports. The

The Athletic Team 1896-97

The Football Team 1897-98

catalogue of 1891-92, in a section entitled "College Athletics," affirmed that "the officers of the institution are heartily in favor of outdoor sports." After the move to Claremont, the students organized an athletic association which managed and financed their sports activities. Although voluntary, the membership by 1892-93 included "nearly all the students and faculty and many outside friends." The trustees set aside ground for a permanent field and provided a building for dressing rooms and baths. The first intercollegiate competitions were field days, now known as track meets, and Pomona enjoyed much success in these contests. Special trains were arranged when the meets were held in Los Angeles. As in oratory and debate, athletic competition was primarily among U.S.C., Occidental, and Pomona.

The greatest athletic change in the late Nineties was the development of football, which after some difficulty found a firm place in American colleges. It was not played at Pomona until the autumn of 1895, as it was felt to be too hazardous. This objection was so strong that the game was not resumed in 1896, but after its revival in 1897 it became a permanent part of Pomona's sports program. While the early teams included players from both the preparatory and the college departments and games were often played with high schools, spirited intercollegiate rivalry developed very quickly with U.S.C. and Occidental. The first game with Occidental, played in 1895 and lost 16 to 0, was characterized as "a very clean game, and one in which no substitutes were required for either team." The first game with U.S.C. was played in 1897 and Pomona lost 6 to 0. Acting on the suggestion of Roger S. Day '94, then a graduate student at Yale, Pomona in 1896-97 adopted from Yale the practice of awarding to anyone who had succeeded in "making the team for a championship game of football or baseball, or had won a first place on an intercollegiate field day, or had won a tennis tournament, the privilege of wearing a letter 'P' on his sweater and shirt."

The broadest intercollegiate outreach in the Nineties came through the Young Men's Christian Association, which not only brought Southern California institutions together but linked their students with other students throughout the United States and overseas. At summer conferences, national leaders portrayed the vast opportunities for unselfish service that awaited the American graduate. The Student Volunteer Movement, which sought to evangelize the world and win it for Christianity in a generation, began in the 1890's to exercise a profound influence on most American campuses. A "Student Volunteer Band for Foreign Missions" was organized at Pomona as early as 1892, and its first activity was to subscribe seventy-five dollars for Armenian relief. The Band pursued a definite line of study each term, such as medical missions, the lives of missionaries, and the history of the American Board of Foreign Missions. At a ten-day conference in May 1896 at Cazadero in the redwoods north of San Francisco, Sherwood Eddy, Yale '91, captivated the two Pomona delegates as he was to inspire thousands of others in an illustrious career then just beginning. In the spring of 1897 Pomona students raised one hundred dollars for missionary work in China.

Most significant in intercollegiate relations were the achievements of Pomona alumni in the great graduate schools of the nation, and the sharing of their experiences with faculty and students in Claremont. Of the class of '94, six of the seven men and two of the four women went to graduate school. Three men of '94 took Ph.D.'s, one at Yale, one at Harvard, and one at Chicago. These earliest Pomona graduates were generally required to take a further undergraduate year at the university where they had been admitted and thereby to receive a second bachelor's degree. George S. Sumner '94, who took a Ph.D. in history at Yale in '97, was fond of recalling that after he was elected to Phi Beta Kappa at the end of his first year there, Yale required no later Pomona graduate to validate his B.A. David Prescott Barrows performed a similar service at the University of California.

These alumni were especially interested in the Pomona Alumni Association which was formed at the commencement of 1895. Seventeen members were enrolled and Arthur V. Stoughton '95, a future distinguished physician, was elected president. The strength of institutional loyalty was shown by the formal vote that "all class distinctions were obliterated forever" and graduates "stood together as pledged comrades in the support of our Alma

Mater." The college officers welcomed the Alumni Association by printing the names of alumni and their addresses in the catalogue for 1895-96 and continued the practice for some years.

Tennis 1897-98

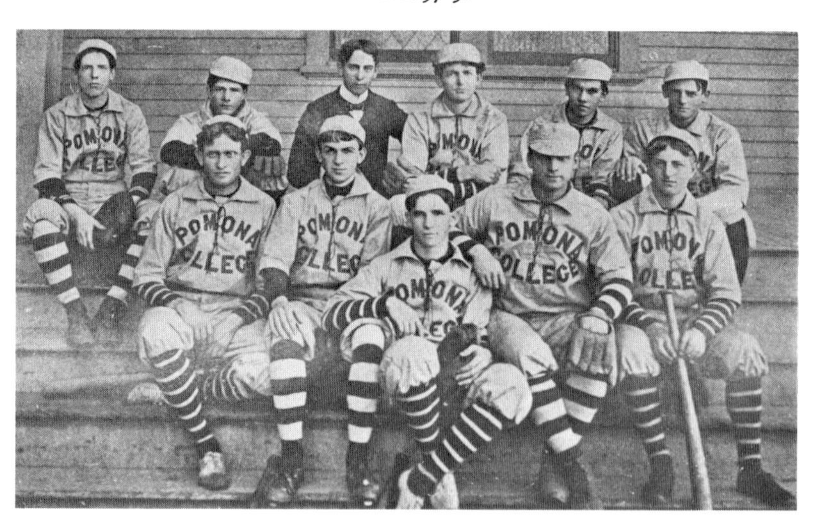

Baseball 1898

CHAPTER III

Years of Crisis, 1894-97

IN ADDITION to his solicitation of western Congregationalists and his work with the Congregational Education Society in Boston, President Baldwin undertook an enterprise unique in college financing, and one which allowed his lively imagination full play. Exploring the San Gabriel Mountains and picnicking there with his family and friends, he discovered in San Antonio Canyon the spot where the Hogsback made a natural dam and produced a lovely waterfall. Baldwin had some knowledge of the growing use of electric power in Europe and the eastern United States, and he thought of lighting the Pomona Valley and the area as far away as San Bernardino by electricity generated from the water power of the canyon. He felt that if a company could be formed to achieve this, with the college participating in the profits, a significant advance would be made in financing Pomona. He reported his enthusiasm to the trustees who by vote on April 14, 1891 approved his plan and urged him "to press the matter to conclusion as rapidly as possible."

For several years Baldwin gave much of his time to this effort. The San Antonio Light and Power Company was organized in 1891, a steep flume was established with a drop of nearly 400 feet to the power house constructed below and the Westinghouse Company in Pittsburgh was persuaded to design and manufacture the necessary generating equipment. The result exceeded expectations both technically and in the low cost of water power.[1]

[1]This historic achievement was honored and its record preserved for posterity on May 7, 1955 in a joint ceremony of the California State Park Commission, the Historical Society of Pomona Valley, Pomona College, Westinghouse Electric Corporation, Los Angeles County, and the California Division of Beaches and

The installation and the process were sound, but unfortunately the water power proved undependable. For four years the snows and the rains were not adequate. "Alas for our hopes!" wrote Baldwin. "The water dropped as low as 230 miner's inches two years ago [he had confidently counted on 1,000] and considerably lower this last year! A steam plant added to the investment, and fuel expenses have eaten up profits." Ultimately the plant and its lines were sold to the San Gabriel Electric Company, which incorporated them permanently into the service of the Pomona Valley, where they constitute today a part of the system of the Southern California Edison Company.

Baldwin had designed a plan by which the college, while not investing itself, could be supported by the San Antonio Light and Power Company. The capital stock of $60,000 was to be sold to the public with the stated understanding that the college would share permanently in the corporation's profits. The stock was preferred and would pay ten per cent annually to its holders. Funds needed beyond the original capital were to be secured through first mortgage bonds. The prospectus stated that, after the expense of operation, interest on the bonds, and the ten per cent dividend to the stockholders, the college would receive one half of "the net surplus to be distributed," which was expected to provide "a considerable income."

The failure of the San Antonio Light and Power Company to meet Baldwin's optimistic hopes was a serious blow to Pomona and to its president.[2] Inevitably the college was criticized and those who lost money in the enterprise were bitter in their disappointment. For Baldwin the failure led to more than personal discour-

---

Parks, culminating in the dedication of an official California Historical Landmark, entitled "Pomona Water Power Plant," which states: "The first hydro-electric installation in California for long distance transmission of alternating current at high voltage was built in 1892 on San Antonio Creek below this spot by the San Antonio Light and Power Company organized by Dr. Cyrus Grandison Baldwin, President of Pomona College. The first high voltage transformers built by George Westinghouse for this installation provided for 10,000 volt transmission of electric service from this plant to Pomona."

[2]While Baldwin failed in his attrempt to endow Pomona through electric power, it is interesting to note that the Duke Trust, established in 1924, made electric power a large source of support for Duke University and the other institutions of higher education which the Trust assists in North and South Carolina.

agement, for first among the trustees, and then among the faculty, there arose serious doubts about his managerial and financial ability. Henceforth, he would be handicapped by a growing lack of confidence in his leadership. This was extremely grave for the college which faced a financial crisis at the end of the academic year 1893-94.

Financial expedients that merely held off a greater crisis were undertaken. When the trustees were unable to meet the salaries of most of the faculty for 1892-93, the individual members were given college notes for two years, beginning July 1, 1893, and bearing ten per cent interest. Illustrative of the crisis were the amounts owed the major members of the faculty: Baldwin, $2,050.78; Norton, $1,388.40; Brackett, $1,178.45; Colcord, $1,114.61; Sumner, $1,539.58; Hitchcock, $725.23; and Bissell, $518.75. For the first five of these, the notes represented essentially a full year's salary. Had not the Claremont of those days been in a semi-subsistence economy in which every family kept a cow and chickens and grew its vegetables and fruit, faculty families could not have remained. Fortunately, the banks made loans on the notes, and a few of the faculty, particularly Baldwin and Sumner, had independent personal resources. The constant financial difficulties and needs of the college also presented major personal problems for the trustees, some of whom had individually signed college notes at the banks. For example, on December 11, 1894 the members of the Executive Committee of the Board signed notes of $500 each with the People's Bank of Pomona

> with the understanding that if the Committee are not joined in this security by the other members of the Board before January 1st, some other provision must be made by the Board of Trustees to relieve us of the responsibility, and further that the credit, so created by the Committee shall not exceed its proportion of the whole credit sought to be established, viz. — $6,000.

As many of the trustees had quite limited resources, men of property, such as Blanchard, were in danger of having to meet personally the financial obligations of the college.

Feverish efforts were undertaken in the summer of 1894. The crisis was so severe that Baldwin went East in June and did not return for the college's first commencement. He reported to the trustees in a meeting in Holmes Hall on July 20 a pledge of $2,000 from his father in Dayton, Ohio, and an additional gift of $5,000 from the Congregational Education Society, stating that these two gifts would cover the total deficit for the year 1893-94. In a resolution of thanks to Baldwin, the trustees received the good news "as a gracious answer to prayer and a great deliverance." Shortly thereafter, Sumner "on account of ill health and pressure of other duties" asked to be relieved as Financial Secretary and Baldwin was requested to assume this responsibility. Sumner went East to recuperate and the trustees expressed the hope he could raise $5,000 there "where he is widely and most favorably known." The trustees, at the same time, looked to Baldwin to raise $9,000 on the Pacific Coast.

The situation was not alleviated when college reconvened in September, and it reached a traumatic crisis before the end of 1894-95. The need for attracting students was as acute as that for gaining funds, and in October "the work of securing new students for the coming year" was placed first in Baldwin's hands, and then in the hands of the members of the faculty. By a formal resolution in December the Board asked that Baldwin be relieved "of every duty, care and responsibility respecting the working of the College at Claremont inconsistent with the work of raising $5,000 for current expenses from California," of which $4,500 was expected to come from Southern California. Baldwin was to go successively to the different churches and "to stay with them until he has secured, in cash or legal subscription all the assistance that can be reasonably expected from these communities." At the same time, the trustees requested the pastors of the Congregational Churches in Southern California "to set apart one Sunday morning service to be occupied by President Baldwin in presenting the claim of the College upon the Churches for financial aid and patronage."

The financial state of the college continued to be so precarious that the trustees at their meeting in Holmes Hall on January 22, 1895, after a very serious discussion, set up a committee of three, one of whom should be George W. Marston, "to make a thorough canvass of the affairs of the College, financial and otherwise and report any needed changes." This meeting was the point at which Marston began to take a major role on the Board. In the previous four years he had been little in attendance, and once had offered his resignation, which had been refused. When this committee reported at a trustee meeting at the Hoffman House in Los Angeles on the afternoon of February 12, a major crisis ensued. Marston presented a plan to raise $20,000 for the current expenses of the college by July 1, 1895 which included securing $10,000 from the College's constituency. Of the latter he offered to give $2,000 personally when the other funds had been received. The Board approved Marston's proposal and adjourned until 8 o'clock the following morning.

When the trustees reconvened, President Baldwin presented a letter of resignation saying "The defect in my work, as we have all agreed, has been my inability as a solicitor to secure the funds needed for the current expenses of the growing institution. . . . The financial plan adopted at your session yesterday is one in which I could not with my present health and courage take the leading part." However, as the trustees had expressed a disinclination orally to accept his resignation and as Sumner had consented "to undertake the leadership in working out the plan adopted," he said he would continue as president until the trustees saw some way to relieve him, but "please consider my resignation in your hands for action at the earliest moment in your judgment possible," he concluded. The Board at the same session unanimously approved a letter to Baldwin expressing "its warm approbation of the ability you have shown in your relation to Faculty, the students and to our constituency at large. While we recognize the motives which led you to this action we do not see our way clear to consummate, at present, this separation you propose."

The trustees proceeded cautiously, well aware of the regard for Baldwin among faculty, students, churchmen and the Board itself. Their wisdom in doing so was soon shown by the strong campus support for the president. On February 19 *The Student Life* in an editorial of great regret at the news of Baldwin's resignation hailed him as one who had shown "a patient Christlike spirit through every vexation," concluding that "even the thought of his not being here is well-nigh unbearable." David P. Barrows, then a graduate student in Berkeley, in a letter published in *The Student Life* of March 5, appealed to the trustees to retain Baldwin.

> Five years ago [he wrote] Pomona College was an institution of the veriest insignificance, unknown outside the town from which it took its name, without a head or leader and of doubtful future. It is impossible for one who was not a student at that time to appreciate the immediate change that his coming brought. . . . He secured, by much personal labor, a student body desirable and enthusiastic. He recognized the imperative value of strong men as instructors and of a high standard of work and he secured both. He made Pomona College known throughout the state.

These strong expressions of student concern were part of a very difficult month for the trustees and the college. The faculty appointed a committee to wait on the Executive Committee to ask that "in consideration of the President's ill health, the plan of sending him at once into the field for money be reconsidered," and to urge the Board "to call early an important meeting to consider important business." The trustees confronted the issue in tense sessions in Holmes Hall on March 12 and 13. Eleven trustees were present. Four papers from the faculty were first presented in a session that began at 7:15 p.m. and occupied the entire evening of March 12. The Board adjourned until 8:50 the following morning and after voting "to take up the matter of President Baldwin's resignation," then "voted to hear the representatives of the students and the citizens of Claremont." Two students and three citizens spoke — all asking that Baldwin be retained. Letters of support for Baldwin from individuals, the Congregational churches of Pasadena and Santa Barbara, and the Congregational Union were presented. "President Baldwin was called upon for a statement and made a request for an investigation, after which prayer was offered by Mr. Ford and adjournment taken to 1 o'clock." The Board reconvened "by itself" and voted that no investigation was necessary "as no charges reflecting on the moral character or business integrity of President Baldwin had been made but the fullest conference with him will be fully and freely granted." Baldwin was then invited to rejoin the Board and the conference "continued until adjournment for supper at 7:15 p.m.," after which the Board again reconvened "by itself." When a motion was made and seconded "that President Baldwin's resignation be accepted" ten trustees voted "no" and one abstained. The crisis thus passed, the Board established "a Committee of three consisting of Messrs. Marston (who was not present), Sumner, and President Baldwin to formulate a financial plan, with full power to act." To reassure the faculty, the Board also reaffirmed its policy "to maintain a high standard of work." *The Student Life* joyously reported the news on March 19.

Marston renewed his offer to give $2,000 on the condition that $10,000 be secured from the Congregational Education Society and $8,000 be raised from other sources — $7,000 from old pledges and $1,000 from Eastern subscriptions. He wrote in his letter of March 21 that he was making his pledge "upon the explicit understanding that President Baldwin shall assume the general responsibility of this financial work." At the same time Marston stated that he could give only "advisory work" to the finance committee and he would have to resign from the committee if it were expected that the chief responsibility for the forthcoming canvass rested upon it. Through the work of others, particularly Sumner, Marston's program attained its goals and further financial crisis was avoided during 1894-95.

But inevitably another year again brought the most serious financial problems. Not only were the two-year notes given to the faculty for their services in 1892-93 due on July 1, 1895, but funds were needed for the new year beginning in September. At this juncture Marston again took the lead and on his motion the Board on June 27, 1895 established the college's first recorded budget. Expenses for the academic year 1895-96 were to be "limited to $21,000." The categories of expense, totalling $20,007.38, illustrate the struggle in keeping Pomona alive: interest on debt $4,085.97, taxes $308.25, office (use of horse, typewriting, postage, mail carrying) $350, repairs and improvements $450, salaries $13,795, and travel $906.92.

The beleaguered president and trustees soon found their efforts to raise funds for current expenses complicated by the necessity of inaugurating a parallel campaign for endowment. Mrs. Nancy M. Field, the sister of Cyrus W. Holmes, Jr., and also a resident of

Monson, Massachusetts, through her close friend, Charles Burt Sumner, had made a contract to give Pomona $5,000 a year for endowment over a ten-year period, provided the college would match this amount. Before the college could begin its own matching efforts, Mrs. Field died, and the matter had to be negotiated with the executors of her estate, who were in Philadelphia, Pennsylvania. Doubtful of the future of the college, the executors sought a firsthand report by sending to Claremont their attorney and Franklin La Du Ferguson, the secretary of the Congregational Education Society. Somewhat reassured by their emissaries' reports, the executors offered to give the college $25,000 for endowment on condition that the institution raise $75,000 by January 15, 1897 and the trustees accepted a contract to this effect on January 15, 1896. Despite this action, very little effort was made on the endowment campaign before the following September.

Beset by the conflicting claims of immediate and long range needs, the Board could not avoid giving primary attention to the mounting crisis of the operating budget. The faculty on March 12, 1896 established a committee of four "to put in form some plan relating to finance from a faculty standpoint." Faculty concern grew to such a degree that on June 21 the faculty voted to make professors Brackett and Hitchcock a committee "to prepare a letter signed by the faculty and presented to the Board stating the feeling of apprehension for the future and the demand that current expense for another year be met." Indicative of the perilous state of the college was the fact that the trustees on June 25, 1896 gave Baldwin a note of $2,000 payable in six months with interest to cover his salary for the past year. Earlier several faculty members had been given, for portions of their salaries, notes due in twelve months with interest at eight per cent. The Board was so dispirited that after electing two new trustees it asked President Baldwin "to inform each, fully and candidly, of the true condition of College affairs, and secure if possible his acceptance."

In the autumn of 1896 Baldwin undertook an eastern journey in search of funds to match the Field legacy, and he achieved considerable success. Chairman Bent also sought the assistance of Ferguson, asking him to be in Philadelphia for final arrangements with the executors of Mrs. Field's estate. Ferguson further bestirred himself in Chicago, whence he wired Bent on January 13 that he had secured a "written subscription for $20,000 from Dr. D. K. Pearsons," a well-known philanthropist.

The trustees held a triumphant session on January 14, Bent reading a series of telegrams between himself and Ferguson, and then wiring Ferguson: "Subscriptions ample including Dr. Pearsons' generous gift. Will carry out your instructions and wire Miller [the Field estate attorney] final action tomorrow. God be praised." Of the list of subscriptions certified to the Field estate, the largest was from President Baldwin's father, C. H. Baldwin, who gave $25,000. The trustee meeting continued into January 15, when Bent telegraphed Miller, "Endowment fund subscriptions completed and formally approved by trustees for seventy-five thousand dollars." Great was the rejoicing among all Pomona's friends. President Baldwin and trustee Frary, pastor of Pilgrim Church in Pomona, sent postal cards announcing the completion of the $100,000 endowment to the pastors of all the Congregational churches in California.

The Student Life, to which President Baldwin had sent a telegram, heralded the great news with front page headlines: "$100,000, Pomona's First Endowment Secured." "This means permanency for Pomona College and guarantees her future in a way most satisfactory," the editor wrote. *The Metate* of 1897 in a page account of the endowment concluded: "Thus the College was put upon a firm foundation, which — please God, may never be shaken."

Alas, "permanency" was so little established that within a few weeks the most serious financial issues arose within college councils. Income from the endowment was not immediately available, obligations for 1896-97 were not being met, and the increasing debt was a matter for apprehension. President Baldwin reported to the trustees on February 25 that the debt and the deficit from 1896-97 would total $61,338.27, and he presented a plan by which he, Thomas Barrows of Claremont, and the trustees would endeavor to raise the full amount by July 1, 1897. In an informal meeting of the Board at the First Congregational Church in Los Angeles on May

17, Baldwin had to report that this plan had failed, and he then estimated the debt at $45,600. To meet the dire situation, he submitted a lowered budget for 1897-98, reducing his own salary to $1,500 and those of the highest paid professors to $1,200. After these economies, he estimated that of the $20,048.67 budget, $6,533.62 must come from gifts.

In his lengthy and detailed report on the financial situation of the college Baldwin also discussed a recent visit of Ferguson to the campus. Ferguson had offered a number of suggestions on administrative and trustee matters, among them a candid proposal that Baldwin give himself "to inside work, retaining the office of President and giving overall financial work to Mr. Sumner." Baldwin told the Board this "was not at all feasible." When a trustee moved to amend the by-laws and create the position of financial agent at a salary of $1,500 with an office in one of the college buildings, Baldwin spoke in vigorous opposition. The mood was not good when the Board adjourned at 11 p.m., and it was ominous that Baldwin was not in attendance when the trustees reconvened on May 18, for a session in which appeals on financial matters were presented by two faculty members.

In unofficial discussions outside the meetings of May 17-18 the trustees began to seek another president for the college. J. H. Williams was authorized informally to sound out President Slocum of Colorado College. A committee of the Board was appointed to inform the Congregational Education Society of "the informal action of the Board of Trustees at their last meeting relative to the presidency of the College."

Tortuously the Board came to a decision in the annual meeting of 1897. Scheduled for June 30, the meeting had to be adjourned to the following day because of lack of a quorum. However, a meeting of the Executive Committee was held on the afternoon of June 30. The committee learned that President Slocum had informed Williams that he could not consider leaving Colorado College. A letter from Ferguson replying to the Board's letter to the Education Society was read.

When the annual meeting was reconvened in Holmes Hall in the afternoon of July 1, nine trustees were in attendance. Baldwin was not present. Sumner, as secretary, read two further letters from Ferguson, one a copy of his letter to the Education Society on his visit to Pomona, the other a letter from Ferguson to Baldwin. These letters were critical of Baldwin's administration, and the afternoon was spent in discussing "what to do with the President." During the recess for supper Bent and Dr. Day talked with Baldwin and they reported that the president felt he could meet all the objections to his administration if he were allowed to present the situation to a committee of three disinterested and unprejudiced persons. The Board responded by inviting him to make a statement that evening.

The president's statement did not remove the doubts that had been growing among the trustees. Baldwin's resignation in 1895 and the continued financial crisis had undermined the confidence of the most active and most influential members of the Board. Among these were Blanchard and Marston. After the president had withdrawn, Marston moved "that it is the sense of the Board that the best interests of the College require the resignation of President Baldwin." The motion was seconded and approved by a vote of five to four, and Bent immediately informed the president. The minutes of the meeting do not indicate the votes of individual trustees, but it is clear from Marston's memoirs and their own subsequent actions that both Bent and Sumner voted for the president's resignation. Marston had acted with a heavy heart for he admired Baldwin and appreciated his integrity and his magnetism.

The close vote in a meeting in which only nine of the fifteen trustees were present left an uneasy situation that continued throughout the summer. President Baldwin presented a formal resignation to the Executive Committee on July 17 but it was not until his supplemental resignation was read to the committee on August 23 that the trustees felt the matter had been concluded. The resignation and the supplemental resignation were accepted by the Board on October 26.

President Baldwin's departure was a traumatic experience for the young college and for those who bore the responsibility for the separation. The president and his wife had given their full energy and devotion to Pomona College and Claremont. They had built a fine three-story house which still stands, on the southwest corner of Warren Avenue and Second Street, and made it a center for faculty, students, and the community. There was much sadness that one so gifted in educational and personal leadership must be lost, but the expressions of regret were more tempered than at the time of President Baldwin's first resignation in 1895. The committee of three sent by the Alumni Association to interview the Executive Committee of the trustees returned convinced that the Board had done what it felt necessary. In its report to the alumni, the committee asked that they "consider the attitude of each trustee as being strictly loyal to the College and ready to set aside all personal feeling and interest." Most of the letters and appeals to the Board were not for the continuance of Baldwin as president but for his retention as a teaching member of the faculty. Petitions to this effect were sent to the trustees by every class in college, as were a resolution from the General Association of Congregational Churches in Southern California and numerous letters from individuals. To all these communications the trustees replied that "circumstances make it impossible to realize this at the present time."

Despite his resignation, President Baldwin and his family maintained close relations with the college and their friends in Claremont. Their daughter and only child, Florence, continued as a student at Pomona and graduated in 1901. Baldwin did not take another position in higher education. Continuing his residence in Claremont for a while and engaging briefly in agriculture, he finally returned to the ministry. From 1902-10 he was the pastor of the Congregational Church in Palo Alto, where he died in 1931 after a long period of ill health. His personal relations were good, even with the trustees who felt impelled to force his resignation, and over the years their differences were mutually forgiven.

Baldwin left a lasting influence at Pomona. He shaped wisely the academic structure and program of both the preparatory and the college departments. He chose able and devoted faculty members, and the "old guard" he left served the college until the 1920's. High standards and integrity governed campus life and the academic program. Had Baldwin lived in an established society or in a more affluent era, he might well have led the college for many years. But he was unable to master the grave financial problems of Pomona in the 1890's, and the trustees had no choice but to seek another leader.

CHAPTER IV

Progress and Conflict, 1897-1901

REGRET FOR THE DEPARTURE of the beloved president did not lead to despair. While the problems of finance and the seeking of a new president rested heavily on the trustees, the faculty and students went on with the work of the college. Seven years of operation had developed a faculty structure and student institutions with enough strength to meet the crisis. Dean Norton, who had been on sabbatical leave during 1895-96 for study and travel in the Middle West and New England, took over the direction of the institution for 1897-98.

In addition to Norton, Brackett, Hitchcock, Colcord, Bissell, and Spalding, the faculty had been strengthened by A. J. Cook, professor of biology and instructor in geology, who was appointed in 1894. Cook, the husband of President Baldwin's sister, had graduated from Michigan Agricultural College in 1862 and had received a Master of Science degree there in 1866. After further study at Harvard, he returned to his alma mater in 1869 as professor of zoology and entomology, whence he was called to Pomona. As early as 1891, Baldwin had sought funds to bring Cook to the college. Finally, Baldwin's father made this possible by paying Cook's salary for a three-year period, and after the president's resignation the trustees defrayed Cook's salary from the income of the $25,000 which C. H. Baldwin had contributed to the endowment. The president had desired Cook, whose services to agriculture in Michigan indicated that he could be invaluable both to the college and the region in the rapidly developing fruit industry of Southern California. Baldwin's expectation was abundantly realized, for Professor Cook aroused great enthusiasm among his students and established the foundations of the biological sciences at Pomona. At the same time, he rendered such services to ranchers that the University of California engaged him to direct agricultural institutes throughout the state. It meant a great deal to Pomona that Professor Cook elected to remain after the resignation of his brother-in-law, and that he served the college so effectively and devotedly in the crucial years that began in 1897. His wide acquaintance among agriculturists brought both students and financial support to Pomona in a time of direst need.

Despite Pomona's financial difficulties, her ideals and the quality of the faculty augured well for the future. Ten years of work both on and off the campus had produced an institution which had the respect and love of a growing group of concerned people. In the crisis of the presidency these were genuine assets which the trustees could offer to a new leader. The man they called was no stranger to them, nor was the college new to him.

As noted above, the field secretary of the Congregational Education Society, Reverend Franklin La Du Ferguson, had visited Pomona College on several occasions and had surveyed the institution on the ground as well as from his vantage point in Boston. In this period the Society played a role in higher education comparable to that of the great philanthropic foundations in our own time, providing both money and advice. Mr. Ferguson's suggestions for the administration of Pomona had been given to President Baldwin and also shared in conversations with some of the trustees. In May, 1897 Chairman Bent, on learning that Ferguson was in Los Angeles, had sent "a hurried notice to such of the trustees as would most likely wish to meet Mr. Ferguson and who were accessible," and Blanchard, Frary, and Sumner joined him for a meeting that began on May 3 and continued through the next day. The conversation touched "the vital interests of the College" with "such recommendations as Mr. Ferguson might see fit to offer," and the attitude of the Educational Society toward Pomona. On this visit to California, Ferguson addressed the Pomona students on a Sunday evening, and *The Student Life* reported him "a forcible and cultural speaker."

Following President Baldwin's resignation, several trustees in-

President Franklin La Du Ferguson

terviewed Ferguson in the East, and others corresponded with him. A letter from Ferguson was read to the Executive Committee on September 16, and the committee on October 4 authorized Sumner "to make inquiries by letter or otherwise as to the record and qualifications of Reverend Frank L. Ferguson" for the presidency. Sumner reported the result of his inquiries to the trustees at an evening meeting on October 26, and Dr. Day and Marston spoke of interviews with Ferguson and Dr. D. K. Pearsons which they had held during the summer. After a two-hour discussion the following morning, Ferguson was unanimously elected president of Pomona College. However, he delayed several months before accepting.

The correspondence and discussions with Ferguson continued, with long lapses, into 1898. Chairman Bent on December 14, 1897 reported the receipt of an appreciative telegram from Ferguson and a letter explaining "his delay in regard to a definite acceptance," saying he expected to visit the college before the close of the year.

The Board voted to pay his expenses and the Executive Committee appointed a special committee of Bent, Sumner, and Dole to meet with him. Ferguson's arrival was further delayed, and it was not until January 6, 1898 that he met with this committee. The trustees on the morning of January 11 appointed a further committee of Dr. Day, Reverend Frary, and Dean Norton to confer with Ferguson, and this committee reported in the early afternoon that he had accepted, a formal letter to follow. The next day Ferguson announced his acceptance of the presidency at a special meeting of the faculty.

Pomona had a president at last and his reception could not have been more cordial. "Every student was in his place congratulating himself that he had come, for Dr. Ferguson was on the platform," *The Student Life* wrote of the chapel services of January 14. After the devotional exercises Dean Norton rose "with the air that betokens an important announcement," saying that after weary months waiting the man "who is in every way fitted for the place has accepted" and hailed him as "President Ferguson." The president of the junior class jumped up and led "the old college yell three times." President Ferguson responded by outlining his plans for immediate development of the campus and for retiring the college debt.

Although a Congregational minister, President Ferguson brought to Pomona a background somewhat different from that of those who had founded and developed the college. The son of a minister of the Methodist Episcopal Church in Canada, he was born in the province of Ontario, where he attended Albert College, later to become a part of the University of Toronto. Leaving college to enter business, he came to the United States and married the daughter of Samuel Maxwell, Chief Justice of Nebraska. After marriage he decided to study for the ministry and he received the Bachelor of Divinity degree from Yale in 1888. Ordained as a Congregational minister, he held a pastorate at the Congregational church of Milford, Connecticut. He was attracted to education and accepted a position as the head of Chadron Academy in Nebraska, where his success in raising money led to his appointment as field secretary of the Congregational Education Society.

Mr. Ferguson's work for the Society kept him in Boston until the summer of 1898, and by the time he assumed his duties in Claremont the interim measures taken by the trustees had stabilized and improved the financial position of the college. Shortly after President Baldwin's resignation, Sumner was again named financial agent, and he threw his full energy into the raising of funds and the improvement of the credit of the college. The year between presidents of the college was also marked by outstanding service by President Henry Kirke White Bent of the Board of Trustees. Bent was persuaded to move to Claremont and to take the position of business manager, for which he received a modest salary. With fund-raising and business affairs in the hands of two such widely known and respected men, prospects for the college improved considerably. Confidence was strengthened further by steps which President Ferguson took in the months before he began his residence in Claremont. When he came to California in January 1898 he brought with him a written pledge from Dr. D. K. Pearsons to build a science hall to cost not less than $25,000, on the condition that the college would raise the funds to liquidate its outstanding debt, then $62,000.

Dr. Pearsons (1820-1912), who had already contributed $20,000 to the Pomona endowment campaign, was an early philanthropist who in his lifetime made donations aggregating $4,000,000 to thirty colleges in twenty states. Born in Vermont, he taught school from age sixteen to twenty-one, and at twenty-two received his M.D. degree from the Medical College in Woodstock, Vermont. After practicing medicine from 1842 to 1857 in Chicopee, Massachusetts, he moved to Illinois and became a farmer in Ogle County, leaving after three years to enter the real estate business in Chicago, in which he continued from 1860 to 1887. He served as director of the Chicago City Railway and other corporations, and from 1873 to 1876 he was a city alderman. He and Mrs. Pearsons had no children, and he devoted his years after 1887 to philanthropy, giving away his fortune in his own lifetime, in the strong belief that "a man is his own best executor."

The news that Dr. Pearsons had offered to build a science hall on condition the college would liquidate its indebtedness was communicated to Pomona's friends by Sumner early in 1898, first in a letter on February 1, and then in a fuller, printed statement on March 22. To meet Dr. Pearsons' condition, Sumner wrote that the president was seeking gifts in the East and that the college was selling scholarships "at a large discount" and building-lots in Claremont at prices from $100 to $250. President Ferguson indeed secured a grant of $12,000 from the Congregational Education Society, to be paid in annual installments of $3,000 from 1898 through 1901, but with the condition that Pomona College would make no further solicitation for its current expenses among the churches of New England and their organizations and donors to the Education Society. The trustees accepted these restrictions.

When President Ferguson arrived for several weeks in late April and early May, the trustees felt encouraged enough to authorize the Executive Committee to purchase a suitable site for the new science hall, and lots on Warren Avenue opposite Holmes Hall were secured. *The Student Life* exulted on May 24, "The Science Hall is assured," Dr. Pearsons having announced that he was satisfied that the gifts and pledges would cover the debt. The Executive Committee on June 28 authorized President Ferguson to engage an architect to prepare plans and specifications for the building. The contract was awarded on August 11, on a basic bid of $22,816, and a plumbing and gas fitting bid of $1,597.

Construction proceeded rapidly under the careful supervision of President Ferguson, and the building was dedicated on January 21, 1899. The cream-colored pressed brick structure with its open hall finished in oak brought a new standard of quality for Pomona buildings. The office and president's room were near the entrance on the main floor, and the library occupied the large room in the southwest corner of that floor. Otherwise, the three floors of the building were given over to science classrooms and laboratories, chemistry on the ground floor, physics in the northwest corner of the main floor, and biology and the museum which Professor Cook was developing, on the third floor. The concrete porch and steps of Pearsons became at once the place for college gatherings, from class photographs to athletic rallies. Pomona had a science hall of which she could be proud, "lighted by gas, heated by steam, and

Pearsons Hall of Science

Renwick Gymnasium

practically fire proof," and sketches of it were included in all the college literature.

The impressive dedicatory exercises of Pearsons Hall constituted a memorable day for the young college. Several hundred visitors were in attendance, among them alumni, educators from many parts of California, notably professors from the University of California and Stanford. President Ferguson gave the address of presentation in behalf of Dr. Pearsons, who was unable to attend. Trustee Warren F. Day accepted the building for the college, and Professor Hitchcock brought the congratulations of the department of science. Trustee L. H. Frary offered the prayer of dedication and the audience joined in singing the hymn, "The Spacious Firmament on High." The audience then moved across the street to the chapel in Holmes Hall, where Thomas R. Bacon, professor of European History at the University of California, spoke on "Natural Science as a Factor in Education." After luncheon Walter Miller, professor of Classical Philology at Stanford University, delivered an address, "The Old and the New in Education."

President Ferguson was responsible for two other major additions to the physical facilities of the college. He responded to the student interest in athletics and took successful steps to secure a gymnasium to replace the inadequate building that provided only a changing room and baths for the college teams. Mrs. Helen Goodwin Renwick of Claremont made a gift of $2,500, the students raised $1,600, and the remaining $1,400 was covered by the college from other sources. The building, placed just east of Holmes Hall and dedicated on March 6, 1900 was named the "William Renwick Gymnasium" in memory of Mrs. Renwick's late husband. Fitted up the following year "with a bowling alley, chest weights, rings, bars, etc., for systematic exercise," the Renwick Gymnasium was hailed by *The Metate* of 1901 as "of inestimable value for developing and training the different college teams." With an improved track, a baseball diamond "in excellent shape," and good tennis courts, the college was experiencing a steady increase in its athletic facilities.

The teams responded with a series of successes that gave the Ferguson years an outstanding record in athletics. Pomona won the intercollegiate field meets with U.S.C. and Occidental in 1900 and 1901, culminating in nine consecutive victories for the Blue and White in these events. In football, U.S.C. was defeated for the first time by a score of 12 to 0 on Thanksgiving in 1899, ending a season in which Pomona lost only one game. In the football season of 1900, Pomona had a record rarely achieved in any intercollegiate sport, an undefeated, untied, unscored-on team; the seven successive victories included a 17 to 0 win over Occidental, and a 10 to 0 Thanksgiving Day conquest of U.S.C., and of course the championship of Southern California.

The third major building achieved by President Ferguson was the President's House. An official residence for the president and his family was a need that had been recognized by the trustees; it was discussed by them at their meeting on March 14, 1899 and referred to the Executive Committee. Mr. Ferguson vigorously pursued the matter, and the Board on October 11 voted to build a president's house at a cost not to exceed $5,500, exclusive of the building site. A very unusual agreement was then approved. President Ferguson was to borrow the money from a private party at an interest not to exceed six per cent and the loan would be carried until such time as a gift could be received to retire it. President Ferguson, in the meantime, was to take the legal responsibility of the loan and pay as rental the interest, insurance, taxes, maintenance, and cost of landscaping of the grounds. The only cost to the college would be the provision and grading of the building lots, which would be deeded to President Ferguson. A further agreement between the Board and Ferguson provided that when a donation might be received to retire the loan, or when he ceased to be president of Pomona College, he would redeed the land and the buildings on it to the college. If he ceased to be president, the Board would assume any portion of the loan remaining unpaid. After first planning to locate the house just north of Pearsons Hall, the trustees on December 28 ratified purchase of three lots on the southwest corner of Warren Avenue and Fourth Street.

With the completion of these negotiations, President Ferguson arranged a loan with his friend, Miss Harriet Cousins of Newton, Massachusetts. Meanwhile the necessary steps for construction had gone forward. C. H. Brown was engaged to prepare plans and specifications; and the contract for $5,280 was awarded to C. C. Bryant on November 21. The house was completed in April 1900, and began its historic role as the home of Pomona's presidents and their families.

The three buildings constructed in the Ferguson administration were evidence of the energy and attention he brought to the developmental and business matters of the college. In published reports for 1897-98, 1898-99, and 1899-1900, he placed the progress and needs of the college before its friends more fully than ever before. He commended the achievements of Bent and Sumner in the interim between Baldwin's resignation and his own assumption of duties, and rejoiced in the gifts of Dr. Pearsons, and the prospect that "the day of deliverance from the bondage of debt has dawned." The assets of the college in June 1898 he listed as a total of $187,000, including an endowment of $100,000, village lots in Claremont, $12,000, and Dr. Pearsons' pledge for the Hall of Science, $25,000. He stated in his report for 1898-99 that the endowment funds had been carefully invested in first mortgages on improved real estate paying six to eight per cent, that the members of the faculty had been paid "the large arrears of their salaries from the previous years and had received their current salaries in such installments and with such regularity as to relieve them of financial embarrassment."

With Ferguson's coming there developed a fundamental change in the president's official relations with the Board of Trustees. Baldwin had suffered some embarrassment and had been handicapped because he was not a member of the Board. While he was awarded the full privilege of attending trustee meetings and of speaking on any matter, he was not a member of the Executive Committee and did not attend it regularly. Thus he was not always in full communication with trustee deliberations and thinking. Ferguson addressed himself to this problem shortly after his election and in a letter read to the Board at its meeting in Los Angeles on February 11, 1898 he set forth the desirability of the president's being a member of the Board. The matter was referred to a committee of Day and Sumner and on June 22, 1898 Ferguson was elected a trustee and a member of the Executive Committee. At the next meeting of the trustees, and the first one at which President Ferguson was in attendance, a letter of resignation from the presidency of the Board was presented from Mr. Bent, whose health was declining rapidly. Ferguson was elected to succeed him. As the president of the Board was also the chairman of the Executive Committee, the initiative in major trustee matters was in President Ferguson's hands. The joining of such trustee leadership to the authority of the president of the college created a hazardous concentration of power.

However, this unwise union of powers was congenial to President Ferguson's concept of administration, and he could have cited Harvard and Brown as examples of institutions where the president of the institution was also head of the Board. In his annual report for 1899-1900, he stated that "unity of plan and purpose and an efficient administration of any corporation is practically impossible without a centralized responsibility." In accordance with this view, he undertook changes in the management and government of the college and in the president's role within the faculty. In a revision of the by-laws he looked to clearer definition of responsibilities between the trustees and the faculty "not inconsistent with the modern and successful commercial and educational organizations which have imposed upon the president the principal task of inaugurating and superintending the plans of operation." Soon there arose at Pomona the classic issue of the extent to which a college can be handled as a business corporation.

There developed between the president and the faculty a situation in which even a more experienced administrator than Ferguson might well have had difficulty. President Baldwin and the faculty had been in such accord on academic matters that the internal management of the institution was largely left to the teaching staff. Furthermore, the leaders of the faculty were men of experience in academic matters, who, having cast their lot with the college, had deep convictions about its nature and its government. The personal contrast between the reserved, businesslike Ferguson and the scholarly, imaginative Baldwin also contributed to the serious friction which began to manifest itself early in President Ferguson's second year in Claremont.

Not surprisingly, the sharpest conflict turned on the authority of the dean, which Norton brought to a head by resigning in December 1899. The matter was considered by the trustees at a meeting in Los Angeles on December 28 which convened for sessions at 10 a.m., 1:30 p.m., and 7:00 p.m., the last continuing until around midnight. Norton was invited to join the Board at the afternoon session, and along with him a committee of the faculty, including Brackett, Colcord, and Hitchcock was received in the evening. The committee presented five resolutions from the faculty expressing "its view of the duties and prerogatives of the president and the dean, most significantly that in the absence of the president, the dean should represent him; that discipline [in which the president had been interfering] should be handled by a standing committee appointed by the faculty; and that announcements to the students should be made by the president," whom the faculty considered "as the executive officer of the faculty." "After a conference of some hours with the representatives of the Faculty," and prolonged discussion within the Board, the issue was resolved by "full assurances of cooperation," with the Board's placing the faculty resolutions in immediate operation, and Dean Norton's withdrawing his resignation.

However, the differences between the faculty and the president were too fundamental to be resolved so easily. At a special meeting on the morning of June 28, 1900, the faculty challenged the president on the key issue in college and university government — the procedure by which academic appointments are made. On that day Ferguson reported to a faculty meeting that the trustees had approved five new appointments and one change of status "subject to faculty approval," which was a reversal of the order in the established process of making academic appointments at Pomona. It was the custom for prospective academic appointments to be first approved by the faculty, after which the president recommended them to the trustees for Board approval. When the president ignored the accepted procedure, the faculty withheld its approval of the appointees reported on June 28 and established a committee of Brackett, Cook, and Colcord to draw up resolutions regarding these appointments. At two o'clock that afternoon, Brackett read a report from the committee which does not appear in the minutes. However, the faculty appointed him chairman of a committee "to confer with the Trustees on behalf of the faculty." A further meeting of the faculty was held the following day but again the resolution passed does not appear in the minutes. However, the text of the actions is not necessary to show how fundamentally the faculty by the end of June 1900 had lost confidence in the president.

The new academic year began in an atmosphere of great uncertainty in faculty-presidential relations. Although faculty meetings occurred on September 25, October 19, and 26, there were no minutes until a meeting of October 30 in which President Ferguson spoke of a paper proposed by Professor Hitchcock pledging confidence and cooperation to one another, a plan which was not carried out. The revision of the by-laws which the faculty undertook in November led to a further conflict of views with the president. The Executive Committee to which the amended by-laws had been forwarded by Dean Norton asked the faculty at the end of February to appoint a committee to meet early in March with the trustees, "to act in conference with the Trustees if needed." Brackett, Hitchcock and Norton were elected by the faculty. When the president asked that an additional faculty member be chosen, Professor Colcord was elected.

President Ferguson's position was weakened further by the fact that after his good beginning he, too, proved unable to secure the funds the college needed. The increase in the plant and improvement in the older buildings in 1898-99 required an outlay of more than $10,000 "for the steam heating plant, the gas plant [to light the college buildings], the painting and papering of Holmes and Sumner Halls, the lots for Pearsons Hall, and cement walks in front of Holmes and Pearsons." Some of the pledges to meet the debt were not paid, and "the great chasm between the regular income and expenses" required annual gifts of at least $10,000 for current operations — a sum, the president pointed out, much larger than individuals and the churches had ever given the college in any single year.

However, in his report for 1899-1900, he expressed confidence that the $11,000 required to avoid a deficit would be donated for

1900-01. When his appeal for funds to liquidate the debt and to meet the annual deficit fell short in the spring of 1901, he found himself unable to "relieve the trustees of the sad duty of serious retrenchment in the modest expenditures which now obtain."

In this dire situation, the Board on January 15, 1901 appointed a trustee committee to consider measures "for reducing current expenses," and this committee on March 1 recommended a reduction of $3,000 which was approved, and the president was instructed, "in conference with the faculty, to take steps to carry out the recommendations." When the president proposed to the faculty on April 20 that the emergency be met by increasing the teaching duties of the faculty by establishing twenty-four hours as the maximum and twenty hours as the minimum load, the assent he secured was a very reluctant one. To their acquiescence, the faculty joined a resolution of remonstrance: "While we willingly take charge of the additional classes necessitated by the reduction of the teaching force, we regard the step as a deliberate lowering of the standards of class-room work and as a temporary measure which should be rescinded at the earliest possible moment." Discussion of the resolution was spirited, however, and it led to the first recorded division which occurs in the faculty minutes. Listed by name were the five who voted for the resolution and President Ferguson and two others who voted against it.

The college was entering a very difficult spring in which the issues between the faculty and the president were to come to a climax. When President Ferguson presented to the faculty nominations for the new members to be appointed for 1901-02, a series of contentious meetings ensued lasting from May 21 to June 7. The sharp discussions, which on one occasion involved the president's ruling a matter out of order and an appeal from the decision of the chair, strained relations already nearing the breaking point.

At this stage the leading trustees finally concluded that the Board could no longer secure effective cooperation between the president and the faculty. It was with heavy hearts that the trustees faced a second presidential crisis within four years, but they could not escape it. A typed memorandum of June 8, 1901 in the college archives, with a long-hand note beneath it signed by H. K.

W. Bent, summarizes the situation: "Seven of the nine department heads of the teaching force have definitely lost confidence in the wisdom of the administration of President Ferguson, and feel its continuance is detrimental to the college." The memorandum also affirmed that the president did not enjoy the "goodwill and cooperation of the people of Claremont and vicinity," and that there was a "serious lack of respect and confidence in the student body." With these presentations the trustees were asked to sign the memorandum, which concluded with this call to action: "We the undersigned members of the Board of Trustees of the Pomona College hereby express our judgment that President Ferguson's resignation should *come* before the board at the annual meeting and that without further discussion his official relations with the college should terminate." Mr. Bent signed "in general agreement." The supporters of the memorandum were in process of preparing for the annual trustee meeting on June 25 when an event at the beginning of the commencement week removed any fear of opposition. The president's baccalaureate sermon on June 23 was the subject of severe faculty criticism. This criticism cannot be assessed accurately or fairly from materials extant today, but it is clear that the sermon was only an incident and not the cause of President Ferguson's resignation.

When the Board met on June 25, its leaders had worked out a terminating agreement with the president. After the essential business of approving the names of students to be graduated the following day and the presentation of the financial report, the president "at some length" presented his formal resignation to the Board on the condition that "untrue charges must be proven or withdrawn" and "that a pecuniary consideration be agreed upon." A committee headed by Marston was asked "to arrange the pecuniary terms of adjustment with President Ferguson." The committee's recommendation of full salary for the following year was approved. Mr. Ferguson was asked to continue the business management of the college until September 1 and was authorized to sign checks.

In a resolution, the trustees expressed their appreciation of the retiring president's "able administration of the financial affairs of the College," his "securing for it much needed buildings and endowment funds," and "his efficient and successful financial management" during his term of office. These commendations were merited, for President Ferguson's leadership did strengthen Pomona in its greatest crisis. It was a misfortune for the college and for him personally that an administration which began so auspiciously should have ended so disastrously.[1]

[1]Following his resignation President Ferguson returned to the East, where he entered the real estate business, first in the Boston area and after 1910 in New York. From 1910-15 he was president of the board of trustees of Plymouth Church in Brooklyn. After 1920 he made his home in Orlando, Florida, where he took an active part in civic affairs and thrice ran unsuccessfully for mayor. Beginning in 1929 Mr. Ferguson published the *Orlando Weekly News.* He died in Orlando on May 28, 1944.

CHAPTER V

The Administration of President Gates

FOR THE SECOND TIME within four years Pomona sought a new president. Disillusioned by their experience with one who was primarily an administrator, the trustees made a careful search for a recognized educator. Secretary Sumner, who was to go east to represent Pomona at the Bicentennial of Yale in September, was also commissioned to make inquiries and to conduct interviews for the new leader. Sumner was successful in his mission, and on November 11, 1901 he recommended the election of Dr. George A. Gates,who was chosen unanimously. The salary was to be $2,500 annually and use of the President's House. Dr. Gates accepted promptly, becoming the president officially in December 1901, and assuming his full duties with the beginning of the winter term that began on January 2, 1902.

President Gates, then fifty-one years of age, brought a combination of qualities and experience unusually well suited to the needs of Pomona. A native of Topsham, Vermont, he had graduated from Dartmouth College in 1873. After two years of teaching and two years as a student at Andover Theological Seminary, he was uncertain of his vocation and decided to accept a position as tutor in a wealthy Boston family. He lived with them for two years in Europe where he enjoyed the opportunity of hearing lectures in theology and philosophy at Neuchâtel, Bonn, and Göttingen. His years abroad confirmed his desire to enter the ministry, and he returned to Andover Seminary, graduating in 1880. Although then denied ordination by a church council in New Hampshire because of his liberalism, he was soon called to an interdenominational church in Montclair, New Jersey, where he had a successful ministry for

President George Augustus Gates

seven years. In 1882, he married Isabel Augusta Smith of Syracuse, New York, who was to be a devoted co-worker in all he undertook.

In 1887 Reverend Gates was called to the presidency of Iowa College, now Grinnell, where he brought new life to the institution. For the students most notable were his short Friday morning chapel talks. As the historian of Grinnell writes: "Not only was he a convincing speaker by the clear impact of his thought and the fearless courage of his utterance but he had the gift of brevity." Students were inspired by the goals he set before them, and by his open and friendly manner. Dr. Gates also showed excellent judgment in the selection of faculty members and those he appointed gave distinction to Grinnell for many years. Having selected able faculty members, he worked cordially and easily with them, leaving educational planning and the operation of the curriculum in their hands.

While some tension ultimately developed at Grinnell because of Gates' liberal theology, his fervent espousal of the social gospel, and his continued support of a highly controversial faculty member, he would have remained at the college had the state of Mrs. Gates' health permitted. Because of her severe asthmatic condition, physicians urged that she move to the high mountain country of the West, and the family went temporarily to Colorado. The western climate proved so helpful for Mrs. Gates that her husband resigned the presidency of Grinnell in June 1900. Returning to the ministry he accepted the pastorate of the Congregational church at Cheyenne, Wyoming, whence he was called to Pomona College.

Coming as a widely known and esteemed minister and an experienced executive, President Gates restored harmony within Pomona and won the warm support of trustees, faculty, and students throughout his administration. His personal integrity, friendly manner, and broad intellectual outlook created a climate of opinion conducive to freedom in teaching and learning. At a time when the conflict between science and religion was a serious source of controversy in many educational and religious institutions President Gates was a wise and enlightened leader. Accepting the theory of evolution, he saw a grand harmony in the universe. As one of his Grinnell colleagues wrote, "He brought a message of reconciliation between the new science and the old religion." He deserves much credit for the fact that Pomona College moved through the early years of the twentieth century with men of science and religion searching for truth together in harmony and mutual respect. President Gates was not a great scholar, but he was a man who understood the thought of his era and communicated it eloquently.

His appointment brought Pomona to the attention of Congregationalists and leaders in education. His New England youth and education, and his residences in the Middle Atlantic region, the Middle West, and the Far West gave him invaluable associations and an understanding of most of the United States. President Gates was in great demand as a speaker, and in addition to countless addresses in California he was honored by invitations to speak on such occasions as the meeting of the National Education Association in St. Louis, and the meeting of the American Board of Commissioners for Foreign Missions at North Adams, Massachusetts.

On December 4, 1901 President Gates, Mrs. Gates and their two sons arrived in Claremont bringing high expectations to the college and its friends. The new president was at once at home with both faculty and students. His initial chapel address, "The Good Success," made an unforgettable impression. Characteristic of his appeal to the students was his message in *The Metate* of 1902 on the "great works a right college ought to do for its students." It should induce a spirit of modesty, set students free, make them reverent, and inspire them with a passion for righteousness. He carried the message of the college in October 1902 to the annual meeting of the General Congregational Association in Ventura, in an address, "Enlargement of Life," emphasizing the role of the Christian college. With him was C. B. Sumner, addressing the Association on college finance, and "presenting to the churches the urgency of substantial aid forthwith to enable the trustees to lift a great financial load and place the institution on a sound financial basis."

Dr. Gates' moving address set the stage for a dramatic and successful campaign among the Southern California Congregational churches. This had been well planned by Sumner; en route to Ventura for the Association meeting he had stopped in Santa Paula for a conference with Nathan Blanchard, who not only supported his plan but volunteered to give two thousand dollars of the amount required. Key to the campaign was a pledge which Gates had received from Dr. D. K. Pearsons to give $50,000 for endowment on condition that the college would raise the funds to liquidate the debt, then $67,000. The morning after President Gates' address, the Association by a rising vote gave its enthusiastic support to the program, resolving to "reaffirm the proportional responsibility of every church in this Association to sustain Pomona College, its own child . . . and to use our best endeavors to have our respective churches, before January 1, 1903, anticipate their gifts to the College for five years, and give their notes, due on or before five years from date, with interest in the amount of six per cent." The implementing of this resolution was ingenious and effective. Representatives of the college met with the trustees of each church, and the church then conducted its own canvass. When the pledges were secured, the church assumed the responsibility for collecting them and gave the college a note from the church for the amount subscribed. The campaign was expeditious and enthusiastic, and on December 30, 1902 the Pomona trustees could record, "Debt fully provided for."

Of even greater value than the funds secured were the resulting sense of unity between the college and the churches and the growing confidence in Pomona's future. At the annual meeting of the Congregational Association in Los Angeles in October 1903, a delegate spoke of Pomona as "the ideal college of the Pacific Coast." When the Association in 1904 held its meeting at Pilgrim Church in the town of Pomona, the delegates were the guests of the college for supper and an evening program in Claremont, at which Professor Brackett spoke on the state of the college. Throughout Gates' presidency this close relationship of the college and the Southern California Congregational churches was an important factor in Pomona's progress. At the meetings of the Association in Claremont in 1906, Riverside in 1907, and Santa Ana in 1908 sessions were devoted to the college, giving President Gates, and often trustees, faculty members, and student groups frequent opportunities to appear on its behalf. Resolutions of praise for "the success attending our beloved college" represented much more than convention rhetoric.

In the characteristic spirit of Congregationalism President Gates and the trustees endeavored to enlist the interest of other Protestant denominations. In particular, they sought the cooperation and financial support of the Disciples of Christ and the Baptists, and each denomination was invited in 1906 to nominate five members to the Board of Trustees. The Disciples accepted promptly, but the Baptists after some months of deliberation finally declined. In anticipation of broadening the religious base of its membership, the Board on February 21, 1907 increased the number of trustees from fifteen to twenty, and five members from the Disciples were elected, two of whom, C. C. Chapman and Reverend A. C. Smither, took a very active part in the work of the Board. While the Disciples ultimately decided to establish their own college, which they named for Mr. Chapman, President Gates felt that their cooperation for a few years on the Pomona Board was an entrance into "the broader sphere of Christian brotherhood which was the original purpose" of those who founded Pomona.

The Board took a further step in this direction on June 15, 1908 by electing as a trustee Joseph Horsfal Johnson, Bishop of the Episcopal Church for Southern California. Bishop Johnson was a graduate of Williams College and of the General Theological Seminary in New York City. After service with Episcopal churches in New York state and Detroit, he came to California, where he was consecrated Bishop of Los Angeles in 1896. Bishop Johnson brought great ability, genuine interest, and much personal charm to the Pomona Board. He served in many capacities, including the vice-presidency, and his counsel and friendship were invaluable to the presidents of the college with whom he served.

President Gates also sought to expand the horizon and reputation of Pomona by bringing to the campus distinguished visitors from the East. The climax of these efforts was a visit by President Theodore Roosevelt, who responded to Gates' invitation to include the college in his Pacific tour in the spring of 1903. Roosevelt, only forty-five years old and at the height of his personal vigor and public influence, arrived on May 8 and was greeted by seven or eight thousand persons who had gathered to hear him. The officers of the college, the student body, and a large group of townspeople met President Roosevelt's train at the Santa Fe station. He was drawn in a carriage by students up College Avenue to Pearsons Hall, where a platform had been built and decorated with the Harvard and Pomona colors. Across the entrance of the building and above the platform hung a large American flag. The students greeted him with the Harvard cheer and the Pomona song. Roosevelt's address reflected his rugged individualism and patriotism. "Every college should strive to bring to development among the students the capacity to do good original work," he declared. His concluding paragraph was a challenge to the young college. "I hail the chance of being met by such a gathering as this because it is of good augury for the republic to see in this mighty Western state, this typically American state, the things of the body and the things of the soul equally cared for." A live-oak which President Roosevelt planted in front of Pearsons Hall grew into a large tree and survived for many years. After the exercises the president was drawn to the station by the students and his train sped westward. Behind him were a faculty and a student body who had *seen* and *heard* a President of the United States! From their memories the visit of Theodore Roosevelt became an imperishable part of Pomona's history.

Campus Expansion and New Buildings

The Gates administration was responsible for a dramatic extension of the campus and for the acquisition of properties which made possible much of the physical development of the later college. In 1902, the campus comprised only twelve acres, most of this east of Warren Avenue between Fourth and Sixth Streets. None of the college-owned property on the west side of Warren Avenue extended to Pearl Avenue, one block west. The east half of the block between Pearsons Hall and the President's House had been reserved for a public park when the Pacific Land Improvement Company laid out the town. The trustees sought to secure this undeveloped park land as a site for a proposed college and community library. As the land company was no longer in existence, the proper procedure was an application to the court for a title, which was granted to the college on November 13, 1902.

Early in the Gates administration the streets of Claremont were renamed in a way that emphasized the centrality of higher education in the city. A town meeting in 1902 voted "that streets running east and west should be designated by numbers while north and south streets should be avenues named for colleges and universities, save that the street bisecting the campus should be called College Avenue." Thus Warren Avenue became College Avenue and the streets immediately west of College Avenue became Harvard Avenue and Yale Avenue.

Initiative in the development and landscaping of the campus was taken by Mr. Marston, who as chairman of the finance committee of the Board had come into a leading position among the trustees. He made an eventful visit to the campus on March 10, 1905 bringing with him Mr. Cooke of Samuel Parsons and Company, landscape architects in New York, and arranging that trustee Albert Smiley and his brother, Daniel Smiley, join them in a meeting with the Executive Committee of the Board. It was an exciting day for the Smileys, Marston, and Cooke as they walked through the small campus and rode over the extensive wash to the east for they were all dedicated to gardening and landscaping. Marston was in the process of constructing his spacious home in San Diego, with its seven-acre garden, and of establishing a park system for the City of San Diego; and the Smiley brothers were developing Smiley Heights in Redlands and their 7,500-acre resort property at Lake Mohonk, New York.

The visit of these enthusiastic landscape planners led to two immediate steps in improving and expanding the Pomona campus. Recognizing the limited extent of the land on which it was proposed to locate a library, Marston urged the acquisition of the west half of that block and offered to give a thousand dollars to plan the area and landscape it. The trustees accepted his offer and acquired the property which with Marston's planting became the wooded park we know today.

A further result of the day was the formulation of a plan for acquiring the large tract adjoining the campus on the east and extending from First Street to Sixth Street. Known to the students as "The Wash," the more than sixty acres comprised the rocky bed of an old mountain stream and a plateau filled with live oaks, shrubs, and wildflowers. From the earliest days of the college the Wash, particularly the tableland, had been a favorite place for picnics and outdoor meetings. When it appeared that this property might be sold for development, the college was alarmed and the trustees took steps to acquire it. Nathan Blanchard had proposed to give $2,500 for developing the Wash into a park if the college would acquire the land. At its campus meeting on March 10 the Executive Committee voted that Marston and Sumner be a committee to visit Mr. Blanchard and propose that if he would purchase the land at a cost of $3,000 and give it to the college, the trustees would expend $2,000 in the development of the park, provide at least

College Avenue in 1905

The Claremont Church

three hundred dollars annually for maintenance, and name the park for him. Blanchard agreed and the Board of Trustees at its meeting on April 3 accepted the sixty-four-acre tract and christened it Blanchard Park. Marston provided funds for the planning of the park by Samuel Parsons and Company.

This expansion of the campus was accompanied by a building program that was continuous from 1904 to 1908 and transformed the appearance and facilities of the college. This marked development was in response to the increase in enrollment. The total enrollment of the preparatory department and the college grew from 245 to 507 during the Gates administration.

The building program began with an enlargement of Holmes Hall. Miss Esther R. Holmes, of Monson, Massachusetts, who earlier had joined with her mother in presenting the building in memory of her father, gave five thousand dollars "for improvements in Holmes and especially the enlargement of the chapel." The work nearly doubled the number of seats on the main floor of the chapel, provided a stage "roomy enough to meet the requirements of a commencement gathering," and added on the east end "two commodious music rooms, which serve as dressing rooms upon occasion." Repainting of both the exterior and interior of the building made it seem "more attractive than when new." The dedication of the enlarged structure was held on September 21, 1904.

The enlargement of Holmes Hall was followed in 1906 by the construction of a sanctuary for the Claremont Church. The church had been organized in the college in 1891 and had conducted its services first in Sumner Hall and then in Holmes Hall after 1893. While the membership was comprised largely of faculty and students, other residents of Claremont had joined, and the Claremont Church was an early and notable example of ecumenicity, a community church which served as the only Protestant church in Claremont until after World War II. Although the new church building was separately financed, it was so much a part of faculty and student life that it seemed in effect a part of the college. This feeling was reinforced by its location on the west side of Harvard Avenue one block from Pearsons Hall.

The Claremont Inn, like the church, was built to serve both town and gown. The college had serious need of a dining hall larger and more commodious than that of Sumner Hall, and the growing community of faculty and townspeople was without the dining and guest facilities that a hotel would provide. A plan for a joint financial undertaking by the college and citizens of the community first came officially before the Executive Committee of the trustees on June 27, 1905 when the committee voted to recommend the formation of a stock company "to erect suitable buildings for a combined Boarding Department and Hotel," and authorized a loan to the company not to exceed $7,000 at interest of six per cent. In addition, the college voted to take stock not to exceed $1,500. It soon became necessary for the college to provide larger support and on December 29, 1905 the trustees made a further stock subscription of $5,000. Included in this sum was $1,500 for the four lots on College Avenue south of the President's House, which the college had secured as the Inn site. The sale contract included provisions under which the college could repurchase the property, and prohibited "the making or sale of liquor as a beverage" on the premises.

The Inn, opened in the autumn of 1906, was an attractive two-story redwood building, designed by the Pasadena architectural firm of Green and Green, whose work, then much in vogue, was to be highly respected by later generations. Erected at the northwest corner of Third Street and College Avenue and fronting on the latter, the Inn occupied an attractive and impressive location where the college and the town joined. Its facilities, which included a student dining room for 250, a guest dining room, a kitchen to serve both, a club room, and rooms for forty overnight guests, added much to the convenience and pleasure of living or studying in Claremont. Nevertheless, the operation of the Inn in the early years was much more difficult than had been envisaged. The students objected to the requirement that they eat at the Inn, and complained at the price of board, feeling they could prepare their own meals for less than the Inn rate. The mood of the campus was sharply expressed in the caption below a photograph of the Inn in *The Metate* of 1907, "Where we are Nothing Inn, but $16.00

The college buildings in 1907

out." While the college continued its control of discipline in the dining hall and "the custom of small tables with members of the faculty or older students acting as heads," several difficult years ensued before the spirit of Sumner Hall could be fully re-established. Contributing to the friction was the fact that the financial management of the student dining hall was in the hands of the Inn Company rather than the college.

When the company was unable to manage the Inn profitably, the college moved to take over the management, and later, assume full ownership, which it achieved in 1910. Assessments against stock were necessary in the summer of 1907, and the college paid the assessments on stock which other owners turned over to it. With this larger share in the enterprise, the college took over full operation of the Inn, which was announced to the public on September 6, 1907 in a printed letter "in behalf of the Faculty" by Dean Norton. "Now that the College is once more in full control of the dining room," he wrote, "it will resume the policy so successfully carried out for over fifteen years of expecting all students not in their own homes or employed in Claremont homes for their board, to eat at the College dining hall unless given specific permission by the Faculty to board elsewhere."

Despite this strong statement of policy, opposition from students continued so vigorously that the trustees felt impelled to act, and upon the recommendation of the Executive Committee the Board voted on January 8, 1908 to "instruct the Faculty to take such measures as in their judgment will best insure the cooperation of the student body in maintaining the College boarding table." To protect its concept of a college commons, the faculty voted disapproval of "the cafeteria system," of boarding clubs of more than twelve members, and of "clubs composed of both sexes." The faculty's firmness succeeded, and most of the students came to enjoy the Inn dining hall and its unifying influence in college life, and to cherish the associations and friendships made there.

The college's acquisition of all the Inn stock, through gift or purchase, not only contributed to effective and pleasant operation of the student dining room but also strengthened the Inn as a college and community guest house. When the Claremont Inn opened on September 24, 1910 after the customary closing for the summer season, the press carried an enthusiastic announcement of enlarged student and guest dining rooms and kitchen improvements, and the good news that "already a number of guests have taken rooms for the winter." The Inn had entered successfully upon its unique role as a college and community institution which would place it at the heart of Claremont life for much of the next sixty years.

With the transfer of the kitchen and student dining to the Inn, Sumner Hall became a more capacious residence hall for women. As renovated in the summer of 1906 Sumner provided rooms for seventy women. These accommodations included single rooms and suites of two rooms, all "light, airy and attractively furnished." The catalogue in 1908 commended particularly the third floor rooms as among the most attractive and desirable, as they had "cozy window seats" and "more commodious closets." Rent for these rooms ranged from forty to seventy dollars a year depending upon location, "desirability of the room and the number of occupants." The social facilities of Sumner were extended and improved and a new recreational room was added to the parlors and reception rooms. As the college assured would-be students in a bulletin of January 1907, the young women congregated "for a social half hour after dinner," and there was "no paucity of young men" in the parlors on "calling days."

While the Inn was under construction, plans for a college library building began to take form. As noted above, the trustees had secured for this purpose the block on the west side of College Avenue between the President's House and Pearsons Hall. The library, which earlier had occupied only the southwest room of Pearsons, had by 1906 taken over the entire south half of the first floor and its resources had grown to 8,000 volumes. If Pomona was to progress, it was imperative to provide a library building and a constantly growing collection of books.

Andrew Carnegie was then engaged in the mammoth program of gifts for library buildings by which he would provide 2505 such buildings by 1918. Naturally, he was the first potential donor to

Carnegie Library

whom Pomona appealed. When making a gift for a library building, Carnegie expected the site and funds for its maintenance to be furnished by the recipient institution. Accordingly, the Pomona trustees led by Marston and Blanchard voted in June 1904 to approve a solicitation of $30,000 to $40,000 for a library, and on December 8 authorized President Gates and Sumner to sign a contract in this spirit with Mr. Carnegie. On April 3, 1905 President Gates read to the trustees an offer from Carnegie to give Pomona $40,000 for a library building on condition that the college would raise $40,000 in new endowment for its maintenance. The Board accepted the offer, with appreciation to Mr. Carnegie and to Albert Shaw, who had rendered "valuable services in securing this proposition from Mr. Carnegie."

For the next two years, issues of the *Pomona College Bulletin*, which Gates had inaugurated, carried to Pomona's growing circle of friends the good news of the Carnegie offer and reports of the college's progress in meeting it. Mr. Marston's gift for grading and planting the library block according to plans made by Samuel Parsons and Company accompanied the initial announcement. The response of friends was heartening and in October 1906 the college reported that the architect's plans had been accepted and the contract let for $37,987. The building was to be of reinforced concrete and to contain two large reading rooms, faculty rooms, the offices of the president, and stack space for 80,000 volumes. In January 1907 the building whose "exterior will, of course, be classic" was under construction. The cornerstone was laid on February 22, 1907 with the principal address by A. S. Phelps, pastor of the Central Baptist Church of Los Angeles.

In using reinforced concrete, the architect, F. P. Burnham of Los Angeles, was employing a then new and little tried type of construction. However, just as work on the library was beginning, a large reinforced concrete hotel in Long Beach collapsed, and a reinforced concrete structure fell in the East, showing, as Dr. Sumner said, with considerable understatement, "that there was much to be learned about reinforced concrete." Construction was halted on the Pomona library, and Edwin Squire, the able engineer whom the college had employed as its own superintendent of the building, made a careful personal investigation of the collapsed Long Beach hotel and studied the report of the committee of investigation of the eastern catastrophe. On Mr. Squire's advice, the architect revised the specifications, strengthening the foundations and the floors. Despite the increased expense, the specifications were promptly accepted, and the strength and permanence of the building were assured. Unfortunately, however, the contractor became bankrupt and gave up the work before its completion, which led to additional expense of $8,860, half of which was borne by the contractor's creditors and half by the college. But vexations in construction could do little to reduce pride in the library or dim the realization that with it Pomona had greatly increased in academic stature. "There is not a college or university in the land," President Gates said at its dedication, "that would not be ornamented by it."

While the Carnegie Library was nearing completion, the college was constructing a dormitory for men. Except for the first two years, when Claremont Hall had been coeducational, male students in both the preparatory and college departments lived in homes within the village. This was the practice in many eastern institutions as well as among the newer institutions of the West. Colleges lacked money to build men's dormitories, and there was also doubt of their desirability, many college officials considering them "prolific of trouble." However, a very different view began to prevail early in the twentieth century, and there was a growing belief that living in residence halls could contribute significantly to the education of men in their undergraduate years. An ardent advocate of this point of view was Pomona's good friend and benefactor, Dr. D. K. Pearsons, who spent the winter of 1907-08 and part of 1908-09 in Claremont. As he studied Pomona, he was deeply impressed with her need of a men's dormitory. By his insistence, "almost a command," President Gates said, and with his generosity, the building was constructed in a hundred days in the summer of 1908. When Dr. Pearsons gave $25,000, he was joined at once by Blanchard and Marston, and most of the $40,000 needed was soon in hand. The architects were Myron Hunt and Elmer Grey.

At the suggestion of Dr. Pearsons, the dormitory was named for Albert K. Smiley (1828-1912) who, except for a two-year absence because of illness, had served Pomona as a trustee since 1893. Smiley, whose development of the beautiful resort community of Lake Mohonk in the Hudson River Valley has been noted above, was a teacher, a botanist and horticulturist, a trustee of several colleges, a worker for the American Indians, and a leader in the movement for international arbitration. In addition to his service to Pomona he was a trustee of Bryn Mawr College, Brown University, and the New York Normal School at New Paltz, near Lake Mohonk. Appointed to the Board of Indian Commissioners by President Hayes in 1879, he did much to reform the Indian Service. The conferences on international arbitration which Smiley held at Mohonk from 1875 to 1910 were encouraged by Andrew Carnegie, and were one of the sources of Carnegie's interest in the Peace Conferences at The Hague in 1899 and 1907. When at his winter home in Redlands Smiley was assiduous in his service to Pomona,

Smiley Hall

Brackett Observatory

and the trustees were delighted to name the new men's residence hall in his honor.

Smiley Hall was placed east of Holmes Hall, where the baseball diamond had been, a location resulting from the master plan for the campus which Myron Hunt had just prepared for the trustees. It was a three-story, reinforced concrete structure with a tile roof and was divided into three sections by two solid concrete walls. There were single rooms, but most of the rooms were in suites of three rooms for two students. The annual rent charge per student was sixty dollars. A feature of the hall was a recreation room with a fireplace, and this room immediately became the center for men's activities. *Student Life* hailed Smiley "as a dormitory which cannot be equalled anywhere in general equipment and conveniences." Its capacity was eighty students; however, in 1908 the north wing was to be occupied by the music department. The trustees had hoped to build a music and art building, but they had been unable to secure the necessary funds.

The third building completed in 1908 was far more significant than its size and cost would indicate, for it was given by a Pomona alumnus and named in honor of a Pomona professor. Astronomy had been taught by Professor Brackett since the acquisition of a six-inch telescope in 1892, but observations could be made only from a rude pier and platform on the west side of College Avenue. As astronomy became increasingly his major academic interest, Dr. Brackett undertook to secure more adequate equipment and an observatory building. His efforts were crowned with success in 1907 when one of his ablest students, Llewellyn Bixby '01, made gifts of $2,300 to pay for an observatory as designed by Brackett, and other friends of the college gave $2,000 for equipment which included a chromograph and a coelostat. The trustees recognized the service of Professor Brackett by naming the observatory in his honor. With Mr. Blanchard's approval, a stone and concrete building surmounted by a dome room and a revolving dome was placed on the western side of developing Blanchard Park, further extending the eastern projection of the campus begun by Alumni Field and Smiley Hall.

The completion of the Carnegie Library, Smiley Hall, and the Frank P. Brackett Observatory climaxed Pomona's celebration of her twentieth anniversary (the founding date was then counted as 1888, the beginning of instruction, rather than 1887, the date of incorporation, now recognized as the founding date), and their dedication was the most momentous event in the young college's history. On the great day, November 21, 1908, an academic procession formed at Pearsons Hall at 10:30 a.m. and marched to each of the three buildings for exercises of "Presentation of Keys," "Reception," and "Commission of Keys," concluding with prayer and a hymn. Proceeding first to Brackett Observatory, the members of the academic procession, students, and guests witnessed the Presentation by donor Llewellyn Bixby, the Reception by President Gates, and Commission of the Keys to Professor Brackett. The evening before, the great astronomer, George Ellery Hale, Director of Mt. Wilson Observatory, had given a lecture in Holmes Hall. At Smiley Hall, the Delivery of Keys was made by the builder, Charles E. Richards; President Gates received them and commissioned them to the president of the Associated Students, acting for Dean Norton who was ill. The keys to the Carnegie Library were delivered by C. B. Sumner to President Gates, and commissioned to Professor Arthur Dart Bissell, chairman of the library committee. The prayer of dedication was offered by former President Cyrus G. Baldwin. In the afternoon, exercises were held in the Claremont Church where the principal address was given by Bishop Joseph Horsfal Johnson. Greetings from other institutions were presented by the presidents of Throop Polytechnic Institute and Whittier College, the deans of the University of Southern California and Occidental College, and a former president of Carleton College.

Evolution of the Instructional Programs

The institution which these excellent facilities would serve was developing rapidly and looking confidently to the future. Of the total enrollment of 507, college students numbered 296. In June 1908, Pomona granted 48 baccalaureate degrees, in comparison

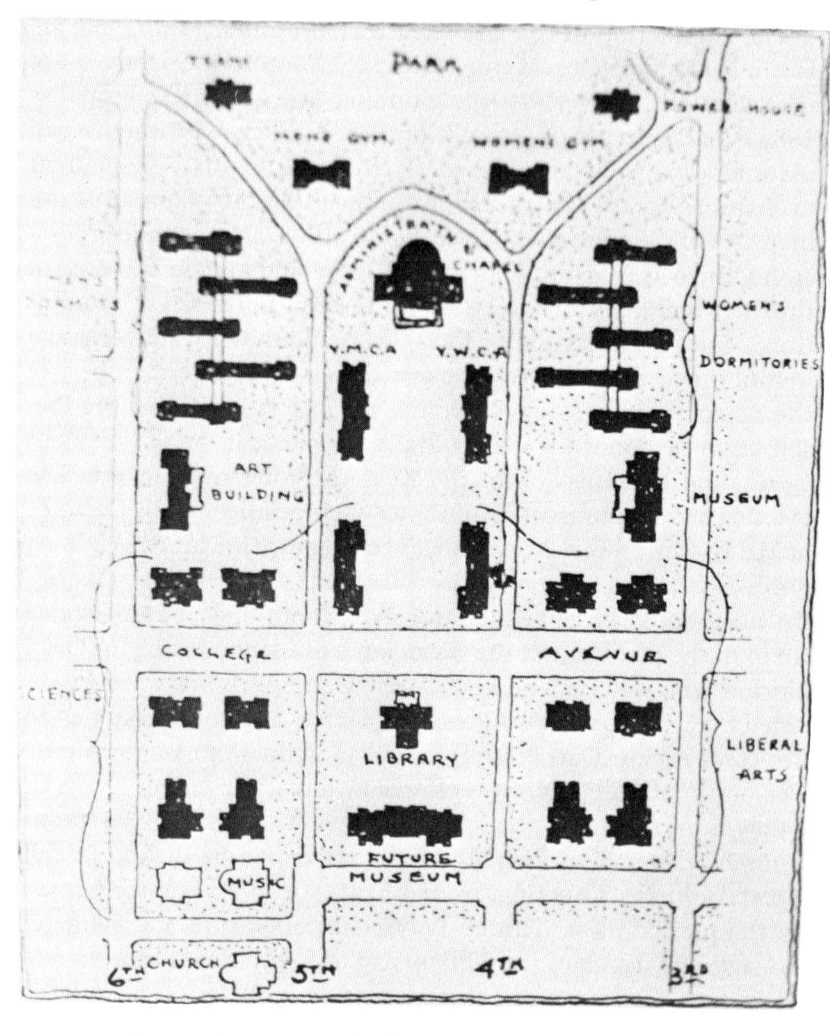

Campus Plan, recommended by Myron Hunt and Elmer Grey, Architects, Los Angeles

with Beloit's 49, Carleton's 46, Grinnell's 45, Knox's 32, and Whitman's 20. The trustees and faculty anticipated that in another five years Pomona would have 500 college students.

The academic calendar and the curriculum established in the Gates administration in many ways shaped the subsequent history of the college. The three-term plan was replaced by the semester system in 1902-03, and within the next six years the catalogues took the form familiar to all subsequent generations of Pomona students and faculty members. The 132 units required for graduation, which included four in physical education and four in advanced rhetoric, were slightly higher than in later years. The College Department continued to give three degrees, with classical, literary, and scientific programs leading respectively to the Bachelor of Arts, Bachelor of Letters, and Bachelor of Science degrees. For each of the three degrees, the admissions requirement of sixteen units prescribed a common core of three years of mathematics, two of English, two of history, and one of physics. Latin was also required for each program, four years for the classical and literary, but only two years for the scientific program. The classical course had the further requirement of three years of Greek. While two years of a modern language were expected for the literary and scientific courses, special arrangements could be made for meeting this requirement.

The total faculty for the College Department, the Preparatory Department, the School of Music, and the School of Art and Design had grown from twenty-one to thirty-eight. The catalogue for 1908-09 listed twenty-one "departments of instruction" in the College Department, although at least four of these were really sub-divisions of larger areas. The expanded curriculum, with the enthusiastic support of the faculty, quickened the intellectual vitality of the campus. Among the new faculty were several who made outstanding and lasting contributions to the college.

There was great development in the biological sciences where Charles Fuller Baker joined Professor Cook. First appointed only for 1903-04, Baker returned to Pomona in 1908 as professor of zoology and curator of the museum. While away he had served as chief of the botany department of the Agronomy Station of Cuba, and then as curator of the Botanical Garden and Herbarium of the Goeldi Museum in Pará, Brazil. A graduate of the Michigan Agricultural College, now Michigan State University, and with a Master's degree at Stanford University, Baker was excited by the developing agriculture and fruit culture of Southern California. He enthusiastically studied fruits and plants new to California and encouraged their propagation and cultivation. The collection of plant materials which he gave the college initiated the Pomona Herbarium which today numbers over 325,000 specimens. Baker's magnetic personality and devotion to his subject made him an inspiring teacher. Although he remained only five years, he left a lasting influence at Pomona.[1]

Work in English language and literature was strengthened in 1904 by the appointment of Mendal Garbutt Frampton as instructor in English language and rhetoric. An alumnus of Illinois College who had done graduate work at the University of Chicago and Harvard, he came to Pomona from the faculty of the University of Wisconsin. Innovative and an ardent advocate of high standards of scholarship, Frampton soon took an important role in the work of the faculty and its committees.

Although music and art were included in the curriculum from the very beginning of Pomona, they were organized as associated "schools," rather than as parts of the College Department. Their finances were separate; the teachers were compensated by the fees of their students and did not receive salaries from the institution.

Music was much better established than art, enjoying a larger staff and enrollment. By 1893-94, the catalogue announced a "School of Music" offering "a thorough and symmetrical musical education." Two courses were arranged: the academic, which led to a teacher's certificate, and the collegiate, which led to a diploma. With the appointment in 1895 of John Comfort Fillmore as head of the school, the basis was laid for the future development of Pomona in music. Professor Fillmore, head of the Milwaukee

[1]Baker was the brother of Newton D. Baker (1871-1937) who was Secretary of War under President Woodrow Wilson. Baker resigned at Pomona in 1913 to accept a professorship at the University of the Philippines, Los Baños, where today a building bears his name.

School of Music, was an experienced teacher who had studied in Europe and had written a widely used *History of Music.* Professor Brackett credited Fillmore with bringing "an entire change in the study of music in Pomona." Combining a good nature and a sparkling humor with a devotion to the best in music, Fillmore won the admiration of students and faculty. It was a tragic loss when he died in 1898 at the age of fifty-five.

The School of Music made little progress in the difficult years that ensued and it was not until the appointment of Fred A. Bacon as director of the school in 1903 that there was further development in the music program. He had come to California in 1891 after study at Oberlin College and in New York and Boston, and for a number of years had served as director of music for both the First Congregational Church of Los Angeles and the University of Southern California, whence he came to Pomona. His leadership was such that by July 1904 a special bulletin on the School of Music could announce a faculty of six, with instruction in voice, piano, pipe organ, violin, violoncello, theory, and history of music. The School of Music proposed "to fit students for the musical profession as composers, theorists, artists, and teachers," and provided for "the study of music as a part of general culture or as an accomplishment." While most students took the diploma, a course in music and literature leading to the degree of Bachelor of Letters was available in the college. Among the faculty was Kate Condit, instructor in piano and voice, who in 1902 organized "The Ladies Glee Club of Pomona College," the first women's glee club in Southern California.

The School of Music grew with the college and from 1904 to 1908 its enrollment increased from 50 to 150. Its facilities were augmented by use of the two rooms added off the stage of Holmes Hall auditorium in the renovation and expansion of that building in 1904. A great addition came in 1907-08 with the installation of a Hope Jones pipe organ in the Claremont Church. Made in Elmira, New York, the organ had "electro-pneumatic action throughout—quicker than that of the best piano-forte." As the college had unlimited use of the organ, it provided new opportunities for both instruction and performance. A college orchestra, augmented by sixteen musicians from Los Angeles, assisted the Choral Union in its concert in June 1909.

Art at Pomona, as in most colleges in the nineteenth century, also began outside the normal academic program and institutional financial structure. Mrs. L. E. Garden-McLeod, head of the Los Angeles School of Art and Design, came to Claremont once a week and gave art lessons to a small group assembled by Professor and Mrs. Brackett. "The School of Art and Design" was announced in 1893, with Mrs. Garden-McLeod as director, and she conducted a painting and sketching class in a "north room."

A decade was to pass, however, before any larger development in art occurred at Pomona. In 1905, a special "Art Number" of the *Pomona College Bulletin* announced that the growing demands of the college "required the attention and direction of a resident teacher," and that Mrs. Hannah Tempest Jenkins had been appointed Associate Professor of Art and Design, and Director of the School. A Pennsylvania Quaker and the widow of an industrialist of means, she had studied at the School of Industrial Art in Philadelphia, the Philadelphia Academy of Fine Arts, and in Amsterdam and Paris. In addition, Mrs. Jenkins had graduated from the course in pedagogy and fine arts at Teachers College, Columbia University. She came to Pomona from the headship of the art department at Mansfield, Pennsylvania, State Normal School. Mrs. Jenkins was "a rare teacher, with an inborn love and enthusiasm for her work" and with a deep interest in her students. Art flourished at Pomona under her direction.

The influence of Mrs. Jenkins was as strong in the general community as within the college. Early in her first year, she organized the Rembrandt Club for the purpose of advancing art education. The membership was at first composed of only students and faculty, and the officers, all students, included two women and two men. The Rembrandt Club soon broadened its outreach, however, and by 1907-08 its membership was drawn from the community, faculty, and "working members of the art department." Although their participation was short-lived, it should be noted that students played an important part in the beginning of the club. The quality of student leadership is indicated by the fact that Alexander C. Judson '07, an editor of *Student Life* and later a distinguished professor of English literature at Indiana University, served as vice-president of the Rembrandt Club, both in 1905-06 and 1906-07, and that Mabel Shaw Bridges '08, was treasurer in 1906-07.

The School of Art and Design introduced programs to meet the needs of three types of art students: the regular program for those considering "professional life in art work," courses for those wishing only to elect some art work, and an art-literary program leading to the Bachelor of Letters degree in Pomona College. This last marked the greatest change, and indicated the direction in which art at Pomona would move ultimately. Art, like music, had been taken into the college curriculum. The next step would be for the School of Art and Design and the School of Music to be brought fully into the curricular and administrative structure of Pomona College.

An Unexpected Resignation

The strengthening of the faculty and the development of an enlarged campus inevitably brought increased financial requirements. As set forth in the twentieth anniversary pamphlet, "Indebtedness, accumulated for indispensable equipment, and overwrought professors are good ground for anxious thought. It is the very prosperity of the College that constitutes its pressing problem." To meet the emergency, the faculty and trustees announced "The Forward Movement," which had been preceded by a year of preparation. The trustees first contemplated a drive for $500,000, but concluding that this was an unattainable goal, voted to raise "at least $300,000," of which $100,000 would be for endowment, $100,000 for new buildings, and $100,000 for indebtedness and new equipment. There were hopes that Mr. Carnegie and the General Education Board, recently established by John D. Rockefeller, would give a significant part of this amount. When Carnegie responded promptly that he would give $50,000 if the College would raise an additional $200,000, the total objective of the Forward Movement was reduced to $250,000.

This goal was to be raised during 1908-09 as the climax of the triumphant celebration of the twentieth anniversary, and Dedication Day for Brackett Observatory, Smiley Hall, and the Carnegie Library was planned as the major public event of the campaign. The college looked confidently to its immediate constituency: "Our Congregational Church membership has multiplied nearly eight times since the organization of the College. . . . Can a lover of humanity and of Christianity find a better channel, one reaching out more widely and touching more deeply the springs of character than Pomona College? . . . [It] is not impotently begging for help; it is offering an opportunity to those who can appreciate and take it [for] rare investment in supreme values."

The pace with which the Forward Movement began justified such confidence and indicated an early realization of the $250,000 goal. Dr. Pearsons subscribed $25,000, members of the Board of Trustees added $50,000, and the "Incorporated Alumni" pledged $10,000. In June 1908, the trustees set up a committee of three headed by Charles B. Sumner, including President Gates and another member they would choose. Sumner was to give full time to the Forward Movement and to receive a salary of $2,000.

There was such enthusiasm for the prospects of the college in 1908-09 that a serious illness which required Sumner to withdraw from the Forward Movement Committee did not seem critical. President Gates succeeded him as chairman of the committee, and Henry Kingman, pastor of the Claremont Church and assistant secretary of the Board, took over Sumner's duties with the trustees. But Sumner's illness proved a turning point. After the high tide of Dedication Day, the campaign lagged, and President Gates, unable to advance it, became deeply discouraged. To the astonishment of the trustees and faculty he abruptly resigned the presidency at the trustee meeting on January 12, 1909.

While those nearest him had noted the tenseness of the president, they expected this to pass. Unlike his two predecessors, he had never been the subject of serious criticism by the faculty or the trustees, and he was loved by the students, who in the *Metate* of 1907 characterized him as one "who combines with the dignity of a leader the kindliness of a friend." But Gates, like Baldwin, could not stand the strain of the constant seeking for funds, which was basic in the development of a new college, particularly one in a newly settled area. After the excitement of completing and dedicating the new buildings, the difficulties of the Forward Movement and the daily pressures of the presidency made it difficult for Gates to sleep, and he sensed himself on the verge of nervous exhaustion. As Mrs. Gates wrote some years later, "He felt impelled to ask for release at once while self-recovery was possible." The trustees, in sorrow and with deepest regret, accepted his resignation, but made it effective only at the close of the college year and placed him on leave of absence with full salary until October 1, 1909.

President Gates had been close personally to everyone in the college and his resignation brought great sorrow among the students and faculty. "His ideals of nobility and honor, his ever simple, ever genuine depth of character, his breadth of view and love of truth," were praised in *Student Life.* Always a minister at heart, Gates enjoyed a pastoral relationship with the students, and his chapel talk following his resignation was a unique moment in the history of the college. "I have long felt," he told the packed chapel, "that my position in reference to any college of which I was President must be as an educator, not as a financier. My position in Pomona is where I am today, when I speak from this platform." He predicted the financial emergency would end, and that his resignation would place "the college's needs more sharply before its friends and new helpers will appear." In the spirit of his first chapel talk, "The Good Success," he told the students not to worry about financial burdens nor allow them to take away "the charm of these days.... My last word to you is that you let nothing rob you of the poetry of life, that is in these college years." A moving testimonial to the esteem in which President Gates was held in the collegiate community of Southern California came in a letter to the president of the Associated Students of Pomona from President John Willis Baer of Occidental College, who wrote, "Occidental will lose a friend beloved by its student body."

As events proved, this January chapel talk was not to be President Gates' "farewell" to the students of Pomona. The long sea voyage to Australia and New Zealand, on which he embarked alone immediately after his resignation, so restored him that he acceded to the urgings of the seniors to return and conduct commencement. *Student Life* reported on May 21, 1909 that Gates would be arriving in San Francisco from Honolulu on the *Alameda* on June 1 and would be in Claremont shortly thereafter. A front page editorial rejoiced that "for three weeks longer President Gates is the head of Pomona College. . . . With him have come gladheartedness, joy, sunshine." The Class of 1909 had commissioned Mrs. Jenkins to paint the president's portrait, which was presented to the college on Class Day and hung in the Carnegie Library. The Gates family left Claremont following commencement. By September 1909 President Gates had been persuaded to accept the presidency of Fisk University, Nashville, Tennessee, a pioneer liberal arts college for black students founded in 1866 by the Congregational Education Society.

Although Pomona trustees, faculty and students were slow to recover from their deep sorrow at President Gates' departure, the college was in better condition than they realized. There was unusual harmony and cooperation among the Board of Trustees, the faculty, and the student body. All parts of the institution had responded to the president's leadership with a resulting pride at home and wider respect for Pomona in California and the East. The editors of the *Metate* of 1909 accurately analyzed the situation: "We do not for a moment think that Pomona is going to falter in her great work. The machinery is unimpaired, and a captain will be found."

CHAPTER VI

Student Organizations and Campus Life, 1901-10

THE EMERGING PRIMACY of the College Department invigorated student activities, and the athletic, literary, and religious organizations moved forward with confidence, scarcely reflecting the serious problems that occupied the faculty and the trustees. Athletics particularly contributed to student pride in Pomona and to the growing intercollegiate community of Southern California. Pomona was a charter member of the Southern California Amateur Athletic Union which was organized in 1901-02 and included the principal colleges and high schools in the region. Professor George S. Sumner represented Pomona in the Union for many years and made a major contribution to the development of a sound athletic program for the college and her friendly competitors.

Within the college, steps were taken to place the Athletic Association on a secure basis and to regularize the operation of the various aspects of the athletic program. When the trustees established an annual athletic fee of five dollars, effective in 1903-04, the *Metate* of 1904 hailed this action as "the greatest boon that has ever come to Pomona in an athletic way." This fee and the gate receipts at games defrayed all athletic expenses, including the salaries of the coaches, who were not members of the faculty and were employed directly by the Pomona College Athletic Association. Although the faculty controlled the schedules of athletic contests in detail and established strict rules of academic eligibility, the Athletic Association was largely autonomous in finance and athletic management.

The college limited its official role to the encouragement of athletics and the provision of playing fields. It was the Athletic Association, therefore, which in 1904 built new "commodious training quarters for the men, thus allowing the young ladies the entire use of Renwick Gymnasium." But it was the trustees who in 1905 provided the land that permitted the expansion of Pomona's athletic program. With the acquisition and development of Blanchard Park, an agreement was made with the donor that an area in the northwest portion of the park be set aside for athletic purposes. The Alumni Association undertook the improvement of the area, securing $2,000 augmented by the personal labor of students and individual alumni. "Alumni Field," when christened, provided a football field, enclosed by a quarter-mile oval track, with a two hundred twenty-yard straightaway within the oval. To the south, space was provided for tennis courts and the baseball field. Bleachers were placed only on the south side of the football field in order that spectators would face north and enjoy the view of "Old Baldy's real majesty and grandeur."

The college enjoyed great success in intercollegiate contests, and the *Metate* had exulted in 1902-03 that Pomona easily stood "first among S. California schools in all lines of athletics, and with such a future before it her position will be maintained." For example, Pomona in 1903 won the track championship from U.S.C. and Occidental for the eighth time in eleven years. Such success in the south led to invitations from the two universities in the north, and in the spring of 1904 the Pomona track team participated in meets with the University of California in Berkeley and with Stanford in Palo Alto. Although Pomona lost to California, 90 to 18, and to Stanford, 83½ to 24½, the meets marked "the first time that any Southern California team had met either of the universities in any branch of sport."

Other contests with California and Stanford soon followed. The great success of the Pomona football team in 1904 (victor over Occidental 42 to 6) earned it an invitation to play the University of California in Berkeley on October 29. This time a determined Pomona "played the part of guests in a way that surprised all" and lost an excellent game by the score of only 5 to 0. In the spring of

1905, Stanford came south for a track meet on the Pomona campus, "an honor never before given to a Southern California College." Although Pomona, fresh from a 72 to 50 victory over Occidental, lost to Stanford 81 to 36, the *Metate* felt the college had shown itself "a worthy rival."

Alumni Field was completed in the spring of 1906. Dedication Day, which featured a track meet with U.S.C., was marked by a Pomona victory. The impetus given to track led to a win over Occidental on their field. In 1907, Pomona won the conference meet, and two members of its team established new all-Coast records, William H. Spurgeon, Jr. '08 in the 120-yard low hurdles, and William B. Himrod '08 in the mile run.

Football had an unusual season in 1906. The University of California and Stanford had decided to play English rugby instead of American football, and Pomona in 1906 sought to meet this competition. The team began the season with rugby and went north for games at Berkeley and Palo Alto, losing 6 to 0 and 26 to 0. Returning south they shifted to American football and lost games with the Sherman Indians, U.S.C., and Occidental. As the *Metate* observed, "The attempt to play British and American football (combined with the loss of experienced men) weakened Pomona's unredoubtable varsity."

The academic year 1908-09 marked a major transition in Pomona athletics. By agreement among the institutions in the conference students in preparatory departments were not permitted to play on the college teams. For the first time Pomona had "college athletics."

"Pomona College is now football champion of the South," exulted *Student Life,* November 26, 1909. "The season has been eminently satisfactory in every way — nobody hurt, none of the squabbling or contesting over eligibility rules, the best financial showing, probably, of any season thus far, and best of all the CHAMPIONSHIP." The season was also one of high drama. Pomona had tied U.S.C. 0 to 0, and Occidental had tied U.S.C. 3 to 3. The day of decision was thus to be the Pomona-Oxy game on Alumni Field. The attendance was unprecedented with the bleachers overflowing, and "over seventy-five automobiles filled the space on the north side of the field." The game lived up to its billing, with Pomona winning 14 to 6.

While track and football claimed greatest student and public attention, other sports were also developed on an intercollegiate basis in the Gates administration. Although baseball had been played with U.S.C. and Occidental as early as 1900, the teams and their records were unimpressive until 1909; then Pomona celebrated the construction of a new diamond by winning the conference championship with an undefeated season. Included were such thrillers as an eleventh inning victory over U.S.C. on Bovard Field and a tenth inning victory over Whittier on Alumni Field in the season's finale. The evening before the Whittier game the first baseball rally in the history of the college was held on the library steps, where speakers addressed the rooters from a "precarious position on the automobile serving as a rostrum." The great season was hailed with a special "Baseball Edition" of *Student Life* featuring articles by Coach Stanton and Captain Lee C. Mahoney '09.

Basketball at Pomona was first played by the women who took a lead in introducing the sport in Southern California colleges. As in the early days of football, the games were often played with high schools. Eight teams formed a league, and a regular schedule was set up for 1903-04. As it was difficult to arrange games even with neighboring institutions, it was not until 1906-07 that basketball was recognized by the Student Association as a regular college sport. The Pomona women played their first intercollegiate game on February 20, 1909, losing to U.S.C. 17 to 13. The men's basketball team, organized in 1906-07, played its first intercollegiate games in 1907-08, losing two to Whittier and winning one from Occidental.

By the end of President Gates' administration Pomona had well established policies in "physical culture," as it was then known, as well as in intercollegiate athletics. "Gymnasium work," required for both men and women, had been part of the college program since shortly after Gates' appointment, and was described in a special bulletin on physical education in July 1904. The problems of intercollegiate athletics led the trustees in 1908 to place the finances and management of the program under the control of the faculty. The athletic fee of five dollars, hitherto separately collected, was included as a part of the tuition fee which was increased from seventy to seventy-five dollars a year. The college then assumed the cost of light, repairs, and equipment for Renwick Gymnasium and the training quarters, handling these as it did other campus buildings. Henceforth the director of physical education would be chosen by the procedure for faculty appointments, but to insure harmony the approval of the joint committee on athletics would be secured. In addition, the joint committee was required to secure the approval of the cabinet of the faculty for the appointment of all coaches. To finance physical education and athletic activities, the trustees voted to set aside annually, in a special fund, three per cent of the income received from tuition fees. While some difficulties would arise in the years ahead, the trustees had established beyond question the fundamental principle that athletics were under the college administration.

The gift of Alumni Field illustrated the growth of the Alumni Association and its increasing contribution to the college. The Association marked its tenth anniversary by an act of legal incorporation in 1905, which greatly facilitated its work. As the number of graduates grew, alumni clubs, known as "Terra Toma Bands," from the already famed college song, were established, first in Berkeley in 1904, then at Stanford, and New York City — the members being primarily graduate students in these university centers. The Pomona Club in Los Angeles was organized in 1905.

All the undergraduate organizations showed appreciation of the alumni, who were notable for their deep and continuing interest in their alma mater. Alumni were listed in the catalogue as soon as the first class was graduated. A "Triennial Register" in January 1908 contained the names of all alumni, together with trustees up to that time, and the current faculty.

Communications from alumni to *Student Life* informed the undergraduates of the exciting life not only at Berkeley, Yale, Harvard, or Columbia, but of Great Britain and Germany. Alexander C. Judson '07 wrote of his studies at the University of Marburg. Earl H. Kennard '07, who had brought distinction to Pomona by becoming its first Rhodes Scholar, wrote not only of his experiences at Oxford, but of his pleasure in seeing Professor and Mrs. Arthur Dart Bissell and their son and daughter in Leipzig, where Professor Bissell was spending a sabbatical leave studying German literature.

The trustees recognized the stature of Pomona's alumni by beginning to elect them to membership on the Board. The first alumnus so honored was Edwin F. Hahn '98, who was elected a Pomona trustee in 1903. His achievement as a young lawyer in Pasadena had matched his distinguished career in college. In 1909 he was joined on the Board by Arthur M. Dole '96, a businessman in the city of Pomona who in college had been a leader in many undergraduate activities and had served as president of the Alumni Association in 1899-1900 and 1900-1901. Each of these men was to serve on the Board for over forty years. Recognizing the growing strength of the Alumni Association, the trustees on February 20, 1909, voted to increase the number of alumni on the Board to five "as soon as practicable" and invited the Alumni Association to nominate one or more alumni each year, from whom a choice would be made by the trustees. Although the Board did not bind itself to elect an alumnus each year, this action was a definitive step in bringing alumni into a greater role in the governance of the college.

The leadership and operation of student activities were enhanced in 1904 by the organization of the Associated Students. Frank Seaver '05, who had been managing editor of the *Metate* and manager of football in 1903-04, was elected its first president. The college provided a large room in the basement of Holmes Hall as headquarters where there were desks for the officers of the Associated Students, the *Student Life* board, and the athletic manager. "All student interests are brought in harmony through the officers chosen by the student body," the catalogue stated. The executive committee included "those prominent in such diverse lines as athletics, oratory, and editorship of the *Student Life*." The role of the Associated Students was strengthened by setting aside each week one of the daily chapel periods for a general assembly of the student body. Membership in the Associated Students, which at first included students from both the College and the Preparatory Department, was limited to college students after 1907-08.

The improved management of student organizations brought a desire for a means of discussing college affairs among representatives of all segments of the institution. The constitution of the Associated Students was amended in May 1909 to provide for an advisory committee of seven to be appointed by the president of the college, who would be its chairman, and to include a member of the Board of Trustees, two alumni who were not faculty members, and three members of the faculty. This advisory committee, meeting with elected student representatives, constituted the Joint Committee. The Joint Committee proved a useful instrument in the critical period of growth in the early part of the century, and it provided valuable experience in governing the college.

The life of the developing college was well presented by the *Metate* and the *Student Life.* The former became a larger book after 1903 and included a literary and humorous section sometimes exceeding fifty pages. "Metate Day" was one of the greatest occasions of the college year. For example, on June 10, 1910,

> at four-thirty, amid clattering hoofs and banging shotguns Claremont awoke to a great fact — the annual was out! Then followed, at the Commons, an incongruous reception-banquet-breakfast at which blue shirted Welakhoos [the juniors] sat restfully beside their trim and tidy classmates all in decorous white, at a long table whose snowy cloth contrasted effectively with the gentlemen's 'cords'. Between classes, up to chapel-time, gay-bedecked tallyhos and autos paraded the streets for the especial benefit of prospective purchasers. Chapel found the whole crew of them [the juniors] marching solemnly down the aisle, triumphant strains issuing from the great organ, while they filed to their wonted rows and seated themselves.

After chapel there was a mad rush of the students to purchase the *Metate* for a dollar and fifty cents.

The *Student Life* reached a high standard of effectiveness in President Gates' last year. With Philip S. Bird '09 as editor-in-chief, it showed maturity in its perceptions of Pomona and in its comments on and news of American higher education. A special "Dedication" issue hailed the new buildings in November 1908, and featured the address by Bishop Johnson. The paper stressed the larger purposes of Pomona and called the students to a college loyalty of "unceasing faithfulness."

As the college grew there was continued interest in public speaking and debate. The coeducational Pomona College Literary Society received large student support, and debating clubs of twenty members each were organized separately for men and women. For the men there were the Pomona College Debating Club, dating from 1898, and the Pomona College Lyceum, established in 1901. Alpha Kappa, also organized in 1898, belonged to the women. Debating, intramural until 1905-06, became intercollegiate when Pomona and Occidental concluded a three-year agreement. Debate topics, such as the annexation of Hawaii and a federal subsidy for the United States merchant marine, reflected public issues of the day. Debate and oratory were held in such regard at Pomona that leaders in these activities were privileged to join athletes in wearing the coveted "P".

Music and dramatics gradually took a more important place in the college. The Men's Glee Club was joined by the "Ladies' Glee Club of Pomona College" in 1902-03. When Professor Bacon became head of the School of Music he built up a stronger Men's Club, and began a new series of tours in California. In the summer of 1906 the Men's Glee Club had a ten-day engagement with the Long Beach Chautauqua. The Choral Union, which sang for major college events, brought in soloists for such programs as *The Messiah* in the commencement season of 1905.

Students were talented in providing their own musical entertainment, and one of their presentations in 1909-10 gave Pomona the song that soon became the college's Alma Mater. A minstrel show, organized to raise funds for baseball uniforms, required an ensemble finale. In a few hours freshman Richard N. Loucks composed *Hail! Pomona, Hail!*

Drama was taken less seriously at this time. It was essentially a class activity, and from its entrance each class looked forward to its own Senior Class Day, with "a chance for the exercise of originality and genius." The Plug Ugly, given by the juniors early in the college year, was comprised of caricatures of students and faculty. The "two real plays of the year" were the athletic farce and the junior farce, the latter usually directed by a member of the faculty.

As indicated by dramatics, the classes were the cohesive organizations of the college. All their social activities were chaperoned and closely regulated by the faculty. The regular closing hour for evening social events was ten o'clock, and only major affairs were allowed the much sought after hour of eleven. Beset with the problem of distinguishing between major and minor events, the dean of women in October 1905 asked the faculty to inform her which social occasions were considered "annual functions with the privilege of continuing until eleven o'clock." The faculty voted these: the annual joint reception of the Y.M.C.A. and Y.W.C.A., the senior reception for the freshmen, the freshman reception for the seniors, the sophomore reception for the seniors, and the football banquet. Exceptions or special privileges were granted only by vote of the entire faculty. A sophomore request in 1905 for a picnic and hay ride to San Antonio Canyon was granted with the understanding that the class would have "seats placed in the wagons." Seniors occupied an especially exalted place in their last semester, and in February 1906, for example, were permitted to hold meetings of the entire class "at any time" provided the meetings did not extend beyond ten p.m.

By the spring of 1908 the question of dancing, then firmly forbidden, had to be faced by the faculty. On March 10 the cabinet, which was the body of full professors, reiterated its opposition to "dancing and single rig driving" and asked Professors Norton and Sumner to present "a formulation of this principle." Their report, which was approved, stated that "promiscuous dancing is not expected in the college buildings nor at college parties or functions, either in term time or in vacations." The attendance of individuals at non-college dances was not forbidden. But there was strong disapproval of "couples driving in single rigs." Despite these firm statements, the question of dancing could not be quieted and in March 1909 separate petitions requesting the privilege of holding annually three college dances were presented to the cabinet by the men and the women. The petitions were laid on the table until each member of the cabinet could present his views in writing. After the discussion, the faculty held the decision over until the following year, and finally in a special cabinet meeting on October

4, 1909 reaffirmed the regulation that "no dances, class or college, shall be given at any time in the name of the college," with college receptions specifically included. The *Student Life* in an editorial, "A New Challenge," called on students to understand the faculty position and stand united in one purpose "that Pomona go ahead."

Along with dancing, the faculty had to face the larger issue of fraternities and sororities. The *Metate* of 1903 carried for the first time a section entitled "Class Fraternities," listing four fraternities: the Cajole Club, Sirocco Club, Kappa Delta, and T.S.P., established respectively in 1900, 1902, 1901, and 1902; and three sororities: Crickets, Phi Upsilon, and Sigma Mu, all established in 1902. Although the fraternities and sororities varied in name and number in succeeding years, they were listed in the *Metate* through 1907, and then omitted in 1908. The one continuous fraternity had been Kappa Delta. Meanwhile, the faculty in March 1906 had established regulations for the formation of new societies. They must secure faculty approval, be registered with the faculty, and present annually the names of their officers and the place and time of their regular meetings. Membership in such societies was restricted to juniors and seniors, and pledging was not permitted until the junior year. Significantly, the faculty ruled out national social fraternities.

At Pomona, as elsewhere, housing was involved in the fraternity question. Since the college had only two residence halls, Sumner for women, and Smiley for men after 1908, most students lived in houses in Claremont, and some of these became, in effect, clubs. The college regulations permitted junior and senior women to take rooms in private homes, subject to the approval of the faculty. Junior and senior women wishing to live together outside Sumner Hall or in a private home were required to secure a woman, preferably a faculty member, to be "in practice and in theory the head of the house."

The regulations for men were more complex. Freshmen could room in a club house only if a faculty member resided in the house. By a special vote of the faculty, sophomore men could be permitted to room in a club house in which either a member of the faculty or some responsible upperclassman resided. Upperclassmen, as a group, could rent houses only after obtaining permission from the faculty. Since the college was so dependent on off-campus housing, the faculty was only accepting reality when it voted in May 1908 that it was "inexpedient to legislate against the existence of so-called fraternity houses." They did, however, restrict approval for groups petitioning to engage houses to those students who needed to make "a material financial saving." While there was no reference to fraternities in the *Metate* of 1908, their activity continued, and ten "secret societies" were listed the following year — five for men and five for women. Furthermore, the members of Kappa Delta in May 1909 completed "their summer cottage" in Bear Canyon.

The faculty realized that major decisions would have to be faced, and the societies were informed in late May "that the matter of fraternities and fraternity houses" would be discussed in the autumn with the newly formed Joint Committee. Previewing the work for this committee for 1909-10, the editor of *Student Life* cited as "imminent questions it must solve" the matter of national fraternities and the related issue "of what the housing system of the institution shall be — Dormitory or Club House." These were questions that would be waiting for the new president whom the trustees were seeking in the autumn of 1909.

Housing for students was available because the Claremont community had grown with the college. After the trustees made the decision to keep the college in Claremont, faculty members built houses there, and they were joined by ranchers. A small business section developed to serve them and the students. The population of Claremont which had been 250 in 1900 had increased to 1114 by 1910.

As the state of California did not provide municipal government for communities of less than 500 inhabitants, local matters in Claremont were at first handled in a voluntary town meeting such as many Claremonters had known in New England. Citizens were notified of meetings, officers were elected, public policies discussed, and funds secured by subscription. The growth that led to the building of the Claremont Church and the Claremont Inn in 1906 also resulted in the incorporation of Claremont as a city which was approved by the electorate by a vote of seventy-three to forty-nine on September 22, 1907. The incorporation of Claremont thus came twenty years after the founding of the college around which it had grown and which had determined its character.

Claremont began to resemble "Claremont the Beautiful," as its promoters had christened it. Streets were improved, and trees and gardens planted. The planting of saplings of *Eucalyptus viminalis* on Warren Avenue in 1890 by H. A. Palmer, president of the Pomona Board of Trustees, and Professor Brackett was assuring the development of one of the finest tree-lined streets on any American campus. Always in the background of the increasingly beautiful town were the grandeur and majesty of the mountains.

CHAPTER VII

A Captain is Found

THE TRUSTEES were slow to realize that Pomona College had entered its most prolonged presidential crisis. Thirteen months were to elapse between the resignation of President Gates and the arrival of his successor. The search committee of Marston, Hahn, Kingman, Chapman and Bishop Johnson, appointed on January 12, 1909, at first felt they had an immediate solution at hand. They counted on the acceptance of their fellow trustee, William Horace Day, pastor of the First Congregational Church of Los Angeles, and nominated him within two weeks. The Board then offered him a salary of $3500, and occupancy of the President's House, with his assumption of the presidency at a convenient date in the summer. To the Board's surprise, Dr. Day in early February not only declined to accept but amplified his official refusal in a public announcement in his Sunday morning sermon and with a letter to the editor of *Student Life*.

To make matters worse, the search for a president was brought to a halt in the spring of 1909 by consideration of a union of Pomona with Occidental College, then planning to move from its Highland Park campus where it lacked room for effective expansion. The idea of a union of colleges of Protestant foundation in Southern California was attractive to many churchmen, and it had been broached on earlier occasions. President Ferguson had been interested in such a union, and as early as 1900 the Pomona trustees had set up a special committee "on the consolidation of the colleges of Southern California." This committee had been asked to ascertain the views of the Occidental trustees "as to the feasibility of uniting the two institutions." What had not proved feasible in

1900 seemed more likely in 1909. Pomona was seeking a president, and Occidental was looking for a new campus. Furthermore, Dr. John Willis Baer, the president of Occidental since 1906, was highly esteemed by both students and faculty at Pomona. Would it not be logical, so some opinion ran, if Occidental came to Claremont, with President Baer heading the resulting larger and more influential institution?

Consequently, the Pomona Board on May 25, 1909 established a committee to canvass the possibilities of such a union with a similar committee of trustees from Occidental, naming as members William Horace Day, Edwin F. Hahn, C. C. Chapman, Charles B. Sumner, and Bishop Joseph H. Johnson. When the actuality and practicality of a union were faced, little progress could be made in the negotiations. The Pomona committee was instructed in a meeting of June 9 to "ask a fuller statement by the Occidental committee of the difficulties in the way" of the merger. Major issues which soon appeared were the reluctance of Occidental to come to Claremont, and the natural disinclination of the Pomona trustees to abandon a campus on the development of which they had just made notable progress. While the definitive decision against union was taken by the Occidental trustees, they obviously articulated the final consensus of both boards. Rejecting "the practicability of uniting the two student bodies upon one campus and merging the two corporations into one," the Occidental trustees in addition affirmed their belief that it would be unwise for their college "to remove from the immediate vicinity of the growing city of Los Angeles." The Occidental trustees expressed their faith in the future of both colleges, foreseeing "that the rapid growth of Southern California will tax each institution to the utmost."

With the presentation of this correspondence at its annual meeting on June 22, 1909, the Pomona Board of Trustees instructed Secretary Charles B. Sumner to go east at his earliest convenience and seek a candidate for the office of president. Dean Norton and the faculty, who on January 12 had been asked to administer the internal affairs of the college according to the provisions of the by-laws, realized that their responsibilities would continue well into the academic year 1909-10. Beset with questions and uncertainties about the selection of a president and the conduct of the dormant endowment campaign, the college in its bulletin of July 1909 testily informed the public that "if no attempt is made to forecast the probabilities for the coming year, it should be borne in mind that the settled policy of Pomona College is to rely upon history rather than prophesy in its published statements." In October, the catalogue carried a stark entry, "__________________________, President." The *Metate* for 1909-10 reflected student concern with a cartoon captioned "Christmas Eve at Pomona." A youth was sleeping in a four-poster bed with this letter attached: "Dear Santa: I want a president. P. C. Trustees."

Meanwhile, Charles B. Sumner had gone forth for the third time to seek a president for Pomona. Beginning in the northwest, he proceeded to New England, where from Congregational House in Boston he began his usual careful and thoughtful procedure, interviewing and making inquiries about those who had been commended to him. We get an insight into his method and his problems in correspondence between him and the distinguished theologian, Dr. E. W. Lyman, then teaching at Bangor Theological Seminary in Maine. Although Dr. Lyman had earlier declined the presidency of Carleton College, Sumner felt that perhaps he could be won for Pomona. Their correspondence portrays the classic dilemma of a man asked to consider a major change in his career and how each of the principals handled such an important matter. Sumner presented to Dr. Lyman the opportunity of continuing his teaching through weekly chapel addresses on subjects of his own choosing before over five hundred students, and a weekly meeting with the senior class (then sixty-five in number) "on the relation of philosophy and religion, or some kindred subject," as had been the practice of President Gates. In addition, all the Congregational churches in Southern California would always be open to him. Sumner pointed out that the population of Southern California already equaled that of Maine and "would no doubt double in five years." "Doesn't it mean something to have a hand in molding the leaders of this great population?" he wrote. "Then too we are in the border land of the great far away East." But Professor Lyman could not be persuaded to relinquish scholarship for administration, and he refused to allow his name to be submitted to the trustees. However, Sumner's enthusiastic advocacy of Pomona College and Southern California was effective with others, and when the Board of Trustees met on September 9 he was able to submit several names for consideration. After discussion, the Board instructed the committee on the choice of a president "to invite Professor Blaisdell if he will accept our terms."

James Arnold Blaisdell, then on the faculty of Beloit College in Wisconsin, was born in Beloit on December 15, 1867. After graduating from Beloit College in 1889, he studied at Hartford Seminary, where he graduated in 1892. Later that year he was ordained as a Congregational minister. After successful pastorates in Waukesha, Wisconsin, and Olivet, Michigan, he was called in 1903 to the faculty of Beloit, where in 1909 he was Professor of Biblical Literature and Ancient Oriental History, and Librarian. Blaisdell was brought to the attention of Pomona by Dr. D. K. Pearsons, who through his many philanthropic activities had acquired wide acquaintance in higher education. Furthermore, as Pearsons had been on the Pomona campus early in 1909, he had intimate knowledge of the financial vicissitudes of the college.

As he knew little of Pomona and had never been in the West, Blaisdell was completely surprised in the late summer of 1909, when vacationing with his wife at Crystal Lake in Northern Michigan, to receive a telegram from Sumner asking whether he would consider an invitation to the presidency of Pomona College. Although Blaisdell allowed his name to be presented, he indicated in his reply that his acceptance "would not be likely." When informed of the trustee action of September 9, he decided to come west in October to see the college and to discuss the matter with the faculty and the trustees. In order to judge the standing and position of the college in California, Blaisdell went first to Berkeley and sought information from faculty members of the University of California. What he learned there was "altogether favorable." "Don't hesitate," said the head of the department of education. "Pomona students are distinguished by their loyalty to a cause."

In Southern California Blaisdell was given a full opportunity to meet those with whom he would be working. En route to Claremont he addressed the Southern California Association of Congregational Churches then meeting in Pasadena. In Claremont he spoke in chapel, met with the faculty, and had long and highly satisfactory talks with Sumner, in whose home he stayed, and with Dean Norton. Everywhere the reception was enthusiastic. *Student Life* reported that seldom had "the power of personality" been felt so strongly as in his chapel talk. The faculty on October 21 drafted a resolution saying it would be a pleasure to cooperate with Professor Blaisdell in case he accepted the presidency. The trustees were delighted with him, and on October 23 expressed their confidence that if he accepted he would be "eminently successful." Thus assured of the strongest support, Blaisdell went home to talk with his family and his Beloit friends and to make his decision.

Unknown to Pomona, there were strong forces working in her favor. Blaisdell had begun to feel that impending academic changes at Beloit would soon reduce the emphasis on Biblical literature and thereby his own role in the college. The growing desire of the faculty to remove the requirement of the freshman Bible course would make it extremely difficult to secure students for advanced courses in his field. He thus faced reduction of the role of his department in the life and work of the college. Blaisdell was also influenced by his experience in serving for nearly three years as the interim pastor of the Second Congregational Church in Beloit, while at the same time continuing his college duties. He appreciated his friendship with the laymen, finding in their society "relief from the constancy of academic relations." While he had felt unable to accept the permanent pastorate when it was offered, his experience in the church left him "hungering for a renewal of those constructive tasks in society" which he had experienced and enjoyed as a pastor. "I wanted to be a builder," he wrote years later, "and to have a larger right of way to that end." The presidency of Pomona offered Blaisdell a chance to work out his "own ideas and ideals" in college education. What could be more challenging than a new college like Pomona, "a small college with ideals, in a new country?"

Rarely were a man and a situation more perfectly matched.

PRESIDENT JAMES A. BLAISDELL

Recognizing the great opportunity that Pomona could be, Blaisdell concluded that he should accept the call to the West, however hard it would be for him and his family to leave their beloved Beloit.

Word of Blaisdell's acceptance of the presidency of Pomona was received with the greatest enthusiasm in California. *Student Life* carried the good news on November 12, 1909, and characterized it as "the beginning of new life, new impulse, new power," for "we believe no man better appreciates the wonderful opportunities of the Christian college in a strong section of the rapidly growing Southwest." This appreciation was revealed in the letter of formal acceptance which Blaisdell wrote to the Pomona trustees on November 19.

> In thus assuming the place to which you have called me I think of myself as becoming partner in a great company already finely organized by those who have served before me, a company among whom life will find deep satisfactions, into the harvest of whose previous toil we shall all alike be privileged to enter and on whose common loyalty to our cause the future will be built.
>
> When one thinks of this company, the combination of so many effective elements, there is an inevitable sense of its capacity and power. There is the body of students among whose generous impulses and fresh ideals it is incomparably inspiring to live and who so much farther than they ever dream make the real character of a college. There is the Faculty who, in Pomona as in so many other institutions, contributing unreservedly of scholarship and life, have given themselves as the sacred human foundations of the institution. There are the Alumni on whose unfailing affection the college is absolutely dependent and by whose suggestion it is kept in near and practical relation to the world we serve. There are the Trustees, finding place for this among the other commanding interests which occupy them, guarding our financial concerns and giving official direction to the college. And finally there is the great company of citizens who share the same ideal of the college, contributing in appreciation to its financial resources, surrounding it with their splendid friendships and enthusiasms, and leaving their names to be treasured among us. When one thinks of the power which, in all these varied forms is included in our common company no college ambition or ideal seems impossible.
>
> And for this company we have a cause which may well enlist the high enthusiasms of every one of us. Could there be a more stirring determination than to set on our Pacific coast an institution peer with the best the world has achieved and growing year by year richly historic with the deeds of the men and women mothered here. This is no empty word. I have touched your united purpose. I have felt your spirit. It will come to pass. To have a part in the building of such an enterprise, to lay its broad foundations, to lift its earliest walls, to give it sufficient endowments, to shape its permanent spirit, to equip it amply for endless human service — these are chances noble enough to

satisfy and occupy great men. They are opportunities worthy enough to bestir all the united power and purpose of Pomona's company of men and women.

In conclusion, allow me to say that I believe with you that the worth of the college is in the fulfillment of the ends for which it was created. In these days when the American church is granting to the colleges their legal freedom we have no right to forget that loyalty is deeper than legality. By all that lies behind us it has become our inherited obligation so far as in us lies to make it sure that we have common cause with every company which is set for Civilization of Righteousness and that to every worker for the new day the name of Pomona is a word of courage. Nor is this simply a matter of loyalty. It is a matter of vitality. In the emphasis of the Christian faith on the deeper values modern education had its birth and we may be sure also that there it will best keep its vigor. We may hope that the church shall receive generously and patiently from us; we may desire increasing trustfulness toward scholarship; but, nevertheless, in that democracy of earnest souls, which the Christian Fellowship is, we too shall preserve our best. From that Fellowship came our richest possessions. In that Fellowship it will be our fortune to abide.

Publication of the letter in *Student Life* and the *Claremont Courier* gave confidence that a greater day for Pomona was at hand. "We have a President," wrote the editor of *Student Life*, "a young man of unquestioned ability and great enthusiasm, whose vision penetrates the future and recognizes the tremendous opportunities Pomona College may have as the world's activities move themselves and all their complexity from the Atlantic to the Pacific."

Such enthusiasm ushered in six months of high drama for the new president and the college. In February 1910 Professor Blaisdell and his wife and little daughter began their journey to Claremont, leaving the three boys to complete the school year in Beloit where they lived with their grandmother Blaisdell. To the Blaisdells' surprise, many students came to the station to see them off. A few days before the editors had dedicated the Beloit annual, the *Codex*, to their departing teacher. "Professor Blaisdell is an idealist," they wrote. "He sees in every man the best of which he is capable. The energy of his preaching, the clearness of his teaching, the charm of his conversation, are warmed by the glow of a human sympathy which lays deep upon the heart." Blaisdell was greatly moved. "Never again," he later wrote, "was I to know so many intimacies, nor any I think quite so deep."

But the reception in California did much to reduce the pain of leaving old friends in Wisconsin. When the Blaisdells arrived in

Claremont on the Santa Fe at 6:48 on the morning of February 11, a group of ninety students and faculty were there to meet them. The family was hurried into "a horseless double-seater and hauled up the hill like lightning express by the surplus energy of every class and character" and taken to the Sumner residence at 105 College Avenue. After a cheer, the students pulled the carriage away rejoicing that "Pomona College was no longer decapitate."

The power of the new president was such that those who heard his first chapel address a few days later never forgot the inspiration of that moment. He congratulated the students on their opportunity to determine the future personality of Pomona and on their being in the college in a time of financial distress when they could put all they had into the enterprise. "In the years that are coming," he said, "it will be a splendid thing for you to have a great cause into which you have already put part of yourselves." In his message in the *Metate* of 1910 he set forth high ideals of service and accomplishment: "Let us today put into our college an irrevocable and dominating tradition of self-sacrifice. So far as in us lies let us make a passion for service the abiding atmosphere of the place. Let us here and now create a perpetual conscience for consecrated scholarship."

President Blaisdell sought to develop such loyalty early in the students' life at Pomona. To this end he instituted matriculation exercises, which honored all new students who had successfully completed their first semester in college. "On last Thursday the class of 1913 matriculated," wrote *Student Life* on March 4, 1910. "In honor of this event was instituted what we hope will become a tradition in the college. At the chapel service the freshmen occupied the middle section of seats ordinarily given to the seniors and juniors. After the reading of the college chapter [I Corinthians, XIII] and the singing of the college hymn [*How Firm a Foundation*] President Blaisdell addressed the freshmen." Matriculation became at once a cherished part of college life and was hailed as "the pledging of loyalty to a new cause," "the acceptance of a new honor," and entry into "all the benefits, rights and heritages of Pomona."

The first task in 1910 was gathering the full force of the college and its friends for completing the financial campaign that President Gates and the trustees had not been able to finish. At his first meeting with the full Board of Trustees, on March 29, 1910, President Blaisdell proposed that the trustees enter at once on a campaign for $130,000 in order to secure the proffered gift from Mr. Carnegie and to pay off the indebtedness of the college, and that the campaign be completed before commencement on June 22. The $130,000 to be raised would retire the debt of $45,000 for previous improvements and interest, and provide the $85,000 still required to secure the grant of $50,000 from Mr. Carnegie. The proposal was approved unanimously and verbal subscriptions of $31,000 were made by individual members of the Board before the meeting adjourned.

Naming the program "The Campaign of the Crisis," President Blaisdell first enlisted the students for the great effort. In his office he placed a blank book, "The Record of a Crisis," in which were to be inscribed the names of all who contributed, thereby giving "those whose lives are written there a certain kind of immortality." The Class of 1910, with which President Blaisdell was to enjoy a rare and lifelong intimacy, took the lead with resolutions of support. *Student Life* in an editorial, "Our President," expressed the enthusiasm of the campus: "Seldom does a man win so quickly the combined loyalty of students, alumni, faculty, trustees and constituency." With such support the president increased his emphasis on the importance of the campaign. If the funds could be secured, he held out a hopeful future for the college; if not, he predicted that Pomona would be "condemned to a long and wearisome struggle with poverty."

President Blaisdell at once coordinated the full force of Pomona for a magnificent and inspiring effort, and by mid-May the tempo of the campaign was intense. On a typical Sunday, he went to Santa Ana, preaching in the morning at the Congregational Church and in the evening in the First Presbyterian Church. On the campus, the women students divided themselves into groups of ten for earning money for the campaign — blacking shoes, dressing hair, cleaning houses, and selling peanuts and popcorn. On June 1 President Blaisdell could write to the *Claremont Courier* that

$30,000 remained to be raised; on June 8 the amount needed had been reduced to $15,000. The following week the Claremont Church added $3,000 to the $15,000 they had given the year before. With less than $5,000 yet to be secured, the *Courier* on June 15 carried a two-column article headed, "Endowment Is Assured."

In anticipation of success, a special number of *Student Life* had been directed to the alumni, with a personal invitation to commencement from President Blaisdell. "Let me feel your hand in mine," he wrote. "On June 22nd there should be a story of victory to recount which will make us glad." It was indeed a memorable commencement. At the close of the graduating exercises, President Blaisdell reported that the total amount of gifts and pledges was $135,650.66. Included were more than $60,000 for establishing two professorships, one to honor Dean Norton, the other to honor Professor Spalding. Most heartening for the future was the fact that two-thirds of the alumni had contributed. Charles Burt Sumner wrote that the campaign had been "pushed with a vigor, sagacity, and persistence never equalled" in Pomona's numerous financial efforts. The Board of Trustees lauded the leader who had made success possible. President Blaisdell in an article in *Student Life* paid a moving tribute to President Gates both for his launching the campaign and for the achievements of his presidency. "It remained for his successor," he wrote, "only to carry to completion the work which he had so largely achieved."

The success of the "Campaign of the Crisis" not only lifted the cloud over Pomona's future; it was decisive in the president's relation to the college. President Blaisdell had had no experience in fund raising or in college administration, and he saw the campaign as the test of his leadership and of the loyalty of trustees, alumni, faculty, students, the Congregational churches, and the Southern California public. Consequently, he refused all consideration of his inauguration until the campaign had been concluded. When the trustees appointed an inaugural committee in their victory meeting of June 21, both they and President Blaisdell knew they were joining in a deep and permanent commitment to a cause greater than themselves. The president saw his own responsibility not primarily as fund-raising but as "guarding the ideals of college genuineness, efficiency, and worth," with "the duty of making quality."

With the satisfaction of this successful beginning, the president with Mrs. Blaisdell and their daughter went to Beloit for a reunion with their sons and a summer with old friends. But no more would he look back to the Middle West with thoughts of returning; henceforth his mind would be on the West and the great future he saw there.

The United States was in an exciting stage of its development, and the magnitude and nature of change would be revealed in the census of 1910. The nation's population had grown to 91,972,266, a gain of twenty-one per cent over 1900. The most significant increase was in California whose population had grown in the decade from 1,485,053 to 2,377,549, a gain of over sixty per cent. More important for Pomona College was the fact that the greatest growth within the state was in Southern California. For example, the population of Los Angeles County had grown from 170,298 to 504,131, the City of Los Angeles from 102,479 to 319,198, Pasadena from 9,117 to 30,291, and San Diego from 17,700 to 39,578.

Furthermore, as the population of the United States increased, her people quickened their interest in education. This was seen most strikingly in the development of high schools. Prior to 1890, the education of most American children ended with the eighth grade, and in that year there were only 43,731 high school graduates. Shortly thereafter, the high school movement became a fundamental part of the American school system, and by 1910 the number of graduates had grown to 156,429. Greater economic resources to support colleges were matched by an ever increasing supply of students to attend them. A wisely led college, and particularly in Southern California, had an opportunity for unprecedented influence both in its own area and in the nation.

This was well understood by President Blaisdell as he with his wife and children and his mother arrived in Claremont in September 1910 and he looked to the opening of his first full academic year at Pomona. The news of the enrollment was good, with a freshman class of 140 showing an increase of 20 over the year before and with substantial increases in the other three classes. For the opening convocation, President Blaisdell had thoughtfully invited former President Baldwin to give the main address. President Blaisdell shaped his own remarks around the high estimates of Pomona made by Dr. Baldwin.

With the new year President Blaisdell turned for the first time to the daily administration and supervision of the college. In the previous semester he had given his time largely to public appearances within the college and in the Southern California community and to the leadership of the "Campaign of the Crisis." The faculty and the college had been under the leadership of Dean Norton since January 1909, and the president perceived at once Norton's great ability and his devotion to all that was best in the institution. From their first meeting the two men had felt a confidence in each other and an ease in their relationship that were to be basic in the future development of the college. Thus Blaisdell felt no necessity to preside or be present at faculty meetings in his early months at Pomona; but he took his place in the chair with the first meeting for 1910-11 and presided regularly thereafter.

Although he could delay certain campus responsibilities, President Blaisdell of necessity had entered fully into his work with the Board of Trustees as soon as he assumed office. He and the trustees were fortunate in the reorganization of the Board which had been made after the resignation of President Gates. Beginning with President Ferguson, the president of the college had also been elected president of the Board of Trustees. While there does not seem to have been any overt oppostion to this practice, it was not constitutionally wise. It deprived the Board of the leadership of an outstanding layman, and imposed excessive and diverse burdens on the president of the college. Doubtless the nature and extent of these responsibilities were factors in the breakdown of Dr. Gates' health. When it had been evident that some months would elapse before the college would have a president again, the trustees decided to return to the practice of their earlier years and choose a president of the Board from their own number.

On October, 23, 1909 they elected George W. Marston. This was a turning point in the history of the Board of Trustees as significant

GEORGE WHITE MARSTON

as was the election of Dr. Blaisdell in the history of the college. As a founding trustee, Marston knew Pomona as few others did. His leadership in the church, in San Diego, and in business was widely recognized. Financially successful, he was liberal in political and social outlook. Generous in spirit, blessed with a kindly humor, he was warm and friendly in his relations with individual trustees and with the Board as a whole. He was a masterful presiding officer, with such skill in handling controversial questions and difficult individuals that he consistently kept the Board's attention focused constructively on the main business of the day.

Interestingly, Marston, like Blaisdell, was born in Beloit. Although he left Wisconsin after high school, he retained deep affection for his boyhood home. While Marston apparently did not suggest Blaisdell for the presidency, he found great pleasure in the selection, and soon the two men were bound in a lifelong friendship. Their mutual understanding was such that the urbane merchant even felt free to advise the minister-educator about his dress and appearance. Blaisdell was grateful to learn from Marston much that widened his horizon and helped him to know men and women of substance and idealism who could assist the college. Marston's tenure as president of the Board throughout Blaisdell's administration, and through much of that of his successor, was one of the greatest factors in Pomona's progress. Together they worked out the pattern of the relationship between president and trustees which continues essentially today. The president of the college would be a voting member of the Board, and could serve as chairman of trustee committees, but he would never again be asked to carry the responsibilities of the president of the Board.

Thus as President Blaisdell faced his work at Pomona, he was blessed in a dean of the faculty and a chairman of the Board of Trustees, each superbly equipped for his responsibilities. He would be advised on faculty and trustee matters by men of wisdom and understanding who in their counsel always thought first of the college. Norton, Marston, and Blaisdell were to be leaders in shaping the course of the college for many years to come.

CHAPTER VIII

Confidence and Growth

UNDER SUCH LEADERSHIP Pomona in September 1910 entered upon a period of unprecedented growth as the grievous uncertainties of earlier years were replaced by confidence and sound progress. Much of the achievement was due to the thoughtful study and effective action of the president.

To his new office Blaisdell brought the experience and perception of a college teacher. Unlike his three predecessors, he had come to the presidency from the classroom, and he understood the function of a faculty, the legitimate hopes of its members, and the nature of academic administration. Above all, he had a love for the American college and a faith in its mission, in which the college and church were united. To him "a Christian college" was "one of the supreme undertakings in which a people may enlist its energy. No enterprise is more far reaching in its perpetual influence. And there are few causes which so definitely call together the far seeing, the public spirited, the enlisted souls of humanity. Reaching through the generations it gathers to itself select men and women."

With remarkable skill and energy he devoted himself to making Pomona such a college, quietly and effectively studying every aspect of her life. At the same time he kept his eyes on the East, where Yale was then restricting its elective system and stiffening the requirements of the junior and senior years, and Princeton was developing a graduate school for which a difference of policy had led to the resignation of its president, Woodrow Wilson. With continuing interest he followed the development of the colleges of his native Middle West and the University of Chicago which had brought new forces and ideas into higher education.

At Dr. Blaisdell's request, his inauguration as president had been deferred from the previous year. With the improvement in Pomona's financial condition, he now felt the inauguration could be a marked step forward in the proclamation of Pomona's ideals and her plans for the future.

The inauguration was conceived also as a celebration of Pomona's past. All the alumni were invited, and the *Student Life* on December 23, 1910 was placed at the disposal of the administration for announcing the events of the two inaugural days, Friday and Saturday, January 20 and 21, 1911. "No inauguration will be representative of the real makers of the college unless it include a full attendance of alumni," the president wrote. Upon the suggestion of President Blaisdell, and the recommendation of the cabinet, the trustees voted to confer Pomona's first honorary degree on Charles Burt Sumner, who more than anyone was founder, builder, preserver, and lifelong leader of the college.

On the memorable weekend, a festive air dominated Claremont and the college. The Inn was overflowing with guests, and the Santa Fe ran a special train from Los Angeles. The visitors would find a greatly improved College Avenue, and on its west side a recently laid eight-foot concrete walk extending from Third Street to Sixth Street. The formal activities began Friday evening in the Claremont Church when Dr. Blaisdell's close friend, President Edward D. Eaton of Beloit College, spoke on "The Historic Service of the American College," and President Henry Augustus Garfield of Williams College gave an address on "The Place of the College in the Educational System of the Future."

Every element of the college participated in the inaugural procession which formed on College Avenue on the following morning. Marching in order were the college choir, the college students, the alumni, the faculty in formal academic attire, the delegates of other institutions, the trustees, the officiating clergyman, the president of the Board of Trustees, and the president-elect of the college. Led by the choir, they marched up College Avenue and along Fifth Street to the Claremont Church. After the Scripture reading, prayer, and a hymn sung by the audience, Mr. Marston, who presided, read a letter from President Gates which was much applauded. He then presented the keys of the college to Dr. Blaisdell and invested him with the presidency.

In his inaugural address, "The Culture of Loyalty in College Life," President Blaisdell stated that loyalty and dedication to learning could be developed best in an institution of limited size. The views he set forth that day were basic in his thinking and planning throughout his administrative career. President Eaton presented greetings from other educational institutions represented by some fifty delegates. As the final act of the morning, Dean Norton presented Charles Burt Sumner for the Honorary Degree of Doctor of Laws, hailing him as a "builder of civilization." President Blaisdell held Pomona's founders in highest esteem, and it delighted him that his first official act after inauguration should be the conferring on Dr. Sumner of the first honorary degree ever awarded by Pomona College.

Following "a noon dinner" at the Inn for the delegates, the exercises of the day continued at the church. Benjamin Ide Wheeler, president of the University of California, emphasized the significance of a college presidency, calling the college "the most instructive element of the American educational system with its trichotomy of high school, college, and university." Following greetings by President Scherer of Throop Institute and President Nash of the Pacific Theological Seminary, President Lasuka Harda of Doshisha College, Kyoto, Japan, brought the congratulations of "a sister college across the Pacific." "Let Japan and America," he counselled, "think of peace, not war, and through education work against the common foes of ignorance, degradation, and corruption." The long to be remembered day ended with an evening in the church with the Choral Union presenting "The Messiah."

Academic Reorganization

After the inauguration, President Blaisdell took steps to effect fundamental changes in the structure of Pomona by bringing about coordination of its instructional programs. Developments over the years had given the institution four related, but separate, units operating on the same campus: the Preparatory Department, the

College Department, the School of Music, and the School of Art and Design. While some faculty members served in more than one of these divisions and all units were administered by the president, who reported on them to the trustees, they attracted different groups of students and had varying admissions requirements and diverse purposes. By 1911 the College Department had come to be the dominant unit of the four, and President Blaisdell felt that steps should be taken to make Pomona into a unified college which would include all instruction given by the institution.

The Preparatory Department, for many years the largest of the four instructional divisions, had essentially fulfilled its purpose. The services which it rendered the College Department for many years had been taken over by the many high schools established in California early in the twentieth century. Thus Pomona could safely follow the practice of colleges in other areas of the country which were closing their preparatory departments and academies, and with the graduation exercises of June 1911 the program of Pomona's Preparatory Department was terminated.

The School of Music, on the other hand, presented some important and urgent questions. Its work had met a need both in the community and in Southern California, and despite its meager physical resources in Sumner, Holmes, Smiley, and then a house in Claremont, it had made a large place for itself. The question was not whether music should be continued, but the direction it would take. In the years immediately preceding President Blaisdell's arrival widely different possibilities began to appear. Although instruction at first was limited to individual lessons in voice and instrumental music and to preparation for certificates for teaching in California public schools, some work in music had been offered toward an academic degree — first toward the Bachelor of Letters degree and, after its discontinuance, toward the Bachelor of Arts degree. There was, however, a countervailing desire for the establishment of the Bachelor of Music degree and directing the work in music to this end. Although this degree had been approved by the faculty and the trustees before President Blaisdell's election, only a few Bachelor of Music degrees had been awarded prior to 1910.

President Blaisdell had a clear and firmly fixed view of the role of music in a college like Pomona. In his published Report in 1911 he stated,

> It seems to me that the Music School should be conceived of as existing wholly to contribute its part to the cultural life of the college, thus maintaining here, as elsewhere, the initial interest of the institution. I believe it is unwise in this department, as in all others, to build up a professional school. To this end I believe the musical opportunities offered by the college, except in unusual cases, may be wisely more and more limited to those who take this work as part of the regular cultural course, and on the basis of the regular entrance conditions. I believe, moreover, that the degree of Mus. B., which is in its nature a professional degree, should be withdrawn save that it might be granted for graduate study in accord with a uniform scheme.

For music so conceived President Blaisdell proposed new facilities and greater opportunities.

This philosophy appealed to both faculty and trustees and steps were taken to conform to it. The trustees adopted a policy which was to become in effect an academic charter for Pomona College, by voting at the annual meeting, June 18, 1912, that

> the Board approves a policy by which the College shall seek distinction as an institution of liberal culture following the general type of those institutions which are distinctively known as Colleges as over against institutions known as universities or vocational schools. It believes that all departments of the College should be organized to contribute to the general culture of the student body rather than to create specialists or to attract a body of students separate from the general College company. In conformity with this ideal, it holds that the College should aim to furnish to its students such training of mind and such an introduction to the larger appreciation of the past and the present as shall be the basis for a broad and intelligent citizenship and shall be, after graduation, a foundation for later specialization.

By a series of actions from 1911 to 1914, the college discontinued the Bachelor of Music degree (last awarded in 1913) and transformed the School of Music into a department of the college. With these decisions, Pomona College developed a new path for itself and a new place for music in higher education. Many colleges with strong interest in music, such as Oberlin or DePauw, followed the policy of establishing schools of music, or conservatories, and awarding their students the Bachelor of Music and Master of Music degrees. Pomona, on the other hand, by integrating a department of music into the liberal arts program sought to bring its music students into the broader life of the institution and to give all of its students an appreciation of both choral and instrumental music. In an age when many colleges and universities did not include music in the curriculum, Pomona led further by allowing a certain amount of work in applied music as credit toward the Bachelor of Arts degree. Pomona's approach to music, unusual in the United States before 1914, would find growing support in the years to follow.

The organization of music as an instructional department in the college brought stability to the program and security to the music faculty. The full-time members were placed on salaries paid from the college budget and thus were no longer dependent on fees paid by students for private lessons. Henceforth, such fees would be paid to the college and handled as a part of the general budget. The full-time members of the music department became members of the college faculty with all of its rights and privileges.

The School of Art and Design, despite the impressive title, could be transformed into a department without great difficulty. The "School" was essentially Mrs. Jenkins with occasional part-time assistants. No specialized degrees in art had been given, nor were they contemplated. There were, therefore, no serious problems of academic organization and administration. However, some faculty and trustees were hesitant to bring art into the college on the basis of full academic and financial support that was being accorded to music. Despite the long record of instruction in art at Pomona, the trustees for financial reasons were slow to give it permanent status. On April 23, 1912, the Board recorded that it "entertained serious question as to the possibility of continuing this department in the midst of the stress and need for the general resources of the college" and was therefore unable "to commit itself more than for the coming year as to the permanence of the department."

These doubts gave way before the support of art by President Blaisdell who saw art like music as a fundamental part of the curriculum under the general administration of the college faculty. Furthermore, there was much support for art through the Rembrandt Club whose members included many influential Claremont women. Their efforts directed toward better facilities and an extension of the art program were to be so successful that an art building would be the first new structure of the Blaisdell administration.

Inspired by the coming of the new president, faculty committees energetically set to work to reorganize the college, taking into account current educational change as well as the work of other educational institutions. The result was a major revision of the curriculum and the college catalogue during the academic year 1910-11. For the courses of study, the faculty and the president took as their guide "an equitable balance of departments." "It is fundamental," President Blaisdell declared, "that all the great fields of learning should have their proper consideration." In a proposed "Scheme of Departments" he suggested as main academic groupings: English, foreign languages (ancient and modern), the natural sciences, the logical sciences, the social sciences, religious science, and the arts (music and art).

Effective academic planning depended, of course, on the number and kind of students desired by the college. Analysis of the total enrollment of 404 for 1911-12, which included thirteen graduate students, 50 seniors, 59 juniors, 111 sophomores, 166 freshmen and five special students, made it obvious that greater effort should be made to hold students through the junior and senior years. Success in this endeavor would result in an enrollment of 500. While President Blaisdell considered this probably "a large enough attendance," he had "an impression" that a college of 700 would be the best medium "for securing an environment sufficiently large to make the strongest pull upon the different sides of personality, offer range and opportunity of friendship," and still retain "that close and intimate personal influence which is the glory of the smaller colleges."

Following the faculty's careful analysis of Pomona's academic needs, the trustees had authorized, effective September 1912, the appointment of nine new faculty members, making possible the addition of many new courses. Among the new faculty were William S. Ament in English, Judge Charles G. Neely in constitutional history and law, Walter A. Allen in music, and Miss Marion Jeannette Ewing in the library.

Much had been accomplished by the autumn of 1912. For its 420 students the college had forty-two faculty members. President Blaisdell could state with pride in his printed annual report that "the differentiation in departments in number and range is well in line with that of the strongest institutions East and West." There was increased emphasis on high scholarship, and the graduation distinctions, *summa cum laude, magna cum laude, cum laude,* and *rite* were introduced in June 1912. A six-day schedule replaced the five-day program which Pomona had known from its foundation. Gone were the leisurely Mondays on which students could study or return from home. While the new schedule made possible the greater availability of the larger number of courses, it also counteracted the growing tendency of students, "owing to the new interurban facilities, to remain out of the college life and atmosphere" for long weekends.

The administrative reorganization which brought the Schools of Music and Art and Design into the structure of the college also required some adjustments within the older academic departments of the institution. For the most part, these adjustments were made speedily and harmoniously, but in the biological sciences the determined resistance of a great teacher resulted in his loss to the college and the major restaffing of instruction in botany and zoology. At issue was the conflict between the interests of the institution as a whole and those of a department led by a brilliant scholar and an inspired teacher. In gratitude for the great services of Professors Cook and Baker to California agriculture, ranchers made gifts which, not surprisingly, were often directed to scientific study and research of immediate interest to the donors. President Blaisdell, while appreciating the value of the work, felt it imperative that all gifts should be made directly to the college which then would control and direct their use. The issue remained unresolved when in 1911 Professor Cook at the age of seventy retired from Pomona to become Commissioner of Horticulture for the State of California, and the college elected him its first emeritus professor. The clash of institutional and departmental interests and control came to a head with the younger and brilliant Professor Baker who took his case to the Board of Trustees. The issues were too fundamental for compromise, and reluctantly President Blaisdell and the trustees accepted Professor Baker's resignation in June 1912. He went that autumn to a professorship at the University of the Philippines, where he continued the career that made him one of the most distinguished botanists of his time. He left a great and permanent influence on Pomona College.

William Atwood Hilton succeeded Baker as Professor of Biology in September 1912. Earlier he had spent three years at Pomona and was aware of its ideals and its opportunities. A Phi Beta Kappa graduate of Cornell University, from which he also took his Ph.D. in zoology, he had taught both at Cornell and the University of Minnesota. Professor Hilton built on the good work of Cook and Baker and also added his own emphasis to Pomona's work in biology. Throughout his professorship he continued publication of *The Journal of Entomology* which they had founded. At the same time he extended the work in zoology and led an increasing number of students into medicine. The development of a summer program in marine biology at Laguna Beach and the building of a laboratory there were valued contributions to Pomona science.

Professor Hilton possessed the qualities that make an outstanding professor and an excellent faculty member. Indefatigable in research, teaching, and his departmental duties, he was equally concerned for the program and life of the college as a whole. He exemplified the spirit of Pomona's early professors in subordinating personal and departmental concerns to the interests of the institution. His good humor and his fund of anecdotes were to become legendary. One of his finest qualities was his constant encouragement of young colleagues.

Pomona's Twenty-Fifth Anniversary

Progress in restructuring the college and strengthening its academic program opened the way for an enthusiastic celebration of Pomona's twenty-fifth anniversary and the inauguration of discussions of a major financial campaign. At a "Home Gathering" of alumni, trustees, and friends on Sunday and Monday, October 13 and 14, 1912, significant steps were taken in the advancement of the college. Religious services on Sunday were followed on Monday by meetings which featured an historical account of the college. This, as Sumner wrote, "led up to a clear, definite statement of the present needs of the college," forcefully given by President Blaisdell. When the president had concluded, the business manager, E. F. Goff, offered a resolution "that we heartily approve right here and now a campaign to raise a million dollars for Pomona College, and that we promise to stand by President Blaisdell *when he sees fit* to inaugurate such a campaign." The motion was carried by a rising vote. Concluding addresses by Marston and Bishop Johnson expressed trustee support for an enterprise which ultimately was to engage the entire college community.

The "Home Gathering" aroused a desire for a broader and more popular celebration of Pomona's Twenty-Fifth Anniversary in which the city of Claremont could join with the college. On January 24, 1913, President Blaisdell, supported by Professor Frampton, presented to the faculty the possibility of holding an historical pageant at commencement, suggesting that such a pageant would be "helpful in the financial campaign which may be on at that time." Within a month both the college and the town had committed themselves to a tremendous dramatic venture, and an executive committee of seven representing the faculty, the city of Claremont, and the trustees was placed in charge.

The setting was the new Greek Theater in Blanchard Park and the date of the production was June 17, 1913. The Pomona College Pageant was given in two parts, one at three-thirty in the afternoon, the other at eight in the evening. The first part dealt with the history of the region from the earliest times. The evening program began with the "Founding of the College," featuring a re-enactment of the opening exercises in the Ayer Cottage on September 12, 1888. Three of the original trustees, C. B. Sumner, J. H. Harwood, and H. A. Palmer, were present to play themselves, and the roles of Henry Kirke White Bent and C. B. Sheldon were taken by their sons. Four of the original students, among them Professor George S. Sumner, also played themselves.

Subsequent scenes portrayed the bringing of water and electricity to the Pomona Valley, and "Greater Pomona," which featured the dedication of the Library and a student celebration with the band and the Men's Glee Club. The concluding scene, "The Look to the Future," suggested "what the valley, the city of Claremont, and the College should mean to the future of our great State." Three processions of students representing the humanities, the sciences, and the social sciences passed in review. The pageant concluded as "The Spirit of Pomona" was met by "The Spirit of California," and the chorus sang a song composed by Alice Anderson '13 and Paul Blaisdell '16, which included this tribute to the college and its future:

> All hail to our Pomona!
> New era hath begun.
> Our hopes in thee fulfilled;
> Our pride in years to come.
> Strength of the mountains, breath of the Valley,
> Gladly we hail thee, Spirit Sublime;
> Ever thy glory, broadened and brightened,
> Lighting our pathway, conquering Time.

The text of the historical pageant was published in a profusely illustrated eighty-two page, hard-cover booklet, which also included two important historical articles: "The Beginnings of Claremont and Pomona," by Professor Brackett, and "Pomona College — An Historical Sketch," by Professor Milton E. Churchill. In the foreword George C. Griswold expressed the spirit in which the pageant had been given:

> We wish you to feel, we wish you would treasure it in your memory that this pageant, presented in the beautiful Greek Theatre in Claremont, June seventeenth, nineteen hundred thirteen, was given with the fervor of youth, in the fullness of the joy of living, in commemoration of the past, in the hope of the future, with good will toward all, and with a feeling of gratitude and a spirit of reverence for Him who for twenty-five years has looked down with favor upon Pomona College and Claremont.

Recognition of Pomona's twenty-five years of sound academic work came in the summer of 1913 when the college was awarded a chapter of Phi Beta Kappa. This had been achieved through the thoughtful effort of President Blaisdell who felt that the problem of the college was "that of accomplishing something genuine educationally and then of securing recognition for it locally and nationally." The winning of a chapter of Phi Beta Kappa would bring such recognition. To one of lesser courage this would have appeared too great and too early an undertaking, but President Blaisdell knew the worth of the faculty and students and the quality of Pomona's scholarship, and he had faith that the national officers of Phi Beta Kappa would recognize these values if they were properly presented.

Preparation began in the faculty committee on scholarship, honors, and prizes, which on May 12, 1911 won the approval of the cabinet to seek to obtain a chapter of Phi Beta Kappa, and toward that end to organize a local society whose rules for membership would be the same at those of Phi Beta Kappa. In March 1912 the members of the Pomona faculty who had been elected to Phi Beta Kappa in their own undergraduate colleges took steps to prepare the searching application required by the national organization. As the biennial national meeting of Phi Beta Kappa was scheduled for the summer of 1913, vigorous efforts were made by the president and the faculty throughout 1912-13. Dr. Blaisdell had canvassed the situation among his friends in the East, and he proceeded carefully in securing the required endorsements from six university and college chapters. On December 6, 1912 he reported to the faculty that the University of California had endorsed Pomona's application. Two weeks later he told them in confidence that Stanford University, Grinnell College, Cornell University, Beloit College, and Colorado College had joined the University of California, and that the application would be up for action in the summer. Oberlin and Amherst had also given Pomona generous help.

When the news came in the summer that Pomona College was one of the four institutions granted a chapter of Phi Beta Kappa, President Blaisdell in a letter to all the students gave the credit to those of earlier years. For this honor he expressed indebtedness "first to a faculty which, through twenty-five years, has maintained unflinchingly and at constant sacrifice a practice of thoroughness," and secondly, "to the most loyal alumni that ever a college had. Every graduate who has done distinguished work in graduate study, not only for his own sake, but also for the sake of the little, unknown far-western college from which he hailed, today has his reward."

The Gamma Chapter of Phi Beta Kappa granted Pomona was the third to be established in California, the first chapter south of the San Francisco Bay area, and the first chapter ever given to any institution west of the Rockies which devoted itself wholly to collegiate work. This national recognition strengthened the college in defining and implementing the role toward which it had worked so long. "More than ever before our college life must focus on the business of thinking," President Blaisdell wrote the students. "Pomona College cannot be everything. It has chosen to be the scholar's college. The college need not be distinguished for its size; but it must be distinguished for its standards."

CHAPTER IX

Achieving the Greater Pomona

BY THE AUTUMN OF 1913 the goals for "the Greater Pomona," formulated in the Gates administration, seemed attainable. Feeling that the past two years had seen "the establishment of the main policies of the college," the president and the trustees officially announced the million dollar campaign suggested at the "Home Gathering" the year before. Behind the announcement lay months of intensive work and two trips East by President Blaisdell. After five individuals in California had subscribed a total of $250,000, the trustees presented an application for $250,000 to the General Education Board, recently established in New York by John D. Rockefeller. Although the Education Board responded by offering only $150,000, and that on condition the college raise $1,000,000 by January 1, 1915, the Pomona trustees accepted these terms at their annual meeting in June 1913 and authorized the opening of the campaign at an appropriate date in the autumn. They felt the grant would be of tremendous value in enlisting other support since Pomona was the first college in "the region west of the Rockies and south of the state of Washington" to receive a gift from the General Education Board.

President Blaisdell had also educated Pomona's friends regarding the resources needed for the college's development. In 1912 he had pointed to "the general consensus of informed opinion that a college of from 500 to 700 students should have an income-producing endowment of $3,000,000." Reed College, then being established in Portland, Oregon, "and purporting to do precisely the same work as Pomona," already had this amount of endowment while Pomona had income-producing funds of only $542,000.

On July 1, 1911, the total assets of Pomona, including all funds and the equipment, buildings and grounds, were $897,125.46. Of the annual income of approximately $120,000 for the academic year 1910-11, over $52,000 had come from gifts and nearly $40,000 had come from student payment of tuition. That Pomona's achievement had been so much greater than its resources was due to the dedication of the faculty of whom the most senior members then received only $1,800 a year.

The campaign goal, when announced in November 1913, was set at $1,100,000, including $700,000 for endowment, $300,000 for buildings and grounds, and $100,000 to retire the college debt. To achieve such a goal the college had larger and better organized human resources than ever before. The members of the Board of Trustees, under the leadership of Mr. Marston as president, were generous donors and also worked zealously among their friends and the churches. A Board of Overseers, constituted from the alumni in 1911, and "charged with the duty of acquainting itself with the life and procedures of the institution," served in an invaluable advisory role to the president and as a proving ground for future trustees. With such trustee and alumni leadership, the college was able to announce total gifts and pledges of $475,000 when the "Million Dollar Campaign," as it was popularly called, was launched. Notable among the trustee gifts were $100,000 from Nathan W. Blanchard, of which $50,000 was for faculty salaries and $50,000 for endowment of Blanchard Park, and $50,000 from Mr. Marston, to be used as determined by the Board.

New Buildings and Campus Improvement

The most dramatic effect of the campaign was the enhancement of the campus and the addition of new buildings. Myron E. Hunt, the architect of Smiley Hall, had made "recommendations to the City of Claremont and to the trustees of Pomona College relating to the future development of the college campus" in 1908, and Hunt's plan as officially approved by the Pomona trustees had been published with six sketches and a text in the college bulletin commemorating the dedication of Brackett Observatory, the Carnegie Library, and Smiley Hall. Although the financial crisis and personal tragedy which terminated Dr. Gates' presidency prevented immediate implementation of Hunt's recommendations, evidence of the trustees' look to the future had been a major factor in Dr. Blaisdell's decision to come to Pomona.

By 1913, Hunt (1868-1952) was well launched in the career that made him one of the most distinguished and influential California architects of the first half of the twentieth century. Following a course of study in architecture at Northwestern University and the Massachusetts Institute of Technology, he had spent two years of study in Europe before beginning the practice of his profession in Chicago. Coming to Pasadena in 1903, he formed a partnership with Elmer Grey, and together they brought much of eastern and European architectural practice to the Southwest. Using reinforced concrete, and a good deal of exposed construction, they emphasized the relationship of the buildings to their surroundings. Gardens were designed as extensions of enclosed areas.

Hunt hoped, in planning for Pomona, to save the college from the grievous mistakes which had marred campus development in so many older American colleges and universities. Citing the foresight of Jefferson for the University of Virginia and the contrasting lack of provision for adequate growth by Harvard and Yale, he undertook to lay out a plan for Pomona that would meet the needs of the generations ahead. The first requirement was the purchase of land in order to permit the expansion of the central campus and to safeguard its future. Most urgent was acquisition of the block on College Avenue facing the President's House and the Inn which was occupied by private residences. Hunt urged the purchase of these and other properties that would give the college ownership of all the land between Third Street and Sixth Street, eastward from Harvard Avenue to Blanchard Park. This would provide forty-two acres for the central campus in addition to the sixty-six acres in Blanchard Park.

While some of the ideas and much of the detail proposed in 1908 were not to be carried out as Hunt had recommended, the basic elements of his plan determined the future development of the Pomona campus. Hunt considered all wooden buildings as tem-

Holmes Hall in 1913, as viewed from Sumner Hall

porary, and among his proposals was the removal of Sumner Hall from its position facing the Carnegie Library and the development of a large quadrangle with an administration and chapel building at its eastern limit on the site now occupied by Bridges Auditorium. Academic buildings were envisaged on both sides of College Avenue and on the east side of Harvard Avenue. The southwestern portion of the campus was to be given to the "liberal arts." A science quadrangle was planned north and west of Pearsons Hall, and a music building was to be placed on Harvard Avenue facing the Claremont Church. Five men's residence halls were to be located eastward from Holmes Hall, and these were to be faced by five women's residence halls placed east of the proposed new academic buildings on College Avenue. The location of Y.M.C.A. and Y.W.C.A. buildings with the respective groups of dormitories emphasized the religious and social roles these organizations then played in Pomona student life.

With foresight and appreciation of the value of campus land, President Blaisdell took steps to acquire the needed properties. By an expenditure of $30,000 the college secured the College Avenue block facing the Inn and the President's House and the block on Harvard Avenue opposite the Claremont Church. The consolidation of these areas was an arduous and protracted task, for local owners were often much attached to their properties, and distant owners were at times difficult to locate and then slow to respond. But the work was essential, for President Blaisdell "soon found that the possession of the necessary ground was quite half the battle in securing the gift of buildings to erect on it."

The acquisition of the land between Third and Fourth Streets on College Avenue opened a new stage in the development of the campus of Pomona College. In the discussions regarding the transformation of the "School of Music" and the "School of Art and Design" into "departments," the faculty had endorsed the provision of adequate buildings and facilities for the two departments, and a building for each department was included in the objectives of the Million Dollar Campaign. It was decided to place the buildings near each other on the newly acquired property and thus to constitute an art and music center. Myron Hunt was engaged as the architect for both buildings.

Through the gifts and the activities of the ladies of the Rembrandt Club the art building was achieved first, and appropriately named Rembrandt Hall. The building, as completed in the spring of 1914, was expected to be only a portion of a larger building, but twenty-three years were to elapse before the anticipated addition. Nevertheless, the significance of the original structure was great indeed. It was the first building devoted to art in the Pomona Valley, and its studios, work rooms, and auditorium were invaluable to both the art department and the Rembrandt Club.

As Rembrandt Hall was being completed, President Blaisdell announced that Mr. and Mrs. Appleton Shaw Bridges of San Diego had given Pomona $100,000 for the construction of a music building as a memorial to their daughter, Mabel Shaw Bridges '08. Music had been a special interest of this radiant young woman who entered Pomona in September 1904. In college she had participated

Mabel Shaw Bridges '08, above, and Bridges Hall of Music

in musical activities and in her junior year was the treasurer of the Rembrandt Club. Her death after a short illness in May 1907 brought great sorrow to the college. A three-page memorial tribute in the *Metate* spoke of "her cheerfulness and loyalty as a classmate; her kindness and sympathy as a friend; and above all, the beauty and sweetness of her character," which made her "an inspiration to all who knew and loved her."

The love which Mabel Shaw Bridges held for Pomona was reflected in the abiding interest and generosity of her parents. At the commencement of 1907, Mr. and Mrs. Bridges had established a scholarship in Mabel's memory. Early in his administration President Blaisdell sensed their desire for a permanent memorial to their daughter and her love of music. They sought, as President Blaisdell wrote, "not only to perpetuate the name of this young woman but to continue her life work in the service of the college."

Myron Hunt achieved a quality in Mabel Shaw Bridges Hall of Music which set it apart from other Pomona buildings. It was one of Hunt's outstanding creations, which included the early buildings of the present campus of Occidental College, the Henry E. Huntington residence (now the Huntington Art Gallery), and the Huntington Library. Hunt explained the architectural influence in Bridges Hall in a letter to Elizabeth Edmunds '34, who wrote him in her student days.

> It was set by the desire of the college to have a room which could hold a thousand people, but could be arranged to look as though there was a real audience if there were only three hundred and fifty. This was done by using the side benches of the parliament type and making the seats of the pit removable. When it came to the character of the detail, we worked back to Mexico, which means to Spain, which means to what the Spanish thought was Renaissance. (It was the latter form of the Renaissance, when it began to reach the rococo, and this influence was carried to Mexico where again it was modified as a result of the materials at hand and the genuinely decorative instinct of some of the Indian workmen used.) The reason for this was because of our local Spanish traditions. Effort was made to spot the ornamental Spanish style, rather than spread it out, Italian style.

Perfectly located and proportioned to its site, Bridges Hall brought to Pomona a beauty which had not existed before. The concert hall, with its fine panelling, decorated ceiling and outstanding acoustics, made attendance a memorable experience. The superb hall and the practice rooms and studios of the two wings on the south set a new standard for music facilities in the Southwest. The building, first generally known as Mabel S. Bridges Hall of Music, was opened on the evening of June 12, 1915 with a memorial concert by the Los Angeles Symphony Orchestra, conducted by Adolph Tandler, and the Pomona College Choral Union, directed by Professor Fred A. Bacon. Mr. and Mrs. Bridges were present and President Blaisdell paid a tribute to their daughter.

While Bridges Hall was under construction, significant steps were taken to improve the grounds. Architectural landscaping brought a pleasant aspect to the older buildings and gave a sense of unity to the campus. The beautification program owed most to William S. Mason, a Chicago businessman, who had become acquainted with Pomona through his friendship with Judge Charles G. Neely, a former Chicagoan recently appointed to the faculty. Mr. Mason made provision for plantings along the south side of Sixth Street from Harvard to Dartmouth.

Sensing that the college needed a central point of unity which would be a clear physical entrance to its life, Mason made a gift for the construction of an impressive gate at College Avenue and Sixth Street. The gate, designed by Hunt and President Blaisdell, brought a new dimension to the campus. The cornerstone was laid on Founders Day, October 14, 1914, and classes were shortened that morning to free a full hour for the ceremony. "This day marks the beginning of a new period of enrichment," said President Blaisdell; "we have struggled through the days of necessities; today, in a certain sense, we begin to glorify and beautify our life."

Classic in design and consisting of concrete block panels and curving iron grilles on each side of College Avenue, the Gate was an expression of the ideals which underlay the building of Pomona. Each panel had a large space for an inscription, and President Blaisdell gave deep thought to the words to be placed there. The inscriptions as completed were of his own composition, and their reception and continuing influence gave him great satisfaction. "By nothing would I more like to be remembered," he wrote of these injunctions to entering and departing Pomona students:

Let only the eager, thoughtful and reverent enter here.
They only are loyal to this college who departing bear their added riches in trust for mankind.[1]

As the central campus was embellished by the building of the Gate and the improvement of College Avenue, the construction of the Greek Theater added a focal point on the east. The theater was an outgrowth of "fun-producing entertainment" which early senior classes had given in the "Wash" on Tuesday afternoons of commencement week, and of somewhat more formal evening entertainment by later classes. As audiences became too large for their members to see or hear the actors conveniently, demand arose for a permanent Greek Theater, which would serve not only for commencement entertainment but on numerous occasions throughout the year. Leadership in the project was taken in its senior year by the Class of 1910 whose members subscribed twenty-five hundred dollars. Myron Hunt was engaged as the architect and, after a visit to the Greek Theater at the University of California in Berkeley, he presented a plan which was adopted by the college. The plan envisaged not only a stage and seats for four thousand people but dressing rooms and stage facilities — all in a structure ornamented by Greek columns and other classic decorations. Although the full plan was never completed, a fine stage among the live oaks and an excellent amphitheater were constructed. The basic concrete structure contained seats for several hundred, and wooden bleachers set on ground supported by concrete retaining walls provided space for some three thousand additional spectators. Work proceeded as funds could be secured, but

[1]In reflection many years later, President Blaisdell considered the first inscription "a trifle too prohibitive," perhaps expecting "too much of the entering student," and he thought it would have been better to have omitted the word "only." On the other hand, the departing injunction, he said, was "exactly as I still would wish it and I hope it may always express the final admonition of the college to its departing sons and daughters." He had clearly thought long about these words, for they occur as the conclusion of one of his earlier and unpublished papers, "The Pomona College Creed":

To give lavishly of myself and what I have,
To love my college, my country and my God;
And departing bear my added riches
In trust for mankind.

the Greek Theater as later generations were to know it was essentially built by the end of 1914.

While new buildings and campus improvements were under way, the college celebrated on March 7, 1914 the installation of its chapter of Phi Beta Kappa. Care had been taken to make the exercises, which were held in the Claremont Church, a gala occasion. Southern California high schools were invited to send delegates and a large number attended. The glee clubs, the trustees, the faculty, those to be initiated into Phi Beta Kappa, and students of the four college classes marched in the academic procession. The installation address was given by Professor George Herbert Palmer, and the charter was presented by Dr. Charles Noble of the University of California. Honorary degrees, Pomona's second and third, were conferred on Dr. James Mann Campbell, a Scot by birth, who was minister of the Congregational Church at Avalon, and David Prescott Barrows '94, the Dean of the Graduate School of the University of California.

The honoring of Dr. Barrows was only one of the awards to alumni on March 7. The new chapter of Phi Beta Kappa was authorized by the national organization to elect the outstanding graduates of earlier years, and forty were so recognized. Seventeen of these were able to be present and were initiated in the exercises held at Rembrandt Hall in the late afternoon, joining the fifteen undergraduates and four faculty members also inducted that day. The undergraduates and these faculty members, together with faculty members elected to Phi Beta Kappa in other institutions, composed the active chapter, Gamma of California, of which Dean Norton was elected president. The great day concluded with a chapter banquet at the Inn.

President Blaisdell had seen in the Phi Beta Kappa initiation an opportunity to bring a distinguished speaker from the East, not only for the exercises of the day but for an extended stay on the campus. In a special meeting on January 5, 1914, the faculty recommended that George Herbert Palmer, Alford Professor Emeritus of Natural Religion, Moral Philosophy and Civic Polity at Harvard University, be invited to spend a month at the college. Professor Palmer was one of the most famous teachers of his generation,

President Blaisdell and Harvard Professor George Herbert Palmer on Carnegie steps, 1915

eloquent on the platform, distinguished in his scholarship, and deeply interested in his students, one of whom, Dr. Willis Parker, was then Professor of Philosophy at Pomona. In his month on the Pomona campus Palmer gave the Phi Beta Kappa and Matriculation Day addresses, regular lectures to the ethics class on "The Ethics of Duty," and a series of lectures on "Phases of English Poetry." He captivated the students; "No man visiting Pomona in years has given us such inspiration and impetus toward high ideals," stated the *Metate* in a full-page salute.

The success of Professor Palmer's visit encouraged President Blaisdell to seek funds to support annually a visit of several weeks by a person of great distinction and national reputation. "The location of the college," he wrote, "in a small village in the far West made it clear that every effort should be made to bring to it the larger cosmopolitanism of the Great World." Through Bishop Joseph H. Johnson of the Board of Trustees he had come to know Miss Ellen Browning Scripps, a distinguished newspaper woman living in retirement in La Jolla. Miss Scripps was a graduate of Knox College; sensing her sympathy and understanding of a college like Pomona, Dr. Blaisdell invited her to establish an endowment of $15,000 for the purpose of bringing a distinguished person to the campus each year. Miss Scripps responded by forwarding $25,000 and requesting that the fund be named for Bishop Johnson. Since its establishment in the autumn of 1914 the Joseph H. Johnson Foundation has made possible visits by a large number of lecturers who have enriched the life of Pomona. Moreover, with this gift, Miss Scripps' first for higher education in Claremont, Pomona gained a benefactor who within the next twelve years would enable the college to enter new and unprecedented paths of academic organization.

The interest of Miss Scripps was representative of the wider outreach of the Board of Trustees. Recognizing its need of more strength for raising the funds required by the college, the trustees early in 1914 voted to increase their membership from twenty to twenty-five. When this change was approved by the State of California, among those added to the Board were two distinguished businessmen, William S. Mason and Seeley W. Mudd. They brought new dimensions to the Board and through their wisdom and generosity they made large and permanent contributions to the advancement of the college.

As noted earlier, Mason (1866-1961) had come to know Pomona College through Judge Neely before the latter moved from Chicago to California and joined the Pomona faculty. Knowledge of the college grew into deep interest when Mason himself established a winter home in Pasadena. A native of Illinois and a graduate of the Sheffield Scientific School of Yale University, Mason began his professional career as an engineer for the Chicago, Minneapolis and St. Paul Railway. After four years with the railway he established a real estate and insurance business in Chicago which he ran with great success throughout the remainder of his active business career. A man of wide intellectual interests, he developed a profound appreciation of American history and formed valuable collections of books and manuscripts, including the largest collection of material on Benjamin Franklin in private hands, a significant library on other literature of the American Revolution, and a remarkable collection of Californiana. These materials he gave in his lifetime to the Yale University Library, the Clements Library of the University of Michigan, and the Pomona College Library, which in the Mason California Collection possesses indispensable materials for the study of the West.

Seeley W. Mudd (1861-1926) was a native of Missouri who, after graduating with honors from the Mining Department of the School of Engineering of Washington University in St. Louis, became in 1887 the highly successful manager of a silver and gold mine in Leadville, Colorado. There he met and married Miss Della Mulock. Following the loss of a daughter, Mr. and Mrs. Mudd sought a milder climate for their three sons and the family moved to Los Angeles in 1903. There Mr. Mudd's career gradually took a new direction. Although he continued the management of mines in Leadville, by journeying to Colorado from Los Angeles, he began to develop mining projects of his own. In 1912 he relinquished his responsibilities in Leadville and devoted his energy to his personal business interests. With an associate, Philip Wiseman, he developed a copper mine in Ray, Arizona, where rich deposits were located and extracted by brilliant sampling and engineering methods. That same year, Mudd and Wiseman backed a prospecting engineer, Charles Godfrey Gunther, who was convinced that some of the abandoned copper mines of the ancient Mediterranean world could be reopened and worked profitably with modern methods. After explorations in the Sinai and Spain, Gunther concluded that the ancient copper mines of northwest Cyprus offered the best prospect. There on the night of July 4, 1914 he discovered large deposits of rich copper ore. The ultimate success of the Cyprus Mines Corporation was tremendous, but more than a decade of faith, courage, hard work, and financial support would be required before it showed a profit.

However, by 1914 Mr. Mudd had reached a period when he could give more time to interests outside his own business. Shortly after their arrival in Los Angeles the Mudd family had joined the First Congregational Church which that year completed a new church building on Hope Street near Ninth Street. The minister until 1913 was Warren Finney Day, who was succeeded by Carl S. Patton. Both were distinguished men who became close friends of the Mudds and their family. They were trustees of Pomona College and from them as well as from the church Mr. and Mrs. Mudd learned of the college in Claremont. Mr. Mudd thus came to know President Blaisdell, and the two men were to develop one of the great friendships of Pomona history. Equally imaginative, Dr. Blaisdell and Mr. Mudd were men of professional and social vision who complemented each other in developing the college which had brought them together. Mr. Mudd, said Marston, was "a perfect trustee, combining educational and spiritual ideals with the wisdom of affairs."

The broader new interests represented by Miss Scripps, Mr. Mason, and Mr. Mudd were invaluable supports in the tough campaign to raise by January 1, 1915, the $1,100,000 required to secure the $150,000 gift from the General Education Board. By mid-summer 1914 the total had reached $900,000, but it required the full energies of President Blaisdell and the leaders of the trustees to secure the remainder. Unfortunately, the period of the campaign was marked by general financial stringency over the country, severe crippling of the orange industry in Southern California due to a serious freeze in 1913, and by the outbreak and increasing seriousness of war in Europe. On December 31, 1914, President Blaisdell announced total gifts and pledges of $1,000,000, but the $100,000 to remove the college debt had still to be raised. As many of the pledges ran for five years and others were in land, which the General Education Board would not accept, it was not until 1919 that all matters arising from the Million Dollar Campaign were concluded.

Despite these vexations and delays, the Million Dollar Campaign made possible a "Greater Pomona." Perhaps more important than any other of the campaign's accomplishments was the realization that Pomona could raise large sums of money and that the future of the college was assured.

Four new buildings financed by the campaign were a visible basis for such confidence. In addition to Rembrandt Hall and Bridges Hall, two science buildings had been added: a marine laboratory at Laguna Beach, and a Hall of Botany on the campus. The marine laboratory constructed in 1913 and largely a gift from interested citizens of Orange County, was the culmination of summer expeditions in which first Professor Cook and then Professor Baker had taken students for study on the coast, first near San Pedro, and after 1911 at Laguna Beach. The work of that summer was of such quality that Professor Baker presented it in a book of 215 pages with accounts of fourteen student projects and three of his own. Such achievement aroused local financial support for a permanent laboratory, and the college made this one of the objectives of the campaign. The resulting two-story wooden building with pillars giving it the appearance of a Greek temple, was placed under the direction of Professor Hilton who for more than thirty years was to conduct summer sessions at Laguna Beach, developing many marine biologists and adding much to the lore of Pomona student life.

With the advance of scientific knowledge, Pearsons Hall could no longer meet the full needs of the college. The Million Dollar Campaign had included $60,000 for a new science hall but in the end funds of such significance were not available. However, Mr. A. P. Harwood made a gift for a hall of botany as a memorial to his son, Alfred. This was constructed west of Pearsons in the summer of 1915. The large lecture hall, offices and laboratories of the new structure, together with the adjoining greenhouse and lath house, contributed much to the brilliant era of instruction and research in botany which soon ensued at Pomona. When the department moved to more modern quarters in Crookshank Hall in 1922, Harwood Hall was converted to other college uses which it served until its demolition in 1968.

The building program of the early Blaisdell administration was climaxed in 1916 by the remodelling of Holmes Hall, a project which had not been included in the objectives of the Million Dollar Campaign. Despite the addition of other structures in the preceding quarter century, Holmes had continued as the main instructional and student center of the college. There were the classrooms for the humanities and the social sciences, the offices of the dean, the registrar, the business manager, and the auditorium which

College Avenue after the renovation of Holmes Hall

served as the chapel and place for most student and college gatherings. A plain wooden building of no architectural pretension, the appearance and facilities of Holmes were no longer adequate to the needs and the standards of the advancing college. Some months after the completion of the Million Dollar Campaign, gifts totalling $20,000 were received for the restoration of the building. Of this amount half was contributed by Miss Esther R. Holmes, daughter of Cyrus W. Holmes.

Confident that they could proceed, the Executive Committee on May 22 invited James P. Jamieson, an architect of St. Louis, to come to Claremont at college expense and begin planning the remodelling. Jamieson's plans were approved on July 14 on which date a contract was also signed with a builder. When the students returned in September, the work was nearing completion. While the entire project eventually cost $45,000, there was no reason to question the wisdom of what had been done. A very Victorian wooden building with gingerbread decorations and an open bell tower had been transformed into a functional grey stucco structure with a mission tile roof, thus harmonizing with Pearsons, the Carnegie Library, Smiley, the new Rembrandt, and Bridges Hall of Music. The closing of the old south entrance and the building of "a new and more stately" west entrance oriented the building toward College Avenue and emphasized the sense of unity marked by the

College Gate. The construction of a covered porch on the south side of the auditorium and the building of a new entrance from the east made a pleasant gathering place before chapel or after classes. The remodelling was so well done that more than thirty years were to pass before major renovation would be necessary. Jamieson's work was so satisfactory that he and his associates were engaged as the supervising architects for the college. With Bridges Hall of Music the new Holmes Hall was expressive of "the Greater Pomona."

CHAPTER X

The College, 1915-17

THE RESOURCES and confidence gained in the success of the Million Dollar Campaign were soon manifest in every area of the college. The enlargement of the faculty and the expansion of the academic program were attracting a larger student body. Through the work of its faculty and students and the leadership of its president Pomona enjoyed growing recognition throughout the country.

To the faculty were brought a number of men who would establish themselves among Pomona's greatest teachers. Ralph H. Lyman, dean of the school of music at the University of Oregon, came in 1917 as professor of applied music and head of the department, positions he would hold for the next thirty years. A graduate of Grinnell College in 1906, with study in Berlin, Lyman brought to Pomona an understanding of the American liberal arts college enriched by his European experience. He was an ideal choice to direct music as "a department," and to integrate it fully into the college.

Bernard Capen Ewer, professor of psychology, and Waldemar Christian Westergaard, assistant professor of history, joined the Pomona faculty in 1916. Ewer, who came from the faculty of Reed College, held B.A. and M.A. degrees from Brown University and a Ph.D. from Harvard. At Pomona he developed a strong psychology department and also won the esteem of his students to whom he and his wife extended warm and frequent hospitality. Waldemar Westergaard, a graduate of the University of North Dakota with a Ph.D. from the University of California, brought the scholarly study of history to Pomona undergraduates. Although he was called to a professorship of history at the new University of

California at Los Angeles in 1925, Westergaard maintained close ties with Pomona throughout his life.[1]

The new faculty members included two young scientists who would bring great distinction to themselves and Pomona. Alfred O. Woodford '13, a graduate student at the University of California, began his lifelong service to his alma mater in 1915 as an instructor in chemistry, but he soon offered courses in geology which in 1919 became a separate department under his direction. Philip A. Munz, assistant professor of botany, came to Pomona in 1917 from Cornell University where he had just completed his Ph.D. A westerner and a graduate of the University of Denver, he brought particular interest in Western flora, and continued the development of the herbarium to which Professor Baker had contributed so much. As young faculty members Woodford and Munz were soon establishing teaching and scholarly traditions that would make Pomona an outstanding center for the study of geology and botany.

The courses of instruction in the college were then organized in three groups: language, literature, and fine arts; mathematics, physical and biological sciences; and history, social sciences, and philosophy. Although students were given "a large range of choice" in the selection of their work, they were required to take introductory courses in "each of the great realms of knowledge"— English, French or German, history, mathematics, a physical or biological science, economics, and philosophy or psychology. In order to provide "concentration along some chosen line of work" the student selected a limited number from certain indicated groups of courses. A student "who had shown special ability in one line of work," and who had secured the permission of the head of the department, could take a "departmental major" consisting of at least eighteen hours in the department with courses in allied subjects and including a reading knowledge of French or German. Physical education was required for all students throughout the

[1]In later years he was a major benefactor of both art and history at the college. Professor Westergaard joined his parents-in-law in 1938 in establishing the Viola Minor Westergaard Fund, an endowment for the Pomona art department in memory of his young wife who died in 1918. Of Danish parentage, Westergaard became a distinguished scholar and author in Scandinavian history, and by bequeathing his library and an endowment to Pomona in 1963, he made the college an important center of Northern European studies.

four years, the time demanded in the first two years being twice that of the junior and senior years.

The first assembly of 1916-17 set the pattern for the opening of college which has been followed essentially since that time. Dean Norton read the college chapter, and President Blaisdell spoke. Following the exercises, the students and faculty gathered on the front steps of Bridges Hall and President Blaisdell and the president of the Associated Students spoke to them informally. The flag was raised and college was declared officially open.

The daily schedule was a full one for both students and faculty. Classes began at 7:30 in the morning, and the final class was scheduled at 3:15. The period from 10:30 to 11:15 in the morning was reserved for those activities which contributed to the life of the whole college community. Within this hour students and faculty gathered for chapel, or students held meetings of their organizations, or visiting lecturers were heard.

The chapel exercises served not only for daily devotionals but as a center for announcements and college information. Students sat by classes and their attendance was checked by proctors. Since seating was rigorously determined "according to the number of hours and credits required for full standing," a student's place in the chapel rows was public announcement of his academic status. "Moving-Up-Day," in which the classes advanced at the end of the year, was an impressive and cherished occasion. The chapel services were led by members of the faculty, but by 1915 this was no longer an obligation in which all faculty members were required to share. Although their attendance was expected, this declined as the faculty grew larger, and the faculty minutes after 1915 contain a number of reminders that faculty members should go to chapel regularly. Scripture reading, a brief devotional talk, and hymns constituted the body of the service. President Blaisdell led chapel regularly on Fridays and he prized this opportunity of meeting with the entire student body. Dean Norton was the most frequent leader from the faculty. While students might complain about the chapel requirement, there was little fundamental objection to it in this period.

The college regularly brought to the students an increasing

group of distinguished speakers and outstanding personalities, President Blaisdell giving much attention to this means of broadening the horizon of the college. Among those who came in 1915-17 were Helen Keller, Booker T. Washington, Alfred Noyes, Rabindranath Tagore, the Hindu poet and philosopher, and Washington Gladden, a well known New York state clergyman and pacifist. On the Johnson Foundation, the college brought Professor John Bates Clark, an economist from Columbia University; George Burton Adams, a distinguished authority on English history then at Yale; and John Douglas Adams, professor of practical theology at Hartford Theological Seminary. The Reverend John Kingsley Birge, of Smyrna, Turkey, who spoke on "Mohammedanism," was brought through the newly established Henry D. Porter Foundation, which provided for a lecture by a prominent worker in the field of Christian Missions. George Herbert Palmer returned for a week in February 1917, and Harry Emerson Fosdick, soon to be known as the most influential American preacher of the twentieth century, gave five lectures at Pomona in May 1917. The following November all classes and activities were cancelled to permit the college to hear Dr. George Parkin, Organizing Secretary of the Rhodes Trust, who had translated the idea and bequest of Cecil Rhodes into a working system of scholarships at the University of Oxford for young men from the British Empire and the United States.

With the opening of Bridges Hall the college inaugurated a Music and Lecture Course in order to give the entire student body opportunity to hear the great artists and lecturers of the day. For these events each student received a ticket without charge. The Music and Lecture Course became immediately one of the most important cultural forces in the college, and it would be extended to a wider audience and influence with its transfer to Bridges Auditorium when that building was constructed in 1931.

An improved library also contributed to the growing maturity of the college. In the period June 1, 1913, to June 1, 1916 the library book holdings increased from 17,873 to 31,000. President Blaisdell's experience as the librarian at Beloit made him an especially effective leader for developing a library.

The enrollment increased with the growing strength and reputation of the college, and when the number of students exceeded 550, the trustees felt it imperative to limit admissions. Their action on March 22, 1915 limiting "the incoming class to two hundred — one hundred men and one hundred women" was evidence not only of progress but of determination to maintain standards by admitting only the number of students whom the college could serve adequately. It was hoped also that more selective admissions would enable the college to hold a greater body of students through graduation, thereby providing a more mature student body. The total enrollments as of November 1915 and November 1916 were respectively 551 and 598. Of these the seniors numbered 80 and 102.

The achievement of the college on a limited budget was remarkable. At their annual meeting in June 1915 the trustees voted that "the expressed policy of this Board is that the expense account for the coming year should be kept within $135,000," and there is no evidence that President Blaisdell exceeded this budget. On March 22, 1915 the trustees had approved a report of its committee on education recommending that it be "the aim of the college, as speedily as possible, to bring full professors to a salary of at least $2,500" and associate professors to a salary of $2,000. Toward this end salary increases of $300 for professors with twenty years' service at the college, increases of $200 for other professors, and increases of $100 for associate professors were voted. Despite these steps, the salary for most twenty-year full professors for the academic year 1917-18 was $2,200, and the top salary for associate professors was $1,800. This continued low level of faculty salaries was of great concern to President Blaisdell.

But the nature of higher education in California at that time made the president and the trustees hesitate to seek adequate funds for faculty salaries by raising tuition. The University of California did not charge tuition, nor then did Stanford, which provided free tuition in return for the privileges which the state had included in its charter. For a number of years tuition at Pomona had remained at $45 per semester. When a modest increase was made, effective 1915-16, the college adopted the Yale system of computing tuition by a general fee and a charge for each semester hour of instruction. At Pomona the plan involved a general charge of $15 a semester plus two dollars for each semester hour. As students took from sixteen to eighteen hours, the semester tuition charge ranged from $47 to $51.

If living was plain for faculty and students alike, both thinking and spirits were high. "The college is preeminently a company of workers," stated the catalogue of 1917-18. "Extravagant social life does not exist at Pomona College and no one should seek the institution who is not willing to make surrender of some personal pleasures in the interests of the common earnestness and simplicity.." While social life was restricted, thought was not, and the college welcomed "all honest expression of opinion," believing "that no student should go out of the college unaware of the throbbing questions of the day or unprepared to face the winds of free discussion."

The college was a community in which faculty and students were in constant and close association. Owning their homes, the faculty lived in the immediate vicinity of the campus, for the most part on College Avenue from First to Third Streets and from Sixth to Tenth Streets, on Harvard and Yale, and a block or so east or west of these avenues. The Claremont Inn, which had been extended, was the social center for the faculty and the community and a residence for eastern visitors.

The Inn was also the college commons where some two hundred students took their meals in the large dining room specially reserved for them. Other students lived at home or were members of boarding clubs in the village. Some prepared their own meals amid Spartan conditions they would love to recall, and doubtless exaggerate, when they returned as prospering alumni. For those who ate there, the commons was a lively place. In 1916 the *Metate* declared,

> The Commons is the center of social life during the week and vies with the college library as a point of departure for "queeners." An orchestra furnished music once a week and the room is filled at every meal with the happy bubbling chatter of divers young men and sundry coeds. "Mixed tables" are a feature of the Commons. Owing to the fact that the men are outnumbered they are distributed gracefully about the room as long as they last.

Class organization was strong and much of a student's social life was with his classmates. Selection of the class name and the banner were very important matters in the freshman year. Each class had its sweater which was worn with pride. Freshman-sophomore rivalry was intense — and a constant source of concern to the faculty.

Social events were banquets, receptions, picnics, or days in the mountains. The students delighted in the natural beauty of the Claremont area, its flowers, the chapparal, the canyons, and above all the mountains. The climbing of Mt. Baldy was almost considered a requirement for graduation. While dancing was forbidden and all groups were chaperoned, students and faculty were adept at making the system work. A quatrain from the *Metate* on Ditch Day 1916, when classes had been "ditched" and the entire college had gone to the mountains, perhaps best reveals the real spirit of the campus:

> Where green are trees and soft are mosses
> Forget the world, its cares and crosses,
> For all the chaperones are snoozing
> And all the younger folks are "Twosing."

Student publications and organizations reflected the strength of the larger enrollment and the growing pride of the college. The *Student Life* began to appear twice a week, still retaining one issue a month as a literary magazine. Beginning in the autumn of 1916, the paper carried the College Gates on its masthead. *The Handbook of Pomona College,* prepared annually by the Young Women's and Young Men's Christian Associations, introduced the new students to Pomona, her regulations, traditions, and songs, and provided all students with essential information for the academic year. The *Metate* reflected the life of the larger college. The Pomona College Literary Society, the first student organization, had limited the range of its interest, and by 1916 devoted its bi-weekly meetings to "the authors and works of English Literature," with papers and "impromptu speeches" by the members.

The discussion of contemporary political, economic and social questions passed to the debating clubs which flourished in a period marked by the domestic reforms of Woodrow Wilson's administration and growing concern over the European war. By the spring of 1916, Pomona had four debating clubs for men, the Pomona College Debating Club, Lyceum, Areopagus, and Adelphi; and two for women, Alpha Kappa and Delta Lambda. The clubs aimed for a membership of twenty to thirty, and gave all their members training and experience in debate, public speaking, and parliamentary drill. There were debates between the clubs within the college, but for the men the great occasions of the year were the debates with Occidental and the liberal arts college of the University of Southern California. The three institutions had a Triangular Debating League which operated through a series of three-year agreements. These were triumphant years for Pomona and in 1915-16 the college won the championship of the Triangular League for the fifth straight year. Among the debate topics of the period were: "Resolved that in the State of California land values should be the only subject of taxation for state and local purposes," and "Granted that further restriction of immigration is desirable, resolved that such restriction should take the form of an illiteracy test."

There was an increase in the number and quality of student organizations related to the academic departments. The glee clubs, the choral union, and the orchestra entered a great period with the building of Bridges Hall and the leadership of Professor Lyman. Initiated in 1916-17 were the history seminar, the chemistry conference, and the society of pure and applied mathematics. The organization of Scribblers, a club for student writers, in 1916 further attested to the widening interests of the students.

Two aspects of student life presented major problems for the college: fraternities and sororities, and intercollegiate athletics. In both the Blaisdell administration made decisions that set the future pattern for Pomona.

For some years a fraternity, Kappa Delta, organized in 1902, and a sorority, Sigma Beta Eta, established in 1905, had been part of Pomona student life. Each group had a faculty member as advisor. Both groups were included in the *Metate,* but not listed with other student organizations in the college catalogue. A second fraternity, Sigma Tau, was organized in 1912. Membership in the fraternities and sororities was limited to juniors and seniors in 1914. The issue of national fraternities came to the fore in February 1915 when a group of men requested the privilege of organizing a local fraternity "with a view to making it later on a chapter of a national fraternity." The faculty authorized the group, Phi Delta, to organize as a local fraternity but with "the understanding that such action was not a commitment on the question of its relation to the national organization."

President Blaisdell's view was decisive in the course Pomona soon chose. He saw college as a "life" which included influential elements beyond the academic program. He hoped that Pomona students could build friendships that would be both pleasurable and character forming. His experience with national fraternities at Beloit convinced him that they both "complicated administrative problems" and narrowed "the range and richness of college friendships," and he sought a better solution for Pomona. Under his guidance Pomona adopted a plan of local fraternities especially adapted to the conditions in which the college had developed. Local fraternities were encouraged, but their charters stipulated that they were not to have fraternity dining tables nor displace the class as the social and guiding unit of the campus. Building by fraternities was limited to cabins in the mountains which were to be enjoyed by both faculty and students. Through these decisions the college retained much of "the simplicity and freedom of its democratic society," and it avoided the loss of social control that beset institutions which authorized national fraternities.

The college came to a different conclusion regarding sororities, although it took nearly two years of faculty discussion to do so. After two months of considering "the status of the sorority in Pomona College," the college life committee reported on April 14, 1915 that it did not seem a wise time "to take definitive action concerning the relations of sororities to Pomona College;" therefore no steps should be taken to create new sororities or to interfere with the one in operation. Accordingly, the faculty refused permission for a new sorority, and again referred the general question of sororities to the committee which nine months later reported its unanimous judgment "that sororities should not be permitted." On April 21, 1916 the faculty voted to discontinue Sigma Beta Eta by forbidding its election of new members, and to prohibit the formation of any new sororities. Realizing that these actions established policy "not only in the present, but for a long future," the faculty in justification cited "the history of other institutions" and "the convictions of leading educators." A year later the members of Sigma Beta Eta petitioned for reconsideration, but the faculty held its position, and the question of sororities at Pomona was never seriously raised again.

Issues of great significance for Pomona were raised by the growing interest in intercollegiate athletics and physical education among American colleges and universities. In athletics greatest interest centered on football which, after rule changes in 1906 making it less hazardous, soon became the major intercollegiate sport throughout the country. At the same time, leaders of the "new physical education" emphasized corrective work for individuals and recreational games in lieu of calisthenics and the mass exercises which had made "gym work" something to be endured rather than enjoyed. Long accepted European programs of physical education were being challenged by American systems pioneered at Harvard and Amherst.

In most institutions full-time appointees in athletics and physical education had replaced the student and part-time coaches who had introduced sports to the American campus. This evolution had occurred at Pomona in the administration of President Gates, and President Blaisdell found an able and extremely successful man in charge. Although William L., "the Fox," Stanton was not the first full-time appointee in athletics and physical education at Pomona, he was the first to raise this post to major status within the college. Coming in 1909 in the uncertain interim between the resignation of President Gates and the arrival of President Blaisdell, Stanton rebuilt confidence in Pomona's athletics and achieved remarkable success: three football championships, and one track championship. Intercollegiate athletics became the largest social and extracurricular interest of the students, and Stanton's popularity was enhanced by his further service as an able director of dramatics.

However, Stanton's work in physical education did not match his remarkable leadership in intercollegiate athletics. Giving his own major concern to coaching football, baseball, and track, he placed the required physical education program in the hands of student assistants. Although a physical education requirement of two semesters for freshmen had been instituted by 1910, "outdoor athletics" could be substituted for "gymnasium," and permission for this substitution was given so freely that it vitiated the program.

While he had not himself participated in intercollegiate athletics, President Blaisdell brought valuable experience for the shaping of athletic and physical education policy at Pomona. As the chairman of a faculty committee on athletics at Beloit, he had gained intimate knowledge of problems and values of intercollegiate sports. While favoring them, he realized that an uncontrolled program could imperil the integrity of an educational institution. Pomona had not succumbed to the corrupting and growing practices of lower standards of admission and special scholarships for athletes, and President Blaisdell took steps to see that she did not. The greatest peril lay in the admission of athletes who would play for a few weeks and then not continue in college; and the relations of American colleges before 1920 were often imperilled by contentions and allegations over "ineligible" players. To forestall this problem President Blaisdell led Pomona in instituting the "freshman rule" on the Pacific Coast. With both student and faculty approval the college announced in 1913 that, beginning in September 1914, freshmen would not be eligible for varsity teams, but would play on specially organized freshman teams.

The public was astonished by this action, but soon Pomona's lead was followed by the University of Southern California and Occidental, and the stage was set for the creation of a new athletic conference based on higher standards. The Southern California Conference, formed in 1908, had collapsed in 1911 when the University of Southern California withdrew because students in its law school were declared ineligible for conference games. For the next several years, the former member colleges made dual arrangements among themselves, but these were often highly unsatisfactory. In April 1914 President Bovard of the University of Southern California invited representatives of Occidental and

Pomona to meet with him to lay plans for a new conference agreement. The three colleges were eager to reestablish their athletic relations on a sound and permanent basis and in September 1914 they announced the formation of the Southern California Intercollegiate Athletic Conference.

The conference charter established new ideals and standards. To be eligible for a varsity team a player must have been in residence for one full year and have completed twenty-four hours of work. The government of the conference was placed primarily in the hands of the college faculties with the provision that two of the three representatives for each institution should be members of its academic faculty, the third being a coach.

Although the original membership of the conference lasted for only a year, the conference was able to reconstitute itself over the years and adapt to the growth of higher education in Southern California. After the University of Southern California withdrew, concluding in 1915 that its own future athletic relations lay with other and larger institutions, the conference was enlarged by the admission of Whittier College, the University of Redlands and Throop College (later to become the California Institute of Technology), these institutions joining Occidental and Pomona in subscribing to the conference principle of "amateur sport coupled with high scholastic standards."

The unexpected resignation of Stanton in the autumn of 1915 and his acceptance of appointment as coach at Occidental, effective September 1916, produced a tense situation within Pomona, but it also offered the faculty an opportunity for change. While the students lamented the loss of "the man who has wrought such miracles" for Pomona, the faculty cabinet recommended that the trustees accept the resignation. The faculty and President Blaisdell were looking toward a more modern physical education program. Two excellent young men were secured, Carl Peter Schott and Eugene White Nixon, each with the rank of assistant professor of physical education for men, Schott primarily to have charge of the work in physical education and Nixon to be coach of most of the athletic teams. Schott had received the Bachelor of Education degree from Nebraska State Normal School and the Bachelor of Physical Education from the Young Men's Christian Association College at Springfield, Massachusetts. Nixon held the Bachelor of Arts degree from Monmouth College, where he had studied the classics, and had done graduate work at the University of Illinois. He came to Pomona after six years at Davenport, Iowa, high school, where the phenomenal record of his football teams (only two defeats in the six years) made him known as the "wizard of Iowa."

Nixon and Schott arrived at an auspicious time. The faculty had shown its support of physical education and athletics by the appointment of two full-time men instead of one. Furthermore, the earlier physical education requirement for freshmen and sophomores had been extended in 1914 to juniors and seniors for both semesters, thus making Pomona one of the few colleges in the nation which provided and required a four-year program in physical education.

The requirement applied to women as well as men and there was a separate physical education department for women. The work for women was led by assistant professor Laura C. Squires '08, who after graduating at Pomona had taken a Master's degree in physical education at Wellesley College, a pioneer in developing instruction in physical education for women in both schools and colleges.

The athletic and physical education facilities for all students were greatly improved. Alumni Field, which had been severely damaged in a storm and flood in 1915-16, had been rebuilt and, with new facilities, was better than ever. Much prized was a new enclosed swimming pool, "the standard size for water polo," which had been provided through the Million Dollar Campaign, largely by student efforts. In accordance with Myron Hunt's campus plan, Renwick Gymnasium was moved eastward from its original location and the pool located beside it. A separate training quarters building was also provided for men, and the baths and dressing rooms in Renwick were given to women students.

Amid the era of good feeling which accompanied the college progress from 1915-17, President Blaisdell had the happy thought of bestowing the title of President Emeritus on former President Baldwin. The suggestion was cordially received by both the faculty and trustees, and there was much satisfaction among the older alumni when this recognition was voted to Pomona's first president. From 1916-17 until his death in 1931, President Emeritus Baldwin was listed in the college catalogue.

The academic and financial building of Pomona required extended travel by the president to the East and Middle West, and long absences from the campus. For example, Dr. Blaisdell departed two days after the opening assembly in September 1916 and did not return until six weeks later. While away, he conferred with architect Jamieson, in St. Louis, spoke to the state Congregational Association in Racine, Wisconsin, represented Pomona at the fiftieth anniversary of Carleton College where he was one of the principal speakers, attended the Congregational National Council in Toledo, Ohio, and spent several days on college business in Boston.

President Blaisdell's outstanding leadership and the growth of the college brought him recognition beyond Congregational circles. He took an active part in the Association of American Colleges, organized in 1914 through the leadership of President Robert L. Kelly of Earlham College who became its first director. At the annual meeting of the Association held in Chicago in January 1917, Dr. Blaisdell delivered an address, "Constructive Criticism of the American College," telling his presidential colleagues that "the college is yet in process; its day, both inner and outer, is still in the morning."

Whether this address crystallized the desire among his former colleagues for his return to Beloit, where President Eaton was about to retire, is not clear; but at a meeting of the Pomona Board of Trustees held in Bridges Hall on January 30, 1917 President Blaisdell "made a full statement of an assured call to the presidency of Beloit College, and the special appeal his Alma Mater made to him." In the full discussion that followed his retirement from the meeting, there was a unanimous feeling of "the urgent necessity of President Blaisdell's remaining at Pomona." The trustees felt that his work had made the college "in such a sense *his college,* that its future very largely depends on him" — a responsibility, in the judgment of the Board, "hardly comparable to any other responsibility." A committee of five, including the chairman of the Board, was appointed to confer with President Blaisdell. A matter of such importance required much thought and consideration, and on February 5 he spoke about it at length to the faculty cabinet, which likewise urged him to remain at Pomona. Dr. Blaisdell's decision to accede to the deeply held desires of the trustees and the faculty and to continue his work at Pomona was significant, indeed crucial, in the life of the college.

CHAPTER XI

The College in World War I

PRESIDENT BLAISDELL'S renewed commitment to Pomona gave the college the assurance of experienced and devoted leadership in a gathering national crisis in which the American people and all their institutions would be severely tested. In the long period from the outbreak of war in Europe in August 1914 to April 1917 the American people became increasingly supportive of the Allied powers whom they saw as the defenders of democratic institutions. Unrestricted submarine warfare against merchant ships in the North Atlantic led Congress to declare war against Germany on April 6, 1917. Lifted by the eloquence of President Wilson, the nation took up arms "to make the world safe for democracy."

At Pomona, as in nearly all other institutions of higher education, exigencies of the war were to be the prime considerations from 1917 to 1919. Four days after the declaration of war, the Executive Committee of the Board of Trustees in a special meeting voted "to proffer to the Government during the war the use of the college grounds and appurtenances to facilitate the purposes of war, and further to apply to the Government, under the Officers Reserve Corps Act, for an officer to drill our students."

The country was so deficient in military supplies that the government could not enlist and arm immediately all the young men eligible for military service. Accordingly the War Department in April urged students to remain in college and to prepare there for the role which would be theirs "when America's new army is mobilized." In May, Secretary Newton D. Baker gave the same message to a national conference of college and university presidents held in Washington which President Blaisdell attended.

While awaiting calls from the government, Pomona instituted its own military training. In accordance with the "Preparedness" program which President Wilson championed from December 1915, the faculty, as early as April 1916, had discussed military drill for Pomona men, and an elective military course taught by Assistant Professor Schott had been instituted in the second semester of 1916-17. The objectives of this move and the action of the trustees a few days earlier were the securing of a unit of the new Reserve Officers Training Program, which Congress authorized on June 3, 1916. The Declaration of War came while the college was on spring vacation, and immediately on their return to the campus the students formed under Mr. Schott three military companies and a Red Cross corps. For learning the use of arms there were available only "about thirty muskets, breech loaders used in the time of the Indian Wars in the West."

The faculty took immediate steps to put the college on a wartime basis. Effective September 1917, the work in physical education for freshman and sophomore men was reduced by half each semester, and in the freed time these men were required to take military training, unless they were excused by the officer in charge of military training, the director of physical education, and the chairman of the faculty committee on physical education. Also instituted, and for academic credit, were an elective course in military drill for juniors and seniors, an elective course in military science (supplementing the drill courses) for sophomores, juniors, and seniors, and Red Cross courses for both men and women.

These provisions did not interfere with the regular work of the college as the academic year drew to a close. However, the May Masque, "The Key," presented by the women of the college before an audience of two thousand in the Greek Theater, was given as a benefit for the Red Cross. A class of 101, the largest in Pomona's history, was graduating, and the customary three days were given to commencement occasions. For the first time, the graduation exercises were held in the Greek Theater. The popular move was occasioned by the pressing need to accommodate larger audiences. Commencement, at six o'clock Monday evening, June 25, according to *Student Life,* differed "somewhat from that of other years in that the martial democratic spirit of the times pervades it in a dominating tone." The topics of the addresses by five members of the class were: "Germany's War Philosophy," "The Basis of Value," "The Education of Women," "The War God," and "The Expansion of Democracy." Seven of the graduates, already in military service, received their degrees *in absentia.*

When college opened in September 1917, Pomona was part of a rapidly arming nation, and under the Selective Service Act of May 18, 1917, all men between the ages of 21 and 30 had registered for military service. Within the college the immediate influence of the Act was limited as only seniors and younger faculty were within these age limits. Furthermore, the college had provided military training on the campus for all able-bodied men. On August 13, President Blaisdell reported to the Executive Committee that he had secured Charles B. Vogdes, a retired major in the United States Army and a graduate of the United States Military Academy, to head the military program of the college at an honorarium of $1,000 a year. Major Vogdes, as Acting Professor of Military Science and Tactics, with an assistant, put into effect the military courses, required and elective, established by the faculty the previous spring. The men under his supervision were known as the Cadet Corps.

Despite the training on the campus, the fervor to enlist brought steady losses of men, and the total enrollment of 544 students in November 1917 represented a decline of fifty-four from the same date a year before. When the seniors made their initial appearance at chapel "in the time honored costume of cap and gown" the class included fifty women and only twenty men. President Blaisdell informed the trustees in January 1918 that seventy-five men had left the college to meet some phase of the war requirement. "The change is marked," he said. "Our rapid growth is checked."

It is a tribute to the stability of the college that President Blaisdell could be absent from the campus for five months in the beginning of 1918. In the autumn of 1917, the American Board of Commissioners for Foreign Missions of the Congregational Churches invited him to go to Japan as a member of a three-man deputation charged with making a fact-finding survey of the

Board's missionary work in that country. Both the faculty and the trustees urged him to go, and on November 9, 1917, *Student Life* announced his acceptance under the headline, "Honor Given to Dr. Blaisdell." President and Mrs. Blaisdell left Claremont on January 21, and returned on June 13. As the entire journey, both going and returning, was made on Japanese vessels, the Blaisdells had exceptional shipboard opportunities to secure some firsthand knowledge of the Japanese people and their culture.

The months in the Orient proved taxing and strenuous. Despite the "unceasing labor of travel and conference," President Blaisdell met every appointment in a program that took him to "all parts of Japan, the whole length of Korea, and three of our (Congregational) stations in North China, including Tientsin and Peking." He found, as he wrote Mr. Marston on April 28 from "a little Japanese hotel on the back side of Japan, seated on a matting floor," that he had "both greatly over-estimated and greatly under-estimated the country and the people. Japan is wretchedly poor — beyond my furthest imagination. In many respects she is most incapable and almost hopelessly lacking. But in other ways she has a most inspiring life. The courage with which she faces the daily task and keeps her lonely leadership in this welter of the East is most impressive. And out of this mass of poverty and commonplace there does flower some of the loveliest saintliness that I have ever looked upon."

This extended and intimate introduction to the Orient and the five months' respite from his duties at the college were both a fulfillment and an inspiration for President Blaisdell. He had long had a keen interest in Asia and the part American higher education could play in its future. This trip, his first journey to any foreign country, was to have a permanent influence in his thinking.

While President Blaisdell was away, the college was granted the R.O.T.C. unit for which it had applied many months before. The primary factor in the long delay was the lack of military supplies, and it is a comment on the problems of the Army that arms were finally provided by the college itself. The equipment thus assured, the War Department telegraphed Dean Norton, as Acting President, on February 21, 1918, granting Pomona an Infantry Unit of the Senior Division of the R.O.T.C. *Student Life* carried the good news on March 5, in a headline across the entire front page, and set above a row of fifteen American flags. Major Vogdes was named Professor of Military Science and Tactics, and the Cadet Corps as a reward for its work became an official unit of the United States Army. The satisfaction and pride with which the college received the R.O.T.C. was indicated by Professor Brackett, who in a signed article in *Student Life,* said that with its coming "Pomona thus takes her place again among the leaders of the nation." The battalion celebrated its new status with a review to which all the college was invited. An editorial in *Student Life* urging the women students to attend the regular Friday ceremonies, observed that "fifty girls in the bleachers puts more ginger and enthusiasm into cadets than as many generals on the field."

The purpose of the R.O.T.C., then and later, was the training of young men to become military officers while they were taking regular civilian college courses. To this end Pomona, in its first contract with the Federal Government, obligated itself to establish a two-year course of military training for its physically qualified male students for whom completion of the two-year program was a requirement for graduation. After the compulsory two years, students so desiring could apply for the advanced program, and those then chosen as officer candidates would receive financial allowances for their subsistence. The R.O.T.C. was featured in the *Metate* of May 1918 of which the theme was military.

There was much college life, however, which was not military. The editors of the *Metate* in seeking to produce a yearbook "worthy of Pomona at war" asked their readers "to bear with them in this attempt to keep alive one of the oldest traditions of the college and yet not lose sight of our larger duty to our country." The glee clubs were active, and the Masquers presented *Othello.* The three debating societies for men and the two for women continued, and intercollegiate debates were held with both Occidental and U.S.C. The Southern California Oratorical Contest was held and was won by Redlands with Pomona taking second. In intercollegiate athletics, football, track, and baseball were played. The football team won the conference championship with an undefeated team, only three points being scored against it. Of the season Coach Nixon said, "I have never known another more satisfactory." A freshman football team was fielded, although its games were all intramural. The track team was strong, winning the dual meet from Occidental but losing to her in the championship meet. The three fraternities, Kappa Delta, Sigma Tau, and Phi Delta were active.

A number of visiting speakers came to Pomona in 1917-18. George Herbert Palmer, en route to Berkeley to give the Earl Lectures at the Pacific School of Religion, returned in February and spoke twice at chapel. Professor William M. Sloane of Columbia University and a former president of the American Historical Association, spent a month at Pomona in February and March 1918 as the Johnson Lecturer, speaking on "Democracy: Its History, Nature and Meaning." The war brought John Masefield, the English poet, Professor Charles Cestre of the University of Bordeaux, who was touring the United States speaking on behalf of France and who lectured in French, and Jane Addams, founder of Hull House in Chicago, who, as a representative of the Federal Food program, spoke on food conservation. Bliss Perry, Professor of Philosophy at Harvard and a Johnson Lecturer at Pomona, spoke at the Claremont Inn to the Phi Beta Kappa alumni of Southern California, who met on May 11, 1918 at the invitation of the Pomona chapter and organized the Phi Beta Kappa Alumni Association of Southern California.

However, neither the arrival of distinguished visitors nor the continuation of civilian instruction could diminish for a moment the essential adjustments of the college to a nation at war. The faculty was constantly occupied with the problems of the institution and of individual students. At the outbreak of the war, immediate steps were taken to facilitate the completion of work in progress for those entering the armed forces. Academic credit was given for the portion of the semester completed, and college credit was allowed for training successfully completed in military camp. As the enrollment of upper classmen decreased, the college abolished the numerical restriction on entering students, the faculty voting "to admit those who give promise of maintaining our standards, regardless of numbers."

Through the personal letters of faculty, general communications from the college, and *Student Life,* Pomona kept in close touch with its men in service. These remembrances were among the happiest recollections of many a Pomonan in camp or overseas. *Student Life* rendered invaluable service, regularly carrying news of men in the armed forces, also preparing special issues for them at Christmas 1917 and Easter 1918. The twelve pages of the Easter issue included a two-page center fold with twelve photographs of the college, including the buildings, the Gate, Alumni Field, the Greek Theater, and the mountains with the "P." Many letters from alumni to *Student Life* gave news of the war and showed how much the regular and special issues of the paper were appreciated. Of value to those who went overseas was the membership which Pomona took in the American University Union, formed in 1917 under the leadership of leading eastern universities. Located on the Rue de Richelieu in the heart of Paris, the Union had eighty rooms, dining halls, and other recreational facilities for the use of alumni and students of the member colleges. The faculty and friends of the college contributed Pomona's annual dues of one hundred dollars. The Union continued for over a decade after the war and, with offices in London, as well as Paris, assumed the role of assisting the large number of American students who came to study in Europe.

The academic year 1917-18 closed with the customary three-day commencement program for which President and Mrs. Blaisdell had just returned. Neither the exercises nor the annual meeting of the Board of Trustees gave evidence of the dramatic change the war would bring to the college in the autumn. The Cadet Corps and the R.O.T.C. had been composed of Pomona students already in college, and 1917-18 was therefore a year of rather easy transition to military life. The situation in 1918-19 would be very different indeed.

In the spring of 1918, the American army, increasingly involved in hostilities on the Western front, required more trained men to meet these heavy responsibilities. The army's need led Congress in August 1918 to amend the Selective Service Act by lowering the age of registration to eighteen and raising it to forty-five. While the government had done a remarkable job in building training camps throughout the country, the War Department could still make full

The faculty in 1918

Student Army Training Corps

use of the residence halls, classrooms, and athletic facilities which would lie idle when all able-bodied college men were called to the colors. Furthermore, such use by the government would assist higher education in its grave financial crisis. Thus was born the Student Army Training Corps.

As early as May 8, Secretary Baker had announced that in September 1918 a comprehensive plan to provide military instruction for college students would be put into effect in every institution of college grade which enrolled as many as a hundred able-bodied male students of age eighteen or over. The government planned to contract with colleges and universities throughout the country to receive 200,000 men for education and training in military tactics, one third of them for three months, one third for six months, and one third for nine months. "These are accepted enlisted men," President Blaisdell told the trustees on August 6, "under military discipline, and subject to governmental plans in their education and training. The college acts for the government in all respects in the care and training of these men in accordance with a temporary contract." The government paid a dollar a day for room and board, provided cots and bedding, and paid the regular tuition. The men were to be lodged together in large numbers and in barracks as soon as these could be constructed. The men themselves would receive a dollar a day. The trustees authorized such a contract with the government, "to incorporate into the college life a scheme for the military training of not to exceed 500 students." At a special meeting of the trustees on September 5, President Blaisdell reported that the government plan called for organizing the academic year on the quarter system. The Board renewed its authorization for a contract, indicating the number of students as "between three hundred and five hundred," using for the first time the official name of the new program, "Student Army Training Corps," and instructing the president and the special committee to adjust the tuition charge to a quarterly basis.

The college soon concluded the contract and prepared to receive two companies of student soldiers. Accommodations available were a dining room at the Claremont Inn, and the rooms of Smiley Hall, which served as quarters for one of the companies. The other company was placed temporarily in Renwick Gymnasium and the adjacent enclosed swimming pool which was covered over to give additional floor space. More permanent housing for this company was to be provided in a large wooden barracks building, upon which construction was begun immediately. With foresight the building was designed so that it could be used later as a gymnasium, the college defraying the extra expense for this purpose.

As the departure of older men and the lowering of the draft age made the R.O.T.C. inoperable at Pomona for the remainder of the war, the Army transferred Major Vogdes to the command of the S.A.T.C. He was assisted by three lieutenants, one of whom was Eugene Nixon who had sought and received a commission.

With the arrival of 246 men in the S.A.T.C., Pomona had a total enrollment of 649, the largest in her history. All but forty-five of the S.A.T.C. were enrolled in one of the college classes, 145 being freshmen. Total freshman and sophomore enrollments of 294 and 134, respectively, gave the college its youngest student body since the closing of the preparatory department.

The Pomona unit of the S.A.T.C., as it was soon known, was

formally instituted with a service in Bridges Hall on October 5. After a welcome by President Blaisdell, the corps and the audience repaired to the flagpole where everyone waited in silence until nine o'clock, when at the sound of the bugle the flag was raised aloft. At that moment, similar exercises were being held in every S.A.T.C. unit in the nation. To conclude, the presidents of the colleges read to the units a message from the War Department emphasizing the importance of the S.A.T.C. program.

Student Life greeted the S.A.T.C. as "the most important factor in our college life." With a touch of humor the paper described the changes in campus daily life: "Almost over night, Pomona has been transformed into a military institution. Everywhere we notice evidences of the changed spirit — the bugle call to meals, the crisp orders sounding through our streets at the break of dawn, the prescribed hours which even the 'queeners' must observe." Dartmouth Avenue, which then ran through the campus, was the dividing line between the S.A.T.C. and the mostly feminine civilian college. A separate instructional program was provided for the S.A.T.C. men who were marched to classes. Social life was minimal, and by a general order of the War Department fraternities were suspended in all colleges with S.A.T.C. units.

Soon there was no social life at all, for in mid-October the world-wide influenza epidemic reached Claremont. The S.A.T.C. was placed under partial quarantine, and Harwood Hall, the botany building west of Pearsons, was converted into an infirmary for the women. In academic subjects, the faculty held separate class sessions for men and women from October 28 to November 18. The epidemic was so serious in Southern California that the college gave only one day for Thanksgiving and students were advised not to leave Claremont. Chapel was not resumed until December 3, and on December 16 the faculty was so disturbed by continuance of the flu that a special meeting was called to review the situation. As late as January 16, 1919, "social and public gatherings" were prohibited in Claremont by the City Board of Health, and students desiring to leave town were required to secure permission from the college authorities.

Through the splendid services of Dr. A. V. Stoughton '95, Dr. J. A.

Latimer, the Claremont Health Officer, the two nurses at Harwood Hall, the ladies of the Claremont Red Cross, and the Pomona Valley Hospital, Pomona College came through the epidemic without the loss of a student life. Tragically, this was not true within the faculty and the city. The faculty was saddened by the death on January 7, 1919 of Viola Minor Westergaard, the young wife of Dr. Waldemar Westergaard. The forty-four year old Dr. Latimer, stricken with double pneumonia, died on January 24.

The triumph of the Allied Forces and the signing of the Armistice on November 11, 1918 produced an outpouring of national thanksgiving and patriotism never to be forgotten. With a one-word headline, "V I C T O R Y," flanked by American flags, *Student Life* said, "World-wide peace was established when the German representatives signed the armistice.... This news, made public by the State Department, reached the coast at an early hour yesterday." The cessation of hostilities led to a rapid demobilization of the S.A.T.C. The Pomona unit was ordered to begin the process on December 4 and to complete it by December 21. Members of the corps were offered opportunity to remain at Pomona as regular students, and the faculty made schedule adjustments to facilitate their transfer from military to academic subjects. In a farewell salute to the Corps, *Student Life* thoughtfully assessed Pomona's participation in this first nationwide experience of the Federal Government in higher education: "An entirely new curriculum was created, a commodious barracks building was erected and a miniature army developed literally under our very eyes. Perhaps one hundred men have gotten a taste of a college education which would have been denied them had it not been for the training corps."

The barracks building, the one physical evidence from the war to remain at Pomona, was never used by the Corps. It was not until December 7 that the building was completed and opened with a reception for the college community. However, its early conversion into a gymnasium brought a large return to the college,which up to that time lacked indoor basketball and volleyball courts. The completed building cost $16,000, of which the government paid $10,000, an individual donor gave $4,000 to help prepare the structure for eventual use as a gymnasium, and the college assumed the remainder, which President Blaisdell estimated at from three to five thousand dollars. The building, placed immediately south of Renwick, soon became known as the "Big Gym," and despite many developments and even a change of name, it remained in continuous service until this writing.

With the cessation of the war and the demobilization of the S.A.T.C. the faculty took swift action to restore the college to the semester basis. The period from December 2, 1918 to February 8, 1919 was considered the second half of the first semester, and a regular second semester was scheduled to begin on February 10. Faculty members were authorized to handle courses prior to February 8 on a quarter or semester basis, as seemed desirable.

Two hundred and ninety-three men from Pomona served in the Armed Forces of the United States during the war. Of these seventy-six were commissioned officers. Five men from the college gave their lives, three on the battlefields of Belgium and France, and two in military hospitals in California. In a building later erected to their memory, Pomona paid homage in these words to her first sons ever to die in war:

> In reverent memory of the brave sons of this college, once comrades in the games on this field who carried on the spirit of devotion which is here traditional and as soldiers of the World War were loyal even unto the supreme sacrifice laying down their lives for Country and for God.
>
> John Edgar Breckingsdale ex '12, August 22, 1917, Ypres, Belgium;
> Albert Howard Hankey '14, July 21, 1919, Letterman Hospital, San Francisco;
> Edmund Sheldon Gerry '17, August 16, 1918, Fismes, France;
> Walter Edgar Stafford '17, May 22, 1918, Mare Island, California;
> Samuel Benjamin Terry ex '18, July 22, 1918, Belleau Wood, France.

CHAPTER XII

Years Of Fulfillment

AFTER THE WAR, rapid and fundamental changes ensued in the United States. Over 3,500,000 young men had entered military service, and of these 2,000,000 had been transported to France. Never had so many young Americans seen so much of their own country or of the world. The larger view with which they returned to civilian life was shared by those on the home front who had done all they could to support them "over there."

The wider horizons of the American people brought increasing interest in colleges and universities and new demands upon them. In the decade from 1920 to 1930, the number of degrees granted annually in all American institutions grew from 53,516 to 139,752. Every institution faced new problems in meeting its enlarging responsibilities.

Pomona College made an early return to peacetime operation. "Welcome to the Pomona of Old" wrote the editor of *Student Life* on January 7, 1919. "Everywhere there is prevalent the feeling that our Alma Mater is really donning civilian clothes, literally and figuratively." Customary student organizations resumed operation, and the fraternities were permitted to pledge again.

One very significant aspect of the war years, however, was retained. Pomona elected to continue its contract with the United States government for a unit of the Reserve Officers Training Corps. Early in 1919 the colleges of Southern California held a conference on military training and forwarded resolutions to the War Department. In accordance with these resolutions, the Pomona faculty voted to resume R.O.T.C. instruction on January 13 and to require enrollment in the unit for all able-bodied freshman and sophomore men. Major Vogdes, who had been reappointed Professor of Military Science and Tactics after the termination of the S.A.T.C., resumed command of the Pomona R.O.T.C. unit.

President Blaisdell had given much thought to the future of Pomona, and in April 1919 he challenged the college with a published report, "The Making of the Adequate College." After reviewing the nine years of his administration, he declared,

> The time has now fully come when we should frankly wish to see that which has been accomplished set in relation to some comprehensive estimate of all that is involved in the whole serious business of the establishment of a modern college . . . After the most careful and deliberate consideration of the matter I cannot believe that in my own position I can satisfy the eagerness of the friends of Pomona by the presentation of any less strenuous vision. With a full consciousness of the burden involved and with the utmost reluctance for the task to be assumed, and yet aware also of the power there is in the call to do a thing splendidly, I am compelled to affirm my conviction that the task in which we have already set ourselves in Pomona College must require, without amplification of our numbers or educational range, and in order to place us abreast of that which is being and will soon be done by institutions of exactly the same range and ambitions as Pomona College, an addition of three million dollars to our resources in the near future.
>
> The whole question of the kind of a college Pomona should be was decided when it was founded. It is not necessary to men and women of Pomona's mold to have an extensive college or a diffuse college, but it is necessary that we have the best college.No other appeal will much count with those among whom Pomona seeks to do its work. I am convinced that in addressing our friends I am speaking to those who see in a college one of the greatest forms of human service, one of the finest investments which has yet been fashioned for the world's blessings. The citizenship of such a constituency will be satisfied with nothing less than the ambition that here in the West shall be developed a college which in its efficiencies and ideals shall be worthy of men and women who desire to crown the best of the past with a still better future.

Pomona had trustees, alumni, and friends who would respond to such a call. Led by President Blaisdell, they made the five years after the war a period of remarkable fulfillment.

There could be no delay if Pomona was to match her opportunity. Large numbers of students desired to attend; the problem was how to provide for them. In November 1919 the college had an enrollment of 685, the largest in its history. "We are greatly perplexed as to how to care for the large numbers coming to us," President Blaisdell wrote Marston on September 19, 1919. "Fearing that we should not have as large upper classes as usual, we took in an extra number of freshmen. Now it appears that the upper classes are over-full and it makes a serious congestion." Although the trustees established a limit of 700 students for September 1920, demand was such that by June they were forced to raise the limit to 750.

To make Pomona adequate for such an enrollment, President Blaisdell felt the college required $2,000,000 for endowment and the library, and $1,000,000 for new buildings and campus improvements. The trustees at their meeting on April 9, 1919 affirmed the needs set forth by the president and questioned "whether it may not be desirable to set a larger goal than three millions." As a plan of action, the trustees on June 24, 1919 determined to raise one million dollars immediately.

New Buildings and Campus Improvements

The inadequacy of campus facilities dictated that priority be given to the building program, and there was agreement that the first building should be a dormitory for women. Although the trustees and faculty had committed themselves in the Gates administration to the principle of college-owned residences for students, the only dormitories yet achieved were Smiley for men and Sumner for women. The latter, a wooden building threatened by fire, was a constant concern to the college authorities.

With such pressing need, the college had made important progress toward a new women's dormitory in the year before the United States entered the war. Jamieson and Spearl, the St. Louis architects, were engaged to prepare preliminary plans which were presented to the trustees at a meeting in Claremont on January 29, 1917. The trustees voted to locate the new building east of College Avenue on the south side of Third Street and authorized the acquisition of land from Third to First Streets. Although building plans were halted by the war, the acquisition of land proceeded and in 1919 the site and additional land had been secured.

The financing of these purchases was made possible by generous gifts from Miss Ellen Scripps, whose admiration for Dr. Blaisdell had grown with the development of the college. She became increasingly interested in the education of women at Pomona and she fully shared Dr. Blaisdell's conviction that ample land should be acquired for a spacious and attractive women's campus. Her gifts of $100,000 for this purpose enabled the college to acquire ultimately all the property between First and Third Streets eastward from College Avenue to Blanchard Park. Miss Scripps' farsighted generosity made possible the purchase of land in this area as late as the 1940's.

Despite the urgency, funds for the women's residence hall were difficult to secure. Judge C. E. Harwood, longtime trustee, provided the necessary momentum with a gift of $50,000, which was announced at the trustee meeting in which President Blaisdell presented his program for "the adequate college." As other large gifts were not forthcoming, the trustees voted that three-fourths of the cost, up to $200,000, could be defrayed by a loan from the college endowment fund. It was estimated that annual room rents of $125 a student would amortize the loan and bring a return of six per cent on the investment, thereby preserving the endowment and the continuity of endowment income. With this assurance, the buildings and grounds committee of the Board proceeded, and Jamieson and Spearl developed plans for a three-unit building, a central portion with reception and social rooms on the first floor, a west wing, and an east wing, with a total capacity of 180 students. Dean Berry was sent to make a study of a number of "recent and well reported dormitories," and many of her suggestions were incorporated by the architects. Financial problems, however, were a continual concern for the trustees. On December 11, 1919 the Executive Committee recommended that only "the central and western units of the dormitory be built now," and until the summer of 1920 this appeared to be the final decision. However, as the result of a gift by Schuyler W. Strong, the trustees were able to proceed with the east unit and to complete the building as originally planned.

Schuyler Strong, a businessman who had recently retired to

California, became interested in the college, and as he learned of the plans for the women's dormitory, saw an opportunity for an appropriate memorial to his late wife. For this purpose Mr. Strong in June 1920 gave the college $140,000 subject to an annuity during his lifetime. His gift consisted of securities realizable in cash, so the trustees could go forward with construction at once. Rooms for a hundred students were ready in September 1920, and the entire building was in use in February 1921.

The completed buildings were named Harwood Court, in memory of Catherine Henry Harwood and in gratitude for her husband's gift and his work and generosity as a trustee over many years, and the east wing was named Strong Hall. The Harwoods' daughter, Aurelia, contributed to the furnishings of the hall.

Harwood Court with its attractive and beautifully landscaped courtyard brought a new standard in student living at Pomona. It also represented a new development in the architecture of the college buildings. Previously these were essentially like college buildings in the East or Middle West, and little attempt had been made to take advantage of the mild and open climate of Southern California. The new dormitory and its courtyard brought rooms and garden together in the way that would become characteristic of California living. The attractiveness of Harwood Court was further enhanced by its architectural relation to Bridges Hall and its outlook across Third Street into the beautiful Bridges courtyard.

At long last the college had a women's dormitory of which it could be proud. The students hailed it in the *Metate* of June 1923 as "probably the most artistic and beautifully appointed women's dormitory in the country." It became at once the center of women's social life at Pomona.

The dedication of Harwood Court was part of impressive exercises that on February 22, 1921 celebrated the tenth anniversary of Dr. Blaisdell's inauguration as president of Pomona. The decennial ceremony was held in the morning in the Greek Theater, with Trustee Edwin F. Hahn '98 presiding. Tributes to Dr. Blaisdell were paid by Dr. David P. Barrows '94 and Mr. Marston, who observed, "He grasped the college, he grasped the trustees and for ten years

Harwood Court, view from Second Street

Memorial Training Quarters

Mason Hall

since that time Pomona has had a president that was well fitted for the place." At the dedication of Harwood Court in the afternoon, Charles Burt Sumner spoke in appreciation of Judge and Mrs. Harwood.

The day was also marked by the beginning of a major building for physical education for men. Prior to the dedication of the dormitory, ground was broken east of Smiley for the training quarters designed to be Pomona's tribute to her sons lost in the war. Funds for the building were raised by the alumni and students, greatly assisted by a gift from the parents of Sheldon Gerry '17. It had been hoped to secure sufficient funds to build both the training quarters and a modern reenforced concrete gymnasium, but the fund of $52,000 subscribed was sufficient only for the former. The Memorial Training Quarters marked, however, the culmination of a notable improvement in the college's physical education facilities. The conversion of the S.A.T.C. barracks into the "Big Gym" had been completed and the building formally opened on March 14, 1919. Renwick Gymnasium, renovated and improved, then became the center for the women's department of physical education.

In this same period, developments of the greatest importance were taking place in science. For several years, trustee William S. Mason had been making plans for new facilities for chemistry. He first thought in terms of an extension of Pearsons Hall, but by the beginning of the war he had come to favor a new and separate chemistry building. Unfortunately, the amount required by 1920 was twice that projected before the war, and President Blaisdell, reviewing the situation with Mr. Mason, asked if he could provide the additional funds. "This is one of the critical moments in the development of the college," Blaisdell wrote.

Mr. Mason was a trustee of great perception and his response indicated how well he understood the value of "befriending the college at vital points and in significant ways." On September 22, 1921 he sent his note for $100,000 beyond the $200,000 he had already given. He stipulated that $200,000 be used for the chemistry building and its equipment and that $50,000 be set up as an endowment for the building. The remaining $50,000 he designated as an endowment for upkeep of the grounds to which he had already contributed so much.

Mr. Mason's munificence opened a new era for science at Pomona. Associate Professor Edward P. Bartlett, who had been on leave for war research with the Chemical Corps of the Army, was soon sent to study the best and newest chemistry buildings in the country. His recommendations led to the construction of one of the finest college science buildings in the United States. The two stories and basement of Mason Hall of Chemistry, with its eighty rooms and an acre of laboratory space, must have seemed a paradise to the students and faculty who previously had known only the chemical laboratories in the basement of Pearsons Hall. The completed building certainly made possible Bartlett's desire that Pomona be "one of the strongholds of chemistry in the Southwest."

Mason Hall of Chemistry was not only an outstanding science building but was also an ornament to the campus and to the city. The massive reenforced concrete structure with its tile roof and tower occupied the full block from Fifth to Sixth Streets on the east side of Harvard Avenue. By extending the college buildings westward Mason defined a rapidly developing science quadrangle.

The north side of the science quadrangle took form surprisingly soon. On October 19, 1921 President Blaisdell wrote Mr. Mason that "a friend of the College has advised me that he will give a building for zoology. This building would front on Sixth Street immediately back of your building. It is his desire to proceed as soon as possible. It would obviously be economical if we could build the two buildings at once as all the cement for both buildings could be poured from one tower."

The friend of the college was David Carnes Crookshank, a local contractor and an important citrus grower. His firm had done such work for Pomona as the renovation of Holmes and the construction of Harwood Court. His extensive citrus acreage in the La Verne Association brought him membership on the board of directors of the California Fruit Growers Exchange. To finance the zoology building Crookshank gave the college common stock and bonds of the Keystone Iron and Steel Works in Los Angeles, valued

Crookshank Hall

Reconstructed and relocated Sumner Hall

at $100,000. Although funds from the gift were not as easily realizable as from the gift of Schuyler Strong, the trustees worked out a financing plan by which funds could be made available for the building while Mason was under construction. On April 25, 1921 the Board authorized a contract to the extent of $100,000 for the zoology building. Events ran ahead of the news, and one day President Blaisdell dramatically announced in chapel that arrangements for the zoology building were complete, that the equipment for construction was in place and that the digging of the foundation would begin in fifteen minutes. "The assembly was excused," reported Charles Burt Sumner, "marched to the ground and at the President's word the steam shovel started the work."

Crookshank Hall of Zoology when completed was a first-rate science laboratory with space for two hundred students working at one time. Its facilities had been planned by Dr. Hilton assisted by Dr. Munz. Zoology would share its space with botany, and Crookshank would become the home of the growing herbarium. As a reenforced concrete building of two stories and a basement, Crookshank with its red tile roof was an attractive, as well as valuable, addition to the campus. With Mason and Crookshank and subsequent changes in Pearsons for physics and mathematics, Pomona developed the science facilities that would serve the college for the next generation.

As new buildings were developed throughout the campus the college began to achieve much of the master plan designed by Myron Hunt in the Gates administration. Essential in that plan was a central campus around which the buildings would be developed. The provision of this central campus was very dear to the heart of Mr. Marston, and in the summer of 1919 he told Dr. Blaisdell that he planned to give $100,000 for the formation and endowment of a central quadrangle. "All through the summer," wrote Dr. Blaisdell to Mr. Marston on September 19, 1919, "I went in the inspiration and joy of the wonderfully generous promise that you gave me regarding the future. Mr. Mason was wonderfully delighted."

Some work on the quadrangle began in the autumn of 1919, and it was with this that Ralph Cornell '14 began the fifty-three years of landscape planning he was to bring to his alma mater. A distinguished student under Professor Charles F. Baker at Pomona, Cornell was an early graduate of the Harvard School of Landscape Architecture. When he returned to Los Angeles in 1919 after discharge from military service, he was the first professional landscape architect to locate in the city, and his first client was Pomona College which engaged him as its supervising landscape architect.

While some preliminary work could be done in 1919, Cornell, Marston, and the college were unable to proceed with the central campus until a decision was made regarding the future of Sumner Hall. The location of this building opposite the Carnegie Library on College Avenue thwarted the realization of the spacious central campus envisaged by Hunt and desired by the trustees. Cherished memories of alumni and faculty made the destruction of Sumner unthinkable. It seemed equally impossible to leave it at its original location. The trustees ultimately resolved the issue constructively by voting on February 21, 1921 to preserve the building and move it to another place on the campus. The area chosen was east of Bridges Hall, where a court could enhance both buildings. The renovation of Holmes in 1916 offered a pattern that was essentially followed. Again a wooden building was turned into an attractive stucco structure with a tile roof.

In 1922 Sumner Hall returned to a central position in the college and in campus life. After sojourns in Pearsons and in Carnegie the president's office was back where it had begun, in the very suite where President Baldwin and his family first lived. Also returning was the dean, now joined by the registrar and other officers of the growing college administration. The offices and classrooms of several academic departments were also included in the building which for more than thirty years would be used for both administration and instruction. From their associations in historic Sumner, succeeding generations of students and faculty have sensed the faith of Pomona's beginnings and the quality of her accomplishments.

As the building program neared its end, the college scheduled a dedication day for the four new structures: the Memorial Training Quarters, Mason Hall of Chemistry, Crookshank Hall of Zoology, and reconstructed Sumner — the first two already in use, the latter two still under construction. On March 24, 1923 guests from the other academic institutions joined in the day of celebration. The plaques in the respective buildings paid tribute to Mrs. Sumner, rendered homage to Pomona's sons lost in the war, and signaled the new opportunities for instruction in science. President Blaisdell expressed the sense of fulfillment which the four buildings brought: "We move in a steady way, but there come certain days when apparently we climb to the peaks and look off into new highlands which are yet to be won."

The pride and confidence of the early 1920's were illustrated in the Ceremony of the Flame. From his associations with Marston, Sumner, Norton and Brackett, Dr. Blaisdell had come to venerate the founders of Pomona. To honor them he instituted the annual celebration of Founders Day on October 14, and a worldwide celebration of Founders Day was held on October 14, 1921. On this occasion "The Ceremony of the Flame" was initiated "as an annual rite to be perpetuated throughout the years. It was inaugurated in commemoration of the Founders of this institution and in symbolism of the spreading spirit of service which is increasingly being carried to the far reaches of the earth by the loyal sons and daughters of Pomona." The moving text written by Professor Robert C. Denison, the passing of the flame from candle to candle in a darkened hall, and the singing of *Torchbearers* and *Hail! Pomona, Hail!* constituted a unique ceremony which would be cherished by succeeding generations of students, faculty, and alumni.

Reorganization of the College Administration

To assist in the winning of "new highlands," the college was in the process of making administrative changes and staff additions that would be completed by September 1923. Before the war Pomona had only two major academic administrators, the president and the dean of the faculty; and the latter also carried heavy teaching responsibilities. Two members of the faculty gave some time to administrative matters. Professor Frampton served as acting registrar for a number of years while also teaching a full load in the English department. Milton E. Churchill, who taught both Greek and German, edited *The Pomona College Magazine* and served as secretary of the faculty.

President Blaisdell first moved to strengthen student services, and William Evan Nicholl was appointed dean of the college and assistant professor of education, effective September 1919. He had come to the attention of Pomona through his work as dean of the Y.M.C.A. Overseas Training School held on the Stanford campus during the war. A Canadian by birth, Nicholl had received his collegiate and professional education in Nebraska where he graduated from Bellevue College in 1904 and the Omaha Theological Seminary in 1907. He had then studied education and psychology for a year at the University of Edinburgh. After the war he completed an M.A. at Teachers College, Columbia University. To Pomona he brought experience as a faculty member at Hastings College, and as professor of education and acting president of Bellevue College. Nicholl was admirably suited to the new position at Pomona and he served until 1948, winning the affection of generations of students.

The growth of the college required more attention to the keeping of student records and the handling of admissions. For these responsibilities Charles Tabor Fitts, assistant professor of English since September 1919, was appointed registrar in 1921. As registrar he worked with the faculty committee on admissions and also handled the reception of new students each autumn. A graduate of Amherst College, Mr. Fitts had spent most of his career in the Hawaiian Islands where he was a teacher of English and principal of Punahou school.

In addition to finding appointees for new positions, the college faced the necessity of replacing the older faculty members who had established Pomona's academic excellence. On January 1, 1921 Dean Norton offered his resignation as professor of Greek and dean of the faculty, effective after June 1921 when he would be sixty-five and would complete thirty-three years at Pomona. The retirement of Dean Norton was a matter of deep concern to President Blaisdell. Norton's experience was so great and his understanding with

Blaisdell so complete that the president could leave him in charge of the college whenever his own duties required absence from the campus. As Blaisdell analyzed Pomona's future he felt the need for a dean whose duties would be primarily administrative and who could also assist the president in his public responsibilities.

Although the appointment was not made until two years after the date at which Dean Norton had asked to retire, President Blaisdell and the faculty made early and valiant attempts to fill the position. Their first choice was Dr. Charles K. Edmunds, president of Canton Christian College in China, who was then in New York working for its trustees and raising funds. Dr. Blaisdell had seen Dr. Edmunds in Southern California in the autumn of 1920 and had discussed with him a possible affiliation with Pomona. In a long letter to Edmunds on June 11, 1921 Blaisdell described the larger role envisaged for the office.

> This new Dean will have very large responsibility in the inner life of the college. The selection of the faculty must very largely fall to him and also the adjustment of the personnel in connection with the needs of the various departments. It would be his work also to gather up the educational facilities of the institution into the most effective forms and to forecast the educational lines of the future. There would also fall to the Dean a large measure of responsibility in presiding at college functions and in administering the daily chapel service. Ample opportunity would be given to impress himself upon the life of the student body. On the other hand, the opportunity would not be simply within the college by any means. The Dean should be an important figure in the life of Southern California — the larger the range, the better.

When Dr. Edmunds concluded that his obligations to Canton Christian College precluded his acceptance of the deanship at Pomona, President Blaisdell turned to Ernest J. Jaqua, dean of men and professor of education at Colorado College, whose career he had followed for some years. After graduating from Grinnell College in 1907 Jaqua had studied at Columbia University and Union Seminary where he had received an M.A. degree in 1910 and a B.D. in 1912. He had returned to Grinnell as assistant to the president when Blaisdell in 1916 offered him a position at Pomona as dean of students and professor of Biblical literature. Jaqua declined, feeling that he should take further graduate work. He pursued his plan and received the Ph.D. degree in education from Harvard in 1919. Dr.

Jaqua then accepted a position with the Rockefeller Foundation in New York, but a nervous breakdown prevented him from assuming it and forced him to take a long period of recuperation which he spent on a farm in Minnesota. From there he wrote Blaisdell on January 28, 1922 that he was "again feeling keen to get back to real work" and asked if "the position for which you once considered me was still open." Blaisdell replied that the deanship of students had been filled but mentioned the possibility of "business comptroller" or "some form of executive work."

Jaqua's interest in Pomona was heightened by the reports of its progress he received from Professor Ralph H. Lyman, whom he had known at Grinnell. "Lyman writes of the buildings that are being erected at Pomona, and of the splendid future he sees for the college," Jaqua reported to Blaisdell on February 20, 1922. "You are really laying the foundations of a great university if you wish to have the college grow in that direction. Pomona is most fortunately located and is developing a unique history and spirit." To which Blaisdell responded, "I cannot but believe that Pomona, in some sense, has a national future and presents, therefore, peculiarly interesting educational prospects." In the summer of 1922 Pomona offered Jaqua a position as dean of the faculty and professor of education, but Jaqua had recently accepted the position at Colorado College from which he could not secure a release.

President Blaisdell marked time with the deanship, and in January 1923 he raised the question again with Dr. Jaqua. After a meeting in Denver and some negotiation, Blaisdell renewed the offer as dean of the faculty and professor of education, on February 21, 1923 saying, "I feel we should know at once what we can rely on next fall. The position is of such consequence to our whole program for the coming year that I cannot have it longer in risk." In accepting a week later, Jaqua wrote, "I shall come with the earnest hope that I may make a real contribution to the splendid spirit of Pomona."

When the long search was over and Norton was finally released from the deanship, he paid a tribute to Blaisdell which is eloquent testimony of the president's leadership of the faculty. "That you would have brought things of great value to pass anyone who knew you might in advance have taken for granted," he wrote the president from Wisconsin in July 1923. "But that you could have entered with such tact and sympathy into the lives of those with whom you were set to work by no choice of your own and whose ways and thoughts could not always meet your approval, this might well have been thought beyond expectation. But it is this that has made these years rich beyond belief and again and again I have been made most grateful and most humble by your repeated kindnesses . . . I do not know how any mortal could have been more generous in thought and deed."

While the academic administration was being strengthened, the college effected an important reorganization of the business office. Earlier all the business matters of the college had been handled by the treasurer. In 1922 these manifold responsibilities were ably directed by Ernest E. Jones '09, who on graduation had entered the service of his alma mater. But the growth of the college's invested funds and the great increase of the annual budget demanded some specialization and a larger business office staff. On the recommendation of the president, the trustees amended the by-laws, on June 20, 1922, to provide for two officers, a treasurer and a controller. Mr. Jones was named treasurer, "confining his efforts largely to the care of the investments of the college," but continuing "the management of the Inn and supervision of the dairy," two college enterprises in which he had demonstrated rare and essential competence.

As the controller was to work closely and continuously with the president, it was essential to have a man with a deep understanding of the college and a high devotion to its purposes. President Blaisdell turned to Dr. George S. Sumner '94, professor of economics and for some years a key man in the faculty. For Professor Sumner, who had had no thought of leaving his teaching and the study of economics, the decision was difficult. He was devoted to his profession but he had an even greater loyalty to Pomona College. He had witnessed its founding and with his father, C. B. Sumner, had experienced its vicissitudes and its triumphs. Dr. Sumner was also keenly aware of President Blaisdell's pressing need of business assistance in meeting the demands of the expanded campus, the increased enrollment, and the larger faculty. Furthermore, relations with the great philanthropic foundations and individual donors required the services and advice of a broadly trained financial officer. Therefore, reluctantly yet wholeheartedly, "Professor" Sumner became "Controller" Sumner on February 2, 1923.

A further administrative change in 1922 was the naming of Robert J. Bernard '17 as executive secretary of the college. As a student Bernard had won President Blaisdell's admiration, and upon graduation he had been appointed assistant to the president. He grew rapidly in the position and the president called on him for numerous duties. When the Artist Course was organized it was placed under his direction. Bernard constantly broadened his associations and became an invaluable aid in fund raising.

While the reorganization of the academic and business administrations was under way, President Blaisdell faced a serious personal dilemma. Beloit College was again seeking a president and in the winter of 1923 his alma mater turned once more to Dr. Blaisdell. Although the offer was little discussed by the trustees or the faculty, letters from Mr. Mudd and Mr. Marston to the president show that he gave the offer serious consideration. The Three Million Dollar campaign had not advanced as Dr. Blaisdell had hoped and the Board as a whole had not taken the leadership the president expected. To his close friends, Mudd and Marston, he expressed concern and disappointment. Mr. Mudd sought to reassure him, writing in November 1922, "You have my greatest respect and confidence. I am ready to carry a part of the deficit if a deficit continues for some years, and my resources continue as good as at present."

Marston took steps to retain Blaisdell for Pomona. To the president, then in Chicago, Marston telegraphed on January 25, 1923: "Both Clark and Mudd share my feeling that we should do everything possible to sustain the college and to retain you as president. Further consideration confirms my conviction that trustees are good for half a million. I beg you not to make a commitment during this absence."

The appeal of Beloit was very real. But in the final analysis, Blaisdell could not leave Pomona and the great cause to which he had committed himself. He heeded Marston, who in joy wrote him on February 17, 1923, "The last meeting of the trustees (February 12) was most important and it was marked by two outstanding points — the hearty support of the 1923 campaign and your announcement of remaining with Pomona.... The majority of the trustees have not realized that you were giving serious consideration to the Beloit call.... You have given up, I doubt not, some cherished hopes and personal desires. And you have done it for the sake of Pomona College, for its students and teachers and friends. We owe you an immeasurable debt of thankfulness and our appreciation of your devotion will grow as time goes on."

The president's rededication to Pomona called for the full energies of the Board, and the Three Million Dollar Campaign began to move forward. The major attainments since the announcement of the campaign in May 1919 had been in new buildings and campus development. In 1923 the two million dollars projected for endowment and the library were largely still to be raised. Marston told the trustees that the time had come when the college must begin an active campaign, and he and Mudd rallied their colleagues for the effort.

The first objective was the securing of a matching grant from the General Education Board then engaged in a wide program of support for higher education. President Blaisdell and Controller Sumner called on the officers of the General Education Board in New York and received a cordial reception. The visit opened negotiations which led in March 1924 to an offer from the General Education Board of $400,000 for endowment, on condition that Pomona raise $800,000 for the same purpose. When the Pomona trustees accepted the proposal on March 28, the way was opened for a vigorous effort. But despite the leadership of Mudd in Los Angeles and the personal generosity of the trustees, it was not until June 16, 1925 that President Blaisdell could announce that the $3,000,000 goal had been reached.

Whatever doubts or problems the trustees and administration may have had, the students never questioned the outcome of the campaign. "For a generation," wrote the editor of the *Metate* of 1923, "men have dreamed of a greater Pomona. That dream is about to become a reality. Fortunate are we who stand on the threshold."

Commencement in the Greek Theater, 1922. President Blaisdell confers the honorary degree of Doctor of Laws on Fong Foo Sec, distinguished leader of the Y. M. C. A. in China and English editor of the Commercial Press, Shanghai. Dr. Fong Foo Sec was a student in the Preparatory Department and Pomona College from 1896 to 1902.

CHAPTER XIII

The College in the Mid-Twenties

WITH ITS new buildings, larger enrollment, and expanding faculty, Pomona entered a period of academic advancement and vigorous student life. National prosperity and unprecedented regional development seemed to assure a most promising and exciting future for the college. Under the direction of dedicated scholarly teachers the instructional program was strengthened and extended.

There was particular excitement in the new science quadrangle. Professor James A. Lyman, who had spent fourteen years on the ground floor of Pearsons, must have moved in wonder each day as he and his students worked in the splendid and spacious chemical laboratories of Mason Hall. He established a foundation for the chemistry department which would make it outstanding among American colleges. After his sudden death in 1926, his younger colleagues and his successor, Professor Charles J. Robinson, went forward in this tradition.

Mason Hall was larger than the chemistry department required, and on its ground floor the newly established department of geology found a spacious and congenial home. There its head, Alfred O. Woodford '13, made for himself and the collge one of the most remarkable records of American science. His father, Pomona trustee Butler A. Woodford, was a citrus grower, and not surprisingly young Woodford's earliest scientific interests were in agricultural chemistry and the soil sciences. He majored in chemistry at Pomona and began his graduate work at Berkeley in this field. In 1915 he received an appointment in chemistry at Pomona and, except for absences for graduate study, remained a member of that department for seven years. In 1919 he was given permission to introduce a course in geology, and its great success led him to transfer to geology as he continued his graduate work at the University of California. Upon Woodford's completion of his doctorate in 1922, Pomona established a separate department of geology under his direction.

Woodford knew how to take advantage of the abundant opportunities which Southern California offered for geological study and research. His enthusiasm and insight awakened the interest of his students. On countless field trips and in research projects students developed with their teacher friendships that were to remain lifelong. The work of the department was advanced by the remarkable library Woodford developed. His early schooling in the classics and his study of Latin and Greek at Pomona gave him a literary and historical approach to science. Often using his own funds, he built a large and valuable collection of books in geology, and established a departmental library in Mason Hall. This library grew constantly under Woodford's care and it soon became a resource for all Southern California geologists.

Although Woodford was the only member of the geology department for most of his career he made Pomona an outstanding center for the education of geologists. His students made major contributions in teaching, research, and the petroleum industry. To date four of his students have received honorary degrees from Pomona. One of these, Charles A. Anderson '24, was head of the United States Geological Survey.

In botany as in geology Pomona learned what one man could accomplish. Philip A. Munz had come to the faculty in 1917 and was well established at Pomona when the construction of Crookshank Hall gave him for the first time adequate laboratories and facilities for his work. He was an indefatigable collector, and building on the work of Baker he developed at Pomona an herbarium of national importance. Munz also built a remarkable departmental library which, like the geology collection, was often consulted by other western scholars.

Munz was gifted both in research and teaching. Centering his scholarly research and writing on the study of western plants, he brought to his work a contagious enthusiasm which won and held his students. A significant number, influenced by his general course and work both in the laboratory and in the field, proceeded to graduate schools and to careers in the field of botany. Foundations laid by Munz would make the college and Claremont one of the most highly respected botanical centers in the United States.

Zoology, like chemistry, entered a new era when it moved from Pearsons to the first-rate laboratories, classrooms, and offices of Crookshank. There Professor William A. Hilton, already a mainstay of the Pomona faculty, developed zoology into one of the most important departments of the college. Indefatigable and enthusiastic, he was extraordinarily appealing to students. The variety of his interests and his publications made him an exceptionally effective teacher. He combined his research with extensive travel and in his long life would explore some of the most remote parts of the world, even the upper reaches of the Amazon.

Hilton was another of those pioneering scientists who did an amazing amount of work. In addition to the normal responsibilities of the department, he continued the *Journal of Entomology,* and its worldwide distribution, in exchange for other scientific journals, brought much recogition to the college. Ever ready with a story, or causing one by his own exploits, he brought a joyous, buoyant quality to this work. He was a valuable counsellor, and his wise and understanding advice led many of his students to graduate work in zoology or to medical school. No one did more to develop Pomona College as a center for the preparation of physicians.

With the moving of chemistry and zoology, all of Pearsons Hall became available for physics and mathematics. In September 1925 Roland R. Tileston succeeded Professor Hitchcock, then nearing retirement, as head of the department. Tileston was a graduate of Dartmouth College where he also took an M.A. and taught while a graduate student. Work in engineering brought him to the West in 1910 and after three years he accepted a position as professor of physics at Colorado College. There he developed a program for physics majors which led a large number of students to go to graduate schools. His appointment at Pomona came at a time when the teaching of physics was entering a new period in the

United States, and Tileston was admirably equipped to lead the department. Tileston was so in love with physics that students caught his fire. He was not a research scientist and he never took a Ph.D., but when the American Physics Society awarded him its Oersted medal for outstanding teaching in 1943, he had sent more students to graduate school than any physicist then teaching in the United States.

The qualities which most distinguished Tileston were his understanding of the respective groups a physics department should serve, and his skill in meeting the needs of each group. He discussed the responsibilities of the department to the general student, the science student, and the physics major in an excellent article in the *Pomona College Quarterly Magazine* for October 1925. The general student should receive "working knowledge of the facts and theories, which shall make him acquainted with the interesting modern developments in the material world." Students in physical chemistry, in biology, music and allied fields "require a grounding in the fundamentals of physical laws and theories." Finally, the department should have the faculty and apparatus "to train thoroughly and with vigor such students as may early choose to devote their lives to research in physics."

Colonel Mudd took the lead in providing funds to implement Tileston's plans for the department. He was joined by William L. Honnold and together the two men financed new physics equipment, costing approximately $13,000, which was placed in use in the autumn of 1925. Tileston looked forward to an expansion that would include a new building. "Southern California," he wrote, "offers exceptional opportunities for a strong undergraduate department in physics. Pomona with its established reputation for high scholarship and for solid character is the logical place for such a department." Tileston attained his objective, and he did it in Pearsons Hall, which remained the home of the physics department throughout his years at Pomona.

In the English department veteran professors Spalding and Frampton were joined by Bruce McCulley in 1921 and Elliott C. Lincoln in 1924. Both remained until their retirement, bringing new courses and new viewpoints while also contributing to the remarkable continuity of the department. McCulley, who came as a professor of English, was a graduate of Hiram College in Ohio, with a Ph.D. from Harvard; for the previous ten years he had been on the faculty of Washington State College. There he had been a colleague of Lincoln, a graduate of Colby College, with an M.A. from Harvard, who came to Pomona as an associate professor.

The faculty in ancient and modern languages had undergone little change. While Dean Norton continued to teach Greek until 1926, the direction of the classics program was under Homer E. Robbins, Ph.D., University of Michigan, who had come to Pomona in 1915 as professor of classical history and languages. Maro B. Jones, a graduate of Boston University who had studied in several European countries, had been professor of Romanic languages since 1911. His research and publications brought wide attention to the college. A most significant development in the modern language program was the appointment in 1925 of Margaret Husson as instructor in Spanish. A young graduate of the University of Kansas with an M.A. from Columbia University, she brought to her teaching an infectious enthusiasm which soon gave Spanish a larger place in the Pomona curriculum.

In art the founding period of the department was drawing to a close. Hannah Tempest Jenkins would retire in 1927 after twenty-two years of teaching art and design. Since 1924 she had been assisted by José Pijoan, a Spanish scholar trained at the University of Barcelona and at the Spanish School in Rome, who had come to North America in 1914 as a lecturer at the University of Toronto. In 1922 he was appointed to an assistant professorship at the University of Southern California, whence he came to Pomona. He was a striking personality who would play a lively role in his years at the college. Upon Mrs. Jenkins' retirement, the direction of the department passed to Thomas M. Beggs,who joined the faculty in 1926. After receiving the B.F.A. degree from Yale, Beggs had studied at the Fontainebleau School of Fine Arts in France. When appointed at Pomona, he was working as a muralist in Florida.

The music department, well established in Bridges Hall under the experienced leadership of Professor Ralph Lyman, had never been so strong. Courses were offered in history, appreciation, harmony, and composition. Individual lessons were available in voice, piano, and violin. While there was training for teaching public school music, the department sought primarily "to permeate the consciousness of all the students and the entire community."

The musical organizations played a major role in the life of the college. Lyman had organized the college choir which in 1924-25 included 137 voices. This was a great period for the glee clubs, the Men's Club conducted by Lyman, and the Women's Club by Arthur Babcock. Pomona enjoyed great success in the annual glee club contest with Southern California colleges, and these competitions, together with the annual tours of the glee clubs, brought wide recognition to the college as a center for the study and performance of music.

The work of the department and the musical traditions of Pomona were to be greatly enhanced in September 1923, when Everett S. Olive, pianist and composer, was appointed associate professor. He was a graduate of Simpson College in Iowa, with further study in Berlin and experience in private and college teaching. Throughout his career at Pomona Olive was closely associated with Lyman in the work of the glee clubs. Writing both words and music and making all the choral arrangements, Olive gave the college four songs: *Primavera* and *The Picture* for the Women's Club and *Chivalry* and *Loyalty* for the Men's Club, which beautifully portray the spirit of the 1920's and live as a cherished part of the Pomona repertoire. Olive's memories of the Mediterranean, evoked by the climate of California and the style of Pomona's buildings, particularly Bridges Hall, inspired the imagery of *Primavera* and *The Picture.* In these words from *The Picture* he expressed the love which he had come to feel for the new college in the West:

> Oh, I see, through the green of the campus,
> Spanish walls and alluring red tiles;
> Stately cypress adorning the angles;
> Blooming hedges whose fragrance beguiles,
> And in the near distance the lofty insistence
> With which San Antonio smiles.

In philosophy, the appointment of Professor Robert C. Denison in 1920 brought to Pomona a teacher whose influence was felt throughout the college. A graduate of Amherst and of Andover Seminary, he was minister of the United Church on the Green at New Haven, Connecticut, when Dr. Blaisdell persuaded him to come to Pomona. By his distinguished teaching and the nobility of his character Denison gave leadership to both students and faculty in the social changes of the 1920's.

Immediately after the war, the trustee requirement for Sunday church attendance came under sharp attack from the students. The issue engaged the cabinet throughout the spring of 1919, and a committee of Brackett, Norton, and Neely conferred with a committee of the trustees; but these discussions were inconclusive and two years went by before a decision was taken. President Blaisdell wished to retain the requirement until the college could establish a department of religious education with an outstanding leader. In the spring of 1921 he was able to get his plan under way; the trustees authorized the new department and Raymond C. Brooks, pastor of the First Congregational Church in Berkeley and a trustee of the college, was appointed professor of religious education.

In the autumn the trustees referred the question of church attendance to the cabinet, with power to act, and that body voted on October 27, 1921 "that the present rule regarding required church attendance be changed, and that church attendance be placed on a voluntary basis." With this action the cabinet requested the committee on college life "to take into earnest consideration things which might interfere with church attendance and the spirit thereof, and to endeavor to devise ways and means of keeping the value of Sunday." The following day President Blaisdell reported the action to the student body.

Dr. Brooks brought wide and exceptionally congenial experience to his important duties at Pomona. After graduating from Tabor College, Iowa, and receiving the Bachelor of Divinity degree from Yale, he had held pastorates in three college towns: Oakland, California, where he was also minister for Mills College; Walla Walla, Washington, the home of Whitman College; and Berkeley, where the First Congregational Church played an important part in student and faculty life at the University of California. At

Pomona Dr. Brooks fulfilled admirably the important roles of teacher, counsellor, and faculty member to which he had been called. His widely elected courses and frequent chapel talks had great influence throughout the college.

While developing the department of religious education, President Blaisdell gave thought to more adequate provision for instruction in public speaking, and when funds made it possible he recommended the addition of a faculty member in this area. Effective September 1923, Benjamin D. Scott, then professor of philosophy at Nebraska Wesleyan University, was appointed professor of public address at Pomona. A graduate of the University of Southern California where he had won the Southern California oratorical contest, Scott had taken a Bachelor of Sacred Theology degree and a Ph.D. in philosophy at Boston University. Before coming to Pomona he had taught philosophy at Simpson College and Nebraska Wesleyan. Dr. Scott brought to Pomona deep devotion to students, a generous spirit, and amazing energy. Through his instructional work and training for oratorical contests and intercollegiate debates he taught a significant portion of the student body. As a leader in chapel and a generous participant in college life he was a great favorite of the students.

Faculty members who would serve for many years were appointed in the social sciences and the humanities. William B. Kirk, B.A., Ph.D., Johns Hopkins University, who came as professor of social economics in 1922, would develop a department of sociology. Earlier the only instruction in sociology had been an introductory course which Dr. George S. Sumner gave in addition to his work in economics.

Waldemar Westergaard was succeeded by Dr. Frank W. Pitman, who had been at Pomona in 1924-25 as acting professor of history. Dr. Pitman held baccalaureate and doctoral degrees from Yale, where he had taught in the history department since 1910. A New Englander by birth as well as education he brought to Pomona standards of high scholarship and academic excellence. Through his own work and the younger men he selected he determined the course of the history department for the next fifty years.

Two new men brought strength to the teaching of political

science and leadership in the governing of the college. George S. Burgess, who was a graduate of the University of Michigan and of its Law School, joined the Pomona faculty in 1918. When Judge Neely retired in 1925, Burgess took over his courses and was promoted to professor of law. His understanding of parliamentary procedure and his deep interest in the work of the faculty were recognized in 1927 by his appointment as Secretary of the Faculty, a position in which he would serve with great effectiveness.

Russell M. Story of Syracuse University was appointed professor of political science. A graduate of Monmouth College, Story had taken his Ph.D. at Harvard. After teaching at Clark University and Monmouth, he spent ten years at the University of Illinois before going to Syracuse. He was an able teacher whose questioning mind, at its best in seminar discussion, stimulated thought and independent work. Active in instructional changes, Story was a leader in curricular innovations. A number of his students went to graduate schools, and their later achievements in government service and teaching brought great distinction to Pomona.

F. Raymond Iredell '21 returned from graduate work at Harvard to become assistant professor of philosophy. In a college career interrupted by military service in France he had been the president of the Pomona College Debating Club, the president of the Y.M.C.A., president of the French Club, a class president, a student body officer, and a member of Sigma Tau fraternity. In his senior year he was elected to Phi Beta Kappa and chosen as a commencement speaker. At Harvard he held a fellowship and a scholarship, and in 1924-25 he had the privilege of a year at the University of Brussels as a Fellow of the Committee for the Relief of Belgium.

As the student body grew and the faculty increased, the strengthening of the library became imperative. At the end of 1922-23, the library holdings comprised 40,000 volumes and over 30,000 pamphlets, and the library was a depository for publications of the United States Government and the Carnegie Institution of Washington. Of special collections the most notable in Carnegie was the Mason Collection on California. Departmental libraries were the Cook-Baker biology library in Crookshank, the astronomy library at Brackett Observatory, the new libraries for chemistry and geology in Mason, and the Viola Minor Westergaard Art Collection in Rembrandt Hall. Victor E. Marriott had served as librarian since 1912, combining the librarianship with other responsibilities. When he decided to resign and study at the Chicago Theological Seminary, the college sought a professional librarian who would lead the expansion which was envisaged.

The choice fell upon Willis H. Kerr, librarian of the Kansas State Teachers College at Emporia. Kerr was a graduate of Bellevue College, Nebraska, of which his father was president and where he took the classics course. After receiving an M.A. in English with minors in philosophy and history at Columbia University, he continued graduate study at the University of Edinburgh. Following a brief period of teaching at Bellevue, he served seven years as librarian and professor of English at Westminster College, Missouri. In his fourteen years at Kansas State he had won the highest respect of his own community and had attained state-wide leadership among librarians. Kerr's distinguished fellow townsman, William Allen White, wrote Dean Jaqua that if Pomona wanted a librarian who would work with students and enlist their use of the library, the college could not find a better person. While the negotiations were under way, Kerr was offered the librarianship of the University of Nebraska, but family ties strengthened the appeal of Pomona, for Mrs. Kerr was a sister of Dean Nicholl. Kerr was appointed librarian of Pomona, with the faculty status of full professor, and in September 1925 he and his accomplished wife (Dean of Women at Emporia College and called by one writer "the outstanding woman of Kansas as a leader and speaker") brought their talents to California. For more than a quarter of a century he would be the major force in the development of libraries at Pomona College and in Claremont.

Pitman, Story, and Kerr took an active part in the advancement of the Honors Program which the faculty had initiated in 1924. In the mid-twenties there arose among American colleges and universities a belief that new teaching methods and more challenging academic programs should be made available for the abler students. One attempt to meet this need was Honors Study which provided greater freedom for the student and the study of a few subjects in greater depth. The most notable and successful example of Honors Study was that of Swarthmore College, where as many as half of the juniors and seniors gave their full time to such a program. Pomona was a pioneer in Honors Study on the Pacific Coast, its program offering "the student to whom the college is primarily an intellectual experience the opportunity for more independent study through a more flexible use of courses." It aimed "toward the mastery of a major subject and the understanding of one or two minor subjects, particularly in their relation to the major." The student was to be "released from as much of academic routine as his instructors may approve." Honors Study as thus designed was kept at Pomona until World War II.

Knowledge of developments in higher education throughout the country was much advanced by Pomona's inclusion in the Exchange Agreement which Harvard University had made with a selected group of western colleges. In 1911 President A. Lawrence Lowell of Harvard had invited Beloit, Knox, Grinnell, and Colorado College to join in a program by which annually Harvard would send a member of its faculty for a semester to the four institutions. The Harvard professor's time was divided among the four institutions as they determined; he taught in regularly scheduled classes in his field, and participated fully in faculty matters. Harvard paid the professor's salary, and the member colleges defrayed his travel expenses and maintenance on the respective campuses. Furthermore, each of the western colleges enjoyed annually the privilege of sending a member of its faculty to Harvard. Younger members who enjoyed this coveted opportunity often continued their graduate work; older faculty members normally used the period for study and research. Young or old could teach a third of a program in Harvard College if they so elected.

The colleges in the Harvard Exchange Agreement were all of Congregational origin, and with the success of the arrangement they looked to the inclusion of their sister institutions, Carleton and Pomona, which were invited to membership in 1914 and 1919, respectively. With the expansion of the group to six colleges, Harvard annually sent two members of its faculty for a semester, and the colleges were arranged in two groups, Pomona being joined with Grinnell and Colorado College. From 1920 through 1932 Pomona was enriched by the Harvard Exchange professors, all of whom were both distinguished scholars and able teachers. Their presence in the daily work of the college brought valuable insights on the rapidly developing graduate programs of the eastern universities and helpful contacts with the academic departments at Harvard. The exchange expanded opportunities for Pomona graduates, and their outstanding performance at Harvard gave the college high standing with the academic departments of the university.

The esteem in which Harvard held the exchange was shown by a comment in the *Harvard Alumni Bulletin* in 1924. "This relation of cooperation and friendly intercourse is of great value to Harvard. It brought interesting young teachers to Harvard. It has encouraged the resort of graduates of these colleges to the Harvard professional schools. Last but not least it has given many members of the Harvard Faculty the opportunity of visiting these fine institutions. They are all liberal in their outlook and preserve the intellectual seriousness and freedom of the New England Congregational tradition. On the other hand, in their strong community spirit and their educational organization, they are characteristic of the American West."[1]

Extracurricular Activities and Social Life

In intercollegiate athletics and physical education there was much progress and achievement. After the war the college reenforced the "strictly amateur" policy which President Blaisdell and the faculty had established in 1915 and 1916. As a further step in this policy and its administration, the trustees voted on April 9, 1919 to place the financial administration of athletics in the hands of the head of the department of physical education. As this action involved a transfer of financial management from the Associated Students and was effected without much consultation, it occasioned some resentment. However, the vote of the trustees appropriating five dollars of each student's tuition fee for athletics and the institution

[1]That President Lowell should have felt it essential, on March 10, 1933, to suspend a program so highly regarded and that Conant would discontine it in February 1935 indicated the gravity of the Great Depression for American higher education.

of an athletic council by the department of physical education allayed student dissatisfaction. The Athletic Council, set up to advise the head of the department, was composed of seven members: three students chosen by the ASPC, three faculty members appointed by the president of the college, and the head of the department of physical education for men who served as chairman. Among its duties were advice on the budget for athletics, the securing and direction of student managers for the various sports, and the recommendation to the faculty of the schedules for the respective sports. The council proved so effective that it became a permanent college body and some years later representatives of the Alumni Association joined the faculty and students as members of the council.

In the early twenties, Eugene Nixon effected a reorganization and restaffing of the department of physical education for men which secured its policies and provided its leadership for nearly forty years. He selected as new faculty members three young alumni whose qualities he had tested on athletic fields and in whose character he had complete confidence. Each of the three had married a Pomona alumna who shared his interest in the work and life of their alma mater.

Colvin Heath '16, who had been freshman football coach when war began, returned to the college in 1922 from Pomona High School where he had been a teacher of history and physical education. To his duties as line coach for football, freshman basketball coach, and teacher of physical education, he brought the record of a great football player, participation in track and baseball, and devotion to the development of young men.

Robert L. Strehle '19, who joined the faculty in 1923, was a star hurdler who held the Pacific Coast record in low hurdles and had been named low hurdler on Walter Camp's All America College Team in 1917. His college career, interrupted by war service and a period of business, included membership in the Men's Glee Club, presidency of both the debating club and the senior men's organization, and managership of the football team.

The alumni trio was completed in September 1925 by the appointment of Earl Jay Merritt, who had graduated that June. Known throughout his career as "Fuzz," Merritt had had a phenomenal athletic career at Pomona, winning letters in football, track, baseball, and basketball. It was then the custom to retain a graduating senior for a year as freshman adviser and Merritt was named to this post and to an instructorship in physical education. As freshman adviser he and his family lived in Smiley Hall where he began the dual career of teacher and coach in physical education and athletics and director of the men's campus.

The intercollegiate athletic program aroused such enthusiasm that annually nearly fifty pages of the *Metate* were given to the varsity and freshman teams in the five major sports: football, track, basketball, baseball, and tennis. The athletic rally, which developed distinctive qualities in Southern California, became at Pomona an elaborate and spirited gathering normally held on the library steps and including "clever stunts by various campus comedians, pertinent speeches by members of the faculty, members of the varsity squad, alumni and campus celebrities, and musical selections by the Men's Glee Club." By 1923 a rooting section had been established with special stunts and the wearing of rooting caps as features of each game. The night before the Oxy football game a climactic rally was held on Alumni Field, with hundreds of alumni, townspeople, and faculty families joining the student body. Spirits rose with the Ghost Dance and the singing of *Torchbearers* by the Men's Glee Club, the illumination of the "P" on the mountain, and the lighting of the bonfire. By its leaping flames Pomonans, young and old, dreamed of defeating the Occidental Tiger on the morrow.

Under Nixon and Heath the football teams won the conference championship in 1922, 1923, and 1924. While almost all games were within the conference, Pomona continued to schedule games with the University of Southern California, and on occasion to send the team north for a game in Berkeley with the University of California. As the undefeated conference champion in 1922 Pomona represented the Southern California colleges in a game with the University of Hawaii in Honolulu, and the following year the University of Hawaii came to Claremont. In 1923 Pomona and U.S.C. played the dedicatory game at the opening of the Los

Conference Championship Football Team, 1923. The varsity with coaches Heath, left, and Nixon, right

Conference Championship Track Team, 1925. Nixon at left and track coach Strehle, right

Angeles Coliseum, "America's finest athletic edifice," U.S.C. winning 23 to 7.

Student organizations were strong and confident. *Student Life* was published on Monday, Wednesday, and Friday. *The Sagehen,* "the first comic magazine put out by Pomona students," was published in January 1923 by seniors Robert V. Edwards and Braven V. Dyer. The Associated Students Cooperative store, established by Derwood Baker '22 in 1918 in the basement of Holmes Hall, had been set on a successful and permanent course by the managerial ability of Morris B. Pendleton '22, ably assisted by Lawrence T. Cooper '23. There were a large number of departmental clubs, and debating and oratory still held great interest.

Debating, which was fostered by four men's societies and one women's club, had an extensive intercollegiate program. For example, in 1922-23 the men held debates locally with the Southern Branch of the University of California, Occidental, Redlands, U.S.C., Whittier and Cal Tech and journeyed to the University of Wyoming, Beloit College, and the University of Arizona. The women met Southern Branch and Occidental. The intercollegiate question for the year was: "Resolved, that the United States should establish a responsible system of cabinet-parliamentary government." The high point of interest in debating was a visit on January 7, 1925 by a team representing the Oxford Union Society of the University of Oxford. Three recent Oxford graduates, J. D. Woodruff, Christopher Hollis, and Malcolm McDonald, who were on a national debating tour in the United States, met Pomona seniors Marshall E. Dimock '25, Paul B. Papazian '25, and R. Blackwell Smith '25. Before a full house in Bridges Hall the Oxford team supported the resolution "That this House is opposed to the principle of Prohibition," and Pomona spoke for Prohibition. The audience constituted the judges, as is customary at the Oxford Union, and of 708 present 602 voted for the Pomona position.

There had been a change in the number and interests of campus organizations. The Y.M.C.A. and the Y.W.C.A. continued to play important roles, but their influence was much less than before the war. There developed a number of new academic and social organizations closely connected with the work of academic departments.

These included the History Club, the Astronomical Club, the Mathematics Society, the Art Club, and the language clubs: Le Cercle Français, El Circulo Español, Il Circolo Italiano, and after 1923, the German Club. The Pomona College Literary Society continued, as did three women's literary societies, Alpha Kappa, Delta Lambda, and Phi Kappa Sigma, but their influence was declining.

The development of the fraternities had followed the guidelines held by President Blaisdell: independence of any national organization, interest in nature and the mountains, and primary loyalty to the college. Two new fraternities were founded: Nu Alpha Phi in 1921, and Sigma Phi Alpha, 1923. Each fraternity owned a mountain cabin which was a center for hiking and climbing and for coed social affairs held under faculty chaperonage.

The greatest change in campus social life was the introduction of ballroom dancing. Earlier student interest in dancing had met firm faculty and administrative resistance. A *Student Life* editorial of December 10, 1918 favoring dancing, concluded in resignation: "The principle of non-dancing has become ingrained into the very fiber of the institution for reasons which the executives can best express and it is worse than futile for us to oppose it." Change came rapidly after the war, and when dancing was permitted, attention turned to the management and control of the college dances. In 1921-22, the faculty urged that the informal Tuesday evening dances be used "for the instruction of those who do not know how to dance." These informal dances were supervised by the physical education department, with a student social manager in charge of a floor committee of four men and four women who had power "to reprimand any undesirable form of dancing or to request any person to leave the floor." The college life committee of the faculty urged that "the social program include some method of training the student body in social manners," and this responsibility was taken seriously by the faculty and the deans. The dance program developed rapidly and by 1922-23 four all-college formal dances were conducted: the senior-freshman dance, the Christmas dance sponsored by the Associated Women Students, the Military Ball, and the Junior Prom. The *Metate* of June 1923 carried a two-page listing of the officers and patrons for these dances. The formals were held in the "Big Gym," always specially decorated for each dance, and general oversight was exercised by the social committee of the Associated Students.

New Forces in California Education

While the students were enjoying the fuller social life of the "Greater Pomona," outside forces were affecting the college curriculum. The passage by the State of California of a law requiring the certification of teachers for the public schools and setting forth the conditions of such certification presented a number of critical academic questions for Pomona and all other California institutions of higher education. How would the required courses in professional education be worked into the curriculum, and what would be displaced? There were two basic state credentials, one for teaching in the elementary schools and the other for teaching in high school. The state assumed that the elementary credential would be given as part of the baccalaureate degree and in the regular four-year period. The credential for high school teaching on the other hand required a fifth year of academic work, consisting primarily of courses in education. The Pomona faculty felt that the compression of the work for both the baccalaureate degree and the elementary credential into four years would reduce the quality of the bachelor of arts degree. Accordingly, Pomona insisted on a fifth year of instruction for the elementary credential, and it was the only institution in California that did so.

The secondary credential, with its requirement of a year of professional work after the B.A. degree, fitted well into the Pomona curriculum. Students were able to combine the courses in education with work in their special fields of interest, and in most cases received an M.A. degree as well as the California Secondary Teaching Credential. Consequently there was a rapid increase in the number of graduate students of whom there were forty-six in the autumn of 1924. Work developed in conjunction with the secondary credential was the foundation on which graduate work would develop at Pomona and in Claremont over the next fifty years.

The growing emphasis upon teaching education was reflected in the appointment of both Dean Nicholl and Dean Jaqua; each had a title in education and gave courses in the field, as did Mr. Fitts. The introduction of the statewide credential system led to the organization of a more systematic department of education, and Aubrey A. Douglass was called to head it in 1926. A graduate of Kansas State Teachers College with a Ph.D. from Clark University, he had been assistant professor of education at Washington State College and lecturer on secondary education at Harvard before coming to Pomona. He would play a large role in the education of western teachers, first in Claremont and then throughout California.

In the early 1920's Pomona was able to take significant steps in improving the financial condition of its faculty. Salaries were increased, and a retirement program was instituted. Earlier, few American colleges or universities had any plan for the retirement of older faculty members. As institutions were unable to provide pensions, they hesitated to establish mandatory retirement ages; thus many teachers continued beyond their best years, sometimes to their personal detriment as well as that of their institutions.

The officers of the Carnegie Corporation and the Carnegie Foundation for the Advancement of Teaching in New York sought to remedy this deplorable national situation. In 1918 the two Carnegie organizations made grants for the establishment of an institution which would manage retirement funds for colleges and universities. The resulting Teachers Insurance and Annuity Association was one of the most significant advances of the twentieth century in the economic progress of the college teaching profession. A nationally applicable retirement program became available to American colleges and universities. After an institution had worked out its retirement plan and had been admitted to membership in the T.I.A.A., as it was soon known, an annuity policy was issued to each eligible individual. Thereafter and until retirement, payments toward the policy were made by both the institution and the individual, each usually paying an amount equivalent to five per cent of the individual's annual salary. As the fund established was the property of the individual and as policies were transferrable from one member institution to another,

T.I.A.A. brought nationwide economic security to college and university faculties.

The success of the Three Million Dollar campaign enabled Pomona to establish a retirement plan, and it was with deep satisfaction that the trustees on March 28, 1924 approved membership in T.I.A.A. The basic plan then approved became the charter upon which the college's subsequent retirement policies have been based. The normal retirement age was established at sixty-five, with provision for continuance on a year by year basis until sixty-eight, upon invitation by the college. Retirement annuities for faculty members were set up on the standard matching basis of five per cent by the individual and five per cent by the college. Special arrangements outside T.I.A.A. were made for those already above fifty-five years of age, the trustees fixing a guaranteed retirement pension for each of them.

Further security for Pomona faculty and staff members came two years later with the establishment of a group life insurance policy to which also both individuals and the college contributed. A particularly valued feature of the policy was protection in case of permanent disability before age sixty. The group insurance policy, like the retirement program, brought a valued benefit to the members of the Pomona faculty.

In the mid-twenties there were developments of long-range significance in the governance of the college. With the growth of the faculty it had become necessary to define more formally membership in the cabinet which acted on all regular appointments to the faculty and on faculty promotions. On March 29, 1924 the trustees approved a revision of the by-laws which defined the cabinet as "all members of the faculty of full professorial rank, who have had one year of service to the college."

This revision of the by-laws took another step of great consequence in the operation of the college by establishing a committee "to assist the President of the College and the Dean of the Faculty in matters of college administration." The committee consisted of the president, the dean, and six members of the faculty, four of whom were elected by the faculty and two appointed by the president. Their terms were so arranged that one person would be elected and one appointed each year; no faculty member could be re-elected or reappointed until an interval of one year had elapsed.

The administration committee was created to meet a critical need and it went to work immediately. Because of the pressures of the financial campaign the Executive Committee of the trustees on April 16, 1924 relieved President Blaisdell, until further action, of "the duties of internal administration" and requested the dean of the faculty "to assume these duties with the advice and assistance of the Administration Committee of the Faculty." The impact of the new arrangement is shown by the fact that Dean Jaqua presided over all but three of the numerous cabinet meetings held from March 28, 1924 through May 1925. As the agenda for a cabinet meeting emanated from discussion in the administration committee, that committee rapidly became the focal point of college government.

Although the administration committee arose from the particular needs of 1924, it was a creation of lasting value. The establishment of an official faculty committee to advise the president and the dean provided a constitutional body in which all important matters of faculty appointments and college administration could be discussed before arriving at recommendations to the cabinet and the faculty. Although the procedure was informal, without recorded minutes, and the committee's function was advisory, the president and the dean almost invariably acted in accord with the sense of the committee discussion. The committee assured cooperation and understanding between the faculty and the administration.

Such improved governance of the college was required by the larger responsibilities which external forces brought so insistently in the mid-1920's. The region Pomona served most directly had grown at a rate and to an extent unparalleled in previous American history. The population of California increased from 3,428,861 in 1920 to 5,677,251 in 1930, and the larger part of this phenomenal increase was in Southern California.

Much of the economic growth of the decade contributed to the development of higher education, and state-supported higher education became an important force in the region. In 1924 the Regents of the University of California raised the Southern Branch, which had been established in 1919 on Vermont Avenue, to a four-year degree-granting institution, named it the University of California at Los Angeles, and took steps to build a new campus for the institution in West Los Angeles.

Great changes also occurred in two of the older institutions of the Los Angeles area. The University of Southern California, at which Rufus B. von KleinSmid began a twenty-five year presidency in 1921, made a rapid transition from its collegiate beginning into a diversified urban university. In Pasadena, George Ellery Hale, the distinguished astronomer who directed the Mt. Wilson Observatory, enlisted wealthy residents of the city in the conversion of Throop College of Technology into a major technological institute. Robert A. Millikan, physicist and Nobel prize winner at the University of Chicago, was secured to head the institution which in 1920 was renamed the California Institute of Technology.

Sensing the need and desirability of cooperation in higher education in Southern California, President Blaisdell took the initiative in organizing the institutions, both old and new, into an association that would provide for regular exchange and annual meetings. Utilizing the structure of the Southern California Athletic Conference he invited administrators and faculty from its member institutions to meet at Pomona College on April 19, 1924. Sixty-eight representatives of Cal Tech, Occidental, Pomona, Redlands, Whittier, and the University of California, Southern Branch, organized the Southern California Conference of Colleges and Universities for the purpose of promoting common academic interests. Dr. Ernest C. Moore, Director of the Southern Branch, was named president and Professor Charles T. Fitts, of Pomona, was elected secretary.

By the time of the second meeting, which was held at Pomona on March 14, 1925, both La Verne College and the University of Southern California had joined the new conference. Thereafter, meetings of the conference were held in rotation on the campuses of the member institutions. A permanent association had been established, one which would maintain continuity with its origins despite great growth in membership and two changes of name.

Today, as the Western College Association, it serves all the institutions of higher education in California and Hawaii. The association owes much of its development to the remarkable and devoted service of Charles T. Fitts who, in addition to his regular responsibilities at Pomona, served as its secretary-treasurer from 1924 to 1954, and attended its meetings until his death in 1977.

CHAPTER XIV

A Bold Venture in Educational Organization

SERIOUS DISCUSSION of the future of Pomona had begun in the faculty as early as June 17, 1921 when the cabinet addressed itself to "the question whether a policy of expansion should prevail or one of intensifying and developing the present lines of work with approximately no increase in numbers." As consideration of this crucial issue proceeded in faculty, trustee, and alumni circles, President Blaisdell sought an approach which would meet the pressing needs of the new age and also preserve the best of the past. He had long been attracted by the collegiate system of the Universities of Oxford and Cambridge and he intensified his study of these institutions.

At the trustee meeting on February 12, 1923 he suggested that "the advantage of close relationship between students and between students and faculty might perhaps be preserved by the developing of a group system." By October 1923 he had begun to formulate his ideas, and he shared them in a letter to Miss Ellen Browning Scripps. "My own very deep hope," he wrote, "is that instead of one great, undifferentiated university, we might have a group of institutions divided into small colleges — somewhat on the Oxford type — around a library and other utilities which they would use in common. In this way I should hope to preserve the inestimable personal values of the small college while securing the facilities of the great university. Such a development would be a new and wonderful contribution to American education."

On March 29, 1924 the trustees charged "the President of the Board together with the trustee Committee on Education with the duty of studying the future organization of this institution and such matters as may be involved in any form of reorganization." This led to the appointment of a special committee consisting of Colonel Mudd and Llewellyn Bixby from the trustees, Dean Jaqua and Professor George S. Burgess from the faculty, and President Blaisdell, with Mudd as chairman. In connection with the work of this committee Dr. Blaisdell called Marston's attention to *Oxford and Oxford Life,* a book by J. Wells of Wadham College whose writings on Oxford had been authoritative since 1892.

However, much of the energy of the president and the trustees for the next twelve months had to be given to the Three Million Dollar Campaign. Colonel Mudd accepted the chairmanship of the Los Angeles committee, and a public drive in the Pomona Valley was begun on November 19, 1924. In addressing the meeting President Blaisdell held out bright prospects for the future. "After Pomona College has met the urgent need for completing the equipment for the present college, the eastern foundations have plans for Pomona College which would put it in the lead with the greatest institutions in the country." These efforts in Southern California were successful and on June 16, 1925 Dr. Blaisdell reported to the trustees that "the goal of $3,000,000 set in 1919 had been attained."

The trustees could turn to the work of the Committee on Future Organization and the momentous decisions its report might require. To this end 1924 had been a year of valuable preparation. President Blaisdell had shared his own thinking fully with Marston and could count on his support of a bold program.

Significantly, Blaisdell found an enthusiastic patron in Miss Scripps,whose satisfaction in her gifts for the Johnson Foundation, the women's campus, and the endowment, had deepened her interest in Pomona and her regard for its president. English by birth, she was pleased at the prospect of bringing Oxford practices and precedents to higher education in California. Early in 1924 she made a gift for the purchase of Indian Hill and adjacent property, approximately 250 acres. The good news brought rejoicing among the alumni. "Indian Hill, famed in song and story, and from which every alumnus has surveyed valley and mountains, shall forever be kept sacred to the high ends of education" stated an article in the

Pomona College Quarterly Magazine. An editorial in the same issue spoke of a plan "in which several colleges, as at Oxford, would be grouped around a larger central institution and make use of common facilities." Envisaged were "a women's college for which a growing demand exists in Southern California" and a graduate college "perhaps after the pattern of the Princeton Graduate School." In such high spirits alumni and faculty gathered on Indian Hill for a dedicatory ceremony on the morning of Alumni Day, 1924, prior to the reunion luncheons. President Blaisdell spoke of Miss Scripps' gift, and when venerable Charles Burt Sumner told something of the plans for the development of Indian Hill, "the spirit of a conquering army seemed to pervade that little assemblage of three hundred."

Miss Scripps' interest in Pomona and knowledge of its operation were much increased by the election of her attorney and agent, Jacob C. Harper, to the Pomona Board of Trustees on March 28, 1924. As a young lawyer in Cincinnati, Harper had attracted the attention of E. W. Scripps, then beginning the expansion of what was to become a newspaper empire. Thereafter, he devoted his career primarily to the interests of the Scripps family and the Scripps newspapers. As the personal attorney of E. W. Scripps and Ellen Browning Scripps, and as general counsel for the Scripps-Howard newspapers, Harper was very successful and participated in his own right in the founding of newspapers in Dallas and Houston.

In 1916 Harper moved to La Jolla where Miss Scripps had established her residence in 1897. Relinquishing his position as general counsel for the newspapers, he thereafter centered his attention on the personal business of E. W. Scripps and his sister; after 1924 he gave his time primarily to the business and philanthropic interests of Miss Scripps. It was to him that President Blaisdell addressed the letter which led to Miss Scripps' gift of Indian Hill and the adjacent land.

Great expectations, aroused by dramatic statements and events, gripped the college in 1925. A preliminary statement which had been submitted to the Committee on Future Organization was discussed by the cabinet on March 2 and 4. Pomona's first

Rhodes Scholar, E. H. Kennard '07, posed the problem and suggested an answer in an article, "Which Way, Pomona" in the *Pomona Quarterly Magazine,* March 1925.

> In the next few years Pomona will have to make a definite choice. Shall Pomona retain for all time the size and coherence of a small college or shall she swell into one more drab university of the usual American type, with a faculty indifferent to student life outside the classroom, with social chaos for the many and the intensely standardizing influence of fraternities for the few? Or shall she dare to be original and strive to develop a new and better organization that will combine the advantages without the disadvantages of both the old forms?

Regarding the pattern of Oxford, Kennard warned that "no particular detail of that historic university is likely to prove satisfactory here if copied outright. Rather one should study Oxford thoroughly and then, burning his notes, face the problem anew and seek to devise a form of organization suitable to America." With great wisdom he foresaw the problems that an adaptation of the Oxford College system would present, and the patience such a development would require in the United States.

> Now it is obvious that such a plan bristles with difficulties. It can be made to succeed only by a group of men and women who believe in its possibilities and will patiently seek the goal through decades of effort. These devoted spirits will have to resist continually the common American passion for seeking the easiest course and the utmost simplicity and the greatest mechanical efficiency. The start must be made in such a way as to commit Pomona definitely to the broad outlines of the plan. The only way to accomplish this would seem to be to walk boldly out into the sagebrush and *stake out college number two.*

When Kennard's article appeared the Executive Committee of the Board had already taken a bold step. On March 9, 1925 the Committee appropriated one thousand dollars to be "placed in the hands of President Blaisdell for work in planning the campus for the greater college." Jamieson and Spearl were engaged to prepare architectural plans which would be presented to the Board at its annual meeting in June.

The commencement exercises of 1925 were used as an occasion for considering the future of the college. The practice of having only seniors speak at commencement, which had been the invariable rule since the first commencement in 1894, was set aside in favor of a distinguished visitor. In the faculty meeting on February

26, 1925 Professor McCulley stated, "There was a strong sentiment in many quarters that it may be to the advantage of all if the present practice of having student commencement speakers were discontinued and a man of national repute as a speaker be secured." He reported that the officers of the senior class had been consulted and were willing to see the change made. McCulley suggested Professor William Bennett Munro, professor of American government at Harvard University, who was then in Southern California. Munro cordially accepted the college's invitation, and thus became the first outside commencement speaker in Pomona's history. The quality and long-range effect of his address were worthy of the momentous departure from established precedent.

Entitling his address, "The College at the Crossroads," Munro posed the great issue then confronting much of American higher education.

> Of all the general problems which are facing the American college today, this one is by far the most important. Shall the college remain a college, with all the intimacy of instruction and fellowship which a simple collegiate status supplies, or shall it prepare to go the way that so many of our colleges have gone; for remember that Yale, Harvard, Princeton, Columbia, all began as small institutions. Or again is there some third alternative? Is the crossroad a three way point at which the wayfarer has a choice between more routes than two? . . . Can we develop in this country an institution which is large in its resources, broad and deep in its intellectual life, with an atmosphere that is stimulating to the highest type of creative scholarship, but which nevertheless preserves the wholesome community ideals of the small college, its rural environment, its religious spirit, its restfulness in the shadow of the hills? . . . In a way the two oldest English universities, Oxford and Cambridge, have done it by grouping a number of small colleges into a large academic center while continuing to keep the college small.

Professor Munro saw Pomona as one of the colleges which had "arrived at the crossroads" and thus had the opportunity "to do a great service not only to her own future but to the future of higher education in general." No college was better situated "to launch out upon the third alternative, to try the plan of creating two or more academic units joined in a common enterprise." The college had an ideal location "with plenty of land for expansion" and was "within easy reach of an area which in a few years will contain more than two million people." Most important, Pomona had a reputation and "sound traditions already created." Now that she had arrived "at the parting of the ways" Pomona must determine whether she would do "just as other colleges have done and are doing" or whether she would do "something new, different, and manifestly superior."

President Blaisdell spoke to the annual meeting of the Alumni Association that commencement week and invited support of "some plan by which it is hoped that Pomona College may be enlarged to meet the demands of its increasing clientele without sacrificing the advantages inherent in the small college," saying that the plans "which will probably contain certain features of the Oxford-Cambridge idea, have not been worked out in detail."

The alumni wished Pomona to lead in meeting the larger educational needs of the Southwest, yet they desired the college to remain the small, personal institution they cherished. Dr. Blaisdell offered a program to achieve both objectives. Accordingly, the members of the Alumni Association voted:

> Whereas President Blaisdell has envisioned a plan of a group of small colleges, each with its own individuality and charm, but all with the high standard and ideals of Pomona, be it resolved by the Alumni of Pomona College that we heartily approve the principle of a group of small colleges centering around and multiplying our Pomona; and we do enthusiastically reaffirm our faith in the President of our College, in its trustees and faculty, and their ability to unfold to success the plans for progressive Pomona.

The Alumni Association was endorsing a concept and a hope rather than a completed plan. In view of its importance the proposal for a group of colleges had had surprisingly little discussion within the college. There is no record that it was ever presented to the entire faculty prior to commencement, 1925. At their meeting on the campus on June 16, 1925 the trustees studied "campus plans, preliminary in character, for a group of colleges," as prepared by Jamieson and Spearl. Following the meeting the trustees lunched with the faculty in the College Club rooms in Sumner Hall, and doubtless the matter of the group plan was discussed then.

The essence of the proposed new organization was contained in the "Preliminary Statement submitted for consideration by the Committee on Future Organization," which Dr. Blaisdell sent to the Committee on March 15, 1925. The covering letter indicates that the Statement was largely his own. "While we have not met as a group," he wrote, "the subject has been in our minds. I have talked with you and with many others informally regarding these possibilities. It seems important that in the near future we should have a meeting and that we should formulate our recommendations."

After commencement the trustees prepared the way for action, requesting the printing of Professor Munro's address, and "any resolutions of the alumni or expressions of other groups on the new form of organization." Following discussion during the summer, the Board felt ready to make a decision. The procedure which the trustees followed was as English in character as the university from which they sought to learn. The Board approved no statement of purpose or written constitution. Instead it met immediate objectives by separate actions, thereby creating a body of precedents for future guidance. Although Dr. Blaisdell's "Preliminary Statement" of March 15 was the only comprehensive draft of the new plan of organization, it was not voted upon and there is no record of it in the minutes of the Board. After due legal notice, a special meeting of the Board was held on the campus in Rembrandt Hall on September 17 and 18, with nineteen of the twenty-five trustees in attendance. The purpose of the meeting was to amend the Articles of Incorporation of Pomona College in a way to authorize the establishment of a group of coordinating colleges. This great power was given on September 17 by adding the following provision to the purposes for which Pomona had been formed: "'To establish, maintain, conduct and assist financially or otherwise, institutions of learning of any nature, the establishment, maintenance and assistance of which is not inconsistent with or contrary to the objects and purposes hereinabove set forth." The amendment became effective when approved by the State of California on October 13, 1925. This fundamental change had been made by simply giving a new power to a long established institution.

It was understood that the first result of the amendment would be the organization of a "central college," which Dr. Blaisdell envisaged would serve "as a clearing house of the interests of the various colleges." The board of trustees of this central college would include substantial membership from the boards of the other colleges. The matter of the incorporation of the central college was referred to a committee consisting of President Blaisdell, Mudd, and Harper, who were to be the nucleus of its board of trustees and were empowered "to complete their number and establish the organization." Although the committee was also empowered to adopt a name for the new corporation, the Pomona Board "tentatively recommended" the name "Claremont Colleges" and this was adopted. The incorporation of Claremont Colleges was appropriately completed on the thirty-eighth anniversary of the founding of Pomona College, October 14, 1925, when Robert J. Bernard '17, executive secretary of Pomona, filed the articles of incorporation with the Secretary of State in Sacramento.

Before this, on October 1, the trustees had made a dramatic announcement of their plans in a testimonial dinner to Dr. Blaisdell at the Biltmore Hotel in Los Angeles. The presidents of other California institutions of higher education and other outstanding citizens were guests for the occasion. Mr. Marston, as the presiding officer, announced the decision of Pomona College to develop a group of coordinated colleges in Claremont. Substance was given to the announcement by the reading of a letter of September 29 from Ellen Browning Scripps to Dr. Blaisdell. The president had talked and corresponded with her regarding a college for women and had suggested that it be named for her. Her letter authorized him to announce at the dinner that she was giving to "the proposed Scripps College for Women at Claremont, California" stock in the Evening News Association of Detroit, Michigan, valued at $500,000. As Robert J. Bernard had hoped, the dinner gave "wings to the whole futuure plan." Kennard's advice "to walk boldly out into the sagebrush and stake out college number two" could be followed.

The Los Angeles dinner was a farewell party for President and Mrs. Blaisdell, who were to be away from Claremont for a year. At the annual meeting on June 16, the trustees had voted Dr. Blaisdell a leave of absence on full salary from September 1, 1925 to September 1, 1926 "with the understanding that he spend a portion of the year studying conditions in other colleges in the United States

President and Mrs. Blaisdell leaving for Europe. From the left, ASPC President Paul Jones, President and Mrs. Blaisdell, Mrs. Ernest J. Jaqua, Dean Jaqua and their young son

and Europe." The Board officially provided the president an expense allowance of $2,500, and members of the Board personally contributed an additional $2,500. A trip to Europe, which he had never visited, had long been dreamed of by Dr. Blaisdell, and he had been much encouraged to go by Marston who with his family had made several extensive European tours.

As early as April 28, 1923 Marston had urged Blaisdell to take an absence of five or six months later that year, observing that current problems seemed "to loom up less formidably to me after getting away from the atmosphere of Pomona College." "Please don't give up on the journey to England," Marston wrote. "It is the place in all the world for rest, recreation and enrichment. The President needs to have his education rounded out! There is Cambridge and Oxford and Winchester, etc., etc." Marston's desire for Blaisdell to make an extended trip to Europe was increased by his concern over the president's health. Dr. Blaisdell was not a strong man and he experienced periods of great exhaustion. He had been seriously ill for three weeks in April 1923 and had just returned to the office when he received Marston's letter of April 28.

It was serious concern for his health that led Dr. Blaisdell to choose 1925-26 as the year for his long anticipated trip to Europe. Writing to Marston in longhand on May 14, 1925 about his own plans for the coming academic year, he confessed, "I don't like to admit it, but I am coming to the end of the year feeling thoroughly worn out. A few hours of work each day leaves me entirely useless. I carry a sense of aimlessness and confusion which would make me very despondent were it not for the hypothesis that it is due to weariness and not to old age!" He felt matters would be such that he could leave at the end of the summer, and suggested a leave for himself until July 1, 1926 and the appointment of Dean Jaqua as acting president.

Personal matters, as well as the future organization of the college, delayed the Blaisdells' departure until the autumn. When the day for departure finally came on October 13 the entire student body went to the Southern Pacific station to see the Blaisdells off, and the president of the student body presented Dr. Blaisdell with a special medallion.

As they stopped for college and family matters in Washington, New York, and New England, it was late November before the Blaisdells sailed for France. Caught in stormy weather they had an uncomfortable voyage, and the further misfortune of a month of continuous rain in Paris. Schools were closed for the holiday season and Dr. Blaisdell could find few of the people he had hoped to see. He was astounded by the slowness of service in the Bibliothèque Nationale and the limited hours of the Sorbonne library. But living in a small family-run hotel he soon became at ease in Paris, and succumbed to the beauty, historic past, and intellectual and artistic excitement of the city. He wrote Mr. Bernard on January 15 that on every hand he found "such opportunities for conversation and friendship as to make every moment invaluable." He enjoyed meeting the Rector Adjunct of the College de France and others in French education. Fortunately, Dr. Henry O. Eversole, the son-in-law of trustee Eli P. Clark, was stationed in Paris on a medical mission for the Rockefeller Foundation, and he and Mrs. Eversole were extremely helpful to the Blaisdells. Paris so captivated the Blaisdells that they retained it as their continental base, and returned for a further visit after a tour that took them to Grenoble, Nice, Northern Italy, and Geneva, where Dr. Blaisdell observed the work of the League of Nations.

Meanwhile, in California those entrusted with the large responsibilities of the college diligently faced their varied duties. Dean Jaqua who had handled the complete internal administration for several months in 1924, and whose role in general administration had been much extended by President Blaisdell, effectively directed the ongoing life of Pomona College. He had taken full charge as acting president on September 1, 1925 and delivered the opening convocation address. Dr. Blaisdell limited his own participation to a brief address at the traditional flag raising ceremony.

The course of Pomona and its campus life were well established, but the organization of a group of cooperating colleges in one academic community in the United States was an uncharted operation. The amendment of the articles of incorporation that empowered Pomona to establish other colleges was no more than an agreement in principle. The lack of a constitution or other formal document of organization was not an oversight but the express desire of Dr. Blaisdell, who felt that decisions should be taken in the light of future needs and opportunities. The implementation of the principle of a group plan, therefore, became a major responsibility for the Pomona trustees, to whom were left the large decisions and the hard work of establishing new colleges. Marston and Charles Burt Sumner could share their experience from the founding of Pomona, but the lead would be taken by younger men. The trustees proved equal to the unprecedented task, and by the end of the academic year 1925-26 they had incorporated two new institutions.

Leadership in the organizing of Claremont Colleges was taken by Colonel Mudd and Jacob Harper, whom with Dr. Blaisdell the Pomona Board had designated trustees of the new corporation, and who were empowered to choose the other founding trustees. In late September the three agreed to invite Marston, Bishop Johnson, William L. Honnold, and Fred M. Wilcox from the Pomona Board.

Before the articles of incorporation of Claremont Colleges were filed two others were chosen: Edward D. Lyman, an attorney in Los Angeles who had greatly assisted in the Three Million Dollar Campaign, and Professor William B. Munro, who soon would leave Harvard for a professorship at the California Institute of Technology.

The organization meeting of Claremont Colleges was held in Claremont on December 9, 1925. In order to emphasize the special nature of Claremont Colleges the by-laws provided that the trustees be known as the Board of Fellows. In accordance with this nomenclature, Dr. Blaisdell was chosen Head Fellow. Colonel Mudd was elected chairman and Mr. Honnold vice-chairman. Robert J. Bernard was named secretary.

The choice of Honnold as a Fellow and his election as vice-chairman of the board would prove of the greatest significance in the development of the Claremont Colleges. Mr. Honnold's introduction to the Pomona College circle had come through Colonel Mudd. Much of Honnold's professional career had been in South Africa where he had made a fortune in mining. In Africa he met and formed a lifelong friendship with another American mining engineer, Herbert Hoover, with whom he later worked in 1915 as a member of the International Commission for the Relief of Belgium. His friendship with Mr. Hoover was a factor in leading him to move to Los Angeles, where through his mining interests he soon made the acquaintance of Colonel Mudd. Their respective offices were located in the Pacific Mutual Building and the two men soon engaged in joint business ventures and became good friends.

Honnold, like Colonel Mudd, had a high sense of obligation to society, and he wished to use his large fortune for the good of his country. This desire was intensified by the fact that he and Mrs. Honnold were without children. As Mudd shared his own interest and enthusiasm for Pomona, he sensed that Honnold would also find fulfillment in its work, and as a member of its Board of Trustees. Elected a trustee on February 24, 1925, Honnold took an immediate and vital interest. By June 1 Mr. Mudd could write Dr. Blaisdell that Mr. Honnold "is enlisted from now on and ready to work at any time. He has shown two distinct interests since he came to California and of these I believe Pomona College is well in the lead."

Claremont Colleges was organized to serve the common interests of the nascent group of colleges and to found new colleges. Of these functions the most immediate in 1925-26 was the establishment of the new college for women. This required land, and Pomona College had been holding the land for such future expansion. As the Board of Fellows planned new colleges, they sought to develop buildings of taste and quality so set in attractive grounds that the whole would give a sense of inspiration and abiding beauty to students and faculty. As a guide and control to this end, the Board of Fellows at its second meeting, on March 8, 1926, established an architectural commission, which included James Spearl of St. Louis, and two Los Angeles architects, David C. Allison and Carleton Winslow. For many years this commission, with its changes in membership, would be a guiding influence in giving quality and beauty to new college buildings and to new colleges.

On December 8, 1925 the Pomona Board made available the land on which new colleges and their buildings could be located. This action, which would provide land for the campus of Scripps College for Women, was a landmark decision in the development of Claremont Colleges and also a basic statement on the nature of the group plan. The motion, made by Colonel Mudd, outlined the Pomona trustees' concept of the future in Claremont and took steps toward its realization. "Whereas, Ellen B. Scripps has purchased and provided for the purchase, in the years 1924 and 1925, of certain lands in and adjacent to Claremont, for the promotion of President Blaisdell's plan for a group of small residential colleges in association with Pomona College, a graduate college, etc., with certain common facilities to be enjoyed by all, . . . (and) whereas Claremont Colleges has, under the authority of this Board, been incorporated under the laws of California as the central and coordinating body for carrying out President Blaisdell's plan," the officers of the Pomona Board were authorized to convey to Claremont Colleges the lands north of Sixth Street, Claremont, purchased or provided by Miss Scripps.

Harper explained that "Miss Scripps cordially approved President Blaisdell's suggestion that Indian Hill be regarded as a special contribution by her to the general project. Therefore the surface and slopes of Indian Hill should go to Claremont Colleges for use by it for a Graduate College or such other uses as the Board of Fellows of Claremont Colleges may hereafter determine will best promote the whole project. The residue of Miss Scripps' real estate purchases made since January 1, 1924 and comprising land north of Sixth Street, Claremont, should be regarded as endowment for Scripps College for Women along lines outlined by President Blaisdell." All these arrangements covering the various lands provided by Miss Scripps were concluded by an agreement between Claremont Colleges and Miss Scripps on May 28, 1926.

Steps for the establishment of the college for women had begun in the autumn of 1925 and to Harper and Dean Jaqua fell the responsibility for the work and communication to the Board of Fellows, the Pomona trustees, and the Pomona faculty. A letter of November 20 from Harper to Dr. Blaisdell, who was in the East awaiting his departure for Europe, reflected the zeal of the two men as they moved to found the new college. Harper reported that he had just spent the greater part of two weeks in Claremont "on land questions, city council, etc.... So much for the generalities. I find Dean Jaqua a most efficient, tactful and untiring worker, with whom it is very delightful to be associated. He and I are both so interested in the work that both of us find it difficult to practice temperance in the hours devoted to it." Miss Scripps, herself, did not go to Claremont, but she enjoyed a pleasant contact with the campus when the Pomona Women's Glee Club, on tour in the San Diego area, called at her home in La Jolla on the afternoon of January 29, 1926 and gave her a special concert.

The Scripps board of trustees and the administration of the college rapidly took form in the spring of 1926. Harper in a letter of April 26 to Dr. Blaisdell in London gave the names of the seventeen trustees selected by that date. He and Dean Jaqua were included as was William B. Munro. At the organization meeting of the trustees on June 18, Harper was elected president of the board and Dean Jaqua vice-president. In addition, Jaqua was appointed temporary director for 1926-27 with the powers of president, and it was announced that permanent academic officers would be named during that year. A freshman class of fifty to sixty students would be received in September 1927, and a similar class each succeeding year, with the first graduation scheduled for June 1931. To provide for the first class, construction of a two-story dormitory, "Spanish-California" in style, for which $150,000 had been given, would begin in December 1926. Harper wrote Blaisdell in London on June 30 that Gordon B. Kaufmann was the choice of the committee as the Scripps College architect. "He is an Englishman," he stated, "who is recognized as possessing imagination and originality coupled with thoroughness of his plans and specifications."

The good news of progress in the organization of Scripps College for Women reached Dr. Blaisdell at the most joyous moment of his year in Europe. With springtime had come the pilgrimage to England — his first acquaintance with London and the long anticipated journey to Oxford. The visit to the University and its colleges was the climax of Dr. Blaisdell's journey abroad. He reveled in the beauty of the ancient English city and the majesty of university and college buildings. Particularly rewarding was his conversation with Francis J. Wylie, a former Oxford tutor who by 1925 had been for twenty-two years the Oxford Secretary of the Rhodes Trust. Among the Rhodes Scholars whom Wylie annually advised and nurtured in Oxford were ninety-six young men from the United States. As these then came from all the states and from a variety of colleges and universities, no man in England was so well acquainted with American higher education, or so capable of explaining Oxford meaningfully to an inquiring college president from the United States. Many years later, Sir Francis Wylie, then knighted, recalled their memorable meeting to the author of this volume. Firsthand knowledge of Oxford confirmed and reenforced Dr. Blaisdell's belief that much from Oxford and its colleges could be a guide for the new organization of higher education being initiated by Pomona College.

After Oxford the Blaisdells travelled to Spain. In that country, whose orange blossoms, vineyards, and red tile roofs gave the California visitor a sense of coming home, Dr. Blaisdell received a staggering blow. A cablegram from Dean Jaqua conveyed the unexpected and overwhelming news that Colonel Mudd had died on May 24.

As Dr. Blaisdell's mail had been held in London, he had not received letters from Claremont that informed him of Colonel Mudd's illness and would have given him some forewarning. Mr. Mudd's health had failed rapidly in the spring and the meeting of the Board of Fellows on March 8 was to be his last. The gravity of his illness was such that, after an operation in Los Angeles in April, it was decided to take him by special train for treatment in New York. He weakened so rapidly en route that the train was stopped at St. Louis where after two operations Mr. Mudd died on May 24.

Few men have been so deeply mourned in Southern California. Colonel Mudd's death was a great loss and it brought profound grief to his colleagues on the Pomona Board. As Honnold said of his friend, "There was so much of the sublime in his character, so much of simplicity and engaging personality, that it was easy and pleasurable for him to enter understandingly and responsively into the lives of others." The trustees had relied on his "calm judgment and quiet leadership," and recognized Colonel Mudd as one who "possessed the emotion essential to daring action, while he submitted to the dictation of a well-trained judgment."

These qualities had led him to support Dr. Blaisdell's plan for the expansion of Pomona and to lead in the development of a group of colleges. The two men worked so closely that they were as one in their hopes and plans for the future of Claremont. They felt no need of a detailed program for they expected to work out the plan together as need and opportunity dictated. Bereft of his great friend, Dr. Blaisdell felt as if he had lost his right arm.

The depth of Colonel Mudd's commitment to higher education in Claremont was attested by the bequest of $1,000,000 which he left to Claremont Colleges for the purpose of advancing the group plan. This bequest was the largest single gift for higher education in California since the founding of Stanford University. But Colonel Mudd left a far greater legacy to society. His sons, Harvey and Seeley, continued his generous concern for civic, cultural, and educational institutions. He had founded one of the great philanthropic families of America, which in serving the nation, would include Claremont among its major benefactions.

CHAPTER XV

The Evolving New Structure in Claremont

THE ACADEMIC YEAR 1926-27 was the watershed between the one college community of the past and the emerging group of colleges that would henceforth characterize Claremont. As college opened, the new order in Claremont began to unfold. On September 17, 1926 a joint meeting of the boards of trustees of Pomona College, Scripps College for Women, and Claremont Colleges was held in Rembrandt Hall, with Mr. Marston presiding. Dr. Blaisdell, recently home, addressed the boards on his study of "educational conditions in Europe." Professor Munro "outlined the educational plan of Scripps College for Women" and reported the progress made in the organization of the college. After discussion, the trustees of Claremont Colleges and Scripps withdrew and the regular meeting of the Pomona trustees was called to order.

The first item of business was a motion by Mr. Honnold that Harvey S. Mudd succeed his father as a trustee of Pomona College. On June 15 Mr. Mudd had been elected a member of the Board of Fellows and there he was to serve under Mr. Honnold who was elected chairman on September 18. The association of the older Mr. Honnold and the thirty-eight-year-old Mr. Mudd would lead to a close personal friendship and incalculable benefits to higher education in Claremont.

The autumn of 1926 brought perplexing problems for the Pomona trustees and faculty. The announcement of the group plan in October 1925 had been followed by sober consideration of the realities of the momentous decision. President Blaisdell's absence in Europe had contributed to unease among trustees and faculty. The trustees faced two major responsibilities: the continued development of Pomona College itself, and the effective launching of the group plan. With Dr. Blaisdell at home, they were sobered by the magnitude of the over-all program which confronted them.

The trustees' concern was reinforced by the shortage of administrative talent at hand for the large undertaking. The Board had relied for so many years on the leadership of Dr. Blaisdell that its members were not prepared for the administrative problems and perplexities implicit in the new organization. Nor was the president. In the autumn of 1926 Dr. Blaisdell was heading both Pomona College and Claremont Colleges, and the dean of the faculty of Pomona was giving much of his time to the organization of Scripps College for Women. Furthermore, Dean Jaqua had worked so well and effectively with the Scripps trustees that they had begun to think of him for the presidency of that institution. Under these circumstances, the Pomona trustees felt impelled to appoint a special committee "to consider officials for Claremont Colleges, Scripps College for Women, and Pomona College."

The committee report, which Mr. Marston presented at a Board meeting in Los Angeles on November 19 "emphasized the importance of determining at an early date who is to head Pomona College and serve as the Dean of the Faculty of Pomona College so that President Blaisdell can be relieved of the responsibility of Pomona College while he is perfecting the organization and advancing the work of Claremont Colleges." "Furthermore," Mr. Marston stated, "in view of the consideration given by the Scripps College Board to the calling of Dean Jaqua to head that institution, it is important that the decision of that body be reached soon, not only on account of the progress of the Scripps College organization and work but to establish the administrative changes faced by Pomona College." The trustees, recognizing that "while deliberation to the point of sureness was required, an early solution of the problem was important," took steps to resolve the administration of their increasingly complex enterprise. They informed Scripps College that it was "free to invite Dean Jaqua" to become its president. A committee of six trustees, with Marston as chairman, was appointed to "consider in detail the selection of officers for Pomona College, in particular the President and the Dean."

Despite the trustee actions, the resolution of these pressing administrative matters proceeded very slowly. The Scripps trustees delayed nearly four months before offering the presidency of the college to Dr. Jaqua. The resolution of the matter was completed at a meeting of the Pomona trustees on March 8, 1927 when Dr. Munro, on behalf of the Scripps trustees, suggested that Dean Jaqua's resignation take effect at once, with leave of absence and full salary from Pomona until June 1, and that thereafter his salary be borne by Scripps. In accepting Jaqua's resignation and approving Dr. Munro's suggestions, the Pomona Board thanked him for a "remarkable development in the quality and efficiency of the entire teaching corps" at Pomona, and expressed its faith that at Scripps he would "do a conspicuous piece of work for the educational life of America." In its farewell resolution, the Pomona faculty spoke of the "atmosphere of unfailing good fellowship and generous appreciation of the varied aspects of our life" which Jaqua had brought to his work at Pomona.

Despite the appointment of the trustee committee on administration on November 19, 1926 President Blaisdell was by no means ready to be "relieved of the responsibility of Pomona College," and he saw need for his carrying the presidencies of both Pomona College and Claremont Colleges. The president had returned to serious problems within Pomona, where the social change characteristic of the United States in the 1920's was felt among both students and faculty. Less regulation and more individual choice were insistently demanded. The issue was pressed most vigorously and continually against the required daily chapel. In a chapel address on October 28, entitled "The Voluntary Principle," Dr. Story presented the argument against the required service. The discussion, which went on all the year, led first to the allowance of a greater number of absences, twenty-four for seniors, and eighteen for other students, and finally to an abolition of required attendance. Although conducted in a religious context with the reading of the Bible, prayer, and hymns, chapel was more than a religious service and not infrequently less. The chapel was the college assembly where announcements, business, and visiting lecturers could be brought to the attention of the academic community.

When the college gave up chapel as a requirement, it sought to preserve its essential values by the institution of regular voluntary religious services and voluntary "college hours," which later became known as assemblies.

Further evidence of change within the college was reflected in the procedure of faculty meetings. Beginning with the first faculty meeting in September 1888, these had always been opened with prayer. The faculty minutes indicate that this was done for the last time on January 10, 1927. No action was taken; the long established practice was simply discontinued.

The new outlook and greater freedom demanded by the students indicated the necessity of the appointment of a younger woman to succeed Miss Berry as dean of women. President Blaisdell himself undertook the search for the new dean. Miss Jessie E. Gibson, who was appointed in May 1927, was a graduate of the University of Idaho and had just completed an M.A. at the University of Washington. After teaching Romance languages in several high schools in Washington she had been, since 1918, dean of girls in the North Central High School, Spokane, where she had shown great understanding of young people. In confirming Miss Gibson's appointment President Blaisdell wrote, "I trust you may be given large wisdom, great patience, and abundant sympathy." All these she both received and shared. She won the affection of Miss Berry, who returned to a full-time teaching position as associate professor of mathematics and continued to serve as a member of the cabinet.

A changing Pomona and the emerging group of colleges tested Dr. Blaisdell severely. His inspirational qualities which had led to his great success were not sufficient for leadership of the new academic community in Claremont. Earlier at Pomona, he had been relieved of much internal administration by outstanding deans of the faculty, and he had been supported throughout his administration by the same chairman of the Board of Trustees. After 1925 he faced a situation in which there would not be the unity of command and counsels that had characterized the administration of Pomona since 1910. The new diversified structure called for a high degree of administrative expertise.

Dr. Blaisdell had expected to work out the organization and

operation of Claremont Colleges in close cooperation with Colonel Mudd. "The passing of Mr. Mudd," he wrote in his memoirs, "resulted in a period of confusion of counsels, and this just at the moment when hearty and confident cooperation under trusted leadership was most imperative." Although Blaisdell recognized his own lack of background and experience for "administrative work in an institution of the proportion of a large university," he had initiated in the group plan and Claremont Colleges an academic venture more exacting than any university.

The University of Oxford to which Blaisdell looked for guidance could be a model in some aspects but offered little assistance in others. The heart of Oxford was its colleges, of which in 1925 there were twenty-one for men and four colleges and a society for women, serving in all some four thousand students. A student's college was the center of his life during his three years at the university. There he lived, had his tutorial instruction, dined in hall, attended chapel, played on sports teams, and joined literary, dramatic or musical organizations. To a considerable degree the values and institutions of Oxford college life could be secured in the small residential college. Moreover, to some extent the tutorial method of instruction characteristic of Oxford could be introduced into an American institution. Thus the example of Oxford had led to the programs of Honors Study such as that developing at Pomona.

However, in governance the University of Oxford and its colleges were bound in a complexity of relationships that could have misled the most sophisticated American administrator. The university, beginning in the twelfth century and a child of the University of Paris, antedated the oldest of its colleges by almost a century, and for over seven hundred years the university and its growing group of colleges had been working out changing relationships. The university, which granted all degrees, had some academic appointees of its own but most of its administrative and instructional work was conducted by members of the colleges who were commonly known as fellows. There were no lay boards of trustees and the governing of Oxford was entirely in the hands of its permanent teaching staff. The university was run by a variety of boards and committees under the general oversight of an elected council which held weekly meetings. The vice-chancellor, who was the administrative head of the university, was elected in rotation from among the senior heads of the colleges. There were, however, many areas of tension between "college" interest and "university" interest. The issues had changed from generation to generation and from century to century but conflicts of interest and consequent arguments persisted. Only in a very limited sense could administrative practices in Oxford be transferred to Claremont.

Home from England, Dr. Blaisdell sought in the autumn of 1926 to move forward with the new organization that he and the Pomona trustees had initiated the year before. He reported to the alumni in the *Pomona College Quarterly Magazine* in October that all he had seen in the United States and England during the past year had

> increased his confidence in the form of organization according to which we have already determined to shape our life. We are seeking to combine the intimacies which are characteristic of small groups of students with the privileges which are only warranted by the presence of a much larger body of students. . . . Such a combination is not only practicable but most promising of rich results and the plan which has been more or less definitely formulated for the reorganization of the educational interests in Claremont is likely to have not only a long history with us but a really profound effect upon all American education.

What was the plan which had been "more or less definitely formulated?" As noted earlier, the only written document was the Preliminary Statement which President Blaisdell had submitted to the Committee on Future Organization on March 15, 1925. In this Dr. Blaisdell had offered a "definition of colleges" which differed from both the Oxford concept and the established pattern of American liberal arts colleges — a "definition of colleges" so particular and unusual that it confused those who attempted to follow it. "In all the discussion which has taken place," he wrote, "an increasing distinction has been made between (1) academic centers, which are understood to be those points at which buildings having distinctly academic utilities are grouped, i.e., laboratories, libraries, recitation halls, gymnasia, etc.; and (2) colleges, which are understood to be residential accommodations, i.e., dormitories, dining hall, common rooms, informal libraries, chapels." "It is conceived," he continued, "that several 'colleges' might be organized around a comparatively small number of academic 'centers.' These colleges should be constructed and equipped to allow the most cultural and stimulating influences to operate upon resident young people. They should be differing types and form, and should gradually develop some distinct traditional qualities." The enrollment of colleges, he suggested, should range between one hundred and fifty and three hundred students, "such as to establish and maintain an individual esprit de corps. Largely this is to be accomplished around a common dining table."

The new colleges at Claremont he foresaw as "organized on substantially the same lines as now obtain in Pomona College, and that the institutions should be distinctly and wholly separate, the administration of each to consist of a board of trustees and a faculty, with their typical powers. While these various college corporations should be separate one from another, they should be held to common standards and to loyal cooperation" through the central college, which would serve the common interests of the group of colleges. Thus he envisaged that Claremont Colleges would hold "the major portion of such property as is used in common." All graduate work and summer school activities would be carried out by it. Generally it would serve as the coordinating institution for the group of colleges.

With the incorporation of Scripps College and the assurance of funds for Claremont Colleges through the $1,000,000 bequest of Colonel Mudd, more specific measures for advancing the group plan were required. The Board of Fellows appointed a "Special Committee on Aims and Purposes," with William B. Munro as chairman and Dr. Blaisdell, a member. The committee's report, approved by the Board of Fellows in April 1927, set forth objectives and procedures for both the academic and coordinating functions of Claremont Colleges. A "primary aim" of Claremont Colleges was to serve "as the agency for determining the conditions under which individual colleges may hereafter enter and remain members of the group." Proposed "physical facilities for common use" were listed in order as: adequate land, a central library, enlargement and completion of the Pomona Science Quadrangle, reconstruction of the Claremont Inn, an auditorium with a seating capacity of 2,000, and a central heating plant. Less urgent but highly desirable facilities were noted as a "Student building, a Faculty Club House, a Museum of Fine Arts, and a Health Center." The enlargement and completion of the Pomona science quadrangle envisaged making it available for common use by the affiliated colleges "under an equitable arrangement with Pomona."

On academic procedure it was proposed that Claremont Colleges "countersign the baccalaureate degrees given by the associated colleges." The report also recommended that Claremont Colleges take over from Pomona the granting of advanced degrees and teachers' certificates and the administration of the summer school.

The Munro report stated that Claremont Colleges, as the central institution, would "not operate with the highest degree of effectiveness until the group includes three colleges at least." For a third undergraduate college the committee proposed a residential college for men with emphasis on "preliminary training for certain male vocations and professions, notably the outstanding business professions and the law." A men's college with such emphasis on the social sciences became henceforth a genuine objective of Claremont Colleges.

While some of its recommendations, such as the countersigning of baccalaureate degrees, and the enlargement of the Pomona science quadrangle, would not be followed, the Munro report presented a series of specific objectives, most of which would ultimately be attained. Together the Board of Fellows and the trustees of Pomona and Scripps laid the basis for the new structure of what was soon to be known as the Associated Colleges. Part of the process was the conversion of certain Pomona offices into joint services and the transfer from Pomona to Claremont Colleges of academic programs beyond the baccalaureate degree. As early as December 1925, the Pomona trustees and the Board of Fellows had agreed that the treasurer and controller of Pomona, E. E. Jones and George S. Sumner, would also hold such offices in Claremont

Colleges. The Pomona business office was then in Holmes Hall and there began the first joint service for the group of colleges. On June 14, 1927 the Pomona Board approved the extension of the joint business office to include Scripps College and all subsidiary corporations of any of the Associated Colleges. That day the Pomona trustees also voted to discontinue giving the master of arts degree and California teaching certificates as soon as Claremont Colleges could take over these responsibilities.

Soon academic events made history. Scripps College received its first students in September 1927, and President Jaqua's inauguration was held in the Greek Theater on the afternoon of October 14, the fortieth anniversary of the founding of Pomona. The academic procession included the visiting delegates, and the trustees and faculties of both Pomona and Scripps. President Blaisdell presided and Newton D. Baker, former Secretary of War, spoke on "Education and the State." Pomona conferred the honorary degree of Doctor of Laws on Miss Scripps, for whom the degree was received by Mrs. Florence Scripps Kellogg. Dr. Jaqua was inducted as president by Jacob B. Harper, chairman of the Scripps Board of Trustees. The day concluded with the fortieth anniversary banquet in the Big Gym.

The inaugural ceremonies and the joint celebration of Pomona's Founders Day were illustrative of the warm and generous cooperation that marked the beginning of Scripps. In addition to President Jaqua, Pomona would release two other members of its faculty to Scripps, Professor William S. Ament from the department of English, and Mary B. Eyre from the department of psychology. After the inauguration the Scripps Board expressed to the Pomona Board its "great appreciation of the unfailing interest and cooperation and invaluable service given by the Trustees, Faculty, officers and employees of Pomona College. . . . But for Pomona College and the constant help given by all connected with it, what has been accomplished would not have been possible."

The winter of 1927 brought the necessity of decision by Dr. Blaisdell regarding his relationship to the Claremont Colleges and to Pomona. Ideas with which he was not in sympathy were developing in the Board of Fellows, and he first concluded that he should not continue as head of Claremont Colleges but should remain at Pomona. Dr. Blaisdell was particularly disturbed by pressure for Claremont Colleges to appoint faculty members for conducting graduate work. He had expected Claremont Colleges to offer only such graduate work in the arts and sciences as could be carried by faculty members on appointment at Pomona and Scripps. His concern and decision at this point are best stated in his own words from his unpublished memoirs. "Mr. Fred Wilcox, a member of the Board of Fellows, and a friend to whom I was long and deeply indebted, insisted that the outcome would be immediately and seriously disastrous unless I accepted the presidency and endeavored as best I could to meet the situation. His influence, and his alone, led me to reconsider my refusal to accede to the request." When he thus committed himself to Claremont Colleges, Dr. Blaisdell and the trustee committee at last began a serious search for a president for Pomona.

Very early the committee turned to Charles K. Edmunds,whom Dr. Blaisdell had kept in mind since the effort to secure him as dean of the faculty in 1921. In the meantime, Dr. Edmunds had completed a seventeen-year presidency of Canton Christian College and had returned to his alma mater, Johns Hopkins University, where he served as provost from 1924 to 1926. Beset with problems arising from the Nationalist revolution in China, the trustees of Canton Christian College, then renamed Lingnan University, persuaded him to return to their service in 1926 and he was the American director of Lingnan in New York when the Pomona committee approached him. On January 9, 1928 Dr. Blaisdell, for the committee on the presidency, reported to the Executive Committee that Dr. Edmunds would be recommended to the Board of Trustees and that the committee had guaranteed the travelling expenses of Dr. and Mrs. Edmunds for a journey from the East to Claremont.

Mrs. Edmunds, the former Sarah Katherine Poorbaugh, had an association with the Far East even longer than that of her husband. Left an orphan in Iowa, she was adopted as a small child by an aunt who was a Christian missionary in Sendai, the principal city of Northern Honshu, Japan. Katherine Poorbaugh had had a remarkable life by the time she returned to America and entered Goucher College in Baltimore. Following her graduation from Goucher she studied music at the Peabody Conservatory and directed the Goucher Glee Club. She met Dr. Edmunds when he was home on leave from Canton Christian College, and they were married in 1909. As her husband had been president of Canton Christian College since 1907, Mrs. Edmunds as a bride assumed the responsibilities of the wife of a college president. To these she brought generous hospitality, a love of young people, and a refreshing freedom of spirit. The Edmunds had two children, Elizabeth and Richard.

Dr. and Mrs. Edmunds visited Claremont, January 24-27, 1928, and Dr. Edmunds met with the Board on January 26 at a special luncheon meeting at the University Club in Los Angeles. He spoke to the trustees of his experiences at Canton Christian College, and after discussion the Board adjourned until February 21. On that date the trustees confirmed the terms which the committee on the presidency had worked out with Dr. Edmunds, and formally elected him the fifth president of Pomona College.

The election of Dr. Edmunds, who was a scientist, marked a significant evolution in the presidency of Pomona. He was the first president of the college who was not an ordained minister. Furthermore, he had spent the greater part of his professional life outside the United States. The financial provisions of the appointment illustrated important changes in American life and in the operation of the college. For the first time, a newly appointed president of Pomona was provided with an automobile, and the terms of his retirement "at or after the age of 65" through the contributory annuity program with the Teachers Insurance and Annuity Association were stipulated.

Dr. Edmunds was to assume the presidency in May, and until that month Dr. Blaisdell remained the titular president. He had divested himself, however, of almost all internal responsibilities at Pomona. As early as September 1927 the combined demands of Pomona and Claremont Colleges were such that something had to be done to give immediate relief. Professor Burgess had been called in to assist Dr. Blaisdell when Dean Jaqua was released to Scripps, and on September 12 the Executive Committee of the Board approved the appointment of Dr. Burgess as secretary of the faculty. Thereafter he gave half his time to this increasingly important office and half to his teaching as professor of law.

However, the appointment of an influential professor as secretary of the faculty could not meet all the pressing administrative needs of Pomona in 1927-28. The Executive Committee took a further step on September 30 by appointing "an interim Executive Committee of the Faculty to have charge of the administrative affairs of the college until other arrangements can be made." Named shortly thereafter to this committee were Professors Brackett, Brooks, Burgess, and Dean Nicholl. The Executive Committee voted that after October 16, Dr. Brackett, as chairman of the interim executive committee of the faculty, "be given authority to sign documents on behalf of the college as Acting Head."

When Dr. Edmunds arrived in May he immediately took over the duties of the presidency. In faculty and cabinet meetings he showed at once the careful attention to academic matters and faculty concerns that would characterize his administration. He met first with the Executive Committee of the trustees on May 14, presenting some recommended faculty appointments for the coming year. He gave the commencement address on June 11, and its title, "A Lesson from China," indicated the wider knowledge of the Far East which his administration would bring to the college.

The commencement of 1928 was a moving occasion and a landmark in the history of Pomona. The college showed its appreciation for the inestimable services of Dr. Blaisdell by conferring on him the honorary degree of Doctor of Laws. The occasion also marked the transfer of the granting of advanced degrees to Claremont Colleges, and Dr. Blaisdell as president of Claremont Colleges conferred three Master of Arts degrees. The 1928 commencement led the editor of the *Pomona College Quarterly Magazine* to write joyously of the present and prophetically of the future. "Now the college is no longer alone in the ceremony, for this year the Claremont Colleges joined with her, and conferred their first degrees. It will be only a few years until Scripps College will take her place in the trinity of kindred schools, to be followed in the more distant future by other institutions which as yet can be only seen by the eye of faith."

CHAPTER XVI

Building the Residential College

PRESIDENT EDMUNDS' appointment took effect on April 16, 1928, and on May 7 he arrived to assume his duties in Claremont. It was characteristic of his outlook that his first official act was to participate in a ceremony of the students — the inauguration on May 10 of the officers of the student body who had been elected for 1928-29. "As the most important feature of the most important student body meeting of the year, President C. K. Edmunds appeared in public. The new President of Pomona College sat on the platform with the other new administrative officers as one of them signifying his close interest in all student body activities," reported *Student Life.* The president expressed his desire "at all times to work with the students where their two spheres of influence overlapped, and even where the students were not directly concerned." Dr. Edmunds' appearance and his statement evoked a cordial editorial on May 12. "We like President Edmunds because instead of standing on his own level and preaching down to us, he stepped to our level and talked to us. No matter how much President Blaisdell wanted to be with the students his many duties kept him from it. We hope that the administration will leave Prexy Edmunds enough time to continue the membership in the Student Body to which he was so enthusiastically received." The students were not to be disappointed, for their first meeting revealed the true measure of their new president. Charles K. Edmunds was an open man, direct and to the point, with a genuine concern for young people. He considered his primary responsibility at Pomona to be the welfare of the students, and he desired to know them well. Throughout his administration President and Mrs. Edmunds

PRESIDENT CHARLES K. EDMUNDS

would entertain at dinner each week from forty to forty-five students and faculty, and for this purpose the college built a large dining room on the north side of the President's House.

Dr. Edmunds was inaugurated on Founders Day, October 13, 1928 in a great gathering of the Pomona family. The students were expressly invited by Dr. Edmunds, and the president of the student body had an important role in planning the arrangements for the day.

Pomona had never had such a joyous inauguration. Its second, third, and fourth presidents had each taken office following a major crisis and amid uncertainty; the college could welcome its fifth president secure in the present and with faith for the future. The weather on October 13 was perfect; the rains had come early that autumn, and the campus was "bathed in mild October sunshine, with snow-capped mountains to the north and with lawns made freshly green." The inaugural exercises were held at 10:30 a.m. in the Greek Theater, the procession forming in front of Bridges Hall. The invocation was given by Holland F. Burr '14, then minister of the Oneonta Congregational Church, South Pasadena. The major address, entitled "The Objectives of Government," was by David Prescott Barrows '94, LL.D. 1914, then professor of political science at the University of California. The president was inducted by Mr. Marston with characteristic charm and wit. In his acceptance Dr. Edmunds said, "Most of all I am attracted by the students and filled with a desire to serve them and the future they represent." Greetings were brought by Dr. Blaisdell as President of Claremont Colleges, President Walter F. Dexter of Whittier College on behalf of the colleges and universities of the state of California, Dr. Morris Slemons for The Johns Hopkins University, and Professor Yan Kong Chee for Lingnan University. The honorary degree of Doctor of Laws was conferred on Max Farrand, the distinguished historian from Yale who in 1927 had come to California as director of research at the Huntington Library.

An afternoon program in Bridges Hall by alumni featured "Pomona in Fields of Thought and Service." The climax of this program was the presentation to the college of portraits of Mr. Marston, Dr. Blaisdell, Dean Norton, Professor Brackett, and Professor Spalding. The initiative for securing the portraits and their presentation had come from President Edmunds. His suggestion, made to the Executive Committee of the trustees on May 28, had been warmly received, and trustee Arthur M. Dole '96 had been asked to head an alumni committee to arrange for the painting of the portraits and their financing. The successful completion of the committee's work was not only a moving tribute to the five who were honored, all of whom were able to be present, but a valuable contribution to posterity's understanding of three pioneer faculty members, a founding trustee, and Dr. Edmunds' distinguished predecessor. At the inaugural and Founders Day dinner in the evening President Edmunds made a major statement of his own educational philosophy and the needs of the college, calling for liberal, rather than specialized education, urging that Pomona should "emphasize the *college*" as a whole rather than any of its parts.

The inaugural ceremonies reflected the mood of confidence prevalent in California in 1928. The unprecedented population growth and the remarkable economic prosperity seemed to make all plans possible. The optimism of Pomona students was reflected in the theme and dedication of the *Metate* of that year. Beginning with engravings of Merton College Chapel and Magdalen Tower, Oxford, the editors dedicated their book to "those great traditions which have made the Universities of Oxford and Cambridge justly famous, with the trust that such traditions may arise here, to make the name of Pomona as famous in the West."

Such optimism was easily shared by the Pomona faculty. Almost as soon as he took office in May 1928, President Edmunds had the pleasure of writing the members of the faculty that their salaries would be significantly increased through funds raised toward the end of the Blaisdell administration.

What did the new president from China and Johns Hopkins find when he analyzed the college and how did he elect to proceed? Above everything, he felt the urgent need to make Pomona a completely residential college. Although for years there had been plans for extensive dormitories for both men and women, only two residence halls had been built by 1928, Smiley Hall for men and

Harwood Court for women. Living and dining facilities were woefully inadequate for a college with an enrollment of 750. Women, other than the freshmen who were housed in Harwood Court, lived in approved private homes or other privately owned facilities in the vicinity of the campus. The student commons at the Claremont Inn, which earlier had brought all students together at meals, no longer sufficed and for some years it had been reserved for the women who lived at Harwood Court. Men took their meals in private homes or formed boarding clubs.

No one deplored this situation more than President Blaisdell, but he had been forced to give priority to the even greater need for classrooms and laboratories. He had told the alumni on his return from England that "if anything has grown upon me in these months of observation it has been an appreciation of the importance of a carefully developed environment as a significant element in the training of youth. We need to exalt the great fact that education is founded primarily in the exposure of youth to noble associates and surroundings in a carefully prepared environment of learning and character." Pomona's need became more evident with the building of the beautiful residence halls at Scripps College, two of which were in operation and a third under construction by October 1928.

At the time of his inauguration President Edmunds had issued the call to complete Pomona as a residential college, and had defined the program which would transform its campus life.

> Our most imperative needs have to do with those physical facilities which would make our life here together truly effective — dormitories, dining halls and college-owned, properly located residences for the president, the dean and some selected members of the faculty. To sleep in one building, go to another for meals, to yet another to entertain guests, and to another to read or to mingle with other members of the family is not a normal or an effective way of living. Properly arranged group life will create and maintain a high *esprit de corps* — a unity of feeling, sympathy and interest that will dominate every member of the group. Such groups should be cross-sections of the whole institution. A great many of the difficulties now constantly confronting us would be ameliorated, if not entirely removed, if we first put our students into healthy, congenial, attractive, well regulated homes.

Fortunately there were some funds at hand and some preliminary steps had been taken toward achieving a men's campus. By a letter of October 12, 1920 to President Blaisdell, Eli P. Clark, vice-president of the Board of Trustees, had conveyed to the college 150 acres of land at the mouth of Las Flores Canyon, property then valued at $10,000. In March 1926, the Board of Trustees sold the property to the Southern Counties Land Company, a corporation owned by William Randolph Hearst, for $600,000. Marston expressed the joy and gratitude of the trustees to Mr. and Mrs. Clark on March 13: "I beg to assure you that the trustees were really overwhelmed by the magnitude of the transaction. It is a noble gift and it will redound to your honor for generations to come." Ernest E. Jones wrote President Blaisdell in Paris that the sale had "pleased Mr. Clark greatly."

The funds set up in the "Clark Trust" provided capital for a major development and had been considered immediately for dormitory construction. At the meeting of the trustees on June 16, 1926 A. J. McFadden '01 suggested that some part of the money from the sale of the E. P. Clark land be used for men's dormitories. Because of Dr. Blaisdell's absence in Europe, the trustees limited their action to the authorization of a committee to consider the matter of men's residence halls, confer with the president, and report at a subsequent meeting. On November 19, 1926 the trustees voted that "Sumner M. Spaulding act as architect for the men's dormitories" and approved a contract with the firm of Webber and Spaulding.

Dr. Blaisdell had met Sumner Spaulding in Europe and was much impressed by the imaginative young architect. On his return he had recommended that Spaulding receive the commission at Pomona. In giving their approval, the trustees had made an inspired choice. A graduate in architecture of the Massachusetts Institute of Technology who had spent some of the years 1921-26 in study in Europe, Spaulding was just beginning his practice in Los Angeles, where his planning of the Civic Center would make possible the remarkable group of city, county, state, and federal buildings which constitute the heart of public life in Southern California today. He would give Pomona a group of the finest residential buildings on any American campus.

Although the trustees hoped to begin work on the men's campus in 1927-28, construction was delayed a year by financing and the choice of a site. Meanwhile, the trustees voted to name the entire group of buildings the Eli P. Clark Dormitories. On November 16, 1928 the Executive Committee confirmed the location of the dormitories as the area between Dartmouth and Amherst Avenues, north from Sixth Street to Eighth Street. At the same meeting the committee approved a contract of $305,000 for one unit of the dormitories and the refectory.

As designed by Spaulding the men's campus would include eight units: four residence halls, a refectory, a lounge, an assembly room, and a tower. The first unit to be constructed was to be a residence hall for freshmen. Ground for the dormitory and the refectory was broken on a combined Matriculation Day-Parents Day, February 9, 1929. Dean Emeritus Norton spoke and the first spadeful of earth was turned by donor Eli P. Clark. It was a tribute to the contractor, Stover Brothers, that both the residence hall and the dining hall were ready for use when the college opened in the autumn of 1929. Unit One of Eli P. Clark Hall then housed 108 freshmen, their faculty adviser, and three instructors. The first meal was served in the dining hall on the evening of September 17 with the freshmen, other new students, and the faculty in attendance.

Dedication ceremonies for the residence hall and the dining hall were held at a dinner on October 12 with both Mr. and Mrs. Clark present. The occasion was scheduled as a part of Founders Day, and the capacity crowd included alumni from San Diego to Santa Barbara. The dining hall, which had been constructed by funds given anonymously by Mr. Marston, was named at his request the Lucien Frary Refectory, in memory of a much beloved former pastor of Pilgrim Congregational Church, Pomona, who had been a most helpful trustee of the college from 1892 to 1903. Mrs. Frary was present for the dedication.

The academic year 1929-30 was one of transition in the life of the men of Pomona College. The freshmen lived in Clark Hall and ate at Frary, as did some sophomores and upperclassmen. Other students, except those in Smiley Hall, continued to take their meals in private homes or the student boarding clubs. During the year the college pressed forward with dormitory construction, and two

Clark Hall and Frary Dining Hall

View of Mt. Baldy from Bosbyshell Court

The First Dinner Dance in Frary Hall

additional units for men were ready for occupancy in September 1930. Thereafter, all Pomona men were expected to live in the dormitories and take their meals at Frary unless they had received permission not to do so from Dean Nicholl. With completion of these units, which were financed by $200,000 from the Clark Trust and a $250,000 interest-bearing loan from endowment to be amortized at the rate of $15,000 a year, construction on the men's campus came to a halt and would not be resumed until 1953.

Although some desirable features, particularly the lounge, were lacking, the handsome group of buildings brought comfort and privacy to students, and impressive beauty to the college. The Clark campus included features that had most impressed Dr. Blaisdell in Oxford. The student rooms, some of which had fireplaces, were grouped around courtyards and for the most part were reached directly from a court or a staircase. Whether in suites or as singles, an individual room was provided for each man and gave him much of the ease of a gentleman's room in the Oxford colleges of the 1920's.

In his European travels, Spaulding had been greatly impressed by Spanish architecture, and the Pomona buildings with their Romanesque arches reflected much of what he had seen in the Balearic Islands. The combination of white reenforced concrete walls, red tiled roofs, spacious courtyards, a cloistered walk, and the enormous plaza with its fountain and steps gave harmony to the three dormitories and the great dining hall where heavy wooden tables added to the distinction of the interior.

When college opened in September 1930, the buildings of the men's campus had been enhanced by a great work of art. Its initiation and achievement were so unusual that, not surprisingly, legend surrounding its creation has outrun fact. As Frary Hall was completed, its extensive and high walls seemed to many to call for further embellishment. Spaulding thought of a fresco by one of the Mexican muralists, and discussed the matter with José Pijoan, adjunct professor of Hispanic civilization and lecturer in the history of art at Pomona. According to Pijoan, Spaulding "pressed him to plan and work this decoration."

Since coming to Pomona in 1924, Pijoan had won wide recognition by his writings, notably the five-volume *Historia del Mundo* and a two-volume *Historia del Arte.* His prestige as an art critic had been enhanced by an invitation from the Spanish government to serve as advisor on art for the twin expositions held in 1929 in Seville and Barcelona, for which Pomona had granted him leave in the autumn of 1928. Pijoan required no "pressing" for an art project that appealed to him and he took immediate steps to follow through on Spaulding's request.

The times were propitious for securing a Mexican artist, for political changes in Mexico had deprived the muralists of financial support at home. In 1930 two of the greatest of these, Diego Rivera and José Clemente Orozco, were expatriates in the United States. Rivera had enjoyed several outstanding commissions, first in California and later in the East, but Orozco, who had gone to New York, had been less successful in America and was in desperate financial need. He hoped to find a wall in some non-commercial institution where he could demonstrate his creativity with a large mural. Pijoan first thought of Rivera for Pomona, assuming he would bring more prestige to the college. However, two Mexican friends of Orozco who were living in Los Angeles learned of the proposed mural in Frary and sought to win the commission for Orozco. Aragón Leiva, contributor to Spanish language film magazines, and Jorge Juan Crespo de la Serna, painter and critic, assembled photographs and slides of Orozco's frescos in Mexico and won Pijoan so completely that he asked Crespo to get in touch immediately with the "New World Michelangelo."

When Crespo began correspondence with Orozco in January 1930, he found the artist eager to come to Pomona, for as his friend and agent, Alma Reed, later wrote, "Mural prospects in New York and elsewhere in the United States were virtually nonexistent. Yet precisely at that bleak hour when the Great Depression, like some cataclysmic tidal wave, was engulfing the hopes of most creative artists, Orozco's genius met a supreme opportunity."[1] A commission for him to paint in Frary Hall was concluded through letters from Crespo and Pijoan, between January and March 1930.

Neither President Edmunds nor the trustees had any part in arranging for Orozco to paint in Frary Hall. The only agreement was between the artist and Pijoan, who expected to raise the funds for the fresco from Pomona students and other donors. Pijoan led Crespo to believe that five thousand dollars were already in hand or guaranteed, and Crespo communicated this to Orozco, who with this understanding took the train for California in late March.

Pijoan first endeavored to secure funds for the mural from the men taking their meals in Frary Hall, asking them to raise a thousand dollars toward a total represented as two thousand dollars. Less than a thousand dollars were in hand when Orozco arrived in Los Angeles. Met at the train by men from Clark Hall, he was told that they and Pijoan had not been able to raise the funds required for the proposed mural. Though shaken by the news, Orozco had come too far and had too great need of the Frary commission to consider withdrawing. "Do you still have the *wall*?" he asked. "Yes, and a very good one," replied the student leader. Crespo suggested that money to make a start would be secured as Pijoan was continuing to solicit support, and offered his own service as Orozco's assistant. The Pomona art department invited Orozco and Crespo to live in Clark Hall and to take their meals in Frary as college guests. In this dramatic change of what he

[1]Most helpful on Orozco were Alma Reed, *Orozco*, Oxford University Press, 1956, and Leopoldo Castedo, *A History of Latin American Art and Architecture*, London, 1969.

thought had been the arrangements, Orozco maintained his dignity and even joked with the students as they drove him from Los Angeles to Claremont. "Orozco, Crespo Mexican Fresco Painters Arrive," "Two Months to be Required for Completion of Frary Mural Decoration," were headlines in *Student Life* on March 22. All students were urged to join the freshmen in raising the needed funds.

Despite multiple and repeated suggestions from Pijoan, Orozco alone was responsible for the theme of the mural. Weeks before leaving New York he had determined that the heroic figure of Prometheus should be the subject of the Pomona mural. During the winter of 1929-30, Orozco had been inspired by a series of programs in which distinguished Hellenists read and interpreted Aeschylus' *Prometheus Bound.* In Claremont, Orozco lost little time in finalizing his theme. As the *Los Angeles Times* reported on April 5, "Passing up the customary pageant of Indians, Padres, Forty-niners and Spanish dancers" Orozco chose "the universal theme of Prometheus bringing the fire to man, as a fitting symbol of education."

As Orozco and Crespo lived in Clark Hall and ate in Frary, Pomona students enjoyed the unique experience of seeing a fresco take form. *Student Life* published a "Fresco Edition" on April 19, in which articles by Professors Denison and Pitman strongly supported the fresco which had begun to receive some faculty and town opposition. F. Raymond Iredell, assistant professor of philosophy, wrote that many had been "dreaming of the time when the walls of the refectory would be covered with some fitting artistic decoration, and we are grateful to Professor Pijoan for taking the initiative in starting such a project, and in giving all of us the opportunity of having some part, however small, in making possible its realization." Pijoan himself thought of an even larger project. In an article headlined "More Frescos Visioned," he wrote, "We have been dreaming to make Frary Hall the hall of the giants. On the arch around the fireplace we would have liked to paint the 'Parents of the Giants'; Tellus, the earth, Oceanus, or the water; Uranus, the heavens, throwing hail and rain down below. On the side walls should go 'Combat of the Gods and the Giants', in each side of every window a god and a giant fighting. And on the wall above the door, the 'Doom of the Giants,' when they tried to escalade Olympus." He proposed a budget of $25,000 and hoped "to be able to nail down Orozco and Crespo for the next year and a half."

There was no prospect of accomplishing such a large undertaking. Funds were not available and it would have been extremely difficult to secure them, for in many quarters the great Mexican muralists were then considered dangerous revolutionaries. The intensity of this feeling was illustrated by the rejection of a work of Diego Rivera which had been commissioned for Rockefeller Center then under construction in New York.

Despite some objections the Prometheus mural was completed amid strong student and faculty approval. The trustees refused to yield to pressure and tabled indefinitely a suggestion for removal of the fresco. When the mural was completed in mid-June, the college gave a dedicatory dinner in Frary Hall. Alma Reed had come out from New York and her account of the evening shows the warmth of feeling with which Pomona had received Orozco and Prometheus. President Edmunds spoke appreciatively of Orozco's work, saying the moral effect of the artist's stay at Pomona was a genuine and incontrovertible benefit to everyone on the campus. He praised the fine example set by Orozco through "his faithful observance of working schedules, rare modesty, his meticulous regard for craftsmanship, integrity, his simplicity, and kindliness of manner, his devotion to purpose, and his high standards of personal conduct." President Edmunds then presented Orozco with the contributions to the mural fund, which were approximately $2500. Professor Pijoan left Claremont in June for European travel, and later to lecture in art at the University of Chicago. His imagination and the genius of Orozco had given Pomona an invaluable work of art which would become known throughout the world.

After the completion of Prometheus, Alma Reed sent newspaper and magazine articles, and statements from architects, educators, writers, and others who were enthusiastic about the mural in Frary Hall, to Professor Artemas Packard, head of the art department at

Dartmouth College, suggesting that "Dartmouth might do well to follow Pomona's example." Her suggestion resulted in the commissioning of Orozco in 1933 to paint frescos on the walls of the reserve book room of the new Baker Library.

The Clark campus was embellished further by the erection of a beautifully proportioned fountain in the plaza west of Frary Hall. The fountain is the outward symbol of a most important gift by Edward P. and Mary G. Bosbyshell. On his death in 1926, Mr. Bosbyshell had bequeathed $50,000 to Pomona to be used as his executors and the college deemed most expedient and beneficial. The executors, who were members of the Bosbyshell family, cordially agreed to President Blaisdell's suggestion that the funds be used to purchase a well to supply water for the college, requesting only that a memorial plaque be placed somewhere on the projected men's campus. The Bosbyshell Fountain, which adds so much to the campus, is also a physical reminder of the valuable well that since 1927 has supplied water for the college buildings and the grounds.

The Pomona administration was successful in developing effectively the educational and social values of the growing residential campus. Great wisdom was shown in the choice of the individuals to whom such large and important responsibilities were entrusted. President Edmunds was assisted by Dean Nicholl and by Dean Gibson, to whom he would look increasingly for counsel and guidance. Mrs. Edna Prescott Davis, for the previous sixteen years director of dormitories at the University of Oregon, was appointed director of dormitories and dining halls at Pomona, effective September 1929. Earl J. "Fuzz" Merritt '25, instructor in physical education and freshman class adviser, was named the social director of the men's campus. Mrs. Davis and Mr. Merritt and his family lived in apartments built as integral parts of Clark Hall and took their meals with the students in Frary. Breakfast and lunch were cafeteria style, but dinner was served and the men were obliged to wear coats and ties. Mr. Merritt, who presided, began dinner with a blessing, later made announcements, and finally indicated when the diners were free to leave.

Living arrangements for men at Pomona College were transformed by September 1930. Almost all the men lived on the campus and dined at Frary Hall. Fraternity rooms, for which the fraternities paid only a small rent to the college, had been constructed in the basements of the new dormitories. Frary, with three smaller dining rooms in addition to the refectory, provided not only a dining hall for men but a place for many smaller college meetings, and for some all-college events which had been held at the Guildhall of the Claremont Church.

An all student-faculty Christmas Supper was instituted and soon became an annual event with its own cherished traditions. The freshman class secured and brought in a large tree, and committees of students decorated the hall. The official hosts were President and Mrs. Edmunds and the Associated Students. All members of faculty families and staff were included and the Associated Women Students provided a special Christmas party for small children. Trustees and their spouses were invited and many attended. For most members of the college community this event became the high point of the year.

The housing of Pomona men on the Eli P. Clark campus, where in Mr. Marston's words "they lived like kings," emphasized the less fortunate position of the Pomona women. Only half of them could be accommodated in college-owned residences and this was made possible by placing 185 women in Harwood Court, which had been built for 135, and by using two nearby cottages which housed eight and thirteen, respectively. The other 200 women lived in approved, privately-run boarding houses in the vicinity of the campus. Miss Gibson described these houses as "often too crowded, with proper heat always a problem, bathroom facilities usually inadequate" and lacking in suitable places for the women to entertain men. These conditions, difficult in themselves, were made more so by the new situation in Claremont after 1930. "The splendid and adequate new residence units for Pomona men and the attractive residence halls for women at Scripps College provide a contrast with the conditions under which Pomona women live which is hard to meet," Dean Gibson reported to the president. Scripps had completed its four residence halls by September 1930, and all of its 200 students were living on the campus and taking their meals in beautiful dining halls.

Dr. Edmunds fully shared Miss Gibson's concern and he was very hopeful that the college would soon be able to secure the urgently needed facilities. Preliminary plans had been drawn for two residence halls, each for ninety women, and two dining halls to be served from one kitchen. These new buildings were to be located to the east of Harwood Court, and the estimated cost was $580,000. At the same time, a kitchen and dining hall to cost $60,000 were proposed for Harwood Court. Ultimately a building program on this general plan would be completed, but the funds were not available in 1930-31 and several years would elapse before any construction could be undertaken east of Harwood Court.

However, the dining hall and kitchen for Harwood Court were constructed and were placed in service in September 1931. Once again the family of Charles E. Harwood, who had served Pomona as a trustee since 1899, had generously come to the assistance of the college. His children, trustee Edward C. Harwood '95 and his wife, and Paul H. Harwood '98, and Mrs. Isabella Harwood Scott, gave the dining hall in memory of their sister, Aurelia Squier Harwood, who had contributed generously to the building of Harwood Court which honored their mother. At the dedication of Aurelia Squier Harwood Memorial Dining Hall on Founders Day, October 14, 1931, with Dean Gibson presiding, tributes were paid to Miss Harwood by Dr. Blaisdell and President Aurelia Reinhardt of Mills College. Miss Harwood, who had died in 1928, was a nature lover and an early conservationist. She was the first woman to serve as president of the Sierra Club. The building, designed by Webber and Spaulding, comprised a main dining room seating approximately 200 and a smaller room for twenty-four which also served as a reception room. With the construction of Harwood Dining Hall the student dining room was discontinued at the Claremont Inn, and thereafter the Inn became a center for the faculty, the community, and the general public. A quarter century of student use of the Inn, with its memories and traditions, had come to an end.

The Growing Role of Claremont Colleges

While Pomona was building its residential campus, the role and evolving functions of Claremont Colleges began to take form. The transitional years, 1928-32, were difficult and exacting, particularly for the college presidents. Claremont Colleges owned no facilities and with the appointment of President Edmunds in 1928 Dr. Blaisdell needed to find another office for himself and a new home for his family. The office problem was solved for 1928-29 by Dr. Blaisdell's remaining in Sumner Hall,where he used a reception room adjacent to the Pomona president's office. With the academic year 1929-30, Claremont Colleges established its administration in a rented house at 818 College Avenue,which continued as the offices of Dr. Blaisdell, Mr. Bernard, and their assistants for the following three years. Early faculty appointees had offices in Sumner or Holmes Hall.

Although they suffered the inconvenience of temporary living arrangements for some eighteen months, the Blaisdell family at the end of 1929 could move into a beautiful new house which had been constructed as the president's house of Claremont Colleges. The Board of Fellows raised funds for a white brick, two-story, ten-room house of "New Orleans architecture," which included a reception room, living room, dining room, maid's room, kitchen, sewing room, and four bedrooms. Located at the southwest corner of Dartmouth Avenue and Ninth Street, this gracious residence with its attractive garden set a high standard for the future buildings of Claremont Colleges.

With full-time presidents in office at Pomona, Scripps, and Claremont Colleges, progress was made in working out constitutional relationships and operational procedures among the three corporations. Since the incorporation of Scripps College, Dr. Blaisdell had enjoyed an ex-officio relationship with its Board of Trustees. Although he continued to attend Pomona board meetings after the coming of President Edmunds, he was present by courtesy rather than right. The situation was regularized when the Pomona trustees on June 18, 1929 voted that "The President of Claremont Colleges be an ex-officio, non-voting member of the Board of Trustees of Pomona College." As the Board of Fellows accorded similar status to the presidents of Pomona and Scripps, and as other trustees of both Pomona and Scripps were voting members of the Board of Fellows, constitutional means of communication were established among the three boards and the three presidents. To improve the growing need for cooperation and communication in Claremont an administrative council composed of the president and one faculty member of each institution was established in 1930.

Claremont Colleges, as conceived by Dr. Blaisdell, would be the colleges acting together for common purposes. This concept was expressed by the Claremont Colleges' motto, *Multa Lumina, Lux Una* (many lamps, one light). From 1928 through 1932, the institutions made impressive progress in determining the means by which they could work together. The terms "joint services" and "joint facilities" entered the Claremont academic vocabulary. Some of these would be amplifications or transfers of long established services at Pomona, such as the business office and graduate work. Others would be new creations made possible by the growing need and strength of the Associated Colleges.

The full professors of the Associated Colleges were constituted as "the General Faculty of Claremont Colleges," and it was upon the recommendation of this body that graduate degrees were granted. At first all graduate instruction was given by members of the Pomona and Scripps faculties, but soon appointments for graduate teaching were made by Claremont Colleges itself. Great impetus was given to graduate instruction when Pomona transferred to Claremont Colleges the granting of California teaching credentials. While Pomona faculty members would continue to offer some courses in education, the administration of credential programs and most instruction in teacher education became the responsibility of Claremont Colleges.

Building on the earlier work of Pomona, Claremont Colleges soon established one of the most respected programs in professional education in California. Professor Aubrey A. Douglass, who had served with distinction at Pomona since 1926, moved to Claremont Colleges in 1929 as head of the work in teacher education. Because much of the work of the summer session was given for teachers in the public schools, the administration of the summer session was transferred from Pomona to Claremont Colleges in 1931. However, Pomona retained the marine biology program which Professor Hilton continued to conduct each summer at the laboratory at Laguna Beach.

Directing attention to the needs and interests of students, Claremont Colleges from 1930 through 1932 began an extensive building program which ranged from a central heating plant to a spectacular auditorium. A joint health service for the colleges was organized in 1928, and Dr. Morrill L. Ilsley, the physician at Colgate University, was appointed head of the medical service of the Associated Colleges. In June 1929, Mr. and Mrs. Hiram T. Cleaver gave Claremont Colleges funds for an infirmary as a memorial to their brother-in-law, Colonel Seeley W. Mudd. Completed in 1931, this building served the growing student bodies of the Associated Colleges.

The building program of Claremont Colleges brought transformation and beautification of the eastern end of Marston Quadrangle where stood the unsightly Pomona heating plant, an enclosed swimming pool, and the Renwick gymnasium which housed the department of physical education for women. Further east was the "Big Gym." The desire of the colleges to build a jointly operated heating plant to serve the group of institutions led to the removal of the old heating plant and the construction of a new plant on First Street. This change provided a prime location for a building of major significance.

After the building of Bridges Hall of Music, President Blaisdell had kept in touch with Mr. and Mrs. Bridges and from time to time informed them of the progress of the music department at Pomona. In a series of letters from August 1924 to July 1925, he spoke of additional building needs for music, particularly a small hall and an additional library. "My hope," he wrote Mr. Bridges on February 17, 1925, "is that this work may be ultimately so consequential here as to compare with the work in Rochester University, which Mr. Eastmen has endowed and which has become so famous throughout the East." Mr. Bridges called on Dr. Blaisdell in Sumner Hall in the spring of 1925 and expressed his continued interest in music at Pomona, suggesting that the college might sometime need a large hall and that possibly he would be able to help. Dr. Blaisdell renewed this conversation on July 9, 1925 and sent Mr. Bridges a diagram of the campus, saying, "Our hope has been that we might have a large auditorium at the head of the quadrangle, thus using, as you may recall, a drop in the land in the east. . . . It would be the central and most commanding building on the campus." Mr. Bridges replied promptly but held out no immediate hope of such a gift. But his interest continued and on May 29, 1928 *Student Life* carried the headline, "Bridges Donate New Auditorium; Will Face Marston Quadrangle." Dr. Blaisdell had just announced that Mr. and Mrs. Bridges had given funds to Claremont Colleges for a large auditorium to seat 2500 people, the building to be a further memorial to their daughter, Mabel Shaw Bridges '08.

More than three years elapsed before the auditorium was completed. William Templeton Johnson, the architect whom the Bridges family desired, was in Spain working on the United States Government buildings for the forthcoming International Exposition at Seville. The death of Mr. Bridges on May 9, 1929, less than a year after making his gift to Claremont Colleges, delayed the beginning of construction until 1930. The building was completed in the autumn of 1931. Mrs. Bridges was present for the dedication service on September 18, which was attended by 1500 students, faculty, and friends of the colleges.

Mabel Shaw Bridges Auditorium, one of the largest and best equipped auditoriums on any American campus, was a dramatic illustration of the value of joint facilities for the Associated Colleges. With outstanding management, the colleges from the beginning took full advantage of the opportunities which the building brought. Primary credit for this achievement was due Robert J. Bernard '17, secretary of the Board of Fellows and assistant to Dr. Blaisdell. Under his direction the earlier Pomona music and art course was succeeded by the Artist Course which brought the world's finest music to Claremont.

In its first year the Artist Course included concerts by the Los Angeles Philharmonic Orchestra; Richard Crooks, operatic tenor;

Gunna Johansen, the leading pianist of Denmark; the Don Cossack Chorus; Sigrid Onegin, a leading contralto; and Paul Robeson, baritone. Students of the colleges were given free tickets, and regulár subscribers to the Artist Course came from Claremont and the surrounding communities. Concert nights were gala occasions with formal dress for both men and women and with special dinners served in the college dining halls, often with pre-concert entertainment.

As "the central and most commanding building on the campus" Bridges Auditorium brought majestic beauty to Marston Quadrangle. To make way for the auditorium, Renwick Gymnasium, "Little Gym" to the students, was moved east and placed north of the "Big Gym." The enclosed swimming pool had to be destroyed but was replaced by a new pool adjacent to the Memorial Training Quarters. A new road, "College Way," beginning between orange groves at the juncture of Eighth Street and Columbia Avenue, curving southward past the Eli P. Clark Campus and terminating east of Sumner Hall, enhanced both the auditorium and the quadrangle.

South of the quadrangle, Pomona designed and landscaped the area between Sumner Hall and Bridges Hall of Music as a Memorial Court, thus creating a place of quiet beauty. Sumner Spaulding's design of the gates and the wall and the landscaping by Ralph Cornell brought Sumner Hall and Bridges Hall into pleasant harmony. The completion of the Memorial Court was marked on May 28, 1929 by a convocation in Bridges Hall addressed by Professor Denison, and by dedicatory exercises in the Court, with participation by President Edmunds and representatives of the four college classes.

The extensive building among the three Claremont institutions made evident the need of Claremont Colleges for administrative and academic facilities. The president's office remained in the rented residence at 818 College Avenue. The joint business office, still in Holmes Hall, required additional space. A graduate library being developed by Willis H. Kerr who, in addition to his duties as librarian at Pomona, was director of libraries for Claremont Colleges, had attained a total of some 8,000 volumes, and these had to be housed in the already crowded Carnegie Library at Pomona. Offices and seminar rooms were also necessary for the growing program of graduate instruction. Moreover, a more imposing physical presence was necessary for the Claremont Colleges administration.

Once again Ellen Browning Scripps led in meeting a great need. Her gift of $75,000 joined with $100,000 from other sources made possible an attractive academic-administration building. An excellent site east of College Avenue, in the block between Ninth and Tenth Streets, was assured by George W. Marston who gave land that could be exchanged for the desired location. Gordon Kaufmann designed the building as a modern adaptation of Italian Renaissance style and in harmony with the buildings of Scripps College. The structure occupied the entire block, with the library wing on Ninth Street, and the business office wing facing Tenth Street. The panelled offices of the administrative suite included an attractive Board of Fellows Room, and the pleasant faculty offices and seminar rooms set a high standard.

The building was named for Jacob C. Harper, who as Miss Scripps' adviser, trustee of Pomona 1925-29, a founding member of the Board of Fellows, and first chairman of the Board of Trustees of Scripps College, had been a leader and devoted worker in the development of the Associated Colleges. Harper Hall was dedicated with impressive ceremonies on February 19, 1932. In his dedicatory address Mr. Marston emphasized that in its "service for all present and future generations" the building represented "the inherent idea of the Claremont Colleges enterprise, the idea of a voluntary unity in an association of colleges and a use in common of certain advantages afforded by a central institution." With faith in the future Marston continued prophetically, "When Claremont Colleges is older and richer and the library rooms are overflowing with books, there will rise on the campus the greater library that is in our plans for the future." William L. Honnold, chairman of the Board of Fellows, was an attentive listener.

The importance of Harper Hall as a functioning library was further emphasized by a conference on libraries held in conjunction with its dedication. Among those who spoke were William

Warner Bishop, librarian of the University of Michigan, and Andrew Keogh, librarian of Yale University. Mr. Kerr speaking on "the Claremont Libraries" reported the combined holdings of Pomona, Scripps, and Claremont Colleges as approximately 100,000 volumes, half of which had been added since 1925.

The celebration and satisfaction of February 19, 1932 could not still the foreboding with which trustees and presidents regarded the immediate future. They knew that with Harper Hall the building program in all the Claremont Colleges had come to a halt. The United States and the Western World were in the depths of the Great Depression.

CHAPTER XVII

Pomona in the Great Depression

BECAUSE THE STATE lacked the diversified economy that characterizes it today, the Great Depression was very severe in California. The loss in values was catastrophic; in 1932 total farm income was only half what it had been in 1929, and there were thousands of mortgage foreclosures. Mass unemployment affected both country and city, and in 1934 more than 1,250,000 people, approximately one-fifth of the population of the state, were on relief. The strain on the economy was widely reflected in many aspects of California's social and economic structure.

The autumn of 1929 had found Pomona College, like the nation, expanding and supremely confident of its future. The pressure for admission was such that the Executive Committee of the Board of Trustees authorized that for the academic year 1929-30 the enrollment be increased from 750 to 800. The class of '33 was thus so large that it was necessary to establish two new college houses for freshman women.

While there was some reduction in 1930-31, the college did not experience a marked loss in enrollment until the following academic year. By September 1931 Pomona was no longer able to hold its normal enrollment of 750. The reduction in numbers was due primarily to the loss of students already in the college who were unable to find the summer work on which they had depended to meet their financial needs. In September 1931 such students numbered 108, many of whom transferred to state universities or other less expensive institutions. Enrollment, which was 729 in September 1931, decreased each semester and by the second semester of 1933-34 only 591 regular students were in attendance.

The college made valiant efforts to meet the grave financial problem of students. Handling of requests for credit, "offering as collateral stocks, bonds and real estate," was entrusted by the trustees to a committee comprised of the controller, the dean of the college, and the dean of women. The trustees enjoined the committee to be "as liberal in attitude as reasonable safety will warrant" and to take "obligations for tuition" that might "prove slower in collection than in normal times." The college increased the student loan fund by $1500, and reduced the minimum room and board charge by twenty-five dollars a year, effective September 1933. The catalogue carried the following table of student expenses for the academic year 1933-34:

	Minimum	Average	Generous
General Tuition	$300	$ 300	$ 300
Board and Room	375	475	550
Books and Fees	35	45	100
Personal Expenses	125	180	300
Total	$835	$1000	$1250

Loss of student income was accompanied by lower endowment income and a marked decrease in gifts. The college deficit, which was $28,000 for 1930-31, mounted to $50,000 for 1931-32 and presented a financial crisis requiring drastic action. The Executive Committee invited the president of the Board and eight senior members of the faculty to meet with it on September 12, 1932 to consider revision of the educational and general budget for 1932-33. It was the conclusion of this meeting that the revised budget should "include a salary reduction of ten per cent to all persons on the payroll." In adopting this recommendation, the trustees set the total educational and general expenditures for 1932-33 at $436,605, a sum $78,701 less than that of 1931-32.

Despite this drastic reduction, the college's financial condition continued to worsen and constantly concerned the trustees. Illustrative of their desperate efforts to save were suggestions that library expense "be confined to income from library endowment" and "the night use of laboratories by students be dispensed with." The budget for 1933-34 was revised downward in October to expenditures of $399,502. A significant portion of the reduction was achieved by a further salary cut of five per cent.

The state and spirit of the college were epitomized by an editorial in the July 1933 issue of the *Pomona College Quarterly Magazine.* "The last Triennium," Professor Clifford Nott Hand wrote, "has been made up, for the most part, of frustrated plans and deferred hopes. In almost every phase of college life the necessity for retrenchment has inhibited the consummation of promising projects for expansion and enrichment. This has been the common experience and the uncomplaining and dignified acceptance of drastic cuts has demonstrated the loyalty and unselfishness of the disappointed." The following year these drastic cuts included the *Pomona College Quarterly Magazine* itself, which was discontinued with the April 1934 number. President Edmunds announced that henceforth college publications would be restricted to official bulletins and news letters for the alumni, a policy that would continue until the early 1960's.

The decline in the Pomona budget continued through 1934-35; expenditures were set at $390,180, and tuition income was based on an enrollment of 625. But the low point of the Depression had been reached at last, and Pomona with the nation began a slow but steady recovery.

In the early years of his administration President Edmunds courageously and effectively presented the capital needs of the college to alumni and friends. Declaring that Pomona had entered "a pivotal period" in its history, he analyzed the situation in the *Pomona College Quarterly Magazine* in February 1930. *Externally* he saw the rapid rise of junior colleges, *locally* "the new responsibilities and privileges and problems which Pomona now faces as one of the group of Associated Colleges in Claremont," and *internally* "the inadequacy of the present resources to develop or maintain either the faculties or the facilities that will enable Pomona to do effectively what she had already undertaken."

Dr. Blaisdell reenforced President Edmunds' interpretation of Pomona's critical needs and emphasized the strength of Pomona as essential to the success of all the Associated Colleges. Dr. Blaisdell was aware of the extensive needs of Pomona, but he had hoped to meet these at the same time that new institutions were being founded. "Pomona, which has given so lavishly to the undertaking," he wrote in the *Pomona College Quarterly Magazine,* March 1930, "should find its burdens lightened by the common organization. New friends have come to Scripps and Claremont Colleges. Their interests are not limited to Scripps and Claremont. . . . There are burdens which Pomona has been obliged to carry alone under the old form which should now be borne by the combined constituency. The time is at hand when we should all sit down together to assess the needs of our common task."

To alumni and faculty who may have doubted the wisdom of the group plan Dr. Blaisdell said, "It was not a question of whether we loved the old separate college. It was a question whether under the conditions of free education and the junior college system of California a small, isolated, four-year college could be a permanent and adequate institution. That both Harvard and Yale with the Harvard House plan and the Yale College plan have now chosen the path which Pomona first announced is certainly significant testimony to our forethought."

Pomona set forth its needs in September 1931 in a comprehensive and attractive brochure, entitled "An Invitation." Its sixty-four pages and many illustrations constituted an outstanding presentation of the history, program, and aspirations of the college. Stating that from its beginning Pomona had been a "creation of sacrifice, affection and idealism," the brochure invited its readers to meet present needs in this spirit.

The total assets of the college in 1931 were $6,500,000, of which $2,250,000 was invested in buildings, equipment, and grounds, $2,500,000 in endowment producing income for college purposes, and $1,750,000 in trust funds and annuities of which the income was not available for college use. President Edmunds felt that added income of $125,000 annually would be needed. The endowment sought for an individual professorship was $100,000. Provision for "steady growth of the library to meet current needs" would require $200,000 in endowment. New academic buildings most desired were an extension of the library building, a botany building, and a new physics building which was considered "the most urgent." For student living greatest emphasis was placed on additional dormitories and dining halls for the women's campus. Additional dormitories, a social hall, an assembly hall, and a gymnasium were sought for the men's campus.

The program presented in "An Invitation" was not designed for a capital gifts campaign comparable to Pomona's earlier Three Million Dollar campaign. This was just as well, for the times proved increasingly unpropitious. Although the college would attain ultimately all the major objectives set forth in "An Invitation," the immediate response was meager. Gifts for all purposes, which were $188,352.97 in 1931-32, dropped to $58,892.88 for 1932-33, and to $28,408.39 for 1933-34. Losses in invested funds had been so severe in 1931-32 that the permanent assets of Pomona at the end of 1933-34 stood at $6,577,397.49, little more than the total of three years before.

The situation in Claremont had become so critical that the three colleges in Claremont united in a joint appeal for current funds for 1934-35. A joint trustee committee with Harvey S. Mudd as chairman and William B. Himrod as vice-chairman sought $50,000, of which $30,000 was for Pomona, and $10,000 each for Scripps and Claremont Colleges. "For four years the colleges have steadily diminished their budgets rather than make such an appeal," Dr. Blaisdell stated. "They have borne quietly the heavy sacrifices which reductions have involved." He warned that the colleges might find it necessary to repeat this appeal for a second and perhaps a third year but he was confident that "in due time funds and student attendance will return, enabling the group of colleges to continue their characteristic development and great service."

A Changing Board of Trustees

While the Board of Trustees was dealing with the serious economic problems of the college, its members gave much thought to the membership and operation of the Board itself. At the first trustee meeting he attended after his election, President Edmunds was asked "to look over the field with a view of finding three women to be later elected to the Board." On March 12, 1929 Mrs. Susanna Bixby Bryant of Los Angeles was elected and became the first woman to serve as a trustee of Pomona. Mrs. Bryant, the spirited wife of Ernest Bryant, a distinguished Los Angeles physician, was the daughter of John W. Bixby, who had established and developed a large ranch in Orange County. She had a deep interest in botany, particularly in the native plants of California. In 1927 she had established on the family property the Rancho Santa Ana Botanical Garden as a memorial to her father. As a Pomona trustee Mrs. Bryant came to know and admire the botanical research of Professor Munz, who in turn was much impressed with the work she had initiated at the Rancho Santa Ana Garden. From their collaboration came valuable encouragement for the Pomona botany department and the development of one of the most significant botanical gardens in the United States.

Mrs. Warren Olney, Jr. of Berkeley, who was elected a trustee on September 20, 1929, brought great ability and much knowledge of the college to her work on the Board. An alumna of the University of California, she had given distinguished leadership to cultural and religious interests in the Bay Area, and had had national recognition by the Y.W.C.A. The daughter of founding trustee John Knox McLean and herself the "Lady Principal" at Pomona in 1898-99, she had known the college from its earliest years. Her ties had been strengthened when her two sons attended Pomona in the early 1920's. As the wife of one of San Francisco's most distinguished attorneys, Mrs. Olney made her home a center of warm hospitality and genuine intellectual excitement.

Mrs. Henry O. Eversole joined Mrs. Bryant and Mrs. Olney on the Pomona Board on March 17, 1931. A daughter of Eli P. Clark, she had followed the development of Pomona since her father became a Pomona trustee in 1910. The wife of a distinguished physician with international interests, she had spent a great deal of time in France, where she and Dr. Eversole had welcomed President and Mrs. Blaisdell in Paris in 1925. She was a woman of discriminating taste, with a continuing interest in France and in the support of the arts.

Mrs. Bryant, Mrs. Olney, and Mrs. Eversole brought a new and valuable emphasis to the Board. As members of the special committee on the women's campus they joined with Dean Gibson in keeping the critical need of women's dormitories and dining halls constantly on the trustees' agenda. When new buildings were constructed, the three women worked with the architects and decorators in establishing a high standard of taste and comfort throughout the women's campus.

As these distinguished women were elected, other significant changes were taking place in the personnel of the Pomona Board. Mr. Marston continued as president with his amazing vitality, esprit, and ever perceptive generosity, but he was the only remaining member of the valiant band of trustees who had begun the college in 1887. The large ministerial group of the early days had gradually given way to ranchers, lawyers, and businessmen. By 1930 the Board included only two ministers, Dr. Luther Freeman, pastor of Pilgrim Congregational Church in Pomona, and Josiah Sibley '99, minister of the Westminster Presbyterian Church in Pasadena. The service of a group of trustees who had carried heavy responsibilities on the Board was drawing to a close. These included businessman William R. H. Weldon of South Pasadena, elected in 1910; financial secretary of the Southern California Congregational Conference, Fred M. Wilcox of Los Angeles, elected in 1912; citrus rancher Butler A. Woodford of Claremont, elected in 1912; and citrus rancher James S. Edwards of East Highlands elected in 1919. Two men entering into great service and influence within the Board were engineering contractor Arthur S. Bent of Los Angeles, son of Henry Kirke White Bent, elected in 1921, and attorney Dell A. Schweitzer of Los Angeles, elected in 1919.

Increasingly the college chose trustees from its alumni. The early group, attorney Edwin F. Hahn '98, businessman Arthur M. Dole '96, rancher and businessman Llewellyn Bixby '01, and rancher Donald G. Aplin '98, had been joined by citrus ranchers Frank H. Harwood '98, Edward C. Harwood '95, C. Stanley Chapman '10, and rancher and attorney A. J. McFadden '01, a citrus, walnut, and persimmon grower. As the Edmunds administration began, two younger alumni who were to make a great contribution to Pomona joined the Board: attorney William B. Himrod '08, and civil engineer Ralph J. Reed '05. Businessmen George L. Eastman and John M. Treanor joined the Board in 1926.

Under President Edmunds' leadership the college sought trustees among the parents of Pomona students. Notable was the election in 1929 of Rudolph J. Wig, scientist and industrialist, whose daughter, Helen, was a member of the class of 1933. Indefatigable in concern for investments and in fund raising, Mr. Wig was the first of a number of parents who came to leadership among the trustees in the generation after the Depression and generously served the college.

The inauguration of the group plan in Claremont brought a new element and new responsibilities to college trusteeship. The Pomona trustees and the trustees of each new institution had, in addition to the work of their individual colleges, an evolving relationship to the other boards of trustees within the Associated Colleges. The countless committee meetings and conferences among the trustees on constitutional questions, property, and academic matters required wisdom, stamina, patience, and often forbearance. The Pomona trustees as the creators of the group plan necessarily carried a heavy load in both discussion and decision. For all the trustees of the Associated Colleges the problems of the nascent plan were compounded by the rigors of the Depression.

These developments imposed such heavy responsibilities on several members of the Pomona Board that they felt impelled to resign. Trustee experience, like administrative talent, was in short supply for directing and leading the new institutions established under the group plan. William L. Honnold, who had succeeded to the chairmanship of the Board of Fellows of Claremont Colleges after the death of Colonel Mudd, asked to be relieved of his responsibilities at Pomona in 1929, continuing, however, as an honorary trustee. Harvey S. Mudd, a member of both the Pomona Board and the Board of Fellows, felt obligated to give most of his time to Claremont Colleges, the grave needs of which had been compounded by the Depression. When he resigned as a Pomona trustee in 1930, he was succeeded by his brother, Dr. Seeley G. Mudd, who as an active trustee and later as an honorary trustee, remained a member of the Pomona Board throughout his life. Jacob C. Harper, much occupied as the first chairman of the Board of Trustees of Scripps College and as a member of the Board of Fellows, resigned as a trustee of Pomona in 1929.

Economic pressure and the development of the Associated Colleges led to creative growth within the Pomona Board. Regular official communication with graduates and former students was instituted in 1929 by inviting the president of the Alumni Association to serve as an ex-officio non-voting member of the Board of Trustees. The first person to serve in this capacity was Charles E. Bent '03, son of Henry Kirke White Bent.

A further and even greater step in alumni relations came with the authorization of the appointment of a full-time alumni secretary. Robert J. Bernard '17, who had rendered great service as alumni secretary from 1919 to 1927, had carried this office as only one of the many duties of the executive secretary of the college. Miss Margaret Maple '26, who was appointed as Pomona's first full-time alumni secretary in 1929, brought the outlook and enthusiasm of a recent graduate together with experience in alumni affairs. An honors student in zoology, she had been vice-president and social chairman of the Associated Students in her senior year. Upon graduation she had entered the alumni office as a secretary under Mr. Bernard. With her appointment as alumni secretary she became a leader of great importance in strengthening Pomona's relations with the growing body of alumni and in increasing their service to the college.

A momentous step was taken in 1929 when the board of directors of the Alumni Association, in cooperation with the college administration, organized the first annual Alumni Fund. Hitherto, Pomona like most independent colleges had solicited alumni in capital campaigns but had not provided a plan for regular support. Consequently alumni were not well informed on the college's needs, and financial appeals were often not effective. "The College will no longer solicit alumni," but through the Alumni Association "every former student will be given an opportunity once a year to contribute as much as he may desire to the maintenance of the College in somewhat the same way that the habit has been formed of contributing to the Community Chest each year," reported the editor of the *Pomona College Quarterly Magazine* in January 1930. The first meeting of class agents was held at a dinner in Frary Hall, February 21, 1930, and the Pomona College Alumni Fund was under way.

Alumni were given a greater sense of community and of Pomona's achievement by the publication in May 1930 of *Pomona College Who's Who, 1894-1930.* This 422-page volume prepared by Miss Maple listed alphabetically all students who had ever attended the college, included biographical data on each individual, and cited his or her activities at Pomona and subsequent professional and business associations. The *Who's Who* also contained an index of all college classes and a geographical index. Furthermore, all faculty members and trustees who had ever been associated with the college were listed, with biographical data. Prized by those for whom it was intended, the *Pomona College Who's Who, 1894-1930,* remains the most comprehensive directory ever published by the college and an invaluable source for its history.

While assisting a program of annual giving by the alumni, the trustees also took steps to establish a similar program among a wider clientele. The California Institute of Technology had achieved spectacular success by forming a group of "Associates," whose members pledged annual support to the Institute and enjoyed special benefits which included lectures, participation in campus events, and the privilege of membership in the Athenaeum, the faculty club. Studying the Cal Tech plan, the Pomona trustees adopted some of its features and in 1930 organized the Pomona College Associates with new trustee R. J. Wig taking the lead.

Despite the budget stringencies of the early 1930's, the college managed to make some valuable improvements in its buildings. Notable was the reconstruction of Pearsons Hall in 1934. The Long Beach earthquake of 1933, which became the landmark for California legislation to make buildings safe from earthquakes, led to questions about the strength of Pearsons Hall. The proposed new physics building, for which preliminary sketches had been made in 1929, had been deferred indefinitely by the Depression. Fortunately, engineering studies indicated that Pearsons Hall could be made earthquake safe for approximately $30,000. Mr. Marston gave $20,000, and the trustees found resources outside the budget to provide the remainder. Professor Tileston spent the entire summer of 1934 working with the contractors in converting Pearsons into a more adequate physics building. The reconstruction was very successful and the building was saved as a permanent college asset.

Valuable improvements were made in 1935 on both the men's campus and the women's campus. To provide a reception room and lounge on the Clark campus, several student rooms off the cloister leading to Frary were converted into a pleasant meeting place for students, faculty, and guests. Progress was being made in the summer of 1935 in providing additional dining facilities on the women's campus. The kitchen for the Aurelia Harwood dining hall was expanded, and a new dining hall with a capacity of 125 was added on the east side of the kitchen. The total cost of remodeling the kitchen and adding a dining room with equipment was less than $12,000.

The prices for which remodelling and new construction could be secured from 1932 to 1936 are illustrative of one virtue of the Depression from the point of view of the college. Much could be accomplished with even very limited funds. Salary cuts, though severe, could be faced because the price of everything to be purchased, notably food, had fallen by much more than a fifteen per cent salary reduction. Academic communities like Claremont, though arrested in their forward planning, underwent less suffering and personal privation than most sectors of American life.

Curricular Changes and New Faculty

The creativity which led to the establishing of a group of colleges was also manifest in curricular planning for Pomona students, and the late 1920's were a period of great academic advance within the college. For guidance the faculty looked to the ancient universities of England and to a few American colleges that were introducing new forms of instruction. The great concern of the Pomona faculty was the motivation of the individual student and a lifting of the intellectual outlook of the entire student body.

When the University of Oxford faced similar problems in the nineteenth century, the faculties met them by the introduction of a new and more demanding baccalaureate degree which led to graduation with honors. Thereafter, Oxford undergraduates elected to take either the honors degree or the traditional "pass" degree. Over the years the honors degree gained such prestige that by 1925 it had become customary and the pass degree was the exception. This profound change in the work and outlook of undergraduates transformed the University of Oxford and was largely responsible for its twentieth century renown.

The organization of subject matter, the greater responsibility of the student, and the methods of instruction and examination that characterized the Oxford honors degree made a strong appeal to those who were seeking a new orientation and greater depth of learning for American undergraduates. Pomona had taken a first step with honors instruction by introducing in 1924 a program of departmental honors to which juniors of special ability were admitted for the remainder of their college course. A more general honors program leading to a degree with honors for a student's entire college course was introduced in September 1927. The new honors degree was adopted on the recommendation of a joint faculty-student committee which had been appointed "to plan for further extension of the Voluntary Principle at Pomona College." Boldly extending its mandate the committee presented a major curricular revision which the faculty accepted with enthusiasm. "The college shall henceforth recognize two planes of academic achievement," the faculty voted, "one meaning advancement to a bachelor's degree in ordinary, or *rite*; the other meaning advancement to the bachelor's degree with honors; the main distinction between them being an enlarged opportunity for individual initiative offered by the one as compared with the other. By this step it is hoped that superior achievement may receive more impressive recognition and that student fellowship in serious undertakings may be more of a reality."

By the end of the freshman year every student had to make a choice between the program for the ordinary degree and that leading to the degree with honors. One of the significant differences between the two degrees was the requirement that honors students take an academic major, either in one department or in a field drawn from two or more closely related departments. According to their academic achievement, honors students were graduated *cum laude, magna cum laude,* or *summa cum laude.* Candidates for the degree with honors had the further opportunity of "reading for honors" and thereby also receiving "honors" or "high honors" in a chosen field. Such students worked under an adviser with whom they had regular conferences. They took both written and oral comprehensive examinations, occasionally with outside examiners participating. All honors students were under the surveillance of the Committee on Honors which admitted students to the program and removed those who failed to attain its objectives.

The honors degree was viewed as a means of deepening the scholarship and the intellectual range of both faculty members and students, bringing thereby "a new way of life in American education." Professor Frank W. Pitman saw it as "a creative adventure in scholarship, scientific discipline and the realm of the mind that challenges the courage, intelligence and loyalty of teachers no less than students." "The voluntary principle has released imagination, energy, interest and responsibility that have been a revelation and inspiration to many despondent teachers. The new spirit of the honors college justifies calling the movement a revival of learning," he wrote in the *Pomona College Quarterly Magazine,* May 1929. Carl B. Swisher '26, M.A. '27, and later a distinguished professor of political science at Johns Hopkins University, on returning to the campus for a few weeks in 1929 found "an unprecedented intellectual alertness at Pomona among the faculty." The clash of new ideas and the questioning of tenets long taken for granted had resulted in "the development of a new intellectual life among the teachers themselves. The students found themselves in contact with teachers who were trying to think." Building on the quest for excellence of the earlier faculties, the new members combined scholarly enthusiasm and achievement.

It was hoped that this wider outlook among the faculty and the example of the honors students would act as a leaven among the larger group of students who elected to take the baccalaureate degree in *rite.* The requirements for this degree permitted wide election of courses and were directed more to breadth than to depth of knowledge. Seven groups of academic subjects were established and the student was required to choose courses from each group. There were regulations applicable to the work of freshmen and sophomores, and further stipulations regarding juniors and seniors. The degree did not provide for a major and the only guarantee of advanced work was the stipulation that thirty-six of the sixty hours of the last two years be courses of junior and senior grade. The earlier foreign language requirement had been discontinued. The only specific requirement was four years of physical education, of which four hours were taken in the first two years and two hours in the junior and senior years. As a whole, the program for the ordinary degree at Pomona was far from arduous.

The quickening of learning at the college owed much to a remarkable group of men and women who joined the faculty between 1924 and 1928. Retirements and expansion brought new and younger men who soon rose to leadership throughout the college. Many of the new faculty were in the social sciences, fields in which the faculty had greatly needed strengthening.

Russell M. Story, as noted above, became almost immediately a a man of great influence among both students and faculty. Dr. Story's contribution to Pomona was enhanced by his bringing of Edward M. Sait as his colleague in political science in 1928. Canadian by birth and a graduate in the honors course of the University of Toronto, Sait had taken a Ph.D. at Columbia University, after which he had taught at Columbia and the University of California. A scholar and an able writer, Sait combined a knowledge of American and European governments with rare and dedicated teaching ability. He and Story constituted a remarkable team and fortunate were the Pomona students who studied under them.

A mature scholar and a brilliant young teacher brought great vigor to the department of economics. Kenneth Duncan, who was appointed Stedman-Sumner Professor of Economics in 1926, came to Pomona after fifteen years of teaching at Lingnan University, Canton, China, of which for the previous nine years he had been both professor of economics and dean of the faculty. On his periods of furlough Duncan had taken an M.A. in economics at the University of Wisconsin and later a Ph.D. at the University of Michigan. A close friend of President Edmunds at Lingnan, Dr. Duncan was fond of saying he had "spied out the land" for Pomona's fourth president. Duncan was an excellent speaker before business and professional groups.

Student interest and public esteem for the work in economics were increased by the appointment of Norman T. Ness as an instructor in 1928. A graduate of Carleton College with an M.A. from the University of California, he would later take a Ph.D. at Harvard. Scholarly and dedicated to his students, Ness soon became one of the most valuable members of the Pomona faculty. Like Story, he was at his best in the classroom and the seminar. Ness could, and did, write scholarly articles, but he gave his energy chiefly to his students and to preparation for his teaching. He was one of the greatest teachers in Pomona's history, and many of those who studied under him in the 1930's later occupied the highest positions in business, government, the professions, and philanthropic foundations.

Younger faculty members brought new interest to the humanities. Harold Davis, a Utah Rhodes Scholar just home with a B.Litt. degree from Oxford, joined the English department in 1927. A vivacious lecturer, a poet, and a pianist, he typified for students both the depth and the breadth of an Oxford education. Much sought by students,he was influential both in the classroom and in college life. Davis was a valuable aid to older scholars, such as Pitman and Story, in instituting both curricular and social change within the college.

Ernest A. Strathmann came to the English department in 1932. A graduate of Johns Hopkins University from which he had also taken his Ph.D., he brought to Pomona a scholarly appreciation of the age of Shakespeare and excellent research experience from his work on the *Variorum* edition of the works of Edmund Spenser. Living in Clark Hall, he was an unofficial counsellor for many

Pomona students. He soon became a leader in shaping the curriculum of the English department.

Three persons destined to give the remainder of their careers to Pomona were appointed in modern languages. James W. Crowell, an experienced teacher, came as associate professor of Spanish in 1929. A graduate of Haverford College with a Ph.D. from Cornell University, he came to Pomona from Colorado College where he had been professor of Romance languages. Emilie Elizabeth Wagner, B.A. Smith College and M.A. Pennsylvania State College, who had been teaching languages in the high school in Pleasantville, New York, came to Pomona in 1928 as instructor in German. Carl Baumann, Ph.D. from the University of Basel in his native Switzerland, who had been studying at the University of Wisconsin, joined the German department in 1931. Baumann was a man of many academic interests which included economics, in which he had taken his doctorate, music, and art, as well as German and comparative literature. His teaching greatly enriched the life of the college.

The science faculty was also fortunate in securing new members who would devote their careers to Pomona. The pressure of teaching and administrative duties required that Brackett have assistance in astronomy and fortunately one of his own students was available. Walter T. Whitney '10, who had taken a Ph.D. in astronomy at the University of Chicago and then served on the staff of Mount Wilson Observatory and the faculty of the California Institute of Technology, was appointed associate professor of astronomy at Pomona in 1929. For the next quarter century he maintained standards of teaching and scholarship which gave Pomona an honored place among liberal arts colleges in the teaching of astronomy.

Chester G. Jaeger, associate professor at Tulane University, succeeded William P. Russell as professor of mathematics and chairman of the department in 1931. A graduate of the University of Missouri where he had also taken his Ph.D., Jaeger was an able administrator and an outstanding teacher. Under his direction instruction in mathematics was strengthened, with consequent enhancement of the work in all the Pomona science departments.

An outgoing man with a great interest in his students and a deep devotion to the life and work of the entire college, he would serve in many capacities, notably on faculty committees concerned with student life and athletics.

Robert S. Ellis, of the faculty of Colorado College, who joined the psychology department in 1931, was a graduate of the University of Arkansas who had taken his Ph.D. at Clark University, then a leader among American universities in research and graduate work in psychology. His emphasis on experimental research complemented the philosophical approach of Professor Ewer and gave balance to the work of the department.

Elizabeth Kelley, appointed in 1928 as associate professor and chairman of the department of physical education for women, would play a large role in the college. A graduate of the University of Wisconsin with an M.A. from New York University, she completed a Ph.D. at Stanford after she came to Pomona. Miss Kelley brought wide experience in the teaching of physical education in secondary schools, first in the Middle West and then in California as head of the department of physical education for girls in Berkeley High School. Her professional standards and her achievements at Pomona would lead to her election as president of the National Association of Physical Education for Women. Within Pomona Miss Kelley worked closely with Dean Gibson in the program for women, and in general college matters she was a valued counsellor to President Edmunds.

In both structure and operation the administration of the college under President Edmunds was very different from that under President Blaisdell. The office of dean of the faculty was discontinued and matters relating to faculty appointments and promotions were handled by President Edmunds. His interest extended beyond official matters and in many ways he showed great personal friendship and concern for members of the faculty and their families. Dr. Edmunds was diligent as the presiding officer of the faculty and gave much thought to the agenda and conduct of faculty meetings. He was careful to work with the cabinet on the academic appointments which were subject to cabinet approval before their presentation to the trustees. Dr. Edmunds' wise use of the administration committee confirmed the role of this advisory committee and the pattern for its work. In his relations to the faculty and its committees and in countless individual matters, President Edmunds strengthened the excellent basic constitution of Pomona.

Furthermore, Dr. Edmunds initiated new practices that became valuable precedents in the governance of the college. As a procedure for granting honorary degrees he recommended to the trustees the authorization of a joint trustee-faculty committee on honorary degrees. The new committee was instituted in the autumn of 1932 with a membership of three trustees and three faculty. Soon it became the practice for all nominations by this committee to go first to the cabinet and then, after its approval, to the Board of Trustees for final action. The joint committee and its procedures were so satisfactory that they became a permanent part of Pomona's constitution.

The president needed a major officer, of course, to assist him in the administration of the college. This was provided by enlarging the duties of the secretary of the faculty and by giving greater stature to that office. Earlier the work of the secretary of the faculty had been limited to keeping the minutes of faculty meetings and handling communications among the faculty. Dr. Burgess who on September 12, 1927, had been appointed secretary of the faculty "for an indefinite period" was entrusted with these and larger responsibilities, such as the chairmanship of the courses of study committee, editing the catalogue, and scheduling public events. President Edmunds found this arrangement highly satisfactory and continued it throughout his administration. He and Dr. Burgess were extremely congenial and they worked in closest harmony.

The small academic administrative team they led was mature and effective. Of these only Dean Nicholl and Dean Gibson were primarily administrators, and each of them did some teaching. Mr. Fitts, the registrar, who was chairman of the admissions committee and handled admissions, also served as assistant professor of English. The only addition to the academic administration in the Edmunds years came with the establishment in 1932 of a full-time director of admissions. Howard H. Pattee '22, dean of personnel at

Pasadena Junior College, was called to this post. The president and his five administrative colleagues, together with treasurer Ernest E. Jones '09 and controller George S. Sumner '94, directed academic affairs, student life, and finance, and brought the college through the difficult years of the Depression.

CHAPTER XVIII

Campus Life in the Early 1930's

FOR POMONA STUDENTS the effects of declining enrollments and their own financial problems were offset by the great increase of facilities for their use and enjoyment. The construction of the men's campus at Pomona, the completion of the Scripps campus, and the erection of Bridges Auditorium initiated a period of lively interest in social and extra-curricular activities.

The mirror and chronicler of these years was *Student Life,* which, more than before, was primarily a newspaper in the best tradition of journalism. In 1926 it had increased its schedule from three issures a week to five, publishing from Tuesday through Saturday. Supported by funds from the Associated Students, whose fee was required and collected for them by the college, and by the large volume of national advertising which became available in the 1920's, *Student Life* was able to continue as a daily until 1937 when it reverted to a tri-weekly. The special appeal of a student daily, maintained elsewhere in California only by the large universities, and the general interest in college activities attracted a large and able staff. The intensive coverage of campus news was supplemented by articles on state, national and international affairs; never before had Pomona students written or published so much.

With the establishment of the group plan *Student Life* extended its coverage to serve both Claremont Colleges and Scripps College. Students from the other colleges were invited to serve on the staff, and an editor for Scripps was selected when the first students of that college were welcomed in 1927. Such cooperation with Scripps, which for a time included a financial contribution by the

Scripps student body, continued until February 1932. Feeling the need of a paper of their own, the Scripps students in February 1931 had established *The Scripture,* a weekly that would serve the college for many years.

The daily issues of *Student Life* provide a valuable insight into the extensive and varied social opportunities that were available to Pomona students. Class spirit was strong and continued so throughout the decade. Soon after arrival each freshman class chose a name. Typical were Nagaraja '31, Aztlan '32, Omayyad '33, Bellerophon '34, and Monoceros '35. A class banner was designed and at an appropriate moment, and conforming to well established regulations, the banner was "sprung" at a public place and in a manner that, it was hoped, would preserve it from capture by the sophomores. The class of '36, for example, sprang its banner in the Fox Theater in the city of Pomona on November 4, 1932. As reported by *Student Life,* the freshman banner spring came as "the climax of a snappy program, ten husky frosh escorting the banner across the stage during the intermission between yells. Sophomores poured out of the theater but were unable to capture the banner." The wearing of green caps, "beanies," by freshmen enhanced their own class spirit and also assisted sophomores in their efforts to enforce long established controls on an entering class. With the completion of the second residence unit of the Eli P. Clark campus the sophomores appropriated its arched entrance from Sixth Street and forbade passage through "the sophomore arch" by freshmen.

The greatest moment of the year for the sophomores was their "sweater spring." The drama attached to this event is shown by an account of the "spring" on October 31, 1932. "Beginning at 8:50 Monday morning and starting at the corner of College Avenue and Tenth Street the motor cavalcade composed of 17 sophomore automobiles hurtled down College Avenue and through the college gates before the startled members of the class of '36 fully realized the impact of the bombs set off at the close of the first class in the morning. A triumphant parade was immediately begun by members of the Monoceros tribe and the remainder of the day was spent in merrymaking and celebration at Camp Baldy and Ice House."

As the "sweater spring" was the high point of the year for the sophomore class, the "Prom" and the "Plug Ugly" expressed the "sophisticated" tastes of the juniors. Their Prom was one of the great social events of the year, and the "Plug Ugly," their amusing and biting satire of campus life and faculty personalities, was eagerly and anxiously anticipated. But the "Plug" was in constant jeopardy, and on occasion the faculty were so incensed by its text and tone that the presentation was forbidden. This had happened in 1929, so there was much rejoicing when the 1930 version, "The Inhibitions of 1930," received the approval of the dean and was given in Holmes Hall on November 14. The reviewer in *Student Life* characterized the "Plug" as "much the better for its officially prescribed year of rest."

Tradition determined much of the activity of the seniors. From the privilege of "ditch day" to the nostalgia of Ivy Chapel the senior year was marked by a number of significant events. Caps and gowns were provided for the seniors and worn on stated occasions, of which the most important was Ivy Chapel held in Bridges Hall of Music toward the end of May. At this service a selected senior spoke for the class, generally with appreciation and affection for the college, but sometimes with sharp criticism. After the service, the seniors and others in attendance proceeded to the traditional planting of the ivy by Bridges Hall. Commencement week included music and a play presented by members of the class.

Much social life centered around the fraternities and their new club rooms in Clark Hall. But fraternity men lived in college residence halls and dined in Frary and they were in no sense isolated from the general student body. Furthermore, the faculty gave special care to making the fraternities an effective part of the college. The regulations for rushing and bidding were carefully drawn, and the bidding process was supervised and managed through Dean Nicholl's office. The eligibility requirement of two completed semesters of college work, which the faculty voted in the autumn of 1930, resulted generally in the pledging of students in the first semester of their sophomore year. However, two rushing, bidding, and initiating periods were established for each academic year, the first being the weeks between the Thanksgiving and Christmas vacations, and the second being a week at the beginning of the second semester.

The costs of individual membership were modest, and after the payment for initiation and a pin, dues among the Pomona fraternities ranged from ten to twenty dollars a semester. Each fraternity had social occasions of its own, and the inter-fraternity dance was a major event in the college social calendar. For the annual observance of Fraternity Day all classes were cancelled. "Old-time Greek letter group members, their wives and offspring" came for entertainment by each fraternity on the campus, in its mountain cabin, or at the beach.

For the classes, the fraternities, and other student organizations the most popular social activity was dancing. Large informal dances could be held in the "Big Gym," and after 1929 in Frary Hall, but as neither had been designed for dancing, students sought off-campus ballrooms for their formal events. The prevalence of automobiles (151 of the 369 men owned cars in 1931) brought the ballrooms of the surrounding area, Pasadena, and Los Angeles within easy reach. Thus formal dances, frequently attended by three hundred couples, were held at such locations as the Oakmont Country Club in Glendale, the Lake Norconian Club in Norco, the Los Serranos Country Club in Chino, the Mission Inn in Riverside, the Ambassador Hotel in Los Angeles, and the Vista Del Arroyo Hotel, the New Civic Auditorium and the Annandale Country Club in Pasadena. Dancing continued until midnight and late permits, sometimes until two a.m., were given women students living in the residence halls. Such an occasion was the sophomore-senior spring formal, the last formal function in 1932-33 and held at the Mission Inn in Riverside. "Pomona Collegians Will Dance Where Padres' Feet Trod" ran a headline in *Student Life.* The last informal dance of that year, "the last fling before finals," was held on the south porch of Bridges Auditorium, such use being permitted for the first time.

Sometimes dancing was included in an occasion which was not solely for entertainment. In May 1931 a student committee arranged a buffet supper dance in conjunction with an art symposium in Frary Hall. Dancing, which began at 4:30, and supper

A Snow Day in the Early Thirties

were followed by an interpretation of the Orozco fresco, which had been arranged by Morgan Padelford of the Scripps art faculty. Participating, in addition to Professor Padelford, were Arthur Millier, art critic of the *Los Angeles Times,* and Professor Robert C. Denison.

One of the most cherished traditions of the 1930's was Snow Day, an occasion when all classes were cancelled and the students as a body went for a day in the San Bernardino Mountains. Held in February or early March, Snow Day was enjoyed in such mountain areas as Lake Arrowhead or Big Pines. Buses left Holmes Hall at 7:15 and 7:30 a.m., arriving at the mountain resort three hours later. "Skis, sleds and skates are available (the eastern colleges have nothing on us)," observed *Student Life* of this period when skiing first became popular among American students. Lunches were prepared by the Frary staff and served without charge to those who ate regularly in the dining halls. The cost of Snow Day declined from $2.75 in 1929 to $1.25 in 1933. The event was best attended in the worst years of the Depression.

Another all-college occasion of the early thirties, the biennial trip to San Diego, was made by facilities long since unavailable in

Labels for citrus boxes when Pomona was "The Oxford of the Orange Belt."
The Carnegie building with a simulation of College Avenue.
Mason Hall and Harwood Hall as seen from the east

Southern California — the electric railroad and the coastwise passenger steamboat. San Diego State College was then a member of the Southern California Intercollegiate Athletic Conference and in alternate years Pomona played football in San Diego. According to an account of the trip for October 1931, at 8:30 and 8:45 on Saturday morning, Pacific Electric cars were boarded at the station on College Avenue and First Street and ridden to the docks of the Pacific Steamship Company at Wilmington, where the students and faculty patrons embarked on the *S.S. Emma Alexander,* which had accommodations for 306 persons in first class cabins holding two or three persons, and third class quarters for twenty-eight. The ship sailed at ten o'clock and luncheon was served in two sittings at 11:30 and 12:30. The *Emma Alexander* arrived in San Diego around 5 p.m. and dinner was served on board at 5:45 and 6:45. The football game was played at 8 p.m. and the ship, "with favors for all," sailed for Wilmington at midnight. After the night and breakfast on board, the students took boat trains which brought them from the dock to College Avenue, where they arrived at 11 o'clock Sunday morning. The cost of the entire trip, first class, was seven dollars and fifty cents, which included six dollars for the boat trip and meals, one dollar for rail fare, and fifty cents for entertainment.

Intercollegiate Athletics

As indicated by the game in San Diego, night football had come to Southern California. Alumni Field at Pomona had been lighted the previous year at a cost of $3,000, and the first night game at the college was played with San Diego State College on September 25, 1930. "Night football is a new feature for both the team and the rooting section," reported *Student Life* on October 3. The following year fourteen of the twenty-five games within the conference were played at night.

Further additions to Pomona sports facilities were the new men's swimming pool adjacent to the Memorial Training Quarters in 1930, and a renovated golf course on Indian Hill in 1931. The swimming pool replaced the enclosed pool which had been demolished to make way for Bridges Auditorium. As the new pool had no dressing facilities for women, coeds were deprived of campus swimming until 1933, when Scripps College constructed a pool and opened it to Pomona women. The golf course, which had sand greens, would be an integral part of the college's athletic program until the course was closed early in World War II.

With campus rallies and by their attendance at games, both at home and away, Pomona students of the 1930's brought great support to their teams, as did many alumni. The Pomona athletic office, for example, had 1600 tickets for sale to alumni and the general public for the football game with Occidental in the Rose Bowl in 1930. On payment of tuition, students received tickets for all athletic contests, but for the Oxy game student tickets provided admission only to the Pomona rooting sections, where no one else was allowed. As in earlier years, the rally and bonfire on the Friday night preceding the Occidental game marked the climax of the students' enthusiastic support for football. The Ghost Dance and the singing of "Torchbearers" by the Men's Glee Club, the illumination of the "P" in the mountains, and the lighting of the great bonfire were cherished Pomona traditions.

A fundamental change was occurring in the structure of intercollegiate athletics in Southern California. The nature of this change was reflected in the schedules for major sports and in the composition of the Southern California Intercollegiate Athletic Conference. At the beginning of the decade Pomona still played an occasional football game with the University of Southern California and with the University of California at Los Angeles, which came to Alumni Field in 1931. However, early in the 1930's the two universities began to restrict their scheduling to fellow members of the Pacific Coast Conference and to occasional intersectional games.

A few years of uncertainty remained before the Southern California Conference took what was to be its permanent form. In the autumn of 1930 the conference members were Cal Tech, La Verne, Occidental, Pomona, Redlands, San Diego State College, and Whittier. Santa Barbara State College applied for membership and was admitted to the conference in December 1930. But disagreements between members in the conference prevented a full conference schedule until some years later. Both Pomona and Cal Tech did not schedule Whittier in football in 1931, and Occidental and Pomona did not schedule La Verne that year. Pomona completed its seven-game season for 1931 by playing the University of Arizona in Tucson and by inviting U.C.L.A. to Claremont. With the growth of public higher education in California, San Diego State and Santa Barbara State found their affinity with the other state colleges and withdrew from the Southern California Conference. La Verne, with its small enrollment, could not meet the conference requirements for teams and resigned. With its five continuing members, Cal Tech, Occidental, Pomona, Redlands, and Whittier, the conference charted a course for small private institutions in intercollegiate athletics, setting high standards for itself and an example for athletic conferences in other regions of the United States.

Pomona took a leading part in this development of the conference. It was enabled to do this not only by faculty regulation but by the quality and continuity of the members of the department of physical education for men. Eugene Nixon saw physical education and athletics as parts of a college program in which primary emphasis was on learning, and he was ably supported by Strehle, Heath and Merritt. His ideal was the participation of the men of the college in athletic teams that tended "toward the acquisition of valuable physical skills, which promoted respect for scholarship, encouraged fine fellowship and love of wholesome sport, and imbued our student body with a finer appreciation of courage, honor, integrity and sportsmanship." Athletes were judged by the same standards as other students, and Pomona gave no athletic scholarships.

Although there was no change in the regular personnel of the department, there was considerable variance in the responsibilities of its members. A program of varsity and freshman teams in football, basketball, baseball, tennis and swimming plus physical education for all the men in college offered plenty of work and variety. Nixon, who had coached varsity football since 1916, turned that responsibility over to Merritt, effective September 1935, taking the freshman team himself. Merritt also handled varsity basketball and varsity tennis, while Heath coached the varsity line in football and varsity baseball. Strehle coached the track team throughout most of his career at the college, also giving much time to physical education. Interest in track and in sports generally in California was greatly stimulated by the holding of the Olympic Games in Los Angeles in 1932.

Pomona won fewer victories and championships than she had enjoyed in the 1920's. But the early thirties were a good period for intercollegiate athletics at the college, and there were high moments in all the major sports. The track season of 1931 opened with a victory over U.C.L.A., 81⅔ to 58⅓, and Pomona won the conference meet in the Coliseum, although the conference championship for the third consecutive year went to Occidental. In 1933 Pomona defeated Oxy in track for the first time since 1927 and went on to win both the conference meet and the conference championship. The tennis team won the conference championship in 1932 for the first time since 1922, defeating Redlands, 9 to 0, and Occidental, 5 to 4, in the deciding match. Football continued as the most popular sport but the teams were less successful than in the 1920's, and Pomona did not win a conference championship from 1927 to 1938. This in no sense diminished the interest in the Oxy game in which Pomona was victorious in 1930, 1931, 1933, and 1935.

The daily conduct of the sports programs was facilitated by a manager system which had been set up by Nixon, Schott, and William P. Russell of the mathematics department. Professor Russell's long service on college and conference committees was an outstanding example of the devotion which many Pomona faculty members gave to physical education and intercollegiate athletics. When he retired from the faculty in 1931 he had served twenty-five years on the college athletic committee, much of this time as chairman, and sixteen years as a Pomona representative in the conference of which he was for many years the secretary. The managerial system which he helped perfect provided for each sport a senior manager who at the end of the season received a regular varsity letter. Under each senior manager were two junior managers and four sophomore assistants, all chosen by the college athletic council. The senior manager appointed eight freshman helpers early in each new season and from these normally came the men who carried on in the succeeding three years.

The successful financial management of the many student organizations on the Pomona campus — publications, classes, athletics — was provided by the graduate manager. As the volume of campus activities grew and financial complications ensued, the Associated Students in 1927 made a study of the graduate manager system then operating in many institutions in the United States, and amended their constitution to provide for a graduate manager at Pomona, effective September 1927. Under this system a college employed a graduating senior, well versed in its extra-curricular activities, to remain for a few years and manage them for the student body.

For Pomona the ideal man was at hand. Glen C. Turner '27 had been auditor of the cooperative store during his junior and senior years. As graduate manager from 1927 to 1935 he established a system which, with necessary modifications as conditions changed, has served Pomona admirably over all the intervening years. Student organizations whose finances were thus managed were of three categories: those supported from the student fee collected by the college, self-sustaining activities such as the glee clubs and the formal dances, and profit and loss activities such as the Associated Students store and the publications. The finances of intercollegiate athletics were also handled, and for this service a payment was made by the college.

It was Turner's office and his wise management that kept the established organizations in sound shape and made possible such occasions as the San Diego boat trips and Snow Days. The semester fee was then five dollars and for the first semester of 1932-33 Turner reported the following apportionments: $1.50 to a fund for a Student Union building, $1.35 to *Student Life,* 60 cents to the social committee, 90 cents to a miscellaneous list including the handbook, and thirty-five cents to salaries. The *Metate* was financed by individual subscriptions and advertising and was not included under the general student fee. There were also separate fees for the Associated Men Students, the Associated Women Students, and the four college classes. For Turner the years at Pomona were preparation for a distinguished career in the business management of higher education. On leaving the college he joined the business office of Colorado State College of Education in Greeley where as controller he became one of the leading college and university business officers in the West.

Independent Study in China

Under Dr. Edmunds Pomona students began to acquire a wider acquaintance with the peoples and cultures of the Far East. Soon the more adventuresome among them thought of travel and study in the Orient and developed one of the most remarkable student undertakings in Pomona's history — the college's first really independent study and its first study-abroad program.

In the spring of 1929, Sik-leong Tsui '31, an Hawaiian of Chinese ancestry, proposed to some of his fellow students at Pomona that they spend the academic year 1929-30 in travel and study in China. Under his dynamic leadership a group of ten was organized, and the sum of $12,000 was raised to finance the trip. In addition to Tsui, the "Oriental Study Expedition" included Relman Morin '29, Warren Scott '29, Carroll Lorbeer '29, Robert Armacost '29, Oliver Haskell '31, Donald Dreher '31, George Gambell '31, Bruce Smith '31, and R. Stanton Avery '32.

The group sailed from San Pedro on October 4 on the Japanese ship *Korea Maru,* which, after calling at San Francisco, proceeded to Honolulu. There they spent two weeks as the guests of Tsui's friends in the Chinese community. The Pomonans then sailed on the *Shinyo Maru* for Yokohama. In Tokyo the expedition had interviews with the president of the House of Peers, a delegate to the London Arms Conference, and the minister and vice-minister of education. Toyohiko Kagawa, the well known Christian social worker, poet, novelist, and essayist, spent an afternoon with them. From Tokyo the group went to Kyoto where they attended the Conference of the Institute of Pacific Relations and enjoyed the beauty of that magnificent city. On November 24 they sailed for China, the primary objective of the study expedition. Debarking at Hong Kong, they took the river boat to Canton.

Their destination was Lingnan University where Dr. Edmunds' service as president assured them a warm welcome. Lingnan was located on Honan Island three miles downstream from Canton, and its campus was a sudden reminder of home to the Pomona students. "First of all, they saw a cluster of sturdy two- and three-storied buildings for dormitories, classrooms, the mess hall, student recreation, and housing," later wrote Relman Morin in his book, *East Wind Rising.* "From a distance the campus could pass for a small Chinese city. A network of paths neatly trimmed and lined with trees cut across wide stretches of lawn. Lingnan looked something like a small midwestern college in Chinese fancy dress." Established by Presbyterians before the end of the nineteenth century, Lingnan had by 1929 four colleges: arts and sciences, business administration, agriculture, and silk-raising, with a total enrollment of three hundred men and sixty women. The faculty members were Chinese and American, with the former in the majority. In this environment the Pomona students spent two months. The college had given each of them a program of study which included a thesis in some field, such as transportation, fine arts, social transformation, or economic change.

From Lingnan the Pomona expedition journeyed to Shanghai where for a month they were in residence at St. John's College. There Relman Morin took a job as a reporter on the *Shanghai Evening Post,* but the other students continued their studies and travel, going as far north as Peking. They then returned to Tokyo for six weeks of study at the Imperial University before sailing home at the end of the summer.

When the men from the Oriental Study Expedition returned, their articles in *Student Life,* addresses to students, and conversations with friends helped the college to comprehend the nature and significance of the civil war in China and the Japanese attack on Manchuria in 1931. The expedition was also a step in the long-range development of Oriental studies at Pomona. These were advanced when Dr. Story, as a result of having received the Seeley G. Mudd fellowship for study in China in 1931-32, introduced a course on the political problems of Eastern Asia in the second semester of 1932-33.

The Leadership of Dean Gibson

The decade of the thirties was a period of great achievement for the women of Pomona College. On every hand there was evidence of the quiet and effective leadership of Dean Gibson, who shared with the students her high ideals for them and for Pomona. Using the facilities of the residential college as opportunities for the personal development of the women, she worked out a remarkably successful program. To bring a closer sense of union among all the women of the college she inaugurated in 1928 an annual banquet of the

President Edmunds and Dean Gibson

Associated Women Students, to be held near the end of the academic year. First given in the Guildhall of the Claremont Church, the banquet in 1930 was brought to Frary Hall, which thereafter the men annually relinquished for this event.

To encourage leadership and service to the college Dean Gibson organized a senior women's honor society. This group petitioned for a chapter of Mortar Board, the national women's honorary society, which had been organized a few years earlier at Swarthmore College and had chapters in the East and Middle West. The petition was granted and the Senior Women's Honorary Society at Pomona was installed on March 28, 1930 as the forty-sixth chapter of Mortar Board.

With their new organizations and increased activities, the women of the college felt the need of a mountain cabin which could serve as a retreat and a place for planning and recreation. Land was secured at Idyllwild, and a sketch of the proposed cabin was carried in the *Pomona College Quarterly Magazine* in January

1929. Little progress was made until the autumn of 1930 when tentative plans and a sketch were carried in *Student Life* and the women inaugurated a financial drive for the required $3000. As part of the drive they raised money on the campus by the sale of Sagehen playing cards, recommended as "excellent Christmas presents," and by the sale of Pomona Christmas cards, which carried a photograph of Marston Quadrangle with the view of Mount Baldy. The women had raised $1100 when trustee R. J. Wig gave $2000 to complete the fund. A committee composed of Mr. Wig, Alumni Secretary Margaret Maple, Professor Elizabeth Kelley, and several students planned a lodge, including a large living room with a big fireplace, a kitchen, and sleeping accommodations for fifteen, with extra beds for large parties. The cabin was dedicated on May 9, 1931 and named "Halona Lodge," meaning "place of happiness," the name suggested by Dean Gibson, who won the contest for choosing a name. Since that date "Halona" has served admirably the purposes that brought it into being.

One of Dean Gibson's most effective ways of promoting responsibility and leadership among the women was her institution of a system of sponsors. Upperclass women, usually juniors, were selected to serve as sponsors for groups of ten or twelve freshman women. The sponsors corresponded with the students during the summer prior to their entering Pomona and returned to college early in September to assist with the freshman orientation week. Throughout the year each sponsor guided her group and assisted its individual members in countless ways. The climax of the year for Pomona women was the annual Women's Day held early in May and retaining some of the features of the traditional English May Day. Large numbers of high school girls were invited for a day which included their participating in athletic events, witnessing the coronation of the popularly chosen May Queen, and attending in the Greek Theater a performance of a student-written and produced May Masque.

In developing the life of the women's campus Miss Gibson was greatly assisted by Miss Kelley and her colleagues in the department of physical education for women. A prominent part was also taken by the student-led Women's Athletic Association. There were opportunities for participation in basketball, hockey, tennis, golf, archery, badminton, speedball, and swimming. Sports were intramural, except for occasional contests with Scripps.

The construction of the Aurelia Harwood Dining Hall in 1931 made Harwood Court more attractive for student living and for the entertainment of visitors. A series of faculty-student dinners were inaugurated for Wednesday evenings in 1932-33. Dean Gibson invited distinguished visitors to dine at Harwood and to meet with the students in the parlor and the dining hall. Dean Yost, the celebrated dean of women at Stanford, visited Pomona as a guest of honor of the Associated Women Students in January 1932 and talked to them at tea and at dinner. President Ellen Fitz Pendleton of Wellesley College visited Pomona in November 1932 and was the dinner guest of President and Mrs. Edmunds and the women of Harwood Court.

While the Depression postponed the prospect of additional residence halls, smaller steps could be taken to enhance the social facilities of the women's campus. Notable was the development of an extended recreation area consisting of a lounge, a dance floor, and a game room on the ground level in the east wing of Harwood Court. This Harwood "Rec Hall" had a long period of useful service.

Effective September 1933, the college discontinued the use of private homes as residences for women students. Henceforth, all Pomona women would reside in college-owned houses on the campus and in Harwood Court. This concentration of housing and dining, made possible by the lower enrollment in the Depression, contributed greatly to the morale of the women's campus. Able house mothers, responsible to the dean of women and working with the Associated Women Students, could administer more satisfactorily the code of conduct for women and the closing hours of the residence halls which they had drawn up and adopted in 1932-33. A notable step had been taken toward the complete and permanent residential campus for women on which Dean Gibson and President Edmunds had set their hearts.

Changes on the Men's Campus and in College Procedures

In some ways, innovations on the men's campus paralleled those among the women. The Ghosts, an upper-class men's organization begun in 1929-30, had become by 1932-33 an invitational group of fifteen men whose special charge was "a rather informal care of the college traditions." They worked with the deans in maintaining the tone of campus life and were ready to help individuals or organizations. Matters of student misconduct on the campus, too slight to come under the censure of the dean, were handled by the Ghosts.

Impressed by the achievement of the Associated Women Students, the men took steps to set up a similar organization. A constitution was drafted and adopted by the men on May 28, 1931. Leaders of the Associated Men Students felt that they should follow the pattern of the AWS in acquainting high school students with Pomona. This was one of the planks in the platform of Robert V. Brown '33, who was elected president of the Associated Students for 1932-33, and he proceeded to carry it into effect. The first Men's Day held on March 25, 1933, with eighty-five students from twenty-six high schools participating, featured tours of the college, a field day program, entertainment in the fraternity rooms, a banquet in Frary Hall with music by the glee clubs, and a play in Holmes Hall.

Despite their zeal in presenting the advantages of the college to potential students, Pomona men and women were not reluctant to suggest changes to administration and faculty. *Student Life* adopted a seven-point program for 1930-31 and carried it on the editorial page of each issue. Heading the list were improved lighting in the library and the beginning of classes at 8 a.m., instead of the long established hour of 7:30. Desired but less urgent were substitution of "passing" or "failing" for the traditional grading system, classes in journalism with academic credit, the early construction of a student union building, increased support for collegiate activities, and student body meetings every other Wednesday for rallies and other activities. At the beginning of the second semester an eighth objective was set forth: a method by which students could grade their professors on teaching ability, presentation, and other phases of their work.

The two most pressing issues were speedily attained. Responding to the campaign by *Student Life* and the Forensic Union, the college began the work on a new lighting system for the library between semesters and completed it early in 1931. The faculty approved the recommendation that classes begin at 8 a.m. rather than 7:30, and made this change, effective September 1931.

The early thirties were the period in which the college established a more regular and effective program of assemblies and religious exercises. After the abolition of required chapel and assemblies at the end of the Blaisdell administration, confusion in both method and purpose marked the public exercises of the college. President Edmunds sought to restore the assemblies as a meeting for large bodies of students and to give vitality to the devotional chapel services. From his first year he brought to the college a group of distinguished scholars and outstanding ministers. In the beginning he experimented with the hours of these meetings, holding assemblies at 8:30 or 9:30 in the morning, or at 7:15 in the evening. By experience the college found and determined a pattern which was well established by 1934 and would last essentially until 1969. The eleven o'clock hours on Tuesdays and Thursdays were reserved for all college purposes and no classes, appointments or conflicting activities were to be scheduled. A voluntary devotional chapel service was held on Tuesday, and a voluntary college assembly was held on Thursday. The latter would be addressed by a visitor or a faculty member, and as often as once a month would be available for student body or class meetings. On five occasions in the year, the opening of each semester, Founders Day, Matriculation Day and Parents Day, and Memorial Day, the assembly hour was used for formal convocations with the faculty in cap and gown. Before the end of the Edmunds administration the Memorial Day Convocation was simplified. Only the participants wore academic regalia and the convocation was held in the afternoon in the Memorial Court.

A National Championship Glee Club

The early 1930's were a period of great achievement by the musical, dramatic, and public speaking groups of the college. Among these the glee clubs were outstandingly successful. The Men's Glee Club, directed by Professor Lyman, and the Women's Glee Club, directed by Professor Arthur Babcock, made separate and extensive tours each year in California.

Interest in the glee clubs had been heightened by the organization of the annual Pacific Southwest Glee Club Competition in 1925. Both the Pomona clubs entered these contests, and with marked success. The achievement of the men's club was truly remarkable as it won first place in six of the first seven competitions. When both the men's club and the women's club won first places in 1931, *Student Life* observed that the double victory established "Pomona's growing supremacy in glee club competition."

The contest in 1932 offered a new challenge and opportunity to the men's club. For some years a national competition had been held among men's glee clubs, generally on the East Coast and beyond the financial range of western students. However, in 1932 the national contest was to be in St. Louis, and this made possible participation by a Far Western institution. Consequently, the Pacific Southwest contest, held that year in San Diego, was staged in February in order to give the winner time to prepare for the national competition. Pomona repeated its double victory for the previous year, with both the men's club and the women's club taking first place. The men's club had won the right to represent the Western states in St. Louis.

A campus-wide and Claremont-wide effort to raise funds for the trip ensued. The executive council of the Associated Students voted $125 and the college appropriated $300; but the objective was $2750 and an intensive drive was required. Articles on the Men's Glee Club dominated the front page of *Student Life* on March 4. "Glee Club Drive Committees Selected," "Student Body To Begin Gigantic Financial Drive," ran the headlines. The paper gave strong editorial support the following day: "It is high time that Pomona cast aside occasionally the academic gown and don the business suit of the modern commercialized higher institutions of learning. There is something admirable in the administration's reticence concerning athletic barnstorming trips but perhaps Pomona may profit by emerging from its almost monastic seclusion and, literally, tooting its own horn. In sending the Glee Club Pomona will be putting its best foot forward." The ASPC declared March 9 Tag Day with twenty-five cents the minimum gift but with the aim of contributions from fifty cents to five dollars. President Edmunds and Dr. Brackett gave strong personal support, as did Dr. Blaisdell and J. C. Harper. The Redlands Glee Club sent fifteen dollars. By March 30 funds had been secured to send the full club to St. Louis.

The contest in St. Louis on April 8 was destined to become one of the great events in the history of Pomona. The other regional winners were: Yale, Dartmouth, Pennsylvania State College, New York University, University of Rochester, University of Oklahoma, Washington University at St. Louis, and University of Utah. In the first session each club sang three numbers, one of which was chosen to be sung in the finals. Pomona sang "Dance of the Gnomes," by MacDowell, "Fight," a student song of Finland, and "Feign Would I Change," by Vaughn Williams. In addition to its own program each club sang a "contest song" selected by the judges. In the finals in the evening, each club sang the contest song, a song of its own choice, and a college song. In these latter categories Pomona chose the "Echo Song" of the Blue and White quartet and "Torchbearers."

With its haunting chant introduced by David Prescott Barrows '94 and Professor Brackett, adapted by Professor Bissell, "Torchbearers" had been cherished and sung at Pomona since the earliest days of the college. However, the words of the song had never matched the quality of the music, and "Torchbearers" had remained a song for a rally or a stunt night rather than for major college occasions. Sensing the larger possibilities of "Torchbearers," which had been arranged for men's voices by Professor Lyman, Ramsay Harris of the English department wrote new lyrics first performed on Founders Day, October 14, 1930. These lyrics,

National Championship Men's Glee Club, 1932.
Professor Lyman and club president Leonard A. Shelton holding the cup

which constitute the text as it has since been known, were sung in the competition at St. Louis, and its enthusiastic reception was the highlight of the final session of the national contest.

When the judges announced their decision to the hushed audience, Pomona College had won first place. Yale was second and Pennsylvania State College was third. The Men's Glee Club, Pomona's oldest student organization, had brought never-to-be-forgotten distinction and success to its members and national recognition to the college. Tales of the men who went to St. Louis by coach and spent three nights on the train would become Pomona legends. Furthermore, with the singing of "Torchbearers" they had given a new song to American glee clubs. Yale included it in its repertoire, as soon did Harvard.

The homecoming reception was worthy of such a triumph. The trip to St. Louis had been made during the spring vacation, and when the glee club returned on April 12, the entire student body and a sizeable deputation from the town of Claremont were at the Santa Fe station to meet them. "Winner of the national contest and accorded the title of the best Men's Glee Club in the Western Hemisphere," reported *Student Life,* "the returning twenty-seven songsters with Professor Ralph Lyman were feted in an automobile parade which wound its way up and down College Avenue finally to deposit the victorious club members on the steps of Holmes Hall."

The club concluded its concert season in triumph and with great support. Standing room was at a premium for the home concerts on April 29 and 30. A later concert by the combined glee clubs, arranged by L. E. Behymer, in the Philharmonic Auditorium in Los Angeles was sold out. Bullock's store showed in its Hill Street windows the cups which Pomona had won in the eight years of competition, and downtown Silverwoods displayed a Pomona exhibit in one of its windows. The concert cleared $1500 which was given for student aid. The Pomona Glee Clubs followed their triumphal concert in Los Angeles by again sweeping to victory in the Pacific Southwest Contest in 1932-33, both the men's club and the women's club taking a first place.

Drama and Public Speaking

While the glee clubs were continuing their remarkable achievements, dramatics made great progress in the quality of its productions and the place of the theater in the life of the college. Until the late 1920's plays had been presented by the Masquers and remained essentially under student management with different directors for the individual plays and little financial support from the college. The fundamental change inaugurated in 1930 and its astounding success were due to the interest of President Edmunds in the theater and to the genius of the woman he chose to head dramatics at the college. The president genuinely loved the theater, attending whenever and wherever he could do so. On business trips to New York he was an ardent theater-goer, and he enjoyed performing in amateur theatricals himself.

Virginia Princehouse '26, who was appointed instructor in dramatics in 1930, had shown great talent in dramatics when an undergraduate. Her performances in Masquers, of which she was a leader, and her interest in the theater had gained her admission to the exciting Yale School of Drama where she studied in 1926-27. After Yale she spent a year in study and performance at the Pasadena Community Playhouse which enjoyed great regional influence. From Pasadena she returned to Claremont to study English in the evolving graduate school of Claremont Colleges from which she took an M.A. degree. While a graduate student, she assisted in dramatics at Pomona and her appointment to the faculty was greeted with enthusiasm. Assuming her responsibilities in the autumn of 1930, Miss Princehouse soon gave new stature to dramatics at Pomona.

The times were propitious for greater student interest in the theater in both study and performance. This was particularly true in a college located only fifty miles from Hollywood, then the world's primary center for the production of motion pictures. Directors for the studios looked to colleges for possible actors, and one Pomona alumnus, Joel McCrea '28, was already launched on what would be an outstanding motion picture career. Students and the public shared an absorbing and universal interest in motion pictures.

At Pomona College Virginia Princehouse utilized these interests with rare creativity and outstanding achievement. The physical facilities and resources that could be placed at her disposal were minimal. The Holmes Hall stage, despite improvements from time to time, was always an inadequate theater from a director's point of view. Yet it never seemed so to those who saw her productions. As Frederick Bracher later wrote, "She performed an annual miracle: on the shallow, ill-equipped stage of Holmes Hall, working with students whose majors in science or economics or literature limited the time and energy they could devote to the theater, she infallibly produced plays of near professional excellence."

From Miss Princehouse's first season, which included Molnar's "The Swan," and "Twelfth Night," drama productions at Pomona won enthusiastic support by students and the Claremont community, with Holmes Hall filled for nearly every performance. She was so quiet and retiring that on first meeting one did not sense the force and control of her direction. Her genius was in casting; she seemed always to find the right person for each part. As Ray Frazer writes, she then "confronted the inexperienced students with the responsibility of conceiving *themselves* how a part should be played. Left with such a major job, they grew up." Students came to love her and soon she was known and revered as "Teach." One of her early students, Arlington Brugh '33, had a great career in motion pictures in which he became known to the world as Robert Taylor. In more serious drama, Norman Philbrick '35 went from study and performance at Pomona to a career that culminated in his direction of the School of Drama at Stanford. For all the college the theater became a source of entertainment and cultural development.

Miss Princehouse worked closely with Benjamin D. Scott, professor of public address, who had joined the faculty in 1923. Tireless and ever generous to both students and faculty, Professor Scott coached young actors to speak distinctly and helped the drama work in a number of other ways. Assistance in drama was an addition to Professor Scott's heavy load in public speaking and debate.

Debating drew large support from both the men and the women and it received much attention in *Student Life* and the *Metate.* The international debates, which had begun with the coming of the team from the Oxford Union in 1925, continued in the 1930's. A team representing the National Student Federation of England, with speakers from the University of Liverpool and St. John's College, Oxford, visited Pomona in November 1930. One of the influences of the English teams was the elimination of judges and the adoption of the custom of "no decision" debates. Of special interest was a debate with a visiting team from the University of Puerto Rico in 1931. In addition to Pomona's debates with colleges in Southern California there were debates with Stanford in some years, with a team from each institution visiting the campus of the other. Debate topics reflected current social and political issues, for example: "Resolved, that the nations of the world should adopt a policy of free trade;" "Resolved, that Congress should pass legislation for the central control of industry;" and "Resolved, that the Republican Party is a major cause of the present financial depression in the United States."

Debating procedure in the 1930's called for an institution to prepare teams on each side of the question, and two debates were held, one on each campus. Debate was thus made more a learning process than a matching of wits. In addition to debating, Pomona participated in the annual conventions of the Pacific Coast Forensic League. In April 1931, Professor Scott, Robert Shelton '32, and Leonard Shelton '32 attended the convention at the University of Washington and "Pomona's famous debating brothers" entered oratorical contests and debated at Stanford en route south.

On the campus Professor Scott and Miss Princehouse joined in directing a faculty show which was presented in Holmes Hall on April 21 and 22, 1933. First suggested by Miss Grace Berry and entitled "Oh, Professor, How Could You!", the production had an all-faculty cast, with Dr. Edmunds taking a leading role. The proceeds went to the scholarship fund and $700 was cleared for this purpose. Dr. Edmunds sought to use amateur dramatics as a way to promote closer student-faculty relations and to strengthen the effectiveness of Pomona as a residential college. The show in 1933 was one of three to be held in the Edmunds administration. Scheduled four years apart, in 1933, 1937, and 1941, they gave each Pomona student an opportunity to see his professors once as thespians.

By the end of the summer of 1933 it was evident that leadership of the college in the Depression had been very demanding for both President and Mrs. Edmunds. At Dr. Edmunds' request the Board of Trustees granted him a leave from October 1933 to February 1934. The administration of the college was entrusted to a committee of three: Professor Burgess as chairman, Dean Nicholl, and Dean Gibson. Dr. Burgess, in effect the acting president, had charge of the general administration, the budget, and relations with the trustees and the faculty. Dean Nicholl presided at faculty meetings, handled student matters, and represented the president in relations with the department of military science. Dean Gibson had full oversight of the personnel committee, of which she was chairman.

The Edmunds planned an extensive sea trip to South America, going down the West Coast, flying across the Andes, then sailing up the East Coast, and returning to the United States via New York. They expected to be in St. Louis for the annual meeting of the Association of American Colleges, on January 18 and 19, 1934, and then to return home. Just a few weeks before their scheduled return, tragedy struck the Edmunds family. Their son, Richard, a junior at Pomona, died in his sleep on the night of January 5. Born in Canton on July 1, 1914, Richard was not a robust young man but the family had had no concern in leaving him and his sister, Elizabeth, a senior at Pomona, in Claremont to continue their college work. Dick was interested in science and the out-of-doors, was active in campus life, and was a popular member of the student body. Reached by cable in Rio de Janeiro, Dr. and Mrs. Edmunds could not return for the funeral, which was conducted by Dr. Stauffacher in the Claremont Church on January 8. Later in 1934, President and Mrs. Edmunds established at Pomona the Richard Poorbaugh Edmunds Scholarship in his memory. This endowed scholarship is held by an upperclassman who is nominated to the scholarship committee by the professor of physics.

CHAPTER XIX

Recovery

WITH THE ACADEMIC YEAR 1935-36, Pomona made a notable recovery from the effects of the Depression and was able to go forward with long-cherished plans in both academic program and campus building. Five years of achievement ensued. Basic was the marked increase in enrollment, which in the autumn of 1935 reached 750, as compared with 681 in 1934. The trustees were so encouraged that in September 1935 they restored five per cent of the fifteen per cent faculty and staff salary reduction which had been voted in earlier years.

Encouraged by the larger enrollment and the reviving economy, the trustees took steps to provide the long desired additional women's residence hall. Once again Mr. Marston by his munificence provided the means for meeting this need. When he offered, anonymously, a $50,000 matching gift toward the residence hall, the trustees in June 1935 authorized the buildings and grounds committee to engage an architect to make preliminary drawings. The Los Angeles firm of Allison and Allison was commissioned, and at the September meeting of the trustees they presented plans for a quadrangle formed by two residence units and a dining room and kitchen, with complete living and dining accommodations for 164 women. A plan so extensive did not seem financially attainable in 1935, and after much consideration the trustees voted on December 10, 1935 to proceed with only one of the residence units. The anticipated cost of the building, including architect fees and furnishings, was $210,000. Half of the cost would be met by gifts, and the remainder would be defrayed by a loan from the college endowment, the loan to be amortized and to bear interest. The

Blaisdell Hall

contract, awarded in March 1936, provided for a reenforced, earthquake-resistant structure to accommodate eighty-two women.

President Edmunds thoughtfully proposed that the new residence hall be named Florence Carrier Blaisdell Hall, in honor of Mrs. James A. Blaisdell, who had been her husband's inspiration and support throughout all his years at Pomona and Claremont Colleges. Although Mrs. Blaisdell was in ill health, both she and Dr. Blaisdell were present for the ground-breaking ceremony on March 12, 1936.

Blaisdell Hall was ready for occupancy in September 1936. Because of the great attention it received from the trustees and the college authorities, the building was a highly successful combination of excellent individual rooms and ample social facilities for group activities, small or large. On each floor there was a room for informal meetings and social affairs. The handsome public rooms included a large living room and a parlor, furnished in Georgian style, conveniently served by a kitchenette. Downstairs was a recreation hall for informal dances and other social events; "Blaisdell Rec Hall" would soon become an integral part of campus life.

The opening of the building was hailed as "a milestone in the social history" of Pomona.

Improving economic conditions also made it possible to go forward with plans for a student union building for which there was a pressing need. Long desired by the administration and the students, such a building had seemed almost at hand in 1930, but the Depression forced its postponement. From the discussions in 1930, however, had come positive steps by both the Board of Trustees and the Associated Students. The trustees had declared themselves in favor of a student union and had approved as its site the area between Holmes and Smiley Halls. The Associated Students, for their part, had requested the trustees to increase the student activity fee from $3.50 a semester to $5.00, with the provision that the additional $1.50 be placed in a reserve fund toward a future student union building.

By 1936 there was a strong desire by the students to find a means to offset the fragmentation of the college community which had been augmented by increasing use of automobiles. A ballroom for both the formal and informal dances was greatly needed. Dependence upon hotel and club ballrooms was unsatisfactory and expensive and also involved the hazards of long automobile trips. The increasing number of automobile accidents involving Pomona students, and repeated *Student Life* editorials calling for safer driving were somber evidence of the dangers of the open cars of that era. Moreover, the concentration of the offices of the graduate manager and of student organizations in a building designed for their use, provision for a larger and more modern store, and the addition of a soda fountain and a sandwich facility were seen as major steps toward a more effective college.

President Edmunds, in cooperation with the Associated Students, revived active consideration of a student union building in the autumn of 1936. The trustees in early October authorized him to prepare a pamphlet on the proposed building and to conduct a campaign among the parents of students. By January 1937 there were enough funds in hand to encourage the trustees to authorize the architects, Marston and Maybury of Pasadena, to prepare the detailed drawings for the building.

Despite campus enthusiasm, student and faculty support, and the hard work of President Edmunds and some of the trustees, notably William B. Himrod, the campaign proved disappointing, and much earnest consideration was required before the Board felt able to authorize construction. The building as designed would cost $128,000, and despite the strenuous efforts of President Edmunds and the parents who assisted him, only $64,000 had been secured. Of this amount $25,740 came from gifts by parents, alumni, and friends. The remaining $31,500 were Associated Students' funds, of which $17,500 represented annual assessments toward a student union building, and $14,000 constituted reserves from the store and other ASPC activities. Confronted with these facts the trustees proceeded as they had often done before — by reducing the scope of the project and by using every available fund at their disposal.

The main building and the west wing were approved, leaving the east wing to be constructed later. To provide the $94,000 required for this reduced program a bequest of $10,000 from the late Florence Riley was placed in the union fund, and finally a loan of $20,000 to be repaid by continued student assessment for the building, was made from college funds. These provisions were approved on March 9, 1937 and a contract was executed with Stover Brothers of Claremont. Construction proceeded rapidly and the building was placed in use in the autumn, a dedicatory dance being held in the ballroom on October 2.

The facilities constructed served the college well and with little change until after World War II. The graduate manager's office was the hub of the activities of the many organizations that made up the vigorous extracurricular life of the college. Nearby were the offices of the Associated Students and the publication offices of *Student Life* and the *Metate*. The cooperative store, moved to the student union building from the basement of Holmes Hall, was an enlarged and profitable undertaking. The fountain, lounges, and the patio were pleasant gathering places. The ballroom was the center for all formal dances, and for some informal occasions.

New academic buildings were harder to achieve than residence halls and social facilities, and the hopes of the 1930's for a new

Student Union Building

Dean Nicholl and E. C. Griffin '41, captain of the 1940 football team

physics building or an additional music building could not be realized. However, the long envisaged expansion of Rembrandt Hall was accomplished in 1936. The growth of the art department had made this imperative. Fortunately Myron Hunt, the architect of Rembrandt in 1914 and Bridges Hall in 1915, was available to design the western addition to Rembrandt.

While these new buildings were being constructed on the Pomona campus, Dr. Blaisdell was nearing the end of his long official service in Claremont. To honor him Pomona, Scripps, and Claremont Colleges held a joint convocation in Bridges Auditorium on February 7, 1936. The occasion celebrated the tenth anniversary of the group plan, the tenth anniversary of Scripps College, and the twenty-fifth anniversary of Dr. Blaisdell's service in Claremont. The featured speaker at the morning convocation was President Robert Gordon Sproul of the University of California, whose address was entitled "The Role of the Privately Endowed College in a State System of Education."

Former President Hoover honored the colleges with his presence and was the featured speaker at the luncheon in Frary Hall. Mr. Hoover's participation was a tribute not only to Dr. Blaisdell, but also to his friend of many years, William L. Honnold, chairman of the Board of Fellows of Claremont Colleges. The closing event was a dinner in Frary Hall honoring Dr. Blaisdell. Mr. Marston presided and greetings were brought by representatives of all the institutions and groups with which Dr. Blaisdell had been intimately associated. As they paid tribute to Dr. Blaisdell on February 7, his friends were well aware that they were also saying official farewell. Then on sabbatical leave and already 68 years of age, Dr. Blaisdell resigned the presidency of Claremont Colleges on March 31, 1936, and soon established his residence in La Jolla.

New Leadership and New Members of the Board

A momentous change in the leadership of the Pomona Board of Trustees followed in June 1936. Mr. Marston, who had served as president of the Board since 1910, insisted that his resignation from that office be accepted. On earlier occasions the trustees had

Frank H. Harwood, new president of
the Board of Trustees

refused to heed his proffered resignation, but they realized this time that they must accede to his wishes. Happily, the Board was not deprived of his counsel and service because he consented to remain as an active trustee and was also named Honorary President. The debt of Pomona College to Mr. Marston cannot be overstated. For nearly fifty years he had given his time, thought, and substance to the developing college. His wise leadership in the Board and his understanding relationship to the successive presidents of the college were essential factors in Pomona's progress as a college of distinction. Through his initiative and generosity came the beauty of the campus and some of the college's finest buildings. Moreover, Mr. Marston was exceptionally happy in the ongoing responsibilities of a trustee. His frequent trips to Claremont gave him close contact with students and faculty who treasured his warm personality and his delightful humor. Certainly he was one of the great American college trustees of the twentieth century.

When Mr. Marston resigned, Pomona was fortunate in being able to turn to an alumnus as president of the Board. Frank H. Harwood '98, vice-president of the Board, who was elected to succeed Mr. Marston, brought loyalty and experience to his high responsibilities. As a member of the Harwood family of Upland, he had known Pomona College all of his life and had seen the members of his family contribute to its advancement. Upon graduation he became active in alumni affairs and as early as 1901-02 he served as president of the Alumni Association. Elected a trustee in 1919, he soon participated in major committees of the Board. He was a member of the buildings and grounds committee when the Eli P. Clark campus was constructed.

Mr. Harwood was a citrus rancher and as such was at the heart of the major economic activity of the San Gabriel Valley in those years. Living in neighboring San Dimas, he was a founder of the San Dimas Lemon Association and for many years was president of the San Dimas Fruit Exchange. His business interests expanded with the growth of the citrus industry in this region and he became a member of the California Fruit Growers Exchange and president of the National Orange Company at Riverside.

Frank Harwood had qualities that made him an outstanding president of the Board. He had the long, steady view of an agriculturist. He was a model of judiciousness as a presiding officer. Moderate in temperament and opinion, he intuitively sensed the best interests of the college. To these qualities he joined a warmth of personality and a hospitality that bespoke genuine friendship. Memorable were the occasions when officers of the college and their families were the guests of Mr. and Mrs. Harwood at "Homeacres," their residence in San Dimas.

The amendment of the by-laws in 1925 which authorized Pomona to establish other educational institutions also provided for increasing the membership of its own Board of Trustees to thirty. This expansion, which took place in the Edmunds administration, brought strength and greater diversity to the Board.

The new trustees were drawn from three groups: alumni, parents of Pomona students, and other business and professional men in Southern California. Nine men from these groups were elected to the Board from 1933 to 1940.

The alumni included Robert P. Jennings '00, Roy E. Thomas '03, and Willis H. Merrill '30. Mr. Jennings, an attorney who had served as president of the Alumni Association in 1918-19, also had intimate family ties to Pomona. Mrs. Jennings '00 was the daughter of Henry Kirke White Bent, and the Jennings' son and daughter were graduates of the college. As a trustee from 1933 to 1955, Mr. Jennings was generous in giving legal assistance and he also rendered valued service as a member of the executive and investment committees.

Roy E. Thomas, a physician who had graduated from the Harvard Medical School, had been active in alumni affairs, serving as president of the Alumni Association in 1922-23. His ties to the college were strengthened by his marriage to Georgia G. Seaver '04 and by the graduation of their daughter Patricia in 1932. Dr. Thomas served the Board in many ways from 1939 to 1963, notably in the development and expansion of the student health service.

Willis H. Merrill, a businessman elected in 1940, was the youngest member of the Board, and as such was a valuable interpreter of student and alumni interests. In college he had edited *Student Life,* as also had his wife, the former Margaret Inglis '30.

Three non-alumni parents of Pomona students joined the Board: William Raymond, Fred W. Smith, and Charles E. Donnelly. Mr. Raymond, a Los Angeles businessman elected a trustee in 1937, was the father of three alumni, a son in the class of '34, and daughters in the classes of '35 and '37. His own large contribution to the Board was cut short by his early death in 1942, but his deep interest was continued by his family, two members of which would later be elected trustees.

Fred W. Smith, rancher and businessman living in Ojai, was elected a trustee in 1939. His son and two daughters were then at Pomona and they would graduate in the classes of '40, '42 and '43. Generously, and often anonymously, Mr. and Mrs. Smith gave financial support to many phases of Pomona's development, notably scholarships, the music department, and the women's campus. The warm hospitality which they extended in their summer home on Lake Arrowhead endeared them to faculty and students.

Charles E. Donnelly, attorney and a graduate of the Law School of the University of Southern California, was elected a trustee in 1940. His son was then attending the college, and his daughter would graduate in 1945. As counsel and vice-president of the California Bank and a director of several other financial and business corporations, Mr. Donnelly played a major role in Los Angeles. He soon became a leader within the Pomona Board. His wisdom in the Executive Committee and his work as a member and chairman of the nominations committee contributed greatly to the good government of the college.

Three other Southern Californians brought a diversity of talents and interests to the Board after 1933. The youngest, Los Angeles attorney Frederick Williamson, was a gifted man of great personal charm who early gained a position of leadership among the trustees. A graduate of Stanford and the Harvard Law School and a trustee of Cal Tech, he had a deep understanding of American higher education. He had special knowledge of Pomona through his wife, the former Ruth Chandler, who had taught physical education at Pomona in 1921-22 and 1922-23.

Paul S. Armstrong, general manager of the California Fruit Growers Exchange, was elected a trustee in 1936. Associated with the Exchange since 1921 he had become a friend of the citrus growers on the Pomona Board. A graduate of Michigan State University, which conferred an honorary degree on him, Mr. Armstrong worked closely with Mr. Harwood and Mr. McFadden in serving Pomona.

James E. MacMurray, who was elected a trustee in 1938, was a retired industrialist and philanthropist from the Middle West, who had moved to Southern California. Amassing a fortune in the steel business he had made such large gifts to Illinois Woman's College that in 1930 the college had been renamed MacMurray College for Women. President Edmunds became acquainted with Mr. MacMurray and he accepted a place on the Pomona Board. Both Mr. and Mrs. MacMurray took great interest in the college, and they contributed generously to its support.

The Fiftieth Anniversary

As Mr. Harwood became president of the Board, the trustees and faculty were involved in planning the celebration of Pomona's Fiftieth Anniversary. The jubilee year, 1937-38, was to be marked by a series of notable events and distinguished speakers. Happily, the trustees could begin the great year by removing a continuing shackle from the worst years of the Depression. The Board restored five per cent of the remaining reduction of faculty salaries in September 1936 and the final five per cent in September 1937, thereby returning faculty and staff salaries to the levels from which they had been reduced in 1932. The funds for these restorations were secured by increasing tuition from $300 to $350 a year, and room and board by amounts ranging from twenty-five to fifty dollars a year, depending on the location of the room.

The interest always inherent in the celebration of the fiftieth anniversary of a college or university was particularly notable in the American Southwest in the first generation of the twentieth century. Prior to 1937 the University of Southern California was the only institution of higher education in Southern California to have commemorated its fiftieth birthday. Pomona sought, therefore, to make the most of the opportunity which age had given it.

The Founders Day Convocation in Bridges Auditorium, which officially opened the Fiftieth Anniversary Year on the morning of October 14, honored those who had established Pomona in faith and had led it with wisdom and devotion. Central in the exercises were presentations to George W. Marston, Edwin Clarence Norton, and Frank Parkhurst Brackett. The trustees had engaged Cyril Jurecka, sculptor in the art department, to design a fiftieth anniversary plaque for each of these beloved founders. The plaque, entitled "Torchbearers," depicted the president of the college holding a torch, toward which a young man and a young woman were looking in search of education. Trustee Mary Clark Eversole, who made the presentation to Mr. Marston, spoke of "the graciousness of spirit that has always distinguished him among his fellowmen." James T. Allen '95, professor of Greek at the University of California, Berkeley, paid tribute to the learning and character of Dean

Professor Brackett, Dean Norton, and Mr. Marston holding the Torchbearer plaques presented to them on Founders Day 1937

Norton: "Your ideal was to combine the spirit of the Greeks with the spirit of Jesus. You came to Pomona with Plato in one hand and in the other the Bible." Llewellyn Bixby '01 praised the lucidity and enthusiasm which Professor Brackett brought to his teaching and his personal interest in students: "Not alone in the classroom did he excel, he was a wise counsellor and friend to us all."

After the ovations to the three revered founders, President Edmunds read greetings and congratulations from alumni in many parts of the United States, including the territories of Hawaii and Alaska. Cables had been received from Brussels, Berlin, Vienna, and from countries as distant as Arabia, India, China and Japan. The convocation ended with the Ceremony of the Flame in which representatives of the entire history of the college participated.

The afternoon of Founders Day was marked by a pilgrimage to the site in the city of Pomona where the college had begun instruction in September 1888. Through the cooperation of the college, the Historical Society of Pomona Valley, Pilgrim Congregational Church, and the City of Pomona, a bronze tablet was unveiled at the four-room cottage at Fifth Street and White Avenue. Dr. David

Prescott Barrows '94 spoke charmingly and affectionately of the months which he and other students had spent in the Ayer Cottage in the autumn of 1888. Later in the Fiftieth Anniversary Year an anonymous donor made a gift for the erection of a replica of the Ayer Cottage on the Pomona campus, and it was placed at the southeast corner of College Way and Fourth Street where it stood for many years.[1]

The Fiftieth Anniversary Founders Day concluded with banquets in Los Angeles and in San Francisco, with Dr. Barrows participating in both places. This novelty was arranged by having Dr. Barrows, who was toastmaster of the Los Angeles banquet at the Biltmore Hotel, speak to the San Francisco banquet by direct telephone and introduce Professor Kenneth Duncan, the San Francisco speaker. The large list of guests in Los Angeles included Governor Merriam, who brought the congratulations of the state; President William O. Mendenhall of Whittier College, who presented the greetings of the Association of Colleges and Universities of the Pacific Southwest; and former Knox College President Albert Britt, who conveyed the good wishes of Pomona's fellow members in the Association of American Colleges. Dean Norton, who gave the main address in Los Angeles, eloquently expressed his hope for Pomona's future: "Amidst all the inevitable changes the only thing that all of us who truly love our college would have remain unchanged forever is its purpose, this all-inclusive aim to be a center of judgment and authority in moral matters, and to send out men and women trained to right judgment regarding the world's needs."

Throughout 1937-38 there were scheduled an unparalleled array of events which affected every area of the college. Thirty-two visiting lecturers came to Pomona in the course of the academic year. A series of lectures in biography by Albert Britt, who had been an editor before he became president of Knox College, were made possible by trustee William L. Honnold. Frederic L. Paxton, professor of history at the University of California, Berkeley, lectured on "Western America During the Last Fifty Years."

[1]With the construction of Oldenborg Center in 1966 the replica was moved to a location south of the baseball field.

Lectures in science were indicative of the developing scientific leadership in California and Pomona's significant part in it. Ernest O. Lawrence, originator of the cyclotron and already considered the foremost of American atomic physicists, lectured in Pearsons Hall on "The Atomic Nucleus." Linus Pauling, professor of chemistry at the California Institute of Technology, whose research would later bring him the Nobel Prize in chemistry, lectured on "Molecular Structure and the Chemical Bond" and "Structural Chemistry of the Blood." Pomona alumni were included among the visiting lecturers in science. H. Victor Neher '26, a research physicist working with Dr. Robert A. Millikan at the California Institute of Technology, lectured on "What Are Cosmic Rays?" Norris Bradbury '29, associate professor of physics at Stanford University and later to become director of the Los Alamos Scientific Laboratory, lectured at Pomona in the spring of 1938.

The second semester began with a convocation address, "The Fifty Years," by the widely read British historian, Philip Guedalla. Other speakers in the social sciences were: William B. Munro, professor of American institutions at the California Institute of Technology, and Pierre de Lanux, a popular French lecturer. As the anniversary year drew to a close, Dr. Robert L. Kelly, Executive Director of the Association of American Colleges, looked to the future in a lecture, "The Next Fifty Years in the College of Liberal Arts in the United States."

In addition to the demanding program which it necessarily carried in the Fiftieth Anniversary events, the music department gave two special concerts. Vladimir Ussachevsky '35, then a Ph.D. student at the Eastman School of Music, wrote a cantata honoring Pomona and this was presented, with the composer in attendance, in Bridges Auditorium on February 13, 1938 by the Pomona choir of 150 voices, directed by Professor Lyman, and a fifty-piece orchestra directed by assistant professor Kenneth G. Fiske. Pomona was host in February for a musical event which involved a hundred instrumentalists from twenty junior colleges and universities, from San Diego to Sacramento. These worked for three days under the famous band leader, Edwin Franko Goldman, who then conducted them in Bridges Auditorium in the first state intercollegiate concert.

As a tribute to Pomona's anniversary President Edmunds was fortunate in securing the Pro Arte String Quartet of Brussels for six performances on Friday evenings and Saturday afternoons in February and March 1938. This excellent series was made possible by the generosity of Elizabeth Sprague Coolidge of Boston, on whom Pomona conferred the honorary degree of Doctor of Music.

The special events of the Fiftieth Anniversary concluded on April 23, 1938 with the presentation in Bridges Auditorium of "The Quest," a symbolic drama. Written by Norman Philbrick '35, who had returned from study at the Yale School of Drama, and directed by Mrs. Allen, with dance director Ada Cowsey as choreographer and Benjamin Scott as general manager, "The Quest" required the participation of over 275 students in its eleven episodes. It was estimated that more than half the student body were involved in the total effort of organization and the preparation of stage scenery. A large group of faculty wives gave essential service in making the costumes.

Philbrick saw Pomona College as an institution that "had kept pace with the years and the changes in them without sacrificing its character. But it is no easy performance, this setting up of a goal and determining a course of progress that aims to keep to the middle of the road." In the drama he presented the universal search of man for an answer and a way, suggesting "that Pomona College becomes a station from which man in his quest can set out, to which he may return in body and in spirit for a renewal of faith and courage when the way seems too hard and long."

New Faculty and Staff

Pomona could celebrate her Fiftieth Anniversary in pride and confidence because she was gaining in academic strength. New courses of instruction had been added, and faculty positions left vacant during the Depression had been restored.

Notable was the creation in 1936 of the department of Oriental affairs, the first new department to be added in many years. Pomona's commitment to the study of the Far East was so significant that President Edmunds was able to secure a grant from the Rockefeller Foundation to support such a department. Charles Burton Fahs, who was appointed instructor in Oriental affairs, brought impressive qualifications for the study of both Japan and China. The son of Christian missionaries, he was a graduate of Northwestern University, from which he had also taken a Ph.D. in Oriental studies. Dr. Fahs had studied at the University of Berlin, in Paris, and at the Imperial Universities of Kyoto and Tokyo in Japan. Few American colleges could offer the range of courses in Oriental affairs that became available to Pomona undergraduates after 1936. The courses given by the departmental staff included "The Development of Oriental Civilization," "History of Far Eastern Diplomacy," and "Contemporary Far Eastern Government." In addition there were "Oriental Philosophy," offered by Dr. Iredell of the philosophy department, and "Economic Problems of the Orient," given by Professor Duncan of the economics department.

Major changes in faculty and curriculum were made in the department of music. Among the students there was a growing desire for more emphasis on instrumental music, the history of music, and music appreciation. Recognizing these needs, the college brought to the faculty three men who would make very significant contributions to the teaching of music at Pomona.

Kenneth G. Fiske, who came in 1936 as teacher of violin and director of the orchestra, transformed instrumental work at Pomona and soon gave the college an orchestra of distinction. He also introduced a much appreciated course in the history of music. A graduate of the American Conservatory of Music in Chicago, from which he also held a master's degree, Fiske was teaching at Dickinson State Teachers College, Dickinson, North Dakota, at the time of his appointment.

William G. Blanchard, also appointed in 1936, first directed the symphonic band and taught courses in orchestration and instrumentation, and music theory. When Joseph Clokey left the department in 1939 to become dean of the College of Fine Arts of Miami University in Ohio, Blanchard became teacher of organ and the college organist. A graduate of DePauw University with a

Backs of the 1938 Conference Champion Football Team: Nixon, Nicholl, Merritt (all sons of faculty members), Hisanaga, and Nagel

Earl J. "Fuzz" Merritt, to whom the 1939 *Metate* was dedicated

master of music degree from the University of Michigan, Blanchard was a gifted musician of rare endowment. His choral compositions and arrangements enriched the life of both the college and the church.

Daryl Dayton, appointed in 1938 as teacher of piano, also contributed a new emphasis to the music program. In addition to his work in piano, Dayton established for the general student a course in "listening to music," providing the student with a rich background for the appreciation of both instrumental and vocal music. Received with enthusiasm, the course attracted a large enrollment. A graduate of the Oberlin Conservatory of Music, with study in New York and Berlin, Dayton came to Pomona from Eastern Washington College of Education.

A major change also occurred in the program of the department of religion. When Raymond C. Brooks retired in 1936, he was succeeded by Bernard Eugene Meland, professor of religion and philosophy at Central College, in Missouri. A graduate of Park College, with a Ph.D. from the University of Chicago, Meland brought a new approach to the teaching of religion at Pomona. His scholarship and leadership of the department are illustrated by the titles of the courses he offered. These were: "Great Personalities in Religious History," "Introduction to the Philosophy of Religion," "Applied Psychology of Religion," "Religion Through the Ages," and "American Philosophies of Religion." Meland was a distinguished scholar, who continued a program of writing and research while carrying his heavy duties at Pomona. In addition to his teaching he was chairman of the faculty-student committee on religious activities, and the director of the voluntary Tuesday morning chapel service. Under his leadership new life and new direction were given to the chapel. A broader range of readings was introduced, and a chapel choir was developed. Chapel speakers included the leaders of the Associated Students as well as faculty members and visitors.

The department of philosophy also underwent a major change in personnel and approach. Dr. Robert C. Denison, the much beloved head of the department, died in January 1936 while still in service. F. Raymond Iredell '20, who had joined the department in 1925, became the chairman of the department and because of his professional orientation brought it into closer contact with the leading graduate schools.

Of great significance was the appointment of W. T. Jones as an instructor in philosophy in 1938. A native of Natchez, Mississippi, he had graduated in the honors program of Swarthmore College. Elected to a Rhodes Scholarship in 1931, he spent the following three years at the University of Oxford from which he received the Bachelor of Letters degree in philosophy. After his return to the United States he entered the Graduate School at Princeton University where he took his Ph.D. in 1937 and whence he came to Pomona. A scholar who was also a superb teacher, Jones soon exercised great influence within the college. He and Iredell conducted a department of distinction.

With the improvement of the financial condition of the college, a full-time appointment in American history, long desired by Professor Pitman and his colleague, W. Henry Cooke, became possible. John Haskell Kemble, a Stanford graduate then completing a Ph.D. at the University of California, Berkeley, was appointed instructor in history in 1936. With research interests in maritime history and the history of the American West, he was the first man trained primarily as an American historian to join the Pomona faculty.

A second opening in the department was occasioned by the resignation of Professor Cooke to accept a position as professor of history and Director of Studies in the Graduate School of Claremont Colleges. W. Henry Cooke '20 had taken a Ph.D. at Stanford and was a specialist in European history. To fill this second opening, John H. Gleason, an instructor at Harvard, came to Pomona in 1939 as assistant professor of history. A Harvard graduate, Gleason had taken a Bachelor of Letters degree in history at the University of Oxford and upon his return from England had completed a Ph.D. at Harvard. Gleason brought a broad understanding of English and continental European history, with research interests in English history of the Tudor and Stuart periods and the early nineteenth century.

Hugh J. Hamilton came as instructor in mathematics in 1936. A graduate of the University of California at Los Angeles with a Ph.D. from Brown University, he was a scholarly teacher, well prepared to guide students in a period when mathematics was entering a new era. He brought strength to a department which under the leadership of Professor Jaeger was developing a larger role in the college.

An older and more experienced teacher was included in the group of new faculty members appointed in the late 1930's. Ray E. Baber, professor of sociology at New York University, came to Pomona as professor of sociology in 1939. His appointment was in response to student desire for a larger and stronger department of sociology, and to a particular demand for a course in "Marriage and the Family," a field in which Dr. Baber was the author of a widely used textbook. With a Ph.D. from the University of Wisconsin, he had taught as a young man at Lingnan University where he had known both President Edmunds and Dr. Duncan.

With financial recovery Pomona did not forget the serious lessons of the Depression. Paramount was the realization that the old methods of raising funds would no longer provide the resources essential for the growing needs of the college. Previously, Pomona, like most other independent American institutions of higher learning, had depended primarily upon the president and a few of the trustees, generally working in intensive campaigns, to raise the essential funds for the institution. In the 1930's colleges and universities began the introduction of officers whose duties would be continuous and directed primarily to securing additional financial resources. There was increased emphasis on support from a wide constituency, and the practice of annual giving was instituted. At Pomona these ideas had led to the organization of the Alumni Fund.

President Edmunds persuaded the trustees to authorize a full-time public relations and fund-raising officer at Pomona, and in 1938 the college appointed Allen F. Hawley '16. Following his study at the Harvard Business School and his service in World War I, Hawley had entered the field of advertising in Los Angeles, working for over a decade for the *Los Angeles Examiner.* Initially appointed at Pomona as director of public relations he also gave assistance to Miss Maple in handling the Alumni Fund. When Miss Maple in 1940 accepted the faculty position of recorder, Mr. Hawley was given full supervision of the alumni office and for many years his title would be director of alumni and public relations.

The appointment of Allen F. Hawley was of far-reaching importance. Hawley brought love and understanding of the college to his duties, and he had the creative ability to develop effectively his uncharted responsibilities. An alumnus who had held many offices, including the presidency of the Associated Students, and who had also been elected to Phi Beta Kappa, he worked easily with both alumni and faculty. He won the immediate confidence of the trustees, who found him an invaluable addition to the college administration.

The Shadow of War

Although American students and faculties had had a growing awareness of ominous developments in Western Europe in the late 1930's, it was not until 1940 that the direct effect of these events reached every college and university campus. Adolph Hitler, in ruthless advances between 1936 and 1939, sent troops into the demilitarized German Rhineland, annexed Austria, and occupied Czechoslovakia. When Germany invaded Poland in September 1939, Great Britain and France came to Poland's defense, and a terrible war that would last six years had begun. The tragedy of the war was experienced at Pomona College, the very day of its declaration. Ray Scott MacFarlane, a member of the class of 1941, was one of thirty Americans lost when a German submarine torpedoed the British passenger ship *Athenia* on September 3.

The United States was singularly unprepared in both thought and arms for a great war. "Never since Jefferson's time," wrote Samuel Eliot Morrison, "had America been in so pacifist a mood as in 1933-39." This opinion had resulted in neutrality acts by Congress between 1935 and 1939 forbidding the sale or transport of arms to a belligerent, private loans to a belligerent, or the entry of American ships into war zones. With this background, the issues of the European war and the consequences of Japanese aggression in Asia were vigorously debated throughout the country. Differences of opinion were often sharp on college campuses, and Pomona was no exception.

With the fall of France in 1940 and Britain's gallant and lone defense against Hitler, American opinion moved toward involvement. "We will extend to opponents of force the material resources of this nation," President Roosevelt told the graduating class at the University of Virginia in June 1940. The gravity of the national situation in the summer of 1940 led Congress to pass on September 14 the Selective Training and Service Act, the first compulsory military training act in peacetime in American history. Men between twenty-one and thirty-five were required to register, but not more than 900,000 were to be trained in the first year. When the first draft numbers were chosen on October 29, a changed way of life had begun for young men in the United States.

In this state of impending national and international crisis Pomona College faced the choice of a new president. Dr. Edmunds would reach the college's retirement age in September 1941, and he had informed the trustees that he did not desire to continue in office beyond that time. A presidential search committee of the Board of Trustees, together with an advisory committee of the faculty, began in the autumn of 1940 a nationwide search for the new president.

PRESIDENT E. WILSON LYON

CHAPTER XX

The College in World War II

A New President

ON APRIL 25, 1941 the Board of Trustees elected Elijah Wilson Lyon, professor of history at Colgate University, as the sixth president of Pomona College. The appointment was the culmination of a thoughtful selection process in which representatives of all elements of the college had participated. The presidential selection committee, primarily concerned for the academic program of the college, had made a careful canvass of possible candidates among college and university professors, and Professor Burgess took an eastern trip in which he met and considered those who had been most highly recommended, including Dr. and Mrs. Lyon. When the Lyons were invited to visit the college in April, they met not only with the trustee committee and the faculty advisory committee but with many individual faculty members and representative students. The trustees, for their part, discussed Dr. Lyon's educational interests, stressing academic leadership as the chief requisite of the new president. His election seemed to assure this.

Dr. Lyon brought to Pomona a wide experience in liberal education. Born in Heidelberg, Mississippi, in 1904, he had studied Latin and Greek, French, English literature, and history at the University of Mississippi, where he received his B.A. degree with special distinction in 1925. That autumn he entered St. John's College, Oxford, as a Rhodes Scholar from Mississippi and received from the University of Oxford the B.A. degree in the Honour School of Modern History in 1927 and the B.Litt. degree in Modern History in 1928. After his return to the United States he took a Ph.D. in modern European history at the University of Chicago in 1932.

Dr. Lyon's teaching career, which began at Louisiana

Polytechnic Institute in 1928, had been primarily at Colgate, where he became assistant professor of history in 1929. Promoted to a professorship and chairmanship of the department of history in 1934, he played a prominent part in the extensive reorganization of the Colgate curriculum and for seven years was chairman of the faculty committee which directed the upperclass concentration program. To his Colgate experience he added summer teaching as a visiting professor at Syracuse University, the University of Rochester, and the University of Missouri.

As a scholar his major interest was in the field of modern European history. His published works dealt primarily with French history and the relation of France to the United States. He was the author of two books: *Louisiana in French Diplomacy, 1759-1804,* published in 1934, and *The Man Who Sold Louisiana, The Career of François Barbé-Marbois,* which would come off the press in his first year at Pomona. His other publications included writings on Franco-American relations in the *Dictionary of American History,* and major articles in such professional journals as *The American Historical Review* and *The Journal of Modern History.*

The president-elect's interests in liberal education and history were fully shared by Mrs. Lyon, née Carolyn Bartel. A native of Richmond, Indiana, she spent her freshman and sophomore years at Earlham College in her home town. Transferring to Wellesley College, she received her B.A. degree with a major in French in 1928. At Wellesley she developed an interest in American history which led her to enter the graduate school of the University of Chicago where she took an M.A. in 1930. She then accepted a position as editorial assistant on *The Journal of Modern History* and *The Library Quarterly,* both published by the University of Chicago Press. She met Wilson Lyon when he was a graduate student at Chicago, and they were married in 1933.

The Lyons had attended institutions that prepared them unusually well for serving Pomona. Their undergraduate educations at the University of Mississippi, Earlham, and Wellesley had been in institutions none of which then exceeded a thousand students. Their graduate work in Oxford and Chicago was in universities and departments in which the enrollments were small, and the relationship of student and professor was close.

Colgate in the late 1920's and the 1930's was an ideal place for the education of a future president of Pomona. Despite its name as a university, which dated from an earlier time when it had had a divinity school, Colgate was a residential liberal arts college with an enrollment limited to a thousand men, offering instruction in all the fields taught at Pomona. Led by an able president, George Barton Cutten, Colgate had undergone a major curricular reorganization which advanced the scholarly quality of the college and attracted national attention. Colgate was so well administered that it maintained near normal enrollment throughout the Depression, and its faculty and staff suffered no salary decreases in those difficult years. President Cutten secured a grant from the Carnegie Corporation which enabled him to expand the faculty and the curriculum, and he brought to Colgate a group of young scholars to whom he entrusted very large responsibilities. It was an exciting and stimulating place, which, in addition to the development of its students and faculty, educated a group of future college presidents. After Dr. Lyon came to Pomona three of his faculty colleagues at Colgate were called to presidencies, at St. Lawrence University, Clark University, and Bates College, respectively.

Dr. and Mrs. Lyon came to Pomona with a deep sense of commitment. Keenly aware of the standards and ideals inherent in the college's New England origins and appreciative of the influence of Oxford on the Associated Colleges, they welcomed the opportunity to participate in developing Pomona as part of a great educational center on the Pacific Coast.

The Lyons and their children, Elizabeth, five, and John, two, arrived in Claremont by train early in September. The president's house had been renovated during the summer, the grounds improved by a wall, and the basis laid for a garden. As they learned of California plants, the Lyons developed a garden of camellias, hibiscus, and roses which became the center for countless college functions.

The trustees had wisely determined that the official transfer of authority from Dr. Edmunds to Dr. Lyon should be delayed until October 1. Thus Dr. Edmunds handled the opening of college, leaving the president-elect free to plan for the inaugural convoca-

Participants in the Ceremony of the Flame at the inauguration of E. Wilson Lyon: Dean Emeritus Edwin C. Norton, Professor Emeritus Frank P. Brackett, President of the Board of Trustees Frank H. Harwood '98, Honorary President of the Board George W. Marston, President Emeritus Charles K. Edmunds, President Lyon, and Eleanor Forbes '41

tion which was scheduled in Bridges Auditorium for Saturday morning, October 18. During the summer a special committee had begun to make arrangements for the inauguration which was also to mark Founders Day at Pomona. Invitations for official delegates had been sent to educational associations, the California colleges and universities with close ties to Pomona, and to institutions where Dr. Lyon had studied or taught. A general invitation had gone to all Pomona alumni, and there were official delegates representing the Pomona College Associates, the Friends of the Colleges at Claremont, and the Women's Campus Club of Pomona College.

The convocation was an inspiring occasion, dignified and festive. Claremont enjoyed a perfect October day, with the campus at its loveliest, and over two thousand people attended the inauguration.

The program, with Dr. Edmunds presiding, emphasized Dr. Lyon's education at the University of Oxford and the influence of Oxford in the development of the Associated Colleges at Claremont. Two distinguished Rhodes Scholars participated in the exercises of the day and received honorary degrees. Frank Aydelotte, Secretary to the Rhodes Scholarships in the United

States, former president of Swarthmore College, and since 1939 director of the Institute for Advanced Study, Princeton, New Jersey, gave the address of the morning, and Bernadotte E. Schmitt, professor of history at the University of Chicago, under whom Dr. Lyon had studied, spoke in the afternoon in the symposium on international relations.

Entitling his address "Liberal Education and the Crisis of Democracy," Aydelotte characterized the time "as a moment when a kind of rededication of our colleges and universities to the ideals of liberal education and democracy is taking place all over the United States. The feeling is widespread that for a generation our educational institutions have not met as fully as they might the demands of higher education in a democracy. We have all worked away in our different specialties without giving enough thought to the fundamental intellectual and spiritual ideals for which our colleges stand and the prevalence of which, indeed, makes such colleges as ours possible." Aydelotte reminded the convocation audience that in 1941 "all the intellectual and spiritual values which we group together when we speak of the democratic way of life are in danger. What is most precious is the opportunity for free thought and discussion of fundamental intellectual and spiritual problems which is the basis of all liberal education. It is no accident that democracy flourishes best in those countries where the ideals of liberal education are cherished and it is quite certain that liberal education as we think of it would be impossible under any kind of totalitarian regime."

Following Dr. Aydelotte's address, Frank H. Harwood, president of the Board of Trustees, inducted Dr. Lyon as the sixth president of Pomona College. Assuring him of the hearty support of faculty, students, alumni, and trustees, he summoned the president to his opportunity and his responsibilities. "I charge you," Mr. Harwood stated, "to fulfill the duties of your high office with all the energy, intelligence and zeal at your command. I charge you to be unswerving in your devotion to the cause of truth; that you be the active enemy of prejudice and intolerance; that you inculcate in the youth of this college a love of clear and precise thinking and of orderly knowledge; that you teach them both by precept and example to be ever loyal to the spirit of service to all mankind as well as to their immediate fellows; that you keep our shield stainless and hold our banner high."

President Lyon accepted these high responsibilities in an address entitled "The Role of the Liberal Arts College in Our Generation." As an historian, he saw "the world in the midst of one of the most far-reaching revolutions in modern history, a period resembling in many ways the religious upheavals of the sixteenth and seventeenth centuries in Europe." Liberal education, he emphasized, must provide the comprehensive view of society essential to master trends of our time, and with them our own destiny. Dr. Lyon felt the greatest responsibility of our colleges was training in public affairs. This would involve a reappraisal of our political and economic institutions and an understanding of the place of the United States in the world. Despite the troubles of the present, he looked to the future with hope and with confidence in the role that would be played by the graduates of American colleges. Among these, Pomona graduates should have a most distinguished place, for he believed that no college in America had a greater opportunity for future accomplishment.

Greetings to the college and the new president were presented from two educational associations of which Pomona was a member, and from three institutions with which President Lyon had intimate ties. The words and enactment of the Pomona College Ceremony of the Flame brought the convocation to an inspiring conclusion. Beginning with Mr. Marston and continuing to the president of the freshman class, the flame passed from candle to candle and symbolized the strength of Pomona's past and faith in her future.

For the Lyons the day was a delightful introduction to the cordial relationship which bound those who led higher education in California. A gala luncheon for over 900 guests was served on Marston Quadrangle, decorated for the occasion with blue and white umbrellas, and with music by the Pomona College Band. The luncheon had all the charm of a leisurely English garden party. In such pleasant circumstances Dr. Lyon met for the first time Dr. Robert A. Millikan, the great physicist under whose brilliant leadership the California Institute of Technology had gained world renown, and President Robert Gordon Sproul, under whom since 1930 the University of California had become the greatest of the American state universities. With these and other acquaintances made that day, Dr. Lyon began the formation of friendships which soon made him feel at home in California.

The new president had been called to a remarkably well-organized and smoothly functioning institution. The college had made great strides forward in the thirteen years under Dr. Edmunds. The building of the residential campus provided not only rooms and dining halls for students but facilities which made possible a remarkable sense of academic community. The student body handled its affairs effectively and provided a well-organized social program for the entire college. The financial affairs of the many student organizations were well handled by the graduate manager. A regular program of public exercises had been developed, with weekly chapel services and all-college assemblies. Following the assembly talk, students and faculty met with the speaker in the private dining room in South Frary, the president of the college normally presiding. The music department offered a student or faculty recital every Monday evening. Formal convocations were held at the opening of each semester, on Founders Day, and on Matriculation and Parents Day, as well as at commencement.

The administration and the faculty functioned with exceptional harmony. Dr. Burgess, as the experienced secretary of the faculty, supervised the day to day operation of the academic program. To facilitate the change of administration, the trustees had re-established the position of dean of the faculty,to which Professor Philip A. Munz had been appointed. The deans of students and the senior faculty had been long in service and were deeply devoted to Pomona. The constitution of the college as set up in the by-laws and the practices of the faculty were admirable, and there were safeguards against the conflicts that often develop in academic institutions.

The faculty included some seventy-five members and the enrollment of the college was approximately 850. To the young faculty who had been appointed since 1936 were added in the autumn of 1941 four others who would spend their professional careers in the Claremont community.

Dr. Ch'en Shou-Yi, formerly professor of history at the National University, Peking, China, and more recently of the University of Hawaii, was named professor of Chinese culture. He was a graduate of Lingnan University, where President Edmunds had known him as an outstanding student. After Lingnan, Professor Ch'en took a Ph.D. in comparative literature at the University of Chicago. Earlier he had taught a semester at Pomona in 1936-37, and it was with much pleasure that the college welcomed him to the permanent faculty.

Three young men were appointed as instructors. Frederick Ludwig Mulhauser, Jr., in English, who came from Northwestern University, was a graduate of the College of Wooster and had taken a Ph.D. at Yale. Charles Shiveley Holmes, also in English, was a graduate of Oberlin College who was completing his Ph.D. at Princeton. Luther J. Lee '33, doctoral candidate at Berkeley, who came as instructor in government, would make a significant contribution to Pomona and the Claremont Graduate School.

The assets of the college on June 30, 1941 were $7,576,821.71, of which $3,491,926.66 was in permanent endowment, the income of which was available for college use. Academic expenditures for 1940-41 were $524,160. The highest faculty salary was $4850.

The Lyons were cordially welcomed by the Pomona alumni. The Los Angeles alumni honored them with a dinner at the University Club the week of the inauguration, and shortly thereafter Mr. Hawley drove Dr. and Mrs. Lyon on a memorable alumni tour, beginning with a meeting in San Diego which Mr. Marston attended, and continuing to Santa Barbara, Fresno, and San Francisco. This introduction to the strength of Pomona's alumni and to the diversity and beauty of California contributed greatly to the Lyons' understanding of the scope and potential of their new responsibilities.

For the young college president the quality of alumni, faculty, and students would be an enormous source of strength as together they faced the crisis of December 7, 1941. On that day the Lyons

Dr. and Mrs. Lyon welcome trustee Arthur J. McFadden '01 and Mrs. McFadden '01 in the garden at the President's House

had driven to La Jolla where, with Dr. and Mrs. Edmunds, they were to discuss with trustee and Mrs. James E. MacMurray a proposed additional women's residence hall. As the Lyons arrived in La Jolla, they were stunned by the radio report that the Japanese had bombed Pearl Harbor.

The Outbreak of Hostilities

The attack on Pearl Harbor ended any serious differences of opinion among Americans regarding the foreign policy of their country. Within a few days the nation entered the war and formed a coalition with Great Britain, Russia, and China. Congress declared war on Japan on December 8 with only one dissenting vote. Germany and Italy declared war on the United States on December 11, and that same day Congress adopted a resolution recognizing a state of war with both countries. On January 1, 1942 representatives of twenty-six nations, including the United States, Great Britain, the Soviet Union, and China, met in Washington and pledged maximum war effort against Germany, Italy, and Japan, each agreeing not to sign a separate armistice or peace treaty. As Churchill had hoped a year and a half before, "In God's good time, the New World, with all its power and might," had come to "the rescue and the liberation of the Old." The American people saw the Second World War in such terms; for them its essential aims were the preservation of freedom and democracy. The nation was united more than it had been in any previous war in American history.

For the colleges and universities, the academic year 1941-42 was a period of fairly slow transition from peace to the conditions of war. Although the selective service age was lowered to twenty and extended to forty-four on December 19, 1941, there was only a small drop in college enrollments. The government needed time to prepare for training the men required and preferred to secure manpower through selective service rather than enlistment. The War Department, therefore, urged students to remain in college until their selective service numbers were called. Consequently Pomona had a loss of only fifty students by the end of the first semester, and the second semester opened with an enrollment of 747. When President Lyon attended the meeting of the Association of American Colleges in Baltimore in early January 1942, he learned that the government then had no plan for using the colleges for general or specific military training. Federal officials stated that the colleges could serve best by continuing their regular programs of instruction.

In Baltimore, however, Dr. Lyon found that there was widespread interest among colleges in accelerated programs and schedules that would make it possible for men to complete their college courses before they were called for military service. When he presented the matter of acceleration to the Pomona faculty, they voted unanimously for a new calendar that would keep the college in operation throughout the year. The Executive Committee of the trustees, in full accord, on January 14, 1942 authorized the president and the faculty to institute an accelerated program for the duration of the war and to establish the academic calendar as they deemed best.

The manner and speed with which Pomona inaugurated its accelerated program was a tribute to the faculty and the administration. The faculty generously offered their services for year-round teaching at no extra compensation. For 1941-42, the calendar was altered to eliminate the spring vacation and to establish a twelve-week summer term, divided into two sessions of six weeks each. Students could take one or both sessions as they preferred. A faculty member taught in only one six-week period. The student response was grateful and encouraging; attendance in the first half of the summer term, 1942, was 234, including 165 men and 69 women, and for the second half, 198, including 146 men and 52 women.

Effective with the autumn of 1942, the academic year was divided into three terms of sixteen weeks each. A term carried the academic work and credit normally given in a semester. The summer term was divided into two periods of eight weeks each, and a faculty member taught in only one period. Thus under the wartime calendar a faculty member would teach forty weeks a year instead of the earlier thirty-six. This year-round program made it possible for students already in college to graduate earlier or to complete certain essential courses before they were called into national service. Students entering Pomona from high school in the autumn of 1942 could graduate in the spring of 1945. The accelerated program was optional, and those who did not desire to accelerate could continue their college course on the basis of only two terms a year.

In the course of the first two years of the war most of the young men of the faculty were called to government service. The loss of faculty had begun as early as 1939-40 when Charles B. Fahs, a specialist in Japanese studies, had been placed on leave for work in the office of Coordinator of Information in Washington. Murray Kirkwood '33, in the government department, left for military service in the summer of 1941. After Pearl Harbor faculty departures were constant. John H. Kemble in history, who held a reserve commission in the Navy, was called to active duty in Washington in February 1942. By the end of the year Shirley Snider '37 in music and William A. Cass '39 in psychology had entered the Army. Norman Ness in economics took a position in Washington with the National Planning Association in January 1942. Three scientists were released for wartime research: Curtis Haupt in physics to the Radiation Laboratory at the Massachusetts Institute of Technology, Norman Elliott in chemistry to the Metallurgical Laboratory which the government had established at the University of Chicago, and Richard Post '40 in physics to the Naval Research Laboratory at Anacostia, Maryland.

A large group of the faculty entered the armed forces in 1942-43. W. T. Jones in philosophy accepted a commission in the Navy in December 1942. Joseph W. Angell in English enlisted in the Air Corps and later was commissioned as a second lieutenant. John H. Gleason in history received a commission as lieutenant in the Navy in July 1943. Charles S. Holmes in English entered the Navy Language Training School at Boulder in July 1943. Frederick L. Mulhauser in English entered the Army in November 1943 and would have long service in Italy. Miss Esther Bristol in physical education for women was given a leave of absence for service as a recruiting officer with the Red Cross in California. The Red Cross in 1944 claimed another faculty member and a key member of the college staff: Earl J. Merritt in physical education for men, was to serve primarily in India; Miss Lucille Gramse, director of dining halls, was stationed with the Red Cross in Great Britain.

While the young men were leaving for war service, Pomona, Claremont Colleges, and Scripps College all suffered grievous losses of older major administrative officers. Dr. George S. Burgess, who had joined the Pomona faculty in 1918 and who had served as secretary of the faculty since 1927, died on July 7, 1942. He had suffered for some months with a painful illness which forced him to give up teaching, but he heroically continued his administrative duties to the end of the college year. As secretary of the faculty, Dr. Burgess was the chief assistant to the young president, and his wise counsel and friendship would be greatly missed.

Only a few months earlier, on March 26, 1942, the Associated Colleges suffered a tragic loss in the death of Russell M. Story,

George S. Burgess, Professor of Law and Secretary of the Faculty

president of Claremont Colleges. Dr. Story had succeeded Dr. Blaisdell as president of Claremont Colleges in 1937. There he had made important contributions in the establishment of graduate work, particularly in the social sciences. Dr. Story had welcomed Dr. Lyon with great cordiality and their mutual understanding had promised much for the future of the Associated Colleges.

Two months after the death of Dr. Story, Dr. Lyon was the only college president in office in Claremont. For some time there had been growing difficulties at Scripps College between the faculty and President Jaqua. In fifteen years he had developed a college known throughout the country for its program in the humanities and the beauty of its buildings and grounds. However, he was less successful in administering the college and in holding the confidence of the faculty. The issues came to a head in the spring of 1942 and led to President Jaqua's resignation on May 27, 1942. Shortly thereafter he took a wartime position in Washington.

With the loss of their presidents, interim administrative arrangements were made by both Claremont Colleges and Scripps.

The Board of Fellows decided not to appoint a president at that time and named Robert J. Bernard, its secretary, as administrative director of Claremont Colleges. Scripps College turned to a member of its Board of Trustees, and on July 9, 1942, elected Mrs. Elbert W. Shirk of Redlands as acting president. A graduate of Smith College and a devoted trustee, she brought to her office, in which she would continue until January 1, 1944, a generosity of spirit and charm of manner that endeared her to all who served with her.

At Pomona President Lyon met the administrative crisis by taking the full academic administration into his own office. The position of secretary of the faculty was left vacant, and when Dr. Munz insisted on returning to full-time teaching the office of the dean of the faculty also was not filled. The president elected to administer the college by working directly with the department chairmen and the chairmen of the major faculty committees. He was ably assisted by Dr. Munz,who agreed to serve as chairman of the courses of study committee. The president also did some teaching in the department of history. He assumed work in the department when Dr. Kemble was called to the Navy, and, beginning with the autumn of 1942, Dr. Lyon introduced a one-term course, "The History of American Foreign Policy," which he taught for several years. Working with the students in this course proved to be one of the most rewarding experiences of Dr. Lyon's teaching career.

Effective administration from the president's office was due to the ability and devotion of the secretary to the president, Miss Agnes M. Johnson. She had served in this capacity throughout the administration of President Edmunds and was thoroughly informed on every aspect of the college. Born in Norway, educated from early childhood in Chicago, she came to California for her health, and joined the staff of Pomona in 1925. Miss Johnson had invaluable aptitudes, ranging from a remarkable skill with figures to a keen editorial sense. These accomplishments were joined with objectivity, wisdom, and total dependability. The president and Miss Johnson made the budget, edited the catalog, drafted the programs for convocations, and arranged for assembly and convocation speakers. They worked every Saturday, and often Sunday as well. In the long absences of the president necessary in the era of train travel, Miss Johnson ran the office to the satisfaction of both the faculty and trustees. Fortunately for both Dr. Lyon and Pomona, she remained as secretary to the president until her retirement in September 1967.

Amid its losses of senior administrators Pomona was able to secure a man who would make an outstanding contribution to the college. When Dr. Lyon took office, Howard H. Pattee '22, director of admissions, had resigned, and one of the president's most urgent responsibilities was the appointment of his successor. Fortunately Dr. Lyon could recommend a highly qualified man. On December 8, 1941, J. Edward Sanders, professor of education and chairman of the department at Hendrix College, Arkansas, was appointed assistant dean of students, in charge of admissions. A graduate of Hendrix with a Ph.D. from Columbia University, Dr. Sanders had joined the faculty at Colgate, where he and Dr. Lyon had been colleagues from 1930 to 1935. Subsequently, he served for two years as admissions officer and director of personnel at the University of Redlands, before going to Hendrix.

The three terms of 1942-43 constituted a period of change and adjustment unique in the history of the college. The fall term opened with a capacity enrollment of civilian students. A year later more than half those instructed on the campus were soldiers in special military training programs.

The loss of civilian students was mitigated by the fact that calls to military service were handled in a manner that allowed some planning by the student and his institution. Most Pomona men enlisted in one of the reserve corps and were permitted additional time in college before going on active duty. Students were normally called at the end of an academic term, and all mass departures from Pomona came at such times. During the year, 239 men left for military service. As Congress, on November 13, 1942, had lowered the draft age to eighteen, few new men entered Pomona; only thirty-six freshman men were enrolled in the spring term of 1944.

Most men's organizations were discontinued after 1942-43,

among them the Men's Glee Club and the Associated Men Students. The fraternities were suspended by the faculty when their members left for military service in 1943. Intercollegiate athletics were discontinued after 1942-43, and the operation of the conference was suspended for the remainder of the war.

While civilian men were leaving, the college was welcoming military units which would spend most of the year on the campus. The government had reversed its earlier decision not to make use of college facilities, and by the autumn of 1943 had established training programs on college and university campuses throughout the country. Pomona was one of the earlier colleges to secure a training program for the armed forces. In the autumn of 1942, President Gordon K. Chalmers of Kenyon College conceived the idea of organizing a group of liberal arts colleges which could undertake a program of training weather officers for the Army Air Forces. Encouraged by the Army authorities, President Chalmers asked a small number of institutions to join in the undertaking and Pomona received an invitation to participate. When constituted, the group included twelve institutions: Amherst College, Bowdoin College, Carleton College, Denison University, Hamilton College, Haverford College, Kenyon College, Pomona College, Reed College, the University of Chicago, Vanderbilt University, and the University of Virginia. These institutions contracted to conduct a basic pre-meteorological training program under the supervision of the University Meteorological Committee which the Army Air Forces had established in Chicago. Cadets were to remain at the colleges for twelve months after which they would spend eight months in an advanced center.

On February 15, 1943 Pomona welcomed a detachment of 225 enlisted men in the pre-meteorological program. In operation the unit was a joint venture for the Air Forces and the college. The cadets were under military discipline and responsible to an officer who directed their training. The academic program was entirely in the hands of the college. Courses of college grade and credit were given in physics, mathematics, vector analysis, geography, American history, and English. Dr. Tileston organized the program and served as its educational director as well as chairman of the courses in physics and vector analysis. Chairmen of the other courses were Dr. Jaeger, mathematics; Dr. Strathmann, history and English; and John S. Shelton '35, geography. Housing and messing were provided by the college on the Clark campus.

In the spring of 1943 the Army and the Navy announced a nation-wide training program to be conducted in college and university facilities. Because of its long experience with the Army Reserve Officers Training Corps, Pomona was grouped with the institutions that were to serve the Army. Three units of the Army Specialized Training Program, providing instruction for some 325 men, were established on the campus on June 14, 1943. The three units and their initial enrollments were: basic engineering, 210; European area and languages (French and Spanish), 88; and Oriental area and languages (Chinese and Japanese), 21. The terms were for twelve weeks. The basic engineering curriculum included chemistry, engineering drawing, English, geography, history, mathematics and physics. In the area and language units, language was taught by the intensive method, placing primary attention on the spoken language and giving little time to writing, a new procedure which would have great influence after the war.

The operation of the units of the Army Specialized Training Program and their relation to the college followed the pattern begun with the pre-meteorology program. Senior faculty members headed the instructional staff for each unit: first Dr. Munz and then Dr. Jaeger for basic engineering, Dr. Crowell for European area and languages, and Dr. Duncan for Oriental area and languages. Dean Nicholl served as coordinator for the entire program. The college by contract provided instruction, housing and messing. The men, in uniform and under military discipline, were under the command of Colonel Raymond C. Baird, who since 1941 had been stationed at Pomona as head of the R.O.T.C. program. His knowledge of the college and his cooperative spirit greatly facilitated the reception and management of the A.S.T.P. units.

Thus, by the summer of 1943, Pomona was operating three separate institutions on its campus: the civilian college, the pre-meteorology program, and the Army Specialized Training Program. Each of the military programs imposed the necessity of hurriedly recruiting large numbers of specialized faculty. In addition to the regular Pomona faculty who participated in the pre-meteorology program, six full-time teachers were engaged for this unit. Ten full-time teachers were employed for the basic engineering unit. Twelve teachers, some of them part-time, were recruited for the foreign area and language programs. The faculty of each military program was separately organized and administered. The employment of each individual was temporary and did not include membership in the faculty of Pomona College.

By the autumn of 1943 the total enrollment was 959, of whom 515 were in the civilian college, 173 in the pre-meteorology program, and 271 in the three units of the Army Specialized Training Program. The pre-meteorology program had been reduced by the return to the ranks of men who failed to meet its academic requirements, and some of the men in the A.S.T.P. had completed their course. To accommodate these large numbers the Clark campus and Frary dining hall were assigned exclusively to the military and operated for them by the college. Smiley Hall was reserved for civilian men. The women, whose numbers had increased to 414, occupied Harwood Court, Blaisdell Hall, and the college-owned houses on the women's campus. All civilian students ate together in Harwood dining hall. Community sense was strong among the civilians who saw much of both fellow students and faculty.

The Student Union was the center of campus social life. Formal dances, each with a theme and decorations, were held in the ballroom throughout the war. "Enough men were accumulated to enable the majority of the student body to attend; thus despite the war," stated the 1945 *Metate,* "dances continued to be the heart of Pomona's social life."

The women kept alive many of the basic activities and traditions of the campus. They edited *Student Life,* reduced for a short period to two pages, and continued the *Metate.* In 1944-45 senior Margaret Boothby became the first woman to be elected president of the Associated Students. The Christmas Supper and May Day were enjoyed. The Pomona College Choir, the Women's Glee Club, and the orchestra gave excellent performances throughout the war years. Notable among the small number of men in the civilian

Cadets of the pre-meteorology unit

A graduation review on Marston Quadrangle, Thanksgiving Day 1943.
President Lyon, Professor Tileston, and Dean Nicholl

Pomona men leave for the Armed Forces, spring 1943, from the Pacific Electric station at First Street and College Avenue

Presidents Blaisdell, Edmunds, and Lyon, Founders Day 1944

college in 1943-44 were two Chinese students, Donald H. Tsai '44 and Raymond H. Chuan '44, who as president of the senior class and president of the Associated Students, respectively, gave leadership in the best Pomona tradition. Memorable was a dinner for the entire faculty given by the class of '44 at Padua Hills. Despite the paucity of men, Mrs. Allen presented each year a series of plays of such quality that they were eagerly awaited not only in the college but by many in the Pomona Valley.

The separation of classes and the intensity of the Army programs left little time during the week for contact between the soldiers and the civilian students. However, the full recreational facilities were available to the men in uniform and on weekends they participated in the social activities of the campus. *Student Life* served as a link among all groups, carrying news of the civilian college and all the Army units.

An extensive program of public exercises continued throughout the war and assemblies of the entire college were held each Thursday morning. The speakers included many distinguished visitors, among whom in 1942-43 were: A. D. Lindsay, Master of Balliol College, Oxford; Edward Weeks, editor of *The Atlantic;* and Halvdan Koht, historian and Foreign Minister of Norway when that country was invaded in 1940, who spent a month on the campus during which he gave a series of lectures and met informally with classes and seminars.

Commencements for the college were held at the end of each term, and several significant public exercises were held in cooperation with Army units. At a military review on Marston Quadrangle on Thanksgiving Day 1943 Colonel Baird presented graduation certificates to the first men completing their work in the Army Specialized Training Program. The pre-meteorology students were graduated in an impressive ceremony in Bridges Hall on February 12, 1944. On the completion of their work, certificates were presented to the men in the three units of the A.S.T.P. on March 2, 1944.

The military programs came to an end early in 1944, the pre-meteorology unit in February as expected, and the Army Specialized Training Program units in March, when the government rather suddenly decided to terminate the program throughout the country. It was a tribute to the administration and the faculty that within a short time the college was able to make an efficient adjustment to the loss of nearly half those being instructed on the campus. As teachers recruited from the outside had been engaged on a month to month basis, the college incurred no financial obligation when the military programs were terminated.

These programs were an important factor in carrying the college through the most critical days of the war. The income they brought enabled the college to avoid a deficit for the first two years of the war and to maintain its fundamental academic structure intact. Except in physical education for men, Pomona had college work in their own fields for all of its faculty members who wished to remain in Claremont. Because the college was coeducational, it was able to preserve the continuity of its work and its basic traditions.

The low points of enrollment were reached in the spring term and summer term of 1944. The spring term began with 465 students and ended with 449. By classes, the opening enrollment of the spring term included: seniors, 18 men and 67 women; juniors, 10 men and 83 women; sophomores, 12 men and 98 women; freshmen, 36 men and 134 women; and special students, 3 men and 4 women. The summer term of 1944 had a total of 142 students for the first half and 100 for the second half, as compared to 271 and 151 in the summer term of 1943.

In contrast to these fluctuations, enrollment was constant in 1944-45, with 575 in the first semester and 556 in the second. A major factor in the increase over the previous year was the decision to admit an additional 100 women and to house them on the men's campus. Units of Clark Hall were skillfully converted into attractive residences for women, and reception and social rooms were provided by removing partitions and throwing several rooms together. These changes were made in the expectation that the converted accommodations would continue to be occupied by women in 1945-46.

In handling the many problems of wartime operation Pomona was strengthened by the close cooperation among California colleges and universities which began in 1941. Earlier there had been little communication between the institutions of higher education in Southern California and those of the San Francisco Bay area. A momentous step was taken in 1941 when first Stanford and then the University of California, Berkeley, joined the Southern California institutions in their Association of Colleges and Universities of the Pacific Southwest. In recognition of its wider membership the name of the association was changed to the Western College Association in March 1942. The significance of the expansion was evident when Dr. Robert Gordon Sproul, the president of the University of California, was elected president of the Western College Association for 1942-43.

As the Association of Colleges and Universities of the Pacific Southwest had begun at Pomona in 1924 and as Professor Charles T. Fitts of the Pomona faculty had been its executive secretary since that time, President Lyon was well informed on its activities. He participated in its semi-annual meetings and strongly supported the expansion into the Bay Area and the change of name.

Dr. Lyon's election as president of the Western College Association for 1943-44 gave him an exceptional opportunity to work with other California educators and to learn of higher education, both public and private, within the state. He was privileged to preside at Berkeley in the autumn of 1943 in the first meeting of the Association to be held in the Bay Area, and in the spring of 1944 to welcome the Western College Association to Pomona for its twentieth anniversary. Dr. Lyon felt enough at home in California to deliver a presidential address entitled "Higher Education in the West from 1924 to 1944." The general topic of the meeting, "Postwar Problems of Higher Education," was foremost in everyone's mind.

CHAPTER XXI

From War to Peace

AS THE AMERICAN, British, and Russian armies advanced in Europe and the American forces moved steadily toward Japan in the summer of 1944, their ultimate victory became clear. Statesmen increasingly turned their thoughts to the reorganization of their own countries and to the establishment of an international structure that could prevent another world war. Within each country the leaders of domestic institutions faced new responsibilities.

In the United States, higher education was given an unprecedented opportunity to serve the nation. On June 22, 1944 President Roosevelt had signed the Servicemen's Readjustment Act which the country soon christened the G.I. Bill of Rights. Noble in plan, wise in its provisions, and practical in application, the bill was one of the most important legislative acts in American history. Those who had been in military service were eligible for educational benefits which included full payment of tuition and fees with a monthly subsistence allowance, and a subsistence allowance for dependents. The full payment of tuition and fees by the government gave the serviceman equal access to both public and private institutions regardless of costs. Never had there been such a forceful national affirmation of the value of higher education in the United States. A new era had begun for American colleges and universities. Nowhere was this truer than in California, where the population would grow from 6,907,387 in 1940 to 10,586,223 in 1950.

Pomona College had prepared for the great opportunity which was now hers. After the military units departed, the faculty, warmly supported by the president, used the time gained to complete a comprehensive revision of the curriculum. For three years the courses of study committee had engaged in a careful study of Pomona's entire academic program. Its recommendations constituted one of the most significant changes in the history of the college. The wisdom of the report and the support of the faculty were attested when the new curriculum was adopted unanimously.

The new regulations for the B.A. degree which went into full effect for the freshman class entering in 1945-46 were only partially occasioned by the war. It was obvious by the autumn of 1941 that the elective system, under which the college had been operating, permitted students to graduate without the common fund of knowledge essential for a free society. The revision, though comprehensive, was not radical. While election was restricted, students were not placed in rigid programs where everything would be prescribed for them.

The new curriculum was dominated by the philosophy that in the first two years the student should acquire certain fundamental skills and information in addition to artistic appreciation. To accomplish this one would be expected to take seven basic year-courses in the fields of English, biological science, physical science, the social sciences, literature, art or music, and philosophy or religion; these were soon known as "the seven pillars of wisdom." Normally the student had a choice from two or more courses in each of these basic fields. A student with exceptional high school preparation might be excused from a course in biological or physical science. As a student generally took five courses, there remained opportunity in the first two years to elect courses in such areas as languages, mathematics, or psychology.

At the end of the sophomore year the student was required to select a field of concentration, for which the minimum and maximum limits were set at twenty-four and thirty-six units, with the expectation that the former would be the normal requirement. The concentration program thus permitted juniors and seniors to elect from two-fifths to three-fifths of their upperclass program in other fields. Concentration might be in a single department or in a unified program involving courses from two or more departments.

At the end of the senior year the student would take a comprehensive examination over his field of concentration, and the successful passing of this examination was a condition of graduation.

Students who had entered Pomona before September 1945 continued under the requirements at the time of their admission. It would not be until September 1949 that nearly all students were proceeding to their degrees under the new curriculum. Once in full operation it continued for twenty years without any major change, meeting uncommonly well the needs of the 1950's and 1960's.

While the college was preparing for peacetime operation, it kept in touch with its alumni and students in the armed services. The alumni office was untiring in its communication with those in uniform. Mr. Hawley wrote a regular letter to all Pomona service men and service women, and his warm personal news from the campus brought countless grateful responses. Individual faculty members carried on extensive correspondence with their students.

The annual Alumni Fund, which was used to help worthy and deserving students attend Pomona, increased steadily throughout the war. It grew from $13,383 in 1941-42 to $48,395 in 1944-45. Illustrative of the support of those in the armed forces were two hundred gifts in 1942-43 from men in military posts in the United States, England, North Africa, China, Australia, New Guinea, and Guadalcanal.

The Alumni Association received national recognition for its action in setting aside $5000 from the Alumni Fund of 1942-43 as a trust fund to provide scholarships after the war for men whose education at Pomona was interrupted by their call to the armed forces. An additional $10,000 was reserved for this purpose from the Alumni Fund of 1943-44.

A further notable step was taken when the Alumni Association established five nationwide four-year scholarships, awarded for the first time in September 1945. To be eligible a student was to be nominated by the principal or headmaster of his secondary school and recommended by this official as a person of outstanding ability who gave promise of being a good student and a leader. The alumni four-year scholarships brought strength where the Pomona scholarship program was weakest. Hitherto, most of the college scholarships were for freshmen, and only limited funds were available for assisting students after their first year. This resulted in the reluctance of many well qualified students to apply to Pomona, and in the withdrawal of students who were unable to secure a scholarship after their freshman year.

Despite such assistance from the alumni and the prospect of peace, the college faced an immediate financial crisis when the military units departed in the spring of 1944. There was no certainty regarding enrollment nor any clear opinion as to the extent that veterans would use the G.I. Bill for attending liberal arts colleges. It appeared that a gap of several years might well ensue before Pomona would again have an enrollment of 800. President Lyon advised the trustees that he foresaw a deficit of $72,000 for 1944-45 and probably a like amount for the two years thereafter.

The Board took impressive action. The ways and means committee, under the vigorous leadership of the vice president of the board, R. J. Wig, recommended the establishment of a Wartime Emergency Fund to cover deficits over a three-year period, and the trustees in a special meeting on June 5, 1944 approved the creation of such a fund in the amount of $225,000. President Harwood said the ways and means committee felt that as much as $100,000 should be raised within the Board.

Success in raising the Wartime Emergency Fund required additional time for each trustee and a reorganization of the college staff. Mr. Hawley was asked to relinquish his other duties and give full time to fund-raising. In order for him to do this Robert L. Strehle '19, associate professor of physical education, took over the work of the alumni office, including the letters to those in military service.

Trustee William B. Himrod '08, gave up the practice of law in Los Angeles and generously accepted at a very modest stipend the position of assistant to the president. With an office in Los Angeles and his wide acquaintance there Mr. Himrod was able to place the needs of the college before a constantly increasing group of his friends. Working closely with Mr. Hawley and the trustees in raising the emergency fund, Mr. Himrod saw the even larger needs that lay ahead for Pomona. The task he undertook in 1944 led him to dedicate the remainder of his life to the financial advancement of his alma mater.

Assistance was also required in the administration of academic matters which President Lyon had handled largely in his own office since the death of Dr. Burgess. It was decided to restore the office of secretary of the faculty and F. Raymond Iredell '21, professor of philosophy, was appointed effective January 1, 1944. As his own college career at Pomona had been interrupted by World War I and service in France, Dr. Iredell had a deep appreciation of the problems of veterans and of a college turning from war to peace. He had established himself as an outstanding teacher and an invaluable member of faculty committees, and had succeeded Dr. Story as chairman of the committee on scholarships. Dr. Lyon had been much impressed by Dr. Iredell's understanding of the entire college, his support of high academic standards, and his devotion to the ideals of Pomona's founders. There was complete understanding between the two men, and they worked together with rare effectiveness.

Rebuilding the Faculty

There was much to be done immediately in rebuilding the faculty. In addition to the departure of young men for war service the faculty had suffered serious losses in six academic departments by death, retirements, and resignation. Dr. Edward McChesney Sait, professor of government since 1928, died on October 25, 1943. Dr. Charles J. Robinson, professor of chemistry since 1927, after a short illness died on February 25, 1944. George N. Tyson '35, assistant professor of chemistry, resigned at the end of the summer term of 1944 to become Director of Research for the new laboratory which the Pacific Coast Borax Company had established in Pasadena. Dr. Bernard C. Ewer, professor of psychology since 1916, retired at the end of 1942-43. Dr. William A. Hilton, professor of zoology and the senior member of the science faculty, retired at the end of the summer term in 1944. Edward Taylor, professor of engineering mathematics since 1916, also retired at the end of the summer term of 1944. Dr. Philip A. Munz, professor of botany, resigned, effective July 1, 1944, to become professor of botany and horticulture at Cornell University.

While there was sufficient staff within the college for the work in the other five departments, at least on a temporary basis, it was essential to find a scholar who could assume the work in botany immediately. Dr. Munz had carried the entire program in botany and had made the department outstanding in the West. Through his wide contacts and with his personal assistance Pomona found a worthy successor. Dr. Lyman Benson, assistant professor of botany at the University of Arizona, was appointed associate professor of botany and chairman of the department, effective September 1, 1944. Then thirty-five years of age, Dr. Benson was a graduate of Stanford University where he had also received his Ph.D. Already a widely recognized scholar, he was an authority on ranunculus and the author of two books, *The Cacti of Arizona* and *Trees and Shrubs of the Southwestern Deserts.* He brought with him a personal herbarium of 21,000 specimens which he gave to Pomona as an addition to the impressive herbarium developed by Dr. Munz.

The crisis in the chemistry department was met by the appointment of Dr. Stanley Davis Wilson, Dean of the College of Natural Science at Yenching University, Peking, China, as a visiting professor of chemistry for 1944-45 and 1945-46. Dr. Wilson, who held B.A., M.A., and honorary D.Sc. degrees from Wesleyan University, Middletown, Connecticut, and a Ph.D. from the University of Chicago, had given years to teaching and administration at Yenching. Interned by the Japanese when they occupied Peking, he was one of the large group of American teachers and missionaries who were repatriated in the dramatic voyage of the Swedish liner *Gripsholm* in March 1943. An excellent scholar and a wonderful person, Dr. Wilson blessed Pomona by his presence, and it was with regret that the college saw him return to Yenching in 1946.

In other departments the vacancies would continue into or throughout 1944-45. Professor Robert S. Ellis succeeded Dr. Ewer as chairman of the department of psychology. Dr. Willis E. Pequegnat, assistant professor of biology, was made chairman of the department of zoology. Luther J. Lee, Jr. '33, instructor in government, was placed in charge of that department following the death of Dr. Sait.

Fortunately the college was able to bring a permanent chairman for the department of government somewhat earlier than expected. By the autumn of 1944, the United States Government could consider releasing some of the large body of political scientists, economists, and historians who had been called for service in Washington. Dr. John Albert Vieg, in the international relations section of the Bureau of the Budget, was able to secure a release, and he was appointed associate professor and chairman of the department of government, effective January 1, 1945. A native of Iowa and forty years of age, Dr. Vieg held a B.A. degree from St. Olaf College, an M.A. in history from the University of Iowa, and a Ph.D. in political science from the University of Chicago. When called to Washington he was an associate professor at Iowa State University, Ames. He was the author of *The Government of Education in Metropolitan Chicago* and co-author of *Wartime Government in Operation.*

In the basic engineering staff of the Army Specialized Training Program Pomona discovered a remarkable scholar and teacher for the permanent faculty of the English department. Frederick Bracher had left the faculty of San Francisco City College to teach in military programs at the Santa Ana Army Air Base, whence he came to the basic engineering staff at Pomona. He was appointed assistant professor of English, effective the autumn of 1944. Thirty-nine years of age and holding a B.S. degree from Oregon State College, and M.A. and Ph.D. degrees from the University of California, Berkeley, Dr. Bracher had taught at the University of California and the University of Wisconsin before going to San Francisco City College. As teacher, author, and a faculty member he was devoted to the whole program of the college and would make a major contribution to its development.

The college was fortunate to secure the services of Louis B. Wright as visiting professor of American Civilization from 1944 to 1948. Then research professor at the Huntington Library, he taught a course in the "History of Ideas in America," until he left to become Director of the Folger Shakespeare Library in Washington, D.C.

In 1945 the joint appointment of Hubert Herring as professor of Latin American Civilization, by Pomona and the Claremont Graduate School, added a new field to the curriculum of each institution. As teacher, lecturer, and writer Mr. Herring made Claremont an important center of Latin American studies.

Changes in the Associated Colleges

While Pomona was occupied with the reorganization of its own faculty and staff, major changes were occurring in the Associated Colleges. Most notable were the election of a permanent president for Scripps College, and a fundamental reorganization of Claremont Colleges by action of the three boards of trustees of the Associated Colleges.

The excellent administration of Acting President Shirk had allowed the Scripps trustees to conduct an unhurried search for a new president. Their choice was Dr. Frederick Hard, who took office on January 1, 1944 and was formally inducted on March 25. A native of Alabama and a graduate of the University of the South, with an M.A. from the University of North Carolina, and a Ph.D. in English literature from Johns Hopkins University, Dr. Hard brought to Scripps long experience as a teacher and administrator. A scholar in English literature, particularly of the Renaissance, he was dean of Sophie Newcomb College, Tulane University, when called to Scripps. The coming of Dr. and Mrs. Hard was extremely congenial to Dr. and Mrs. Lyon. The two men had grown up in neighboring states and had many mutual associations in the South. Mrs. Hard, a native of Louisiana, like Mrs. Lyon was an alumna of Wellesley College. The Lyons and the Hards and their families formed a lifelong friendship which they would be privileged to enjoy in Claremont for the next twenty years.

Two basic changes in the inter-relationships of the Associated Colleges were enacted during the war years. The first, the Operating Agreement of 1942, was the result of mounting difficulties dating from the 1930's and had no relationship to the war. The second, the Reorganization of Claremont Colleges in the autumn of 1944, though occasioned by the consequences of the war was also addressed to the long-range operation of the Associated Colleges.

When Dr. Lyon visited Claremont in April 1941, he was told that an operating agreement on the relations of the Associated Colleges had been drafted by a committee consisting of the president and two faculty members of each institution and that it would be adopted in the autumn. The committee, which had been appointed in the spring of 1940, had been greatly encouraged by President Story. "The fundamental weakness of the Claremont Colleges plan lies in the absence of a known delineation of functions which serve as a basis for effective and authoritative jurisdiction," he reported to the Board of Fellows on May 4, 1940. "No time should be lost in the effort to provide effective implementation of constitutional arrangements acceptable to all concerned." The committee saw its mission as the drafting of a constitution "to govern the relationships between Claremont Colleges, Pomona College and Scripps College and such other institutions as may later be brought within this group, and to clarify the procedures and responsibilities of their respective administrations in relation to each other."

When the committee report was submitted to the three boards of trustees, a joint trustee committee was created to study its provisions and to make recommendations to the respective boards. After many meetings and much rewriting of the document, the joint committee unanimously recommended it to the trustees of the three institutions, all of which promptly voted approval. The agreement went into effect on July 1, 1942.

Although the document as enacted was entitled an "operating agreement," rather than a constitution, its provisions were constitutional in nature, and of fundamental effect in the evolution of the group plan. It was "the first written plan of operations which was unconditionally agreed to by the trustees of the three institutions," wrote William W. Clary '11 who, as a member of the Board of Fellows and as a member of the joint trustee committee, was one of the chief drafters of the Operating Agreement.

The key feature of the Operating Agreement was the creation of a new Intercollegiate Council composed of the chairmen of the boards of trustees, the presidents of the colleges, and one faculty member of "professorial rank" from each institution, nominated by its faculty and serving for two years. In the handling of matters of inter-institutional concern the Intercollegiate Council replaced the Board of Fellows and became the coordinating body for the group of institutions. Entrusted to the Intercollegiate Council were "supervision of the administration of all joint budgets such as those of the Joint Committee on Ways and Means, the business office, the superintendency of plant and grounds, the health service, auditorium events which may be offered in common, library purchasing, cataloguing and service, and such other functions as shall be assigned to the Council by agreement of the member institutions." The Council was also empowered to supervise the personnel of these agencies and officers and to nominate the controller, the superintendent of plant and grounds, and the college physician. No new college could be admitted to the group without the approval of the Council.

The Operating Agreement defined the nature and function of the members of the Associated Colleges. Pomona's responsibility was maintenance of a coeducational undergraduate college for approximately 800 students in the liberal arts and sciences. Scripps' responsibility was the maintenance of a college for approximately 225 women, with special curricular emphasis on the humanities. Claremont Colleges was entrusted with the graduate program and the awarding of higher degrees, the support of research activities in the group of institutions, and conduct of the summer session.

Furthermore, there were a valuable series of agreements regarding inter-institutional services among the Associated Colleges. Payment for instructional services between and among the institutions was discontinued, and the principle of reciprocity of services was established. Normal gratuitous intercollegiate services included the teaching of one seminar per semester in the graduate school by an undergraduate teacher, if he were released for this purpose by his college, and the teaching of one undergraduate course per semester by a teacher on graduate appointment, if released to do so by the graduate school. There was confirmation in the Operating Agreement of the long established principle of opening courses in the respective colleges without charge to students from the other institutions.

The enactment of the Operating Agreement was a great disappointment to Dr. Blaisdell, who objected to the delegation of powers to the new Intercollegiate Council. He wrote a letter of opposition to Dr. George S. Sumner, with a copy to Mr. Harvey S. Mudd. Prior to their voting, this letter was communicated to both the Pomona Board of Trustees and the Board of Fellows. A week after the Operating Agreement had been approved by all the boards of trustees Mr. Clary, on behalf of the Board of Fellows, responded to Dr. Blaisdell. "The change is more in the machinery by which we function than in the essential character of the enterprise," he wrote. This was a sound judgment. In effect Claremont Colleges continued to hold legal title to the joint facilities; the Board of Fellows had merely recognized a new principle in their management. Furthermore, Claremont Colleges retained the right to take the lead in the organization of new colleges and the establishment of new facilities for the graduate school and the Associated Colleges. Mr. Clary wisely saw the Operating Agreement as "a necessary step in the evolution of the group plan."

Dr. Story, who had contributed so much to the development of the Operating Agreement, died within two months of its enactment and before it went into effect. The sudden loss of its president came at a time when the problems of Claremont Colleges were being compounded by the war. Its graduate school was particularly vulnerable, for nearly all male students were within the ages to be called for military service, and gifts to meet the recurring annual deficits were difficult to secure:

Despite the magnitude of these problems, there was no talk of dissolving the Claremont Colleges corporation and distributing its assets to the separate colleges as had been seriously considered in 1934-36. Robert J. Bernard, secretary of the Board of Fellows, was appointed to the interim position of administrative director "with the functions formerly exercised by the President." He brought much understanding and great diligence to his extremely demanding duties.

In the spring of 1944 the Board of Fellows appointed a special committee of its members to consider the future leadership of Claremont Colleges. This committee determined to use the crisis as a means of bringing the Associated Colleges more closely together and of strengthening the role of Claremont Colleges in serving the group. As a first step Harvey S. Mudd, chairman of the Board of Fellows and a member of the special committee, came to see Dr. Lyon at his home in Claremont and asked if he would accept the presidency of Claremont Colleges in addition to his responsibilities at Pomona.

Dr. Lyon replied that he would be pleased to do so if the headship of Claremont Colleges would be alternated with the president of Scripps College. This would introduce at Claremont, he said, an administrative plan like that of the University of Oxford, where the vice-chancellor was chosen from among the heads of the colleges. This practice provided effective administration of the university and also kept the colleges involved in the policies and operations. Mr. Mudd was cordial to the idea and the special committee favored it, as did a special faculty committee and the Educational Council. This concept of a rotating headship was basic in the reorganization of Claremont Colleges, which was approved by the three boards of trustees and put into effect in the autumn of 1944.

The reorganization involved a change of name as well as a new plan of administration. From its beginning the name "Claremont Colleges" had proved difficult to explain — even to faculty, let alone the general public. As its graduate work developed, the plural name seemed a misnomer for an institution conducting an instructional program. These criticisms were met by changing the corporate name to Claremont College with the provision that its educational work be conducted under the name of the Claremont Graduate School.

The official head of Claremont College was given the title of provost, rather than president, and the office was to be held in rotation by the presidents of Pomona College and Scripps College. The term of office was three years, and it was provided that the heads of any future colleges would be included in the rotation. The provost received no personal emolument for his services. It was estimated that he would give a fourth of his time to Claremont

College, which accordingly paid to the college of which he was president a sum equivalent to a fourth of his own salary and a fourth of that of his secretary. The provost, made "responsible for leadership in all the educational interests of the institution," exercised the customary responsibilities of a college president, such as the recommendation of faculty appointments, presiding at commencement and awarding degrees, and the preparation and presentation of the annual budget. Provision was made for the appointment of a dean of the Graduate School, and, effective September 1945, Dr. Harold W. Bradley '25, associate professor of history at Stanford, would be appointed to this important post.

The assumption of the provostship by the presidents of the undergraduate colleges was facilitated by the placing of the corporate and group responsibilities of Claremont College under an officer to be known as the "managing director." These responsibilities included oversight of Claremont College buildings, the operation of Bridges Auditorium concerts and lectures, the raising of funds for Claremont College, operation of the joint committee on ways and means and its activities, and the oversight of budget items and personnel in these areas. The position of managing director was admirably filled by Mr. Bernard, who already had these responsibilities very much in hand.

Cooperation among the Associated Colleges was strengthened by the provision that not only the provost but the president of the undergraduate college not then serving as provost be requested to attend all meetings of the Board of Fellows of Claremont College. The managing director should likewise be invited to attend meetings of the boards of trustees of the undergraduate colleges and to make reports on areas within his jurisdiction.

The discussions of the reorganization had been conducted throughout with such cordiality that the plan was approved without modification or objection by each of the three boards of trustees. On October 20, 1944 President Lyon was elected provost of Claremont College and Mr. Bernard was elected managing director. They were inducted into their new offices on November 14 at a special meeting of the faculties of the three colleges and the officers of the three boards of trustees held on the Scripps campus. Mr. Clary, as chairman of the committee, spoke on the background and provisions of the reorganization. Provost Lyon stressed the opportunities for more meaningful cooperation which the new plan could bring.

Public announcement of the plan of reorganization of Claremont Colleges was made the following evening at a dinner meeting of the Friends of the Colleges at Claremont. To this group of committed supporters Mr. Clary explained the changes and their objectives. Messrs. Bernard, Hard, and Lyon spoke on developments in education and the future responsibilities and opportunities of the Associated Colleges. The addresses of the evening, published under the general title, "Graduate and Undergraduate Developments in the War and Post-War Periods," constitute an excellent portrayal of wartime Claremont and the faith of trustees and administrators in the future of its colleges.

In Claremont Provost Lyon and Managing Director Bernard had already begun to exercise their mandate to reduce the deficits of Claremont College and to preserve its graduate program for future strengthening. The two men worked together congenially and wholeheartedly in their enlarged responsibility. They were guided and steadily supported by Harvey Mudd, who amid the vast expansion of his business, the Cyprus Mines, and its problems of wartime operation, always found time for Claremont College. Meetings of the Executive Committee and of other Claremont College and Associated Colleges committees were held in his office in the Pacific Mutual Building in Los Angeles. Adjacent to Mr. Mudd's office was the office of William L. Honnold. The young provost soon enjoyed the warm friendship of Mr. Mudd, Mr. Honnold, Mr. Clary, and Irving M. Walker, chairman of the Scripps Board. It was a rewarding responsibility for Dr. Lyon to work closely with both the Board of Fellows of Claremont College and the Board of Trustees of Pomona College and to sense their devotion to the development and expansion of higher education in Claremont as the nation turned from war to peace. "Claremont will be one of the great academic centers of the world," Mr. Honnold often said.

The Operating Agreement of 1942 and the Reorganization of the Administration of Claremont Colleges in 1944 provided constitutional bases upon which the Associated Colleges could work effectively and wholeheartedly. An era of good feeling ensued among both trustees and faculties.

Della Mulock Mudd Hall

Afternoon tea in Mudd Hall

CHAPTER XXII

The Veterans Return

"THEY CAME BACK by twos and threes at first, with their field jackets and ruptured ducks. From the frosh dormitory, they spread to Eversole, filled Smiley," so wrote the editors in dedicating the 1946 *Metate* "to the men who brought diversity and experience to a waiting campus." The arrival of the veterans, many of whom were former Pomona students, was the dominant factor in the operation of the college and in the life of the campus in 1945-46, 1946-47, and 1947-48. Enrollment rose from 659 in the first semester of 1945-46 to 1110 in the first semester of 1947-48. At its height the enrollment of veterans was 488. Their presence and their achievement were evidence of the greater value the American people were placing on higher education.

Pomona had adopted a transitional schedule for the summer of 1945 and thereafter the accelerated program was discontinued. An eight weeks summer session was held from May 7 to June 29 with the entire faculty in residence. Instruction was resumed on September 13 on the pre-war two-semester calendar. As a wartime measure the accelerated program had contributed greatly to the college, enabling several hundred students to receive instruction they would otherwise have been denied, and bringing income which was a major factor in the college's financial stability at the end of the war.

Transcending all problems was the matter of housing. The college had markedly increased its enrollment of women. In 1945-46 they occupied not only a unit of Clark Hall but also the north section of Smiley, a masculine citadel since its construction in 1908. With the return of large numbers of veterans, this would no longer be feasible.

The crisis presented, however, the opportunity to build the long desired additional residence hall, with accommodations for 98 women. If this could be done, both the immediate emergency and a long-range need of the college could be met. As preliminary sketches had been prepared by the architect when Blaisdell Hall was constructed, and as the architect was free to work on the new building immediately, valuable time would be gained if the trustees could find a way to proceed. The gravity of the housing crisis was particularly felt by Pomona's newest trustee, attorney Paul Fussell, who had joined the Board in September 1943. As a veteran whose own career at the University of California had been interrupted by World War I and as the father of two Pomona sons in combat duty in World War II, he had a personal as well as institutional understanding of the need for action by the trustees.

When Dr. Lyon presented the matter to the trustees at their meeting on the campus in August 1945, Mr. Fussell moved that the architect be authorized to make the working drawings for the new hall, and approval was voted. A few days later trustee Seeley G. Mudd telephoned Dr. Lyon that the Mudd family would make a gift that would enable construction to begin as soon as the drawings were ready.

Without this foresight and action by the trustees in the late summer of 1945 the building would never have been completed by 1946-47. In the year after the war there were acute shortages in all building materials. The federal government in March 1946 ordered that such materials as were available be directed exclusively to housing. However, since the residence hall was already under construction, a permit to proceed was granted. But even a federal permit did not produce materials when they were needed, and the contractor and the buildings and grounds committee worked with extraordinary energy and foresight to secure cement and other supplies. Despite the many problems and delays, two-thirds of the rooms were ready for occupancy when college opened in September 1946, and all the remaining private rooms were ready at the end of the Thanksgiving recess. The shortage of materials delayed until the spring the completion of the parlors and the long connecting corridor with Blaisdell Hall. When finished, the new building was a structure of the highest quality.

The building was named in memory of Mrs. Della Mulock Mudd and dedicated on April 20, 1947. Three members of Mrs. Mudd's family had served as trustees of Pomona: her husband, the late Colonel Seeley W. Mudd, from 1914 to 1926; and her sons, Harvey S. Mudd from 1926 to 1930, and Dr. Seeley G. Mudd, since 1930. Both sons and their families were present for the dedication. Participants in the moving exercises included Dr. Blaisdell, trustee Arthur M. Dole '96, Dean Gibson, Miss Marjorie Belknap, president of the Associated Women Students, and Mrs. William L. Honnold, who paid a beautiful tribute to Mrs. Mudd, her close friend for many years.

While Della Mulock Mudd Hall was under construction, the college faced serious problems in housing married veterans. Like most American colleges Pomona had no houses or apartments for married students. When temporary housing for veterans was made available by the federal government, the college elected to take its entire quota in units for married couples. In May 1946 the area east of Clark Hall from Sixth to Eighth Streets was graded, and sewer and utility mains put in by the college. The government then transported fifty-two units from the Kaiser Shipyards in Vancouver, Washington, and during the summer and fall erected them on this site. These quarters were plain and simple but the rent was low, and they provided housing which could not have been obtained otherwise. The government retained title to the units which were ultimately given to the college.

The Search for New Faculty

As the veterans returned in increasing numbers, the administration was in a race to secure enough faculty members to instruct them. The appointment of faculty was the function of the presidency which Dr. Lyon considered of highest importance, and throughout his tenure he would make it so. His aim was to build at Pomona a faculty as strong as that of any college in the United States, and he was tireless in support of this ideal. He sought men and women of character, teaching ability, and scholarly interest. The president looked primarily for young people who appreciated the special values of the residential liberal arts college. He believed that the development of Pomona and the Associated Colleges, which he foresaw, would lead such young faculty members to remain for long periods of service. Beginning in 1945 he traveled throughout the East, the upper Middle West, and California in search of men and women who would bring strength and long service to the Pomona faculty. His most rewarding visits were at Yale, Harvard, Princeton, Columbia, the University of Chicago, Stanford, and the University of California, Berkeley.

The rebuilding of the Pomona faculty was a formidable undertaking. Some faculty members who had gone into war service elected not to return. Furthermore Pomona required a much enlarged faculty to teach the more than 1100 students who were enrolled by the first semester of 1946-47. Thirty-seven full-time and eleven part-time appointees were added to the faculty from February 1946 to September 1947.

Fortunately most of the young faculty members who had left for the armed forces did return. It was most encouraging to welcome home W. T. Jones in philosophy, John H. Gleason and John H. Kemble in history, and Frederick Mulhauser, Charles S. Holmes and Joseph W. Angell in English.

However, most of those who had left the faculty for non-military war service elected not to return to Pomona. These losses were felt particularly in the natural sciences, where resignations, deaths, and retirement required a fundamental reorganization of three departments: chemistry, physics, and zoology.

In chemistry a totally new staff had to be secured. The death of Dr. Robinson and the resignations of assistant professors Elliott and Tyson deprived the college of every pre-war member of the department. Working in consultation with distinguished Pomona alumni in the field of chemistry President Lyon was able to appoint three men whose teaching and research achievements would win recognition throughout the scientific world.

Dr. Willis Conway Pierce, associate professor of chemistry at the University of Chicago, was appointed professor of chemistry and chairman of the department at Pomona, effective September 1945. A graduate of Georgetown College, Kentucky, with M.S. and Ph.D.

degrees from the University of Chicago, Dr. Pierce had been on leave during the war in order to direct the National Defense Research Committee Laboratory at the Technological Institute of Northwestern University, from which post he came to Pomona. His research interests were in analytical and physical chemistry. A first-rate teacher and scholar, he was an ideal department chairman. Selfless, he sought always to encourage and advance his younger colleagues. In his relations with the other science departments he was so understanding that a new spirit of cooperation developed in the science quadrangle.

Two young men who had been engaged in research with the atomic bomb project at Richland, Washington, were appointed as assistant professors of chemistry. R. Nelson Smith '38, whose appointment was effective September 1945, had been recommended to President Lyon by Pomona alumni, and Dr. Pierce heartily approved his appointment. After graduating with highest honors in chemistry and election to Phi Beta Kappa at Pomona, Mr. Smith took his Ph.D. at Stanford in 1942. He had taught at Stanford and the Missouri School of Mines before entering war research in 1944. Corwin H. Hansch, B.S. University of Illinois, and Ph.D. New York University, a specialist in organic chemistry, who was appointed assistant professor of chemistry effective February 1946, was brought to the attention of the college by Dr. Smith. In the months immediately preceding his coming to Pomona, Dr. Hansch was a research chemist at the Du Pont Experimental Station, Wilmington, Delaware.

The problem of restaffing in physics was accentuated by the early retirement of Dr. Tileston for reasons of health in 1946. For advice President Lyon turned to the renowned physics department at the University of California, Berkeley, from whose chairman he received the most helpful guidance. However, the needs of the university were such that the permanent reorganization of the Pomona department could not be completed until September 1947. Dr. Charles A. Fowler, who was appointed chairman and Seeley W. Mudd associate professor, brought teaching ability, research interest, and rare administrative skill. A graduate of the University of Utah from which he held B.A. and M.S. degrees, he had received his Ph.D. in 1940 from the University of California, where as a member of the Berkeley faculty he won recognition both in teaching and research. Fortunately, Dr. Edward M. Fryer '37, who was appointed assistant professor of physics at Pomona, was able to secure release from wartime service in time to begin his work at Pomona in February 1946. Following a distinguished career at Pomona, he had gone to Stanford, where he took a degree in mechanical engineering and a Ph.D. in physics. During the war he had been stationed as Naval Liaison Officer at the Radio Research Laboratory at Harvard University.

The zoology department, with only one faculty member from the pre-war years remaining, also required a major reorganization. The college had been able to go through the later years of the war with a limited staff because none of the army programs had included the biological sciences. Dr. Willis E. Pequegnat, who had come to the college in 1940 from graduate work at the University of California at Los Angeles, and who had carried most of the work of the department following Dr. Hilton's retirement in 1944, was promoted to associate professor of zoology and made chairman of the department.

Two other young men joined the zoology department in September 1946. Assistant professor Dwight L. Ryerson, who held B.A. and M.S. degrees from the University of Arizona, and a Ph.D. in zoology from the University of California at Los Angeles, came from the University of Arkansas Medical School, where he was assistant professor of anatomy. Assistant professor Miles D. McCarthy, a graduate of West Chester State Teachers College, had taken his Ph.D. at the University of Pennsylvania, where he studied under Professor Charles Metz '11. Dr. McCarthy had conducted surgical research and he brought a strong interest in premedical education.

While no other academic division of the college required reorganization comparable to that in the natural sciences, there were major vacancies in a number of other departments. In religion and classics entirely new staffs had to be secured. Two of the four appointees in physical education for women had resigned. Retirements required new faculty members in music, sociology, and history.

Dr. Bernard E. Meland, professor of religion since 1936, resigned effective July 1, 1945 to accept appointment as professor of constructive theology at the University of Chicago. His leaving was a great loss, for his scholarly teaching, his writings, and the chapel service he had developed had had profound influence throughout the college. Furthermore, interest in courses in religion was increasing and the college felt two members of the department would be required after the war. John von Rohr, Bachelor of Business Administration, University of Minnesota, Bachelor of Divinity, Chicago Theological Seminary, and a candidtate for the Ph.D. degree at the Yale Divinity School, was appointed as instructor in religion, effective September 1945.

Dr. Merrimon Cuninggim, formerly professor of religion at Denison University, was appointed chairman of the department and John Knox McLean professor of religion, effective September 1946. A graduate of Vanderbilt, with an M.A. in English from Duke University, he was elected to a Rhodes Scholarship and from 1933 to 1936 was at the University of Oxford, where he received a B.A. degree in the Honour School of Modern History and a diploma in Theology. Later he took the B.D. and Ph.D. degrees at Yale. During the war he served two years as a chaplain in the Navy. A man of vitality and personal charm, he led in giving the department of religion a greatly enlarged role in the college, and he also participated widely in both student and faculty life. A varsity tennis player at Oxford, he assisted in athletics by coaching the Pomona-Claremont tennis team which enjoyed several outstanding years under his leadership.

The classics department faced an uncertain future after the death of Professor Homer E. Robbins on October 31, 1946. The enrollment in Latin and Greek had declined, and since 1940 Dr. Robbins had served as the college librarian. In addition, he had been mayor of Claremont since 1938. Amid the competing demands for college funds after the war, there was serious danger that the classics department would be discontinued.

President Lyon was determined to rebuild this department, but three years were required before a permanent reorganization could be effected. During this period, students took Greek and Latin under Professor Louis Lord, emeritus professor at Oberlin College, whom President Hard had brought to Scripps College. On the suggestion of Dr. Lord, Pomona in 1948 invited Dr. George Karo, formerly director of the German Archaeological Institute at Athens, to serve as a visiting professor and to give courses in ancient art and archaeology and Greek and Roman history. Dr. Karo was one of that large body of German intellectuals whom Hitler dismissed from their positions and who, to the great advantage of our country, found refuge in the United States. Though much beyond the normal retirement age, this distinguished scholar and superb teacher gave four enriching years to Pomona.

Meanwhile, Dr. Lyon searched intensively for a man who could teach Greek, Latin, ancient history, and classical art and archaeology. Princeton and Harvard were the best sources for such a person in the postwar years, and after many interviews Dr. Lyon found in 1948 the man who met the college's exacting requirements. Harry J. Carroll, Jr., a graduate of the University of Akron, was completing his Ph.D. at Harvard, to which he had returned following service in the Army from 1942 to 1946. When Pomona offered him an appointment Harvard had just awarded him its prized Charles Eliot Norton Traveling Fellowship, and Mr. Carroll was planning a year of study and research at the American School for Classical Studies at Athens. Pomona met the situation by appointing him and placing him on leave for 1948-49. With Mr. Carroll's arrival in September 1949, classics again had an assured place in the college.

The death of Professor Robbins also forced a decision regarding the library, for the enlarged college could no longer be served by a part-time librarian. David W. Davies, director of libraries at the University of Vermont, was appointed librarian of Pomona College and associate librarian of Claremont College, beginning November 1, 1947. A graduate of the University of California at Los Angeles and a holder of an M.A. in history from the University of California, Berkeley, Mr. Davies had done graduate work at the University of Chicago, from which he would receive his Ph.D. in library science soon after coming to Pomona. His earlier library experience included work in the Los Angeles Public Library, the Huntington Library, and the Bancroft Library of the University of

California. During the war he saw service with the Army in France and Germany. Pending Mr. Davies' arrival at Pomona, Miss Marion J. Ewing, assistant librarian, who had served Pomona since 1912, was named acting librarian.

It was with great regret that the college on July 1, 1946 accepted the resignation of Miss Elizabeth Kelley, professor of physical education for women and chairman of the department, who left Pomona to become health education consultant in the California State Department of Education. At Pomona she had won national recognition for herself and the college, resulting in her election as president of the National Association of Directors of Physical Education for College Women for the academic years 1940-41 and 1941-42.

The resignation of Miss Kelley and that of assistant professor Esther G. Bristol '26, who had been on leave for service with the American Red Cross, reflected basic changes in the role of the department of physical education for women. Fewer Pomona students were interested in teaching physical education and in a physical education major. Henceforth, courses in the department would be directed primarily to the health and recreational needs of students. This was the nature of the responsibility entrusted to assistant professor Elizabeth Cawthorne, first appointed in 1935, who succeeded to the chairmanship of the department in September 1946.

The retirement of Professor Frank W. Pitman in history and Professor William Kirk in sociology required new appointments in these two departments. Henry Cord Meyer, who had served with the Navy and the Office of Strategic Services, was named assistant professor of history effective September 1946. A graduate of the University of Colorado, with an M.A. from the University of Iowa, and a Ph.D. from Yale in 1941, he had also spent a year at the University of Vienna. His field of special interest was modern European history. In sociology, Professor Baber succeeded Dr. Kirk as chairman of the department, and Alvin H. Scaff, doctoral candidate and instructor at the University of Texas, was appointed instructor. Before the war Mr. Scaff had taken a B.D. degree at the Chicago Theological Seminary, and under the American Board of

Women arriving at Harwood Court

Commissioners for Foreign Missions had gone to the Philippines, where he taught at Silliman University. After the Japanese invasion he and his family had spent nearly two years in the mountains with Filipino guerrillas; eventually captured, they were held for fifteen months in Japanese concentration camps.

Campus Life

As the veterans returned and professors old and new assumed their duties, an unprecedented excitement prevailed on the campus. None felt this more than Dr. and Mrs. Lyon, who saw the opportunity to make Pomona an institution of unsurpassed quality in every respect. Above all they desired to know students and faculty. They attended most campus events — athletic contests, plays, dances, and musical programs, and countless unscheduled occasions. Students were welcomed at the president's house throughout the year, in freshman and senior receptions and at small dinners, which were often meetings with distinguished guests.

Mrs. Lyon amplified the annual reception for new faculty which had been given by President and Mrs. Edmunds. The dinner for the Pomona faculty which honored the new appointees was followed by a formal dance in Edmunds Union. Over the years this party, complete with Grand March and Virginia Reel to the tune of a good orchestra, marked the beginning of the academic year. Faculty members and their spouses of all the Associated Colleges and a large number of friends from Claremont were invited. These happy occasions contributed greatly to the growing college and Claremont community.

Men came home from the war eager to learn and to build for themselves better places in society. Those who had been in college before the war returned with a new sense of purpose. Those for whom the G.I. Bill made college possible eagerly opened their minds to new learning and a fuller life. Students had never worked so hard at Pomona, and never had faculty members had more satisfaction in their work.

Liberal education in the United States was in a very different position from what many had predicted in the early years of the war. As the conflict progressed, the necessity of liberal education became increasingly urgent and apparent. It was clear that the great questions of society required, not only technical training, but also a broad understanding of the humanities and the social sciences. Such education was emphasized for the country in 1945 by the widely heralded report of the Harvard faculty, *General Education in a Free Society,* which called for "the infusion of the liberal and humane tradition into our entire educational system," and the cultivation "in the largest possible number of our future citizens of an appreciation of both the responsibilities and benefits which come to them because they are Americans and free."

Deeply impressed by the great changes on the Pacific Coast, President Lyon, in his convocation addresses in Bridges Auditorium in 1946 and 1947, stressed the new opportunity of the western scholar and the larger role of California in national affairs. Asserting that intellectually and culturally the West had come of age and that its academic colonial days were over, he saw the western scholar looking eastward across the country with "the power and the vision to speak with a truly national voice."

For Pomona students greater concentration on their academic programs was accompanied by an enthusiastic revival of social life and institutions as they had existed before the war. While overseas, Pomona students had cherished the college as they remembered it, grateful for news from the alumni association and the faculty. Both the returning veterans and the women desired to re-establish student life and activities as they had existed in 1941, and this was effected in 1946-47. As the 1946 *Metate* wrote, Pomona men who came back from the armed forces "found some things are permanent, like the Quad or College Avenue. Our traditions remained, juniors presented the flag, frosh built the Oxy bonfire, in winter the Christmas Supper, in spring the May Day." The college was unusually fortunate in having as president of the Associated Students in 1946-47, Jack A. Bradford, a former lieutenant in the Marine Corps, who had originally entered Pomona with the class of 1945. Under his able leadership student organizations operated much more easily than one would have thought possible. There was a pervading spirit of good will in which both new and old students were soon working together effectively.

The large enrollment of men brought expansion of activities in both music and drama. The Men's Glee Club, reduced to a double quartet in the war, returned to strength and in the spring vacation made an extended tour en route to San Francisco and the Bay Area, its first since 1941. For the first time in their history the Men's Glee Club and the Women's Glee Club gave their annual program together, setting a tradition that has continued. Among the veterans were men with dramatic talent that Mrs. Allen would direct in an outstanding period of the college theater. Inspired by William B. Sanborn '48, faculty and students wrote and produced an original musical play, "Genie on the Spot," which delighted the college.

Although there had been an increase in athletic activities since the autumn of 1945, it was not until 1946-47 that full programs in all sports were restored and the Southern California Intercollegiate Athletic Conference was reactivated. Nixon was again joined by Messrs. Strehle, Heath, and Merritt.

There was some hesitancy among the faculty in reviving the six social fraternities, which had been suspended in 1943. However, after careful consideration the faculty voted to reactivate them, and the first pledges were bid in December 1946. The fraternity rooms, which had been used as classrooms by the military units, were redecorated and refurnished.

A New College

While Pomona was welcoming veterans and organizing for an expanded operation, President Lyon, as the provost of Claremont College, was also occupied with the development of a new college within the Claremont group. The idea of a men's college in Claremont had been held from the inauguration of the group plan in 1925, and it had been expected that such a college would follow soon after the founding of Scripps. But the Great Depression had made this impossible.

However, by 1936 hopes had kindled again and the Intercollegiate Council formulated a report entitled "On the Question of Founding a New College for Men in Claremont." The report proposed "a particular type of collegiate training for young men of great ability interested in careers of public service, whether in the employ of the state or of great private enterprises, or in independent professional practice," and to this purpose called for "a broad, liberal historical outlook coupled with a deep conviction regarding the contribution which men of vision, scholarship, broad training and moral courage can make to the secure establishment of the commonwealth."

In language reminiscent of the boom of the 1880's in Southern California, the report noted that "competent observers in increasing numbers have remarked that the location of Claremont is ideal, being near a center of growing population and wealth, yet far enough away to assure a degree of serenity and reflection necessary for prolonged, intensive study. In this respect it compares favorably with Oxford and Cambridge, both of which are just conveniently beyond the business skyline of London." Neither this appeal, nor a leaflet in 1938 entitled "A College for Men in Claremont

— How Soon?" found financial response in years overshadowed by impending war.

The return of veterans and the provision for their education under the G.I. Bill of Rights revived the idea of a men's college for Claremont. But large questions had to be resolved. Would a new college draw away from Pomona the men it needed for effective operation? Or would a new and more specialized college attract a new body of men from the rapidly growing population of Southern California? In the spring of 1946 there were no certain answers to these questions. The veterans had just begun to return and colleges generally were still below their pre-war strength. A decision regarding a new college in Claremont could be made only by following one's judgment and being aware that a significant risk was involved. Under the Operating Agreement of 1942 and the Reorganization of Claremont College in 1944 a college for men had been authorized. The question in the spring of 1946 was to determine whether that was the time to launch it.

Within eight weeks the crucial decisions had been made. The Intercollegiate Council on April 12 authorized Harvey Mudd, chairman of the Board of Fellows, to appoint two committees: an organization committee of trustees and a faculty committee on academic program. The following day Mr. Mudd forwarded his choices for these committees to Provost Lyon. Much work had been done by each committee when the executive committee of the Board of Fellows met on May 7. Before the executive committee was a recommendation from the faculty committee "that we look to the establishment of a four-year college with emphasis upon the social sciences with the purpose of training men for business and public administration" and that "as an immediate expedient we begin this autumn under the administration of Claremont College."

The key to proceeding lay in the provision of first-rate leadership. Provost Lyon had been reassured on this point when he learned that Dr. George C. S. Benson '28, professor of political science at Northwestern University, who had just been released from service as a major in the Army, could be secured for an appointment at Claremont College. He learned further that Dr.

Benson had in mind an academic program in public administration which could be developed in a new men's college. Upon Provost Lyon's recommendation, Dr. Benson was appointed professor of public administration, with the hope that the recommended program for men could be organized in Claremont College. If this could not be done, it was planned that Professor Benson give courses in public administration in the Claremont Graduate School and Pomona.

The final decisions were taken by the Board of Fellows on June 4. Assured of academic leadership, the organizing committee of the Board undertook the raising of the $175,000 considered essential for capital equipment and an underwriting of the budget for five years. Mr. Mudd crystallized the thinking of the meeting by saying that if this step were undertaken "the program should be announced as an Undergraduate School for Men under Claremont College without making it at this time a separate college." All present participated in this historic discussion, after which on a motion of Irving Walker, chairman of the Scripps Board, seconded by Frank Harwood, president of the Pomona Board, it was voted unanimously "that an Undergraduate School for Men with emphasis on Business and Public Administration be undertaken under Claremont College." Dr. Benson was then appointed director under the general supervision of the provost, and it was voted to begin the school in September 1946.

By heroic steps in which Managing Director Bernard took a large part, the desired funds were secured and facilities were made available. Pomona alumni, notably Russell K. Pitzer '00 and Donald C. McKenna '29, were key to the financial success of the undertaking. The former University Club was made available and christened Story House in memory of the late Russell Story, from whose thinking had come much of the program for the new school. Government-owned housing was brought down from the Kaiser Shipyards in Washington, and government buildings from a Southern California army camp were secured for classrooms. Rooms for students were set up in the wings of Bridges Auditorium. Meanwhile, Dr. Benson, who was fulfilling an earlier commitment for summer teaching at Harvard, assembled the core of a distinguished faculty. In September, 88 students were enrolled.

The response of veterans for enrollment at both Pomona and the Undergraduate School for Men for the first semester of 1946-47 convinced the colleges and the Board of Fellows that they should proceed to incorporate the Undergraduate School as a third undergraduate college under the Claremont group plan. Steps were taken to select a board of trustees and on March 28, 1947 the institution was incorporated under the laws of California as Claremont Men's College. Shortly thereafter, the Board of Fellows made available a fund of $1,125,000, of which $500,000 had come through a matching gift by R. K. Pitzer, and $625,000 from the Chauncey Clarke Fellowship Trust, of which the income was assigned to Claremont Men's College.

After its organization the first act of the Board of Trustees of Claremont Men's College was to elect Dr. Benson president of the college. He had already demonstrated in high degree the professional and personal qualities demanded in a founding president. From service on the faculties of Harvard, the University of Michigan, and Northwestern he brought experience as a teacher and scholar in the field of public administration, to which he added wartime experience in military government in Italy and Austria. The son of a minister and raised on a farm at Ukiah, California, he knew how to value a dollar and how to use it when acquired. Better than most college presidents, Dr. Benson understood the world of business and of politics and knew where to find the support demanded for a new college. As a Pomona alumnus, who was the grandson of Dr. Charles Burt Sumner and son of graduates in Pomona's first class, he brought to his presidential duties a deep appreciation of the tradition of Pomona and of the idealism that led to the establishment of the group plan. His own knowledge of Claremont had been reenforced during the war when Mrs. Benson and their two sons came to live in the Sumner residence on College Avenue while Dr. Benson was overseas. A scholar in English literature, Mrs. Benson was invited to teach in the Pomona English department, and she and her family had established a warm friendship with the Lyons when Dr. Benson returned from military service.

Dr. Benson had been called to an arduous undertaking. Unlike Scripps, the new college had to begin with limited time for planning and with much of its work in temporary quarters. Pomona helped in many ways. In addition to informal assistance by members of the faculty and the administration, the college performed certain special services for Claremont Men's College. The physics department conducted the science survey course required of all its students. Pomona received the students of Claremont Men's College into its physical education department and invited them to participate on its athletic teams. This arrangement, with the combined teams playing under the name Pomona-Claremont continued until September 1958.

CHAPTER XXIII

Reorganizing the College in Years of Cold War

THE YEARS AFTER WORLD WAR II were not the period of peace abroad and harmony at home which the American people had anticipated. The fear of Russian communism was revived, and the nation bore the burden and anxiety created by the atomic bomb. Although the United Nations Charter, drafted in San Francisco during the spring and early summer of 1945, was signed by fifty nations, and went into effect on October 24, 1945, fundamental differences soon developed between the Soviet Union and its wartime allies. On March 5, 1946 Winston Churchill stated at Westminster College, Missouri, to an audience which included President Truman, that "from Stettin in the Baltic to Trieste in the Adriatic an iron curtain has descended across the Continent." Stalin, who a month earlier had issued an ultimatum to the West, was then brutally oppressing Poland and Czechoslovakia, supporting a civil war against the government of Greece, and threatening both Turkey and Iran. His actions led President Truman, on March 12, 1947, to request from Congress support for Greece and Turkey, and to set forth what soon became known as the Truman Doctrine. "I believe that it must be the policy of the United States," he stated, "to support free peoples who are resisting attempted subjugation by armed minorities or by outside pressures. I believe that we must assist free peoples to work out their own destinies in their own way." The divergence between the policies of the United States and the Soviet Union widened in late 1947, when Stalin refused to cooperate in the establishment of the Marshall Plan and forbade Czechoslovakia to participate in it.

The Cold War which ensued bore heavily on American colleges and their students. Selective Service, which had been discontinued in 1946, was reenacted by Congress on June 24, 1948 in order to provide manpower for the occupation of Germany and Italy and for expanding military aid programs. Men from nineteen to twenty-five were subject to induction for twenty-one months service, and men of eighteen could volunteer for one year in any of the regular military services. The reestablishment of Selective Service was followed in 1949 by the formation of the North Atlantic Treaty Organization.

While the United States was building defenses against the spread of Communist power from the Soviet Union, the Chinese Communists were winning the upper hand in their long struggle with Chiang Kai-shek and the Nationalists. After repeated defeats the Nationalists fled to Taiwan, where they established a government on December 9, 1949. The changes in China had grave consequences for American foreign policy and divisive influence on public opinion in the United States.

The significance of the Communist victory in China was soon seen in Korea. That country, like Germany, had been divided by World War II, the demarcation line being the 38th parallel. To the south was the Republic of Korea supported by a small American military mission helping to create an army. To the north was the People's Republic of Korea with a large, well trained army which had been supplied by the Soviet Union. On June 24, 1950 a North Korean force of 70,000 with tanks and armor moved into South Korea. President Truman took the crisis to the Security Council of the United Nations,which accepted the conflict as a United Nations war and called on its members to provide assistance. General Douglas MacArthur was named United Nations commander, and ten nations sent troops, of whom the larger number came from the United States. When an armistice was finally signed on March 5, 1953 a total of 54,246 young Americans had given their lives and 103,284 others had been wounded in the Korean War.

The high tide of veteran enrollment at the undergraduate level had passed by 1950 and most men then in American colleges had been too young to serve in World War II. They were liable, therefore, for military service under the Act of 1948, and two years of uncertainty and confusion followed for them and for American higher education. Ultimately, the Selective Service administration in 1951-52 established deferment procedures which allowed students who were carrying their academic work successfully to continue in college until graduation.

Throughout the Korean War, national morale and the very structure of American academic life were threatened by the unscrupulous attacks on the government led by Senator Joseph McCarthy of Wisconsin. In a speech in Wheeling, West Virginia, in 1950, McCarthy declared that the State Department was "thoroughly infested with Communists" and that he held in his hand "fifty-seven cases of individuals who would appear to be either card-carrying members or certainly loyal to the Communist Party, but who nevertheless are still helping to shape our foreign policy." Although McCarthy never produced any evidence to support his allegations he aroused such popular support that in 1951 he was emboldened to attack General George C. Marshall, former Chief of Staff, who had been Secretary of State from 1947 to 1949. Re-elected to the Senate in 1952 McCarthy secured the chairmanship of the Permanent Subcommittee on Investigations and for the two following years was constantly in the news, investigating the State Department, the Voice of America, and innumerable individuals, many of whom in consequence lost their jobs. The near reign of terror he led added "McCarthyism" to the English language before he was finally halted. A special committee of the United States Senate censured McCarthy on December 2, 1954, and he was formally condemned by the Senate by a vote of 67 to 22.

All institutions of thought and opinion were profoundly affected by the forces which took expression in McCarthy. This was particularly true for colleges and universities. Free speech and free thought were in jeopardy, and individual faculty members were often the targets of unfair criticism.

This was especially true in California, where after 1949 the hysteria over security led to a plethora of loyalty oaths. To avoid the imposition by the legislature of such an oath on University personnel, the Regents of the University of California voted in

March 1949, to institute their own loyalty oath for faculty members and the staff of the University. The "Oath Controversy" which ensued resulted in the dismissal of twenty-six faculty members who refused to take the oath, the resignation of others, and years of serious dissension on the various campuses of the University. Ultimately the California Supreme Court, in October 1952, declared the oath invalid and ordered that those dismissed be restored to their posts in the faculty. After further litigation they also received back salaries for the period when they were denied their positions. The tragic and protracted "Oath Controversy," which brought incalculable damage to the University of California, cast its shadow over higher education throughout the state.

In this period of state and national tension Pomona faced a reorganization of unprecedented proportions. Unfortunately reorganization within the college coincided with a reorganization of the Board of Trustees. Mr. Harwood's retirement as president of the Board in 1948, and his death in 1949, ended the paternal leadership of the trustees which had begun with the presidency of Mr. Marston in 1909. Over this forty-year period the affairs of the Board were handled primarily in monthly meetings of the Executive Committee and approved by the Board. Endowment funds were supervised by an investment committee which met fortnightly and was advised by professional counsel. The seven other trustee committees, buildings and grounds, education, honorary degrees, library, student health, ways and means, and nominations met only when they had specific business.

Some of these committees were organized only for the referral of possible problems or business and were not expected to meet unless such arose. This was particularly true with the education committee which provided an avenue through which an individual faculty member could appeal a tenure question not resolved by the normal administrative process. The president of the college was chairman of the education committee, and Mr. Harwood advised Dr. Lyon that the committee functioned rarely.

Mr. Wig, who succeeded Mr. Harwood as president of the Board, had long felt that the individual trustees should be more active in the work of the Board, and he saw committees as a means to that end. Indefatigable, and at age sixty-five free to give much of his time to the college, he launched the Board into unprecedented activity. There was hardly a day that he did not work for Pomona or think of her affairs. There was much to be said for this invigoration of the work of the Board and for its extension. Fund-raising and the public relations program were greatly strengthened. However, there were hazards for the college when individual trustees began to concern themselves with the details of academic matters and campus life.

These hazards manifested themselves in the reorganization of the education committee and the establishment of a regular schedule of meetings. This committee, soon renamed the academic affairs and library committee, became the avenue through which the president presented faculty appointments to the Executive Committee and the Board. A program for the review of academic departments by visiting committees was initiated. It was a difficult time for such a change in the relationship of the trustees to academic matters, and the members of the committee found themselves under much pressure. The tensions and fears of the McCarthy period led to unfair criticism of the economic and political views of faculty members, attempted interference with academic appointments, and objections to distinguished outside speakers. The resulting differences of opinion among the trustees made the early 1950's a very difficult period within the Board.

These years were a severe test for President Lyon. There could be no compromise of academic freedom to which he was dedicated and of which Pomona College was a notable example. He kept constantly in mind the injunction with which Mr. Harwood had inducted him into the presidency on October 18, 1941: "I charge you to be unswerving in your devotion to the cause of truth; that you be the active enemy of prejudice and intolerance; that you inculcate in the youth of this college a love of clear and precise thinking; . . . that you keep our shield stainless and hold our banner high." Objectively and patiently the president talked with individual trustees, committees, and the Board, taking care never to be personal and always leaving a conversation so that it could be resumed without rancor. Despite sharp criticism from some individual trustees, the difficult issues of the McCarthy period were resolved within the Board without once compromising the fundamental principles of the college.

Furthermore, the grave problems were handled so discreetly by both the president and the trustees that the faculty and students were totally unaware of them. Feeling that the issues were a responsibility to be borne first by the president alone, Dr. Lyon never communicated to his faculty colleagues any of the problems of these years. He knew that revelation of the matters he had to handle would have resulted in tension between the faculty and the trustees and would have seriously damaged the college. In retrospect the president felt that one of his greatest services to Pomona had been the guiding of the college steadily through the 1950's. His differences with individuals had never been personal, and he was gratified that some of those with whom he had differed most strongly came to be his warm friends.

Under the leadership of Mr. Wig, steps were taken to strengthen the personal bonds within the Board and to form a closer relationship between the trustees and the faculty. On his recommendation and through his generosity a retreat of members of the Board and of the senior faculty was held in 1951 at the Kemper Campbell Ranch at Victorville. The trustees defrayed their own expenses, but the faculty were all the guests of Mr. Wig. This retreat set a pattern which was to become traditional. As trustees and faculty roomed together, played golf, swam, and discussed college policy they developed a clearer sense of purpose and better personal understanding.

The Board took measures to give its members a broader and more objective view of educational questions and the operation of the college. It decided to seek a trustee from the teaching faculty of another institution, and Dr. John W. Dodds, professor of English and director of special programs in the humanities at Stanford University, was elected in 1955. A graduate of the College of Wooster from which he held also an honorary degree, he had received his Ph.D. in English from Yale. A distinguished scholar in Victorian literature, he was the author of several books, the most recent being *The Age of Paradox: A Biography of England, 1841-*

1851. Dr. Dodds had taken wide interest in higher education beyond his own campus, serving as president of the Western College Association, chairman of the Pacific Coast Committee for the Humanities, of which President Lyon was also a founding member, and trustee of Mills College, 1943-53.

Problems of the Cold War and McCarthyism from 1948 to 1955 took time and energy of the president that were sorely needed for the internal reorganization of the college. Pomona had to establish a broader base for its student body, appoint a number of key administrative officers, and greatly enlarge its faculty. In order to serve its students and faculty the college had to provide additional buildings and facilities.

Rebuilding the Student Body

The first priority for every institution of higher education in the United States after 1945 was the rebuilding of its student body. In the West, and particularly California, this involved far more than the resumption of old relations with well established secondary schools. The population of California which would grow to 15,863,000 by 1960, brought millions with little or no knowledge of California institutions, especially independent colleges. The California colleges would offer great opportunities to these new citizens, but much hard and intelligent work was necessary to acquaint future students, their teachers, and parents with the academic possibilities available to them.

For this important work Pomona was greatly aided by the Alumni Association and the Women's Campus Club. Led by able and vigorous presidents, the Alumni Council was constantly alert to ways in which Pomona could be brought to the attention of the widening California community. Through its meetings on the campus and its local councils in California the Women's Campus Club presented Pomona to prospective students and their families. As most of the members of the Campus Club were the mothers of present or recent students, they were excellent interpreters of the college.

Pomona was superbly prepared for securing new students. The

college had a new academic program to offer and an experienced man to lead in presenting it. Edward Sanders, whose title had been changed to director of admissions and assistant dean of students in 1943-44, had mastered the operations of his office and had become well informed on admissions both in California and throughout the country. A notable advance in the selection of students was made in 1947-48 when Pomona joined the College Entrance Examination Board,which was extending its activities to the West Coast. As of September 1948, all students applying for admission to the college were required to take the aptitude tests set by the College Board. These examinations, used in conjunction with high school records, afforded objective bases for judging individuals, and for comparing students from different sections of the country and from varying types and sizes of secondary schools.

Through the leadership of the admissions office and the support of alumni, Campus Club, and friends, the college moved into the fortunate position of having far more applicants than it could admit. The selection process was arduous, requiring lengthy and exacting work by the director of admissions and the faculty admissions committee. Travelling throughout California and to selected schools on the Pacific Coast, in the Middle West, and the Northeast, Dr. Sanders won recognition as one of the nation's outstanding admissions officers.

In the postwar years Pomona faced a serious decision regarding the size of its future enrollment. Fulfillment of the college's obligation to veterans raised the enrollment to 1150 by the first semester of 1948-49. There was general agreement within the faculty and the trustees that this was too large, and equal agreement that it was impractical to return to the pre-war enrollment of 800. A study of the financial structure of the college and its new academic program convinced Dr. Lyon that for financial reasons Pomona could not at that time reduce its enrollment below 1000, and that for educational reasons it would be unwise to reduce enrollment below 900. He stressed that such an enrollment provided for a larger and more diversified faculty, with adequate size for the necessary academic departments, and also provided enough concentrators for mutual intellectual stimulation in all the departments. Furthermore, the larger enrollment would enable Pomona to continue assisting all the Associated Colleges by maintaining departments and courses not available elsewhere in Claremont.

As the size of Pomona was stated as 800 in the Operating Agreement, any permanent change required an amendment to that document. The Pomona Board requested in June 1949 that an inter-board committee of the presidents and board chairmen of the four colleges be appointed to consider "the size of the colleges and also some revision of the Operating Agreement." It was not until June 25, 1950 that the inter-board committee could complete and agree on its report. The issues were important, and on the size of enrollment there were strong differences of opinion. Dr. Lyon felt it essential that Pomona's enrollment not be reduced to 800 and he held this position unwaveringly. Others felt that to allow Pomona to increase would imperil the group plan.

Finally agreement and recommendations to the boards of trustees were reached unanimously. With amendments as added by the Pomona Board and the Board of Claremont Men's College, the report made important changes in the Operating Agreement. Effective in 1951-52 Pomona would restrict its student body "to not to exceed approximately 1000." Claremont Men's College, effective 1951-52 would restrict its student body "to not to exceed approximately 350." Scripps was permitted to expand to 325 whenever it chose. Pomona agreed further that "when endowment income increases sufficiently, or when expenses are reduced sufficiently to offset the loss of tuition income, Pomona College shall consider reducing its enrollment to a number approaching 900." Although neither of these conditions would be met, the college moved immediately to reduce the enrollment to approximately 1000. At the end of the second semester of 1951-52 the enrollment was 1006.

New Faculty and Staff

As the student body grew, there were major changes in the administrative officers of the college. Dr. Iredell, who had served as secretary of the faculty with great effectiveness since 1944, was

F. Raymond Iredell, Dean of the Faculty

J. Edward Sanders, Dean of Admissions

Jean B. Walton, Dean of Women

Shelton L. Beatty, Dean of Men

THE DEANS

entrusted with larger responsibilities and named dean of the faculty in November 1948. As dean and chairman of the courses of study committee, he had oversight of the operation of the academic program and the innumerable day to day matters which this involved. On the occasions when Dr. Lyon was away, Dean Iredell served as the acting president of the college. With Dr. Iredell's appointment as dean, the position of secretary of the faculty was discontinued.

Major changes occurred in the other offices in the academic administration. Dean Nicholl retired as dean of students on July 1, 1948, after nearly thirty years of service in which he had conducted his difficult office with rare insight and understanding. He had been loyally assisted by Mrs. Nicholl, and together they won the lasting affection of thousands of students.

Dr. Sanders succeeded Dean Nicholl and also continued as dean of admissions. Such large duties required additional staff, and the office of dean of men was established. The president persuaded W. T. Jones, associate professor of philosophy, to accept appointment to the new deanship and Dr. Jones served with great success until the end of the academic year 1948-49. As a veteran he brought understanding and consideration to the special and often pressing problems of students who had returned from military service. However, Dr. Jones' greater interests were in teaching and scholarship and when he asked to return to full-time work in the department of philosophy, the college decided to look beyond its own faculty for his successor.

Shelton L. Beatty, chief counselor for men at Stanford University, was named dean of men at Pomona, effective September 1949. A graduate of the University of Tennessee, he held an M.A. in comparative literature from Cornell University, and later completed a doctorate in higher education at Stanford. Dean Beatty brought to Pomona valuable experience which included service as dean of men and assistant professor of English at Grinnell College from 1929 to 1941. During the war he had served as an officer with a Naval V-12 unit at Notre Dame University, leaving military service as a lieutenant commander.

Dean Jessie E. Gibson, whose integrity, wisdom, and human

understanding had contributed so much to the life of the college, retired on July 1, 1949. She had the satisfaction of seeing the realization of her dream of a complete residential campus for both men and women, an ideal for which she worked untiringly during her twenty-two years at Pomona.

Miss Gibson was succeeded as dean of women by Dr. Jean B. Walton, a member of the mathematics department of the University of Pennsylvania. A graduate of Swarthmore College, where she took highest honors in the division of the natural sciences, Miss Walton held an M.A. from Brown University, and a Ph.D. in mathematics from the University of Pennsylvania. Before joining the faculty at the University of Pennsylvania she had taught at Swarthmore where she was assistant to the deans and then acting dean of women.

Deans Iredell, Sanders, Beatty, and Walton worked together with rare effectiveness. Their high academic standards, commitment to the best interests of the students, and devotion to Pomona added greatly to the stature of the college. Students thought of the four deans and the president as a working team, with "Sumner Hall" standing for unified and well enunciated policies.

Mr. Hawley's work in fund raising required him to relinquish most of his responsibilities with the alumni office, and William L. Wheaton '34 was appointed Alumni Secretary effective September 1949. Following his graduation from Pomona, Wheaton had taken an M.A. degree from the New York University School of Education and had taught at the Chadwick School. During the war he served for four years as a major in the infantry. Mrs. Wheaton, the former Elizabeth Edmunds '34, was the daughter of President Charles K. Edmunds. After three years in the alumni office, Mr. Wheaton was named assistant dean of admissions, and he entered upon long and distinguished service in the admissions office.

Restaffing was required for the department of economics. At the end of the war Norman Ness had decided to remain in Washington as adviser on Latin America to the Export-Import Bank. Dr. Duncan had recruited younger men and reorganized the department when he was stricken by a heart attack and died on September 23, 1947. Dr. Floyd A. Bond, associate professor of economics at Carleton College, was appointed professor of economics and chairman of the department, effective September 1948. He had been brought to Dr. Lyon's attention by the University of Michigan, from which he held B.A., M.A., and Ph.D. degrees, and where he had taught before going to Carleton. A distinguished teacher and dedicated to his students and his field, Dr. Bond gave outstanding leadership to the department. He found two able colleagues already at the college: assistant professor Philip Neff, B.A., Ph.D. University of California, who had been appointed in 1945; and instructor Louis B. Perry, a veteran and graduate of the University of California at Los Angeles where he was a doctoral candidate, who had joined the Pomona department in 1947. Gerhard N. Rostvold, B.A., M.A., and doctoral candidate at Stanford University, would be appointed instructor in 1952.

Retirement brought major changes in the department of music, which, unlike most other departments, had retained essentially the pre-war membership of its faculty. Professor Ralph H. Lyman, who had shaped and guided the music department since the opening of Bridges Hall, retired on July 1, 1948. The appointment of both a department chairman and a choral director would be required. Fortunately it was not necessary to seek a teacher of voice as well, for this work was in the capable hands of Margery Smith Briggs, who had come to the department in September 1943. She was a graduate of the Chicago College of Music where she had also received the Master of Music degree. However, the department had to prepare for the approaching retirement of Walter A. Allen, professor of musical theory and appreciation and senior member of the college faculty. Several years were required to complete the restaffing and reorganization of the department.

Carl Parrish, professor of musicology and director of graduate studies at Westminster Choir College, Princeton, New Jersey, was named professor of music and chairman of the department, effective September 1949. A graduate of the MacPhail School of Music in Minneapolis, with an M.A. at Cornell and a Ph.D. at Harvard, he had taught at Wells College and at Fisk University. Dr. Parrish's special interests were the history and literature of music.

Three young men were brought to the department from 1948 to

1951. Richard N. Loucks '42, was appointed instructor in 1948. A veteran with a distinguished record as an officer in the Army, Loucks had entered the Eastman School of Music of the University of Rochester, where he had taken an M.A. degree and would complete his Ph.D. He taught piano and theory and prepared to assume the work given by Professor Allen. Dr. Parrish rendered great service to Pomona by recommending for the music department two young men at Harvard: Karl George Kohn, appointed as instructor in 1950, and William F. Russell, appointed as assistant professor in 1951. Kohn, who had just completed his B.A. *summa cum laude* at Harvard, was a native of Austria who had come to the United States in 1939. He became an American citizen and served as a bandmaster with the United States Army in the war. He had also been on the staff of the Berkshire Music Center. At Pomona he would teach piano, composition, and theory. Russell had served four years in the Army, one of them as a bandmaster in the South Pacific. A graduate of Columbia, he also held M.A. degrees from Harvard in both English and music. When appointed at Pomona, Russell was assistant director of the Harvard University Glee Club, the Harvard Choir, and the Radcliffe Choral Society. At Pomona he was given charge of all the choral work. When Dr. Parrish resigned at the end of 1952-53 to accept the chairmanship of the department of music at Vassar, Mr. Russell succeeded him as chairman of the Pomona department. He was an effective administrator who gave stability to the department, and as director of the college choir and the glee clubs, won the admiration and loyalty of the students.

The art department also went through a series of staff changes from 1948 to 1954. Mr. Beggs, who had done so much to establish the modern department, resigned at the end of 1947-48 to become Director of the National Collection of Fine Arts of the Smithsonian Institution in Washington. The retirement in 1949 of Cyril Jurecka, who had initiated instruction in sculpture at Pomona in 1932, removed the other long-time member of the department. Charles Lawler, a distinguished sculptor who after graduation from the University of California had studied in Paris, succeeded Mr. Jurecka and brought strength to the art department in these difficult years. The chairmanship of the department was handled briefly by Kenneth E. Foster, a specialist in Oriental art who had joined the department in 1946 and who remained until 1950.

With the appointment of Seymour Slive in 1951, the study of art at Pomona received impetus and permanent direction. A graduate of the University of Chicago, from which he also held M.A. and Ph.D. degrees, he was an historian of art with special interest in the art of the Netherlands. A veteran of the United States Navy, Slive had commanded small craft in the South Pacific and the Atlantic in World War II. When approached by Pomona he was at Oberlin College taking the place of a faculty member on leave. While discussions were proceeding, Slive was awarded a Fulbright fellowship for a year's study in the Netherlands. Pomona responded, as it had done earlier for Dr. Carroll, by appointing Slive and placing him on leave for the year of his fellowship. Slive began his service at Pomona in September 1952 as assistant professor of art and chairman of the department.

When Dr. Slive arrived, Pomona had already done much to strengthen its program in art. Dr. Carroll was offering work in the art and archaeology of Greece and Rome. A distinguished German scholar, Dr. Alois J. Schardt, former Director of the National Gallery in Berlin, who had been secured in 1950 as visiting professor on a part-time basis, was giving courses in medieval art and renaissance and baroque art. To these courses Dr. Slive added an introductory course in the history of art and advanced courses in art since 1700, and problems in the history of art. His own teaching and his leadership gave Pomona an art department of distinction.

These courses in the history of art were accompanied by excellent work in painting and sculpture. James E. Grant, a young painter who had taken an M.F.A. degree at the University of Southern California and had studied at the Jepson Art Institute, joined the faculty in 1950 and was so effective that he soon drew unprecedented enrollments. In sculpture, Mr. Lawler was admired for his own work and for his teaching; students found him a very helpful adviser. In addition, the extensive offerings in applied art at Scripps College were open to Pomona students.

Retirements and the increased enrollment necessitated continuous search for new faculty members in other departments in the humanities. Changes in the English department included the retirement of Professor Elliott C. Lincoln and the appointment of four young members. Mr. Lincoln had developed work in American literature and in creative writing. Gretchen Graf Pahl, B.A., M.A., Ohio State University and Ph.D., University of California at Los Angeles, came as an instructor in 1947. Edward Weismiller, a graduate of Cornell College and a Rhodes Scholar from Iowa, was appointed assistant professor in 1949 and placed on leave for 1949-50 to work on his D.Phil. at the University of Oxford. A veteran who received the Bronze Star, he had won Guggenheim fellowships for creative writing in 1946-47 and 1947-48. Edwin S. Fussell '43, M.A. and Ph.D. Harvard University, instructor at the University of California, Berkeley, was named assistant professor of English in 1951. A Phi Beta Kappa graduate from Pomona, he had served as a lieutenant in the Navy during the war. Ray Frazer '47, a veteran whose career at Pomona had been interrupted by the war, and who was completing his Ph.D. at the University of California, Berkeley, was appointed instructor in English in 1952.

Important appointments were made in modern languages. Robert F. Leggewie, B.S. Loyola University of Los Angeles, M.A. University of Southern California, M.A. and Ph.D. Harvard University, was named assistant professor of Romance languages in 1951. A veteran with three years service in the Army, he was resident tutor of the Modern Language Center at Harvard when appointed at Pomona. The teaching of the Russian language was introduced into the curriculum in 1950 and Ernest H. Ein, formerly professor of law and dean of the law faculty at Tartu University in Estonia, was appointed lecturer in Russian. Holder of the degree of Doctor of Jurisprudence from Tartu, he had also studied in Paris and Rome. He had been Minister of Justice and Judge of the Supreme Court of the Estonian Lutheran Church before World War II had made him a refugee from his native land.

New appointments were made in the departments of history and government. Vincent H. Learnihan, B.A., MA., and doctoral candidate at the University of California at Los Angeles was named instructor in history in 1949. Herbert B. Smith, B.A., MA. State

University of Iowa and Ph.D., University of California, Berkeley, who had served with the Army in the European area, was appointed assistant professor of history in 1952. Lee C. McDonald '48, also a veteran, M.A., University of California at Los Angeles, who would complete a Ph.D. at Harvard, came as assistant professor of government in 1952. William C. Olson, B.A., University of Denver, and completing a Ph.D. in international relations at Yale University, who had served in the Army Air Corps, was appointed instructor in government in 1953.

New faculty members also came in philosophy and psychology. The faculty in philosophy was expanded and Frederick Sontag, B.A. Stanford University and Ph.D. Yale University, was named assistant professor in 1952. William L. Faust, B.A. University of Chicago, B.A., M.A. and doctoral candidate, Stanford University, was appointed instructor in psychology in the second semester of 1952-53.

A number of new faculty were added in the natural sciences. Assistant professor of botany Edwin A. Phillips, appointed in 1948, had served as an officer in the Navy. A graduate of Colgate, with M.A. and Ph.D. degrees from the University of Michigan, he was an instructor at Colgate when called to Pomona. Burton Henke, who came as an instructor in physics in 1948, was a graduate of Miami University, Ohio, and a doctoral candidate at the California Institute of Technology. Jack C. Miller '47, appointed instructor in physics in 1952, had received an M.A. at the University of California, Berkeley, and was a doctoral candidate at the University of Oxford. Elmer B. Tolsted, instructor at Brown University, was named assistant professor of mathematics in 1947. A Phi Beta Kappa graduate from the University of Chicago where he also received his M.S. degree, he had taken a Ph.D. at Brown. An accomplished cellist, he would contribute much to music as well as to mathematics at Pomona. In zoology, Yost U. Amrein was appointed as an instructor in 1951. A native of Switzerland, he had graduated from the University of California at Los Angeles from which he also held a Ph.D.

The postwar years at Pomona were marked by a significant increase in interest in courses in religion and in religious activities.

The department of religion, expanded to two full-time faculty members in 1946, drew large enrollments, and had great influence throughout the Associated Colleges. A group of students and faculty from the four colleges recommended the introduction of a regular Sunday morning worship hour on the campus, and with the support of the trustees and administrations of all the colleges the College Church was organized in the spring of 1949.

The faculty of the Pomona department of religion took a leading part in the establishment of the church. Dr. Cuninggim accepted the chaplaincy and, in addition to his full teaching load, carried its duties through 1949-50. The four colleges appointed Miss Joan Reed '43 as director of religious activities to assist the chaplain, and the church with its own choir, committees, and benevolence program became a major force in the life of the students and faculty. The services held at eleven each Sunday morning in Bridges Hall had large congregations. The meetings there and in the after-church coffee period contributed greatly to wide and pleasurable acquaintance among administrators, faculty and students of all the Associated Colleges.

The organization of the College Church was followed by the four colleges' uniting in a joint baccalaureate service for the first time at the commencement of 1949. The service was held in Bridges Auditorium and Dr. Blaisdell was the minister. His inspiring sermon, "Demanding One's Citizenship," was published by the Friends of the Associated Colleges at Claremont.

Pomona and the Claremont Colleges suffered a great loss when Professor Cuninggim resigned in 1951 to become Dean of the Perkins School of Theology, Southern Methodist University, but the work he had begun was ably conducted by his successors. Dr. von Rohr became chairman of the department of religion at Pomona and W. Robert Rankin was appointed chaplain of the Associated Colleges, effective September 1951. Mr. Rankin, then director of religious activities at Oberlin College, was a graduate of the State University of Iowa and had received B.D. and M.A. degrees at Yale University. He had served as a chaplain in the Army during World War II.

Retirements

In this period of great faculty and staff change Pomona lost by retirement three men, and one woman, each of whom occupied a distinctive place in her history. Since his appointment in 1919, Charles T. Fitts,who retired in 1948, had had a variety of teaching and administrative posts, among them teacher of English, registrar, and professor of education. As secretary-treasurer of the Western College Association since 1924, a position he would continue to 1954, he rendered immeasurable service to all its member institutions. As a teacher of education Professor Fitts was succeeded by Gordon C. Lee,who was appointed assistant professor of education in 1948. A graduate of the University of California, Berkeley, where he majored in history, Lee had taken M.A. and Ph.D. degrees at Columbia University, whence he came to Pomona. Prior to the war he had taught in Beverly Hills High School, and from 1943 to 1946 he served in the Army.

Marion J. Ewing, assistant librarian, who retired in 1948, had served Pomona for thirty-six years. A graduate of Olivet College she had received library training at Simmons College, Boston; after coming to Pomona she took an M.A. in English literature at Boston University. Miss Ewing served the library in various capacities, and for many years as reference librarian. On several occasions she was Acting Librarian. The development and use of the Pomona library owed much to her work and spirit.

With the retirement of Eugene W. Nixon in 1950 as professor of physical education for men, chairman of the department, and director of athletics, Pomona lost the man who had shaped its physical education program for men and intercollegiate athletic policy. An able writer, he also enjoyed national influence through his articles and textbooks. Nixon was an effective administrator and he prepared a worthy successor. Professor Robert L. Strehle '19, who was appointed chairman of the department and director of athletics, continued the sound policies Nixon had formulated. A young alumnus, Edward W. Malan '48, who had served as graduate assistant while completing an M.A. at the Claremont Graduate School and who would later receive the degree of Ed.D. at the

University of California, Los Angeles, joined the department as an instructor.

Ernest E. Jones '09, who retired as treasurer in 1950, had served Pomona throughout his entire career. By successive stages in the business office he had risen to be treasurer of Pomona in 1922. As they were founded, he was also elected treasurer of Claremont Colleges, Scripps College, and Claremont Men's College. When the controller resigned in World War II, Mr. Jones assumed that office, too. Ably and devotedly assisted by Miss Marjorie B. Woodford '16 as assistant treasurer, Miss Elizabeth Draper, a graduate of the University of Washington, and Miss Amelia Smith '26, he directed the business operations of the four colleges until 1949. Mr. Jones had succeeded Charles B. Sumner as secretary of the Pomona Board of Trustees in 1927, and except for a brief period after 1950, he would continue in this important office until 1962. Ernest Jones was a quiet, able counsellor of administrative officers and trustees. President Lyon greatly valued his advice and judgment and learned from him much of the heritage of the college.

The growth of the financial and business affairs of Pomona and the other colleges required a larger staff for the business office. William V. Shannon, a graduate of Virginia Military Institute and an investment officer at the Security-First National Bank in Los Angeles, who had been named assistant treasurer of the colleges in 1946, was promoted to treasurer. In anticipation of Mr. Jones' retirement, Paul H. Burton, a graduate of Western Reserve University who had been assistant controller at George Washington University in Washington, D.C., was appointed controller of the colleges in 1949. When Mr. Jones retired, Mr. Burton was placed in charge of the growing personnel of the business office. These officers managed the investment, budgetary, and real estate interests of the colleges in the unprecedented expansion of the Associated Colleges that followed in the 1950's and early 1960's. Their wise direction of their offices undergirded the enlarged instructional programs in the colleges.

CHAPTER XXIV

New Buildings for the Postwar College

THE FEELING that Pomona's financial strength was assured, which the trustees had held in 1941, was shattered by the war. The requirements of the expanding college and the rise in prices in the late 1940's produced a need for larger sums than the college had ever envisaged. Long-planned developments would cost much more than contemplated, and unexpected needs made pressing and expensive demands.

Large funds were required in three areas: for buildings, instruction, and student aid. Most of the building needs had been recognized before the war, but planning was necessarily altered by the increased enrollment of the college. The larger instructional costs had not been foreseen. The rapid increase in the cost of living dictated a new scale for faculty salaries. Furthermore, the reorganized college required a larger faculty, and in some departments, especially the natural sciences, there were unprecedented demands for expensive equipment. For a brief period, student aid was not a pressing problem, as the G.I. Bill provided funds adequate for both tuition and room and board at Pomona. But larger funds for student aid would be a genuine need for 1950.

The college gave high priority to building needs, primarily to structures that would complete the residential campus as planned before the war. A new dining hall for the residents of Blaisdell Hall and Mudd Hall, which would form a quadrangle with these buildings, was required. For the men's campus, the college looked to the construction of the additional residence hall and the central lounge, included in the master plan which had been prepared by architect Sumner Spaulding some twenty years earlier. The increased enrollment gave impetus to the completion of the student union by the addition of the long-desired east wing.

It was tragic that Dr. Edmunds, who in many ways had inspired this building program, should have died on the eve of the realization of his plans. Already somewhat impaired in health, he was instantly killed when struck by an automobile while crossing Foothill Boulevard on January 5, 1949. A few weeks earlier, on December 18, 1948, the Board of Trustees, as an expression of the gratitude of the college to Dr. and Mrs. Edmunds voted to name the student union building the Charles Keyser Edmunds and Katherine Poorbaugh Edmunds Union, and Dr. and Mrs. Edmunds knew of that decision. Less than a month later, at a memorial service for Dr. Edmunds held in Bridges Hall on January 11, Dr. Lyon, Mr. Wig, and Dr. Ch'en Shou-yi paid tribute to Dr. Edmunds' wise leadership of the college. The love which the students felt for him is expressed in the plaque of the Edmunds Union, unveiled on Associates Day, May 15, 1949: "This building is named in honor of President and Mrs. Charles Keyser Edmunds who from 1928 to 1941 served with devotion the students of Pomona College."

Changes in the Board of Trustees

The Board of Trustees which faced the large responsibility of developing Pomona after the war was undergoing major changes in its membership. Llewellyn Bixby, who had served in many capacities since 1909, died in 1942. Edward C. Harwood of Pasadena, who had so ably continued the tradition of service set by his father, Judge Charles E. Harwood, had died on April 24, 1944. For many years he was chairman of the buildings and grounds committee, through which he instituted many campus improvements. Mrs. Susanna Bixby Bryant died after a brief illness on October 2, 1946.

On May 31, 1946 the long and wonderful life of George W. Marston came to a close. Mr. Marston was the embodiment of Pomona's highest ideals, and he left an incomparable legacy to the college he loved so deeply. Tribute was paid Mr. Marston on Founders Day, 1946. Judge Charles C. Haines '02, of San Diego, spoke on "Mr. Marston as a Civic Leader," and Dr. Blaisdell gave a moving address, "Mr. Marston: The Investment of a Life." The charm of Mr. Marston's personality and the strength of his character were beautifully portrayed in a booklet, *The Education of George W. Marston,* which Professor Hubert Herring had written and which the college published on that day.

With the death of older trustees a significant change occurred in the composition of the Board. Earlier the predominance of ministers had given way to citrus ranchers and business and professional men. The war and its consequences brought an economic revolution in which citrus growing declined and the expansion of industry made Southern California one of the great industrial centers of the nation. These changes were reflected in elections to the Pomona Board as the war neared its end. George R. Martin, vice president of the Security-First National Bank of Los Angeles, was elected in 1944. Mr. Martin, who attended the University of Chicago, was a former president of Town Hall, Los Angeles, a director of the Hollywood Bowl Association, and the Southern California Symphony Association. At the time of his election to the Pomona Board he was serving as president of the Friends of the Colleges at Claremont. Frederick S. Bale, an Amherst graduate and former alumni trustee, who was a retired New York banker, joined the Board in 1945. At the same time Robert H. Craig, businessman and civic worker, was elected a Pomona trustee. A graduate of the University of California, Berkeley, Mr. Craig had become interested in Pomona through his son, who graduated in 1943.

The college also turned increasingly to its alumni for the election of trustees. Yale B. Griffith '25 of Santa Barbara was elected in 1946, and Frank R. Seaver '05 of Los Angeles and Morris B. Pendleton '22 of San Marino were elected in 1947. Mr. Griffith, a graduate of the Harvard Law School, was an attorney who had held many professional and civic responsibilities. Mr. Seaver, who also had studied at the Harvard Law School, was an attorney who had combined the practice of law and the petroleum business with great success. He was president of the Hydril Company and the Texford Manufacturing Company. Few alumni have ever had such close ties to the college. Mr. Seaver had grown up in Claremont and the city of Pomona and he was one of six brothers and sisters who were Pomona alumni. He had been president of the Alumni Association in 1910-11. Mr. Pendleton, president of the Plomb Tool Company, had developed a business begun by his father into a major industrial enterprise. His knowledge of western business was recognized by his election to the national board of trustees of the Committee for Economic Development, for which he served as regional chairman for the Pacific Southwest. Under his presidency in 1946-47 the Pomona Alumni Association had enjoyed one of its finest years.

Mrs. Victor Montgomery of Beverly Hills was elected a trustee in 1948. A Phi Beta Kappa graduate of the University of California, Berkeley, she had served as a director of the Beverly Hills Garden Club and the Beverly Hills Woman's Club. She was a leading member of the Women's Committee of the Los Angeles Philharmonic Orchestra. Mrs. Montgomery's association with Pomona began when her daughter and son entered the college. She was one of the founders of the Women's Campus Club and as its first president firmly established that new organization in service to the college.

Two businessmen whose tenures on the Board were of shorter duration also knew the college through their children. George W. Bryant of San Marino, president of the Bryant Oil Company, who was elected a trustee in 1947, resigned for reasons of health as an active trustee in 1952. Mark H. Harrington of Pasadena, who headed his own investment company in Pasadena, was elected a trustee in 1951. He was soon placed on the investment committee, of which he was serving as chairman, when he died suddenly in 1957. A third businessman, William A. Johnson of Balboa, president of the American Pipe and Construction Company, elected in 1949, was entering a period of great service when he died unexpectedly in 1956.

Three alumni attorneys were elected to the Board from 1949 to 1952: Elmo H. Conley '17 of Pasadena, Carl I. Wheat '15, San Francisco, and William W. Clary '11, Pasadena. Mr. Conley was a graduate of the Harvard Law School; through his legal practice in Los Angeles he had become a leader in business and civic affairs.

Carl I. Wheat, also a graduate of the Harvard Law School, had maintained offices in both San Francisco and Washington since 1940. In the course of his busy career he somehow found time for extensive scholarly research and writing in the history of California, on which he was a leading authority. Mr. Clary, who had long been a member of the Board of Fellows of Claremont College, brought to the Pomona Board assistance and understanding in the continuing development of the group plan. The service of Mr. Conley was cut short by his death in 1957, and Mr. Wheat resigned that year because of illness.

Two alumni, who were to show great interest in campus development, joined the Board in the early fifties. Herbert S. Rempel '23 of Pasadena, elected in 1951, was secretary-treasurer of the Rempel Investment Company which had large agricultural holdings in the Middle West. Mr. Rempel would give long service to the Board and its committees. Clarence T. Stover '21, a building contractor in Claremont, was elected a trustee in 1952. Placed immediately on the buildings and grounds committee,he became its chairman in 1954 and reorganized the management of the grounds before his untimely death in 1955.

Charles Detoy of Pasadena, elected a trustee in 1952, had come into the Pomona circle when his son entered the college. A graduate of the University of California, Berkeley, Mr. Detoy was a partner in the real estate firm of Coldwell, Banker and Company. His concern for the future development of Southern California was reflected in his service to the college.

As president of the Board Mr. Wig gave vigorous leadership to his fellow trustees in the financial advancement of the college, and their work was advanced by the capable college staff which had been developed. Mr. Hawley, who had gained a thorough knowledge of the college and an ability to present its needs convincingly, was ably assisted by trustee William B. Himrod. Mr. Hawley had searched for an effective and continuous way to finance an independent college. Since 1893 Pomona had received gifts on which a stated annual income was guaranteed the donor during his lifetime, with the principal becoming available for college purposes on the death of the donor. Mr. Hawley believed that this could be the basis for a program of life income contracts in which the donor's annual income would be calculated at the rate of earning of the college's invested funds. He felt further that the gift deduction allowable under the income tax laws would make such gifts attractive to donors. When his views were confirmed by legal counsel and by a ruling of the Internal Revenue Service, Mr. Hawley prepared a pamphlet, *Income for Life with a Living Memorial in Your Name,* which the college had begun publishing as early as 1944. A decision of greatest significance had been made in financing Pomona. The life income contract program provided the basis for long-range financing but other means to meet the urgent capital needs of the postwar college were necessary.

A Dining Hall For Women

Dr. Lyon gave immediate attention to building the dining hall and kitchen which would serve the women of Blaisdell Hall and Mudd Hall and complete a quadrangle with these two buildings. Ardently supported by Dean Gibson, he convinced the trustees of the necessity of the dining hall. The Campus Club then took the leadership in seeking the funds for the building. In December 1946 the club made a formal offer to assume the responsibility of raising the funds for the dining hall, and the trustees gratefully approved.

The Women's Campus Club, which had been founded in 1940 through the efforts of President Edmunds, was an organization of mothers of Pomona students, alumnae, and friends of the college. Inspired by Mrs. Victor Montgomery and Mrs. Edmunds, the club was originally established to assist in the development of the women's campus, but it also concerned itself with the general needs of the college. As its members were for the most part parents of current students, the Campus Club was particularly responsive to immediate needs. Each year the club held three full-day meetings on the campus, each comprising a morning session in Bridges Hall, a luncheon program in Frary Hall, and a tea in Harwood Court or Blaisdell Hall. Regularly President Lyon gave an address on the state of the college at the autumn meeting in Bridges Hall. The work of the Campus Club was extended under the presidency of

Mrs. Frank G. Swain of Whittier by the organization of local councils in communities whence came significant numbers of Pomona students. There was a close liaison between the councils and the campus through the deans' offices and faculty members. Mrs. Lyon, who served on the board of the Campus Club throughout Dr. Lyon's administration, and worked continually with the club and its councils, often spoke at council meetings. By 1947-48 the membership of the Campus Club exceeded 1000, and local councils had been established in thirteen California cities, from San Diego to the Bay Area. Through solicitation of their members, benefits in the local councils and sponsorship of a concert in Bridges Auditorium by the Pomona Department of music, the Campus Club raised nearly $97,000 for the dining hall.

This achievement convinced the trustees that they could prudently make an amortized loan from other college funds to provide the remainder required for the building and its equipment. Working drawings had already been made by the architectural firm of Allison and Rible, and on December 14, 1948 the Board authorized the Executive Committee to call for bids. Ground was broken on March 5, 1949 and the first meal was served in the building on September 23. Featuring round tables, and seating 238 in the main dining room and twenty-four in the private dining room, the building soon became very popular among the students. The officers of the college made extensive use of the private dining room which was attractively decorated with water colors by Milford Zornes.

As the dining hall neared completion, the trustees voted to name it for Dean Gibson. Her retirement on July 1, 1949 had been marked by a great outpouring of affection by the Associated Women Students and the Alumni Association. The christening of the new building as the Jessie Edith Gibson Hall was a crowning tribute to the "Beloved Dean of Women at Pomona College, 1927-1949."

The dedicatory exercises were held on the afternoon of October 21, in connection with the annual autumn meeting of the Women's Campus Club. Robert H. Craig, chairman of the committee on buildings and grounds, spoke on behalf of the trustees. Mrs. Paul E. Lobanoff, president of the Women's Campus Club, and Mrs. F.

Gibson Dining Hall

Four Deans of Women, 1950. Miss Grace E. Berry, 1909-27; Mrs. Warren Olney, Jr., 1898-99; Dean Jean B. Walton, and Dean Jessie E. Gibson, 1927-49

Raymond Iredell '23 paid beautiful tributes to Miss Gibson on behalf of the Campus Club and the alumni. Miss Patricia Aldrich, president of the Associated Women Students, expressed the esteem and affection of the students.

A year after the opening of Gibson, the college had the privilege of honoring another distinguished woman whose life had spanned the history of the college from the very beginning. In a simple ceremony on September 22, 1950 the dining hall east of Harwood dining hall and formerly known as "Blaisdell," was dedicated as Mary McLean Olney Hall, in honor of Mrs. Warren Olney, Jr., who had become an honorary trustee of Pomona in 1949. Mrs. Olney was present and spoke delightfully of the early days of the college and the work of her father, founding trustee Reverend John Knox McLean. Present to honor Mrs. Olney were three of her successors as Dean of Women: Miss Grace E. Berry, 1909-27, Miss Jessie E. Gibson, 1927-49, and incumbent Jean B. Walton.

The Memorial Gymnasium

During World War II seventy-seven men and two women from Pomona College died in combat or war-related service. Within the college a strong desire to establish a worthy memorial developed, and in March 1945 the Board of Trustees approved "the enlargement of the physical education plant as a war memorial to Pomona men and women in service." Moreover, it seemed appropriate to join the memorial to these men and women to the memorial to the five Pomona men who gave their lives in World War I. Accordingly, in the spring of 1946 it was agreed that the college would seek funds for a memorial building, a gymnasium for men which would include some facilities for women.

This decision cleared the way for a campaign among alumni, parents of students, trustees, and other friends of the college. Under the leadership of Mr. Hawley, who prepared a brochure entitled "To Honor Those Who Served," alumni responded loyally and affectionately. The Alumni Association made the War Memorial Gymnasium the first priority of the Alumni Fund of 1947, 1948, 1949 and 1950. There were a few large gifts, but never before

Rudolph J. Wig, President of the Board of Trustees

Allen F. Hawley planning a publication with Willard G. Gregory '24

The Memorial Gymnasium

had so many alumni joined in financing a building for the college. The campaign was sustained and carried to ultimate success by the idealism and devotion of Mr. Hawley and Mr. Himrod.

While funds were being raised, the buildings and grounds committee encountered a serious problem in the location of the building. The trustees had assumed that the memorial gymnasium would be placed east of Smiley Hall and would incorporate the existing memorial training quarters. This site was questioned when the committee began preliminary discussions with architects. The buildings and grounds committee, in a quandary, learned that Wallace Neff, a Los Angeles architect, had just completed at Loyola University a building which attractively incorporated an older structure. Consultation with Mr. Neff convinced the buildings and grounds committee that he could design a building which would conform to the original intention of the trustees, and on March 19, 1948 Mr. Craig reported to the trustees that the site east of Smiley had been definitely chosen and that Neff had been engaged as the architect.

Eighteen months elapsed before the Board felt able to authorize a contract for construction. The total cost of the gymnasium, including equipment, landscaping, and architectural fees was approximately $350,000. Ground was broken on January 5, 1950 with representatives of the trustees, the alumni, the administration, the faculty, the students, and parents participating. The dedicatory exercises were held in Bridges Auditorium on Armistice Day, 1950. The address was given by William W. Clary '11, who paid a beautiful tribute to the men and women of Pomona who gave their lives in the war.

Prior to the convocation a religious service was held in the gymnasium before the memorial plaque, with only the relatives of those honored in attendance. The impressive plaque includes the names of the men and women of Pomona College from World War I and World War II who made the supreme sacrifice for their country. The plaque occupies the central position in the hallway, reminding all who enter that:

This Building Is Dedicated to the Memory of
The Men and Women of Pomona College

Who Gave Their Lives In Defense of Freedom.
O Valiant Hearts, Your Spirit Still Lives
Wherever Free Men Tread This Earth.

Two areas within the building are special memorials: the library in memory of Lieutenant Robert Jewett Cowger '41, and the varsity locker room in memory of Ensign J. Carlyle (Bud) Bryant '45.

The completed gymnasium, with its 27,233 square feet of floor space, included every facility which the college then required for its physical education and athletic program for men. By skillful adaptation Mr. Neff had included the memorial training quarters and the existing swimming pool as integral parts of the new structure, thereby not only preserving but increasing the value of these facilities. Much appreciated was a new dressing and shower room for women, with direct access to the swimming pool. The combined buildings were enhanced by a covered entrance from Sixth Street. A new west entrance for Alumni Field, comprising a wall, an attractive gateway and ticket office, generously provided by the class of 1916, contributed much to the appearance of the gymnasium and its grounds.

Erection of the Memorial Gymnasium brought a need for a distinctive name for the two wooden buildings which were commonly known as the "Big Gym" and the "Little Gym." The former had been constructed as a military barracks in World War I. The latter, the original Pomona gymnasium constructed in 1899, had been named the William Renwick Gymnasium in memory of an early patron of the college. When this building was moved from its original location in the vicinity of Holmes Hall to a location east of Bridges Auditorium, its name had dropped out of use. The two buildings, joined in 1950, were the home of the department of physical education for women. The trustees voted to christen the combined buildings as the William Renwick Gymnasium and thus preserve a name intimately associated with Pomona's early days.

While the Memorial Gymnasium was under construction, President Lyon developed a plan for adding the much-needed east wing to the Edmunds Union, financing it with surplus funds from the Associated Students, a portion of future store profits, and continuance of the dollar and fifty cent charge in the semester dues.

Mrs. Helen T. Throne '30, who had been appointed graduate manager in 1943, worked the plan out with the Associated Students, and it was approved by the trustees on March 14, 1950.

Construction was begun in May, and the east wing was completed early in 1951. Wallace I. Neff was engaged as the architect and he designed the new wing in relation to the Gymnasium and the memorial gate to Alumni Field. An extensive porch, with a curving canopy, and an all-glass east front for the new wing gave a more pleasing outlook on College Way. The transfer of the soda fountain from the west wing freed that entire wing for expansion of the profitable book and supply store. Space, convenience, and attractiveness had been added to the student union, enhancing its role in the college.

Completing the Men's Campus

While Gibson Hall and the Memorial Gymnasium were being constructed Pomona faced an impending crisis in housing for men. The combined capacity of Smiley and the Clark campus was 350, and the college anticipated an enrollment of at least 575 men. Dean Sanders reported that even by crowding and using some temporary facilities, the college could not accommodate more than 425 men on the campus. Furthermore, he felt that a new residence hall for men was needed to assure the proper development of the college.

Dr. Lyon pressed the trustees to complete the men's campus as designed by Sumner Spaulding in the late 1920's. Impressed by the administration's concern, the trustees on June 12, 1950 authorized a contract with Mr. Spaulding for preliminary architectural drawings for a residence hall and a central lounge. On September 21, 1950 the trustees approved a contract with Spaulding and his partner, John Rex, for working drawings and specifications for the proposed residence hall. Spaulding proposed a building in three wings,each accommodating thirty-five men. Under the direction of the buildings and grounds committee and in close cooperation with Dean Sanders and Dean Beatty the architects completed their drawings during 1950-51.

Helen R. Walker Hall

The immediate fulfillment of these plans would not have been possible had it not been for the generosity of Mrs. Helen R. Walker of Glendale. In the late summer of 1951, the trustees learned that she had left the major portion of her estate to Pomona College for a new building. Mrs. Walker's bequest was heartwarming evidence of the support a highly respected college can receive from those who quietly observe its work and influence. It does not appear that Mrs. Walker had ever visited the Pomona campus, but she knew Pomona alumni whom she greatly admired, and her regard for them led her to leave her estate to their alma mater. The estate, which brought over $700,000 to the college, was the largest gift Pomona had received up to that time.

The trustees without hesitation voted to use the funds for the construction of the men's residence hall. Fortunately the funds were large enough to provide also for the central lounge. Sumner Spaulding did not live long enough to learn of Mrs. Walker's bequest, but he had finished the working drawings of the residence hall before his death, and John Rex could complete the men's campus in accordance with his plans. Construction was begun in

1952 and the building was completed in the late autumn of 1953. Named in memory of its donor, Helen R. Walker Hall was dedicated in impressive exercises in 1954.

Walker Hall set a high standard in comfort and conditions for study. Incorporating many valuable ideas from Dean Beatty, Walker was made the chief residence for freshmen. Each wing with its own common room and kitchenette housed two sponsor groups and their upperclass sponsors.

The great lounge at the east end of Walker Hall brought the central reception, social and communications center which the men's campus had needed so badly. Its facilities included offices, a game room, mail boxes, a library and several conference areas, and a large lounge that could accommodate several hundred people. With its all-glass north wall affording a view of the mountains, the lounge soon became the reception center for many occasions.

The addition of Walker Hall transformed the appearance of the men's campus. Its site had been occupied earlier by several old and not very attractive residences. North and east of the residences had been an orange grove remaining from an earlier citrus planting. Walker formed an attractive quadrangle with the unit of Clark Hall to the south. Landscaping converted the area north of Walker into a lovely garden which was developed by his many friends as a memorial to Frank H. Harwood. The area was planted as a lawn and a wall was constructed along College Way, providing a lovely setting for Walker Hall as well as a recreational field. The Pomona men's campus had become the place of convenience, comfort, and beauty which those who first dreamed of it in the 1920's had so ardently desired.

However, there was still urgent need of further rooms for men. The trustees therefore authorized a loan from college funds for the construction of thirty-six single rooms. These were built around a courtyard which was an extension of Clark Hall along Sixth Street. Basically conforming to the architecture of the men's campus, the new unit was an attractive addition to the campus. The rooms were ready for occupancy in November 1956 and the building was dedicated on Alumni Day 1957. The hearts of alumni were warmed by the decision of the trustees to name the new residence unit for Dean Norton. The memorial plaque conveys to succeeding generations the unique place of the Dean in the history of their college: "This building and its Court honor the memory of Edwin Clarence Norton 1856-1943, Professor of Greek and Dean of the Faculty, who in 1888 was appointed as the first member of the original Pomona College Faculty."

The completion of the men's campus at Pomona also contributed greatly to the attractiveness of all the Associated Colleges. Harwood Garden extended northward to Claremont Men's College,which had built its campus in the block immediately south of Scripps College. After 1954 there was a continuity of college buildings and gardens from Second Street to Foothill Boulevard. With three undergraduate colleges and a coordinating college with its graduate school, Claremont had indeed taken on some aspects of Oxford. A central library would bring further resemblance to that ancient English university.

A Central Library Building

Well before the end of President Blaisdell's administration Pomona faced serious problems with its library. The Carnegie Library was inadequate in space for readers and for books, and the problems of the library were a recurring theme in student complaints. President Edmunds gave vigorous and continuous attention to the library and he planned the addition of wings on the north and south sides of the building. Architectural studies were commmissioned, but in the 1930's the necessary funds were not forthcoming.

The idea of a central library for the Associated Colleges had been implicit in the group plan but no tangible progress had been made toward its fulfillment. As president of Pomona and provost of Claremont College Dr. Lyon was strategically situated for advancing the idea with both the Pomona trustees and the Board of Fellows of Claremont College in the crucial years 1944 to 1947. In December 1945 he suggested to the Pomona trustees that the college join in a central library for the Associated Colleges. The Board requested its library committee and the president to examine the idea and report at a later meeting. The library committee, under the chairmanship of Willis H. Merrill, devoted itself zealously to the future of the library and in March 1946, the committee recommended that "Pomona go on record as approving a combined library housing program with Claremont College." The trustees voted approval of "joining in the library project with Claremont College in the development of a central library, subject to the development and adoption of an operating agreement regarding the ownership of books housed and the administration of the library." With this vote the Pomona trustees made a basic commitment from which they never wavered. Thereafter they looked upon a future library building as a facility to be jointly used and operated.

Claremont College did not engage in a campaign for the library because it was believed that Mr. and Mrs. William L. Honnold would supply the large funds required. A wide reader with a remarkable personal library in his home, Mr. Honnold was much interested in libraries and in scholarship. In the administration of President Story, he had given funds for plans and had considered building a library building for Claremont Colleges. This was to have been a building of modest size which would have been coordinated with an enlarged library at Pomona and the Scripps library. Although the Great Depression and then the war prevented the construction of this building, Mr. Honnold's continuing interest gave substantial hope that he would make a significant gift for library development in Claremont.

Determining factors in leading Mr. Honnold to leave a large gift from his estate to Claremont College were the careful administration of the graduate program and the cordial cooperation of all the Claremont colleges in Dr. Lyon's first provostship 1944-47. Working diligently and in close harmony, Provost Lyon and Managing Director Bernard were able to place the operations of Claremont College on a sound financial basis. As early as 1944 Mr. Honnold had told Mr. Lyon and Mr. Bernard that he planned to give a library to Claremont College.

Despite this declaration of his intention, Mr. Honnold did not move immediately to make a gift for the library. His health failed and for the last several years of his life he was confined to his home. But before his death in 1950 Mr. Honnold made special provision for the library, leaving the remainder of his fortune in a trust with his wife, Mrs. Caroline Honnold, as sole trustee. Mrs. Honnold wrote the Board of Fellows, in 1951, that in accordance with the desires of Mr. Honnold and her own wishes she was donating $1,000,000 to be added to the earlier fund he had established for the library. "The erection of the Library will fulfill the long cherished aims of my husband and myself," she wrote. "As you know, we have planned for many years to seek to enrich and strengthen the Claremont Plan by providing such a building for common use."

In anticipation of its funding the Associated Colleges had made the essential decisions regarding the location of the library building, its administration, and its constitutional relationship to the respective colleges. Steps were taken to reserve the block east of Dartmouth Avenue and north from Seventh Street to Foothill Boulevard as a center for future Associated Colleges buildings. Provision of a site for the library was determinative in securing this large and convenient area. Pomona donated several lots and others were purchased. The decision was made to place the library building in the southern portion of the area, and the city gave permission to close Eighth and Ninth Streets. As in the case of Walker Hall, an orange grove had to be removed to make way for the library.

Fortunately the colleges had in office highly qualified librarians who could advise on planning the building, establish the respective libraries within it, and conduct the ongoing operation of the functioning library. Willis Kerr, as librarian of Claremont College, was asked to take the lead in planning the new building. Mr. Kerr spent several years in study and in visiting selected libraries in the United States, observing particularly the new library at Princeton University and the joint university libraries in Nashville, Tennessee. David W. Davies, the Pomona librarian who was also associate librarian of Claremont College, worked closely with Mr. Kerr. When Mr. Kerr retired in 1948, Dr. Davies was named the librarian of Claremont College, and to him fell the responsibilities involved in the construction of the new building and establishing the books of the respective colleges as a central library.

The experience in Nashville provided a model for the organization and operation of a central library for the Associated Colleges. There three institutions, Vanderbilt Universtity, Peabody College, and Scarritt Biblical Institute, had brought their three libraries into one building and had organized them as a functioning library, but had retained the ownership of the books by the respective colleges. This basic concept was followed in Claremont. Although books were catalogued and handled as one operating library, they were the property of the individual colleges and were marked by the bookplate of the college purchasing them.

This fundamental provision and matters of management were included in an operating agreement drafted by a trustee committee headed by Paul Fussell of the Pomona Board and Joseph P. Loeb of the Board of Fellows. The agreement was approved by the boards of trustees of the four colleges in the spring of 1951. In gratitude to Mr. and Mrs. Honnold the building was to be named the Honnold Library for the Associated Colleges at Claremont. All letterheads and publications referring to the library should indicate that it was for the Associated Colleges and that it housed the libraries of Pomona College, Claremont Men's College, Claremont College, and in part the library of Scripps College. (Scripps continued its Denison Library, but in close cooperation with Honnold.) Future colleges were to be included as they might be founded. Very important were the formulae for assessing the respective colleges for the costs of library operation and the maintenance of the building. However, each college determined independently, and in the light of its own needs and budget, how much it would spend annually for books. The United States Government Depository and the California Depository remained in the name of Pomona. The government of the library was entrusted to a committee composed of the presidents of Pomona, Scripps, and Claremont Men's College and the Managing Director of Claremont College, with the provost as chairman, and the librarian was responsible to these officers.

The architects, Kaufmann and Stanton, had completed the working drawings while the trustees were ratifying the operating agreement, and construction began in the summer of 1951. The Ford J. Twaits Company, which was awarded the contract, made excellent progress, and the Honnold Library was placed in full operation with the beginning of the academic year 1952-53. The tremendous task of moving the Pomona books from the Carnegie Library and the Claremont College library from Harper Hall was conducted with great expertise by Dr. Davies and his associates. From late May to early August some 10,000 boxes containing nearly 230,000 books and 156,000 documents were transported to the new building and placed in the stacks. Of these materials the Pomona College library consisted of 132,803 books and 146,621 documents. The other books and documents were those of the Claremont College library, the new library of Claremont Men's College, and some research materials from the Scripps College library. As the books were moved into the building while it was being completed, a new and fully functioning central library awaited students when they returned in September.

The dedication of the Honnold Library on October 23, 1952 marked a new era in scholarship and learning in the Associated Colleges. No previous event so emphasized the commitment of the colleges to academic excellence and to mutual cooperation in achieving it.

The dedicatory exercises were held in the morning in the foyer of the building with a group of specially invited guests in attendance. Harvey S. Mudd, chairman of the Board of Fellows who presided, hailed the occasion as "the most significant event in the history of Claremont College," marking "the fulfillment of a prime objective that brought the founders together to launch the plan of a federation of colleges. One of the keystones of that plan was a central and common library to serve the Associated Colleges." Dr. Blaisdell paid tribute to the donors for a building "glorious in all its appointments, hospitable in all its welcome, wealthy in all the thinking of the ages." Dr. Davies rejoiced in "the possibility that the boy or girl or professor who persists in coming here may end by being liberally educated." Dr. Lyon, serving his second term as provost, accepted the building for Claremont College. The plaque was then unveiled by representatives of the student bodies of the four colleges.

A convocation of the Associated Colleges, with the faculties in cap and gown, followed at eleven o'clock in Bridges Auditorium, which was filled with students, faculty, trustees, and friends of the colleges. Mr. Mudd, who presided, spoke of the lives of Mr. and Mrs. Honnold in the Middle West, South Africa, and California. "Mr. Honnold," he said, "was a great man in his ability to see into the future and to plan for it. He placed his faith in young people and the Library is evidence of that faith." William S. Rosecrans, chairman of the building committee, welcomed the library "as a further spiritual bond, uniting our various colleges and increasing their capacity to serve the educational needs of Southern California." Claremont College conferred the honorary degree of Doctor of Letters on librarian emeritus Willis H. Kerr. The convocation address was given by Louis B. Wright, director of the Folger Shakespeare Library in Washington, who had formed many friendships in Claremont while at the Huntington Library from 1932-48 and as visiting professor at Pomona from 1944 to 1948. Speaking on "Libraries and the Advancement of Learning," Dr. Wright noted the correlation between liberty and free research in libraries, ascribing the astounding progress of American libraries to the determination of American scholars and the zeal of philanthropists like Mr. and Mrs. Honnold. In welcoming the Honnold Library to the group of important American libraries, he was joined by the Bodleian Library of the University of Oxford, which cabled its congratulations.

A Social Science Center for Pomona

With the opening of the Honnold Library the Carnegie Library became available to Pomona for a greatly needed academic building. Despite the increase in enrollment there had been no new classroom construction at the college since 1925. Some of the pressing need could now be met by remodeling the Carnegie Library building. Under the leadership of Dean Iredell a faculty committee formulated a plan for making Carnegie a classroom and office building for the social sciences. A special fund was sought for this purpose, and the work was completed in the summer of 1953. The total cost of the improvements and equipment was $75,891.

The excellent new facilities provided a social science building of which the college could be proud. The departments of economics, government, education, sociology, and Oriental affairs moved into Carnegie from their respective offices in Sumner and Holmes. The foyer, with attractive paneling and portraits of President Baldwin and Dr. Charles Burt Sumner, gave a pleasant sense of historical continuity. After forty-four years as a library, Carnegie entered a new period of service to students and faculty.

The remodeling of Carnegie was the climax of a series of lesser building changes that had been made since 1946. A renovation of the basement of Sumner Hall turned a full floor of unused space into offices for the faculty and the staff and placed that area in permanent use. Notable were the remodeling and redecorating of the Holmes Hall auditorium and the installation of a new lighting and ventilating system, made possible by a special alumni fund. In Crookshank Hall the zoology laboratories were modernized, and the facilities of the botany department were much improved. A new laboratory for general geology was established in Mason Hall.

The construction of new buildings and the renovation of older ones were accompanied by steps which consolidated the campus and added much to its beauty. By moving the former shops and stores buildings east of Clark Hall on Sixth Street to a new location on First Street a more attractive approach to the campus was provided. The removal of a group of old houses along Sixth and Seventh Streets and College Way and Dartmouth enhanced the appearance of the Men's Campus at Pomona and the view toward the Honnold Library, and opened this area for two new central buildings which came to the Associated Colleges in the early 1950's.

Other Buildings for the Associated Colleges

On February 9, 1951 Chairman Harvey S. Mudd told the Executive Committee of the Board of Fellows that Claremont College had received a gift to build a new dispensary for the Associated Colleges. This would replace a converted wooden residence which had served as a dispensary and stood on the site occupied by the Honnold Library. The donor, revealed later, was Dr. George E. Baxter of Glendora, vice-chairman of the Board of Fellows. Dr. Baxter was a distinguished physician who on retiring from his practice in Chicago had moved to California. In Illinois he had taken an active interest in higher education and for many years he was chairman of the board of trustees of his alma mater, Illinois College in Jacksonville. His experience in higher education and his residence in neighboring Glendora led to acquaintance in Claremont and his election to the Board of Fellows. Dr. Baxter was an ideal trustee, congenial and stimulating to his colleagues, perceptive of real college needs, and generous in time and funds.

The Baxter Medical Building, which was dedicated on March 14, 1952 was an expression of the loving concern of Dr. and Mrs. Baxter for the health and welfare of the students of the Associated Colleges. Located on Sixth Street and provided with excellent equipment, the building became, and continues today, the center of the medical services of the colleges.

In 1954 Mr. and Mrs. Harvey S. Mudd and the Seeley W. Mudd Foundation generously made a gift to Claremont College for a Faculty House, which would include facilities for meals, committee meetings, reading, and recreation, and rooms for college visitors. As a trustee of the California Institute of Technology, Mr. Mudd had been impressed by the contribution which the Athenaeum, with its lounges, library, dining hall, private dining rooms, and rooms for visiting scholars, had made to that institution. How much more essential, Mr. Mudd reasoned, was such a building in a group of colleges which were working together in a series of complex relationships and where the growth of the colleges, in number and in size, had complicated communication and personal acquaintance among their faculties. The building was to be the property of Claremont College, but it would be operated by the members of a faculty club, in which membership was open to the faculties of all the colleges upon payment of modest dues.

Mr. Mudd did not live to see the building completed. At the time of his death on April 12, 1955, construction of the Faculty House, located south of Honnold Library and west of Walker Hall, was in its early stages. However, Mrs. Mudd, who had shared this dream for the colleges with her husband, took great interest in the building and its furnishings and contributed additional sums to the project. When it was placed in operation in January 1956, the Faculty House was a model of taste and comfort. Those who shared Mr. Mudd's planning and hopes for the Associated Colleges were grateful for his generosity in making this farsighted contribution to the Claremont academic community.

CHAPTER XXV

Science in a New Era

IN THE POSTWAR PERIOD no aspect of American academic life changed more dramatically than the teaching of science. The tremendous wartime support for research and its resulting achievements had created a new age in science, starkly revealed when the first atomic bombs were dropped on Hiroshima and Nagasaki in 1945. The changes from the 1930's were so vast as to constitute in effect a scientific revolution.

In the postwar period, scientific rivalry became a part of the Cold War between the United States and the Soviet Union. Believing that their country and its British ally alone had the secret of the atomic bomb, the American public was stunned when the Soviet Union exploded its first atomic bomb in 1949. The race between the world's two superpowers was intensified when the United States exploded its first hydrogen bomb in 1951 and the Soviet Union followed with its first hydrogen bomb in 1953. The climax came when Soviet scientists achieved a *first* and on October 4, 1957 launched into orbit "Sputnik," the first rocket-powered artificial earth satellite. With this evidence of the achievement of Soviet science the public in the United States urged wider and more intensive study of basic science in schools and colleges. In the decade that followed the American people gave unprecedented thought and support to science. The period was marked by growing enrollments in science courses, large federal funds for research, and expanding facilities throughout the entire educational system. Pomona College and the Associated Colleges immediately responded to these developments.

Until the 1950's Pomona, with its well established programs in physics, mathematics, astronomy, chemistry, geology, botany, and zoology, had carried essentially all the instruction in science for the other Associated Colleges. Scripps students were welcomed into Pomona courses, as were students of Claremont Men's College. In addition, the Pomona faculty organized and conducted a special course for Claremont Men's College. With the increase in the number of colleges and in enrollments this arrangement was questioned by the other colleges, particularly by Claremont Men's College. President Benson suggested in 1953 that "Claremont College take over the use of the science buildings as a university type function," and that if this could not be done Claremont Men's College would construct a building of its own for basic science and pre-engineering. Discussion regarding science in the Board of Fellows in 1954 led to a proposal that a common science center be constructed on Sixth Street just across from the Pomona campus. The first unit would be a physics building, then being actively sought by Pomona. Although the proposal was favored by Claremont College, Scripps, and Claremont Men's College, it was resolutely opposed by the Pomona faculty and the Pomona trustees.

Pomona College had a long and distinguished tradition in science. To relinquish any control of its science facilities and instruction was unthinkable to its faculty and trustees. More than ever the natural sciences were an integral part of a liberal arts college, and Pomona was unwilling to take any step that might diminish the place of science and the members of the science faculty in the life of the college.

President Lyon, who had worked zealously for the central library, the medical service, and the central shops and stores, strongly supported the position of the Pomona faculty and trustees on the control of science facilities and instruction. He felt that the analogy with Oxford, offered in support of a common science center, was misleading. Oxford, he pointed out, was a university which prescribed a common curriculum for each of its honour schools, and the members of all the colleges received similar preparation for their degrees, which were granted by the University. The Associated Colleges, on the other hand, had an academic diversity in which each college determined the program for its baccalaureate degree. The colleges in Claremont were liberal arts colleges with their roots in New England, each giving its own degree. While they had drawn valuable precedents from Oxford in collegiate organization, residence facilities, teaching, and a central library, they had an autonomy unknown in modern Oxford. To Dr. Lyon diversity and competitiveness among the Associated Colleges were sources of strength lacking in the structures of both Oxford and Cambridge. He saw the construction of a joint science center as an irreversible step in weakening the vitality of the colleges at Claremont and destroying the uniqueness of the group plan.

The Pomona Board in June 1954 made the decision "to own and control its own physics, mathematics and pre-engineering building and facilities and to control its own teaching." This action guaranteed the integrity of the Pomona College curriculum and assured for the physical and biological sciences in Claremont the diversity of approach that characterized instruction in the social sciences and the humanities. In 1955, Claremont College and Claremont Men's College constructed a science building for their joint use, naming it the Baxter Science Laboratories in honor of the donors, Dr. and Mrs. George E. Baxter. That same year a college of science and engineering was incorporated as the fourth undergraduate college in the Claremont group.

The new college was a response to the industrial development of Southern California. Interest in such a college had grown as the California Institute of Technology decreased its emphasis on engineering. Harvey S. Mudd had given thought to the establishment of a college of science and engineering in Claremont.

The organization of a college of science and engineering in the Associated Colleges came to fruition in a series of rapid developments in October and November 1955. President Benson, who was then serving as provost of Claremont College, and Managing Director Bernard secured the support of R. K. Pitzer, who made a gift of $250,000 for an addition to Pitzer Hall at Claremont Men's College, this addition to be available also for the proposed college. Mr. Pitzer's gift was conditional on two actions by Claremont College: the permanent allocation to the new college of the income on $500,000 of endowment, and the securing of additional assets of $250,000. These conditions were met. Claremont College allocated the income from $500,000 of endowment, and Mrs. Harvey S. Mudd made a gift of $250,000. The Board of Fellows approved the formation of the college on November 15 and on November 30 the Executive Committee of the Board recommended that the new college should be named "Harvey Mudd College." It was incorporated on December 14, 1955 as "a liberal arts college of engineering and science."

Unlike Scripps College and Claremont Men's College, Harvey Mudd College had been founded without full discussion and consideration among the Associated Colleges. The Committee on Future Colleges of the Board of Fellows, which had been established in 1954, did not share its deliberations until it had determined its recommendation. The presidents of the colleges were not members of the Committee on Future Colleges, and thus Dr. Lyon, the Pomona faculty, and most of the Pomona trustees were not informed until the basic decision had been made.

The founding of Harvey Mudd College gave clear evidence that changes were needed in the procedure for the founding of new colleges in the group. The Pomona Board recommended that changes be made, and as a result the Board of Fellows voted in 1959 to include the presidents of all the colleges as regular members of the Committee on Future Colleges. The Board further voted that recommendations from this committee be placed first before the Intercollegiate Council (comprised of the chairmen of all the boards of trustees, the presidents, and a faculty member from each college) "for consideration and comments before being presented to the Board of Fellows of Clarement College for action."

Provost Benson was entrusted with the responsibility of searching for a president for Harvey Mudd College. After much travel on his part and the visits of several candidates to Claremont, Dr. Benson recommended Dr. Joseph B. Platt, who was elected in May 1956 and assumed his duties in Claremont the following September. Dr. Platt, then associate chairman of the department of physics at the University of Rochester, was a Rochester graduate who had taken his Ph.D. at Cornell. During World War II he had served in the Radiation Laboratory at the Massachusetts Institute of Technology, which had been directed by Dr. Lee A. DuBridge, his former teacher at Rochester. Dr. Platt was superbly prepared for leadership of a new college in Claremont. He would be greatly assisted by his wife, a graduate of Miami University, Ohio, whose cordial hospitality and generous service would endear her to the trustees, faculty, and students of Harvey Mudd College and to the Claremont community. The college received its first students in September 1957 and it quickly became a distinguished member of the Associated Colleges.

A New Science Center For Pomona

The late 1950's brought unprecedented development in science for Pomona College. It received laboratories and equipment unsurpassed in any undergraduate college in the United States. This dramatic advance in the science facilities of the college was due to the devotion of an alumnus trustee, the perception and energy of a board chairman, and the outstanding quality of a young science faculty. Their productive association began with the planning of a physics building.

Physics was the science which had changed most since the 1930's, and it was the science in which Pomona's laboratories were most inadequate. While much had been done to improve Pearsons Hall, the building could not meet the demands of physics in the nuclear age. As a scientist and an industrialist, Mr. Wig was particularly aware of the need for a new physics building, and he fully sympathized with President Lyon's giving it the highest priority. As chairman of the Board, Mr. Wig set out to raise the required funds among his business friends. These discussions led to a closer association with his fellow Pomona trustee, Frank R. Seaver '05, and remarkable developments ensued.

Mr. Seaver, for many years a generous and devoted alumnus, had shown increasing interest in the college after his election to the Board of Trustees in 1947. He had given funds for laboratory equipment in chemistry, and in 1950 he had provided a laboratory for astronomy at the Brackett Observatory. Through the trustee-

Frank Roger Seaver '05

faculty retreats, initiated by Mr. Wig in 1951 and made possible by his generosity, Mr. and Mrs. Seaver had come to know many of the faculty. At the retreat held at the Hotel Del Coronado in the spring of 1956 Mr. Seaver and Dr. Fowler, chairman of the physics department, were able to confer regarding a physics building for the college.

Some months later Mr. Seaver informed Mr. Wig that he was ready to contribute the entire cost of a new building and its equipment for the departments of physics, mathematics, and astronomy. The firm of Herbert J. Powell, Los Angeles, was engaged as architects, and planning began early in 1957. Mr. Seaver soon came to feel that the site on Fifth Street, between College Avenue and Harvard Avenue, which had been held for the physics building, was inadequate. On his urging it was decided to locate the building on the northeast corner of Sixth Street and College Avenue.

Even in the planning stages the construction of this building brought to the faculty, administration, and trustees an altogether new experience, thanks to the foresight and generosity of Mr. Seaver. As the Pomona scientists discussed the physics, mathematics, astronomy building with him, he invariably asked if they were suggesting "the best" equipment, and urged them to purchase the latest and most advanced scientific instruments. The building could proceed unhampered by undesirable economies which had frequently beset other projects. Through the excellent supervision of the trustee buildings and grounds committee led by chairman L. A. Shelton, the constant encouragement of Mr. Seaver, and endless hours of planning by the faculty, the building was ready for occupancy in September 1958.

As this building was nearing completion, Mr. Seaver informed Mr. Wig that he would like to give a second science building to Pomona. It was determined that this building would serve the departments of zoology and geology in which Mr. Seaver had special interest. Property at the northwest corner of Sixth Street and College Avenue was purchased as the site for the building. Mr. Powell was engaged as the architect, and construction was begun in the summer of 1958. Grateful Pomona conferred the honorary degree of Doctor of Laws on Mr. Seaver on Founders Day 1958, and thereafter he was affectionately known as Dr. Seaver by his faculty friends.

Dr. Seaver's gifts had come to his alma mater at the best possible time. Pomona had a young science faculty who knew how to make the most of the great opportunities which were theirs. Educated in the world's greatest scientific centers, they brought the latest knowledge of their disciplines. To this they joined an understanding of the role of science in a liberal arts college and a devotion to teaching. These qualities, which Professors Fowler and Fryer and

Millikan Laboratory

Seaver Laboratory for Biology and Geology

their younger colleagues, Burton Henke and Jack Miller, exemplified in the physics department, were characteristic of the faculty members in the other science departments.

Leadership in planning the facilities for zoology was given to Professor Miles D. McCarthy, who in ten years at Pomona had established an outstanding record in teaching and research. He was ably supported by Professors Pequegnat and Ryerson and their younger colleague, Yost U. Amrein. The zoologists had worked together for a number of years and responded to the challenge of planning new quarters and facilities for their department.

In geology, Professor Woodford had retired in 1955, but before doing so he made a great contribution in the selection of his successor. He had been much impressed by a young Scot, Donald B. McIntyre, who was a Fulbright Fellow at the University of California, Berkeley, in 1952-53. Woodford told President Lyon that McIntyre would be "tremendous" for Pomona but he held out little hope of securing him. The president urged him to communicate with McIntyre, who had returned to his position at the University of Edinburgh. When McIntyre replied that he would be willing to discuss an appointment at Pomona, Dr. Lyon arranged to see him in Oxford in the summer of 1953, when the Lyons were there for the Fiftieth Anniversary Reunion of Rhodes Scholars. The meeting resulted in McIntyre's appointment, and he came to Pomona as associate professor of geology, effective September 1954. After a year, Dr. Woodford retired and McIntyre became chairman of the department. The holder of three degrees from the University of Edinburgh, B.Sc. with first honors in geology, Ph.D. and D.Sc. in geology, he had been for six years a member of its geology faculty. It was soon clear that geology at Pomona was in excellent hands. McIntyre was named chairman of the department in 1955 and in 1957 was promoted to a professorship. He was ready and qualified when the opportunity came to plan the geology facilities in the new biology-geology building.

The progress of the biology-geology building was such that it could be dedicated with the physics building on December 6, 1958. Beginning with a convocation in Bridges Auditorium, the day included dedication ceremonies at the two buildings on Sixth

Street and College Avenue, and a luncheon in Frary Hall. At the convocation Dr. Detlev W. Bronk, president of the Rockefeller Institute in New York and president of the National Academy of Sciences gave an address entitled "Science for the Individual and the State." With the recessional the academic procession marched across the campus to the new buildings. There Mr. Wig spoke for the trustees, Professor Fowler for the faculty, and Suzanne Sperling '60 and Thomas K. Hunt '59 for the students.

When Mr. Seaver gave the funds for the physics building, he made only one request — that the trustees name the building for his friend, the late Robert A. Millikan, the distinguished physicist under whose leadership the California Institute of Technology had won international recognition. The plaque unveiled on December 6 records for posterity Mr. Seaver's devotion to his alma mater and his love for his friend:

> This building was dedicated to Pomona College by Frank Roger Seaver, '05 in memory of his friend Robert Andrews Millikan 1868-1953, Professor of Physics at the University of Chicago, Chairman of the Executive Council of the California Institute of Technology, Nobel Prize Winner, profound Christian, who made Southern California a world-renowned center of education in science.

The luncheon honored the memory of Dr. Millikan, and the college was pleased to have as its special guest his son, Dr. Clark Millikan, Director of the Guggenheim Aeronautical Laboratory at the California Institute of Technology. The luncheon speaker was Dr. Ernest C. Watson, dean of the faculty of the California Institute of Technology, who had also worked with Dr. Millikan at the University of Chicago.

The trustees persuaded Mr. Seaver that the biology-geology building be named for him, and it was christened the "Seaver Laboratory." The dedicatory plaque records Pomona's debt to her generous son:

> In recognition of his outstanding services to his Alma Mater this building is named for Frank Roger Seaver, '05, devoted alumnus and valued trustee, a son of Claremont, who at Pomona College received inspiration for his distinguished industrial career.

The departments of zoology and geology moved into Seaver Laboratory during the summer and instruction began in the new building in September 1959. Seaver Laboratory was formally opened to the public on October 6. Dr. George W. Beadle, Nobel Prize winner, chairman of the division of biological sciences at the California Institute of Technology, and recently elected a Pomona trustee, spoke on "Geo-Chemistry and Organic Evolution" at morning exercises in Bridges Hall, and open house was held in the laboratory in the afternoon and evening.

Facing each other on College Avenue, Millikan Laboratory and Seaver Laboratory improved and beautified the entrance to the campus. Of matching design, each with two stories, a full basement, and a mission tile roof, they provided approximately 40,000 square feet of usable space in Millikan and over 46,000 square feet in Seaver. The cost of the buildings and their equipment was over $3,250,000.

The two buildings, soon known collectively as the Seaver Science Center, were designed to provide facilities in which undergraduate majors could engage in research and work with faculty members in the relationship of junior and senior scholars. This approach, which had been followed in the older buildings with their limited facilities, could be greatly expanded in the new laboratories. The Seaver Science Center gave Pomona the best facilities in the nation for teaching physics, zoology and geology at the undergraduate level.

Illustrative of the equipment provided in Millikan was a nuclear physics laboratory with a 2,000,000 volt cyclotron specially designed for the college. There was an atomic and molecular physics laboratory, and an electronic laboratory equipped with audio-frequency and microwave equipment. Millikan also included the college's first computer laboratory. A feature which was enjoyed by non-scientists as well as astrophysicists was a Spitz Planetarium in which the main stellar projector simulates the sky as seen by the naked eye.

For zoology the Seaver Laboratory provided electron, phase, and Baker interference microscopes, the first for the study of living cells. Other facilities for zoology included a radioactive-isotope laboratory, patterned after that at Oak Ridge. Experimental aquaria using sea water provided for marine life study under controlled salinity and temperature conditions. There was a controlled-temperature animal house.

For geology, the microscope room was equipped with specially designed Zeiss and Leitz instruments with four-axis universal stages for three-dimensional measuring purposes; these were fitted for observation with polarized light and convergent lights. Other geology facilities included an X-ray spectrograph for rapid chemical analyses of rocks and materials, a gravity meter for measuring earth tides, an ultrasonic separator for breaking up rock material, an experimental laboratory in which clay was used to simulate the earth's crust, and a rock-slicing room with diamond saws.

Both Millikan and Seaver included departmental libraries worthy of their equipment. Millikan had separate libraries in physics and mathematics, and Seaver had libraries in both zoology and geology. To the collections which professors Tileston, Hilton, and Woodford had developed with such care was added a growing list of books and journals. While these materials were catalogued at Honnold and overseen by Honnold's staff they were housed in attractive libraries near the offices and laboratories of the respective departments.

Mr. Seaver's generosity did not end with the provision of the two buildings and their equipment. The operation of Millikan Laboratory and Seaver Laboratory required expenditures of a magnitude Pomona had never known. Annually these were discussed with Mr. Seaver, who not only met them but often provided funds for additional valuable equipment. He was willing and ready to give Pomona whatever her scientists felt the college needed.

The Seaver Science Center also inspired other private donors to support science at Pomona. Notable were the Robbins Lectures founded in 1962. Fred J. Robbins, metallurgical engineer and president of Bliss Laughlin Industries, Chicago, established an annual lecture series in chemistry. The lecturer spends several days on the campus, lecturing on his current research and meeting for discussions and meals with students and faculty. The wise administration of the Robbins Lectures by professors Smith and Hansch has brought to the campus some of the most distinguished American, British, and French scientists, many of them being Nobel laureates.

The facilities of the Seaver Center enhanced Pomona's participation in the large program of federally sponsored research that marked the 1950's and 1960's. On application, the Armed Services and the National Science Foundation made grants to colleges and universities for research conducted on their campuses by members of their faculties. A number of Pomona faculty had won such grants before 1959, and thereafter most of the members of the physics, zoology, geology, chemistry, and botany departments engaged in federally sponsored research. Such projects were carried on intensively during the summer and often provided for the employment of students. The federal agency made a grant to the college which provided for overhead, equipment, and compensation for the necessary personnel. For the summer, faculty members were compensated at the rate of two-ninths of their annual college salary. These projects involved significant numbers of students who, in close association with faculty members, were given an early start in their scientific careers.

The construction of Seaver Laboratory provided additional space for science departments remaining in the older buildings. The chemistry department took over the area which the geology department had occupied in Mason Hall and thus used the entire building. With the removal of the zoology department Crookshank Hall underwent a major renovation. The basement and first floor were reworked for the botany department, which remained in the building with amplified quarters. The third floor was given to the department of psychology,which at last enjoyed adequate offices and laboratories. Thus the older science center at Pomona had been strengthened by the building of the new one.

Construction of the Seaver Science Center made building space available for the humanities, the social sciences, and the college administration. When physics, mathematics and astronomy moved from Pearsons Hall in the summer of 1958, that historic building was renovated to provide offices, classrooms, and seminar rooms for the departments of classics, history, philosophy, and religion. The moving of the departments previously domiciled in Sumner Hall permitted needed changes and expansion in the administrative offices. The registrar's office was moved to the first floor south of the arcade, and the registrar's former area was reorganized, redecorated, and refurnished for offices and for the work of the dean of students and dean of admissions. These arrangements for the first floor of Sumner remain essentially unchanged today. On the second floor, the area formerly occupied by the history department was reorganized for the alumni offices. These would continue there for many years — until the renovation of another historic building would provide a more attractive and commodious alumni center.

CHAPTER XXVI

The College in the Late Fifties

THE ARMISTICE in Korea was followed by a decade of remarkable development in American higher education which received unprecedented financial support from individuals, federal, state and local governments, business corporations, and philanthropic foundations. The number of degrees granted by colleges and universities increased from 356,608 in 1953-54 to 476,704 in 1959-60.

Congress greatly extended the role of the federal government in higher education by enacting a new G.I. Bill which provided educational benefits for Korean veterans. Funds were also appropriated for low interest loans for the construction of dormitories and academic buildings. The National Defense Education Act of 1958 authorized low-interest, long-term tuition loans to both undergraduate and graduate students, with the provision that half the loan would be cancelled if the recipient gave five years to teaching. The act also included grants for graduate programs, fellowships for graduate students, funds for area and language centers, support for language institutes, and funds for counselling.

Additional support for higher education came through the National Science Foundation, established in 1950. With the leadership of such men as President Conant of Harvard, President Bronk of Johns Hopkins, and President DuBridge of the California Institute of Technology, the work of the National Science Foundation was directed to meeting "the preeminent need, from a long term viewpoint, for advancing basic scientific knowledge." To this end the foundation sought "to provide in every section of the country educational and research facilities which will assist the development of scientific pioneers," and to promote "all over the United

States intense efforts to discover latent scientific talent and provide for its adequate development." To advance these aims the foundation established fellowships for graduate students, research fellowships for faculty members, and research grants to institutions. The benefits of these grants extended from the undergraduate to the most senior research scientist.

A significant new source of financial support for higher education came from the nation's great business corporations. After World War II, Frank W. Abrams, of the Standard Oil Company of New Jersey, and Irving S. Olds, of the United States Steel Corporation, had appealed to their fellow industrialists and stockholders throughout America to inaugurate a program of systematic giving to colleges and universities, and especially to those institutions which were not tax supported. When the courts held that corporate income could be so used, the way was opened for new and continuous assistance to higher education. Corporate support was first notable on the Atlantic seaboard, but it had become significant in the West by 1955-56. The most frequent forms of corporate contributions were scholarship programs which included a payment to the college budget as well as to the student, and unrestricted grants for general institutional support.

The Ford Foundation, which had embarked on a wide program of philanthropy in 1951, took steps to assist the teaching profession. When price and wage controls were removed after World War II, the rapid increase in the cost of living bore most heavily on salaried groups not employed in business or industry. Particularly hard hit were college and university teachers whose salaries even before the inflation were seriously inadequate. The Foundation addressed itself to this critical problem and in the largest and most dramatic act of philanthropy in the history of American higher education fixed the eyes of the nation upon the necessity of improving faculty salaries.

The Ford Foundation announced on December 12, 1955 that it was appropriating $260,000,000 to be given in the succeeding eighteen months to the accredited non-tax-supported colleges and universities of the United States. Of this sum, $210,000,000 was allocated among these institutions on the basis of sums equal to their annual instructional salary budgets. These funds were to be held as endowment for at least ten years and the income was to be used only for increasing faculty salaries. The other $50,000,000 appropriated by the foundation was awarded in the form of accomplishment grants to 125 colleges and universities which in their areas had taken leadership in raising faculty salaries. The use of such grants was left to the discretion of the recipient colleges and universities.

Pomona was awarded a regular grant of $497,000 from Ford funds and an accomplishment grant of $308,500. These funds were made available by payments from the Ford Foundation in the summers of 1956 and 1957. As further evidence of their concern for faculty salaries the Pomona trustees placed both the regular grant and the accomplishment grant in the college's permanent endowment. Thus the Pomona endowment was increased by $805,500, and the additional income from these funds was a tremendous resource in strengthening the faculty and developing the instructional program of the college.

The Faculty 1954-61

The Ford faculty salary grants came in a very important period in building and maintaining the Pomona faculty. The new facilities and increased enrollments made unprecedented demands and in the late 1950's the president, the dean of the faculty, department chairmen, and the administration committee were constantly occupied in making new appointments. Permanent faculty members were sought for the newly created positions and to replace older members who were retiring. In addition, a large number of temporary faculty were required each year to carry the courses of regular faculty members who were on leave for study and research. The extent of the correspondence, conferring, and interviewing is illustrated by the numbers that were appointed: nineteen full-time and six part-time faculty members effective September 1958, and thirteen full-time members effective September 1959.

The faculty, which included 111 full-time and twenty-one part-time members on July 1, 1960, had a healthy balance between experience and youth. The distribution of the full-time members among the respective ranks was: academic administrators, eleven; professors, thirty-two; associate professors, twenty-nine; assistant professors, twenty-one; and instructors, eighteen. The faculty included men and women drawn from many foreign countries and from every section of the United States. The diversity of academic backgrounds of the full professors and associate professors was illustrated by the distinguished universities from which they held their doctorates: Harvard-Radcliffe eight, Yale eight, University of California, Stanford and Chicago seven each, Princeton six, U.C.L.A. five, Columbia, Northwestern, and Wisconsin three each, Brown, Michigan, Tulane, Oxford, and California Institute of Technology two each, and one each from Basel, Edinburgh, New York University, Missouri, University of Washington, Johns Hopkins, Massachusetts Institute of Technology, the University of Rochester, University of Texas, and the University of Pennsylvania. The diversity of undergraduate backgrounds among the faculty was even greater.

After World War II faculty members in American colleges and universities enjoyed unparalleled opportunities for research and study, often with travel abroad. Earlier, outside financial support available for faculty research had been restricted to the Guggenheim fellowships and the fellowships and research grants of the American Council of Learned Societies and the Social Science Research Council. To these were now added extensive programs established by the federal government. The Fulbright Act passed by Congress in 1946 allotted funds from the sale of surplus war material to finance an educational exchange program between the United States and many foreign countries. The National Science Foundation provided large sums for fellowships and scholarships. The Rockefeller Foundation, the Ford Foundation, and the Danforth Foundation inaugurated new grant and fellowship programs, as did also many local and regional foundations.

By 1960 such fellowships had been received by nineteen of the full professors, nine of the associate professors, and four of the deans, with consequent enrichment of their teaching and the intellectual life of the campus. As far as possible, leaves for such fellowships were fitted into the regular sabbatical program of the college. Often this was not feasible, and a significant number of faculty requested and received leaves of absence. In 1959-60 there were nine sabbatical leaves and five leaves of absence.

Summer fellowships were available for shorter periods of study and research. The Board of Trustees provided funds for a total of ten awards of $750 each during 1956, 1957, and 1958. Beginning in 1957, trustee Yale B. Griffith supported a summer fellowship in the amount of $1500 for a member of the modern language faculty to study in the country whose language he taught. From 1957 the John Randolph Haynes and Dora B. Haynes Foundation of Los Angeles granted Pomona annually two summer fellowships of $750 each, to be awarded to members of the social science faculty.

Board chairman R. J. Wig and Mrs. Wig established an endowment for a program of Trustees' Distinguished Professorship Awards, available to faculty members of full professorial standing. The donors wished to assist outstanding teachers and scholars and to encourage leadership in the faculty. The first Trustees' Distinguished Professorship Awards, of $3000 each, were made in 1955 to Ernest A. Strathmann, professor of English, and Floyd A. Bond, professor of economics. In subsequent years the awards were increased in number, varied in amount, and were made available to all regular faculty members above the rank of instructor. The endowment was enlarged through Mr. Wig's further generosity, and the Distinguished Professorship Awards, announced annually at commencement, constitute a continuing encouragement to the faculty.

In art and religion, Pomona failed to achieve the stability that marked most other academic departments. In art the galleries and research libraries of the Boston-New York area were lures against which the college could not compete. Dr. Slive was called to Harvard University in 1954. After a year of interim arrangements, Peter H. Selz, assistant professor of art history at the Institute of Design of the Illinois Institute of Technology in Chicago was appointed associate professor of art and chairman of the department. Mr. Selz held a Ph.D. degree in the history of art from the University of Chicago.

The department of religion suffered frequent changes in its chairmanship. Desire to participate in the work of a divinity school was a continuing factor in drawing teachers of religion away from Pomona. Dr. von Rohr, who had joined the faculty in 1945, and who succeeded Dr. Cuninggim as chairman, resigned at the end of 1954-55 to become professor of historical theology and the history of Christianity at the Pacific School of Religion in Berkeley. Assistant professor Gordon D. Kaufman accepted an associate professorship of theology at Vanderbilt University in 1958. The trend had seemed to be reversed in 1957 when Roger Hazelton, Abbot Professor of Christian Theology in the Andover Newton Theological School, came to Pomona as John Knox McLean Professor of Religion and chairman of the department, but he resigned at the end of 1959-60 to accept the deanship of the Graduate School of Religion at Oberlin College. Robert L. Ferm, who held B.D. and Ph.D. degrees from Yale and had been appointed in 1958, succeeded Dr. Hazelton and led the department in a period of growth and influence within the college.

Greatly increased enrollments led to the expansion of the department of philosophy. W. T. Jones, Dean Iredell, and Frederick Sontag were joined by Morton O. Beckner in 1957 and Robert J. Fogelin in 1958. Beckner, a member of the philosophy department at Brooklyn College, was a graduate of the University of California, Santa Barbara, who was completing his Ph.D. at Columbia University. Fogelin, a graduate of the University of Rochester, was completing his Ph.D. at Yale.

There was further growth in the department of romance languages, where Robert F. Leggewie had become chairman with the retirement of Professor Crowell in 1954. Howard T. Young came that year from Columbia where he had received his undergraduate education and was completing a Ph.D. in Spanish. Leonard C. Pronko, with a Ph.D. from Tulane University, was appointed in 1958. Vladimir G. Ulitin, appointed instructor in 1960, taught Russian language and literature.

Mrs. Allen became chairman of the department of speech and drama when Dr. Scott retired in 1953, and she continued her masterful direction of the theater. Several years were to ensue, however, before a satisfactory arrangement could be made for instruction in speech. This was secured in 1956 by the appointment of Howard H. Martin, a member of the faculty of Allegheny College who held a Ph.D. degree from Northwestern University. The English department expanded its staff and Richard G. Barnes '54, Ph.D. Claremont Graduate School, was appointed instructor in 1961.

In the social sciences important additions were made in history, economics, sociology, and government. The department of history was strengthened by the appointment of Burdette C. Poland as assistant professor in 1957 and by the appointment of Mrs. Margaret Gay Davies as associate professor in 1958. Poland, a veteran, was a graduate of Swarthmore College who had received his Ph.D. from Princeton. His field was modern European history, with special interest in France. Mrs. Davies, a specialist in English history, held B.A. and Ph.D. degrees from Radcliffe.

Lorne C. Cook, who would play a large part in the department of economics, was appointed assistant professor in 1954. A veteran of both World War II and the Korean War, he came to Pomona from the University of Michigan where he was an instructor and had received his Ph.D. degree. Gordon K. Douglass '50, a doctoral candidate at M.I.T. and instructor at the California Institute of Technology, joined the department in 1959.

The curriculum in the department of government was expanded, and Houston I. Flournoy, Ph.D. Princeton University, was appointed assistant professor in 1957. At the time of his appointment he was serving in Washington as an assistant to Senator H. Alexander Smith of New Jersey.

The department of sociology lost its chairman with the retirement of Professor Ray E. Baber in 1956. Dr. Baber enjoyed a national reputation among sociologists who had accorded him many honors, among them the presidency of the Pacific Sociological Society. He was succeeded as chairman by associate professor Alvin H. Scaff. Work in anthropology was introduced through the department of sociology in 1956, and Charles M. Leslie, doctoral candidate at the University of Chicago, was appointed instructor. Robert D. Herman '51, Ph.D. University of Wisconsin, was appointed assistant professor of sociology in 1960.

In the natural sciences there were new chairmen of the chemistry department, the astronomy department, and the psychology department, and additional appointments in chemistry, geology, and mathematics. W. Conway Pierce, who had rendered distinguished service as chairman of the chemistry department, resigned at the end of 1952-53 to become head of the Division of Physical Sciences in the College of Letters and Science, University of California at Riverside. Thereafter the chairmanship of the Pomona department alternated between Dr. R. Nelson Smith and Dr. Corwin H. Hansch.

Three new appointments were made in chemistry. With Dr. Pierce's resignation, Charles Freeman Allen, who had taken his Ph.D. at the University of Wisconsin, was named assistant professor in 1954. John E. Quinlan and Alvin Beilby were appointed as instructors in 1958. Dr. Quinlan held a Ph.D. from the University of Wisconsin, where he had been a National Science Foundation Fellow. Dr. Beilby had taken his Ph.D. at the University of Washington.

New men came in astronomy and geology. Professor Walter Whitney, who had advanced the work in astronomy begun at Pomona by Professor Brackett, retired in 1954 after twenty-five years of service. He was succeeded by assistant professor Paul McRae Routly, research fellow at the California Institute of Technology, who held a Ph.D. in astrophysics from Princeton. Alexander K. Baird '54, who was completing his Ph.D. at the University of California, Berkeley, was appointed instructor in geology in 1958. Appointments in physics and zoology were also made in 1960. Walter T. Ogier, who held a Ph.D. from California Institute of Technology, came as assistant professor of physics. William D. Andrus, doctoral candidate at Stanford, and Richard E. MacMillen '54, Ph.D. University of California at Los Angeles, came as instructors in zoology.

Professor Robert S. Ellis, chairman of the department of psychology, retired in 1956 and was succeeded by Graham B. Bell, associate professor at Louisiana State University. A veteran, Dr. Bell had taken his Ph.D. from Northwestern University.

There were major changes in mathematics. Chester G. Jaeger,

professor and chairman of the department, retired in 1961. He was a distinguished teacher whose interests comprehended the entire college, from faculty business to campus life. For many years he was a faculty representative in the Southern California Intercollegiate Athletic Conference. A number of Dr. Jaeger's students had gone to graduate school and one of these, Kenneth L. Cooke '47, returned to Pomona as an assistant professor in 1957. It was with great satisfaction that Dr. Jaeger saw Dr. Cooke promoted to an associate professorship and chosen as his successor as chairman of the department. Paul B. Yale, Ph.D. Harvard University, was appointed assistant professor in 1961.

Two young women were appointed as instructors in the department of physical education for women. Mrs. Jeannette Hypes, a graduate of Bowling Green University, came in 1957. Miss Anne Bages, a graduate of the University of Illinois, was appointed in 1959.

In physical education for men there was a basic reorganization of the program in intercollegiate athletics and in the faculty of the department. At the end of 1957-58 Pomona and Claremont Men's College discontinued the joint athletic program they had maintained since 1946. Pomona returned to its pre-war organization, and Claremont Men's College formed a new joint program with Harvey Mudd College. Although these decisions were dictated by the unwillingness of the Southern California Intercollegiate Athletic Conference to permit combined teams of three colleges in conference competition, the inauguration of a second program of physical education and intercollegiate athletics in Claremont was in the tradition of the group plan. Individuals in each of the colleges were offered greater opportunities for participation in intercollegiate sports.

Through retirement, Pomona lost the services of the three alumni who had developed the department of physical education for men under Eugene Nixon. Heath retired in 1956, and Strehle and Merritt followed in 1961. To generations of Pomona men they had imparted a love of sports and the highest ideals of intercollegiate athletics. Associate professor Edward Malan succeeded Strehle as chairman of the department and director of athletics. He was assisted by two younger colleagues: Walter E. Ambord, B.A. Los Angeles State College, appointed instructor in 1960; and Mike Riskas, B.S. University of California at Los Angeles, appointed instructor in 1961. Together they continued the department in the great tradition of their predecessors.

Dr. James A. Blaisdell died on January 29, 1957. After his second marriage he had returned to Claremont where he and Mrs. Blaisdell enjoyed ten years with old and new friends. Tributes were paid to him in a memorial service in Bridges Auditorium. His great legacy was the assurance that college education in Claremont would be for the individual student and in a center of academic distinction.

The Academic Administration

There were major changes in the offices of the registrar, dean of admissions, and dean of the faculty. Miss Margaret Maple '26, registrar since 1940, resigned at the end of 1954-55. In this office and in her earlier thirteen years in the alumni office Miss Maple had endeared herself to thousands of students and alumni. Her successor as registrar was Masago Armstrong, B.A., M.A. Stanford University, who had served as acting registrar while Miss Maple was on leave for part of 1954-55. Mrs. Armstrong, formerly secretary to the dean of the School of Education at Stanford, had also worked in New York for the National Citizens Committee for the Public Schools. The ability, diligence, and phenomenal memory which she brought to her duties as registrar assured the effectiveness of this key office and soon made her a campus legend.

The increasing number of applications and the demanding task of assessing each application required major additions in the admissions office. William L. Wheaton '34, appointed assistant dean of admissions in 1952, was promoted to associate dean in 1954. When still further assistance was required in admissions, Herbert B. Smith, assistant professor of history, was asked in 1957 to serve as assistant director of admissions on a part-time basis. In 1959 Dr. Smith accepted further responsibility as director of financial aid for students, and he administered the growing scholarship and grant program for the next decade.

The new appointees in the academic administration were exceptionally fortunate choices. Counselled by Deans Iredell and Sanders they were soon at home in their positions, and by their own long tenures they would contribute greatly to the administrative stability of the college in a period of expansion and change. Their experience and devotion were all the more valuable as the college faced the appointment of a new dean of the faculty.

The retirement of F. Raymond Iredell as dean of the faculty and professor of philosophy in 1959 was the first change among the administrators that President Lyon had assembled for the postwar college. Dr. Iredell's retirement also deprived Pomona of a distinguished and much loved teacher who had given thirty-four years of his life to Pomona, her students, and her faculty. Exemplar of the best in the American academic profession, Raymond Iredell held the highest standards of integrity and scholarship. In their attainment he was selfless, indefatigable, and sound in judgment. As dean and as chairman of the courses of study committee he administered the instructional program objectively and with understanding of all areas of the curriculum. On faculty personnel matters he was a wise counsellor to the president and the administration committee.

Dean Iredell had great proficiency in two special areas that stood him and the college in good stead. He had a practical knowledge of building matters which was invaluable, and he deserved great credit for the renovations of Sumner, Carnegie, Pearsons and Crookshank. Dr. Iredell had a knowledge of the Orient rare among American philosophers. He had taught the first undergraduate course in Oriental philosophy ever given in the United States, and by study and travel he developed a personal understanding of the peoples of Asia. On his retirement, this knowledge of the Orient won him appointment as Director of the Vietnamese-American Association in Saigon where he served with distinction from 1959 to 1963.

Mrs. Iredell's devotion to Pomona matched that of her husband. Also a graduate of the college, and with an M.A. from Radcliffe, she was a leader in the college and in Claremont. From its beginning in 1940 she was the treasurer and a guiding spirit in the Women's

Ernest A. Strathmann, Dean of the Faculty. William L. Wheaton, Associate Dean of Admissions

Campus Club. As the wife of a professor and a dean she made the Iredell home a gracious center in which she extended the hospitality she had enjoyed in faculty homes in her own student days. The family attachment to Pomona was strengthened by their two sons, both of whom were graduates of the college.

Fortunately Pomona had within its own faculty a man who could give continuity to the dean's office and also meet the new and increasing demands upon it. Ernest A. Strathmann, Phebe Estelle Spalding Professor of English, who was appointed to succeed Dean Iredell, was a graduate of Johns Hopkins University where he had taken a Ph. D. in English literature. Dr. Strathmann had been a member of the Pomona faculty since 1932 when he came as an assistant professor. Outstanding as a teacher and scholar, he won early recognition within the faculty and in 1944 was named a full professor. A specialist in the literature of the Renaissance he was assistant editor of *The Works of Edmund Spenser: A Variorum Edition,* the author of numerous scholarly articles, and of a volume, *Sir Walter Raleigh: A Study in Elizabethan Skepticism.* Dr. Strathmann had received two Guggenheim fellowships, and fellowships at the Folger Shakespeare Library in Washington and the Huntington Library in San Marino. He had been a visiting professor at the University of Rochester and at Northwestern University.

For some years Dr. Strathmann had been the chairman of the English department where his wise leadership and his recommendations for appointments had made the department outstanding within Pomona and among English departments throughout the country. Always considerate of others, patient but firm, he brought to the dean's office remarkable understanding of liberal education and the academic profession.

Dean Strathmann would enjoy and extend the wider recognition Pomona had won in the postwar period. He took an active part in national organizations and was a leader in the annual Conference of American Academic Deans and in the Western College Association. His experience and wisdom were of special value in Claremont where the expansion of the Associated Colleges brought new challenges at both the undergraduate and graduate level. From the multifold activities of his office Dean Strathmann brought sound counsel to President Lyon. Sharing a common approach to liberal education and a warm personal friendship the dean and the president worked in harmony and with a sense of personal fulfillment.

Dean Strathmann was greatly helped by the understanding which Mrs. Strathmann '34 always brought to his work. Active in Pomona campus life in her student days, Mrs. Strathmann shared her husband's deep commitment to the college and to the joys and responsibilities of academic life. For the Strathmanns, as for the Iredells, family devotion to the college was strengthened by the attendance of their sons, both of whom would become Pomona graduates.

New Trustees 1954-61

Diversified talents and experience were brought to the Board by W. P. Fuller Brawner and James M. Gerstley, who were elected in 1960, and Karl B. Rodi '29 and Valley M. Knudsen, elected in 1961.

Mr. Brawner, an executive with the Fuller Paint Company in San Francisco, gave valued leadership in the Bay Area. As a Princeton graduate, a trustee of Mills College, and the father of a Pomona alumna, he had appreciation and understanding of the duties of a college trustee. Mr. Gerstley, president of U.S. Borax and Chemical Company, Los Angeles, was born in London, and had been an undergraduate at Peterhouse College, Cambridge. To his British experience he added knowledge of the American college which came when his daughter entered Pomona. Karl B. Rodi '29, an attorney in Beverly Hills, had graduated from the Harvard Law School. As president of the Alumni Association in 1948-49, he had given generous service to the college. Mrs. Knudsen was a beloved civic leader in Los Angeles.

The Board had been strengthened by the election of a number of new trustees who would give devoted service to the college. Cyril Chappellet, elected in 1954, and A. J. Gock, elected in 1955, brought valuable support from the Los Angeles business community. Mr. Chappellet, an aerospace manufacturer, was one of the small group that developed the Lockheed Aircraft Corporation. A Stanford alumnus, he had come to know Pomona through his son and daughter, both of whom graduated from the college. Mr. Gock, a native of San Francisco, had spent his entire career with the Bank of America, of which he was a vice-president.

Three other parents of Pomona students joined the Board, Alden S. Mosshammer in 1956, and Robert B. Coons and Dr. S. Rodman Irvine in 1957. Mr. Mosshammer, pastor of the First Congregational Church in Pasadena, was a graduate of Amherst College and Union Theological Seminary. His daughter was a member of the Pomona class of 1957. Mr. Coons, vice-president of the American Potash and Chemical Company, Los Angeles, was a graduate of the University of California, Berkeley, where he had edited *The Daily Californian.* Mr. Coons' sons were members of the classes of 1953 and 1959 at Pomona. Dr. Irvine, a physician in Beverly Hills and a member of the faculty of the School of Medicine at the University of California, Los Angeles, was a Stanford graduate who had received his M.D. from Harvard. One of his sons had graduated at Pomona in 1953, and a second would graduate in 1962.

Four alumni who had unusually close ties to Pomona began in 1956 and 1957 long and distinguished careers as trustees. Leonard A. Shelton '32, an attorney in the city of Pomona, was one of four brothers who were graduates of the college. After Pomona Mr. Shelton took his LL.B. degree from the Law School of the University of California, Berkeley. Mrs. Shelton graduated from Pomona in 1934. Samuel R. Raymond '34 was the son of a former trustee, the husband of a Pomona alumna, and the father of a sophomore son. Since college Mr. Raymond had been in the investment business in Los Angeles. Ranney C. Draper '25, an attorney and civic leader in Monrovia, who had been an outstanding president of the Alumni Association, was elected a trustee in 1957. His elder son was a sophomore at Pomona. Lawrence T. Cooper '23, assistant vice-president of the Pacific Telephone and Telegraph Company, who had also given distinguished leadership as president of the Alumni Association, was elected a trustee in 1957. His daughter had graduated from Pomona. When Mr. Cooper joined the Pomona Board he was also serving as president of the board of trustees of the Southern California School of Theology which was in process of moving to Claremont.

A Nobel laureate in science and two alumni businessmen were elected trustees in 1958. George W. Beadle, professor of biology and chairman of the Division of Biology at the California Institute of Technology, was a renowned geneticist. Named a Nobel Prize winner in 1958, he would serve in 1958-59 as Eastman Professor at the University of Oxford. Rollin Eckis '27, geologist and executive vice-president of the Richfield Oil Company, had long been a leader in the petroleum industry. Robert V. Edwards '23, president of the American Pipe and Construction Company, Los Angeles, had served Pomona in numerous ways, notably as president of the Alumni Association. Both his son and his daughter were graduates of the college.

New Buildings and Campus Embellishment

While the Seaver Science Center was under construction, other buildings were added for Pomona and the Associated Colleges. A new art center and a new residence hall for women were completed at Pomona. Claremont College acquired a new business building and a center for religious activities for the Associated Colleges.

The Montgomery Art Center

The art department was in desperate need of new and enlarged facilities. Dr. Selz maintained the high level of teaching established by Dr. Slive and also arranged outstanding exhibitions. The result was an increased enrollment in art and wide public interest in larger space for exhibitions. Dr. Lyon arranged for Dr. Selz to discuss the work and requirements of the art department with the academic affairs committee of the Board of which Mrs. Victor Montgomery was then chairman. She was much impressed with the need of the department and shared her interest with her husband. Shortly thereafter Mr. Montgomery informed Dr. Lyon that he wished to give Pomona a new art building in honor of Mrs. Montgomery.

Inspired by Mr. Montgomery's offer, the college moved rapidly and effectively to erect the new building. Herbert Powell was engaged as architect and with Dr. Selz he developed plans that were ready for bids in late 1957. Construction was begun in January 1958 and the building was placed in use at the opening of college in September. The new building joined Rembrandt on the south and extended to College Avenue. It contained a lecture room and gallery, a second gallery, a room for the growing permanent collection of the college, a sculpture studio, offices, and rooms for slides and storage. The building was constructed around a patio which it formed with the western side of Rembrandt Hall. The patio was enhanced by a piece of sculpture by Charles Lawler, given by the Rembrandt Club.

The dedication of the Gladys K. Montgomery Art Center on October 10, 1958 was a festive occasion in which a number of cultural organizations joined Pomona in an expression of gratitude to Mr. and Mrs. Montgomery. In naming the Montgomery Art Center, Pomona was paying tribute to a distinguished trustee who had given years of service to the arts in Los Angeles. With her

Montgomery Art Center

Mr. and Mrs. Montgomery at the dedication of the Montgomery Art Center

husband she was active in the Hollywood Bowl Association and gave continuing support to music in Southern California. When her elder daughter and her son were students at Pomona, she became deeply interested in the college. As a patron and trustee Mrs. Montgomery was a perceptive, wise, generous, and loving leader in Pomona's development. The plaque unveiled at the dedication expressed the gratitude and affection of the college for which she had done so much:

> This Art Center is named in honor of
> Gladys K. Montgomery
> First President of the
> Women's Campus Club of Pomona College
> Devoted Trustee of the College
> Beloved Civic and Cultural Leader
> of Southern California.

To mark the opening of the Montgomery Art Center Dr. Selz arranged an outstanding exhibition, "The Stieglitz Circle," which included works of six painters, Demuth, Dove, Hartley, Marin, O'Keefe, and Weber. The lecture opening the exhibition was given in Bridges Hall by Seymour Slive, who had returned from Harvard for the dedication of the Art Center.

Unfortunately, Dr. Selz had also been attracted to the East and shortly after the dedication of the Montgomery Art Center he left for New York, where he had accepted the position of director of exhibitions at the Museum of Modern Art. He was succeeded in September 1959 by Bates Lowry, assistant professor in the Institute of Fine Arts of New York University, who was appointed associate professor of art and chairman of the department. Lowry, like both Slive and Selz, had been educated at the University of Chicago, where he had been an undergraduate and had taken a Ph.D. During 1953-54 he had held a Fulbright Research fellowship in France.

Anna May Wig Hall

By the mid 1950's Pomona required an additional residence for women. When the college enrollment was established at 1000, Harwood Court, Blaisdell Hall, and Mudd Hall no longer sufficed. The college continued, therefore, to use former private homes which it had acquired on College Avenue, filled the residence halls to absolute capacity, and from time to time made temporary arrangements with the Claremont Inn. Once again the Women's Campus Club gave strong support to the construction of a new residence hall for Pomona women.

Mr. Wig took the lead in providing the building. As the father of three daughters he had shown special interest in the development of the women's campus. In 1957 he joined with his daughter Mary and her husband, Stanley Johnson, in a generous gift to the residence hall fund in memory of Mrs. Wig, who had died on September 6, 1956. The Board felt able to proceed, and Mr. Powell was engaged to make the working drawings for a building to accommodate ninety-six students. Construction was begun in June 1958 and the hall was ready for occupancy when college opened in September 1959.

The building was designed to form a quadrangle with Harwood Court. The residences west of Harwood, on College Avenue, were removed, and the new hall occupied the full block from Second Street to Third Street. An attractive courtyard was developed, with access to Aurelia Harwood Dining Hall where residents of the new hall would take their meals. The building provided excellent living and social facilities for its occupants, and also made an attractive addition to the campus. It was in harmony with neighboring structures, and it transformed the entrance to the college at Third Street.

In naming the building in memory of Mrs. Wig, the college was commemorating the life of a gracious woman who was loved and admired by all who knew her. Anna May Bartlett, the daughter of a Chicago physician, and Rudolph Wig were classmates at West Division High School, Chicago, from which they graduated in 1903. A talented pianist, Miss Bartlett studied music for a year at

Anna May Wig Hall, the view from College Avenue

Oberlin College and then taught music in Chicago until she and Mr. Wig were married in 1910. To their home Mrs. Wig brought her love of music which was shared by her daughters. With her husband Mrs. Wig took a prominent part in the Pasadena Presbyterian Church. Central in her life and thought was her family, to which as wife, mother, and grandmother she brought strength, inspiration, and love.

The dedication of Anna May Wig Hall on Founders Day, October 13, 1959 focused on the education of women. After a ceremony in the courtyard, in which tribute was paid to Mrs. Wig by Dr. Ganse Little of the Pasadena Presbyterian Church, a formal convocation was held in Bridges Auditorium. The speaker was Mildred McAfee Horton, former president of Wellesley College and director of the United States Women's Naval Reserve during World War II. In the afternoon a conference on the education of women was held in Bridges Hall, with Nevitt Sanford, professor of psychology at the University of California, Berkeley, as the featured speaker.

New Buildings for the Associated Colleges

Pomona shared with the other colleges two much needed buildings which were constructed by Claremont College for the Associated Colleges and placed in use in November 1959. The McAlister Center for Religious Activities, located to the northeast of the Honnold Library, was expected to be the first unit of a development that would eventually include a chapel. The center contained the office of the chaplain of the Associated Colleges and other offices of the College Church. Also included were a small chapel, a room with a capacity of 125, and a kitchen. The building was named for Amelie McAlister Upshur, the trustees of whose estate made it possible. A resident of Pasadena, she had been a patron of Pomona, to which she bequeathed $100,000 to endow the Amelie Augustine McAlister Scholarships for Women.

With the growth of the Associated Colleges and their financial assets after World War II the business office in Harper was no longer adequate and new quarters were required. When a new building was proposed, Pomona trustee Morris B. Pendleton made a number of suggestions that led to substantial economies. He became so interested that he and Mrs. Pendleton, both Pomona alumni of the class of 1922, generously made a gift for the building. Centrally located at the corner of Eighth Street and Dartmouth Avenue, the new building provided all the services required by the financial officers of the five colleges. Ample room for expansion assured the permanency of the location. The Pendleton Business Building, named in honor of Mr. and Mrs. Pendleton, was dedicated in a ceremony in the foyer on Pomona's Homecoming Day, November 21, 1959. The immediate members of the Pendleton family, all of them Pomona alumni, were joined by trustees, presidents, and faculty members from all the Associated Colleges.

Campus Embellishment

For many years an unpaved portion of the former Fifth Street, extending east from College Avenue to College Way, had constituted an unsightly and unpleasant division within the central campus. Although lined by beautiful live oak trees planted in the

1920's, the street itself was alternately dusty or muddy. The family and friends of Clarence T. Stover '21, late chairman of the buildings and grounds committee, made gifts for developing this area in his memory. The unfinished street was transformed into a wide and handsomely lighted walk leading from College Avenue to College Way, and with a low wall at each end. A memorial court with sculpture by Albert Stewart of the Scripps art faculty faced Marston Quadrangle and Bridges Hall. A wide patio on the east joined the walk to the Edmunds Union, constituting a large area suitable for many college gatherings. The area between Holmes Hall and Edmunds Union was landscaped attractively. Stover Walk, dedicated on Alumni Day 1958, is a memorial to a trustee to whom Pomona is indebted for much of the beauty of its campus.

The grounds were further improved in 1958 by the construction of a new athletic field in the area east of Clark Hall. These earlier unused, rocky acres had been the site of the veterans' units after World War II, and with the removal of the units the college sought funds to improve the area. Early in 1958 Dr. Lyon was surprised to receive a telephone call from a businessman in New York informing him that he and his associates wished to make anonymously a gift in memory of the late Fred G. Athearn, a member of the class of 1900 at Pomona, in gratitude for the contribution which Mr. Athearn, a prominent attorney in San Francisco, had made to the development of their company. The donors responded cordially to the suggestion of an athletic field and contributed $30,000 for it. When the work was completed, the area included two fields for soccer, touch football, softball, and other recreational uses. Athearn Field was dedicated in exercises held on the field at the opening of college on September 25, 1958. Lee A. Wood '00 of Fresno, paid tribute to his classmate, and Mr. Athearn's son, Leigh, and his wife, of San Francisco, were present.

Two embellishments of exceptional merit and interest were completed on the men's campus. The first of these was a mural by Rico Lebrun, a distinguished painter then living in Los Angeles. Lebrun, who had come to know Pomona through Dr. Selz, had spoken in the college assembly and to art classes. Selz learned that Lebrun had long thought of painting a large mural and that he would be interested in doing it at Pomona, if a suitable wall could be found. Careful study of the college buildings convinced Lebrun that the east side of the wall at the steps to Frary Hall would be ideal. At Dr. Selz' invitation, Mr. and Mrs. Donald Winston, art patrons in Los Angeles, agreed to defray the cost.

Leonard A. Shelton, chairman of the trustee buildings and grounds committee, was much interested in the proposed mural and following conversations with Dr. Lyon, Dr. Selz, and Mr. Lebrun he drafted an agreement which was approved by the committee in the spring of 1958. Lebrun had commitments to spend 1958-59 at Yale University and 1959-60 at the American Academy at Rome. He agreed that when these obligations were discharged he would paint a mural at Frary Hall, the subject to be developed in consultation with the college. While in Rome, Lebrun studied the Sistine Chapel and formulated plans for the mural at Pomona. He decided to call the mural "Genesis" and to develop an Old Testament theme. To avoid undesirable competition with "Prometheus" he chose to paint in tones of subdued black and gray. In accordance with Lebrun's instructions, architect John Rex in the winter of 1959-60 prepared a surface on the selected wall by attaching a new wall and leaving an air space between this and the old wall.

Lebrun had planned to paint the mural during the summer of 1960 and arrived in June with drawings so extensive that they covered most of the tables of Frary Hall. The drawings which Lebrun had made in Rome did not satisfy him when he studied them before the wall, and he spent the entire summer redesigning the mural. It was not until late September, just as college was opening, that he began to paint. From then until the Christmas vacation the men of Frary Hall walked to their meals under a high scaffold and watched Lebrun and his assistants at their work. Lebrun was grateful for their cooperation and understanding and he enjoyed the warm relationship that developed between him and the students.

The completed mural, twenty-nine feet high and twenty-five feet wide, dominates the westward view from the south portico of Frary Hall. Central, and occupying half of the wall, are the ribs of the Ark from which a giant figure of Noah reaches down to embrace and comfort a young boy. Surrounding the Ark are five biblical scenes, all but one of them from the Book of Genesis. The panel to the north of the Ark depicts Adam and Eve leaving the Garden of Eden, Cain and Abel, and the destruction of Sodom and Gomorrah. The panel on the south side of the Ark has large human figures endeavoring to climb over each other and find safety in the Ark. Job, the only figure not drawn from Genesis, looks down from above and toward the Ark. As Martha Davidson wrote, Job is "a mutilated, anguished human wracked by pain and despairing of justice," and Noah, "triumphant and protective symbolizes the renewal of life and hope."

With "Genesis" Lebrun found the fulfillment he had sought in a large mural. As he finished his work, one sensed the deep spiritual experience of the artist. Like Orozco, Lebrun had given Pomona a work of art that was recognized as one of the great murals of the twentieth century.

The distinction of the Clark Campus was further enhanced in this period by the building of a tower. Sumner Spaulding had included a tower in his master plan for the Clark Campus, but need took priority over embellishment and for years there seemed little prospect of completing the architect's design. In the late 1950's impetus for the tower came quite unexpectedly from Mr. and Mrs. Edwin S. Smith of San Diego, whom Mr. Hawley had met through the life income contract program and who became substantial donors to Pomona. The Smiths were much interested in a memorial tower and asked if they could give funds for this purpose as well as for the endowment. Through their generosity a sum adequate for a tower was available in 1959.

The buildings and grounds committee, deeply aware of its responsibility in placing a tower on the men's campus, took great care in its planning. It was decided to hold an architectural competition in accordance with the regulations and procedures of the American Institute of Architects. Notice of the competition was published and a jury of non-participating architects rendered the decision. The competition was won by the firm of Rex and Honnold.

Smith Tower

John Rex recognized the outstanding architectural quality of the men's campus and he sought to design a tower that would be the culmination of the master plan established by Spaulding in the 1920's. He elected to place the tower in the southwest corner of the fountain court where, without attachment to any building, it would coordinate all the structures and emphasize their unity. Rex designed a tower 125 feet high with a base sixteen feet square. The east and west sides were finished concrete and the north and south sides were precast grilles of a color harmonizing with the mission tile roofs of the surrounding buildings. The tower had an eight-foot clock and was designed to support a carillon. Completed in 1961, the Smith Memorial Tower became at once a landmark for locating Claremont from the freeway and the air.

Campus Life

The 1950's were an outstanding period in the life of the college. Incoming students were selected from an increasing number of applicants; 1714 students applied for the 260 places in the freshman class entering in September 1950, and 125 others competed for advanced standing. Measured by College Board scores, secondary school records, and their performance in college, the achievement of Pomona students was remarkable. There were fewer withdrawals, fewer failures, and fewer students in academic difficulties in 1959-60 than at any time during the previous decade.

To a high degree the students of the fifties sought liberal education in preparation for becoming teachers, physicians, research scientists, lawyers, ministers, or business executives. In their pursuit of these educational objectives they brought to the faculty an opportunity for building a stronger and more scholarly college. In 1959 the president emphasized the nature of this opportunity in his opening convocation address, "This Household of Learning." "I perceived here," he said, "the foundations, the traditions, and the resources for a household of learning that would lead and illumine a great area. Over the years Pomona has come a long way toward that ideal. The deep needs of our country and of the world now require that we quicken our pace. This is what our predecessors on this campus would have expected us to do. This is what the invincible spirits who opened the West would have expected. This is what America of this decade demands of us."

To this end the college provided many intellectual and cultural experiences beyond the classroom. Regular weekly assemblies were addressed by members of the faculty or by visiting speakers. Funds were provided for bringing distinguished men and women from our own country and from abroad. Lecturers on the Joseph Horsfall Johnson Foundation spent several days on the campus and gave a series of lectures. Among the Johnson lecturers were: Clinton Rossiter, professor of government at Cornell University; Henri Peyre, professor of French Literature at Yale; Barbara Ward, the British economist; and Germaine Brée, a distinguished authority on modern French literature. Among the notable visitors who came for shorter periods, or single appearances were: Senator Hubert Humphrey, of Minnesota; Senator Mike Mansfield, of Montana; Senator Charles E. Potter, of Michigan; William David Ormsby-Gore, British delegate to the United Nations; Hans J. Morgenthau, professor of political science at the University of Chicago; Edward Weeks, editor of *The Atlantic;* Lee A. DuBridge, president of the California Institute of Technology; and W. H. Auden, the British poet. The Arthur O. Clark Lectures in Religion were given by Merrimon Cuninggim, former professor at Pomona and Dean of the Perkins School of Theology, Southern Methodist University; Julian Hartt, professor of Philosophical Theology at Yale Divinity School; George Hedley, chaplain of Mills College; John S. Whale, English theologian; and Theodore P. Ferris, Rector of the Trinity Church, Boston.

Throughout the 1950's the College Church of the Associated Colleges was a major force in the lives of Pomona students and those of the other colleges. W. Robert Rankin, who succeeded Merrimon Cuninggim as chaplain in 1951, led the College Church in a period of significant development for both students and faculty. The services in Bridges Hall at eleven on Sunday mornings were regularly attended by some two hundred persons, generally including the presidents of the five colleges. When Mr. Rankin resigned in 1958 to become Associate Director of the Danforth Foundation, he was succeeded by Edgar C. Reckard, chaplain at

Brown University, under whom the College Church continued to play a major role in the academic community. The work of the chaplain was facilitated by the removal of the church offices in 1959 from Sumner Hall to the new McAlister Center for Religious Activities.

The increasing cost of attending Pomona was mitigated by the availability of larger funds for financial aid to students. Tuition which had been $600 a year in 1949-50 grew to $1100 for 1959-60. Room and board increased from $625 to $875 a year. To assist students in meeting these costs, there were larger Pomona College funds, and newly established corporate and state scholarship programs. College funds expended for financial aid grew from $64,576 in 1949-50 to $244,315 in 1959-60.

Two scholarship programs of great significance to Pomona made their first grants to students entering college in September 1956. One of these, the National Merit Corporation, was the largest private scholarship program in American history. With headquarters in Chicago, the corporation was an agency through which American business corporations made scholarships available to outstanding young men and women throughout the country. With its expenses underwritten by the Ford Foundation and the Carnegie Corporation, the National Merit program immediately became a strengthening influence in higher education. National Merit Scholars, chosen in nationwide competition, were free to take their scholarships to the college of their choice. Twenty National Merit Scholars were enrolled at Pomona in 1959-60.

The state of California established a scholarship program, effective September 1956, that was to be a major force at Pomona. Tuition grants, first limited to $600 annually, were made available to graduates of California high schools for use in colleges and universities of their choice, within the state. The State Scholarship Commission, administered with distinction, won enthusiastic support throughout the state, and soon became a permanent institution. In September 1959, 152 students held state scholarships at Pomona. An initial member of the Commission was Mr. Wig, president of the Pomona Board, who had been a leader in the successful establishment of the state scholarship program.

Virginia Princehouse Allen, Associate Professor of Dramatics

Richard Chamberlain, Ray Spencer, and Ann Eldridge in *Winslow Boy* in 1954-55

Director William F. Russell, and the Men's and Women's Glee Clubs in 1954-55

The achievements of graduating students indicate the excellent use Pomona students made of their many opportunities at the college. Of the 215 graduates in 1958 nearly eighty per cent planned to take graduate work. Eighty members of the class expected to go into teaching, sixteen into medicine, six into medical technology, seventeen into science or scientific research, fifteen into business, and eight into law. Eighteen men went immediately into military service. Members of the class of 1958 won forty-six fellowships, scholarships, or assistantships for graduate study. These included four Woodrow Wilson Fellowships, for preparation as college teachers, three Fulbright awards, four National Science Fellowships, and a Rhodes Scholarship. The class of 1960, with 223 graduates, achieved an equally outstanding record. Seventy-five per cent of the class planned to take graduate or professional work. Forty-five members of the class received fellowships or scholarships. These awards included two Marshall Scholarships for study at the University of Oxford, two fellowships at the Rockefeller Institute in New York, five National Science Foundation Fellowships, and twelve Woodrow Wilson Fellowships. In each of these categories the class of 1960 placed Pomona at the top, or very near the top, of liberal arts colleges throughout the country. Pomona students enjoyed great distinction in winning fellowships for future college teachers which the Danforth Foundation inaugurated in 1951. By 1958 Pomona had won nine Danforth Fellowships, exceeded only by Duke University with twelve.

The outstanding accomplishments of Pomona graduates in the late fifties owed much to the well-structured campus life. The college maintained its residence halls and dining halls as homes for its students. The high standard which Miss May C. Frank had established in the direction of the residence halls was continued by her successor, Mrs. Dorothy Metzger. Mrs. Lucille McCarthy, the former Miss Gramse, continued her superb direction of the dining halls, providing Pomona students with the best of food, pleasantly served in friendly circumstances. Much of the work, and all the serving in the dining halls, was done by college students who, like earlier waiters at the Claremont Inn, considered themselves a special and privileged group.

ASPC Executive Board 1959-60: Mrs. Throne, Robert Kennan, president, David Morgan, John Crawford, Anita Frank, Martin Olson, David Wallerstein

Founders of KSPC, Ronald H. McDonald '57, and Terrell T. Drinkwater '58

The college provided and maintained an excellent physical plant but it took student leadership to make it work. From entrance the student had a sense of "belonging." First it was the class, which took a name, engaged in rivalry with the sophomores, and continued closely together throughout the four years, making the class a continuing, important unit of college life. The Associated Women Students and the Associated Men Students, through committees, governed the respective campuses, assisted by Mortar Board and the Ghosts. On each campus sponsors, chosen through the dean's office, advised and assisted freshmen throughout their first year, and sponsor groups were often continuing social units.

The Associated Students of Pomona College controlled and guided campus-wide student organizations and institutions. Aided and advised by Helen Throne, the able and devoted graduate manager, the officers of the ASPC approved an annual budget, supervised its operation, and considered the countless matters that came up each year. Elections were spirited and there was continuing effort to improve the ASPC. This led to the adoption of a new constitution in April 1959, under which the president of the ASPC was assisted by five elected commissioners who respectively supervised finance, communications, social activities, academic interests, and athletics.

Communication among students and faculty was provided by *Student Life,* which because of increased printing costs reduced its schedule to one issue a week. As in earlier years, its editors did not spare criticism of the college or student institutions. "Whether it be championing student rights in the face of faculty oppression," wrote the *Metate* of 1960, "reviling Judiciary or scooping the campus police on the latest crime, the *Student Life* always backs up its reputation as the most vociferously expressive of the school's publications." Under the leadership of Ronald H. McDonald '57 and Terrell T. Drinkwater '58 an FM Radio Station, KSPC, was installed in the Replica Building and went on the air on February 12, 1956.

The variety and vigor of campus activities were portrayed annually by the *Metate.* It showed a student community with many interests, but a genuine concern for the whole. The Social Com-

Christmas Supper 1950

Conference Champion Pomona-Claremont Football Team, 1954

mittee provided and supervised a social program in which all could participate. Informal and formal dances were scheduled throughout the year. Through the enlarged Edmunds Union, with its offices, store, and fountain, Pomona students met each other and conducted the business of their numerous organizations.

Students gave wide and organized support to athletic teams, particularly football. The Rally Committee was an important part of the ASPC, holding pre-game night rallies, auto caravans, and after-game parties. Interest in athletic participation was such that rugby and soccer were added to the traditional sports. Both freshman and varsity teams were fielded in football, basketball, baseball, cross country, track, swimming, water polo, and tennis.

In addition to the management of ASPC, AWS, and AMS matters, students participated with the faculty on joint committees, and on certain important faculty committees. The College Life Council, which had general oversight of campus life, was composed of faculty members and nine students, with an elected chairman. Led by Dean Sanders the faculty had extended the participation of students on faculty committees to include the admission committee, the personnel committee, the public events committee, and the student affairs committee.

The administration and the faculty were seeking to create a college commuunity in which every member had responsible participation. Their achievement was soon recognized beyond the campus. In September 1958 Dr. Lyon received one of the most cherished awards of his presidency, an honorary degree from the University of California. He was saluted as: "Historian, humanist and able president of our highly esteemed sister institution of learning, Pomona College, one of the leading private colleges in the nation: under your judicious guidance, it has enriched the educational opportunities available in California to the ablest young men and women of this and other states."

An extremely happy and rewarding period had begun for the Lyons and their family. Elizabeth graduated from Wellesley in 1958 and John from Amherst in 1961. At the time of Elizabeth's graduation Mrs. Lyon was elected an alumnae trustee of Wellesley and she continued on the Wellesley Board for the ensuing seven years, journeying to the college three or four times a year. Meanwhile, Dr. Lyon was increasing his own ties with the University of Oxford by editing, from 1956 to 1962, *The American Oxonian,* the quarterly journal of the Association of American Rhodes Scholars. The president's outreach in American higher education was extended by service on important committees of the American Council on Education. He served as chairman of the Commission on the College Student, as a member of the Committee on Relationships with the Federal Government, and as a member of the Overseas Liaison Committee. With a group from the latter he made a three weeks' trip to the Federation of Rhodesia and Nyasaland in 1962.

The College Gates

CHAPTER XXVII

The Seventy-Fifth Anniversary

Higher Education in California

THE SPECTACULAR DEVELOPMENT of higher education in the United States that followed World War II reached its culmination in the 1960's. The number of degrees of all kinds conferred by American colleges and universities increased from 476,704 in 1959-60 to 1,065,391 in 1969-70. The forces that produced such growth were most notable in California, which in 1960 became the most populous state in the Union. In the early 1960's California won universal recognition as the leader in American higher education. Its extensive public system of junior colleges, state colleges, the University of California, and the large number of independent colleges and universities offered diversity and opportunity to young men and women throughout the state.

The public system in California took a great step forward in 1960 with the establishment of a master plan for its development, expansion, and institutional integration. Growth had been so rapid and had presented so many problems that the legislature asked the liaison committee of the Regents of the University and the State Board of Education to prepare a master plan for the future of public higher education in California. This responsibility was entrusted to a Master Plan Survey Team of eight members, two from the state colleges, two from the junior colleges, two from the university, one from the independent colleges, and Arthur G. Coons, the distinguished president of Occidental College, as chairman.[1]

The Master Plan, enacted into law in 1960, determined the functions and interrelationships of the university, the state col-

[1]From 1938 to 1943 Arthur Coons had been professor of economics at Claremont Colleges.

leges, and the junior colleges. A new board of trustees was created for the state colleges, which were removed from the jurisdiction of the State Board of Education. To advise the trustees of the state colleges and the Regents of the University, the legislature created a Coordinating Council for Higher Education. This council, which included members from the university, the state colleges, the junior colleges, and the independent colleges and universities, broke new ground in the history of higher education in the United States. Its functions, though advisory, touched all segments of higher education in California and contributed immeasurably to the wise development of the public system and to its relations with non-tax supported institutions.

The independent colleges and universities of California increased in stature with the growth and maturity of public higher education within the state. This was particularly true of Pomona, whose president, trustees, and faculty saw the opportunity for unprecedented accomplishment.

The greater international outreach, which air travel and the growth of California made possible, was reflected in the life of the college. The number of students from overseas, which was thirty-six in 1959-60, grew to fifty-one in 1965-66. Of these students normally about half were Americans living abroad and the others were citizens of foreign countries. Many of the latter came on scholarships from American sources. Notable was the African Scholarship Program of American Universities, located at Harvard University, in which Pomona joined with 141 colleges and universities. Conceived by David D. Henry of the Harvard admissions office, ASPAU, as it was popularly known, was a brilliantly designed plan, in which the student's own country paid his transportation to the United States, the United States Government provided funds for his room and board, and the American institution that accepted the student gave him a scholarship for full tuition and fees. Through ASPAU, American institutions in the 1960's made a great contribution to newly independent countries in Africa, especially Nigeria, Ghana, Uganda, and Kenya. ASPAU students in turn brought a better understanding of African countries to Pomona students and faculty.

For American students, Pomona in 1961-62 initiated a semester abroad program, which featured independent study and at least a month's home stay with a foreign family. Applicants, normally juniors or seniors, were accepted for the program when they and their programs of study were approved by their department of concentration. The department evaluated the student's work when he returned to the college and determined grades and credit through examinations and essays. Travel and family home stays were arranged under a college contract with the Experiment in International Living. The semester abroad proved effective and popular and laid a basis for later and more extensive "study abroad" programs for Pomona students.

The stimulation which Pomona experienced by the reception of faculty members from abroad and by the opportunities which its own faculty enjoyed for studying and teaching overseas was evident in 1961-62. The college welcomed Professor Maurice Shock from the University of Oxford as a visiting member of the department of government. Six members of the Pomona faculty returned to their classes from leaves which included study and research at the University of Grenoble, the University of Cologne, the University of Freiburg, and work in Madrid, an assignment with the United Nations in Ethiopia, and teaching and administering the Fulbright program in Pakistan.

The College Bowl Team

The lively intellectual life of Pomona's students in this period was brought to the attention of millions of Americans by television which, between 1950 and 1960, had transformed communication in the United States. Among the most popular programs was the College Bowl contest, sponsored by the General Electric Company, which was broadcast over nationwide television at 5:30 on Sunday afternoons. Two teams of four students each vied in the speed and correctness of their answers to questions posed on any subject and asked in rapid-fire fashion by the moderator. The winning team in each contest received $1500 for the scholarship fund of its institution and the loser received $500. After each contest the winning team continued in the weekly competition

The College Bowl Team: Left to right, Dr. Robert J. Fogelin, Dallas Holmes, David Renaker, Matthew Cartmill, Richard Wilsnack, and Dr. Morton O. Beckner. Below: part of the reception crowd on College Avenue

until it was defeated or had won five consecutive contests. A five-time winner was retired with honors and its college received a silver bowl. The weekly programs were broadcast live from New York City, and the travel expenses of the teams and their coaches were paid by General Electric.

Pomona students were eager to enter the competition and Dean Sanders applied to the General Electric Company on behalf of the college. When a Pomona team was scheduled for the autumn of 1961, two outstanding members of the philosophy department, assistant professors Morton O. Beckner and Robert J. Fogelin, were asked to select the team and to serve as coaches. The four students chosen represented the wide range of interests essential for successful competition. Dallas Holmes '62 was concentrating in government, David Renaker '63 in English literature, and Matthew Cartmill '64 and Richard Wilsnack '64 in sociology and anthropology. With Holmes as captain, the team and the coaches worked zealously in preparation.

The test came when the Pomona team and one of the coaches flew to New York for a contest with Texas Christian University, a three-time winner. Behind at half time, Pomona pulled ahead and won a spirited game 230 to 170. When the victors returned, 200 Pomona students awaited them at the Los Angeles International Airport. The team then began the rigorous schedule of flying to New York for the weekend and then returning to the campus for classes. Pomona won the second game, with Washington University, St. Louis, by a wider margin, 200 to 105. In the third contest Pomona overwhelmed Hood College, 325 to 20.

The tempo quickened for the fourth game, in which Amherst College was the challenger. Cartmill, Wilsnack, Renaker and Holmes performed as the veterans they had become and vanquished Amherst, 270-120. The following Sunday afternoon Pomona defeated Washington and Lee University 330 to 110, and with this fifth victory retired undefeated. In becoming the fifth college to win five victories, Pomona with 1355 points had amassed the highest score to date in the College Bowl. In addition to the silver bowl, which is to be seen today in an honored place at the admissions office in Sumner Hall, the team had won $9000 for

Pomona's scholarship fund. The college elected to place this in the permanent endowment whence it provides annually a General Electric College Bowl Scholarship.

No one who was at Pomona in the autumn of 1961 will ever forget the thrill and pride the whole college experienced in the masterful triumphs of its College Bowl team. A large delegation met the returning heroes at the Los Angeles Airport and escorted them to Claremont. On the campus they were received on the porch of the Carnegie Building and greeted by the Mayor of Claremont, President Lyon, and the President of the Associated Students in ceremonies for which College Avenue was closed and occupied by most of the student body. In Pomona's history only the victory of the Men's Glee Club in St. Louis in 1932 could be compared to the success of the College Bowl team. Their achievement was recognized by the Pomona trustees, who presented each member of the team with a book and an especially designed scroll, and by Los Angeles County, with a citation of honor. Governor Edmund G. Brown wrote President Lyon saying, "Inasmuch as they are all Californians and were retired undefeated they have brought much credit to your college and to the State of California."

The Anniversary Celebration

Reflecting this period of great accomplishment by American higher education, Pomona College prepared to celebrate its seventy-fifth anniversary in 1962-63. A trustee, faculty, alumni committee, with Lawrence T. Cooper '23 as chairman, developed a program which included a convocation, a banquet in Los Angeles, a conference on the arts, an invitational conference on science, an art exhibit, and a seventy-fifth anniversary concert by the Pomona College Choir and Symphony Orchestra.

The seventy-fifth anniversary convocation was scheduled for Founders Day and held on the morning of October 16, 1962. During the summer invitations had gone to those colleges and universities with which Pomona and its faculty enjoyed the closest associations. The response was enthusiastic and the delegates constituted the largest academic assemblage in the history of Claremont. Present were 149 delegates of colleges and universities, which listed by the order of their founding ranged from the University of Oxford, founded in the 12th century, to the University of California at Santa Cruz, which had been established in 1961. There were fourteen representatives of civic, church, and educational groups, and the faculties of all of the Associated Colleges joined in the celebration.

President Lyon welcomed the delegates and the audience by expressing Pomona's appreciation for the common heritage from which all colleges and universities are nourished. "Our Congregational founders looked to New England for inspiration and example," he noted. "A Yale man of great leadership and wise foresight was the determining force in Pomona's establishment. The earliest faculty members were drawn from Amherst and Dartmouth. Their deep Christian faith, their devotion to intellectual freedom, their high standard of scholarship, and their joy in their work flowered in the accomplishment of Pomona's graduates." However, Dr. Lyon continued, respect for educational tradition had not impeded innovation in a new and developing region. The four Associated Colleges which joined Pomona in celebrating her seventy-fifth anniversary gave impressive witness to the new and imaginative plan for the organization of higher education which Pomona had inaugurated in the 1920's.

Henry Steele Commager, American historian and professor of history and American studies at Amherst College, gave the main address, entitled "The Emancipation of the College." He interpreted the evolution of the college, "a distinctively American institution," from colonial days to the present. With the rise of the university and the establishment of graduate and professional work there had come, he noted, "an increasing distinction between the work of the college and the work of the university. . . . It is, in a very real sense, a kind of emancipation from all the improper things the colleges have been called upon to do in the past, a kind of declaration of independence from the burdens that have been fastened upon them." The independent college is now free to perform the tasks for which it is so admirably equipped: "imaginative transmission of the heritage of the past," "discipline of mind, character, and body," and an "understanding of and acquaintance

Paul Fussell, Chairman of the Board of Trustees

Seventy-Fifth Anniversary Convocation: President Lyon, Dr. George S. Sumner, Professor Henry Steele Commager

with the seamless web of knowledge, delight in music, art, literature, and science." In contrast to the university, the college can remain small in size and simple in structure, and "subject the whole educational process to continuous exposure and criticism." The college is freer to fix and maintain academic standards, and to experiment. Commager concluded:

> What presents itself to us is an exhilarating prospect. First, to do on a larger scale, for a far more numerous citizenry, what the small colleges of 18th and 19th century America did so well: that is, to encourage the service to the commonwealth which animated the generation of Jefferson, Madison, John Adams, Hamilton, Mason, Jay and other products of the infant colleges of America. Second, to discourage the narrow nationalism and that parochial culture which is urged upon us stridently from almost all quarters, and to encourage the restoration of that larger community of learning that flourished in the 18th century — not least in America. And third, to encourage and participate in what is surely the most enthralling educational enterprise — perhaps I should say intellectual and social enterprise — of modern times: that of spreading the college and university of the West to three-quarters of the globe that has not heretofore known such institutions, and that now desperately needs and wants them. Just as in the early days of the Republic the young men of the New England colleges carried the torch of learning to the new West, so your generation will see a more sophisticated but no less idealistic group carrying to the far corners of the globe the institutions and practices of American higher education.

Although Professor Commager had never heard the Ceremony of the Flame, his peroration seemed a part of it as the enactment of this traditional exercise concluded the convocation. The torchbearers were led by Dr. George S. Sumner '94 who represented the first graduating class. A gala luncheon in Frary Hall concluded the morning's festivities.

A program of visiting speakers and special events marked the second semester of the anniversary year. J. Robert Schaetzel '39, Deputy Assistant Secretary of State for Atlantic Affairs, addressed the opening convocation for the second semester in Bridges Auditorium on "Tides of Change." On February 21 and 22 a conference on "The Arts in a Technological World" was held in Bridges Hall. Participating were: August Heckscher, Special White House Consultant on the Arts, and Director, Twentieth Century Fund; W. McNeil Lowry, Director of the Ford Foundation Program in Humanities and the Arts; Dennis Flanagan, editor *The Scientific*

American; Alfed Kazin, writer and visiting professor, University of California, Berkeley; and Richard Lippold, sculptor, Hunter College.

The Pomona science departments used their new strength and their tradition to lead a nationwide discussion of the problems of the liberal arts college in the new era of American science. With a grant from the National Science Foundation, an invitational conference attended by representatives of twenty-nine colleges from all sections of the country was held on the campus on March 28 and 29. The keynote address was given by Roger Revelle '29, University Dean of Research, University of California and Director of the Scripps Institution of Oceanography. The title of the conference, "Crisis: The Small College as a Source of Scientists" succinctly stated a grave problem in American higher education. By discussing their own research-oriented program and by showing the facilities and equipment of Millikan Laboratory and Seaver Laboratory, Pomona scientists were able to make a contribution to their scientific colleagues elsewhere. The conference was a dramatic presentation of Pomona's leadership in the education of scientists.

The program for the seventy-fifth anniversary year stressed the ongoing educational life of the college, and therefore, most events were held on the campus. It was felt, however, that one major anniversary occasion should be scheduled in Los Angeles in order to acquaint the larger community with the progress of the college. With assistance of a special trustee-faculty committee a banquet was held at the Beverly Hilton Hotel on March 29.

The banquet was as successful as the seventy-fifth anniversary convocation had been. More than a thousand alumni, faculty, trustees, parents, and friends attended. Paul Fussell, chairman of the Board of Trustees, presided masterfully. The combined Glee Clubs, conducted by Mr. Russell, sang Debussy's "Trois Chansons" and Ramsey Harris' Pomona song "Over the Years." The trustees announced four Diamond Anniversary awards for long and outstanding service to Pomona. Etchings of Sumner Hall with plaques of appreciation were presented to Dr. George S. Sumner '94, whose entire professional life had been given to Pomona as

First row: Frank R. Seavor '05, George S. Summer '94. Second row: Paul Fussell, Dr. Lyon, R. J. Wig

Mrs. E. Wilson Lyon, Dr. Lyon, and Paul Fussell

AWARDS PRESENTED AT THE 75th ANNIVERSARY DINNER

teacher and controller; trustee Frank R. Seaver '05 and Mrs. Seaver, whose munificence had brought a new era in science; Rudolph J. Wig, trustee, former president of the Board, and indefatigable worker for the college; and President and Mrs. Lyon.

The address of the evening was given by Lord Franks, Provost of Worcester College, University of Oxford, who had been British Ambassador to the United States, 1948-1952, and Chairman of Lloyd's Bank Limited, 1954-1962. In 1949, while Ambassador to the United States, Lord Franks had received an honorary Doctor of Laws degree from Pomona, and he honored that association by accepting the college's invitation to participate in its seventy-fifth anniversary celebration. Coming as lecturer on the Johnson Foundation, he addressed a campus convocation as well as the anniversary banquet. His main theme was the Atlantic World and within it the closer and more important relations of the United States and Great Britain. To the banquet audience he held forth the larger role of American higher education in "The Future of the Atlantic Community." His brilliant address, like that of Commager, stressed the greater significance of liberal education and Pomona's opportunity and responsibility in the new commonwealth of learning.

The seventy-fifth anniversary program continued on the campus with a remarkable exhibition of French paintings entitled "1887: The Salon and the Ateliers," and with three outstanding performances of Mendelssohn's *Elijah* by the Pomona College Symphony Orchestra and the College Choir. To conclude its year of celebration Pomona welcomed as the commencement speaker John B. Oakes, editor of the editorial page of *The New York Times.* A graduate of Princeton, where he had edited *The Daily Princetonian,* and a Rhodes Scholar at Queen's College, Oxford, Oakes gave an address of special appeal to the members of the graduating class. Under the title, "Smashing the Cliché," he told them that they were starting "their careers at the very beginning of what will surely be the most exciting era the human race has known since the Age of Discovery. You are at the beginning of the Age of Space, where man will soon be searching, not by proxy, but in person, the pathways of the stars." He called for "a receptivity to new ideas; a skepticism toward dogma or rote of any kind, a free, unfettered approach to life and learning that builds on the past but is not bound by it."

The seventy-fifth anniversary had given the college a deeper appreciation of itself, had increased its stature among colleges and universities throughout the nation, and had extended its influence with the discriminating public. Most significantly, the legacy of the past had become an inspiration for future accomplishment.

Financial Planning

The anniversary events on the campus were paralleled by a tremendous effort by the trustees and college officers to meet Pomona's need for additional facilities and higher faculty salaries. Despite the notable advances of the postwar period, Pomona was approaching a point where her progress demanded a large increase in plant and in endowment for support of instruction. As early as the late 1950's President Lyon had urged the Board to begin a capital gifts campaign, but the trustees were hesitant. As Pomona had not conducted a capital gifts campaign since 1924, there was no one on the Board who could bring personal experience to the undertaking. Some trustees felt that the very successful life income contract program would meet the college's need. But this income lay in the future and could not supply the pressing current demands. Over several years the Board studied the needs of the college and assessed the extent to which the trustees could raise the required funds.

The improved structure and operation of the Board did much to make a capital gifts campaign possible. New trustees had brought valuable experience in corporate practice and in the government of non-profit corporations. With their assistance the procedures and organization of the Pomona Board had been improved and clarified. The former concentration of most college business in the Executive Committee was modified by devolving major functions to other committees. A budget committee had been established and entrusted with acting first on the president's budget recommendations. The postwar building program and oversight of the enlarged campus increased the work of the buildings and grounds committee, and the growth of the college's endowment gave greater responsibility to the investment committee. The growing financial needs of the college gave a new dimension to the role of the ways and means committee. Through the wider use of these and other committees all the members of the Board learned the nature and extent of Pomona's problems and needs.

Paul Fussell was early convinced that Pomona must conduct a capital gifts campaign if the college was to advance, and he worked to secure trustee support. When he succeeded Mr. Wig as chairman of the Board in 1961, he took the lead in planning for such a campaign.[1] Thoughtfully and always patiently he promoted discussions within the Board and its major committees. When these discussions reached the point of decision, he took the initiative by making the first major financial contribution to the campaign. By his leadership Mr. Fussell was able to unite the Board in enthusiastic support of the largest financial effort in the history of the college.

Dr. Lyon presented three projected ten-year budgets at the trustee meeting on September 28, 1961. On the basis of the size of the enrollment and the number of faculty he estimated that, to avoid annual deficits, the college would require additional capital from $8,250,000 to $10,080,000. After a very full discussion, the président's report was referred for study to four key trustee committees: academic affairs and library, buildings and grounds, budget, and ways and means. When these committees reported on November 30, 1961, each of them recommended a fund-raising program. At this meeting the Board voted unanimously "that Pomona College celebrate its seventy-fifth anniversary by inaugurating a three-year program to raise six million dollars in capital gifts, over and above the current program." This momentous decision was implemented by establishing a special fund for anniversary events and the employment of fund-raising counsel.

One cannot overstate what such an effort requires on the part of those most responsible. The willingness of business and professional men and women to give of their substance and countless days of their time in the service of educational and charitable institutions, which is one of the finest qualities of American society, would be amply illustrated in Pomona's campaign.

[1]The title of "president" of the Board was changed to "chairman," effective July 1, 1961.

CHAPTER XXVIII

A Capital Gifts Campaign

THE CONDUCT of a major financial campaign required a reorganization of Pomona's fund-raising staff. Vice-president Allen F. Hawley was retiring in 1962, after having served four years beyond the normal retirement age. The programs which he had developed were the bases upon which a capital gifts campaign could be launched. The life income program had won such recognition that it was nationally known as "the Pomona Plan," and had been emulated in a number of colleges and universities. By July 1962, Pomona had received $12,971,023 in annuities and life income contracts. The annual Pomona Alumni Fund brought increasing support and was the means of informing alumni of the needs of their alma mater. John F. Moulds, who following his retirement at the University of Chicago had worked with Mr. Hawley in the bequest and life income programs, also retired in 1962.

Richard T. Nimmons '35 succeeded Mr. Hawley as Vice-president for Administration and Development in the summer of 1962. To his large duties he brought long experience in fund raising and public relations, and great devotion to Pomona. As an undergraduate he had edited *Student Life* and after graduation he remained for three years as director of the Pomona College News Service. While at Pomona he married Virginia Friedman '37. Subsequently Mr. Nimmons had worked with the American City Bureau, a fund-raising firm with headquarters in Chicago, served four years as an officer in the Army in World War II, and spent five years as public relations director for the Hawaii Employers Council. When appointed at Pomona, he was a partner in a public relations counselling firm in New York.

VICE-PRESIDENTS

Richard T. Nimmons

Allen F. Hawley

Mr. Nimmons would be supported by experienced staff members who could carry on the well-established fund-raising programs of the college. William B. Dunseth, who had come from Hampden-Sidney College in 1960, had been trained by Mr. Hawley and could take over the estate-planning office with its bequest, annuity, and life income contract programs. Orlando R. Davidson, former director of the University of Chicago Alumni Foundation, who had been director of development at Pomona since 1958, was in charge of annual giving. Working with him was Morton C. Johnson '42, the experienced and congenial director of Alumni Relations. Continuing in his remarkable and successful service to his alma mater was William B. Himrod '08, who as assistant to the president would work in all aspects of the capital gifts campaign. In addition to the college staff, professional fund-raising counsel was engaged, and with Mr. Nimmons as coordinator preparation for the great effort moved forward on schedule.

"The Advancement Program," as it was named, was officially announced in Los Angeles on October 30, 1963 at a dinner in the

California Club attended by three hundred alumni and friends. The featured speaker, Dr. Norris E. Bradbury '29, Director of the Los Alamos Scientific Laboratory, made an eloquent statement on the achievements of Pomona and its role in higher education. Mr. Fussell presided and presented the plans of the trustees. President Lyon stressed the quality of Pomona and its dedication to excellence for undergraduates.

This emphasis upon the quality of undergraduate education was central in *The Strength of Independence,* the thirty-two page brochure which Dr. Lyon wrote and which was widely distributed early in 1964. "Excellence for undergraduates at Pomona derives in large measure from the college's freedom from outside control," the brochure affirmed. "Pomona is a tribute to private philanthropy and to the non-tax-supported tradition in which American higher education began over three hundred years ago. This tradition must remain strong." The Advancement Program was an appeal for the support essential to maintain Pomona's independence.

During the two years of planning the trustees had doubled the original goal, and the objective announced for the Advancement Program was $12,936,000. Of this amount $5,585,000 was for the support of instruction, $1,200,000 for scholarships and loan funds, $5,551,000 for buildings, and $600,000 for contingency and other purposes. The buildings sought were a new chemistry building, a new music building, a residence center for students of modern languages and international relations, and a physical education center for women. Provision was made for renovation of Bridges Hall and for remodeling Mason Hall as a classroom and office building. Although the amount of the campaign had been doubled, the time for completion remained three years.

Major responsibility was taken by a committee of sixteen trustees, organized as the Steering Committee in 1962 and renamed the Advancement Committee after the official announcement of the campaign in 1963. The chairman throughout the crucial years of the campaign was Robert B. Coons. The Alumni Association, the Women's Campus Club, and the Associates brought their support to the undertaking. The National Council of Pomona

College was formed to advise the college on matters of general policy and planning, and over sixty distinguished alumni and friends in educational, cultural and civic affairs, business, and religion accepted membership and attended its meetings at the college.

Better communication with all these groups was provided by the establishment of a new magazine, *Pomona Today*. Since 1934 the college had depended upon the *News Letter* as its primary publication. The Advancement Program gave the impetus for much needed fuller accounts of the program of the college and the accomplishments of its alumni. Many individuals cooperated in launching the magazine, but the college was most indebted to Frederick Bracher, professor of English, who served as chairman of the initial editorial board. Under Ray Frazer '47, professor of English, who was editor 1964-68, and his successor, Gordon J. Hazlitt '54, *Pomona Today* became one of the outstanding alumni magazines in the United States.

New Trustees

Great help in the Advancement Program came from the ten trustees who were elected to the Board from 1962-64. Of these, four joined the Board in 1962. H. Russell Smith '36, president of Avery Products Corporation in San Marino, was an outstanding leader in civic and cultural affairs in the Los Angeles area. Edwin F. Hahn, Jr. '24, a leading attorney in Pasadena, was the son of the first alumnus elected a trustee of Pomona. Robert R. Sprague, president of Pioneer Savings and Loan Association, was the father of a Pomona son. John H. Burt, rector of All Saints Episcopal Church, Pasadena, succeeded Dr. Mosshammer, who had resigned to accept a pastorate in New York state. Two Southern Californians were elected in 1963. Louis B. Lundborg, a Stanford alumnus, was executive vice-president of the Bank of America in Los Angeles. Maurice H. Stans, investment banker and senior partner in William R. Staats Company, had been Director of the Budget of the United States from 1958-61.

The Board of Trustees voted in 1963 to increase the number of its members from thirty to thirty-five, and in order to secure national representation, provided that as many as five members could be chosen from areas other than California. Albert H. MacLeod '39, vice-president of the Harris Trust and Savings Bank of Chicago, and Charles B. Stauffacher '37, executive vice-president of the Continental Can Company of New York, were the first trustees elected under this provision.

Two Southern Californians who would play a large role in the Board were elected trustees in 1964. Edward E. Tuttle, of Pasadena, attorney and president of Essick Manufacturing Company, whose son had attended Pomona, had served as chairman of the Pomona Associates. William H. Fellows '33, of San Marino, president of Old Colony Paint and Chemical Company, was a former president of the Alumni Association. Mrs. Fellows was a Pomona alumna.

A Greater Seaver Science Center

A dramatic development in science came in the early stages of the planning for the capital gifts campaign. Previously the college had felt that Mason Hall and its laboratories would suffice for the department of chemistry. However, the spectacular impetus to physics, zoology, and geology given by the Millikan Laboratory and Seaver Laboratory indicated that a new building was also required in chemistry. Accordingly, this was incorporated in the first proposals for a capital gifts program which were forwarded to the members of the Board of Trustees late in the summer of 1962.

The day before college opened in September Dr. Frank R. Seaver informed Dr. Lyon that he planned to give the chemistry building to the college. On October 12 he telephoned Dr. Lyon and asked that he and Dr. Nelson Smith meet him at an hour he named in front of Mason Hall and be prepared to go immediately to the treasurer's office. He arrived as scheduled bringing a check for a million dollars which he instructed the treasurer to place at interest before the bank closed that afternoon! Dr. Seaver was a man of few words. When the excited president thanked him for being such a wonderful trustee, he was silent for a moment and said quietly, "Every man is a trustee." The million-dollar gift was

Above: Dr. Lyon, Mrs. Frank Roger Seaver, Dr. Frank Roger Seaver, and Professor R. Nelson Smith examine plans for Seaver Laboratory for Chemistry. Below: ground breaking for Seaver Laboratory, left to right, Michael B. Wardell '64, President of the Associated Students, Mrs. Seaver, Professor Smith, Ranney C. Draper, Dr. Seaver, President Lyon, and Paul Fussell

announced at the meeting of the Pomona College Associates held in Gibson Dining Hall, Sunday, November 18, 1962. Dr. and Mrs. Seaver were both present for the joyous occasion.

Dr. Seaver's munificence for the chemistry building continued in this manner and degree until it was completed. The first projected cost had been $1,500,000 but as the architects, Smith, Powell and Morgridge, were completing the working drawings in the summer of 1963 it was clear that the building would cost over $2,000,000. When the bids were received on August 7, the low bid was $2,470,155. The buildings and grounds committee, of which Ranney C. Draper was then chairman, laid the facts before Dr. Seaver and indicated what changes and economies would be required to stay within the earlier estimates. Dr. Seaver informed the committee that he wished to leave the building essentially as it had been designed.

Announcement of Dr. Seaver's decision was made at a meeting of the Executive Committee on September 3. The contract was accordingly approved and the meeting was on the point of adjourning when Dr. Seaver arose and called the group to order. He said that the year before he had presented the college a check for a million dollars for the chemistry building and that his one stipulation at that time was that the money go immediately to the bank and begin drawing interest. He then overwhelmed the committee by saying he had in his hand a check for $1,600,000 and he wanted the man responsible for getting it to the bank to see that it was deposited before the end of the day. As he finished, the trustees were on their feet, giving him a standing and thunderous ovation. It was an historic moment in which the trustees were bound in gratitude, friendship and service to higher education. The treasurer, Mr. William V. Shannon, rushed to the bank and deposited the check nine minutes before closing time.

Ground breaking ceremonies for the building were scheduled for the opening day of college, September 26, 1963, when the Board of Trustees would be on the campus for their autumn meeting which followed the morning convocation in Bridges Auditorium. In the afternoon the trustees proceeded to the site, the southwest corner of Seventh Street and College Avenue, where they were joined by many faculty members and a group of students. Dr. Seaver and Mrs. Seaver turned the first shovels of earth, followed by trustee chairman Paul Fussell, Dr. Lyon, Mr. Draper, Professor Nelson Smith, and Michael B. Wardell, president of the Associated Students. The announcement of the building, released that day, received wide newspaper coverage. The *Los Angeles Times* in an editorial, "An Investment in Higher Education," praised Dr. Seaver, "for the construction of a three-building science complex at the college," and for the seriousness with which he took "the responsibility of maintaining the strength of America's independent universities and colleges."

The Seaver Laboratory for chemistry was the largest and most complex of the three buildings in the Seaver Science Center and its construction continued throughout the academic year 1963-64 and until the end of the first semester of 1964-65. From the beginning of the architectural drawings in the autumn of 1962, the development of the building required the constant attention of the faculty of the chemistry department. Leadership was taken by R. Nelson Smith '38 who, as chairman of the department, gave the greater part of three academic years to planning the building and working with the architects. Dr. Smith's professional understanding of the requirements of a chemistry building and his devotion to the task greatly facilitated the work of the architect, the planning of the donor, and the wisest use of his funds by the college. When it was found that the chemistry building would require $650,000 in instrumentation, above what had been planned, Dr. Seaver on March 17, 1964 sent the college through Dr. Smith a check from the Seaver Institute for this amount, "to buy all the items shown on the 21-page list which you furnished, making whatever changes or substitutions you may find advisable."

The building proceeded on schedule and the chemistry department moved in during the Christmas vacation of 1964-65. For months the college had been planning to make the dedicatory convocation one of the most significant occasions in Pomona's history. Dr. Seaver took great interest in the convocation and by the opening of college in September he and Dr. Lyon had completed the plans for the day. Dr. Seaver was desirous that the speaker be President Lee A. DuBridge of the California Institute of Technology, and Dr. DuBridge was pleased to accept. The date was set for January 19, 1965. But Dr. Seaver did not live to participate in the convocation and to see the completion of his great provision for science at Pomona. His health failed in the autumn of 1964 and he died on October 31.

Dedication day was worthy of the achievement it celebrated and of the donor who made it possible. Speaking on "The Sciences and the Liberal Arts College," President DuBridge paid eloquent tribute to the planning and generosity which had given Pomona such a distinguished place in science:

> Pomona College decided more than ten years ago that it would try a new approach to undergraduate education in science. It would create a center in which faculty research and undergraduate teaching would go hand in hand. Research opportunities would attract able young scientist-teachers, and research activities would stimulate students and enormously enrich the learning process. Fine laboratories would aid both teacher and students. And today — with the Seaver Center now complete — Pomona's preeminence is assured for years to come. The facilities are here; the equipment is here — the finest that can be found. The faculty is here — and they will now continue to come. The students are here — and more are on the way.

The honorary degree of Doctor of Science was conferred on Dr. DuBridge and four distinguished Pomona alumni in fields of science: Francis E. Blacet '22, Dean of the Division of Physical Sciences of the College of Letters and Science at the University of California, Los Angeles; John M. Ide '27, Director of the Division of Engineering of the National Science Foundation; Victor L. Klee, Jr., '45, Professor of Mathematics at the University of Washington and Consultant to the Boeing Research Laboratiories in Seattle; and Per K. Kofstad '50, Senior Research Scientist for the Central Institute for Industrial Research, Oslo, Norway. These honorees joined with three hundred college and personal guests in honoring Mrs. Seaver at a luncheon in Frary Hall.

The Seaver Laboratory for Chemistry, which with its equipment had cost $3,379,334, included unusual features and facilities, some of them rarely found even in graduate schools. The main floor contained a 246-seat lecture room with closed circuit and commercial television and slide and movie projectors, two freshman laboratories, and one of the finest chemical libraries on the West

Coast. The top floor was designed primarily as the organic and biochemical area. All of the research and teaching laboratories in the building were equipped with huge stainless steel distillation hoods with safety glass partitions to protect students working in the laboratories. On order was a $268,000 IBM System/360 computer, one of the first to be purchased by any college or university in the nation.

In wisdom and devotion Dr. Seaver had taken steps to safeguard for the future the equipment and the three buildings of the Center by bequeathing to Pomona a large interest in a trust fund. Mrs. Seaver had shared all his planning for the three buildings, and many of her ideas on design and landscaping had been incorporated in the Center. As president of the Seaver Institute, through which Dr. Seaver had directed much of his philanthropy, she continued his annual support of the scientific operation of the Center. She accepted membership on the Pomona Board of Trustees in 1965 and there worked further in fulfillment of her husband's dream for his beloved alma mater. For generations of students the noble vision and inspiring generosity of Frank Roger Seaver have made "science" and "Seaver" synonymous at Pomona College.

An Eventful Quinquennium in Claremont

For the Associated Colleges the years 1959-64 were one of the most significant periods since the inauguration of the group plan. They were marked by the reorganization of Claremont College, a new constitutional structure for the colleges, the establishment of a new college, and changes in the presidency at two of the institutions.

The marked growth of the undergraduate colleges and the graduate school led to a reexamination of the organization of Claremont College, where since 1944 academic leadership had been entrusted to the provost and the corporate and group responsibilities had been handled by the managing director. By unanimous action the boards of trustees of the five colleges in 1959 effected a reorganization of Claremont College, reestablishing the presidency of that institution and transferring to it the academic leadership of the college. Dr. Robert J. Bernard, who had served as managing director since the reorganization of 1944, was elected president and took office on July 1, 1959. With his election as president the office of managing director was discontinued.

The retention and reshaping of the office of provost continued the close relationship of the colleges that had come from the reorganization of 1944. By the changes of 1959 the office of provost of Claremont College was abolished, and the office of provost of the Associated Colleges was established to be held in rotation for a term of one year by the presidents of each of the colleges. The provost, who was responsible to the Board of Fellows, provided leadership in the coordination of educational interests, particularly between the undergraduate colleges and the graduate school, and supervised the preparation of the budgets of the joint services. Once these budgets were approved it was the responsibility of the provost to administer their operation. The provost was chairman of the committee of presidents, the presiding officer at joint convocations, the chairman of all joint meetings of faculties, and representative and spokesman for the group of colleges at all public, civic, and academic meetings. A permanent secretary aided the provost and the committee of presidents. Robert W. Cooper, Captain, U.S. Navy, retired, was the first to hold this office. By carrying these multiple responsibilities for annual terms the presidents acquired an intimate knowledge of the operations of the Associated Colleges and greater comprehension of the possibilities of making Claremont a greater center of learning.

The reorganization of Claremont College was soon followed by other helpful constitutional changes. These emanated from an address, "Proposed Reorganization of the Associated Colleges," which William W. Clary gave to a joint meeting of the five boards of trustees in October 1960. The proposed changes involved nomenclature, the nature and functions of Claremont College, the enrollment of each undergraduate college, and the relations of the boards of trustees. After much consideration the boards of trustees in 1961 made important changes in the name of the group and in the name of the central coordinating institution. "The Associated Colleges" were renamed "The Claremont Colleges," and

"Claremont College" became "Claremont University College."

As Mr. Clary wrote, "For the first time it was agreed in writing that the central institution (renamed Claremont University College) is and shall be the central coordinating institution of the Claremont Colleges." Its functions included "holding title to all central facilities which are operated by joint budgets of all the member colleges," and the acquisition or construction of new central facilities, the promotion and founding of additional colleges, the conduct of the Claremont Graduate School, and the awarding of all higher degrees other than honorary degrees.

While these basic matters were under discussion among the boards of trustees, the Pomona Board requested approval to increase the enrollment of the college from 1000 to 1100. The other undergraduate colleges also requested permission to increase their enrollments: Claremont Men's College from 350 to 600, Scripps from 325 to 400, and Harvey Mudd from 350 to 400. These new maximum enrollments were approved. To secure adherence to these limits there was a provision that over-registration in any one year must be balanced by a mandatory decrease the following year.

The creation of the Board of Overseers, which included all the boards of the colleges, brought all the trustees of the Claremont Colleges into one body for the first time. While the Board of Overseers exercised only advisory functions, it provided an official and regular way for all the boards to meet together, and served as a valuable instrument of communication as the colleges grew in number and in size.

Effective operation of intercollegiate matters was secured through the provostship and the body of college presidents, officially constituted as the Executive Committee of the Intercollegiate Council. The ECIC, as it was familiarly known, met fortnightly and aided by a full-time assistant to the provost dispatched the large volume of business that was invariably at hand. For the consideration of the annual joint budgets the presidents were joined by the chairmen of the five boards of trustees; after the approval of the budgets by this enlarged executive committee the appropriate portion of each joint budget was included in each college budget and acted upon by its board of trustees. The enlarged executive committee met from time to time to consider general policy questions, and the close association of the chairmen and the presidents greatly facilitated the operation and progress of the colleges.

When all the above procedural changes had been approved by the respective boards of trustees, they were included in a new document which also updated and combined the existing intercollegiate agreements. Edited by William W. Clary, entitled *Articles of Affiliation of the Claremont Colleges,* and printed in 1962, this was the first intercollegiate agreement made easily available to trustees, administrators, faculties and the general public. Thirty-seven years after the inauguration of the group plan there was at last at hand a document setting forth the agreements under which the colleges in Claremont conducted their group activities and responsibilities.

In this fruitful period the Claremont Colleges were able to add a much needed joint facility. Led by a large gift from Catherine and Robert H. Garrison the colleges joined in constructing the Garrison Theater, which seats seven hundred people. The new building faced the Honnold Library, with which it formed an attractive quadrangle. The Garrison Theater opened in December, 1963.

A Sixth College

The continued rapid growth in the population of California inevitably brought consideration of expansion by the Claremont Colleges. While Pomona and Claremont Men's College moved to enroll, respectively, the maximums of 1100 and 600 permitted under the Articles of Affiliation of 1961, both Scripps and Harvey Mudd elected to hold their enrollments at 300 and not to expand to their permissible maximums of 400.

With the increased enrollments at Pomona and Claremont Men's College the number of men in the undergraduate colleges in September 1962 outnumbered the women by some 700. To maintain essentially the same number of men and women in the total enrollment of the colleges, two possible procedures were discussed: enlarging the enrollment of Scripps, and the founding of a new women's college. These discussions reached resolution early in 1963.

As early as November 30, 1959, the Future Colleges Committee considered the nature of the next college at Claremont. While no action was taken, there was consensus that the next college should be a women's college and might be established within five years. To advise and assist it the Future Colleges Committee appointed two subcommittees: a joint trustee-faculty committee to consider whether the next college should be for men, women or coeducational, and a faculty committee to review the need for an additional women's college. If it deemed a new women's college desirable, the faculty committee was requested to recommend the field of emphasis and the general outlines of its curriculum. The two committees met, both separately and jointly, over nearly a year.

During this time the presidents of the colleges and the subcommittees of the Future Colleges Committee were careful to ascertain the plans and wishes of Scripps College. When it was clear that Scripps did not plan to expand its enrollment beyond 300, the subcommittees submitted their reports. The faculty subcommittee recommended the establishment of a residential "liberal arts college for women, with emphasis on the social and behavioral sciences" with an enrollment of approximately 300, and the faculty-trustee committee concurred. These reports were approved by the Intercollegiate Council on January 24, 1961 and on February 1 the Board of Fellows endorsed the establishment of a women's college.

As no funds were in sight for a new college, it was first thought that the institution could be begun as the Undergraduate School for Women of Claremont College, following the procedure for the beginning of Claremont Men's College in 1946. That this proved unnecessary owed much to the work of President Bernard and the able support of President Benson. Fortunately, there were programs of the United States government which made available large sums for capital expenditures by institutions of higher education. These included forty-year loans for dormitories at 3½% interest, and outright grants of as much as a third of the cost of academic buildings. When Dr. Bernard had secured a site for the new college with a twenty-acre tract east of Mills Avenue, the Board of Fellows applied for a federal loan to construct a dormitory for 207 women, and in November 1962 received a loan of $1,091,000.

The search for the additional funds required to complete and furnish the dormitory soon opened the way to further financing and the establishment of the new college. Russell K. Pitzer, whose gifts had been determining forces in the foundation of both Claremont Men's College and Harvey Mudd College, again generously assisted the new venture. After providing $75,000 toward the dormitory, he indicated in January 1963 that he and Mrs. Pitzer would contribute $1,500,000 to the new college for women, of which $350,000 would be available for the immediate construction of an academic building.

With such financial assistance the Board of Fellows took steps to incorporate the sixth college, and this was accomplished on February 21, 1963. It was named Pitzer College, in honor of Mr. and Mrs. Russell Pitzer and in gratitude for their long, generous interest in all the Claremont Colleges. The advisory board became the first board of trustees of Pitzer College, and the new board elected Dr. Bernard, who had retired as president of Claremont University College on February 1, 1963, as its first chairman.

The five colleges united in financial assistance to the sixth college during its first five years. Upon the recommendation of the college presidents, the overhead service charges to Pitzer College for the Honnold Library, the business office, the health service, the College Church, and other joint services were waived entirely for the college's first year, reduced by fifty per cent for the next two years, and reduced by twenty-five per cent for the following two years. More than $250,000 was thus contributed to Pitzer by the five colleges, the portion borne by each college depending on its size and the extent of its use of the joint facilities and services.

Following the precedent set at the founding of Scripps, the trustees of Pitzer College called a dean from one of the Claremont Colleges to be the first president of their college. Dr. John W. Atherton, dean of the faculty at Claremont Men's College, was elected president of Pitzer College on June 1, 1963. By background and experience he was highly qualified for his new and exacting responsibilities. A graduate of Amherst College with a Ph.D. from the University of Chicago, he had come to Claremont Men's College to teach English literature, and his success led to his promotion to a professorship and subsequent election as dean of the faculty. His knowledge of the Claremont Colleges and of their relationships greatly facilitated the establishment of the new college.

Presidential Changes in the Claremont Colleges

While Pitzer College was being organized, presidential changes were imminent in two of the Claremont Colleges. As noted above, Dr. Bernard had retired as president of Claremont University College in February 1963. Although retiring as president, Dr. Bernard remained a member of the Board of Fellows and chairman of the Pitzer board, thereby in many ways continuing to serve the Claremont Colleges to which he had committed his entire professional life.

In the period following the retirement of Dr. Bernard, William W. Clary '11, who had been chairman of the Board of Fellows since 1953, served for seven months as acting president of Claremont Graduate School and University Center — the new name of the central institution. This was a beneficent period to which Mr. Clary brought a lifetime of work for Pomona and the Claremont Colleges. His constitutional mind, nurtured by years of legal practice, and his sense of history helped his fellow presidents see the group plan in perspective. His brief presidency gave him in turn a better appreciation of the operation of the colleges and the forces at work among them. Mr. Clary's service as acting president from February 1 to August 1 bore further fruit in his book, *The Claremont Colleges, A History of the Claremont Group Plan,* which he published in 1970.

As acting president Mr. Clary did much to prepare the way for Dr. Louis T. Benezet, who took office as president of Claremont Graduate School and University Center on August 1, 1963. Dr. Benezet brought a deep appreciation of liberal education and the independent liberal arts college. Born in LaCrosse, Wisconsin, in 1915, he had graduated from Dartmouth College in 1936. After two years of teaching at the Hill School, he went as an associate in psychology to Reed College where he met and married Mildred Jean Twohy in June 1940. Returning to the East, he took a Ph.D. in psychology at Columbia University in 1942. After three years as a naval officer in World War II, he resumed his educational career at Syracuse University, where his success in administrative positions, notably as assistant to the chancellor, led to his election as president of Allegheny College in 1948. As one of the youngest American college presidents he received national attention.

After seven successful years at Allegheny, Dr. Benezet in 1955 accepted the presidency of Colorado College at Colorado Springs. In his eight years at Colorado College he led a remarkable revival of that historic college, strengthening its faculty, constructing new buildings, and raising large funds, which included grants from the Ford Foundation. Active in national education associations, Dr. Benezet brought vigorous and imaginative leadership to Claremont. Already well known to the presidents of the Claremont Colleges, he made an easy transition to his complex, new responsibilities.

While the Claremont Graduate School and University Center was installing its new president, there was an impending change in the presidency of Scripps College. President Hard had announced his retirement for the summer of 1964 when he would complete twenty years at the college and reach the statutory retirement age of sixty-five. In his long tenure Dr. Hard had brought unity to the Scripps faculty and had given vigorous leadership to its nationally acclaimed programs in the humanities and in art. His work was recognized by the award of a chapter of Phi Beta Kappa to Scripps.

As Dr. Hard's successor, the Scripps trustees elected Dr. Mark Hubert Curtis, associate professor of history and associate dean of the graduate division of the University of California at Los Angeles. Born in Medford, Minnesota, in 1920 Dr. Curtis had graduated from Yale University in 1942. After service in World War II he met and married Maria Isabel Byrd y Zalduondo of Puerto Rico in 1945. Returning to Yale, he completed a Ph.D. in history and served three years as an instructor in history at Williams College. In 1953 he joined the history department at U.C.L.A. He was the author of a volume, *Oxford and Cambridge in Transition, 1558-1642,* and he had held a fellowship at the Folger Shakespeare Library in Washington, D.C. Like President Hard, a scholar in renaissance studies, Dr. Curtis appreciated the emphasis of the academic program of Scripps.

The three veteran presidents and the three appointed in 1963 and 1964 formed an exceptionally congenial team for the Claremont Colleges. They worked hard to develop the Claremont Colleges as an outstanding center of learning and they achieved marked success.

CHAPTER XXIX

Years of Great Progress

TEN WEEKS AFTER the dedication of the Seaver Laboratory of Chemistry, Pomona was able to join with the other Claremont Colleges in the largest fund-raising effort ever envisaged for the group of institutions. On March 31, 1965 the Ford Foundation granted the Claremont Colleges $5,000,000 on condition that they raise collectively $15,000,000 by March 31, 1968. This grant was a part of the Special Education Program the foundation had inaugurated and under which a large number of colleges and universities had benefited by 1965. The unique structure of the Claremont Colleges had presented problems to the foundation, and an earlier application from the colleges had not been successful. However, the foundation had indicated receptivity to a second application which would emphasize the interrelationships of the colleges and their joint services. After months of work in each president's office and with the leadership of President Benezet of the University Center, to whom joint appeals were entrusted, the Claremont Colleges were able to present a convincing and successful application.

The funds of the Ford grant were to be available for current use over a period of five years, and they thus would give the maximum support to the work of each of the colleges. The major designations of the grant were as follows: academic and physical resources, $2,885,000, of which $1,260,000 was for the purchase of books and periodicals for the Honnold Library; the academic program, including faculty salary increases, faculty fellowships and research grants, undergraduate and graduate student programs, $1,965,000; and planning and coordination, $150,000. The faculty salary funds and the fellowship and research funds were to be distributed among the colleges in proportion to the numbers of their faculties.

The Ford Challenge Grant was the catalyst for a much larger campaign than the required $15,000,000. The colleges were so encouraged that they shaped a greater and longer development program in which each college sought resources to meet its own greatest needs, and also cooperated in raising funds for the common purposes of the group. Together the six colleges announced on June 21, 1965 a Challenge Program including the $5,000,000 Ford grant, totalling $86,000,000, to be raised over a period of seven years. The goals of the respective colleges were: Pomona, $23,966,000; Claremont Graduate School and University Center, $11,204,000; Claremont Men's College, $13,000,000; Harvey Mudd College, $18,750,000; Scripps College, $6,930,000; and Pitzer College, $7,150,000.

Pomona's two-year experience with its Advancement Program gave the college courage to undertake such an enlargement of its original goal. In amplifying the amount and extending the time of the Advancement Program the Pomona trustees sought $19,641,000 on a campaign basis by April 1, 1968, which was the end of the Ford Foundation matching period. The trustees anticipated that the further $4,325,000 of their goal could be secured from 1968 to 1972 through the regular development program of the college. It should be emphasized that only funds immediately available for college use were credited to the Pomona Advancement Program. The annuity and life income program, which provided funds that would be released for college use in future years, continued separately with great success, and such gifts averaged over $2,300,000 annually throughout the period of the Advancement Program.

Led by Robert B. Coons, who had become chairman of the Board with the retirement of Paul Fussell on July 1, 1964, the trustees worked with great devotion to achieve the objectives of the enlarged Advancement Program. As their work progressed, instruction was strengthened, facilities were expanded, and the beauty of the campus enhanced.

Substantial increases were made in faculty salaries. The average

Paul Fussell transfers the chairmanship of the Board of Trustees to Robert B. Coons

faculty compensation, which included salary and college payments for retirement, social security, and insurance, rose for the respective academic ranks as follows:

Academic Years	*1964-65*	*1965-66*	*1966-67*	*1967-68*
Professors	$14,541	$16,261	$16,537	$17,368
Associate Professors	11,291	12,696	12,955	12,958
Assistant Professors	9,583	10,070	10,595	10,218
Instructors	7,528	7,534	8,196	8,458

Valuable assistance in the Advancement Program was given by six new trustees. Edward Lasker, an attorney in Beverly Hills elected in 1966, brought experience in business and motion picture production. He was a graduage of Yale University and the Law School of the University of California at Los Angeles. Adam Y. Bennion, James D. Stewart, and Francis M. Wheat '42 were elected in 1967. Mr. Bennion, an attorney in Los Angeles, was a graduate of the University of Utah and the George Washington University Law School. Mr. Stewart, vice-president and general manager of the Hollywood Turf Club, had attended Pomona before transferring to Stanford, from which he graduated. Mr. Wheat, a Los Angeles attorney, was a member of the United States Securities and Exchange Commission in Washington when he was elected to the Pomona Board. He had already served the college in many capacities, notably as President of the Alumni Association in 1964-65. M. Carl Haddon and Mrs. John W. Myers '35 were elected trustees in 1968. Mr. Haddon, a graduate in aeronautical engineering from the University of Michigan, was also a trustee of the School of Theology at Claremont. Mrs. Myers, the former Lucia Raymond, had continued in Los Angeles the leadership that marked her undergraduate years at Pomona. Active in civic affairs and education, she was chairman of the board of trustees of the Marlborough School. Many family ties bound Mrs. Myers to Pomona. Her father had been a trustee, her brother was a current trustee, and her son was a recent graduate.

New Facilities and Buildings

The constant addition of facilities, construction of new buildings and the renovation of old structures, from the autumn of 1963 to the spring of 1970, made this one of the greatest building periods in Pomona's history. Two alumni made valuable gifts for physical education and recreation. Trustee Morris B. Pendleton '22 gave a swimming pool for the women's athletic department. Named in honor of Mrs. Pendleton '22, the Gladys Shepard Pendleton Pool was placed in use in the spring of 1965. New athletic facilities at the east end of the women's athletic field and in Blanchard Park were given by Carlton M. Rogers '37. Five tennis courts, named for Mr. Rogers' mother, were built on the women's field. A new athletic field named for Earl J. Merritt '25, beloved emeritus professor of physical education, was developed on the east side of Blanchard Park.

When the chemistry department moved to its new Seaver Laboratory, Mason Hall was reconstructed throughout as a home for the departments of Modern European languages, Chinese language and literature, and psychology. Construction began in June 1965 and the building was placed in use in March 1966. Attractive offices, seminar rooms, and laboratories were developed at a cost of $525,000, contributed by alumni, other friends of the college, corporations, and foundations. The successful conversion of Mason Hall set a standard for subsequent reconstruction of other historic Pomona buildings.

The department of psychology, which had acquired improved facilities in Crookshank when the zoology department went to Seaver Laboratory for Biology and Geology, finally had a worthy home. Occupying approximately half of the new Mason, the department enjoyed facilities that included seminar and research rooms, a physiological psychology laboratory, an animal colony, and a social and child research laboratory comparable to the very best in the country.

The other half of Mason Hall was developed for instruction in languages. The department of Chinese language and literature was located on the second floor where the new Henrietta V. Frank Memorial Center was a beautiful addition to the work of the department.

The entire third floor was devoted to instruction in European languages and literature. In anticipation of the new facilities in Mason Hall, the former departments of German and Romance Languages and Russian had been combined in a department of Modern European Languages and Literature and placed under a unified administration, effective 1965-66. The beautifully furnished, spacious offices and seminar rooms in Mason were in dramatic contrast to the plain, crowded quarters the language faculty had formerly occupied in Holmes Hall. Moreover, the new Beverly M. Stauffer Language Laboratory, given by the John and Beverly Stauffer Foundation of Los Angeles, provided the most modern equipment available. Its thirty-six stations were served by a full-time director.

The reconstruction of Mason Hall was also a contribution to the beauty of the campus and of the city of Claremont. The quadrangle to the east, which Mason formed with Crookshank and Pearsons, was greatly improved. To the west, Mason and the impressive sanctuary of the Claremont United Church of Christ, which had been constructed in 1954, combined to give beauty and dignity to Harvard Avenue.

Oldenborg Center

Dr. and Mrs. Lyon and Professor Leonard Pronko at a Pomona alumni meeting at the Imperial Hotel, Tokyo, summer 1963

Oldenborg Center

The new facilities in Mason Hall were but part of Pomona's plan for extending its work in foreign languages. One of the most imaginative objectives of the Advancement Program was a residence center for students of foreign languages and international relations. It was proposed to go beyond the usual concept of a "language house" and to build a unique coeducational residence hall which would serve as a language and international relations center for the entire college. There would be separate areas for those studying French, German, and Spanish, and provision would be made for other languages, if there should be sufficient interest. Faculty members and nationals of the respective countries would be in residence. A coeducational dining room would be an integral part of the center. The idea of such a center was developed with great care by the department of Modern European Languages and Literature and by Deans Sanders, Beatty, and Walton, with the strong support of President Lyon. The projected plan for the center was set forth with an architect's illustration in *The Strength of Independence.*

The concept of a residence center for students of foreign languages and international relations was warmly received by D. C. Oldenborg, a retired businessman who had come to know Pomona through Mr. Hawley and the annuity and life income contract program. Both Mr. and Mrs. Oldenborg visited the campus, and Mr. Hawley and President Lyon were able to show them the college and discuss its plans for the future. Mr. Oldenborg then expressed interest and stated that, while for the present his gifts were through the life income contract plan, he expected at some future date to make a gift for immediate use by the college.

Early in the Advancement Program Mr. and Mrs. Oldenborg, then living temporarily in Santa Monica, invited Dr. Lyon to call upon them and made their decision to give to Pomona the foreign language and international relations center as described in *The Strength of Independence.* The estimated cost set forth in the brochure was $1,100,000. As Mr. Oldenborg was eager to begin the building as soon as possible, he authorized the college to proceed with the architect's working drawings, and took steps to provide the full $1,100,000 when it would be needed.

Mr. Oldenborg was a world traveller with a knowledge of many lands, and in embracing so enthusiastically and so generously the concept of a center for students of foreign languages and international relations he was expressing a deep and long held personal interest. Of Danish background, he had been brought up in New York City whence he had gone to Yale University. His business career after graduation took him to the American West and to China, and then back to New York, where he very successfully went into the investment business. From his extensive overseas experience gained through business and wide travel with Mrs. Oldenborg and their two daughters, he had an appreciation of the role that higher education could play in developing a better understanding among peoples.

Oldenborg Center was the most significant addition to Pomona's residence facilities since the construction of the Clark Campus and Frary Dining Hall. Located east of Sumner Hall and south of Bridges Auditorium, and attractively designed by Architect John Rex, the center was an impressive addition to the campus as well as a great contribution to both the academic and residential life of the college. The capacity of the center was increased as planning proceeded and the completed building included rooms for seventy-four men and seventy women. With its dining hall for two hundred, and a separate residence for its director, Oldenborg had many of the qualities of a small Oxford college.

Oldenborg combined residence and teaching facilities in a creative way. Students roomed in the area where the language of their choice was used under the direction of a resident national. This resident oversaw the daily use of the language, arranged language tables in the dining hall, and held group meetings in the social lounge in each of the four main areas. In planning the center, the faculty took full advantage of the most modern methods for teaching languages. Each room had a connection with a central broadcasting unit within the building, from which tapes of programs in the respective languages were played. Stereo-radio and phonograph facilities were installed in each language lounge. There were frequent films and lectures in the multi-purpose room. In its first year Oldenborg had five language groups, French, German, Spanish, Chinese, and Russian. The center was conducted by a full-time director who coordinated its work with the curricular programs in foreign languages and international relations.

The expanded plans for Oldenborg Center increased its cost to over $2,300,000. The greater part of the amount required beyond the gift of Mr. and Mrs. Oldenborg was provided by the college as an interest-bearing loan from the endowment, as had been done with earlier residence halls. Memorial gifts were received for some facilities within the building. The Virginia Glass Library, a memorial to a much-loved member of the Class of '65, was a gift of her parents, friends, and Pomona classmates.

Named for Mr. and Mrs. Oldenborg, the center was dedicated with an impressive convocation in Bridges Auditorium on Founders Day, October 18, 1966. The convocation speaker was Professor Henri Peyre of Yale University, the distinguished leader of French studies in the United States, who gave a brilliant address, entitled "France in 1966: Achievements, Problems, Prospects." Honorary degrees were conferred on three alumni: J. Robert Schaetzel '39, Ambassador of the United States to the European Communities, doctor of laws; Dana Adams Schmidt '37, foreign correspondent of the *New York Times,* doctor of letters; and James Robert Squire '44, Executive Secretary of the National Council of Teachers of English, doctor of letters.

Mr. Oldenborg did not live to see the completion of the building he had made possible. But at the luncheon following the convocation, Mrs. Oldenborg was the guest of honor, accompanied by her daughter Elizabeth, her daughter and son-in-law, Mr. and Mrs. George Barber, and their daughters, Nancy, Virginia, and Christine. Ambassador Schaetzel spoke at the luncheon, and the Los Angeles consuls of the countries whose languages were taught at Pomona joined in this significant occasion.

A Presidential Twenty-fifth Anniversary

The autumn of 1966 marked the twenty-fifth anniversary of Dr. Lyon's presidency and the college honored the Lyons with a convocation and dinner on November 1. The convocation was held in Bridges Auditorium at 4:30, with Robert B. Coons, chairman of the Board of Trustees presiding. Greetings from the Claremont Colleges were brought by the provost, President John W. Atherton of Pitzer College. W. T. Jones, professor of philosophy, who had come to the college three years before Dr. Lyon, spoke for the Pomona faculty.

Dr. Lyon responded to the greetings of Provost Atherton and Professor Jones with appreciation of the past and a confident outlook for the future:

> The quarter century we note this afternoon has seen changes of a magnitude marked by no other twenty-five years in all human history. The revolutions in international relations, in science, communications, industry, and higher education would have seemed inconceivable to a previous generation. My heart is filled with gratitude for the privilege of having served Pomona in such an eventful quarter century.
>
> Mrs. Lyon and I had the good fortune to come to Pomona when some of the Founders of the college were still alive. What a privilege was ours in knowing Mr. Marston, Dean Norton, Dr. Brackett, and Dr. George S. Sumner. To receive from them the living fire of Pomona's flame was an inspiration beyond description. This college was founded by men of faith, of intellect, and of vision. Across the continent they brought the great traditions of our nation — belief in freedom, education, and the brotherhood of man. Pomona has always been great in concept and aspiration.
>
> This convocation should be seen primarily as a call to us all to advance Pomona further in meeting the tremendous responsibilities of higher education today. Twenty-five years from now we should be able to say that Pomona College has created in itself, and through the group of colleges it initiated, one of the great academic communities of the world. This is the call to which I dedicate myself and to which I invite all of you.

The convocation speaker was Francis Keppel, former dean of the School of Education at Harvard University, who from 1962 to 1965 had served in Washington as United States Commissioner of Education. In 1966 he had become chairman of the board of the General Learning Corporation, which had been established by *Time*, Inc. and the General Electric Company. His address, entitled "The

Sharing Concept: New Roles for a Tested Idea," was an interpretation of the past quarter century in higher education and a projection of likely developments in the years ahead. "Knowledge itself," he said, had come to serve "as a focal point of national growth," with the result that "almost half of our material growth has been the consequence of greater education and improved technology, which is largely a product of education." Keppel saw higher education with such extended participation in society, "running the risk of being weakened in its traditional role as a critic and leavening agent among the diverse forces of our society." He commended Pomona and the other Claremont Colleges for placing their focus where it belonged — "on the advancement of knowledge, on preparing the young for a more complex and more diversified future, and on the economic use of resources."

The commemorative dinner, which had been planned by a committee made up of trustees, faculty, alumni and students, was held in the Memorial gymnasium. This unique location added to the festivity of the occasion, which was enjoyed by 500 guests who included the trustees, the faculty, the presidents of the other Claremont Colleges, Pomona alumni representing all the classes that had graduated since 1941, and student representatives. It was an evening of nostalgia, humor, and affection. The master of ceremonies was trustee Ranney C. Draper '25, of whose Pomona class Dr. Lyon was an honorary member. Speaking for the faculty was Lee C. McDonald '48, professor of government, who had been a member of the faculty since 1952. Dr. McDonald emphasized that throughout his administration the president had given the highest priority to the recruitment and development of the faculty, which had been strengthened by his dedication to academic freedom, his support of curricular innovation, his personal concern for students, and his sense of community for Pomona.

The trustees, with Mrs. Lyon as accomplice, had invited Myres S. McDougal, Sterling Professor of Law at Yale University, and one of Dr. Lyon's oldest and closest personal friends as a surprise guest and speaker for the dinner. The two men had been friends since they first met at a conference of 4H Club members in their native Mississippi in the summer of 1921. Subsequently they were fellow

Mrs. Victor Montgomery, Dr. Lyon, and Professor Myres S. McDougal
at the Commerative Dinner

students at the University of Mississippi, from which first Dr. Lyon and then Dr. McDougal had gone as Rhodes Scholars to St. John's College, Oxford.

With her characteristic thoughtfulness and generosity Mrs. Victor Montgomery had anticipated Dr. Lyon's twenty-fifth anniversary at Pomona by engaging Charles P. Cross, a Los Angeles artist, to paint a portrait of Dr. Lyon. This was completed well ahead of November 1, and at the dinner Mrs. Montgomery lovingly presented the portrait to the college, for which it was accepted by Douglas G. McConnell '67, president of the Associated Students. Appropriately, the portrait was hung in Sumner Hall.

Two publications by the college recorded the events of November 1 and shared them with alumni and friends throughout the country. Addresses from the convocation were presented in a brochure entitled, "A Quarter Century of Distinctive Leadership." The November issue of *Pomona Today* featured the celebration and also carried an article, "Dr. Lyon: His Record," by trustee Paul

Fussell. Mrs. Lyon, who had been honored in all the functions of November 1, was the subject of a sensitive and perceptive article, "Carolyn Lyon: The President's Wife," by Mrs. Ernest A. Strathmann '34.

Academic Accomplishment

The years of building expansion, 1963-70, were also a period of great development and achievement within the college. When the Articles of Affiliation of the Claremont Colleges were amended to permit larger enrollments, effective September 1965, the trustees authorized increasing the enrollment of Pomona to 1200. The number of applicants was so large that there was no difficulty in securing outstanding students for this expansion. As the college became more widely known, students were drawn from increasingly distant areas. Those who attended in 1966-67 included American citizens from forty-one states and seventeen overseas areas, and foreign nationals from twenty-two countries.

Significant curricular changes contributed to the academic accomplishment of Pomona students. In 1961 the number of courses taken by a student in a semester had been reduced from five to four, a total of thirty-two courses being required for graduation. Breadth was sought by a distribution requirement of ten courses, and depth by concentration in a department or combination of departments. The distribution requirements were: a course in English, two courses in science, three courses in the social sciences, a course in literature, art, or music, a course in philosophy or religion, and two courses outside the field of concentration to be taken in the junior or senior year. Knowledge of a foreign language was added as a graduation requirement in 1963.

Pomona students were among the ablest in any American college. Guides on colleges, such as that of Cass and Birnbaum, characterized Pomona as "most selective," a category in which only some thirty institutions were annually listed. The quality of the students was a central factor in every aspect of the life of the college.

Most encouraging was the marked increase in the number of

freshmen who remained to graduate. The classes which entered in 1962 and 1963 and graduated in 1966 and 1967 established new college records for the retention and graduation of their members. The class of 1966 graduated approximately seventy-eight per cent of those who entered. The class of 1967 established a college record by graduating approximately eighty-two per cent of its entering freshmen. The presence of larger numbers of seniors gave greater maturity to college life. Further academic maturity was given by the wide range of concentration programs and the balance of choices which students made among the three divisions under which the academic departments were grouped. For example, the concentration choices of the classes of 1966 and 1967 for the respective divisions were: humanities 83 and 97, natural sciences 101 and 107, and social sciences 92 and 92.

Over two-thirds of the graduates in the 1960's went on to graduate or professional schools, from which they received numerous scholarships and fellowships. The class of 1967 matched its retention record by the accomplishments of its individual members. The 280 graduating seniors included forty-eight members of Phi Beta Kappa, the largest number in the history of the chapter. Among national distinctions gained by the class were a Rhodes Scholarship, ten Woodrow Wilson Fellowships, five National Science Foundation Fellowships, four Fulbright Fellowships for graduate work abroad, two Danforth Fellowships, two Rockefeller Brothers Theological Fellowships, and thirteen National Defense Education Fellowships. Thirty-two other scholarships and assistantships were awarded to members of the class by individual universities.

Commencements were happy occasions in which distinguished visitors addressed the graduating classes. Bayless Manning, Dean of the Stanford Law School, spoke in 1965, and Hedley W. Donovan, editor-in-chief of *Time,* came in 1966. Maurice Shock, Fellow of University College, Oxford, and a member of the Commission of Inquiry on the University, of which Lord Franks was chairman, was the speaker in 1967.

In teaching, research, travel and general academic advancement this was also an outstanding period for the Pomona faculty. The activities and achievements of its members were so extensive that the faculty and staff section occupied thirty-two pages of the eighty pages of the *Report of the President for 1965-66 and 1966-67*. Fourteen members of the faculty were promoted effective July 1, 1966, and ten were granted leave for 1966-67. Great encouragement came with the first awards from the faculty research and fellowship fund in the Ford Foundation grant. Fellowships of $1500 each were awarded to seventeen members of the Pomona faculty for the summer of 1967. The continuance of such grants for four additional years marked the high point in college financial support of research.

New Faculty

The faculty was strengthened by the appointment of a large number of young men and women. Many of these appointments were in the division of the humanities. Three were made in the English department. Thomas C. Pinney, Ph.D. Yale University, came as assistant professor in 1962. Darcy G. O'Brien, Ph.D. University of California, Berkeley, and Stephen C. Young, doctoral candidate University of California, Berkeley, were appointed instructors in English in 1965 and 1967, respectively. Andrew Doe, doctoral candidate University of Iowa, came as assistant professor of English and director of the theater in 1966. The department of Modern European Languages welcomed two assistant professors of German: Hans-Dieter Brueckner, Ph.D. University of California, Berkeley, in 1962 and Richard M. Sheirich, Ph.D. Harvard University, in 1965. The department also received three new instructors of Romance Languages: Virginia Crosby, doctoral candidate University of Southern California, in 1963; Phyllis Anne Johnson '59, doctoral candidate University of California, Los Angeles, in 1964, and Monique Jacobson, also a doctoral candidate at University of California, Los Angeles, in 1965.

In the humanities there were important appointments in art, music, philosophy, and religion. Nicolai Cikovsky, Jr. was named assistant professor of art and chairman of the department effective September 1964, succeeding Bates Lowry, who had resigned to accept a professorship at Brown University. Formerly an assistant professor at Skidmore College, Dr. Cikovsky had taken his Ph.D. at Harvard. Four appointments were made in music: John S. Ritter, a graduate of the Curtis Institute of Music with the Master of Music degree from Northwestern University, was appointed instructor in music in 1963. Concert artist Elwood Peterson, B.A. Roosevelt College and License, École Normale de Musique, Paris, was appointed assistant professor of music in 1966. Concert pianist Peter Hewitt, B.A. San Fernando State College, was named instructor in 1966. Giora G. Bernstein, D.M.A. Boston University and violinist with the Boston Symphony Orchestra, was appointed assistant professor and director of the orchestra in 1967. Stephen A. Erickson, Ph.D. Yale University, was appointed instructor in philosophy in 1964. Robert T. Voelkel, Th.D. Union Theological Seminary, had come as an instructor in religion in 1962. J. William Whedbee, doctoral candidate Yale University, was appointed instructor in religion in 1966.

There were important changes in the social sciences. Associate professor Robert D. Herman became chairman of the sociology department when Professor Alvin Scaff resigned in 1966 to become associate dean of the graduate college of the University of Iowa. Hans Palmer, doctoral candidate University of California, Berkeley, came as instructor in economics in 1962. Three instructors were appointed in government: Michael H. Armacost, doctoral candidate Columbia University, in 1962; Leo J. Flynn, doctoral candidate University of California, Santa Barbara, in 1967; and Franklin Tugwell, doctoral candidate Columbia University, effective February 1968. In physical education Lester R. Nagler, M.A. Los Angeles State College, came as assistant professor in the department for men in 1963, and Nancy Louise Breitenstein, B.A. University of Kentucky, as instructor in the women's department in 1967.

The impetus given to science was reflected in the appointment of faculty members in geology, astronomy, chemistry, mathematics, physics, and zoology. Donald H. Zenger, Ph.D. Cornell University, was appointed instructor in geology in 1962. Robert J. Chambers, doctoral candidate University of California, was appointed instructor in astronomy and director of the observatory in 1963. Neil W. Cornell, Ph.D. University of California, Los Angeles, was appointed assistant professor of chemistry in 1966. Two men came in mathematics: Donald L. Bentley, Ph.D. Stanford University, as assistant professor in 1964; and R. Stanton Hales, Jr. '64, doctoral candidate Harvard University, as instructor in 1967. Catalin D. Mitescu, doctoral candidate at California Institute of Technology, was appointed instructor in physics in 1965. Larry W. Cohen, Ph.D. University of California, Los Angeles, came as assistant professor of zoology in 1967. Roger E. Vogler, Ph.D. University of Arizona, was appointed assistant professor of psychology in 1967.

Resignations and Retirements

In this period, Pomona suffered by resignation and retirement the loss of seven faculty members who had served the college with distinction. Dean Edward Sanders, who had been on leave as dean of students from March 1965 to July 1966 to assume the new position of director of financial aid to students in the U.S. Office of Education in Washington, resigned from the college and the government, effective July 1, 1966, to open a new office in Washington for the College Entrance Examination Board. By his sensitivity to the students' viewpoint, "Sandy," as his colleagues affectionately knew him, made a major contribution to the life of Pomona. His wise handling of admissions was a determining factor in the reestablishment of the student body after World War II, and his creative development of the plan of faculty-student government contributed immeasurably to an effective campus community. By their friendship and hospitality Dean and Mrs. Sanders endeared themselves to generations of students.

Burton Henke, professor of physics and a member of the faculty since 1948, resigned for reasons of family health and went to the University of Hawaii in September 1967. A distinguished teacher and internationally known for his work in soft X-rays, Dr. Henke was one of the leaders in the great development of science at Pomona after World War II.

The five faculty members who retired on July 1, 1967 illustrated the qualities that have given the college its quality and stability. Carl Baumann, professor of German, had been a member of the faculty since 1931. Swiss by background and education and with a diversity of intellectual interests, he had long been one of the most popular and influential teachers on the faculty. In addition to his courses in German he developed work in comparative European literature, which he offered in translation, and which many students prized most from their years at Pomona.

Kenneth G. Fiske, professor of music, had come to the faculty in 1936. As the creator of the modern Pomona College orchestra, he brought a new dimension to the music department. In addition to his contribution to Pomona, he played a significant part in the development of orchestral music in Southern California.

Ch'en Shou-yi, professor of Chinese culture, who came in 1941, had given Pomona an international reputation as a center of Chinese studies. An ideal interpreter of the east to the west, he generously shared his learning and insights with students, faculty, and audiences throughout Southern California.

Shelton L. Beatty, dean of men since 1949 and dean of students since 1965, set a standard of caring for students that made him a legend. Blessed with an incredible memory, he never forgot a student. He and Mrs. Beatty, formerly a member of the department of political science at Grinnell, found in Pomona their ideal college and they sought to make it that for others. Dean Beatty knew students as well as had Dean Norton, and in a more complex time gave a sense of personal warmth and community to the college.

Mrs. Margaret Gay Davies, professor of history, had joined the faculty in 1952, but teaching at Scripps College in its earlier years had given her long acquaintance with Pomona. Educated at Radcliffe College, from which she had received her B.A. and Ph.D. degrees, she shared a rich tradition and a deep personal love of scholarship with her students, and gave wise counsel to the faculty.

In a year of so many retirements the college suffered a grievous loss in the death on December 17, 1966 of Lorne D. Cook, Elden Smith Professor of Economics and chairman of the department.

Dr. Cooke was one of the younger men brought to Pomona by Professor Floyd A. Bond in the great development of the department of economics in the early 1950's. Dr. Cook was a leader both in the college and in the city of Claremont. As a member of the planning commission and later as a member of the city council he enjoyed the esteem and affection of both town and gown. Associate professor Gordon K. Douglass was named the new chairman of the department of economics.

The college sustained a further great loss on October 23, 1968 by the death at forty-five of Graham B. Bell, professor of psychology and chairman of the department. Dr. Bell had built the modern pyschology department, developing its staff and then planning the new quarters in Mason Hall. Most of all he loved teaching and his students held him in deep affection. Professor William L. Faust succeeded Dr. Bell as chairman of the department.

The Constitution of the Claremont Colleges

These were years of warm cooperation and great achievement among the colleges in Claremont. In April 1966 The Friends of The Claremont Colleges chartered a plane and 120 of their members, including the six college presidents, flew to Great Britain to celebrate at the University of Oxford the fortieth anniversary of the founding of the Claremont group plan. The Claremont visitors lived in Oxford colleges for several days, were welcomed by the Vice-Chancellor, and addressed by leaders of the university in a three-day program which had been arranged by Maurice Shock of University College, who had taught at Pomona in 1961-62. President Lyon had the pleasure of entertaining the entire Claremont group in a sherry party in the Hall of his old college, St. John's. After their visit to Oxford the Claremont group returned to London for a conference of trustees, presidents, and officials of the six Claremont Colleges and a group of distinguished British educators, drawn primarily from universities other than Oxford and Cambridge. Dr. Lyon wrote an article on the trip, "Claremont Goes to Oxford," for *The American Oxonian,* and the Claremont Colleges published a booklet, *Dialogue on Higher Education,* containing the addresses at Oxford and the proceedings of the conference in London.

The Ford Foundation grant and the Challenge Campaign it inspired brought remarkable achievement for the Claremont Colleges as a group. In September 1967 the total enrollment of the five undergraduate colleges was 3400 and the full-time equivalent enrollment of the graduate school was 600. It is interesting to note that this was approximately the enrollment of the University of Oxford in the years when President Blaisdell was developing the group plan for Claremont. In the academic year 1923-24 Oxford had enrolled 3709 undergraduates and 439 graduate students.

This growth of the Claremont Colleges imposed heavy responsibilities upon the University Center for providing the facilities and buildings required for the joint services and the graduate school. Fortunately, funds from the Ford Foundation grant made possible doubling the size of the Pendleton Business Building, which served all the students and through which also were handled both the current budgets and the investments of the six institutions. By 1966-67 the budgets totalled $17,664,632, and on June 30, 1967 the permanent assets of the six colleges were $135,000,000.

The Claremont Graduate School had expanded its program and the Ph.D. degree was offered in thirteen fields. Consequently Harper Hall and the facilities available in the undergraduate colleges could no longer meet the need for seminar rooms and offices. Under the leadership of President Benezet necessary buildings and facilities were provided, and the Graduate School was given an imposing physical presence. Gifts from the William S. Rosecrans Foundation, the McManus Foundation, and other donors made possible the construction of two connecting buildings just east of Harper Hall. The resulting McManus Hall of Graduate Studies and Harper Hall East, ornamented by the Rosecrans Tower, provided attractive offices for faculty members, the registrar and dean of the Graduate School, and the president of the Claremont University Center.

After the completion of these new structures in 1966, the University Center began a major reconstruction of the interior of the original Harper Hall. This historic building was rededicated in impressive exercises on February 18, 1968. Two of those present, Robert J. Bernard and William W. Clary, had been present at the original dedication in 1932. The exterior of Harper Hall was unchanged, and its architectural harmony with the new buildings to the east made the area from College Avenue to Dartmouth Avenue, between Ninth and Tenth Streets, an attractive and unifying development of the central campus of the Claremont Colleges.

In this same period, the Claremont Colleges were strengthening their association and clarifying the procedures and practices within the group of institutions. A forward step had been taken in 1962 with *The Articles of Affiliation of the Claremont Colleges.* The coming of the sixth college and the growth of the group indicated the pressing need for further consideration of the intercollegiate structure. Earnest discussions among the presidents, led by Dr. Benezet, brought an agreement on general principles, and the question of an examination of existing arrangements was referred to the Board of Fellows on June 6, 1966. A joint committee of trustees and college presidents was then authorized to review *The Articles of Affiliation,* and to make recommendations for their amendment. Their report, *The Constitution of the Claremont Colleges,* was approved by the six boards of trustees in their respective meetings in June 1967.

As the use of the term "constitution" indicated, the document marked an effective advance in the coordination of the group of colleges and in the management of their joint services. The culmination of over forty years of academic governance in Claremont, it was adopted by the six colleges "for the purpose of defining and regulating their mutual interests and objectives in the promotion of higher education."

The colleges committed themselves to develop and maintain at Claremont "a center of undergraduate and graduate learning made up of independent undergraduate colleges of liberal arts and sciences, cooperating with each other and with a central coordinating institution." The ways by which this purpose could be achieved were specified, and much needed clarification was brought to nomenclature. Henceforth, the group would be known as The

Claremont Colleges, and the central coordinating institution was named The Claremont University Center. The constitution, as William W. Clary wrote, recognized that The Claremont Colleges were "more than a cluster" and were "for many purposes a unified center of learning."

This sense of common purpose was fostered by the services which the University Center rendered the group. It conducted the Claremont Graduate School as a collective enterprise of the six institutions. The president of the Claremont University Center also supervised the joint services, such as the medical service, the counselling service, the College Church, the business office, campus security, the engineer's office, and the library. The president of the University Center was responsible for these matters in the first instance to the administrative council composed of the presidents of the six institutions, of whom the provost was chairman. The office of general secretary was established for assistance to the president of the University Center and the presidents of the colleges in the management of their joint enterprises.

Significant changes were made in the office of provost. Henceforth the annual rotation of the office was restricted to the presidents of the five undergraduate colleges. There was clear definition between the planning and ceremonial functions of the provost of the Claremont Colleges and the operational duties of the president of the Claremont University Center. The provost was expected to provide leadership in the coordination of the common educational interests, programs, and services of the Claremont Colleges; to supervise the preparation of the joint service budgets; to preside at joint convocations and joint faculty meetings; and to be the representative and spokesman for the Claremont Colleges at public, civic, and academic meetings at which the group should be represented as a whole.

Important advances were made in the coordination of the six boards of trustees, with consequent expedition of action on joint matters. The chairman of the board, the president, and one other trustee from each undergraduate college served as voting members of the Board of Fellows. The executive committee of the Board of Fellows, which included the chairman of the board and the president of each college, was responsible for the adoption of joint budgets for submission to the respective boards of trustees.

More clearly defined procedures were designed to avoid the tension which had often come with the founding of new colleges in the group. The membership of the Board of Fellows' standing committee on new colleges was reconstituted to include the board chairman and president of each undergraduate college in the group. Further check on the founding of new colleges was the provision in the constitution that "any proposal for the addition of a new college to membership in The Claremont Colleges or for the location in Claremont of any college or other educational institution" must be submitted to the Intercollegiate Council for its consideration before any action could be taken. As the Intercollegiate Council included the chairman of the board, president, and dean of the faculty of each of the colleges, its membership guaranteed that the views of each college would be heard in the admission of new institutions to the Claremont Colleges.

The ratification and publication of *The Constitution of the Claremont Colleges* was a further contribution to the progress of the colleges and to goodwill among the six institutions. The constitution took effect on July 1, 1967, and Dr. Lyon had the privilege of serving as the first provost under the new instrument. The meetings that led to the constitution and the inauguration of its provisions brought mutual understanding and new insights among trustees, administrators, and faculties of the colleges that would be of great value in the unforeseen, difficult years that lay just ahead.

CHAPTER XXX

The College in Years of National Tension

THE CONFIDENCE in the mission of American higher education and the faith in its future, that had been so marked throughout the country since World War II, were severely tested in the decade of the 1960's. The assassination of President John F. Kennedy in 1963 shook the academic community where students had felt a particularly close identification with the young president. The stability and structure of American society came under closer student scrutiny than ever before.

Early in the autumn of 1964 the American Council on Education held its annual meeting in San Francisco, coming to California in recognition of the leadership of the state in higher education, particularly through the widely acclaimed Master Plan. As college and university presidents convened in San Francisco and were welcomed by Governor Edmund G. Brown and President Clark Kerr of the University of California, a stormy student protest erupted on the Berkeley campus of the university. The protest, soon known as "the Free Speech Movement," was originally a criticism of the impersonality and bureaucratic organization which had come to the Berkeley campus with an enrollment increased to over 20,000. There were also accusations of the faculty's neglect of teaching. Protests soon followed in other large universities across the land, revealing, as Jacques Barzun would write in his book, *The American University,* that "the new functions it has taken on and the methods it has improvised in a decade and a half have torn apart the fabric of the former single-minded, easily defined American university."

Agitation that had begun as criticism of the internal organization and operation of universities grew into a movement concerned with national issues, notably the rights of minorities and the war in Vietnam. Deeply concerned, both personally and generally, college and university students reacted with unprecedented intensity. Indignation over the continuance and acceleration of the war in Vietnam was directed at President Lyndon Johnson and his administration. Protests regarding civil rights were directed against state and local governments in the South, segregation practices in housing and schools throughout the country, and ultimately against the policies of colleges and universities.

On the Pomona campus the civil rights movement had a growing influence from the late 1950's. Pomona established a student exchange program with Fisk University in 1952-53; and when Candice Anderson '61 was arrested for "sitting in" at a lunch counter in Nashville, the reality of the civil rights struggle was brought home to Pomona students. *Student Life* sent Andrew Jaffe '60, later a staff member of *Newsweek,* to Nashville and carried full accounts of Candice's experiences. Pomona students were among the large numbers of college students who went to the South in the summers of the 1960's.

Concern for civil rights led to what remains to date the most impressive and influential student conference ever held at the college. Under the direction of Mike Wood '66 a Human Relations Council was organized and its major activity was a three-day Conference on Civil Equality, February 28-March 1, 1964. The committee led by Wood and Carol Popper '64 and aided by Dean Sanders, assembled a group of black and white speakers who represented various groups in the civil rights movement. Plenary sessions were held in Bridges Auditorium, and a number of discussion groups met in seminar and lecture rooms. Among the speakers were James Farmer, national director of the Conference on Racial Equality; James Forman, executive secretary of the Students Non-violent Coordinating Committee; S. I. Hayakawa, then professor of Language Arts, San Francisco State College; Louis Lomax, author; Peter Countryman, past executive director of the National Student Movement; Will Campbell, director of the Committee of Southern Churchmen; and John Doar, Director of the Civil Rights Division of the United States Department of Justice. The conference was an outpouring of racial cooperation and understanding in the spirit of Martin Luther King. From the initial meeting in Bridges Auditorium to the final session in Bridges Hall, when the audience joined hands and sang "We Shall Overcome," the campus was caught up in an experience of far reaching influence.

By 1964 black students from Africa had brought Pomona students some acquaintance with the newly independent countries of that continent. Under the African Scholarship Program for American Universities young men and women from Nigeria, Ghana, Kenya, and Rhodesia were active members of the student body and proceeded to take Pomona degrees. Since the summer of 1961 Pomona students had participated in the Crossroads Africa program, under which they were members of a work project team in an African country. Funds were raised among the student body and by a Claremont Citizens Committee.

The desire of students to assist developing countries led many Pomona graduates to enter the Peace Corps which, on President Kennedy's recommendation, was approved by Congress in September 1961. The Peace Corps evoked a spirit of service analogous to the earlier Student Volunteer Movement, and for its size Pomona contributed one of the largest groups of Peace Corps Volunteers of any college in the country.

There was great interest in off-campus study programs for students still in college. The Semester Abroad Program, which was initiated in 1961-62, grew constantly in numbers and popularity. The long-established Washington semester program had increased appeal. Pomona students developed a plan for a semester exchange with students of Swarthmore College and persuaded the administrations of both colleges to approve it. Begun in 1961-62 it continues as a permanent part of the program of the two colleges.

There was an intensification of interest in American politics. Democratic, Republican, and Conservative Clubs were organized. A Student Lecture Committee, with funds from the Associated Students, sponsored visiting and local speakers. During the gubernatorial campaign in California in 1962, both incumbent Governor

Edmund G. Brown and challenger Richard Nixon spoke in Bridges Auditorium under the auspices of the Student Lecture Committee.

Two years after the Conference on Civil Equality Pomona students held a three-day conference on "Communist China in the World Order," February 10-12, 1966. A group of distinguished authorities from U.C.L.A., Stanford, the Rand Corporation, and Columbia University joined faculty members from Pomona, Claremont Men's College, and the Claremont Graduate School as participants. The concluding address was given by William P. Bundy, assistant secretary for Far Eastern Affairs, United States Department of State. "Interested students of Pomona College," stated the program, "feel that a careful analysis of the internal workings of mainland China and of its cultural traditions and recent history will render Chinese actions more rational to Americans. A deeper understanding of China in addition to a greater knowledge of the foreign policy alternatives open to the United States will form the basis for realistic appraisal and constructive criticism of this subject by members of public and academic circles."

Graduate Manager Helen Throne '30 reflected the spirit and outlook of the students in the *Metate* of 1966:

> Principally the students are my leaven. Those of foreign background, like Tutti Toelle and Afolabi Ajayi, bring new charm to the campus. There are our own natives who leave their mark. Their projects may create problems and extra work, but the results are often memorable and lasting. KSPC harks back to Leonard Lupo and has long been growing to its present status, but the students involved have overcome all obstacles, even mine. The Conference on Civil Equality, student inspired and administered, engendered the Human Relations Council and its tutorial program, a real community service. As I write we approach the Conference on Communist China; students have made a proposal for implementation and management of a central book store to serve the Claremont Colleges; and have had accepted a program of interdisciplinary courses of study. Along the way we have our fun — Gilbert and Sullivan productions, Spring Sings, "How the West Was Lost," and so on. Life is not dull!

As these activities indicate, national and international concerns found constructive expression on the Pomona campus. Students had no basic dissatisfaction with the college, or its academic program. The personal relations of students and faculty and the residential nature of the college contributed to the essential harmony of the academic community. When organized protest came in 1968, the issues were basically matters of national policy.

The Shadow of the War in Vietnam

College opened in September 1967 after a spring and summer of tragic rioting in a number of American cities. In his convocation address, "The College in a Troubled Land," President Lyon characterized the urban crisis as a testing of "the very fiber of our national life." For Pomona College, however, there was much encouragement in its own affairs. The Advancement Program had brought new resources and the Constitution of the Claremont Colleges which had become effective on July 1 marked closer and more fruitful cooperation among the six colleges. Particularly gratifying at Pomona was the college's achievement in securing for the entering class an increased number of students from each of California's two large minorities.

Although the first semester proceeded without incident, the shadow of the war in Vietnam lengthened over the campus, bringing anguish even to those least touched in their personal lives. No war in American history had presented so many problems or had been so divisive. What had begun with sending American advisers to the government of Vietnam in the early 1950's had grown into an undeclared war of tremendous proportions. Young men were asked to risk their lives in a struggle toward which they were increasingly skeptical and hostile, and to follow national leaders in whom they had lost confidence.

At Pomona there was a significant decline in academic accomplishment and fifty-three students withdrew from Pomona during the semester. Throughout the country college students intensified their opposition to the war by protesting the campus visits of recruiters for war-related industries and the armed services, often obstructing the operation of college vocational placement offices. On many campuses there was also a growing opposition to the Reserve Officers Training Corps.

These issues from the war laid heavy responsibilities on the college administration, particularly the deans and the director of placement. Miss Walton, who continued as dean of women, had succeeded Dean Beatty as dean of students. Roger J. Bell, doctoral candidate at the University of Washington, had come as the new dean of men. Miss Elva F. Brown had served as the able director of placement since 1963.

The College Council, which was a joint student-faculty group with considerable power delegated to it by the faculty, studied the matter of possible obstructive demonstrations at Pomona. After many meetings and much thought the council formulated its policy, and its chairman, Dean Walton, forwarded a copy to each Pomona student on February 16, 1968. Emphasizing its "belief in the importance of freedom of expression," the council stated "that demonstrations of protest or support should be conducted in such a way that those participating do not infringe on the rights of others in the college."

It was hoped that the enunciation of this policy would calm the mounting student unrest. However, with the approaching visit of two Air Force recruiters scheduled for the placement office in Sumner Hall on February 21, campus feeling intensified. At the opening convocation of the second semester on February 20 President Lyon sought to steady the students by delivering a major address entitled "The Purpose of the College." Following the convocation, which was held in Bridges Auditorium and attended by almost the entire college, the president spoke further and answered questions from approximately 125 persons at a luncheon in Olney Dining Hall, to which he had invited the executive council of the Associated Students, the members of Mortar Board, the Ghosts, the sponsors on the men's campus, the officers of the four classes, the editor of *Student Life,* representatives of *The Collegian,* the members of the student body who had requested to attend, as well as the officers of the college and the faculty committees on administration and student affairs.

The president emphasized "the steps and the wisdom from which have come the priceless freedom which characterizes Pomona." He pointed out how the college had resisted "the suspicion, lack of faith, and irresponsible accusation" of McCarthyism in the 1950's and in so doing had developed a deeper understanding of its essential purpose — "the maintenance of an atmosphere of learning and freedom in which students and faculty can search for truth and express it as they individually see it." "We must not let problems of this agonizing period of American history weaken the purpose of the college and our seeking its attainment," Dr. Lyon concluded.

The policy of the College Council and the convocation address of the president did not prevent an obstructive demonstration on February 21, but they were mitigating factors. When the Air Force recruiters arrived, some 150 students marched around Sumner Hall, and seventy-nine students occupied the placement office and the adjacent corridor. Of these, forty-nine were from Pomona and some thirty from the other five colleges. While there was no violence, no property damage, and no personal discourtesy to the Air Force recruiters and college officials, the demonstration imposed a heavy burden on the judiciaries at Pomona and each of the other Claremont Colleges.

At Pomona, judiciary councils of the Associated Men Students and the Associated Women Students had administered regulations concerning conduct in the residence halls on the respective campuses since 1959. For campus-wide matters the two judiciaries met as a joint judiciary. The organization and procedure of the judiciaries did not envisage infractions by large numbers of students or obstruction motivated by disagreement with national policies. It was not surprising, therefore, that the joint judiciary when confronted with handling forty-nine individuals who had sat in the placement office should have needed most of the semester for the hearings. At the end of the long and wearisome sessions the judiciary voted to suspend the students involved but also suspended the punishment.

The immediate consequence of the sit-in on February 21 was the cancellation of the visits of all recruiters to the Pomona placement office. Following the demonstration President Lyon asked a special trustee, faculty, student committee to study the placement office and to make a recommendation regarding its operation. This committee, of which Lee C. McDonald '48, professor of government, was chairman, recommended that the office cancel its remaining interviews for career employment and schedule no campus interviews for the immediate future. The office would continue to provide information and advice on career and summer employment, and would arrange off-campus interviews for interested students. Upon receipt of the committee's recommendation in April, Dr. Lyon placed it in effect, and the office would remain closed to visiting recruiters until February 3, 1969.

One further obstructive demonstration marked the academic year 1967-68. On May 27 some eighty students from the Claremont Colleges assembled on Alumni Field where the annual Presidents' Review and Award Ceremony of the R.O.T.C. unit of Pomona and Claremont Men's College was to be held. When advised by the deans of the two colleges that they were engaging in an obstructive demonstration, all but five of the students withdrew and the ceremony proceeded as scheduled. Colonel Bowen N. Smith and his fellow officers deserve great credit for the way they handled this and later demonstrations.

Although the campus was tense, the commencement of 1968 was concluded without a difficult incident. The major address was by Dr. Peter B. Clark '52, publisher of the *Detroit News* and president of the Evening News Association. A novel feature of the commencement was the inclusion of a student speaker for the first time since 1924. Earlier in the spring the seniors had requested that a member of the class speak at commencement. When their request was granted by the college administration, the class elected Alan Davis, who had been president of the Associated Students during the year. In his address he stressed that the changes desired by students were "no more than the embodiment of the ideas for which we in America have always claimed to stand." Honorary degrees were conferred on Robert B. Coons, chairman of the Board of Trustees; Rollin Eckis '27, executive vice-president of the Atlantic Richfield Company; and H. Victor Neher '26, professor of physics at the California Institute of Technology.

The manner in which Pomona met the crises of the spring of 1968 revealed both the strength and character of the college, and also some weaknesses that needed attention. At the request of the Student Affairs Committee President Lyon appointed a special faculty-student committee to review the judicial procedures of the college. With Dr. Ray Frazer '47, professor of English, as chairman, this committee devoted the summer to the consideration of campus government. At the same time the Board of Trustees established a special trustee-faculty committee with H. Russell Smith '36 as chairman, "to take appropriate steps to propose standards of conduct for the administration, faculty, and students and methods of handling thereof; all to be reported back for action by the Board." The two committees kept in close touch through their faculty representatives and from their common work emerged sound and workable procedures for meeting the campus problems arising from turmoil and crisis in national life.

From the trustee-faculty committee came a resolution adopted by the Board and transmitted by Dr. Lyon to every Pomona student a week before college opened in September. Reaffirming the dedication of Pomona "to intellectual freedom and to the fullest inquiry into ideas and institutions," the resolution of the trustees stated that "in these times of change it is important for all elements of the college community, in initiating or reacting to proposals for change, to do so in ways consistent with intellectual freedom and the essential educational purpose of the college." The administration, faculty and students were urged to make full use of the channels of communication open to them "and to devise such additional avenues of communication as may be helpful."

In response to this invitation the student-faculty committee stated that what Pomona needed most was a new advisory body on which all elements of the college would be represented. This proposal was well received and approved by the trustees, the faculty, and the Associated Students. The resulting College Policy Review Council was comprised of a faculty chairman and an administrator appointed by the president of the college, three members elected by the faculty, two trustees appointed by the chairman of the Board, four students elected by the student body, and an alumni member chosen by the Alumni Council. The new council was authorized to review such policies of the college as were questioned by a significant part of the community and to make recommendations to the appropriate body or officer of the college.

When the council was constituted, and Professor Lee C. McDonald had been named chairman, it was asked to study the R.O.T.C. and to make recommendations regarding its status at Pomona. This posed a difficult problem: the R.O.T.C. had come under attack as the most accessible example of "militarism" available to students; yet its whole purpose had always been to leaven the military with well-educated civilian leaders. In a thoughtful report the council recommended the continuance of the R.O.T.C., but without academic credit for students entering the program in September 1969, and thereafter, which was approved by the faculty. Since many Pomona R.O.T.C. students carried their R.O.T.C. work as an extra course, the new regulation imposed no hardship on those who desired to take officer training in the college.

When the College Policy Review Council had completed its report on the R.O.T.C., it was asked to consider the question of which recruiters should be permitted to come to the Pomona placement office. The council recommended to the president that all legally qualified employers be permitted to send recruiters to the office. This open policy was put into effect on February 3, 1969 and with it the placement office resumed its full service to Pomona students, and to many others in the Claremont Colleges.

The College Policy Review Council was an innovation in college government and a valuable addition to the excellent constitution of Pomona. The establishment of the College Policy Review Council owed much to the wisdom and energy of Ray Frazer who, as an alumnus, faculty member since 1952, and editor of *Pomona Today* had a rare comprehension of the college and great devotion to its welfare. The importance of his service in the summer of 1968 was recognized in September of that year when he was appointed to the newly created position of associate dean of the faculty. Dr. Lyon then asked Dr. Frazer to serve as the first representative of the administration on the College Policy Review Council.

While suggesting the advisory committee that eventuated in the College Policy Review Council, the special student-faculty committee, of which Dr. Frazer was chairman, worked diligently at its own special assignment of revising the judiciary. However, this was only one of the issues that needed to be considered. The direction of residence hall life also required attention. Through the cooperation of the deans, faculty, and student officers in the College Council, two other faculty-student bodies were created. The Residence Halls Council was given authority over residence matters. A new Judiciary Council had primary responsibility for the discipline of students and "was empowered to take action up to and including expulsion from the College." An appeal board to which decisions of the Judiciary Council could be appealed was instituted. Thus a major reorganization of campus government was effected in the autumn of 1968 and the spring of 1969.

Meeting the Challenge of a Changing California

Pomona College had been founded to serve the new settlers of the Pacific Southwest, most of whom were white and had come from New England and the Middle West. The Spanish-speaking minority from the Mexican regime faded from view, "in part," writes historian John W. Caughey, "because many were assimilated and with some honorable recognition into the general population." When the railroads early in the twentieth century began to look to Mexico for track laborers, and later, when ranchers sought labor gangs for their groves and fields, a constantly increasing Mexican-American minority was created. The Mexican-American population of California grew from 120,000 in 1920 to 368,000 in 1930 and by 1945 Los Angeles had a Mexican population second only to Mexico City. By the end of the 1960's over two million Mexican-Americans were living in California.

After the 1940's, black immigration from the southern states became an important factor in the population of California. Earlier there had been few blacks in the state, the census of 1900 recording only 11,045. By 1940 the number had grown to some 115,000, of whom 75,000 resided in the greater Los Angeles area. Jobs provided by World War II brought a large and continuing migration, and by the late 1960's California had a black population of 1,400,000, of which the major centers were Los Angeles and the cities around San Francisco Bay.

Pomona College, founded by the Congregationalists, was by tradition a part of the nineteenth century commitment of that denomination to the full participation of black Americans in our national life. Congregationalists were leaders in the abolition movement and after the Civil War they were the first to establish colleges for blacks in the southern states. Pomona had never had any racial barrier to admission and there had been black students at the college from early in the twentieth century, although they were very few in number.

Congregationalists had also established churches and schools on the west coast of Mexico, and from these a group of Mexican students had come to Pomona in the 1920's and 1930's. However, very few students of Mexican descent residing in the United States had attended the college before the 1960's.

The academic year 1967-68 was the decisive breakthrough in the entrance of blacks and Mexican-Americans to Pomona. Through the devoted efforts of director of admissions William L. Wheaton, significant groups of American black students and Mexican-American students entered Pomona in September 1967. At the same time there were increased enrollments from each of these minorities at Claremont Men's College and Pitzer College.

Furthermore, in 1967 the Claremont Colleges as a group, under the leadership of Chaplain Edgar C. Reckard, had sought and secured a grant of $750,000 from the Rockefeller Foundation, and undertook to find additional funds to make a total of $2,000,000, for a program of studies for able young men and women from economically disadvantaged backgrounds who were capable of taking degrees in Claremont, although they lacked the traditional requirements for admission. The Program of Special Directed Studies for Transition to College was established and under it a group of forty students, of whom twelve were at Pomona, came to the Claremont Colleges in September 1968.

In the meantime, black students already enrolled had led a strong movement for a marked increase in the admission of black students in the Claremont Colleges. They contended that large numbers of qualified black students who could pay their college expenses were available, provided the Claremont Colleges would make the effort to find them. The transcending nature of the question and the emotionalism of the campus were such that resolution was required on a Claremont-wide basis. Following a period of campus meetings and tense conferences, the presidents of the Claremont Colleges agreed to seek to build student bodies which would reflect the ethnic distribution within the nation, and to ask the admissions officers to try to find and offer admission to a ten per cent minimum of black students for the class entering in September 1969. However, no black student would be admitted with less than the minimum qualifications that had been expected of entering students. At the same time efforts were undertaken to secure an equal number of Mexican-American students. A Center of Educational Opportunity was organized, a recruiting staff was engaged, and Mr. Reckard was appointed director.

When these steps in admissions had been taken, intercollegiate faculty-student committees in the autumn of 1968 began consideration of the personal needs of minority students in Claremont, the introduction in the curriculum of courses in their cultures, and the appointment of black and Mexican-American faculty members. Professor Alden Pixley of Harvey Mudd College and Professor Morton O. Beckner of Pomona rendered great service in the difficult deliberations of these committees. Serious tension had developed when at the end of December a group of black students presented a plan for a Center for Black Studies. Later the Mexican-American students submitted a request for a program of Mexican-American studies. The two student groups were invited to explain their programs to the faculty of each college, and the faculties then made recommendations to the boards of trustees.

Considerations of issues presented by the black students and the Mexican-American students were made difficult by the fact that early in 1967-68 each group had developed an intercollegiate organization. The Black Student Union and the United Mexican-American Students had group loyalties which transcended their members' attachment to their colleges. Thus administrators and faculties in the individual colleges found themselves dealing with students whom they did not know, and discussion of the difficult issues at stake was exacerbated by the lack of personal acquaintance that normally characterized relations within the respective colleges.

In this critical period the centralization of the student newspapers further handicapped the administrations and faculties in relation to their own students. This was particularly true at Pomona where in January 1966 *Student Life* had been merged with *The Associate,* which served the other undergraduate colleges, to form the *Claremont Collegian.* Although a determined body of Pomona students eventually preserved *Student Life,* it could not play its former major role in 1968-69.

As extended discussions continued, great tension developed and for a few days in February and March 1969, the Claremont Colleges, as James Reston wrote of the country, entered "a time of strong passions and weak reason." Daily mass demonstrations were held, generally in the physical center of the colleges, and many students were swayed by emotional appeals. On February 25, a person or persons still unknown, planted bombs which exploded simultaneously in a women's rest room at Scripps College and in the foyer of the ground floor in the Carnegie Building at Pomona. No one was injured at Scripps, but at Pomona a young secretary in the department of government, Mrs. Mary Ann Keatley, lost two fingers of her right hand and suffered serious injury to her eyes. The reaction throughout the shocked academic community was one of profound grief, felt with particular intensity by all in authority at Pomona. However, strong reason did return, and as Ray Frazer wrote in *Pomona Today* for July 1969, aside from this tragedy "there was only one brief interruption of the academic program (a disruption which was stopped by the students themselves), and there was no mass violence, no damage to property, no seizure of buildings. There was 'pressure' on the colleges to act as they finally did, but on the whole it was pressure of nearly unanimous opinion."

A crucial issue in the discussions was the desire of the black students that the Black Studies Center be "a permanent autonomous part of the Claremont Colleges." Wisdom and their legal responsibilities dictated to the trustees that they could not establish within the colleges an organization over which they did not retain final authority, and on this issue they held firm. Pomona trustees played a large part in these weeks so critical for the Claremont Colleges. Robert B. Coons, chairman of the Pomona Board, was a tower of strength to trustees from all the six colleges. He was in constant communication as they turned to him for counsel and advice. Experienced, thoughtful, and calm, he was throughout the crisis a moderating, stabilizing leader. Mr. Coons received much help from Ranney C. Draper '25 and particularly from H. Russell Smith '36, vice-chairmen of the Pomona Board, whose wisdom, knowledge of the colleges, and deep understanding of contemporary America contributed greatly to the resolution of the crisis.

While all the six college presidents were continuously involved in the discussions in the winter and spring of 1969, the brunt of the pressure on the campuses was borne by President Curtis of Scripps College, who as provost of the Claremont Colleges for 1968-69, and thereby spokesman for the presidents, had to deal with the demands and representations of the students. The courage, patience, and endurance which he maintained throughout the unprecedented and prolonged meetings and confrontations did much to secure a solution of the crisis. President Curtis served as chairman of a special intercollegiate committee of trustees, faculty, and black students which worked out a far-reaching plan that was announced on April 3 and, after certain qualifications added by the boards of trustees, was approved by the board of each of the six colleges during the month of April.

The results of the intensive discussions were more comprehensive than anyone had foreseen at their beginning. At the suggestion of H. Russell Smith, a Human Resources Institute was established in the Claremont University Center, whose president, under the authority of the Board of Fellows, would administer the Institute on behalf of the six colleges. The Human Resources Institute would contain a Black Studies Center, a Mexican-American Studies Center,[1] and a Center of Urban Studies, which would be devoted to research in the problems of the inner cities. Under the leadership of President Louis T. Benezet, able directors were appointed for each of the three divisions of the Institute, and a budget of $365,000 was

[1]The name was changed to Center of Chicano Studies, effective 1972-73.

established for 1969-70. Each college would bear its proportionate share of this expenditure and would seek to secure gifts to meet this additional expense.

The programs in Black Studies and Mexican-American Studies were desired among the student bodies, and there was reason to believe that the courses would be widely elected. As Professor Frazer wrote, the Human Resources Institute was established "as an obligation to the country and to our students, for whom the college can now provide a microcosm of the world they live in and a chance to learn from minority teachers as well as minority students." The colleges felt they had established Centers of Black Studies and Mexican-American Studies that could give sorely needed leadership to the nation. Unfortunately, the development and operation of the two centers would be much more complicated and difficult than was foreseen in the year of their inauguration.

New and Improved Buildings

While the administration and faculty were occupied with tensions arising from national policy and social change in Southern California, Pomona was engaged in one of the greatest building periods of its history. Under way were four construction projects bringing additions to the instructional resources of the college: a building addition, a building renovation, and two new buildings.

Through the generosity of trustee Mrs. Victor Montgomery, additions and improvements to the Montgomery Art Center, costing $280,000, nearly doubled its facilities. The additions included a second story on the eastern half of the building and a room on the north. A new entrance from College Avenue enhanced both the attractiveness and accessibility of the Center. The enlarged Center was dedicated on May 25, 1968, with Mrs. Montgomery and members of her family present.

The reconstruction of the Carnegie Building, one of the objectives of the Advancement Program, was accomplished in the summer of 1969 and the building was ready for use in September. A social science building since 1952, the former library was no longer adequate for the enlarged and strengthened departments of economics, government, sociology and anthropology. But historic Carnegie was strong and with the architectural design of Claremont architects Criley and McDowell and the construction skill of Noyes Roach, it made a splendid home for the three departments. The reorganization of space, air-conditioning throughout, and the addition of an enclosed stairway at the west were achieved by an expenditure of over $400,000. An attractive reading room and library in the economics department was established as a memorial to Professor Lorne D. Cook.

The new music building and the new physical education building for women were nearing completion in the autumn of 1969. The funding of these long desired buildings had been arduous. By the spring of 1966 no large gift had been secured for either building. President Lyon realized that if significant gifts could not be secured soon for the two buildings, hopes which had been nourished since the beginning of President Edmunds' administration would again not come to fruition. In the spring of 1966 he began to see clearly that the only way to move forward the campaigns for the music building and the women's physical education center was to secure grants from the United States Government under the Higher Education Facilities Act. This would require a change in college policy, for hitherto the Pomona trustees had not sought federal funds for buildings, preferring to finance them fully from private sources.

At the annual meeting of the trustees on June 2, 1966, the president pointed out that one third of the cost of each of these buildings could be covered by federal grants, which would be outright gifts to the college, without any federal control once the buildings were constructed. He proposed that the chairman of the Board be empowered to appoint a committee to consider the relations of the college with the federal government. This was voted and the committee, of which Morris B. Pendleton '22 was chairman, met on June 21 and unanimously recommended to the Executive Committee "that appropriate steps be taken to explore the opportunities of federal aid under the Higher Education Facilities Act." The Executive Committee approved, and the trustees on September 29 authorized an application for federal grants toward a music building estimated to cost $1,200,000 and a women's physical education center to cost $500,000. The trustees further authorized the Executive Committee, at its discretion, to approve the preparation of architectural plans for the two buildings.

The applications for both buildings were successful, the college receiving for the music building $462,218 toward an estimated cost of $1,386,654, and for the physical education center $160,681 toward an estimated cost of $482,043. The firm of Powell, Morgridge, Richards and Coghlan was engaged to proceed with architectural drawings for the physical education center, and the firm of Allison, Rible, Robinson and Ziegler was authorized to complete its plans for the music building. Much hard work remained in raising the remaining two thirds of the cost of each building, but the way had been opened and there could be no turning back. Following receipt of the federal grants, large private contributions were secured to bear the remaining cost of the two buildings and their furnishings.

Most significant in the funding of the music building were the benefactions of Madge Rice Thatcher and her husband, the late Harry S. Thatcher for whom the music building would be named. The Thatchers, residents of Oxnard, had developed a 200-acre citrus ranch, which they gave to Pomona on a life income basis. On March 20, 1969 the college sold the ranch for $1,755,775. The trustees later voted to apply $500,000 of this amount to the music building and to devote the remainder to the establishment of endowed professorships honoring Mr. and Mrs. Thatcher.

The Thatcher Music Building, located just west of Bridges Hall, formed a fine arts quadrangle with Rembrandt Hall and the Montgomery Art Center to the south and Bridges Hall to the east. While the auditorium of cherished Bridges Hall remained the center for major concerts and musical events, the department offices, studios, practice rooms, listening rooms and other instructional facilities were all transferred to the new building. Within it were a number of memorials to patrons of music and benefactors of Pomona. The Victor Montgomery Library had been given by Mrs. Montgomery in memory of her husband, who had been president of the Hollywood Bowl Association. The foyer was given in memory of Katherine Poorbaugh Edmunds, wife of President Charles K. Edmunds, a pianist for whom music at the college and in the Southern California community was a major interest. Bryant Hall for orchestra and band is a memorial to Dr. and Mrs. D. C. Bryant of Claremont, who left a benefaction for a Pomona building. Alumni and other friends gave Ralph H. Lyman Hall, a small, handsome auditorium and choral rehearsal room, in memory of the much-loved director of Pomona's glee clubs and choir.

The long overdue new center for physical education for women was also nearing completion. Since the loss of the original Renwick gymnasium by fire in 1952 the department had been forced to operate under lamentable conditions. The new center, attractively designed by Architect Herbert Powell, did much to make up for the long neglect. Located on the north side of the women's playing fields and adjacent to the Gladys Shepard Swimming Pool, the new center included offices for the department, a dance studio, corrective rooms, dressing rooms, and a multi-purpose room with playing fields both west and east. The building with its Japanese roof lines made an attractive addition to the campus and was particularly striking when viewed from College Avenue. Major gifts for the building came from alumni. Mr. and Mrs. Morris B. Pendleton, both of the class of 1922, continued their interest in women's physical education with a large gift, and the new building was named the Gladys Shepard Pendleton Women's Physical Education Center in honor of Mrs. Pendleton. Mrs. Howard S. Wilson '30 gave the multi-purpose room in memory of her parents.

While plans were being formulated for the restoration of Carnegie, Pomona was facing the loss of a building which had been a landmark on the campus and a social center for the college and the community since 1906. The Claremont Inn was a redwood structure which did not meet the new safety codes of the state, and the engineers and architects consulted did not feel the building could be made to comply. The Inn's bedrooms were closed in 1965, but dining and banquet services had been continued pending study of the Inn by a special trustee committee. Reluctantly, the committee concluded that the Inn should be demolished, and it was razed

The Claremont Inn

and the ground levelled in July 1968. At that time, the trustees expected to build a new Inn on the site, and preliminary architectural plans for such a building were completed. However, building costs were such that the trustees concluded that a new building was not feasible.

For sixty-two years the Inn had symbolized the relationship of college and city which gave Claremont its special quality. "Meeting at the Inn" was the way Claremonters carried on business, whether academic or commercial, and entertained their friends. The warm hospitality of the Inn, for over twenty years under the gracious management of Paul Scott, is a treasured memory for thousands of alumni and friends of Pomona.

As additions to the academic facilities of the college were being developed, the trustees and the Associated Students were working together on a major reconstruction and reorganization of Edmunds Union. New student interests and thirty-two years of use called for fundamental changes in the building. A student committee headed by James W. Bean, Jr. '69 and advised by assistant dean of students,

Daryl Sue Goldgraben, drafted a program which was approved by the trustees. Of the total estimated cost of $407,000 the Associated Students would pay $166,000 and the trustees were providing $241,000. The work, which began in August 1969, involved a fundamental reorganization of the building. The offices were transferred to the north side of the Union, and the south wing was converted into restaurant and fountain facilities, opening on a porch which faced Stover Walk and Marston Quadrangle. The east wing was converted into a large lounge. The west wing which had housed the student store was reorganized into a large game room and a smaller store. The change in the store was occasioned by the discontinuance of its book business and its retention as a center for only sundries and supplies.

For some years there had been a hope that a large and complete bookstore could be developed to serve all the Claremont Colleges. When this became a genuine possibility in 1968, Pomona students agreed to cooperate by relinquishing their handling of books, and the Pomona trustees made a site available on the northwest corner of Dartmouth Avenue and Eighth Street. Plans were developed by the University Center, which would own the building on behalf of the six colleges. When these were ready, Earl J. Huntley of San Marino, a long-time member of the Board of Fellows, and his wife made a large gift for the construction of the store. Named for its donors, the Huntley Bookstore was placed in operation as college opened in September 1969. A dream long held for the Claremont Colleges had become a reality.

A new library building was under construction east of Honnold and joined to it as part of the great central library of the Claremont Colleges. For some years more library space had been needed and the Ford Foundation grant included some funds for this purpose, but these were not enough. As the plans progressed Dr. Seeley G. Mudd expressed interest, and he became the primary individual donor. The colleges were delighted to join in his desire that the library be named for his father, Seeley Wintersmith Mudd. With this library the name of Colonel Mudd was placed again at the heart of the Claremont Colleges of which he had been a moving force in his lifetime. Furthermore, it was joined permanently with the name of his friend, William L. Honnold, whom he had brought to the Pomona Board and with whom he had worked for the development of the Claremont Colleges.

The hard work necessary to finance the music building and women's physical education center were illustrative of the effort and devotion necessary to achieve the objectives of the Advancement Program. The leadership given by Paul Fussell and Robert B. Coons was shared by other members of the Board. William H. Fellows '33 succeeded Mr. Coons as chairman of the Advancement Program, when Mr. Coons succeeded Mr. Fussell as chairman of the Board of Trustees in 1964. Ranney C. Draper '25, vice-chairman of the Board, was chairman of a general campaign among all alumni in 1966-67.

Among the gifts for endowment were three professorships which were established by members of the Pomona family. Trustee Russell H. Smith '33 and Mrs. Smith in 1966 gave $400,000 to endow fully the Elden Smith Professorship of Economics in memory of his brother who had been vice-chairman of the board of the Security First National Bank in Los Angeles and a trustee of the Claremont Graduate School and University Center.

The William Atwood Hilton Professorship of Zoology was established in 1967 by his former students in honor of the distinguished teacher who served Pomona from 1912 to 1944 and created the college's modern department of zoology.

The Blanche and Frank R. Seaver Professorship in Science was established in 1969 by the Board of Trustees of Pomona in deep gratitude to Dr. and Mrs. Seaver for their contribution to excellence through the building and continued support of the Seaver Science Center.

The Search for a New President

As Dr. Lyon would reach the retirement age of sixty-five in the summer of 1969, the Pomona trustees were facing their largest single responsibility, the selection of a president. With Chairman Coons taking the initiative, the trustees on December 1, 1966 authorized the appointment of "a small committee of the Board to work on the matter of selection of a new president of the college." When constituted, the committee included Leonard A. Shelton '32 as chairman, Robert B. Coons, Ranney C. Draper '25, Paul Fussell, and H. Russell Smith '36. This committee worked closely with a faculty advisory committee composed of Dean Ernest A. Strathmann as chairman, and professors Robert L. Ferm, religion, Lee C. McDonald, government, and R. Nelson Smith, chemistry. The trustee and faculty committees worked together so cordially that, as Mr. Shelton said, "if a stranger had sat in on those meetings he wouldn't have known who was a trustee and who was a professor."

The first months of the committees' deliberations were given to ascertaining and agreeing on the qualities required in the new president. These were determined to be a strong academic background, experience in a liberal arts college, and dedication to the place of the independent liberal arts college in the United States. It was hoped in addition that the committee could find a man with some administrative experience. These qualifications limited the search to men engaged in higher education and at no time did the committee consider candidates from any other field.

On the personal side the committee sought a man of highest character, who would be sympathetic to the ideals and purposes of Pomona. He should be young enough to give a long period of service to the college. His wife should be an educated woman, gracious in hospitality, and understanding of the demands the presidency would make on her and her family life.

When the committees agreed on the qualifications desired in the new president, nominations were sought from officers of universities, colleges, and foundations. Names were suggested by Pomona faculty members, and some came from alumni and students. The trustee committee then sought information on 150 of the individuals suggested. When the trustee committee was ready to begin the interviewing of candidates, it was expanded to include John W. Dodds, Robert V. Edwards '23, James M. Gerstley, Louis B. Lundborg, and Morris B. Pendleton '22. Interviews were begun in the spring of 1968 and continued throughout the year. Later, student members were added to the search committee.

In the autumn of 1968 the committee found its man, and on January 13, 1969 Dr. John David Alexander, the thirty-six year-old president of Southwestern at Memphis, was elected the seventh president of Pomona College. Though his name had been suggested at the beginning of the trustees' search it was assumed that he was not available, and therefore he had not been approached. When Dr. Lyon ascertained in October 1968 that Dr. Alexander would be interested, the trustees moved immediately to interview him. Chairman Coons and Professor Lee C. McDonald flew to Memphis to meet Dr. and Mrs. Alexander, and after their enthusiastic report the Alexanders came to Claremont for meetings with faculty, students and the student advisory committee which had been instituted. A special meeting of the Board of Trustees was held at the Jonathan Club in Los Angeles on January 13, and following luncheon Dr. Alexander spoke at some length of his background, experience, and educational philosophy, emphasizing his faith in young people and his commitment to the independent liberal arts college. After Dr. Alexander had answered questions from the trustees, he and the other guests retired, and the Board went into executive session. The response of the trustees to Dr. Alexander had been enthusiastic, and after Mr. Shelton had reported for the presidential selection committee and Professor R. Nelson Smith '38 for the faculty advisory committee, Dr. Alexander was unanimously elected president of Pomona College, effective September 1, 1969.

By character, outlook, and experience Dr. Alexander was superbly suited for leadership at Pomona and in the Claremont Colleges. Born in Springfield, Tennessee, and raised in Kentucky, he received his B.A. degree from Southwestern at Memphis in 1953 with honors in Greek and election to Phi Beta Kappa. After a year at the Louisville Presbyterian Seminary he entered Christ Church, the University of Oxford as a Rhodes Scholar in 1954. At Oxford he studied the ancient languages of the Near East and received the doctor of philosophy degree in 1957. Upon returning to the United States he was ordained as a Presbyterian minister and joined the faculty of the San Francisco Theological Seminary where he served as associate professor of Old Testament from 1957 through 1964.

Dr. and Mrs. John David Alexander in Claremont, January 1969

Called to the presidency of his alma mater, he had given oustanding leadership to Southwestern where he had gained experience particularly valuable for Pomona and the Claremont Colleges. After moving from Clarksville, Tennessee, to Memphis in 1925, Southwestern had brought a large number of Rhodes Scholars to its faculty, and had emulated Oxford both in academic matters and the architecture of its campus.

Mrs. Alexander, the former Catharine Coleman of Whitehaven, Tennessee, graduated from Southwestern with election to Phi Beta Kappa in 1955. After a year of teaching, she married Mr. Alexander in the summer of 1956, and they spent the following academic year in Oxford. The family had three children: Catharine, age ten and a half; John, age nine; and Julia, almost two. A delightful young family would be coming to the President's House at Pomona.

PRESIDENT JOHN DAVID ALEXANDER

The Retirement of President Lyon

Commencement on June 8, 1969 was preceded by a round of festivities marking the retirement of President Lyon, whose administration of twenty-eight years was the longest in Pomona's history. The salute from the faculty, presented as a scroll signed by the members of the faculty and administration, emphasized the president's devotion to the college. "Through twenty-eight years," the faculty statement read, "he has been tireless in his service to the college. Constant in resolution, judicious in counsel, he has labored with consummate skill to harness our talents and energies to the attainment of our common goal. He has defended the college with calm reason and quiet courage against irrational forces which have at times threatened, whether from within or without. Responding to every challenge with vision, uncompromising in his quest for excellence, yet compassionate toward everyone, he has enriched the life of our community in ways deserving the respect of all."

With a special flair, Alumni Day on Saturday, June 7, was a gala farewell to the Lyons. Marston Quadrangle, center of the festivities, was decorated with large banners showing an enormous lion placing a paw on a giant "P". Luncheon tables throughout the quadrangle, a colorful marquee for the Lyons and the Alumni Council party, and a stage with a lion banner reflected the happy spirit of the day. After luncheon Dr. and Mrs. Lyon were honored with tributes by Dr. Robert E. Tranquada '51, president of the Alumni Association, and Robert B. Coons, chairman of the Board of Trustees. Mr. Coons announced that the trustees, with the assistance of many alumni and David J. Fishman of the graduating class, had established and fully endowed the E. Wilson Lyon Professorship in the Humanities. He also stated that the fine arts quadrangle formed by Bridges Hall, Rembrandt Hall, the Montgomery Art Center, and the Thatcher Music Building would be developed with the assistance of the Women's Campus Club and named the Carolyn Bartel Lyon Garden, in grateful appreciation of Mrs. Lyon's loving service to Pomona and its students. The trustees, alumni, and the Campus Club could not have honored

Dean Strathmann presents Dr. Lyon with a copy of his opening convocation addresses: Dean Strathmann, Mrs. Lyon, Dr. Lyon, Dean Walton, Mrs. William L. Faust

The Alumni honor Dr. and Mrs. Lyon: Chairman of the Board of Trustees Robert B. Coons and President of the Alumni Association Dr. Robert E. Tranquada

the Lyons more appropriately. For the president, teaching and scholarship were the heart of the academic experience, and Mrs. Lyon's love of music at the college and her development of the garden at the President's House would be reflected in the garden bearing her name.

Alumni Day was a happy recollection of the past, with its friendships for classmates and years of devotion to the college. But commencement, which followed the next day, Sunday, June 8, embodied the tensions and uncertainties of young men and women leaving college in a terrible period of their nation's history. For many the grave problems facing them on the national scene transcended the customary pleasure in commencement ceremonies and the satisfaction of graduation. Only twenty-five members of the class had come to the meeting to elect the student commencement speaker. These were so divided that they asked permission for two speakers to represent the class, and the administration granted the request.

Despite the campus tensions, the customary exercises and occasions of commencement day began harmoniously. W. Robert Rankin, former Chaplain of the Claremont Colleges who had become associate director of the Danforth Foundation, returned from St. Louis to speak at the morning baccalaureate service in Bridges Auditorium, and delivered an excellent sermon entitled "Darkness amidst the Children of Light." After giving a luncheon for the trustees and their wives at the President's House, Dr. and Mrs. Lyon held the annual reception for the graduates and their families in the Memorial Court, between Bridges and Sumner Halls. The commencement exercises followed at the end of the afternoon.

For the trustees and faculty, the commencement marked the closing months of Pomona's longest presidential administration and they saw it as an occasion to note the past of the college and to look forward to its future. The trustees had asked Dr. Lyon to give the commencement address and chairman Robert Coons had come to introduce him. Mr. Coons brought the good news that the Advancement Program had been carried to a successful conclusion. Exceeding the program's goal of $19,641,000 the college had received $21,176,565.

Mr. Coons then introduced Dr. Lyon, who had prepared a valedictory address entitled "The College of the Future." Looking back upon his forty years as a teacher and administrator the president said that his confidence in the vitality of the liberal arts college was greater than ever:

> My faith rests on the basic fact that the independent liberal arts college is manageable. It can be encompassed by its president, understood by its faculty, and reasonably well comprehended by its students. It has the transcending merit of independence from any outside body — whether church, local, state, or national government. Solely responsible for itself, its wisdom and progress can be limited only by its own members. What happens to Pomona in the future lies in the hands of its trustees, its faculty, its students, and its alumni.

Noting the great crisis in American higher education, the president warned that effective operation of the college depended on mutual confidence among those who are partners in its work. "Higher education," he stated, "rests on a belief in reason, an exchange of ideas with mutual respect and faith in the fundamental processes of American government and society. When these give way to confrontations and violence, true learning is the first casualty."

Robert Berke and James E. Rosenberg, both members of Phi Beta Kappa, spoke for the class. Each denounced contemporary American society and the actions of the national government, Berke in prose and Rosenberg in verse. Both reflected the frustrations and impatience of their generation over social problems beyond their immediate control. Many of their class responded with cheers, but expressions of opposition came from some members of the deeply offended audience. Despite these sobering circumstances, the traditional ceremony proceeded without further incident. Dean Strathmann presented the 243 candidates and Dr. Lyon conferred the degrees on the members of the class and congratulated them individually as they came across the stage. The final singing of *Hail Pomona, Hail*! was a release and a reminder of the strength and stability of the college in a time of tension.

The College in 1969

To conclude his administration, Dr. Lyon published a major report on the state of the college, including a record of the past two academic years, a reflection on his years as president, and some suggestions for Pomona's future. Most of all, he wished to express his gratitude for the privilege of working with so many dedicated people in the development of Pomona. He paid tribute to the "four chairmen of the Board who led the trustees and guided me through our many problems;" and to the faculty, "who led the academic program and the students with great sense of responsibility, and always in warm cooperation with the president's office." "The privilege of working with selected students in a personal environment," he wrote, "was the greatest factor that led me to leave the teaching of history at Colgate and to accept the call to the presidency of Pomona. To see students on the campus, to have them in our home, and to work with them in an infinite variety of ways have been sources of deep satisfaction." He was particularly grateful to the alumni, both of the earlier years and of his own period, "who brought such understanding and devotion to the college that my work with the Alumni Council and with the alumni body as a whole has been one of the most pleasant aspects of my tenure. Pomona alumni understand the purpose of the college, and direct their concern toward significant questions." Dr. Lyon had enjoyed an unparalleled opportunity to know alumni closely, for of the 14,000 living alumni 9262 had attended Pomona in his administration.

Through the cooperation of alumni, faculty, trustees and friends, Pomona had made remarkable progress. Its physical resources had grown amazingly. Except for the original Renwick Gymnasium which had been lost by fire, and Harwood Hall which had been demolished, all the academic buildings of 1940-41 were still in use. To them had been added the Memorial Gymnasium; the three buildings of the Seaver Science Center — Millikan Laboratory, the Seaver Laboratory for Biology and Geology, and the Seaver Laboratory for Chemistry; the Montgomery Art Center; the reconstructed Mason Hall and Carnegie Building; the Thatcher

Music Building, and the Gladys Shepard Pendleton Physical Education Center for Women, both nearing completion. Five new residence halls and two dining halls had been built: Mudd Hall, Gibson Dining Hall, Walker Hall, Norton Hall, Wig Hall, and Oldenborg Center, which was both a residence and a dining hall.

The total book value of Pomona's assets had grown to approximately $69,000,000 in July 1969. Of this sum $23,605,000 was in annuity and life income contract funds on which the income was paid to the respective donors during their lifetime. Endowment funds on which the income was available for the support of the college were $22,619,000.

In an age when California was losing much of its natural beauty Pomona could be proud of the development and improvement of its campus and grounds. The spirit of George W. Marston, who pioneered in beautifying the campus, had guided his successors. With attractive landscaping for each new building and the planting of flowering shrubs, particularly camellias, the campus had become a group of green quadrangles and lovely gardens. Added since 1941 were the Harwood Garden north of Walker Hall, Athearn Field east of Clark Hall, the landscaping of the Seaver Science Center, the women's athletic field on College Avenue with the Pendleton pool in the center and the Rogers tennis courts to the east, the Stover Memorial Walk, which unified the central campus, Merritt Field in Blanchard Park, the Pearsons-Crookshank-Mason Quadrangle, and the Carolyn Bartel Lyon Garden in the fine arts quadrangle. The harmonious beauty of these quadrangles and gardens had been developed by Ralph D. Cornell '14, distinguished Southern California landscape architect, who served his alma mater with great affection for over fifty years.

Looking ahead, Dr. Lyon made recommendations for providing new academic and residence facilities for the college. Two departments, botany and English with its program of theater arts, would need new locations. He suggested that all these needs could be met by moving botany from Crookshank Hall and erecting a new botany building just west of the Seaver Laboratory of Biology and Geology. Crookshank could then be reconstructed for the English department. If a small teaching theater were desired, it could be placed in the space just east of Crookshank. With these changes and developments Crookshank, Mason, and Pearsons, which should be renovated, would form a humanities quadrangle. The sciences, except for psychology in Mason, would be located in the Seaver Center.

With an enrollment of over 1250 students Pomona had been forced to find housing for 150 to 175 students in Claremont and the surrounding communities. Never desirable, this dependence on the community had become increasingly difficult. Dr. Lyon urged the building of additional student housing, suggesting that there were convenient campus locations east of Blaisdell Hall and on the south side of Seventh Street, east of College Avenue.

A number of young faculty members who would give long service to Pomona had been appointed in 1968 and 1969. In the humanities were: Charles King, Ph.D. Harvard University, assistant professor of philosophy; Margaret H. Dornish, Ph.D. Claremont Graduate School, assistant professor of religion; and David N. Flaten, doctoral candidate University of California, Santa Barbara, instructor in theater arts. In the natural sciences were: Harry C. Mullikin, Ph.D. University of Wisconsin, assistant professor of mathematics; Larry C. Oglesby, Ph.D. University of California, Berkeley, and William O. Wirtz, Ph.D. Cornell University, assistant professors of zoology; William Preas Banks, Ph.D. Johns Hopkins University, assistant professor of psychology; Theodore A. Weissbach, doctoral candidate, University of Colorado, instructor in psychology; and Richard A. Fass, Ph.D. University of Wisconsin, assistant professor of chemistry. In the social sciences were: Frank C. Wykoff, Ph.D. University of California, Berkeley, and James D. Likens, doctoral candidate, University of Minnesota, assistant professors of economics; Steven S. Koblik, doctoral candidate, Northwestern University, instructor in history; and George K. Hesslink, Ph.D. University of Chicago, assistant professor of sociology.

As Dr. Lyon's administration drew to a close the Board of Trustees made a careful study of the college and looked to its future. In November 1967 the Board had authorized an ad hoc trustee-alumni-faculty committee to review the academic life of the college under the general supervision of the Academic Affairs Committee of the Board. A committee of nine under the chairmanship of trustee Robert V. Edwards '23 worked so effectively that printed copies of the report were in the hands of the trustees and faculty in early June 1969. Entitled *Pomona: An Academic Review,* the report treated the character of the student body, morality standards, the curriculum, the faculty, the Board of Trustees, and Pomona's concern with community problems, particularly racial. Recognizing the heavy national responsibility of institutions of higher learning, the committee concluded that a large share of this responsibility fell "on privately endowed institutions of higher education as these institutions enjoy a unique position of independence and leadership. Pomona, as one such institution, has a special responsibility to the society it serves."

As the Board of Trustees welcomed a new president of the college it faced a change in its own leadership. When the presidential search had come to its successful conclusion, Mr. Coons asked to be relieved of the chairmanship following the inauguration but consented to accept a vice-chairmanship. For their new chairman the trustees turned to vice-chairman H. Russell Smith '36, whose participation had contributed greatly to the effectiveness of the Board in the critical decisions of 1969. When elected chairman of the Pomona Board he was also serving as president of the Southern California Symphony — Hollywood Bowl Association and chairman of the board of Community Television of Southern California (Channel 28). President of the Associated Students while in college, Mr. Smith had continued his deep interest in Pomona throughout his career. One of his sons graduated from Pomona in 1968 and the other would do so in 1971. His success in business, rare wisdom in human affairs, and dedication to the cultural advancement of Southern California made him an ideal chairman.

Mr. Smith and the Board would be greatly assisted by Dr. Robert E. Tranquada '51, who was elected a trustee in 1969, following his outstanding leadership of the Pomona Alumni Association.

Robert B. Coons transfers the chairmanship of the Board of Trustees to H. Russell Smith '36

Dr. Lyon congratulates President Alexander on his inauguration

The Inauguration of President Alexander

Plans for the transfer of the presidency were carried out easily and on schedule. The Alexanders arrived in August and found the President's House ready for them. Dr. Lyon brought Dr. Alexander up-to-date on the operations of the summer and relinquished his official duties at the meeting of the Executive Committee on September 8. The Alexanders were welcomed by the faculty with a reception given by Dean and Mrs. Strathmann. Meanwhile Dr. Alexander turned to the business of beginning the new academic year. His opening convocation address, "Who Owns the College," in which he examined the nature of Pomona, was enthusiastically received.

Preparations for President Alexander's inauguration had been under way since the spring. Following the tradition established by the inaugurations of Dr. Edmunds and Dr. Lyon, the ceremony was scheduled for Founders Day, which was October 18. It was a pleasant coincidence that the day also marked Dr. Alexander's thirty-seventh birthday. The colleges and universities invited to send delegates were those with which Pomona or Dr. Alexander had a particularly close relationship. An alumnus or alumna of Pomona received each delegate with whom he marched in the academic procession. Leading the delegates of forty-four colleges and universities were the representatives of Yale, Dartmouth, Amherst, Oberlin, and Grinnell — institutions that had played such a large part in Pomona's founding and early years. Delegates from fifteen church, civic and educational groups also honored the college by their attendance.

In addition to the delegates, faculty, and trustees, the academic procession included the participants in the Ceremony of the Flame, representatives of the Associated Students, the presidents of Claremont University Center, Scripps College, Claremont Men's College, Harvey Mudd College, Pitzer College, the president emeritus of Pomona College, and President Alexander. Robert B. Coons, chairman of the Board, presided. After the singing of the National Anthem, the invocation, and Palestrina's *Sicut Cervus* by the college choir, President Platt of Harvey Mudd College, provost for 1969-70, brought the greetings and congratulations of the Claremont Colleges.

Dr. Alexander was then inducted as the seventh president of Pomona College by the chairman of the Board who charged him with the high responsibilities of his office. "We are sure," Mr. Coons said, "that under you the students who emerge from the portals of our college will have learned to abhor mediocrity and sham and to espouse the spirit of service to both their fellows and society."

President Alexander's address, "A Perspective on Renewal," showed in content and delivery that Pomona had a leader of great perception, courage, and eloquence. Looking at the critical state of American society he found in the war in Vietnam "a sense of frustration and lack of clarity of purpose that have brutalized the American people to a point of some danger that authority will collapse .... Unless the war can be ended soon," he warned, "massive dislocations will continue to shake society and threaten all authority." Reflecting on the state of the nation he affirmed the role of Pomona: "Our task now is to winnow from the welter of changing values those transcendent values for which this college exists, so that while trying to move with society Pomona College will help move society through education." He pledged the highest priority for teaching and the close personal relationships of students and faculty.

Dr. Alexander welcomed the more open decision-making process developing in colleges and universities. He applauded the creation of the College Policy Review Council at Pomona, with its trustee, faculty, student and alumni membership, and Pomona's long standing policy of student membership on faculty committees. He looked to maintaining the diversity of American higher education through strong independent liberal arts colleges. He challenged the college:

> We must see if we can be as adept at self-renewal as our predecessors have been. War dealt the new administration of Pomona College in 1941 a grievous setback, but it also opened an opportunity which was seized to make Pomona, already a good college, an even better one. This capacity for self-renewal has been the most distinguished characteristic of Pomona College throughout its history. Such re-

newal of inner resources comes from the ability to ask the right questions about oneself and to act firmly when the answers are reached. Such self-renewal disclaims complacency and pride of accomplishment and clings to its transcendent goals.

The convocation closed with the enactment of the Ceremony of the Flame, which had been traditional for Founders Day celebrations since 1921.

The problems that confronted Dr. Alexander were unique. The difficulties of his earlier predecessors came primarily from financial crises, local or national. The crisis from abroad that met his immediate predecessor in 1941 brought unity in war and laid the basis for unprecedented national progress. The war in Vietnam, on the other hand, had produced disunity, bitterness, and violence. To chart Pomona's course under such circumstances would not be easy.

But Dr. Alexander and the college could look to the future with confidence. Pomona's faculty was strong, her students were gifted, and able administrators were at hand to acquaint the new president with his duties and to interpret the college to him. The members of the Board of Trustees were experienced in the affairs of the college and wise and understanding in its control. The alumni were deeply interested in their alma mater and supportive of her development. Like their predecessors, able men and women working together in search of a liberal education would assure Pomona's ability and will to serve and to lead amid the increasing complexities of American life.

APPENDIX

An Essay on the Sources

THE FOUNDERS of Pomona College were aware of the historical significance of their establishing a college of the New England type in the Pacific Southwest. From the beginning they kept records of their plans and actions, and this practice was followed conscientiously by succeeding generations. As a result there is abundant data for every stage and phase of Pomona's history. The earliest sources are the Records of the General Congregational Association of Southern California which are to be found in the Conference office of the United Church of Christ in Pasadena. The Congregational Year Books, published in Boston, also contain valuable information on Pomona. The major depositories at the college are the president's office, the alumni office, and the Special Collections section of the Honnold Library.

The records in the president's office are exceptionally complete. There are individual files on most of the men and women who have been appointed to the faculty and the administration. Correspondence of all types, both internal and external, has been preserved. The minutes and correspondence of all trustee committees are kept in the president's office. Typed copies of the minutes of the Board of Trustees and its Executive Committee are also available there.

Few colleges have such extensive and complete records of their alumni and alumni organizations. From the very beginning Pomona alumni kept in close touch with their alma mater, sending accounts of their activities. These materials were carefully preserved and today the alumni office has files on nearly all of the men and women who have attended Pomona. One can find in these files information that will throw light on any period or phase of the college.

The Pomoniana Collection in the Honnold Library presents the wide range of the college's history. The collection is the culmination of work begun in Pomona's early years. The original faculty assembled materials about themselves and the college and after 1908 these were deposited in the Carnegie Library. There the materials were systematized and lovingly tended, particularly by Miss Marion J. Ewing, who joined the library staff in 1912. The collection was moved to the Honnold Library in 1952, and it has been steadily augmented since that time. Offices of the college now transfer to this collection materials that are not essential in current operation.

The manuscript sources of the Pomoniana Collection in Honnold include the minutes of the faculty from 1889, minutes of the faculty cabinet, and files on individual faculty members, academic departments, campus events, and buildings and grounds. A large file of photographs is a valuable resource for every period of Pomona's history.

The printed sources in the collection in Honnold are rich in official materials and in records of college life. There are copies of all the college catalogues from 1888 to the present. Complete files of the student paper and the yearbook portray all eras in Pomona's history. Complete files of the *Pomona College Quarterly Magazine*, 1912-34, and its successors, the *News Letter* and *Pomona Today*, are preserved. In addition the collection includes most of the literature published by Pomona in its quests for students and for funds. The college endeavors to acquire and preserve the publications of its faculty and alumni, and a large number of their books are to be found in the Pomoniana Collection.

Materials from the other Claremont Colleges have also been deposited in the Special Collections section in Honnold, and these provide data on Pomona's intercollegiate relations in Claremont. Notable in this respect are the papers of Dr. Blaisdell as president of Claremont Colleges, 1926-36.

The records of Pomona's financial development and the custody of its resources are kept in the business office in the Pendleton Business Building. There also are to be found the original minutes of the Board of Trustees and of the Executive Committee.

Materials of historic value are available in many other offices on the campus. The records of all students who ever attended Pomona are on file in the registrar's office. The offices of the deans, the academic departments, the vice-president for development, the business manager of the Associated Students, the director of athletics, and the news bureau all house materials that throw light on the rich spectrum of Pomona life.

Early news of the college was carried by newspapers in Pomona, notably by the *Pomona Times* and the *Pomona Progress*, which began as weeklies but developed into dailies. In 1927, the *Pomona Progress* joined with the *Pomona Daily Bulletin* (which had earlier purchased the *Pomona Times*) to establish the *Progress Bulletin* which gives excellent coverage of college news. The *Claremont Courier*, which published its first issue on September 16, 1908, is indispensable for the subsequent history of Pomona College and Claremont.

Books, Brochures, and Dissertations

Charles Burt Sumner, *The Story of Pomona College*, Boston, 1914. An account of the first twenty-five years of the college.

Frank Parkhurst Brackett, *Granite and Sagebrush, Reminiscences of the First Fifty Years of Pomona College*, Los Angeles, 1944.

William W. Clary, *The Claremont Colleges, A History of the Group Plan*, Claremont, 1970. An account by a Pomona alumnus who had served as a member of the Board of Fellows, as a Pomona trustee, and as acting president of Claremont College.

Over The Years: Recollections of George White Marston, Claremont, 1937. A brochure prepared by Mr. Marston for the Fiftieth Anniversary of Pomona College.

Harold W. Davis, editor, *This is Claremont*, Claremont, 1941. A delightful volume which commemorated the Fiftieth Anniversary of the Claremont Congregational Church.

Natalie Joy Stromberg Ward, *James Arnold Blaisdell: A Study of His Professional Career*. Dissertation for the degree of Doctor of Education, University of California, Los Angeles, April 1960.

George Harvey Sage, *A History of Physical Education at Pomona College (1887-1960).* Dissertation for the degree of Doctor of Education, University of California, Los Angeles. 1962.

Song Books

Pomona College Song and Verse, published by the Alumni and Students, 1906. Twenty-two songs and twenty-seven pages of verse. Includes Class Songs for every class except '95.

Pomona College Song Book, compiled by the Class of 1914. Published in 1912.

Pomona College Song Book, published by the Pomona College Alumni Association, 1925.

The Songs We Sing at Pomona, compiled and edited by William G. Blanchard, published by the Pomona College Alumni Association, 1943.

The Songs We Sing at Pomona. Second edition. Carl Olson '66, general editor; William G. Blanchard, music editor. Published by the Associated Students, Pomona College, 1968. Helpful comments by the editors and a valuable essay, "About the Songs," by William F. Russell and William G. Blanchard.

Biographical Works

Isabel Smith Gates, *The Life of George Augustus Gates,* Boston, 1915. A biography of President Gates by his wife.

Hubert Herring, *The Education of George W. Marston,* Claremont, 1946.

Mary Gilman Marston, editor, *George White Marston: A Family Chronicle,* 2 volumes, Los Angeles, 1956.

Edith Parker Hinckley and Katharine Norton Benner, editors, *The Dean Speaks Again,* Claremont, 1955. Hitherto unpublished excerpts from the personal papers of Edwin Clarence Norton.

Jane Werner Watson, *The Seaver Story,* Claremont, 1960. A duo-biography of Dr. and Mrs. Frank Roger Seaver.

Clifford Merrill Drury, *Rudolph James Wig, Engineer, Pomona College Trustee, Presbyterian Layman*, Glendale, 1968.

Albert Britt, *Ellen Browning Scripps, Journalist and Idealist*, Scripps College, 1960.

David Lavender, *The Story of Cyprus Mines Corporation*, San Marino, 1962. For Seeley W. Mudd and Harvey S. Mudd.

E. Wilson Lyon, "Seeley Wintersmith Mudd," *Honnold Library Record*, Fall 1970.

Histories of Colleges and Universities

Andrew F. Rolle, *Occidental College*, Los Angeles, 1962.

Manuel P. Servin and Iris Higbie Wilson, *Southern California and its University, a History of USC, 1880-1964*, Los Angeles, 1969.

Verne A. Stadtman, *The University of California*, New York, 1970.

John S. Nollen, *Grinnell College*, State Historical Society, Iowa City, Iowa, 1953. For information on President Gates.

Histories of Education and of California

Information on American history and international relations has been drawn from well-known sources. For the history of higher education and the history of California, the most helpful works were:

Frederick Rudolph, *The American College and University, a History*, New York, 1962.

Arthur G. Coons, *Crises In California Higher Education*, Los Angeles, 1968.

E. Wilson Lyon, "Higher Education for the West, 1924-74," in *Addresses and Proceedings of the Fiftieth Anniversary Meeting of the Western College Association*, 1974.

Glenn S. Dumke, *The Boom of the Eighties in Southern California*, San Marino, 1944.

Robert Glass Cleland, *California in Our Time, 1900-1940*, New York, 1947.

John W. Caughey, *California, A Remarkable State's Life History*, Englewood Cliffs, New Jersey. Third edition 1970.

David Lavender, *California, A Bicentennial History*, New York, 1976.

INDEX